UNDERSTANDING THE GRACE AND COVENANT OF GOD

The Masterpiece...the Controversies...the Counterfeit

BY TED ROUSE

UNDERSTANDING THE GRACE AND COVENANT OF GOD

Milestones International Publishers
4410 University Dr., Ste. 113
Huntsville, AL 35816
(256) 536-9402   Fax: (256) 536-4530
www.milestonesintl.com

ISBN: 0-924748-60-5
UPC: 88571300030-7

Printed in the United States of America
© 2005 by Ted Rouse

Cover design by: Tony Laidig, www.thirstydirt.com

1 2 3 4 5 6 7 8 9 10 11 / 09 08 07 06 05

Exposing Counterfeit Grace—

Satan's Master Deception

God's Masterpiece is Salvation by Grace
Satan's Master Deception is Counterfeit Grace

As we begin this study, please realize that the New Covenant is God's new contract with the human race. It is an everlasting Covenant (Heb. 13:20-21). In it are all the terms, agreements, and conditions of the Covenant. No one part of it nullifies another, for God, the author of this matchless document, is not the *"author of confusion."* If it is rightly divided as it says in the Covenant we should do (2 Tim. 2:15), then all parts of it are in perfect harmony with each other, and the admonitions recorded in it to follow after holiness, keep the commandments, and walk righteously, or suffer the consequences, do not contradict God's true teaching on grace, as we shall point out. We will clearly show you how all of this New Covenant harmonizes with itself, and how only if we accept it all, will we clearly see the real grace and Covenant of God complete with all of its warnings as well as its wonderful benefits.

Before we get into some life-changing facts about *the real grace of God*, we will first take a look at the counterfeiter and counterfeit grace.

The scripture reveals that Satan is a counterfeiter and that he always comes bringing darkness, but craftily works to make it appear as light (2 Cor. 11:14-15).

He brings lies and cleverly disguises them as the truth. He is a master deceiver and has succeeded in deceiving everyone on earth at one time or another (Rev. 12:9; Titus 3:3). He has deceived mankind with everything from Evolutionism to Islam. He makes evil look good and good, evil, and puts darkness for light and says that light is darkness (Gen. 3:4-5; Isa. 5:20). So, we must recognize the fact that our great adversary, the father of lies, is a counterfeiter and he is always at work to twist the truth and mislead others. Only God's real truth rightly divided, as is recorded in all of the Holy Scriptures, is our shield and our defense (Eph. 6:14,16; Ps. 91:4). The apostle Paul wrote, *"**Finally, my brethren**, be strong in the Lord, and in the power of his might. Put on the whole armor of God, that ye may be able to stand against the wiles of the devil"* (Eph. 6:10-12). The word "wiles" is synonymous with the word "tricks." This word means something that is "designed to deceive, cheat, and outwit others. An illusion to blind others as to one's real intentions in order to outwit or trap one's enemies and ensnare them;" "a military strategy" (Webster's Dictionary).

Influences, Influences Everywhere

Understand this, that all of the influences in this world which are contrary to God's laws of love, righteousness, and truth, have originated with the adversary and his kingdom, whether they come in the form of obvious evil, or in more subtle forms of nice sounding religious teachings or doctrines.

"Now the [Holy] Spirit speaketh expressly, that in the latter times some shall depart from the faith [our most holy faith], giving heed to seducing spirits, and doctrines of devils" (1 Tim. 4:1; Jude 20). John, under inspiration of the Holy Spirit wrote, *"Love not the world, neither the things that are in the world. If any man love the world, the love of the Father is not in him. **For all that is in the world** [connected with], the lust of the flesh, and the lust of the eyes, and the pride of life, **is not of the Father, but is of the world** [which is walking according to Satan, Eph. 2:2-3]. And the world passeth away, and the lust thereof: but he that doeth the will of God abideth for ever"* (1 John 2:15-17). Jesus said, *"Either make the tree good, and his fruit good; or else make the tree corrupt, and his fruit corrupt: for the tree is known by his fruit"* (Matt. 12:33).

Every bit of the evil or unrighteousness then, whether great or small, that goes on in this world, is from the influence of the evil one, and is tied up with his kingdom. So then, whatever, or whomever in this world that would lead one into sin, condone sin, excuse sin, or says there is any kind

CONTENTS

INTRODUCTION

⟹⊶⊷⟸

According to scripture, it has always taken faith to please God. The Bible says, *"But without faith it is impossible to please Him"* (Heb. 11:6). And, *"Whatsoever is not of faith is sin"* (Rom. 14:23). The Scriptures say that Jesus is *"the author and finisher of our faith"*; and *also* that He was *"full of grace and truth"* (John 1:14). It reveals that He never sinned but He always did those things that pleased the Father (John 8:29). So then, we can conclude that all of the actions of His life were the actions of faith, and none were legalism or dead works. Scripture reveals that He *"loved righteousness and hated iniquity."* It reveals that He prayed, obeyed the written Word of God, fasted, resisted sin and the devil, fulfilled all righteousness, and kept His Father's commandments (John 15:10). Jesus did His Father's will, He tithed (Matt. 23:23), did good works and the work that God gave Him to do (John 17:4), and He lived a holy and separated life. Therefore, this lifestyle and all of these types of activities when based on God's written Word is real faith in action (Heb. 11). The very author of faith left us an example that we should walk in His steps (1 Pet. 2:21-24). These kinds of things then are not legalism, self-righteousness, or the legalistic works of the law in the least, for again scripture says, "For the (works of) the law are not of faith" (Gal. 3:10-12). Yet Jesus, in all of His activities of life, always operated in faith as we've stated, for He always pleased the Father (Heb. 11:6). His life then, while on the earth, is the true example of the life of faith that we too, as Christians, are supposed to live, for *"the just shall live by faith"* (Rom. 1:17). The apostle John wrote, "He that saith he abideth in him ought himself also [then] so to walk, even as he walked."…"He that saith, I know him, and keepeth not his commandments, is a liar, and the truth is not in him" (1 John 2:4). John, a close friend and traveling companion of Jesus, clearly understood the results of a true life of faith, for he learned it first-hand from the Master, Himself. Abraham also, with his faith, did these same kinds of works and obeyed God's commandments. In Genesis 26:5 God says, He blessed Abraham, *"Because that Abraham obeyed my voice, and kept my charge, my commandments, my statutes, and my laws."* This is living faith. God obviously then gave Abraham things to obey, and revealed to him the true way of the Lord over four hundred years before the legalistic law of Moses ever came along, and Abraham responded in faith and by faith obeyed God (Heb. 11:8). God said, *"For I know him, that he will command his children and his household after him, and they shall **keep the way of the LORD, to do justice and judgment;** [so] that the LORD may bring upon Abraham that which he hath spoken of him"* (Gen. 18:19).

Yes, we are Abraham's children if we are the children of faith, but scripture makes it clear that we are not just to say we are the children of Abraham like the Pharisees did who were hypocrites, but we are to *"walk in the steps of that faith of our father Abraham"* (Rom. 4:12). Jesus said, *"If ye were Abraham's children, ye would do the works of Abraham"* (John 8:39). This means obey God's commands as he did. Many have not rightly divided God's Word and have erroneously thought that obedience to God's Word and living righteously is somehow legalism, and that it takes away from faith and grace, but it does not. The fact of the matter is that real grace and faith produce a life of obedience and a walk of righteousness, as we shall clearly point out in this book. Let it be known that there are many different kinds of *works* recorded in the New Covenant, but only one is the *"works of the law."* We need to rightly divide the Word of God here. Legalistic works have to do with the Old Testament's outward laws and carnal, religious ordinances; while grace, which also produces works and a change of life, is God's influence in our lives enabling us and empowering us to do what we couldn't do on our own, by our own efforts. Scripture says, ***"And God is able to make all grace abound toward you; that ye,*** *always having all sufficiency in all things,* ***may abound to every good work"*** (2 Cor. 9:8). *"For we are his workmanship, created in Christ Jesus **unto good works,** which God hath before ordained that we should walk in them"* (Eph. 2:10). Real grace then, we will see, brings us into a walk of righteousness and empowers us to do good. *"That the righteousness of the [moral] law might be fulfilled in us, who walk not after the flesh, but after the Spirit"* (Rom. 8:4). We encourage you to read through this book. Invest the time and it will prove to be a great benefit to you in understanding God's plan of salvation. So, let's take a look into the real grace and Covenant of God.

of an automatic cloak for known sin, is under the influence of Satan and deceiving spirits. For sin is rebellion against the moral government of God, and Jesus came to free us from sin and lead us into paths of righteousness (John 8:34-36). Therefore, God would never condone, or automatically excuse, known sin in any form for He *"loveth righteousness and hateth iniquity"* (Heb. 1:9).

"For the kingdom of God is not meat and drink; but righteousness, and peace, and joy in the Holy Ghost" (Rom. 14:17). Paul wrote that God gave us the Spirit, *"That the righteousness of the [moral] law might be fulfilled in us, who walk not after the flesh, but after the Spirit"* (Rom. 8:4).

Any influences then, which are contrary to righteousness and holiness, could not have come from God, for God's Holy Spirit, the Spirit of Truth, is leading us into holiness, and will never lead contrary to truth or holiness. *"As obedient children, not fashioning yourselves according to the former lusts in your ignorance: But as he which hath called you is holy, so be ye holy in all manner of conversation; Because it is written, Be ye holy; for I am holy"* (1 Pet. 1:14-16). And remember, there are only two kingdoms from which influences can come. There is no third kingdom. So, *"...if the firstfruit be holy, the lump is also holy: and if the root be holy, so are the branches"* (Rom. 11:16). (That is, whatever comes forth out of it.) But, if the root is unholy, so (also) will be the branches and its fruit. So, there are two kingdoms: Satan's and God's, and they are direct opposites, and the fruit of each one is self evident. Either "the fruits of righteousness, which are by Jesus Christ," or the "unfruitful works of darkness" from the enemy. Everything falls under one of the two categories (Phil. 1:11; Eph. 5:11-12).

Jesus Christ said in Matthew 7:15-21, *"Beware of false prophets [and false teachers, 2 Pet. 2:1], which come to you in sheep's clothing, but inwardly they are ravening wolves. Ye shall know them by their fruits. Do men gather grapes of thorns, or figs of thistles? Even so every good tree bringeth forth good fruit; but a corrupt tree bringeth forth evil fruit. A **good tree cannot** bring forth evil fruit, neither can a corrupt tree bring forth good fruit. Every tree that bringeth not forth good fruit is hewn down, and cast into the fire. Wherefore by their fruits ye shall know them. Not every one that saith unto me, Lord, Lord, shall enter into the kingdom of heaven; but he that doeth the will of my Father which is in heaven."* Their fruit is what they say, teach, and do, and tell others they can do. Anyone who doesn't teach holiness and righteousness in agreement with the Apostolic Doctrine, but teaches that grace will **automatically** cover for known sin, is being used by the serpent to influence people to disobey God and what His Word actually says (Jude 3,4).

First John 3:7-8 says, *"Little children, let no man deceive you: he that doeth righteousness is righteous, even as he is righteous. He that committeth sin is of the devil; for the devil sinneth from the beginning. For this purpose the Son of God was manifested, that he might destroy the works of the devil."* Jesus, as we've stated, came to set us totally free from a life of sin and Satan (John 8:34-36; Titus 2:11-14).

Paul wrote to Christians, *"Know ye not, that to whom ye yield yourselves servants to obey,* **his servants ye are** *to whom ye obey; whether of sin unto death, or of obedience unto righteousness? But God be thanked, that ye were the servants of sin, but ye have obeyed from the heart that form of doctrine which was delivered you. Being then made free from sin, ye became the servants of righteousness"* (Rom. 6:16-18). Christians then, are free from slavery to a life of sin, and so must stand fast in this liberty (2 Pet. 2:20-21).

Christianity is people using their God-given free will to turn from Satan back to God; from a life of sin to a life of righteousness, empowered by the Holy Spirit, the Spirit of Grace, to do so. It is living a new life following after the Spirit and no longer following or living a life after the flesh, for *"if ye live [a sinful life] after the flesh, ye shall die"* (Rom. 8:1-14).

"For the flesh lusteth against the Spirit, and the Spirit against the flesh: and these are contrary the one to the other: so that ye cannot do the things that ye would. But if ye be led of the Spirit, ye are not under the law. Now the works of the flesh are manifest, which are these; Adultery, fornication, uncleanness, lasciviousness, idolatry, witchcraft, hatred, variance, emulations, wrath, strife, seditions, heresies, envyings, murders, drunkenness, revellings, and such like: of the which I tell you before, as I have also told you in time past, that **they which do such things shall not inherit the kingdom of God.** *But the fruit of the Spirit is love, joy, peace, longsuffering, gentleness, goodness, faith, meekness, temperance: against such there is no law. And they that are Christ's have crucified the flesh with the affections and lusts. If we live in the Spirit, let us also walk in the Spirit"* (Gal. 5:17-25).

To be saved and stay saved, a person must turn to the Lord, and then follow Him throughout their life. *"For ye were as sheep going astray; but are now returned unto the Shepherd and Bishop of your souls"* (1 Pet. 2:25). And He, the Good Shepherd, *"leads us in paths of righteousness for his name's sake"* (Ps. 23:3). And He said in John's Gospel that His real sheep follow Him, and whoever really follows Him in these paths of righteousness enabled by His grace, will have eternal life. He says to them, *"Be thou faithful unto death and I will give you a crown of life"* (Rev. 2:10).

*"For [the apostle writes] we are made partakers of Christ, **if** we hold the beginning of our confidence stedfast unto the end"* (Heb. 3:14). (Of course, we know a prodigal could also repent and return.) *"Then said one unto him, Lord, are there few that be saved? And he said unto them, Strive to enter in at the strait gate: for many, I say unto you, will seek to enter in, and shall not be able"* (Luke 13:23-24). *"Wherefore we receiving a kingdom which cannot be moved, let us have grace, whereby we may serve God acceptably with reverence and godly fear: For our God is a consuming fire"* (Heb. 12:28-29). Christians are followers of Christ.

The Covenant Agreement

God said, *"**For this is the covenant** that I will make with the house of Israel after those days, saith the Lord; **I will put my laws into their mind, and write them in their hearts:** and I will be to them a God, and they shall be to me a people"* (Heb. 8:10). *"A new heart also will I give you, and a new spirit will I put within you: and I will take away the stony heart out of your flesh, and I will give you an heart of flesh. And I will put my spirit within you, **and cause you to walk in my statutes, and ye shall keep my judgments, and do them**"*(Ezek. 36:26-27). This is the New Covenant. *"That the righteousness of the law might be fulfilled in us, who walk not after the flesh, but after the Spirit"* (Rom. 8:4). Scripture says in the book of Revelation, *"And the dragon was wroth with the woman, and went to make war [using deceptions, wiles and false beliefs] with the remnant of her seed, **which keep the commandments of God, and have the testimony of Jesus Christ** "* (Rev. 12:17). Satan is ever working to deceive the world, and he especially hates and works to deceive the body of Christ, to try and persuade them to not keep the commandments of God (as are recorded in the New Covenant), just as he did in the beginning with Adam and Eve, the first created son and daughter of God.

Four thousand or so years after Adam and Eve failed to keep God's commandment and lost out on the tree of life, the New Covenant says, *"**Blessed are they that do his commandments, that they may have right to the tree of life,** and may enter in through the gates into the city"* (Rev. 22:14). God's plan, then, has not changed. Scripture also says, *"Here is the patience of the saints: here are they **that keep the commandments of God, and the faith of Jesus**"* (Rev. 14:12). And again, *"He that hath an ear, let him **hear what the Spirit saith unto the churches;** To him that overcometh [the devil, the pollutions of the world, and the flesh] will I give to eat of the tree of life, which is in the midst of the paradise of God"* (Rev. 2:7). (See also Rom. 8:12-13; 2 Pet. 2:20-21; 1 John 2:14-17, 5:4; Rev. 12:11.) You can see by these above passages that the commandments of God and the faith of Jesus are directly connected to one another, and keeping them by faith is what will give us the privilege of partaking of the tree of life.

Dear Reader, the same battle rages today as in the beginning. Satan, being the father of sin and of all rebels, is ever working through lies, deceptions, and false doctrines, to not only keep the world deceived, but also to get men who had turned away from him and turned to God to use their wills and submit to his authority once again. He has started many false doctrines in the professing church world that okay sin, or imply that men do not need to repent of sin knowingly committed. For he knows that for a person to submit to a lifestyle of sin is to yield them-selves to him as an authority in their life just as Adam did in the begin-ning (Rom. 5:12; Heb. 2:14; John 8:44; 1 John 3:4-18). This he knows will tie them to his miserable, final judgment. As we've said, Paul wrote to Christians, *"Know ye not, that to whom ye yield yourselves servants to obey,* **his servants ye are to whom ye obey"** (Rom. 6:16). Jesus said, *"Verily, verily, I say unto you, Whosoever committeth sin is **the servant of sin**.... If the Son therefore shall make you free [from being sin's servant], ye shall be free indeed"* (John 8:34,36). Scripture states, *"Who His own self bare our sins in his own body on the tree, **that we, being dead to sins, should live unto righteousness: by whose stripes ye were healed"*** (1 Pet. 2:24).

Sin is rebellion against God and there is no such thing as a God-given grace that will automatically cover for rebellion against God, or automatically cover for future rebellion against God as some imply. Things have not changed. No man can serve two masters. Jesus came to set us free from the power of sin and Satan, and to give us the grace we'd need so we would be able to keep His commandments, walk in His ways, and serve Him. Christ said, *"My grace is sufficient for thee, my strength is made perfect in weakness"* (2 Cor. 12:9). The apostle John wrote, *"And hereby [by this] we do know that we [really] know Him, if we keep his com-mandments. He that saith, I know him, and keepeth not his commandments, is a liar, and the truth is not in him"* (1 John 2:3-4). So everything we believe to be true about grace and the New Covenant must also line up with these, as well as all of the other scriptures in the New Covenant, which are in this new contract that God has given to mankind.

The apostle Peter wrote to Christians, *"Be sober, be vigilant; because your adversary the devil, as a roaring lion, walketh about, seeking whom he may devour: Whom resist steadfast in the faith"* (1 Pet. 5:8-9). How does he destroy people? God said, *"My people are destroyed for lack of knowledge..."* (Hosea

4:6). That is a lack of the true knowledge of God (2 Pet. 1:2-4). Satan preys upon ignorance. The apostle Peter, in his epistle to the church, warned against false teachings and false teachers who were sent out by the enemy to deceive the church, and to lead them astray from the true way of God, which is the way of righteousness and holiness, *"And many shall follow their pernicious ways; by reason of whom the way of truth shall be evil spoken of"* (2 Pet. 2:2). (See 2 Peter 2:19-22.) Scripture says, *"And an highway shall be there, and a way, and it shall be called **The way of holiness;** the unclean shall not pass over it [to Zion]; but it shall be for those: the wayfaring men, though fools, shall not err therein. No lion shall be there, nor any ravenous beast shall go up thereon, it shall not be found there; **but the redeemed shall walk there: And the ransomed of the** LORD **shall return [on this highway],** and come to Zion with songs and everlasting joy upon their heads: they shall obtain joy and gladness, and sorrow and sighing shall flee away"* (Isa. 35:8-10). Paul wrote that "Without (pursuing) holiness **no man** shall see the Lord" (Heb. 12:14). For "Narrow is the road that leads to life" (Matt. 7:14).

The apostle Peter made it clear that false teachers influenced by deceiving spirits are here among us, just as there were false prophets in Israel sent out to deceive the people and to turn them away from the words and counsel of God (Deut. 13:1-6). The apostle further says, *"Ye therefore, beloved, seeing ye know these things before, beware lest ye also, being led away with the error of the wicked [who teach that you could live wrong and still go to heaven, 2 Pet. 2:1-22], fall from your own steadfastness. But grow in grace, and in the [true] knowledge of our Lord and Savior Jesus Christ. To him be glory both now and for ever. Amen"* (2 Pet. 3:17-18). This was Peter's warning to the church about false teachers who were sent out by the enemy to deceive the church. Knowing that our adversary, Satan, is a master deceiver and a counterfeiter, and is still up to his same old tricks; and knowing that he has sent out into the professing church world, numerous false prophets and teachers with many false teachings and doctrines, let's look at the word "counterfeit", and see what it means. For it is vitally important for us to expose his workings and his doctrines.

Counterfeit

A counterfeit is "an imitation of something genuine so as to deceive or defraud"; "Something false that seemingly, on the surface, so closely resembles something true that it can deceive those who are not skilled at detecting it"; "Something that assumes the appearance of something else, but is deceptive, fraudulent, and a deluding unreality." Satan works to *"capture the imagination,"* and blind people's minds to the (real) truth that sets men free from him and his kingdom; and he mostly does his works through men that he's already deceived (2 Cor. 4:3-4). In speaking to Christians, Paul writes, *"For though we walk in the flesh, we do not war after the flesh: (For the weapons of our warfare are not carnal, but mighty through God to the pulling down of strong holds.) Casting down imaginations [reasonings], and every high thing [and false teaching] that exalteth itself against the [whole] knowledge of God, and bringing into captivity every thought to the obedience of Christ"* (2 Cor. 10:3-5). We can see then that the real battleground is the mind, and that this is where Satan works to plant his wrong beliefs. We are to cast down everything that comes to us, regardless of the source, that is contrary to the true knowledge of God as is found in *all* of the scriptures in the New Covenant. We are admonished to overcome the devil and his schemes, just like Jesus did with what is actually "written" (Matt. 4:1-11).

Dear Reader, there are multitudes of false beliefs in the earth coming clothed as the way of God or as the truth, deceiving billions of people right now, at this very moment, and none of these people would want to admit that they were one of those who were deceived. The old serpent is still preying on ignorance and destroying Adam's seed with lies, just as he did with the father and mother of the human race (Gen. 3:20). Let us then be sober and be on guard.

Lucifer

Lucifer, (also called Satan and the devil), since the time of his downfall has always desired to be in the position of God. God says in scripture, *"How art thou fallen from heaven, O Lucifer, son of the morning! How art thou cut down to the ground, which didst weaken the nations! For thou hast said in thine heart,* **I will** *ascend into heaven,* **I will** *exalt my throne above the stars of God:* **I will** *sit also upon the mount of the congregation, in the sides of the north:* **I will** *ascend above the heights of the clouds;* **I will be like the most High***. Yet thou shalt be brought down to hell, to the sides of the pit"* (Isa. 14:12-15).

Since the time he set his will in opposition to God's will, Satan has not only desired worship from others (Luke 4:7), but in wanting to be in the position of God, he has sought to counterfeit all that God does. The difference is, Satan perverts and corrupts all that he touches, while all that comes from God is pure and holy (James 3:17-18). Paul wrote, *"If the root be holy, so are the branches."* (That is, whatever comes out from it, Rom. 11:16.) Jesus said, *"Even so every good tree bringeth forth good fruit;*

*but a corrupt tree bringeth forth evil fruit. A good tree **cannot** bring forth evil fruit; neither **can a corrupt** tree bring forth good fruit. Every tree that bringeth not forth good fruit is hewn down, and cast into the fire. Wherefore by their fruits ye shall know them. Not every one **that** [just] **saith** unto me, Lord, Lord, shall enter into the kingdom of heaven; **but he that** [produces good fruit and] **doeth the will** of my Father which is in heaven"* (Matt. 7:17-21). What is the final product of a person's or church's teaching? Does it agree with the fruit of the (Holy) Spirit and the righteousness of God (Gal. 5:22-24), or does it produce or okay the unfruitful *works* of darkness? (Eph. 5:11). Does it exhort you to be obedient to God's Word and will, or give you excuses as to why you could live unrighteously? By this you can tell its real source, for the real truth will never lead you into believing you could live in moral pollution, and each tree is clearly recognized and known by its fruit (2 Pet. 1:3-4).

God has His Son, the Lord Jesus Christ, and Satan will have his *antichrist*. God gave us the (Holy) Bible, and Satan has produced, through evil and deceived men, a satanic bible, and other seemingly spiritual books and false religions in order to obtain worship. God has apostles and ministers, and Satan has sent out false apostles and false ministers. The apostle Paul wrote, *"For such are false apostles, deceitful workers, transforming themselves into the apostles of Christ. And no marvel; for Satan himself is transformed into an angel of light. Therefore it is no great thing if **his ministers** also be transformed [and come masquerading] as the ministers of righteousness; whose end shall be according to their works"* (2 Cor. 11:13-15). These so-called ministers, Paul revealed, came preaching "another" Jesus and "another" gospel, different from what he preached (2 Cor. 11:4). And the apostle wrote, *"But I fear (that just) as Eve was beguiled by the craftiness of the serpent, so your mind's (and imaginations) should be corrupted (with false beliefs about things) and you should (thereby) be seduced (away by the serpent) from your single-minded faithfulness to Christ"* (Conybeare's Translation of Paul's Epistles). Paul further wrote, *"But though we, or an angel from heaven, preach any other gospel unto you than that which we have [already] preached unto you, let him be accursed"* (Gal. 1:8). You see, it has always really been a battle of good against evil, lies against the truth, and counterfeits against the real. God sends His Holy Word to free us from sin and the negative effects of the Fall, and Satan works to steal, twist, or pervert it to keep people bound in sin and bondage.

The apostle Peter wrote, *"But there were false prophets [influenced by the devil] among the people [in the Old Covenant trying to lead the people astray from the true way of the Lord, Deut. 13:1-6] even as **there shall be false***

teachers among you [the church, who will try to persuade you to believe false doctrines, and persuade you to depart from the true *"way of right-eousness"*] 2 Pet. 2:1-2, 19-21. *"Now the [Holy] Spirit speaketh expressly, that **in the latter times some shall depart from the faith** [the whole Word and counsel of God], **giving heed [instead] to seducing spirits,** and doctrines of devils"* (1 Tim. 4:1; Prov. 19:21). Satan is still at work in the twenty-first century.

Scripture says, *"Woe to the inhabitants of the earth and of the sea for the devil is come down unto you having great wrath because he knoweth that he hath but a short time"* (Rev. 12:12). And remember, his main method of destruction is deception. There will, therefore, be much deception at the end of this age (Matt. 24:3, 5-11). Paul wrote, *"But evil men and seducers shall wax worse and worse, deceiving, and being deceived"* (2 Tim. 3:13).

Yes, Satan seems to be working overtime to corrupt and destroy all that is good and holy, and even more so now that we are drawing near-er to the end of this world as we know it (Isa. 60:2). He is ever working to discredit Christianity and the right ways of the Lord.

Let's continue.

Satan never ceases to pervert the right ways of the Lord. I'll point out a few more examples.

God, in His goodness, gave sex for marriage, and Satan perverts it and gets people into all manner of fornication, adultery and other per-versions telling them that this is okay. He says, "Do what you want, it's your life. You don't need to obey God's will. If it feels good it can't be wrong; this is just making *love*. Ssssss." And by their believing that it's okay to do as they please, he has ruined families, destroyed multitudes with disease, caused emotional breakdowns, and has brought about mil-lions of abortions of unwanted infants. He persuades people that sin and bondage is freedom. God sent the Holy Spirit with His spiritual gifts and placed them in the church for the benefit of mankind, and Satan has sent out his evil spirits to work all manner of deception through fortune tellers, psychics, divination, New Age activity, and so on, and then he works to persuade the professing church world that the true gifts of the Holy Spirit have all passed away (1 Cor. 12:1-11). God sent out true apos-tles. Satan sent out false ones. God sent out true teachers. Satan sent out false ones. God sent out real prophets, and Satan, in turn, has sent out false ones or denied the reality of God-ordained prophets (Eph. 4:11-12).

Satan does the same kind of thing with the wonderful life-changing grace of God, which delivers us from our state of moral weakness and enables us to live for God and His will (Heb. 12:28). Satan has perverted it, changed its meaning, and has promoted a counterfeit grace that doesn't produce holiness, but, rather, tells people that grace means they can now live in sin, disobey God's commands, grieve the Holy Spirit, and still remain secure with God, for they say, it's "unmerited favor" (Jude 3-4,12; James 4:4; Rom. 11:22). He says to people now, as he implied to Adam and Eve in days gone by, that obedience to God is not *really* necessary in order to receive from, and be like, God (Heb. 5:9; 2 Thess. 1:7-8), but, the scriptures of truth clearly teach otherwise. (See also 2 Pet. 1:3-12.) Let me remind you again of what Jesus said, *"A good tree cannot bring forth evil fruit, neither can a corrupt tree bring forth good fruit.... Wherefore by their fruits ye shall know them"* (Matt. 7:18,20). *"And now also the axe is laid unto the root of the trees: therefore every tree which bringeth not forth good fruit is hewn down, and cast into the fire"* (Matt. 3:10). Every tree (and doctrine) therefore, is known by its fruits (what grows out of it), and by this, we can tell its true source.

Grace and Sin, Opposing Forces
Studying God's Word with an Open Heart

In order to find out the truth, Jesus admonished us to *"search the scriptures,"* and to continue in His Word. We should then be like those in Berea, *"These were more noble than those in Thessalonica, in that they received the word with all readiness of mind, and searched the scriptures daily, whether those things were so"* (Acts 17:11). All we ask is that you search the scriptures with us concerning this important, biblical topic and take a clearer look at what the scriptures truly say about God's wonderful grace. If you do so, you will see that grace and sin are opposing forces from opposite sources and you will clearly understand what God's grace really is and what it can do for you. Grace, we will see, is the unmerited power of God working on our behalf to bring about good fruit in one's life; while sin, an opposite force, is directly connected to the power and working of the devil who is ever working to corrupt and pollute human beings. He is called, *"The prince of the power of the air, the spirit that now worketh in the children of disobedience"* (that is, disobedient people, Eph. 2:2; 1 John 3:8; John 8:44). This is the mystery of iniquity. It is Satan who works to produce *"the unfruitful works of darkness"* (Eph. 5:11). Where you see iniquity, you see Satan at work. It is vitally important then that one have the clear and full definition of a Bible topic if he is to end up with the truth. For if a person builds his belief on a wrong or partial definition of a word in scripture, then everything else they say from that point on, is either wrong or just partially true. They then build all their discourses on a wrong foundation, and if their foundation is not truly on the Rock of God's Word, it is built on shifting sand (Matt. 7:24-27).

We will prove to you by the scriptures that grace is the unmerited provision, power, and influence of God, which can totally change us and make us strong where before we were weak, and that grace is not unmerited or unconditional favor, as has been widely accepted in a certain portion of professing Christendom (1 Cor. 15:10). This full definition of Bible grace makes all the difference in the world in understanding the Bible doctrine about grace. By seeing grace as such, you will also see how all of the New Testament harmonizes, and how every statement and warning made by Christ and the apostles is absolutely true and binding. None of them can be discarded. No part of this Covenant is insignificant.

When reading this treatise on true grace and false grace, please realize that we fully believe in God's great kindness toward us; we believe in being born again by the work of the Holy Spirit; and we also have faith in His longsuffering, His love, and His abundant mercy. We know that God instantly forgives every prodigal that repents and that He will forgive His people seventy times seven, even in a single day, if they ask Him to. We fully realize that we can only be saved by mercy and grace, for no one could ever merit what God has given to us in this New Covenant. It is also obvious that no man can spiritually regenerate and deliver himself from the power of Satan and sin, regardless of how many religious works he does in his unregenerate state. We understand that God has provided the blood of Jesus to wash away sins and set up Christ as our great High Priest and Advocate in the event a Christian does sin (1 John 2:1). We don't believe that one unconfessed sin will send a Christian to hell, nor that every time a Christian misses it that God withdraws from their lives as some thought was being said.

We know that scripture says that He gives, *"space to repent"*; *"His goodness leadeth us to repentance"*; and He is *"longsuffering to usward not willing that any should perish but that all should come to repentance."* We understand that He has great love toward us for He *"demonstrated His love toward us in that while we were yet sinners, Christ died for us."* We know that as long as a person is willing to walk with Him, He will walk with them (John 6:66); and that if we *"draw nigh unto God,"* He will *"draw nigh unto us."* Furthermore, we believe that we are saved by grace; kept by grace; overcome sin by grace; work by grace; and serve God by grace. But in any study of God's Word we must ask ourselves, "Am I willing to take every statement in the teaching of Christ at face value?" Can we read all of His teachings on every subject in the Gospels and His teaching through the apostles and look at every verse and say, "I believe that"? This is an important question (Jude 3), for all the teaching in scripture comes from the same Lord who is *"the same yesterday, and today, and forever."* And if the Christ of Christianity never changes, then true Christianity is exactly the same today as is recorded in all of the scriptures (1 Cor. 14:37; 1 Tim. 6:3-4). And although professing Christendom is divided into numerous groups, there really is only *"one Lord,"* and *"one faith,"* and *"one hope,"* of our calling, and Jesus is both *"the author and the finisher of our faith"* (Eph. 4:4-6; Heb. 12:2; Matt. 28:20). If a person cannot believe *every* statement made by Christ and the apostles as true and binding, then they have wrongly divided God's Word. For God's truth, when rightly divided, will never contradict itself. The New Testament in its entirety then is *"the faith"* that was once delivered to the saints (Jude 3). Nothing whatsoever can be added to it nor taken away from it. It is a complete Covenant and document that must stand as is, given to us by a perfect God who has given to us all we need to know about the mystery of His will in it (Eph. 1:9; Heb. 13:20-21). It reveals both what He's done for us and what His present will and requirements are concerning us (Matt. 28:20, 24:14).

A Problem in the Body

A big problem seen in the body of Christ or in professing Christendom, is that certain groups of people, denominations, teachers, or leaders will systematically take out of the Bible all of the verses that they, or their group like, such as John 3:16 or Ephesians 2:8, along with other verses that promise something, or reveal what God said He would do, and they build all of their doctrines on them. But they also systematically leave out or reject all the other verses that present the conditions of the Covenant and the commands of Jesus Christ that do not agree with them. So, they thereby leave out the responsibility of man to obey God and His Word in order to obtain the promised blessings. James 1:22 says, *"But be ye doers of the word, and not hearers only, deceiving your own selves."* So, leaving out man's responsibility to obey God's Word will never work in God's sight. Such teachings that leave out man's responsibility to obey the Word produce a lopsided view of things, but sadly, gain numerous followers who are ignorant of the whole counsel of God as is revealed in the whole Covenant in the scriptures; and they will, because of their ignorance, even fight for their right to remain in darkness and error (Hosea 4:6; 2 Tim. 2:24-26). Many seem to want to take the broad and easy road of sin and no responsibility, rather than obey God and keep their body in subjection as the apostles did.

Seeing that there are so many views on grace in different camps within professing Christendom, only one can really be true. Two plus two can never equal five. Any view of grace that doesn't believe in, nor accept, all of the teachings, instructions, conditions, and warnings of the New Covenant as absolute facts in all of the scriptures is wrong. No certain scripture or groups of passages are an island to themselves, nor does any one passage *or word* paint the whole picture of the Covenant and its conditions. It is all together one complete picture. We cannot trust one passage of scripture while ignoring or rejecting others. You cannot therefore, base all of your beliefs on just one word. For as we've stated, the scriptures never contradict themselves. *"All scripture is given by inspiration of [the same] God, and is profitable **for doctrine, for reproof, for correction, for instruction in righteousness: that the man of God may be perfect, thoroughly furnished unto all good works"*** (2 Tim. 3:16-17). Christ said, *"He that rejecteth me, and receiveth not my words, hath one that judgeth him: the word that I have spoken, the same shall judge him in the last day"* (John 12:48). He also said, *"The scriptures cannot be broken."* He further said, *"Heaven and earth shall pass away, but my words shall not pass away"* (Matt. 24:35). So it is vitally important that we believe the Word, the whole Word, and nothing but the Word, to really be safe and secure. Seeing then, that we face such a formidable foe, who, coming clothed as an angel of light, constantly works to deceive men away from the true way of the Lord, we have had it on our heart to write this book. All we ask is that you believe all of what the New Covenant says, and take the scriptures at face value, and realize that all of it must harmonize or something is wrong with one's belief, for *"God is not the author of confusion"* (1 Cor. 14:33).

Heresies

Let me explain what heresies are, as far as the Christian faith is concerned, and how people get into them.

Obviously, no one with right motives wants to be involved in heresy, or be called a heretic, and so most of the time it is unintentional. Usually people are deceived into believing them through a lack of knowledge of the real truth of God's Word (Matt. 13:18-19). The definition of heresy is "a religious belief opposed to the orthodox doctrines of Christianity"; "a rejection of a belief that is a part of the Christian faith as is revealed in scripture"; "any opinion or philosophy opposed to the teachings of Christ or the Apostles' Doctrine." I believe every true Christian can agree with this definition.

The true starting point for any church or Christian then should be that the whole New Covenant is true and that it's all for us today (Matt. 24:14, 28:19-20); that it's given to us by God to obey (Rom. 10:16; Heb. 5:9; 2 Thess. 1:8); and that it is *the faith that was once delivered to the saints* (Jude 3). If one will not accept the whole counsel of God in this way, they are building their beliefs on just a partial foundation, and Satan will use this to his advantage (1 Pet. 1:23-25).

Referring again to what the apostle Peter wrote in his letter to the church, let us quote this scripture, *"But there were false prophets also among the people, even as there shall be false teachers among you [Christians], who privily shall bring in damnable heresies, even denying the Lord that bought them, and bring upon themselves swift destruction. And **many** shall follow their pernicious [morally loose and fatal] ways; by reason of whom the [real] way of truth shall be evil spoken of"* (2 Pet. 2:1-2). Weys translation says that these false teachers will "cunningly introduce (and bring into the church) fatal heresies." Notice, he also said, *many* will follow these false teachers and their fatal heresies thinking they are being taught the truth, and will even speak evil of God's true way of righteousness because of this. (See Matt. 23:13-28.) This is not a small issue but a major problem in the professing body of Christ. Perhaps millions will end up in hell thinking they were going to heaven because of fatal heresies.

The Doctrine of Christ

John the Apostle wrote, *"Whosoever transgresseth, and abideth not in the doctrine of Christ, hath not God. He that abideth in the doctrine of Christ, he hath both the Father and the Son"* (2 John 9).

Let's look at three words in this passage: "Transgresses" means "overstepping, or going beyond the limits set by the Word"; "to violate (God's) law": saying things contrary to what Christ taught, or assuming things beyond what's actually written. Remember, Christ's words are *the truth*," and "***the perfect law of liberty***," so anything contrary to them is a lie and will bring bondage (John 8:12, 31-32; James 1:22-25; 2 Tim. 2:24-26).

"Doctrine" means "instructions, teachings, and principles."

"Abideth" means "to continue on in without changing"; "to remain in and agree with"; "to adhere to."

Let's look at it now all together. *"Whosoever [whatever man or group of people] transgresseth [oversteps and goes beyond the limits set by the Word of God saying things contrary to what Christ and the apostles actually taught] and abideth not in [doesn't remain in agreement with and adhere to) the doctrine (instructions, teachings and principles] of Christ hath not God. He that abideth in [remains in agreement with and adheres to] the doctrines [teachings, instructions and principles] of Christ, he hath both the Father and the Son"* (2 John 9).

Jesus told His followers to beware of the leaven (the manmade religious doctrines) of the Pharisees and Sadducees (that is, the religious leaders and teachers). They were supposedly God's representatives and the spiritual teachers of Israel, but they exchanged the truth of God's Word for their own ideas and doctrines, and by this led multitudes into so much darkness that they even rejected and crucified the Messiah whom they professed to believe in. This warning is the same today as always, so beware: for men and their committees still add to, and take away from, God's written Word, just as the Pharisees of old did. Human beings have not changed.

True Doctrine

Read carefully these following scriptures concerning the Lord's true doctrine that He left us. *"Jesus answered them, and said, **My doctrine is not mine, but his that sent me. If any man will do his will, he shall know** of the doctrine, whether it be of God, or whether I speak of myself. He that speaketh of himself seeketh his own glory: but he that seeketh his glory that sent him, the same is true, and no unrighteousness is in him"* (John 7:16-18). Notice, He revealed that if any man is truly willing to obey God's will, this man will know of the doctrine and that it's really from God. A willingness to obey the truth received is a prerequisite to seeing the Lord's true doctrine. Solomon wrote under inspiration of God, instructions from God concerning how to receive light from His Word, *"My son, if thou wilt receive my words, and hide my commandments with thee; So that thou incline thine ear unto wisdom, and apply thine heart to understanding; **Yea, if thou criest after knowledge, and liftest up thy voice for understanding; If thou seekest her as silver, and searchest for her as for hid treasures; Then shalt thou understand** the fear of the Lord, **and find** the knowledge of God. For the Lord giveth wisdom: out of his mouth cometh knowledge and understanding. He layeth up sound wisdom for the righteous: He is a buckler **to them that walk uprightly**. He keepeth the paths of judgment, and preserveth the way of his saints [His separated ones]. **Then shalt thou understand righteousness, and*** *judgment, and equity; yea, every good path"* (Prov. 2:1-9). Now, if people teach things contrary to Christ and the apostles and what is actually written in the scriptures, or leave out whole portions of scripture, they knowingly, or ignorantly, are influencing you to follow them and their sect and belief, and not Christ, the true light. They, therefore, that leave Christ's and the apostles' actual sayings, seek not God's glory but their own, and seek to hold you captive to their denomination, group, or system of beliefs, rather than give to you the true knowledge and counsel of God.

If a person fulfills the condition of having a willingness to obey all of God's will as is recorded in the scriptures, then that person will find the true knowledge of God's Word, and will see and receive the light of the real truth that is in it (James 1:21). The Word will then be a lamp unto his feet, and a light unto his path. Scripture says, *"Light is sown for the righteous."* The Bible also says, *"Blessed are they which do hunger and thirst after righteousness: **for they** [alone] shall be filled"* (Matt. 5:6). On the other hand scripture says, *"And for this cause God shall send them [who are not willing] strong delusion, that they should believe a lie: That they all might be damned who believed not the [real] truth [which Paul said is always according to godliness], **but had pleasure in unrighteousness"*** (2 Thess. 2:11-12). If your heart desires to live a life of sin and unrighteousness, you will be in position to be deceived by teachers that will tickle your ears (2 Tim. 4:1-4). God will permit to come to you what you want. You must realize that God's real truth always produces godliness (Titus 1:1), and this is what the scriptures say we are to follow after, in order to lay hold on eternal life (1 Tim. 6:11-12; Heb. 12:14). Friend, we must continue to pursue God, His will, and a life of holiness in order to receive more light from God. If we don't continue to pursue these things, we are, as Peter said, *"blind and cannot see afar off,"* and are headed for more and more darkness. (See 2 Pet. 1:4-9 for proof of this.)

Jesus' Words Still Stand True

Jesus said, *"He that rejecteth me, and receiveth not my words, hath one that judgeth him: **the word that I have spoken, the same shall judge him in the last day.** For I have not spoken of myself; but the Father which sent me, he gave me a commandment, what I should say, and what I should speak"* (John 12:48-49). What Christ said then, in both the Gospels and the epistles, is of utmost importance for He will have the final word in the last day. His Word is unchangeable. The Lord says, *"My covenant will I not break, nor alter the thing that is gone out of my lips"* (Ps. 89:34). When people contradict or nullify any of the words of God, they are then, not following God, but rather, opposing God. Some influenced by wrong teaching have even said that we need not obey Jesus, yet God said, *"This is my beloved Son, **hear him.**"* After the resurrection of Christ, Peter testified to the people, *"For Moses truly said unto the fathers, A prophet shall the Lord your God raise up unto you of your brethren, like unto me; **him shall ye hear in all things whatsoever he shall say unto you**.*

*"And it shall come to pass, that every soul, which will not hear that prophet, **shall be destroyed** from among the people"* (Acts 3:22-23). (See also Matt. 7:24-27, where Jesus admonished us to obey what He said, or be a fool heading for destruction and ruin.)

Jesus, **after His resurrection** said to His disciples, *"Go ye therefore, and teach all nations, baptizing them in the name of the Father, and of the Son, and of the Holy Ghost: **Teaching them to observe** [adhere to and abide by] **all things whatsoever I have commanded you**: and, lo, I am with you alway, even unto the end of the world. Amen"* (Matt. 28:19-20). All things that Christ commanded the early church and disciples then, we are also to obey and teach others word for word, and never contradict anything that He taught. We are only given authority to say exactly what He said about any Bible subject. No more, no less. When His disciples asked Him about **His second coming and the end of the world**, He said, *"**This gospel** of the kingdom [the same Gospel that He was preaching and is recorded in the Gospels] shall be preached in all the world for a witness unto all nations; and then shall the end come"* (Matt. 24:14).

Luke wrote, *"The former treatise have I made, O Theophilus, of all that Jesus began both to do and teach, **Until the day in which he was taken up, after that he through the Holy Ghost had given commandments** unto the apostles whom he had chosen"* (Acts 1:1-2). He gave His chosen apostles *His commandments* both before and after His resurrection to instruct His church even unto the end of the world and here is the result: *"And they [the disciples] **continued steadfastly in the apostles' doctrine**"* (Acts 2:42). Always check out what you're believing and make sure it's in complete agreement with all of Christ and the Apostles' Doctrine. For there is, on the one hand, the true teaching and doctrine of Christ, while anything contrary to it, or that adds to it, or takes away anything from it, is a doctrine of devils, or the doctrines and commandments of men. Rituals, clichés, ceremonies, and statements of belief not actually found in God's Word, are man's doing and not God's. Christ said, *"But in vain they do worship me, teaching for doctrines commandments of men"* (Matt. 15:9). The same would go for those who omit whole portions of scripture in order to hold fast to their own beliefs (Deut. 4:2).

The Doctrine of God

*"Now I beseech you, brethren, **mark them which cause divisions and offences contrary to the doctrine** [of the apostles] which ye have learned; and **avoid them. For they that are such serve not our Lord Jesus Christ**, but their own belly [their own selfish motives]; and by good words and fair speeches deceive the hearts of the simple"* (Rom. 16:17-18). If they are not willing to stay right with all Christ taught then they are not His servants, but really want to gather their own followers, just as the apostle Paul said some would in Acts 20:30: *"Also of your own selves shall men arise, speaking perverse things, to draw away disciples after them."* And in 2 Corinthians, *"And no marvel; for Satan himself is transformed into an angel of light. Therefore it is no great thing if his ministers also be transformed [and come masquerading] as the ministers of righteousness; whose end shall be according to their works"* (2 Cor. 11:14-15). There are many that fall into this category.

Paul said that we need to grow up in Christ and be established in the truth, *"That we henceforth be no more children, tossed to and fro, and carried about with every **wind of doctrine**, by the sleight of men [and their ability to deceive others], and [their] cunning craftiness [their sly ingenuity at inventing errors and making it look like truth], whereby they lie in wait [like a hungry lion waiting for its prey] to deceive"* (Eph. 4:14), and devour the unsuspecting, (1 Pet. 5:8). Paul wrote, *"As I besought thee to abide still at Ephesus, when I went into Macedonia, that thou mightest charge some that they **teach no other doctrine**"* (1 Tim. 1:3). Do not teach anything other than what is actually written, but teach people to believe all that is written (Luke 24:25). Because men or their religious committees have chosen to believe just certain parts of the Bible while rejecting other things in scripture, there has come great divisions in the body of Christ, and these lopsided, false doctrines then control the beliefs of multitudes, and are sending many people to hell. Woe be to those teachers who are responsible for causing people to stumble away from the right ways of the Lord (Ezek. 3:18-19).

God says through His apostle, *"Take heed unto thyself, and unto the doctrine; continue in them: for in doing this thou shalt both save thyself, and them that hear thee"* (1 Tim. 4:16). We can see then how important it is to continue in the true doctrine of the Lord. We are not to continue in a certain person's, or denomination's doctrine, but in Christ and the Apostles' Doctrine. Only this alone guarantees salvation. No man can save you on that day, so we must live by God's instructions and not man's. We are admonished by the apostle to *"Prove all things; hold fast that which is good"* (1 Thess. 5:21).

The apostle Paul wrote, ***"If any man teach otherwise, and consent not to wholesome words**, even the words of our Lord Jesus Christ, **and to the doctrine which is [always] according to godliness; He is proud, knowing nothing**, but doting about questions and strifes of words, whereof cometh envy, strife, railings, evil surmisings"* (1 Tim. 6:3-4). Christ's doctrine always promotes godliness. Anything contrary to the doctrine of godliness then, is not from Him. Anyone who tries to say that you could live ungodly, without repentance, and still go to heaven (Luke 13:3), or that speaks things which are contrary to Christ and His doctrine of godliness (which is the truth), is proud, and knows nothing about Christ's true teaching. The Bible says, *"Having a form of godliness, but denying the [life-changing] power thereof: from such [men] turn away"* (2 Tim. 3:5). Mere outward pretense or profession of faith alone is not enough (1 Sam. 16:7; Titus 1:16; James 2:14). Faith must be lived (Rom. 1:17). *"He answered and said unto them, Well hath Esaias prophesied of you hypocrites, as it is written, This people honoureth me with their lips, but their heart is far from me"* (Mark 7:6).

More Scriptures

"All scripture is given by inspiration of God, and is profitable for doctrine, for reproof, for correction, for instruction in [the way of] righteousness" (2 Tim. 3:16). All scripture therefore, needs to harmonize.

The apostle Paul wrote, *"I charge thee therefore before God, and the Lord Jesus Christ, who shall judge the quick and the dead at his appearing and His kingdom; **Preach the word**; be instant in season, out of season; **reprove, rebuke, exhort** with all longsuffering and doctrine. **For the time will come when they will not endure sound doctrine**; but after their own lusts shall they heap to themselves teachers, having itching ears; and they shall turn away their ears from the truth, and shall be turned unto fables"* (2 Tim. 4:1-4). People have a tendency to want doctrines and teachers that will okay their living in sin and lust, rather than the truth, which is always according to godliness, and if they willingly choose this, these false teachings cannot save them, but they will only further blind and delude them and give them a false hope.

Scripture says, *"Therefore leaving the [foundational] principles of the doctrine [the teachings and instructions] of Christ, let us go on unto perfection [maturity]; not laying again the foundation of repentance from dead works, and of faith toward God, of the doctrine of baptisms, and of laying on of hands, and of the resurrection of the dead, and of eternal judgment"* (Heb. 6:1-2). Repentance of a life of sin; living faith that obeys God; the doctrine of three baptisms for every New Testament believer; laying on of hands for healing and the imparting of the Holy Ghost; the resurrection of the dead; and eternal judgment for all rebels, are foundational doctrines recorded in scripture. Never leave this foundation. These are Christian basics as can be clearly seen, if one simply studies and believes God's Word just as it is written.

"Whosoever transgresseth [then], and abideth not in the doctrine of Christ, hath not God. He that abideth in [all of] the doctrine of Christ, he hath both the Father and the Son. If there come any unto you, and bring not this doctrine [that is recorded in the apostolic record] receive him not into your house, neither bid him God speed" (2 John 9-10). It's not how eloquent or charismatic a teacher is, nor how long a church or denomination has been around, the real question is, have they stayed true to the Apostolic Doctrine or not. The Pharisees of Jesus' day were supposed to have been the Keepers of the Faith and Word, but instead they made the Word of God of none effect by their traditions and manmade doctrines, and even wanted to kill Christ. If people get away from what's actually written, they can get into all manner of presumptions, wrong ideas, and false religious beliefs even to the point of hating the real truth and doctrine of God, and yet still be very religious.

Jesus said to one church in scripture, *"But I have a few things against thee, because thou hast there them* **that hold** *[onto]* **the doctrine of Balaam**, *who taught Balac to cast a stumbling block before the children of Israel, to eat things sacrificed unto idols, and to commit fornication. So hast thou also them that hold the* **doctrine of the Nicolaitans**, *which thing I hate.* **Repent**; *or else I will come unto thee quickly, and will fight against them [that hold on to such things] with the sword of my mouth. He that hath an ear, let him hear what the Spirit* **saith unto the churches; To him that overcometh** *will I give to eat of the hidden manna, and will give him a white stone, and in the stone a new name written, which no man knoweth saving he that receiveth it"* (Rev. 2:14-17). Balaam and the Nicolaitane brought the teaching to God's people that their sin wouldn't be punished by God. Do you have them that hold this doctrine? (We will look more at these things later.) So then, churches can have wrong, sinful doctrines in them, even sinful doctrines that the Lord hates. To these churches He commands they repent, or suffer the consequences as is recorded in Revelation chapters two and three in the letters to the churches.

Obviously, we are supposed to stay right with what is written and never come up with our own philosophies, opinions, traditions of men, nor preach what we think. We are to preach the "Word," for *"He whom God hath sent speaketh the words of God"* (John 3:34); and there is only one Lord and one faith. And the entire New Testament is, as stated, *"The faith that was once delivered to the saints"* (Jude 3). No counsel, no committee, no seminary, no Bible school, no church, no professing minister, no pope, no bishop, no denomination, nor anyone else should ever tell you that any of Christ's or the apostles' words or doctrines are not for us today. And if they do, they are found to be a false or misled teacher and an unfaithful witness to our Lord who told us to *"observe [and do] all things whatsoever"* He *"commanded"* the early disciples *"even unto the end of the world"* (Matt. 28:18-20). Anyone who does such things and willingly contradicts any of the teaching of Christ, or the apostles that are clearly and simply written, should not be in a pulpit until he repents and acknowledges that the scriptures in their entirety are the truth, and should be obeyed. Teachers who teach partial truths while ignoring or rejecting many scriptures are the main reason for all the division in the body of Christ today (James 3:1).

Jesus said, *"To those Jews which believed on him, **If ye continue in My word, then are ye my disciples** indeed; And ye shall know the truth, and the truth shall make you free"* (John 8:31-32).

So, let's make sure we are Christ's disciples and not someone else's disciples, for only Christ can take us to heaven (John 14:6; Heb. 5:9). There are not two ways to get there.

*"Then spake Jesus again unto them, saying, I am the light of the world: **he that followeth me** shall not walk in darkness, but shall have the light of life"* (John 8:12). Many people follow a denomination's doctrine or some person's teachings, rather than checking out everything with what is actually written in God's Word. In this they greatly error. Only Jesus is the way, the truth, and the life. No denomination, or group, or religious teacher of the past can save you, and only the real truth of Christ can truly set you free.

Now, it's okay to follow someone's teaching as long as they don't contradict what is written in the New Covenant, for God set pastors and other ministries in the church for this very purpose, to feed His sheep (Jer. 3:15). But if you follow someone and they say things contrary to Christ, the Great Shepherd and Head of the church, or nullify anything that is written, it is not light then, but darkness that you will be receiving from them. Jesus said, *"If the light [then] that is in thee be [really] darkness, how great is that darkness"* (that you are in).

Characteristics of Heresy

There are certain characteristics concerning those that teach heresy and those who get deceived by it. Let's look at them now.

All heresy involves all, or some of, the following:

1) Those under heresy get more allied to some sect, denomination, or man's teaching than they are to Christ and the apostles' complete doctrine and what is actually written in the pages of the New Covenant. Paul wrote, *"O foolish Galatians, **who hath bewitched you, that ye should not obey the truth**, before whose eyes Jesus Christ hath been evidently set forth, crucified among you?"* (Gal. 3:1). If these Galatians that Paul himself had led to Christ, later came under wrong teaching and were influenced by it, so can others. *"Wherefore let him that thinketh he standeth take heed lest he fall"* (1 Cor. 10:12).

2) These teachers of heresy teach others the reasonings and philosophies of men clothed in spiritual terms as though they were the actual words of Christ, or the things of God. (If it's a belief or system of beliefs that is not actually written in the Word, or is in any way, contrary to other clear scriptures in the Covenant, don't believe it, Col. 2:8.) *"For they that are such serve not our Lord Jesus Christ, but their own belly; and by good words and fair speeches deceive the hearts of the simple"* (Rom. 16:18).

3) Sometimes misled teachers don't want to have to obey all of the scriptures so they take out the passages that they want, such as passages that refer to God's promises, God's love, God's grace, and what He has done; and they leave out all of the conditions, commands, and warnings of Christ, for this would place some of the responsibility upon them. They then teach others their lopsided perspectives, and everyone who sits under their teaching and receives it as truth becomes lopsided as well, and they too, just like their teacher, become blinded.

4) Teachers of heresy don't compare their beliefs with all of the writings of the apostles and the Gospels to show that they are true, but will leave out much of the doctrines and teachings of the New Testament. Anything that doesn't agree with **their personal belief** they waterdown, nullify, ignore, or conveniently say it's passed away.

5) They do not use all of the scriptures, nor do they take their literal meaning, but spiritualize or twist whatever doesn't agree with them;

and also, many times, attach new meanings to the apostles' words, different from what the apostles meant, and so do just as the apostle Peter said, twisting the scriptures to their own destruction (2 Pet. 3:14-18).

6) Whatever they desire to say passed away, as far as God's Word is concerned, they just teach their followers it passed away with no clear scriptural proof at all, taking perhaps, a lone scripture out of context to justify their teaching. With this method, you could make God's Word say anything.

7) They, many times, remove God's conditions and man's responsibility as is actually stated in scripture to obtain the promised blessings of the Covenant (Heb. 3:14, 5:9; Matt 7:21).

8) They will take a few obscure passages and put them in opposition to the great, many, clear scriptures which prove their opinion wrong. They therefore, set a few passages against many and the obscure against the perfectly clear.

9) People follow heretics because many times, they teach that the easy way and the broad road is the way to go instead of the narrow road as Christ taught. This is easy on the flesh and so their belief is by preference. So they fall into the category, of those the apostle speaks of when he said, *"For the time will come when they will not endure sound doctrine; but after their own lusts shall they heap to themselves teachers [who will teach them what they want to hear], having itching ears"* (2 Tim. 4:3; Jude 17-20).

10) They will at times, like Cain who persecuted righteous Abel, vigorously persecute those who teach that you must live as Christ; and the apostles said, in order to inherit eternal life. Jesus said, *"Remember the word that I said unto you, The servant is not greater than his lord. If they have persecuted me, they will also persecute you; **if they have kept my saying**, they will keep yours also"* (John 15:20; 1 John 3:12). *"Yea, and all that will **live godly** in Christ Jesus shall suffer persecution"* (2 Tim. 3:12). Most of the early disciples' persecution came from religious people who weren't obeying God, but just had an outward form and profession of godliness (Matt. 3:9-10). And so it is today.

11) Sometimes heretics will do away with the righteous judgment of God towards unrepentant sinners, saying how you live doesn't make any difference for it's all by grace (1 Pet. 3:12; 2 Pet. 2:6). In this, they nullify hundreds of scriptures and the clear warnings of Christ and the apostles with the stroke of a pen. (See 1 Cor. 10:5-11.) Some also teach

contrary to scripture that God is a respecter of persons, and is only willing to save some (Rom. 2:11; Acts 10:34; Mark 16:15; 1 John 2:2). This too is a heresy, as we shall later clearly show you (2 Pet. 3:9; 1 Tim. 2:4).

12) They will not line up their teachings with the life, teaching, and ministry of Jesus Christ, our Lord and Master, who is the way, the truth, and the life; but teach and believe many things contrary to the Lord Himself and what He actually did and taught in His ministry on the earth. Compare what you're being taught with the life, the teachings, and the actions of Christ. He is the true way. Jesus said, *"For I have given you an example, that ye should do as I have done to you"* (John 13:15). Let Jesus be your role model for living (Matt. 28:18-20).

13) *They will deny* one or more of the foundational doctrines of Christ spoken of by Paul in Hebrews 6:1-3.

(A) **Repentance of a life of sin** (Luke 13:3, 24:46-47). The apostle Paul said that the Lord appeared to him and said, *"But rise, and stand upon thy feet: for I have appeared unto thee for this purpose, to make thee a minister and a witness both of these things which thou hast seen, and of those things in the which I will appear unto thee; delivering thee from the people, and from the Gentiles, unto whom now I send thee, To open their eyes, and **to turn them from darkness to light, and from the power of Satan unto God [so], that they may receive forgiveness of sins**, and inheritance among them which are sanctified by faith that is in me. Whereupon, O king Agrippa, I was not disobedient unto the heavenly vision: But shewed first unto them of Damacus, and at Jerusalem, and throughout all the coasts of Judaea, and then to the Gentiles, **that they should repent [that is, turn from sin and Satan] and turn to God and do works meet for repentance"** (Acts 26:16-20),

(B) **Living faith towards God.** Heretics will teach that a dead faith that just *professes* it believes but doesn't obey, is enough to be saved (James 2:14-26). Jesus, the author of our faith said.

> *"Not every one that saith unto me, Lord, Lord, shall enter into the kingdom of heaven; but he that doeth the will of my Father which is in heaven"* (Matt. 7:21). *"And why call ye Me, Lord, Lord, and do not the things which I say?"* (Luke 6:46). (See also Heb. 5:9.) *"But wilt thou know, O vain man, that faith without works is dead?"* (James 2:20).

(C) *Heretics will change the Doctrine of Baptisms.* There is the Baptism into Christ (1 Cor. 12:13); the Baptism with the Holy Spirit which empowers one for service (Acts 1:4-5,8, 2:4); and Water Baptism by a minister

(Acts 8:36). (Repentance and faith always comes before Water Baptism.) Water Baptism alone cannot save (John 3:1-8; Acts 8:13-23). Jesus said, *"Ye must be born again."*

14) Once heresy has overtaken the mind, people will outright deny clear, plain passages of scripture. The apostle says, *"And the servant of the Lord must not strive; but be gentle unto all men, apt to teach, patient, in meekness instructing those that oppose themselves; if God peradventure will give them repentance to the acknowledging of the truth [so perhaps they will return and acknowledge what the Word actually says]; And that they may [by this] recover themselves out of the snare of the devil, who are taken captive by him at his will"* (2 Tim. 2:24-26). To believe contrary to the truth is to be taken captive by the devil in that area (John 8:31-32). *"In whom the god of this world hath **blinded the minds of them which believe not**, lest the light of the glorious gospel of Christ, who is the image of God, should shine unto them"* (2 Cor. 4:4). The Gospel is full of the light of God's truth, but whatever parts you don't believe, you will be blinded in that area by unbelief. *"So we see that they could not enter in because of unbelief"* (Heb. 3:19).

15) They will not, and cannot, openly tell you to believe *everything* in this New Covenant, for they know that if they told you to do so, you'd see they were wrong. So, they themselves, qualify what you are to believe and are not to believe, so that you don't wander away from their opinion. The Bible reveals, *"as is the priest, so are the people;"* and therefore everyone who is taught, shall be as his teacher.

16) Some will substitute manmade rituals, commandments, teachings, human requirements, and so on, in place of the Word of God (Mark 7:5-12). Paul wrote, *"**Beware lest any man spoil you** [that is, defeat you and make your faith stop functioning and rob you] through philosophy [theories based on human speculations] and vain deceit [a deliberate twisting of the facts], after the traditions [the beliefs and handed down stories] of men, after the rudiments [the undeveloped ideas] of the world, and not after Christ"* and what He taught (Col. 2:8).

17) They will have people do religious looking things and rituals that are not actually found written in God's Word and say, this is the way. Substituting man-made rituals not found in the scriptures for the truth of God, they are the blind leading the blind. They will change the Gospel from what's actually written. They cannot just read every passage and say that it's true, and that it is true today (2 Tim. 3:16-17). And almost all of it is because of a lack of a sincere open study, and willingness to obey God's Word. Jesus said, *"And this is the condemnation, [the basis for the*

judgment] that light is come into the world, and men loved darkness rather than light, because their deeds were evil. For every one that doeth evil hateth the [true] light, neither cometh [he] to the [real] light, lest his deeds [his life's behavior] should be [exposed and] reproved" (John 3:19-20). Unwillingness to obey God then hinders people from coming to the true light.

The apostle said, *"But though we, or an angel from heaven, preach **any other gospel** unto you than that which we have [already] preached unto you, let him be accursed. As we said before, so say I now again, **if any man preach any other gospel** [message] unto you than that ye have received, let him be accursed"* (Gal. 1:8-9). Do you understand? We are to believe the whole New Testament, and that everything in this New Covenant is for us today, even unto the End of the Age (Matt. 24:14, 28:20). We are to preach *no other gospel* than what's actually written in the Gospels, the epistles, and the book of Revelation. God gave us *all* that is written so we'd believe *all* that is written, and He wants us to believe it all, ***just as it is written***. Beware then of the serpent working through men who always come to twist and to *"steal the Word."* He has stolen whole portions and sections of God's written Word from multitudes of professing believers and they don't even know it (Mark 4:1-23). If God would have wanted us to believe it any other way, He would have had it written differently.

Much Division Is Caused by Unbelief

There are multitudes of splits in the Lord's church because of heresy; yet there is really only one Lord, one faith, and one hope of our calling. The apostle wrote, *"For what if some did not believe? Shall their unbelief make the faith of God without effect? God forbid: yea, let God be true, but every man [who contradicts Him be] a liar; as it is written, that thou might-est be justified in thy sayings, and mightest overcome when thou art judged"* (Rom. 3:3-4). Stay right with what is actually written and you will overcome when you are judged. Don't believe anyone who tells you that part of God's Word in the New Covenant is not for us today. That is only their unbelief talking. It is heresy to say that the Word of the Lord that endures forever is partially passed away. It is Satan who wants to divide the body of Christ, and it is he who always comes to blind people to the truth (Mark 4:13-15; Gen. 3:1-2). So let's all make sure that we are staying right with the Bible and the whole New Covenant, for remember that God's truth is our only shield against the wiles of the devil.

Jesus again said, *"Heaven and earth shall pass away, **but my words shall not pass away"*** (Matt. 24:35).

Scripture says, *"For all flesh is as grass, and all the glory of man as the flower of grass. The grass withereth, and the flower thereof falleth away: **But the word of the Lord endureth forever.** And this is the word which by the gospel is preached unto you"* (1 Pet. 1:24-25).

Heresy, Paul said, is a work of the flesh (Gal. 5:17-21), and sometimes the work of demons (1 Tim. 4:1).

"Howbeit when he, the Spirit of truth, is come, he will guide you into all truth: for he shall not speak of himself; but whatsoever he shall hear, that shall he speak: and he will shew you things to come" (John 16:13). The Holy Spirit will only work with God's Word of Truth (John 17:17). He will never contradict it.

So, any teacher speaking under the inspiration of the Holy Spirit will never teach you to not believe, or to not obey any part of God's written Word. If you teach that people should believe and obey the whole New Testament, the religious heretics who refuse to believe God's whole Covenant will, many times, charge you with heresy. That is because you don't believe *their* heresy, just as the deceived religious leaders of Jesus' day called Him a deceiver and said He was of Beelzebub, even though He simply came to confirm the truth of the Covenant. They were upset with Him, because they had taught that much of it wasn't really binding and that much of it had passed away, but He proved otherwise (Rom. 15:8). The truth was that they were the deceivers and were being used by Satan to deceive the people and didn't even know it. *"Jesus answered and said unto them, Ye do err, not knowing the scriptures, nor the power of God"* (Matt. 22:29). Paul said in the book of Acts that the religious leaders called what he taught "heresy," even though he was teaching the truth of Christ.

People, especially religious people, are very protective of their beliefs, whether they are true or not. And we should be protective concerning that which is right, but we should *prove* all things that we are believing by God's Word. Over and over the scriptures admonish us with such things as, *"Let no man deceive you"* (with vain words); and, *"Take heed what you hear."* If you stay right with the whole Word, it will be a lamp unto your feet and a light to your path, but in many cases in professing Christendom, it is the blind leading the blind because people don't read and believe the whole Bible for themselves. It's just that some, in professing Christendom, have gotten so far away from all that is actually written, that they can no longer believe it even though it's clearly written right there before their eyes in the scriptures. They are, many times, rooted and grounded instead in a different set of beliefs not really found in scripture, or they are believing half truths. Even Satan himself will use *some* scriptures if it's to his advantage (Luke 4:8-13). Being blinded by false doctrines, people read right over whole portions of scriptures and their warnings and conditions as though they mean nothing, and stop only at the ones that they are taught to believe and say.

Unless one understands that Satan has succeeded at one time or another in deceiving the whole world (Rev. 12:9; 2 Cor. 4:3-4), it is almost unbelievable to see the extent which he has led much of the professing church world away from what is actually written. He, who at one time, *"sealed up the sum of wisdom,"* is a master deceiver, counterfeiter, and a foe to be reckoned with (Ezek. 28:12). And yes, people can be led astray like sheep. (They sometimes use goats to lead sheep to the slaughter.) Make sure then, that your teacher is a shepherd and not a wolf in sheep's clothing (or a goat).

So then, if anyone's teaching nullifies any of Christ's clear doctrine; nullifies or makes of no effect any of the apostles' commands or clear warnings; nullifies any clear scriptural statements or conditions spoken of in God's Word; or removes from the Word any of the gifts or ministries, or graces of the Holy Spirit, it is a heresy. Some heresies, as the apostle Peter said, are *"damnable heresies,"* and some are less significant and not damnable, but, yet, no heresy is good (2 Pet. 2:1). But always remember where there is a counterfeit, there is also the genuine, and the genuine is always *"according to godliness."* It will always stay right with the whole Word and teachings of Christ and the apostles just exactly as it is written, word for word, line for line, in this New Covenant. Make sure then, whomever you call your minister is willing to do this. Let us continue on now in our study on grace.

The Scriptures Reveal God's Truth

I believe that if you are open and look closely at God's Word, you too, will see by the scriptures as we go through this study that although God has great love toward us, He clearly warns us that as the moral governor of the universe, He must eventually deal with all unrepented of known sin and rebellion once His longsuffering has run its course and given space to repent (Rom. 2:1-6; Rev. 2:21-22). He has also revealed that He will not bless an unwilling soul, but gives grace only to the humble. For justice, holiness, and righteousness is also His nature, just as love and mercy is and He cannot change. And it is these things His Word teaches us to pursue (1 Tim. 6:11; Heb. 12:14; Rom. 2:1-11). The scriptures clearly reveal a balance in the perfect character of God. Paul, in scripture, not only spoke of His grace and mercy, but he also said in 2

Corinthians, *"Knowing the terror of the Lord [against evil] we persuade men"* to repent; and, again, *"Behold the goodness and severity of God"* (Rom. 11:22). God is extremely merciful to the repentant soul, but He's also extremely righteous, just, and holy in dealing with all things. Every area of His perfect nature must be satisfied in dealing with man, or with any free moral agent. He can never change nor vary and is the same God today as He ever was, and therefore deals with souls in the same way in both Covenants. Scripture says concerning them who were His people in the Old Covenant, *"But with many of them God was not well pleased: for they [whom He delivered out of Egypt] were [later] overthrown in the wilderness. **Now these things were [written as] our examples, to the intent that we** [in this New Covenant] should not lust after evil things, as they also lusted. **Neither be ye** idolaters, **as were some of them**; as it is written, The people sat down to eat and drink, and rose up to play. **Neither let us commit fornication, as some of them committed**, and fell in one day three and twenty thousand. **Neither let us tempt Christ, as some of them** also tempted, and were destroyed of serpents. **Neither murmur ye, as some of them also murmured**, and were destroyed of the destroyer. **Now all these things happened unto them for samples: and they are written [down in scripture] for our admonition [and warning]**, upon whom the ends of the world are come"* (1 Cor. 10:5-11).

Notice that the apostle Paul said these things were written down as examples to warn and admonish those who now profess to be His people, concerning how God always works. Paul knew that God deals with people the same way in the New Covenant as He did with Old Testament Israel; so He therefore, wrote this as a warning and caution to Christians (Eph. 5:5-10). You can also see in scripture that Jude too, made it abundantly clear that God's dealings are the same today as in days gone by. He writes, *"Beloved, when I gave all diligence to write unto you of the common salvation, it was needful for me to write unto you, and exhort you that ye should earnestly contend for the faith [which he called, "our most holy faith"] which was once delivered unto the saints. For there are certain men crept in (to the church] unawares, who were before of old ordained to this condemnation, ungodly men, turning the grace of our God into lasciviousness [an excuse to continue in lustful and sinful desires], and denying the only Lord God, and our Lord Jesus Christ. **I will therefore put you in remembrance, though ye once knew this, how that the Lord, having saved the people** out of the land of Egypt, **afterward destroyed them** that believed not. **And the angels** which kept not their first estate, but left their own habitation, **he hath reserved [them] in everlasting chains** under darkness unto the judgment of the great day. Even as Sodom and Gomorrha, and the cities about them in like manner, giving themselves over to fornication, and going after strange flesh, **are set forth for an*** *example [to all future generations], suffering the vengeance of eternal fire"* (Jude 3-7). God has therefore, given us the scriptures and recorded examples of His dealings with free moral agents in it. He did this so that we might adjust ourselves accordingly, and make no mistake about His workings, and therefore, not deal foolishly with the lives He has given to us by turning back and following after sin and Satan again, thereby leaving our proper God-ordained boundaries. For to follow Satan would be to lose out on the tree of life and on heaven (Rev. 2:7, 22:14). The apostle Peter therefore says in his doctrine, *"And if ye call on the Father, who, without respect of persons judgeth according to every man's work, pass the time of your sojourning here [on earth] in [reverential] fear,"* knowing by the scriptures how He deals with people, and the many warnings and examples He has given us, (1 Pet. 1:17).

The truth is, God's promises are to overcomers (Rev. 2–3), and God will only give grace to those who are willing, for He never forces or compels anyone to receive what He freely offers (Rev. 22:17; John 5:6). If we are willing to hunger and thirst after righteousness, His grace will give us the ability to live righteously (Matt. 5:6), and to walk down the narrow road to the city whose builder and maker is God. If we are not willing to *"continue in the grace of God,"* but will to go back into a life of bondage to sin, He will withdraw the power of His grace and we will wither away morally and spiritually, and once again, head down the broad road towards destruction (John 15:6), and eventually be cut off from the Covenant if we persist (Rom. 11:22). Now we can only live pleasing to Him as we are grafted into Christ and empowered by His grace (2 Cor. 12:9), and He will only empower to do good those who are willing, for He will not force His will upon any man (Rev. 22:17; John 10:9). And in the end as the New Testament states over and over again, everyone will be judged according to their works, which is according to what his, or her, life deserves, and whether or not they repented of evil deeds done, and thereby, received His mercy or not (Rom. 14:12).

Jesus, in His doctrine of truth said, *"Marvel not at this: for the hour is coming, in the which all that are in the graves shall hear his voice, And shall come forth;* **they that have done good, unto the resurrection of life;** *and* **they that have done evil, unto the resurrection of damnation"** (John 5:28-29). " ... **then all the churches shall know** *that I am he that searcheth the reins and hearts and* **I will give unto every one of you according to your works"** (Rev. 2:23). *"He that hath an ear let him hear what the Spirit saith unto the churches"* (Rev. 2:29). Christ's Word is the word of truth and He means exactly what He says. Let us further explain why we are saved by grace, but will be judged by our works.

Grace, the Power to Do Good

Paul says, "*Wherefore we receiving a kingdom which cannot be moved, **let us have grace, whereby [by which means] we may serve God acceptably with reverence and godly fear**: For our God is a consuming fire*" against evil (Heb. 12:28-29). Grace then in us, according to the apostle, gives us the ability to live right and serve God, as I will prove by God's Word. Then you will see how the *whole* New Testament ties together, that salvation is by grace alone, and yet we'll be judged by our works (our actions and deeds). Paul saying that Abraham was justified by faith, and James saying that Abraham was justified by works, are both right. What Paul mentioned was concerning the beginning of his life of faith, for when God's Word came to Abraham, Abraham's faith moved him to turn from his old way of life and to follow and obey God (Heb. 11:8). He was not justified by anything he had done up to that point, but rather, repentance and faith only. He believed God. James' statement was about his continuation in faith, and his showing that he really had life-changing faith in God by the changed works and actions of his life. There obviously has to be a starting point for each person's restoration, and that starting point is repentance (a turning away from a life of sin, Luke 13:3), and faith toward God. When a person does such, God forgives and erases their past sins. This is so in both Covenants.

God's Word says, "*The soul that sinneth, it shall die. The son shall not bear the iniquity of the father, neither shall the father bear the iniquity of the son: the righteousness of the righteous shall be upon him, and the wickedness of the wicked shall be upon him. But if the wicked will turn from all his sins that he hath committed, and keep all my statutes, and do that which is lawful and right, he shall surely live, he shall not die. All his transgressions that he hath committed, they shall not be mentioned unto him: in his righteousness that he hath done he shall live. **Have I any pleasure at all that the wicked should die? saith the Lord God: and not that he should return from his ways, and live?** But when the righteous turneth away from his righteousness, and committeth iniquity, and doeth according to all the abominations that the wicked man doeth, shall he live? All his righteousness that he hath done shall not be mentioned: in his trespass that he hath trespassed, and in his sin that he hath sinned, in them shall he die. Yet ye say, The way of the* Lord *is not equal. Now, O house of Israel; Is not my way equal? are not your ways unequal? When a righteous man turneth away from his righteousness, and committeth iniquity, and dieth in them; for his iniquity that he hath done shall he die. Again, when the wicked man turneth away from his wickedness that he hath committed, and doeth that which is lawful and right, he shall save his soul alive. Because* *he considereth, and turneth away from all his transgressions that he hath committed, he shall surely live, he shall not die. Yet saith the house of Israel, The way of the LORD is not equal. O house of Israel, are not my ways equal? are not your ways unequal? Therefore, I will judge you, O house of Israel, every one according to his ways, saith the Lord God. Repent, and turn yourselves from all your transgressions; so [that] iniquity shall not be your ruin. Cast away from you all your transgressions, whereby ye have transgressed; and make you a new heart and a new spirit: for why will ye die, O house of Israel?* **For I have no pleasure in the death of him that dieth, saith the Lord God: wherefore turn yourselves, and live ye**" (Ezek. 18:20-32).

It is the same in the Apostles' Doctrine. "*Repent ye therefore, and be converted,* **that your sins may be blotted out**, *when the times of refreshing shall come from the presence of the Lord.... For Moses truly said unto the fathers, A prophet shall the Lord your God raise up unto you of your brethren, like unto me; him shall ye hear in all things whatsoever he shall say unto you. And it shall come to pass, that every soul, which will not hear that prophet, shall be destroyed from among the people*" (Acts 3:19,22-23). (See also Heb. 10:26-31 and James 5:19-20 for further proof.)

How be it, people could only be born again after Jesus came and paid the sacrifice, for He is **the firstborn from the dead** (Eph. 2:5; Col. 1:18, 2:12; Rev. 1:17-18; Heb. 11:40, 12:22-23). After this initial turning from sin and Satan, to God, a person must "*continue in the faith*" as scripture says, and show by his changed life that he is a follower of Christ (Matt. 16:24). Jesus said, " *... If ye were Abraham's children, ye would do the works of Abraham*" (and live for God and His will as Abraham did). James wrote, "*Show me thy faith without thy works, and I will show thee my faith by my works.*" Both what Paul said then, and what James said, are scriptural and help to paint the whole picture. These things do not contradict one another and there was never the need for Christians to fight one another about this if they would have just believed all of God's Word. One inspired teacher, then, is speaking of the works of a person *before* he is saved and forgiven; and the other teacher is speaking of the works of a person *after* one is saved and empowered by grace to change. Paul simply was saying that you could never be good enough, nor be changed, nor be regenerated by human effort, righteousness, the works of the law, or by will power alone (these things had no power in themselves to save you or erase your past); while James was saying that if you truly have repented and now have living faith and God's grace is now in you, you will change, and everyone will see it by the way you live. Paul believed and preached the exact same thing as James did. (See Titus 1:16; Acts 26:18-20; 2 Thess. 1:7-8.)

Just stay with me and you will clearly see that only grace can break sin's power, and once it does, God expects us to go on from glory to glory, and faith to faith, and never become the slave of a life of sin again (John 8:34-36; 2 Pet. 2:20-21). First justified by faith and then our faith is declared and shown to be righteous by how we live from that point on, just as Abraham's faith brought him into union with God and then changed him and his whole way of life after his initial step of faith. God said that He blessed Abraham. *"Because that Abraham obeyed my voice, and kept my charge, my commandments, my statutes, and my laws"* (Gen. 26:5). But there had to be a starting point and it obviously wasn't Abraham's past that justified him. He started with repentance and faith and was declared righteous, because God erases the sins of the past when a person repents, but then he continued on in faith obeying God more and more as he learned His will. And for this reason, he was called, *"a friend of God."* Scripture says, *"But wilt thou know, O vain man, that faith without works is dead? Was not Abraham our father justified by works, when he had offered Isaac his son upon the altar? Seest thou how faith wrought with his works, and by works was faith made perfect? [Complete]* **And [then] the scripture was fulfilled which saith, Abraham believed God, and it was imputed unto him for righteousness: and he was called the friend** *of God. Ye see then how that by works a man is justified, and not by [saying he has] faith only"* (James 2:20-24). Jesus said to His disciples, **"Ye are my friends, if ye do whatsoever I command you"** (John 15:14). And remember, Jesus only spoke what the Father commanded Him to say. So then, James' commentary just took up from where Paul left off.

Paul too, not only got saved on the road to Damascus as a young man, but years later when he was old he wrote, *"I have fought a good fight, I have finished my course, I have kept the faith: Henceforth [because of this], there is laid up for me a crown of righteousness, which the Lord, the righteous judge, shall give me at that day: and not to me only, but unto all them also that love his appearing"* (2 Tim. 4:7-8). He didn't go back to a life of sin and of following Satan and say, *"Christ's finished work is all I need. I don't need to obey Him."* No, Paul lived for the will of God and taught others to do the same. We will get to heaven, Jesus said, only by living for the will of God (Matt. 7:21), and only grace can give us the ability to do so. So, we need His mercy and grace to give us a new start and we need the power of His grace to continue. Therefore, it is truly by grace, but not a grace that is a cloak for us to go back into what is evil, but a grace that delivers us from evil, if we are willing (Deut. 5:29; Rev. 22:14). This is the true freedom and liberty that grace gives.

*"**Jesus answered them**, Verily, verily, I say unto you, Whosoever committeth sin is the servant of sin. And the servant [of sin] abideth not in the [Master's] house forever: **but the Son abideth [for] ever. If the Son therefore shall make you free [from being slaves of sin], ye shall be free indeed"** (John 8:34-36). This is the real law of liberty. Jesus said, *"My grace is sufficient for thee for my strength is made perfect in [your] weakness"* (2 Cor. 12:9). Christ has made the real believer free from the power and control of sin. Christ said, *"I am the vine, ye are the branches: He that abideth in me, and I in him, the same bringeth forth much [good] fruit: for without me ye can do nothing. If a man abide not in me [in Christ], he is cast forth as a branch, and is withered; and men gather them (dead branches that produce no fruit), and cast them into the fire, and they are burned"* (John 15:5-6). Real Christians are grafted into Him. Before being grafted into Him, we could not produce a life of good fruit inwardly from our hearts, but now that we are grafted into Him and drawing from His life and strength, we must now produce good fruit. Jesus said, *"Every tree that bringeth not forth good fruit is hewn down, and cast into the fire"* (Matt. 7:19); and, " … *every branch **IN ME** that beareth not [any good] fruit [from its union with me] [he] the husbandman taketh away"* (prunes it off, John 15:2). We, as Christians, are saved from a life of sin by being grafted into Christ's grace and life. *"He [therefore] that saith he abideth in him ought himself also so to walk, even as He walked"* (1 John 2:6). Therefore, God said through James, *"So speak ye, and so do, as they that shall be judged by the law of liberty"* (James 2:12). For the Son set us free from our past life of bondage.

In the dispensation of conscience, men were judged by the law of conscience, and the light they had (Rom. 2:15-16), and still are today, where the law or the light of the Gospel has not yet come (Rom. 2:14-16; James 4:17; Matt. 7:12). In the dispensation of law, those under the law who did not have faith as Abraham did are to be judged by the Law of Moses. *"For not the hearers of the law are just before God, **but the doers** of the law shall be justified"* (Rom. 2:13). In this dispensation of grace, we will be judged, the scripture says, by the law of liberty, for Christ has truly freed us to do good and to live right (Luke 1:74-75); and *"to whom much is given is much **required**."* *"But be ye doers of the word, and not hearers only, deceiving your own selves"* (James 1:22). *"What doth it profit [then], my brethren, though a man say he hath faith, and have not works? [A changed life] can [that kind of] faith save him? For as the body without the spirit is dead, so faith without works is dead also"* (James 2:14, 26). It's not always easy but we are to press on and fight the good fight of faith (Phil. 3:13-14; Acts 14:22), and continue in the race to the finish line, empowered by the grace of God. The Bible says, *"Better is the end of a thing than the beginning thereof"* (Eccl. 7:8). And *"Receiving **the end** [the goal] of your faith, even the salvation of your souls"* (1 Pet. 1:9). *"He that endureth to **the end** shall be saved"* (Matt. 10:22). Keep walking and running then with Jesus all the way to the finish line to receive the salvation of your soul (Ps. 23:3). *"Wherefore seeing we also are compassed about with so great a cloud of witnesses, let us lay aside every weight, and the sin which doth so easily beset us, and let us run with patience the race that is set before us, Looking unto Jesus the author and finisher of our faith; who for the joy that was set before Him endured the cross, despising the shame, and is set down at the right hand of the throne of God. For consider him that endured such contradiction of sinners against Himself, lest ye be wearied and faint in your minds. Ye have not yet resisted unto blood, **striving** [in your battle] **against sin"*** (Heb. 12:1-4).

God Is Unchangeable

So, let us then realize that certain things satisfy certain areas of God's perfect nature. But never presume He gives warnings in the scriptures for naught, for the outcome of everything and every individual's life will be just exactly as He said in His written Word. The *"scriptures cannot be broken."* No man by any wrong teaching can save you from judgment on that day (Rom. 14:12). There will be no acceptable excuses for people as to why they refused to walk in the light they had, or why they refused to repent and judge themselves. So, stay right with what is written. This is serious business. His Word is *"forever settled in heaven,"* so it cannot be otherwise. In view of this, God says, *"let no man deceive you,"* with their cunning, crafty, intellectual, religious arguments, which sound nice and are convincing, but are really opposed to God's Word and the whole counsel of God (Rom. 16:18-19), We must all give account of our lives to God, *"Wherefore we labor, that, whether present or absent, we may be accepted of him. For we must all appear before the judgment seat of Christ; that every one may receive the things done in his body, according to that he hath done, whether it be good or bad"* (2 Cor. 5:9-10). You are admonished and responsible to *"prove all things,"* and to *"hold fast to that which is good."* Any version of grace that says that you can live in sin and still be okay with God is not Bible grace at all, but rather, a human philosophy, or, as Jude said in his epistle, it is turning God's grace into lasciviousness, and is a doctrine of devils leading people back to spiritual death (Jude 12; 1 Tim. 4:1). Let us beware then of what the apostle called *"damnable heresies"* in the church (2 Pet. 2:1).

CHAPTER TWO

God's Revelation of Sin and Its Effects

Before we look more clearly at what grace is and our need for it, we need to take a look at the biblical perspective of sin and its effects. Sin, after all, is the only thing in all of creation that God is against, and it is sin alone that has brought about all of the death, suffering, corruption, evil, and misery into God's creation. Sin is not just a little behavior problem. All sin is rebellion by free moral agents against the moral government, righteousness, and love of God. If we look at what the scriptures say concerning man's fallen condition and departure from God because of sin, then we will clearly understand the awfulness of sin and its effects in people's lives. We'll see clearly why sinful men who were following Satan and the course of this world (Eph. 2:2-3), could never save themselves by their own righteousness or works, but could only be saved out of their polluted, fallen condition by God's mercy and grace (Titus 3:5; Eph. 2:8-9). This will help clear up what it really means to be saved by grace.

The Power of Sin

Sin caused men and some of the angels to turn against God. It changed their hearts, their attitudes, and their perspective on life. It moved them to reject God's will and become self-willed, and made them to be creatures that wanted to be their own self-made gods by rejecting God and His will and not allowing His will to be a part of their daily lives. The Bible states that men in this condition are therefore *"without God and without hope in this world"* (Eph. 2:12). Sin made men and other beings, *"Lovers of pleasure more than lovers of God."* This has always been the devil's lie from the beginning that men do not really need to obey God or His will. Satan wants others to believe, like he does, that they can be the gods of their own destiny, do their own thing, and do not have to be subject to God, His will, or His commands in their lives (Isa. 14:12-14; Matt. 7:21; 1 John 2:4-6). For he knows that by rejecting God's will, a person automatically accepts his will (2 Tim. 2:24-26). There is no third area of neutral ground, and Satan himself, knows that the wages of unrepented of sin is death and subjection to him. Satan will, therefore, craftily provide many good sounding arguments as to why a person should be able to continue in sin and rebellion against God's moral government without repentance, and still be accepted by God. He does this in order to get a person to believe wrong, live wrong, and thereby put themselves in a position where they will eventually have to be rejected by God, and *"eat the fruit of their own ways"* (Prov. 1:29-33). Satan knows it is *impossible* for God to lie and that God always means exactly what He says in His Word, so he works to twist what God has revealed. In this case, he has craftily twisted the biblical definition of grace and produced a rebellion against God, which cleverly comes disguised as God's own grace.

Remember, Satan is the deceiver *of the whole world,* and many of his wrong teachings come clothed as something from God, supposedly magnifying God's goodness or grace, but in reality, are opposed to God, His moral government, His Word, and the true way of righteousness, as is revealed in the scriptures.

Satan's Goal

Think about this. Satan's temptation to Adam and Eve was not to get them to worship him directly, or to do sacrifice to him, but Satan's goal was simply to get them to use their wills to go contrary to God's known will and commandment. He knew that they would then be submitted to, and subject to, him. He craftily got them to do their own thing and believe that they could receive good, and be their own self-made gods apart from God and His will for their lives, and that it wouldn't cut them off from God. He persuaded them that they would not die, even though God said they would. He brought them the reasonings of darkness and persuaded them that what he said was a greater light and a greater truth than what God, Himself, actually said. This is what Lucifer himself did in his own fall, for he corrupted his own wisdom by reasoning, and thought he could exalt himself above God without being subject to God and His will (Ezek. 28:17). This type of reasoning is how he persuades and gets other beings to join in, in his rebellion. This departing from God and His will in such a way is the essence of Satanism. To walk then according to the course of this world (Eph. 2:2-3), and to not submit one's life to God, is to be a follower of Satan (Isa. 53:6; 1 Tim. 5:15). On the other hand, to know and love God, to be His sheep, and His people, is to keep and obey His commandments and follow Jesus. Jesus said, *"My sheep hear my voice, and I know them, and they follow me"* (John 10:27); and, of course, Christ only leads us in paths of righteousness (Ps. 23).

Christ further instructed His followers saying in His doctrine of truth, *"If ye keep my commandments, ye shall abide in my love; even as I have kept My Father's commandments, and abide in his love … Ye are my friends, if ye do whatsoever I command you … He that hath my commandments, and keepeth them, he it is that loveth me: and he that loveth me shall be loved of my Father, and I will love him, and will manifest myself to him"* (John 15:10,14,21). (See these scriptures also: 1 Cor. 7:19; 1 John 2:3-4, 5:1-3; Rev. 12:17, 14:12, 22:14.) Jesus then said, ***"He that loveth me not keepeth not my sayings: and the word which ye hear is not mine, but the Father's which sent me"*** (John 14:24). The Father reveals the same thing to us as He revealed to Adam. Since the beginning of man's creation on the earth, this principle has remained the same. To follow God is to obey His commandments. To follow Satan is to reject God's commandments and not obey them. This is the one way to tell if one is a Christian and is in the faith or not, for by their fruits ye shall know them. That is, what is being produced by their lives reveals what kind of a tree they are, and who they are really following, for *"every tree is known by its own fruit."* All you need to do is to look up in Strong's Concordance the word, "commandments," in the Old and New Testaments and this will all become perfectly clear. *"Then said Jesus [the author of our faith] unto His disciples [His followers], If any man will come after me [and be My follower], let him deny himself [all that's contrary to God's will], and take up his cross [crucifying his flesh with its passions and lusts, Gal. 5:24], and follow me"* (Matt. 16:24). These statements are absolutely clear and mean just what they say. This is the true way of New Testament faith, which restores to us what was lost at the Fall; a returning back to obey God's will and commandments (1 John 5:3-4). *"But whoso keepeth his word, in him verily is the love of God perfected: hereby know we that we are in him"* (1 John 2:5).

The Bible says, *"Let everyone that nameth the name of Christ depart from iniquity"* (2 Tim. 2:19). It's either that or hear Him say, *"Depart from me all ye workers of iniquity"* (Luke 13:27). Christ said, *"Strive to enter in at the strait gate: for many, I say unto you, will seek to enter in, and shall not be able"* (Luke 13:24). There is no such thing as a saving faith that professes one thing and lives another (James 1:22, 2:14-26). That would be nothing more than hypocrisy (Mark 7:6). God still commands obedience to His commandments, and the serpent is still telling people not to obey them (1 Cor. 7:19). The scripture says to us, *"And the dragon was wroth with the woman, **and went to make war with the remnant of her seed, which keep the commandments of God, and have the testimony of Jesus Christ"** (Rev. 12:17). "Here is the patience of the saints: here are they that **keep the commandments of God, and the faith of Jesus"** (Rev. 14:12). And the Bible still says, *"Blessed are they that **do his commandments, that they may have right to the tree of life**, and may enter in through the gates into the city"* (Rev. 22:14).

John the Apostle revealed that anyone who says they know God or have fellowship with God and yet does not keep His commandments or walk in the light is a liar. *"If we say that we have fellowship with him, and walk in darkness, we lie, and do not [know] the truth"* (1 John 1:6). *"He that saith, I know Him, and keepeth not his commandments, is a liar, and the [real] truth is not in him"* (1 John 2:4). In other words, if they profess to know God yet their lives are not lived for the will of God (1 Pet. 4:2; Matt. 7:21), they are lying and their faith is not genuine; or, perhaps, they have what Paul called *"shipwrecked faith."* They once walked with the Lord, but now no longer walk with Him (Amos 3:3; 1 John 3:8-10). Grace, again, as we shall see, is what gives us the ability to keep God's commandments.

Beware of any man that tells you that you can live a life disobedient to God and still have God's favor (1 Pet. 3:12). He is being used as a mouthpiece for the devil just as the serpent was in the garden. Things really have not changed all that much. John spoke of obeying God's commands, confessing our sins, and walking in righteousness, and said that some left this path. *"They went out from us, but they were not of us; for if they had been of us, they would no doubt have continued with us: but they went out, that they might be made manifest that they were not all of us"* (1 John 2:19). It is not going to a so-called church once a week, and a profession with the mouth that matters; it's how you live your life every day of the year. Are you living for God's will, or for your will alone?

Rebellion

Rebellion, scripture says, is as *"the sin of witchcraft,"* and what is rebellion but refusal to submit to God and His moral government. Now we understand that a person can choose to repent of a life of sin and follow the Good Shepherd, and yet that person may struggle and sin at times because of weakness of the flesh and ignorance, but can ask forgiveness, be instantly cleansed, and still continue to be a follower of the

Lord (1 John 2:1, 1:9; 2 Cor. 12:20-21; Rev. 2:1,5,12,16,18-29). That doesn't at all mean that he has made a decision of his will to turn away from God. They may be carnal but are still a Christian and in Christ (1 Cor. 3:1-3). But when a person who was once called a Christian chooses again to love this world and live in such a way that they choose to live their lives independent of God's will and commandments, and goes back to live in the lusts of the world, he has then once again *"turned aside after Satan"* (1 Tim. 4:1, 5:15; 2 Pet. 2:20-21). Their God then is, as Paul said, *"their own belly"* and they are *"enemies of the cross of Christ"* (Phil. 3:18-19). When they stop living by faith for the will of God, they have then departed *"from the faith,"* and departed *from* *"the living God"* (Heb. 3:12-14). For a person to depart from God is to depart from living for God and to live only for one's self once again, just like he did before he was saved. God has said that if people forsake Him, He will forsake them (Deut. 3:16-17). But He has also testified, *"Return unto me, and I will return unto you"* (Mal. 3:6-7). *"Be not (then) deceived; God is not mocked: for whatsoever a man soweth, that shall he also reap"* (Gal. 6:7). (See also Lev. 26:23-24.)

To live apart from God and His will is the false way of life. This was Satan's sin, and again, it is the essence of Satanism (it's what he does), for *the whole*, unsaved world is following Satan's pattern and are called children of the devil and children of wrath because of it (Eph. 2:2-3). So were we all until we repented and turned away from Satan to follow Jesus and His will for our lives (Isa. 53:6; 1 Pet. 2:25). Satan still says, "You do not really need to live for God nor obey His will or commandments. You shall not surely die." "Go ahead, live your life the way you want. Just say you believe and heaven will be your eternal home." This though is really dead faith the Bible says, and is doing no more than the demons do who profess to believe in God and tremble (James 2:19). We confidently say that anyone who teaches that you do not have to live for God, nor love God, nor obey His commandments, and yet all is well with your soul, is teaching a form of Satanism, and is either a very deluded, or an intentionally false, teacher (2 Pet. 2:1-4).

Now, in saying these things about obedience to God, we do not advocate any form of legalism or legalistic works of the Old Testament Law. At present, legalism has to do with outward ordinances, propagated by men, such as, "Don't cut your hair"; "Don't listen to this or that style of Christian music"; or, "You must be circumcised"; or, "Keep our Sabbath"; etc. The obedience we speak of which is necessary to follow is the moral commandments and instructions that God has given to us in His Word in the New Covenant through Christ and the apostles (Matt.

28:20; Acts 2:42). These commandments are all fulfilled by obeying the law of love. *"For this is the love of God,* ***that we keep his commandments****: and his commandments are not grievous"* (1 John 5:3). *"And* ***this is love, that we walk after his commandments****"* (2 John 6). *"Therefore, love is the fulfilling of the law"* (Rom. 13:9-10), for love will not break any of God's commandments. Paul asked, *"Do we then make void the law through faith? God forbid: yea, we establish the law"* (Rom. 3:31).

Paul wrote that Christ is *"the author of eternal salvation to all* ***that obey him****"* (Heb. 5:9). And we know we could never obey Him acceptably without the power of His grace (Heb. 12:28). This is not self-righteousness. This is the true fruit of righteousness, which comes by really being grafted into Christ (John 15:1-6; Phil. 1:11, 2:12-13). It is a product of grace in one's life.

The Sin Problem

The sin problem, and our bondage to it, has always been the only problem. It is a work of the devil (1 John 3:8). This is what Christ came to free us from (John 8:34-36). Sin at work, can be easily known by its characteristics and fruit. *"Now the works of the flesh are manifest [clearly seen], which are these; adultery, fornication, uncleanness, lasciviousness, idolatry, witchcraft, hatred, variance, emulations, wrath, strife, seditions, heresies, envyings, murders, drunkenness, revellings,* ***and such like****: of the which I tell you before, as I have also told you in time past, that* ***they which do such things shall not inherit the kingdom of God****"* (Gal. 5:19-21). In Genesis, chapter 3, Scripture reveals that it was through the influence and teaching of the serpent that Adam and Eve sinned and acted contrary to God. When they chose to attempt to live their lives and be gods without obeying God's will, then death, fear, guilt, shame, condemnation, spiritual separation from God, loss of faith, loss of paradise, loss of ease, loss of health, loss of peace, and numerous other evils then entered into this world (Rom. 5:12; 1 Cor. 15:26). Sin caused these effects, not righteousness or obedience to God. Adam and Eve through their act of unrighteousness, gave place to the devil. They then lost eternal life (John 17:3), and were driven from the garden of God. They no longer had the right to partake of the tree of life. Once they chose this course and refused to judge themselves and confess they were wrong, there was no grace or unconditional love that *automatically* spared them the consequences of their actions.

Then in Genesis, chapter 4, the Lord said to Cain, Adam's first-born, who didn't follow God's Word and revelation about the way of His Covenant as Abel did (Heb. 11:4), *"Why art thou wroth? [angry] and why is* *thy countenance fallen? **If you do well**, you can hold your head up, but if not, sin is a demon lurking at the door [like a beast hungering for you] and you will be mastered by it."* (Compilation of translations.) Sin is portrayed in scripture almost as a force with personality. It is something that works to get hold of free moral agents to try and get them to go contrary to God and His Word, to displease God by departing from Him and His commandments, and thereby, not only give place to the devil, but also eventually, if persisted in without repentance, will incur God's wrath against evil. (See John 8:44; Eph. 5:5-11; Rom. 7:7-9; Luke 13:3.) John points out that all sin is of the devil, *"For sin is transgression of the [known moral] law"* (of God, 1 John 3:4). It is a form of rebellion against God's will.

Sin is whatever is contrary to God and His moral government. *"For whatsoever is not of faith is sin"; and "all unrighteousness is sin."* Sin (the devil's influence) turned holy angels into devils and other upright beings into evil spirits. Sin is the only problem with the human race and with all fallen creatures. Actually, the only problem in all of creation is a sin problem, caused by free moral agents yielding to it and not willingly submitting to God and His grace. Satan is the father of sin and rebellion (John 8:44; 1 John 3:8). The only thing then that God forbids is sin. And the only thing that God will judge is sin. Sin is the only thing that God commands men to repent of (Acts 17:30); and God sent Christ to free us from sin (John 8:34-36; Acts 3:26; Rom. 6:1-23, 8:1-4). Repentance is still absolutely necessary for each individual even though Jesus paid for the sins of the world already. They must, by faith, partake of what He has done, and to do so, they must turn from Satan to God.

God reveals in scripture that sin is evil and that it blinds the mind, hardens the heart, sears the conscience, wars against the soul, grieves the Holy Spirit, and that it is doing the will of Satan. All sin gives place to the devil to legally operate in one's life (Eph. 4:27; John 14:30; James 3:14-16).

God reveals that sin alone brought fear, death, pain, suffering, moral darkness, and moral pollution into His creation. God calls sin in scripture, *"wickedness"; "very grievous"; "an abomination"; "frowardness"; "perverseness"; "pollution"; "uncleanness"; "detestable"*; and that it *"makes a person act like a beast"* (2 Pet. 2:12); *"a dog"; "a vulture"; "a hog"* (2 Pet. 2:22); *"a cow"* (Jonah 4:11); *"a venomous serpent"* (Rom. 3:13); *"a fox"* (Luke 13:32); and so on, with the worst part of their characteristics.... (Example: 2 Pet. 2:20-22.) These creatures have no spiritual discernment whatsoever, and neither do those who live in sin, or who teach that sin cannot affect your relationship with God. God reveals that sin pollutes people, and that it's like vomit. It defiles men and women who were originally created in righteousness and true holiness when they were made in His image (Eph. 4:24). Sin, and a life lived apart from God's will, is Satan's work in people (1 John 3:8). Whenever they willfully sin to that degree, they act like Satan and yield to him. Does grace then, as some teach, come to allow this kind of behavior? God forbid! For it really came to free us from such things. If grace came to cover for us while we willingly lived in sin, then it, itself, would be a part of the moral pollution problem in the world. Peter said that God's grace and provision is that you "*might escape the corruption that is in the world through lust*" (2 Pet. 1:3-4). In John 8:44, Jesus said to some religious people, "*Ye are of your father the devil, **and the lusts of your father ye will do.** He was a murderer from the beginning, and abode not in the truth, because there is no truth in him. When he speaketh a lie, he speaketh of his own: for he is a liar, and the father of it.*" Sin then, is yielding to the devil. It is carrying out his lusts and desires. It is opposition to the known will of God. The power of sin that people came under at the fall was "*the power of darkness*" and sin (Rom. 3:9; Col. 1:13). Satan had gained control over man's flesh and it became "*sinful flesh.*" But Jesus came to condemn sin's operation in the flesh and to set us free from sin's power by His grace (2 Cor. 12:9), and to destroy this work of the devil in our lives (1 John 3:8). Redemption did not come to free us to follow Satan and a life of sin with no condemnation. It came to free us *from* Satan and a life of sin, and, "*There is therefore now no condemnation to them which are in Christ Jesus, who walk not after the flesh, but after the Spirit*" (Rom. 8:1-4). We are no longer to follow the flesh as in the past, but the Spirit, and then as we do, there is no condemnation for us. "*But the fruit of the Spirit is love, joy, peace, longsuffering, gentleness, goodness, faith, meekness, temperance: **against such there is no law. And they that are [really] Christ's have crucified the flesh with the affections and lusts**"* (Gal. 5:22-24). A righteous man therefore, lives according to the fruit of the Spirit. In this sense, Paul says, "*Knowing this, that the law is not made for a righteous man [who lives righteously following the Holy Spirit], but for the lawless and disobedient, for the ungodly and for sinners, for unholy and profane, for murderers of fathers and murderers of mothers, for manslayers, For whoremongers, for them that defile themselves with mankind, for men stealers, for liars, for perjured persons, and if there be any other thing that is contrary to sound doctrine*" (1 Tim. 1:9-10). He therefore says, "*but if ye be led of the Spirit [then] ye are not under the law*" (Gal. 5:18).

Sin Is of the Devil

Because all sin is of the devil, all sin, therefore, grieves the Holy Spirit. Known sin causes people to break fellowship with, and eventually relationship with, God forever if it's not repented of. It is an abomination to the Lord. He hates it. He cannot look upon it (Hab. 1:13). It is contrary to God and His righteousness and because its source is God's adversary, sin grieves God; and it grieved Him so much that He repented that He ever made man upon the earth (Gen. 6:1-11). He compares it in scripture to a plague, leprosy, gangrene, cancer, disease, and sickness (Matt. 9:12-13). It is also called corruption. All sin, or compromise with it, in any shape or form then must be of the devil (1 John 3:4-10). Sin fights against God, refuses to be subject to God, doesn't want God to rule, nor does it want people to acknowledge to God that it's wrong. It's called enmity, rebellion, evil, and is contrary to God's nature. It denies God the position of being able to satisfy His own creation; it forms religions that turn His grace into lawlessness; rejects Christ's rightful Lordship; and refuses to acknowledge God's justice in judging it. It will come up with any lie or false religious doctrine it can to get you to side in with it, and tell you that you need not repent of it. As stated, sin has its own form of religion which says that grace will automatically cover for sin, which sadly, many people deceived by it, ignorantly follow after it, and by doing so, are no longer following the Good Shepherd in paths of righteousness, but rather, the angel of light into paths of darkness. This is the great subtlety of the serpent (2 Cor. 11:3; 2 Pet. 2:1-8). (See also 2 Tim. 4:3-4.) He gets people to follow darkness and think that it's light and then says, "Isn't God's grace wonderful? It even automatically covers for my wickedness and rebellion against Him." Oh how deceived people are (1 John 1:9; 1 Cor. 11:31).

All of sin's religions and doctrines still tell people what Satan told man in the beginning, that they need not really love nor obey the Lord, or they set up false gods. This is the bottom line and the goal of sin. Sin alone then, has brought all the ruin and misery into this world. It rejects God's work, God's will, God's way, God's character, God's government, and God's holiness. People are held by the cords of their sins and are slaves to sin and Satan until God's grace frees them from its power. Sin drives, seduces, and leads people to produce the unfruitful works of darkness and causes them to be blind and to be led by blind guides (2 Pet. 1:9; Eph. 5:5-12). It has destroyed homes, children, families, and nations. God says, *"Righteousness exalteth a nation: but sin **is a reproach to any people**"* (Prov. 14:34). If sin is a reproach to any people, then certainly it is to the people of God who are called to be a *"holy nation"* (1 Pet. 2:9-11). It has made men and angels to be proud, haughty, greedy, idolatrous, lovers of pleasure more than lovers of God, liars, deceivers, extortionists, robbers, rapists, fornicators, murderers, backbiters, and every other awful thing in existence, carried out by men and fallen angels. Sin's only goal is to kill, steal, and destroy; to enslave, and to lead men and angels down the broad road to destruction. Sin is aggressively against God, against creation, and against all that is good.

Unrepented of sin and not submitting to Jesus' Lordship is the only thing that will send people to hell. Sin alone destroys the soul (Ezek. 18:4; James 5:19-20). Sin alone displeases God, so God is only against one thing: Sin! God hates sin (Heb. 1:9). It is the only thing that makes Him speak in wrath, when by nature, He is a God of peace. It is absolutely repulsive to Him. The only reason God will condemn men and angels to eternal fire is because of unrepented of sin, and because of their choosing to follow after Satan and his ways rather than God. The cross, the cold, dark tomb, and eternal fire is what God thinks of sin and where it deserves to go. Sin alone leads free moral agents to come to a place where their hearts become so hardened that they no longer are willing to have God, their own Creator, nor His will, in their lives. And when sin has accomplished its work, it brings forth death, both spiritual and eternal (Rom. 8:12-13; James 1:12-15). Like Lucifer, it is pride, selfishness, and rebellion that moves men to be disobedient to God and to promote doctrines that okay sin. God, by His grace, would *never ever* have provided a cloak for something that grieves Him so much, but He is willing to be very merciful to the repentant soul (2 Pet. 3:9). Oh, how great is His mercy towards man! Therefore, turn to Him for forgiveness and mercy while there is still time.

Sin Brings Death

Paul said that the person who is not born again, *"even their mind and conscience is defiled,"* and that *"we, ourselves"* also like the rest of them, once were (in times past), foolish (living recklessly), disobedient (rebellious and hardhearted lives), deceived (the dupes of error, misled, gone astray from the way of the Lord), the slaves of various cravings, passions, vices, and wicked desires; our lives full of jealousy, envy, meanness, hatefulness, and hating one another (Titus 3:3). He said that we too were once corrupted by *"deceitful lusts,"* and that tribulation, anguish and wrath is due to every man who practices a life of such things. He said, *"And even as they did not like to retain God [and His true way] in their knowledge, God* *gave them over to a reprobate mind, to do those things which are not conven- ient [to indecent conduct]; being filled with all [kinds of] unrighteousness [filled with evil things such as], fornication, wickedness [moral depravity], covetous- ness, maliciousness; full of envy, murder, debate, deceit, malignity; whisperers, backbiters, haters of God, despiteful, proud, [haughty] boasters, inventors of evil things, disobedient to parents, without understanding, Covenant breakers, without natural affection, implacable, unmerciful: Who knowing the judgment of God, that they **which commit** (and practice) such things [as these] **are wor- thy of death**, not only do the same, but have pleasure in them that do them"* (Rom. 1:28-32). He said that every one (on earth) (therefore that is involved in these things) is *"guilty before God"*; that *"all have sinned and come short of the glory of God"*; that all were dead in their trespasses and sins because of these very things. There was therefore none righteous. *"As it is written there is none righteous, no, not one: There is none that under- standeth, there is none that seeketh after God. **They are all gone out of the way**, they are together become unprofitable; **there is none that doeth good, no, not one**"* (Rom. 3:10-12). These types of evil things are the main works of the devil and his image in man that Christ came to destroy (1 John 3:8-10).

So then, as we've said, grace would never provide a cloak for some- one to live in these things, and of course, all of our works then, done in our unsaved condition were dead, defiled works by people who were children of the devil and polluted by sin. Paul said, *"We were enemies [of God] in our minds,"* by these evil works, so let us never turn back to live again in these things which made us God's enemies in times past (Col. 1:21), and let us never believe any man or doctrine that says these things are now okay because of grace, or, that it's just a little behavioral prob- lem. Oh, how all men need the real truth of the Savior! Who then could save himself from spiritual death and the power of Satan and sin? What works could we possibly have done in our defiled, polluted, weak con- dition to regenerate ourselves spiritually, wash away our sins, and free us from the punishment due them and the wrath to come?

Paul writes, *"Wherein **in time past** ye walked [lived your life] according to the course of this world, according to the prince of the power of the air, the spirit that now worketh in the children of disobedience [those who live for sin- ful ways]: among whom also **we all** had our conversation **in times past** [before we were Christians] in the lusts of our flesh, fulfilling the desires of the flesh and of the mind; and were by nature the children of wrath, even as others"* (as the rest of mankind because of these things, Eph. 2:2-3). And again, Paul writes, *"Now the works of the flesh [the sins of the flesh which eventually bring*

about spiritual death if not repented of when committed] are manifest [can eas-
ily be seen], which are these; adultery, fornication [sexual impurity], unclean-
ness, lasciviousness, idolatry, witchcraft, hatred, variance, emulation's, wrath
[uncontrolled anger], strife, seditions [a divisive spirit], heresies, envyings, mur-
ders, drunkenness, revellings, and such like: of the which I tell you before, as I
have also told you in time past, that they which do [and practice] such things
[without repentance] **shall not** *inherit the kingdom of God"* (Gal. 5:19-21).
Who is the apostle speaking to? He is writing to brethren in the church
reminding them of the truth (Rom. 8:12-13). Concerning Christ, the Bible
says, *"Who his own self bare our sins in his own body on the tree,* **that we,**
being dead to sins*,* **should live unto righteousness***: by whose stripes ye were*
healed. For ye were as sheep going astray; but are now returned unto the
Shepherd and Bishop of your souls" (1 Pet. 2:24-25).

Certainly, in view of such powerful truths as these, it can be seen
that grace would never provide an automatic cloak for such evil things
(as some have mistakenly been led to believe grace means). God warns
us in Hebrews, chapter 10, *"if we sin willfully,"* rejecting Christ's Lordship
over us and going back into these things, following Satan and the course
of this world again without repentance, after we've received the knowledge of the truth, that there remains no more sacrifice for sins (that will
automatically cover for us). Just a *"certain fearful looking for of judgment*
and fiery indignation," which will devour all of God's adversaries (James
4:4; Heb. 10:26-31). Do not let a false interpretation of grace blind you
to these clear warnings, for remember, if you believe false teachings, it
will blind you to the truth, and if you persist in that which is contrary to
God without repentance, you will suffer the consequences.

Brethren, we could go on and on to show you God's perspective on
sin and its awful effects and consequences, both temporal and eternal,
but I believe that for now, we have shown you enough. With the foundation of this understanding, we believe you will not only clearly see
why we need to be saved by His mercy and grace but you will truly
understand why our works in times past, religious or not, could never
have been good enough to justify us Gentiles, nor the Jews, nor did they
have in them the power to free us. You will also see that true grace has
now provided that we would no longer have to live in these evil things
and follow Satan. We are to, as the scripture says, *"awake to righteousness*
and sin not" for we are now *"dead to sin,"* *"freed from sin,"* and are no
longer to produce its fruit *"unto death,"* nor are we to be its servants, for
sin's wages, Paul said, is still death to anyone who serves it (Rom. 6:16,
23). It's just that now, because of Christ's grace, we no longer have to

serve sin and thereby not receive the wages of unrighteousness. *"He whom the Son sets free is free indeed"* (John 8:34-36).

We are now to be *"servants of righteousness,"* and the end result is eternal life (Rom. 6:22). Scripture says, *" ... that they might be trees of righteousness, the planting of the Lord, that he might be glorified"* (Isa. 61:1-3). Righteous trees produce righteous fruit. *"Being filled with the fruits of righteousness, which are by Jesus Christ, unto the glory and praise of God"* (Phil. 1:11). *"If ye know (then) that he is righteous, ye know [then] that every one **that doeth righteousness** is born of him"* (1 John 2:29).The Bible says, we are *called* out of darkness into His marvelous light. We are called to be saints (separated ones). Scripture says that He called us into the grace of Christ (Gal. 1:6); called us into a life of liberty, both from the works of the law and the works of the flesh (Gal. 5:13). He called us to holiness (1 Thess. 4:7); called you to glory and moral uprightness and integrity (2 Pet. 1:3); and *"called us with a holy calling"* (2 Tim. 1:9). Peter wrote, *"But as he which hath called you is holy, **so be ye holy** in all manner of conversation; because it is written, Be ye holy; for I am holy"* (1 Pet. 1:15-16).

The Importance of Repentance

"Let the wicked forsake his way, and the unrighteous man his thoughts: and let him return unto the Lord, and He will have mercy upon him; and to our God, for he will abundantly pardon" (Isaiah 55:7).

God assures us that although He hates sin and all evil behavior, *"if we judge ourselves"* (when we transgress, the light we've received), *"we will not be judged."* *"**IF** we confess our sins [to Him if we do stumble]; he is faithful and just to forgive us our sins and to cleanse us from all unrighteousness"* (1 John 1:9). But His word to us is to *"sin not,"* and to not let sin deceive us any more, nor let it harden our hearts, blind our minds, or sear our consciences, nor should we let it reign in our mortal bodies, for Jesus has destroyed the yoke of bondage to sin (Acts. 3:26). We Christians are free. *"For, brethren, ye have been called unto liberty; only use not liberty for an occasion to the flesh, but by love serve one another"* (Gal. 5:13). The first step into the kingdom of God is to *"repent."* Jesus said, *"Except ye repent ye shall all likewise perish"* (Luke 13:3). The first message that Jesus preached and the last instructions that He gave to His disciples was a message of repentance (Matt. 4:17; Luke 24:47), that they should go forth and preach that men must repent. God's promise is that if men will repent of their evil lives and behavior and turn to Him, they then will be forgiven of all past sins (Rom. 3:25), and so God commands *all men everywhere* to repent (Acts 17:30; 2 Pet. 3:9). This is God's great mercy. Paul's message also was that men should repent (Acts 26). And the apostle Peter, knowing Christ's command, preached that men needed to repent and be converted (Acts 2:36-38, 3:19). And, dear Reader, all you need to do to see the enduring place the Scriptures give to the doctrine of repentance, is to look and see for yourself that Jesus' final message *to the churches* in the book of Revelation,was for them to repent of evil committed, or suffer the consequences (Rev. 2–3). This too then, is His message to us today for Jesus Christ is *"the same yesterday, today, and forever"* (Heb. 13:8). And what was necessary for the early church is just as needful for us today for there is only one Lord, one faith, and one church.

Why Repentance Is Right

Repentance acknowledges God's justice in judging sin, and although God is willing to forgive all manner of sin, God will not make peace with any sinner until he repents and accepts His Son as Lord. He wills that all would repent so that He can have mercy on them (2 Pet. 3:9; Exod. 34:6-7), but He will not make them obey His command. If they don't turn from a life of sin, they will most certainly perish, not because of God's will, but because of their own stubborn will (Luke 13:3; Rom. 2:4-5).

Whenever we knowingly sin, we need to repent and judge ourselves, and His promise is that He will abundantly pardon; but don't ever believe anyone who tells you that there is no need for repentance. There is no such thing *in scripture* as all future sins being *automatically* forgiven. That is just another doctrine of devils to keep people in sin. When we do repent, we humble ourselves, acknowledge His righteousness, and agree with Him and the truth, and He then gives grace to the humble. But He will never give grace to the willfully rebellious, but will rather, resist them. *"Wherefore he saith, God resisteth the proud, but giveth grace unto the humble. Submit yourselves therefore to God. Resist the devil, and he will flee from you"* (James 4:6-7).

The apostle Paul wrote to Timothy, *"And the servant of the Lord must not strive; but be gentle unto all men, apt to teach, patient, In meekness instructing those **that oppose themselves**; if God peradventure will give them **repentance to the acknowledging of the truth**; And that they may recover themselves out of the snare of the devil, who are taken captive by him at his will"* (2 Tim. 2:24-26).

Only by repentance and acknowledging the truth, can a person recover themselves out of the darkness they've gone into and come back into the light. And only when we walk in the light can we have fellowship with God. *"This then is the message which we have heard of him, and declare unto you, that God is light, and in him is no darkness at all. If we say that we have fellowship with him, and walk in darkness [sin], we lie, and do not the truth: But if we walk in the light, as he is in the light, we have fellowship one with another, and the blood of Jesus Christ his Son cleanseth us from all sin"* (1 John 1:5-7). Once we repent of known sin committed, we can be assured by the scripture that He totally accepts us, and we can know that the blood of Jesus has washed that sin away. Furthermore, His blood also cleanses us of things we've done ignorantly. You are only responsible to walk in all the light that you, personally, have (2 Cor. 8:12), but only the repentant soul is the forgiven soul. (See these scriptures: Acts 5:31, 17:30; Jer. 8:6; 2 Pet. 3:9; Matt. 3:2, 4:17; Heb. 6:1; Luke 24:47; Zech. 12:10.)

Paul said, *"Whereupon, O king Agrippa, I was not disobedient unto the heavenly vision: But shewed first unto them of Damascus, and at Jerusalem, and throughout all the coasts of Judaea, and then to the Gentiles [these things], **that they should repent** and turn to God, and do works meet for repentance"* (Acts 26:19-20). That is, live lives consistent with their repentance.

Scripture says, *"Repent ye therefore, and be converted [so], that your sins may be blotted out, when the times of refreshing shall come from the presence of the Lord"* (Acts 3:19).

Repentance, according to the Gospel, is necessary for anyone who sins, professing Christians or not. That is, if they want God's forgiveness (Luke 17:3-4; 2 Cor. 12:21; Rev. 2–3). This area of grace is provided for us by God's great mercy, and when you repent and acknowledge your sin God says, *"I will be merciful to their unrighteousness, and their sins and their iniquities will I remember no more"* (Heb. 8:12).

*"And they went out, and preached that **men should repent**"* (Mark 6.12). To repent in scripture means to turn *from* a life of sin, and to turn *to* a life of righteousness. This is the beginning of a life of faith. It means to turn from darkness to light, from Satan to God. God only saves the repentant. It is an indispensable part of the Gospel message, for God only promises to forgive those who repent and confess their known sins (1 John 1:9). All one needs to do is to look up all the scriptures in the New Covenant on repent, repentance, and repented, to see the truth. It's either repent now, or stand before God and give account of your sins

later. If you repent, there is abundant mercy, but if not, there is just a *"certain fearful looking for of judgment"* (Heb. 10:26-31).

God says, *"I call heaven and earth to record this day against you, that I have set before you life and death, blessing and cursing: **therefore choose life**, that both thou and thy seed may live: That thou mayest love the Lord thy God, **and that thou mayest obey his voice, and that thou mayest cleave unto him: for he is thy life**, and the length of thy days"* (Deut. 30:19-20).

*"Take heed [then], **brethren**, lest there be **in any of you** an evil heart of unbelief, in departing from the living God. But exhort one another daily, while it is called to day; lest **any of you** be hardened through the deceitfulness of sin. For we are made partakers of Christ, [and are His elect, on this condition] **if we** hold the beginning of our confidence steadfast unto the end"* (Heb. 3:12-14); for the apostle Paul wrote, *"He [Jesus] became the author of eternal salvation unto all them **that obey him**"* (Heb. 5:9). James wrote, *"Brethren, **if any of you** do err from the truth, and one convert him; Let him know, that he which converteth the sinner [the brother that's gone astray] from the error of his way shall save **a soul** from death, and shall hide a multitude of sins"* (James 5:19-20). No man can serve two masters. It's either follow sin and Satan, *or* Christ and righteousness. There is no in between. As Christians, we are not free to do our own thing, but we have just changed masters (Lords) and yokes (Matt. 11:28-30). This has always been the war that rages.

A life lived apart from God and His will must also spend eternity apart from God and heaven. Not because of God's choice, but man's (2 Pet. 3:9; 1 Tim. 2:4). As we have stated, God says that if we forsake Him, He will forsake us (Deut. 31:16-17); if we return to Him, He will return to us (Mal. 3:7); if we walk contrary to Him, He will walk contrary to us (Lev. 26:23-24). *"Be not [then] deceived; God is not mocked: for whatsoever a man soweth, that shall he also reap. For he that soweth to his flesh shall of the flesh reap corruption (and that alone); he that soweth [His life] to [follow] the Spirit shall of the Spirit reap life everlasting"* (Gal. 6:7-8). Who then will you follow? Actions, many times, speak louder than words (James 2:14). Repent then whenever necessary, for God's desire is to help, forgive, and bless you, and this gives Him that opportunity to do so, for He will never go contrary to His own righteous nature.

Delivered from Sin's Power

The Bible says that Jesus came *"to save his people **FROM** their sins"* (Matt. 1:21, not **IN** them). And *"Unto you first God, having raised up His Son Jesus, sent him to bless you, **in turning away every one of you from his** *iniquities"* (Acts 3:26). Jesus' message was always *"Repent [of a life of sin] and believe the Gospel."* There has to be first a sorrow and a turning away from sin and Satan before we can turn to God for His grace and mercy (Acts 26:16-18). The apostle Peter not only told men to repent in order to be saved in his first sermon on the day of Pentecost, but he later wrote to believers, *"As obedient children, not fashioning yourselves according to the former lusts in your ignorance: But as he which hath called you is holy, so be ye holy in all manner of conversation; Because it is written, Be ye holy; for I am holy. And if ye call on the Father, who without respect of persons judgeth according to every man's work, pass the time of your sojourning here in fear"* (1 Pet. 1:14-17). Paul too, revealed in his gospel message that if people don't repent, their hardened and *unrepentant heart* stores up wrath for itself against the day of wrath and revelation of the righteous judgment of God. *"Who will render **to every man according to his deeds**: to them who by **patient continuance in well doing** [who] seek for glory and honor and immortality [He will grant], eternal life: but unto them that are contentious, and **do not obey** the truth, but obey unrighteousness [that is, a life of sin], indignation and wrath [will be given to them], tribulation and anguish (will be), upon **every soul of man** that doeth evil [that lives in sin], of the Jew first, and also of the Gentile; but glory, honor, and peace [will be], to every man that wor-keth good [and lives for God, 1 John 2:17], to the Jew first, and also to the Gentile: **for there is no respect of persons with God**"* (Rom. 2:6-11). This is a vital part of Paul's theology. Read it over again, for any of his real teach-ing on grace is in perfect harmony with what he said here.

Paul preached that we must turn *"from the power of Satan to God,"* and from the power of sin to the power of God's grace which enables us to live right. This was Paul's Gospel message given to him by Christ, and everything he taught afterwards was in agreement with this. This is *"the [true] gospel of the grace of God"* which reveals that God gives us grace to overcome what before overcame us. None of us could have ever possi-bly been saved by our own efforts or works in our fallen condition, for all of our righteousness in our lost condition was as *"filthy rags"* to God, and we were *"yet without strength."* We all deserved one thing only, wrath, because of our sinful lives and following after God's adversary (John 3:36). We were all bound by, controlled by, and under the power of, sin, but we repented and then God saved us. *" ... not by works of righ-teousness which we have done [obviously], but according to his mercy He saved us, by the washing of regeneration, and renewing of the Holy Ghost"* (Titus 3:4-5). But once He washes us and saves us from our sins and our spiritu-ally dead condition by the power of His grace, He then empowers us to live for His will and do good works (Eph. 2:10; Phil. 2:13). Our ties with Satan and his bondage are severed (Col. 1:13).

We then need, according to God's own Word, to obey Jesus and stay on the narrow road that leads to life (Rom. 8:12-13, 11:21-22; Col. 1:21-23), never turning back again to a life of sin and Satan, which is a life lived apart from God and His will. For said He, *"If you live after the flesh ye shall die."* And again, God's Word says, *"For if after they have escaped the pollutions of the world through the knowledge of the Lord and Savior Jesus Christ, they are **again entangled** therein, and overcome [by a life of sin], the latter end is worse with them than the beginning. For it had been better for them not to have known the way of righteousness, than, after they have known it, to turn from the holy commandment delivered unto them. But it is happened unto them [who do turn back to the pollutions of the world and stay there] according to the true proverb, The dog is turned to his own vomit again; and the sow that was washed to her wallowing in the mire"* (2 Pet. 2:20-21). That would be repentance in reverse: A turning away from God back to Satan. Paul said, *"For some are already turned aside after Satan"* (I Tim. 5:15). And Jesus said, *"Sin no more lest a worse thing come unto thee"* (John 5:14). Jesus said, *"When the unclean spirit is gone out of a man, he walketh through dry places, seeking rest, and findeth none. Then he saith, I will return into my house from whence I came out; and when he is come, he findeth it empty, swept, and garnished. Then goeth he, and taketh with himself seven other spirits more wicked than himself, and they enter in and dwell there: and the last state of that man is worse than the first. Even so shall it be also unto this wicked generation"* (Matt. 12:43-45). It's important then that once we are cleansed from our old sins that we don't turn back to them. *"And the times of this ignorance **God** winked at; but now **commandeth all men every where to repent**: Because he hath appointed a day, in the which he will judge the world in righteousness by that man whom he hath ordained; whereof he **hath given assurance unto all men** [that this is so], in that he hath raised him from the dead"* (Acts 17:30-31).

It certainly is then, only mercy and grace that saved us from our lost, spiritually dead and blinded condition, and it's only His grace that can enable us to serve God acceptably and produce good works acceptable to Him (Heb. 12:28; 2 Cor. 9:8). Paul taught grace frees us from the dominion of sin and Satan. *"For sin shall not have dominion over you: for ye are not under [the Old Testament] law [and its rituals], but under grace"* (Rom. 6:14). *"Giving thanks unto the Father, which hath made us meet to be partakers of the inheritance of the saints in light: **Who hath delivered us from the power of darkness**, and hath translated us into the kingdom of his dear Son"*

(Col. 1:12-13). God has given us, as children of His kingdom, a grace that empowers us to live lives separated from this world's fallen system (1 John 2:14-17) and to serve God. We are *"in this world, but not of this world"* (John 17:15-17); and should no longer *"be conformed to this world"* (Rom. 12:2-3), which lives according to Satan (Eph. 2:2-3). God says, *"Be ye not unequally yoked together with unbelievers: for what fellowship hath righteousness with unrighteousness? And what communion hath light with darkness? And what concord hath Christ with Belial? Or what part hath he that believeth with an infidel? And what agreement hath the temple of God with idols? for ye are the temple of the living God; as God hath said, I will dwell in them, and walk in them; and I will be their God, and they shall be my people. Wherefore come out from among them, and be ye separate, saith the Lord, and touch not the unclean thing; and I will receive you, and will be a Father unto you, and ye shall be my sons and daughters, saith the Lord Almighty"* (2 Cor. 6:14-18). This then is the true meaning of the dispensation of grace, as we shall further clearly reveal: Grace, wonderful, freeing grace (1 Pet. 1:5). By grace, ye are delivered and saved from the Fall and its effects. *"For ye were sometimes [in times past in] darkness, but now are ye light in the Lord: walk [now] as children of light"* (Eph. 5:8).

CHAPTER THREE

WHAT IS REAL GRACE?

What then is Bible grace? What is it given for? What does it do for, or in us? Let's look at some of the New Testament scriptures on grace and take a look at the true operation of grace. By doing so, we will see its true effects in the lives of those who have really received grace and understand it. *"By their fruits ye shall know them"* (Matt. 7:20). For sinners can only live sinful, self-centered lives apart from God's will (Rom. 8:8); while those who are grafted into Christ, produce His fruit and live for God, just as Christ, who was full of grace and truth, lived to please His Father and fulfill His commands (John 15:10; 1 John 2:6). Grace and sin, we shall clearly see, are opposing forces from different sources and never will the two agree, nor will they work in conjunction with one another. Grace, as we've stated, certainly will not be a cloak for sin, which is Satan's work, for Christ came to destroy the works of the devil, not to cover for them. Jesus said, *"Now they have no cloak for their sin"* (John 15:22). (See also John 7:7.)

Grace is from God; sin is of the devil. Grace is given to free us from sin. That is simple enough to understand. God's plan was to deliver man by the power of His grace from the evil force that enslaved man since the fall, called "sin" (Phil. 2:12-13). Grace broke sin's chains and opened its prison doors. Now we can change for the better, all by grace, if our wills will only turn to God and choose to follow Him (Deut. 30:19-20; Rom. 6:14). We've seen sin's effects.

We will now look at a number of clear statements from God's Word concerning Bible grace and its effects in one's life.

Grace and Its Effects

The scriptures teach us that we are saved out of our lost state of spiritual death and Satan's kingdom, not by human effort, human willpower, or by religious works, but by grace (God's power). *"Even when we were dead in sins [God], hath quickened us [made us alive spiritually] together with Christ, (by grace ye are saved;)"* (Eph. 2:5; Col. 1:12-13). To be saved then, is to have our spirit quickened and made alive. It is to be "regenerated," and delivered from Satan's authority, and to have the veil caused by sin, removed. So then, we are not saved out of spiritual death, and out of a life of sin and bondage to Satan without grace, but because of it. It is *"by my spirit, saith the LORD"* (Zech. 4:6). Grace then, is God's power given to us by the Spirit of Grace which has quickened us, regenerated us, and saved us from our sins and from sin's dominating power (Matt. 1:21). That same Spirit that raised Christ from the dead gives us a rebirth and frees us from sin's power and our death of trespasses and sins (Rom. 8:13). He does not free us to sin, but He enables us to walk in *"newness of life"*; in a *"new and living way"*; and to *"fulfill the righteousness of the law."* He has come, the scripture says, to empower us to *"mortify the deeds of the body."* This was something we could not have done on our own, but now the Spirit of Grace has come to deliver us (Rom. 8:1-13).

"Mortify therefore your members which are upon the earth; fornication, uncleanness, inordinate affection, evil concupiscence, and covetousness, which is idolatry: For which things' sake the wrath of God cometh on the children of disobedience: In the which ye also walked some time, when ye lived in them. But now [that you're a Christian] ye also put off all these; anger, wrath, malice, blasphemy, filthy communication out of your mouth. Lie not one to another, seeing that ye have put off the old man with his deeds; and have put on the new man, which is renewed in knowledge after the image of him that created him" (Col. 3:5-10). He wouldn't be telling us to put off all of these corrupt things if we couldn't now do it. Is it any wonder then that Jude called it, *"our most holy faith"*; and said that we are *"to hate even the garment spotted by the flesh"* (Jude 1:24). And why he strongly warned against false teachers who would teach a false version of grace that says grace would automatically cover for a life of unrepented sin; and thereby, change the whole meaning and purpose of grace, thereby overthrowing much of the Holy Spirit's work in a person's life?

The Manifold Operation of Grace

Let's see what the Holy Scriptures really teach about grace. Ready?

Point 1: *Grace is given so that we can serve God acceptably* with reverence and godly fear. The apostle Paul writes, *"Wherefore we receiving a Kingdom which cannot be moved, let us have grace, whereby [by which power] we may serve God acceptably with reverence and godly fear: For our God is a consuming fire"* (Heb. 12:28-29). We don't serve God without grace, but we now serve and reverence God because of His grace that we've received in our hearts, and by its power. Those who truly have grace in their hearts from God serve, obey, and submit to God reverently; they no longer serve Satan. For no man can serve, nor obey, two opposite masters. You cannot serve God and Satan (sin) at the same time. You cannot sit at the Lord's Table and the table of demons. Grace frees you to walk in God's ways and to keep His commandments (1 John 2:3; Rev. 22:14; 1 John 2:17). This is why Christians change when they really are saved by grace. Only those who live for God will go to heaven and only those who have grace can live for God acceptably. Therefore, we can only be saved by grace. But if we are saved by grace, we are saved and delivered from Satan and his kingdom and the unfruitful *works* of darkness (Col. 1:13; Eph. 5:11).

Point 2: *Grace is given to us by God so that we can be victorious over a life of sin.* *"For sin shall not have dominion over you: for ye are not under the [Old Testament] law [which were just carnal ordinances carried out by human effort, and could never free them from a life of sin], but [you] under grace"* (the power and influence of God, Rom. 6:14). So, we aren't free from a life of sin because of human effort, rituals, or ability, but because of the power of God's grace. Those who have received grace into their hearts then are also victorious over a lifestyle of sin (1 John 3:4-10). Victory over sin is a clear evidence of grace at work. Grace is God's unmerited power made available to us through the redemptive work of Christ. God gives grace to help the humble and repentant soul (Heb. 4:16). If someone lives in sin, it's evident that grace is not at work there. They are either resisting or frustrating the grace of God, or are blinded by Satan to God's glorious Gospel of grace. They need then to repent, humble themselves, and turn back to God and He will give grace to help (James 4:4-8).

Point 3: *Grace imparts Christ's strength to us* wherever we are humanly weak. *"And he said unto me,* **my grace** *is sufficient for thee: for* **my strength** *is made perfect in [your] weakness. Most gladly therefore will I rather glory in my infirmities [human weaknesses], that* **the power of Christ** *[which is the grace of Christ] may rest upon me. Therefore I take pleasure in infirmities (human weaknesses), in reproaches, in necessities, in persecutions, in distresses for Christ's sake: for when I am [humanly] weak, then am I strong"* (2 Cor. 12:9-

10). Paul, in his theology given to him by Christ, realized that God's unmerited grace was given to make us strong. The grace of Christ and the power of Christ are synonymous. So then, we aren't spiritually and morally strong *without* grace, but *because* of it. Grace empowers one morally to be freed from a life of sin. Scriptures say, *"be strong in the grace that is in Christ Jesus"* and *"be strong in the Lord and the power of his might."* Grace is His power in us that makes us strong where we were, at one time, naturally weak. *"For when we were yet without strength, in due time Christ died for the ungodly"* (Rom. 5:6). He died to make grace available so that the ungodly could become godly. *"But as he which hath called you is holy, so be ye holy in all manner of conversation; because it is written, be ye holy; for I am holy"* (1 Pet. 1:15-16). *"For what the law could not do, in that it was weak through the flesh, God sending his own Son in the likeness of sinful flesh, and for sin, condemned sin [and its operations] in the flesh: [By bearing our sins in His own flesh on the cross, He dealt with sin's legal right to reign in our flesh once and for all, and legally canceled out Satan's work.] That the righteousness of the law might [now] be fulfilled in us, who walk not after the flesh, but after the Spirit"* (Rom. 8:3-4).

Now He says, *"As obedient children, not fashioning yourselves according to the former lusts in your ignorance"* (1 Pet. 1:14). We were, in times past, grafted into a wild olive tree (and were hooked up to the devil) and were wild by nature, but now we are grafted into Christ. It is His grace that flows from the true vine (Christ) into (us) the branches, which enables us to produce His holy fruit. It strengthens us morally and spiritually, and those who have it and understand its operations are thereby strengthened by it to live right (Phil. 1:11). If you're born again, this overcoming power is in you. Believe in it. Trust in it. This is what is meant by being saved and kept by grace (1 Pet. 1:5). It is a lie of Satan that says grace means that you can live in sin under the devil's power and influence and still be okay with God. Grace does just the opposite. It frees us from sin and disobedience. Christ hath *"delivered us from the authority of darkness"* (Col. 1:13). Satan gained dominion over man's flesh at the fall. Christ canceled this operation of sin and put grace in our spirits to deliver us and to give us power over the devil, so that we can now be obedient children (1 Pet. 1:14-15).

Point 4: *Grace is given so that we can have the needed empowerment* to abound to every good work and labor for the Lord and His Kingdom. Paul wrote, *"And God is able to make all grace abound toward you; that ye, always having all sufficiency in all things, may abound **to every good work**"* (2 Cor. 9:8). And again, *"But by the grace of God I am what I am: **and his**

grace which was bestowed upon me was not in vain; but I labored more abundantly than they all: yet not I, but the grace of God which was with me.... Therefore, my beloved brethren, be ye stedfast, unmovable, always abounding in the work of the Lord, for as much as ye know that your labor is not in vain in the Lord" (1 Cor. 15:10, 58). Grace cannot possibly then be contrary to all kinds of works. It's only contrary to human efforts apart from it, and yet Peter taught that even life was a certain operation of grace (1 Pet. 3:7). Do we not have to work then? Scripture says that if you don't work, you shouldn't eat. Grace is given to us but we must cooperate with it. Our rewards will come because of our willing cooperation with His grace. (His grace is not irresistible, as some have erroneously said. If it was, those who say such things would themselves be living perfectly holy lives.)

Now, God will only give grace to us to work if we are willing to work and be as Christ desires; that is, *"zealous of good works."* If we don't want to work, He won't give us the grace to do it because He compels no free moral agent. We, then, don't work without grace but because we believe in grace's energizing power, we are motivated and empowered by it to step out in faith and work for His kingdom. If a person has faith in this empowering grace as Paul said, and they are willing to work for God's kingdom, they will abound in good works and in *"the work of the ministry,"* in proportion to their faith in it and the grace supplied (1 Pet. 4:10-11). This, too, is the result of His grace in one's life. Grace then, is not contrary to good works and the work of the ministry as some have presumed, but it is what produces it. Jesus said, *"Let your light so shine before men, that they may **see your good works**, and glorify your Father which is in heaven"* (Matt. 5:16). God is glorified by our good works. (See also Rom. 12:4-8.) *Jesus being full of grace* and truth abounded in good works and Paul also abounded in good works and said that grace produced it. Paul simply taught that no one could be saved by their dead, defiled works in their unregenerate state without mercy and grace, and that no man could save himself from the controlling power and guilt of sin (Rom. 7:14-8:2). Only the grace that is in Christ Jesus can do this, so we all needed to be saved from our lost, sinful condition by this energizing grace, and we all needed God to be merciful to us concerning our past when we were sinners. Thank God He instantly forgives all sin that's repented of and is willing to give the needed grace to overcome, for those who humble themselves (Heb. 4:16).

Point 5: *Grace is not given as a cloak for unconfessed sin* (Jude 3-12). In writing to Christians, Paul says, *"What shall we say then? Shall we continue in sin, that grace [the unmerited power that saved us out of sin], may* *abound? [Or that God's unmerited power then can keep us even while we live in sin?] God forbid!"* (May we never think such a thing!) *"Know ye not, that to whom ye yield yourselves servants to obey, his servants ye are to whom ye obey; whether of sin unto death, or of obedience unto righteousness?"* (Rom. 6:1,16) Do you not realize that *"No man can serve two masters."*? Paul pointed out that grace was given in order to free you from serving sin and to make you servants of God and righteousness (Rom. 6:22), just as Jude wrote in his letter to the church, *"Beloved, when I gave all diligence to write unto you of the common salvation, it was needful for me to write unto you, and exhort you that ye should earnestly contend for the faith [our most holy faith as he called it, for grace makes us holy] which was once delivered unto the saints. For there are certain men crept in [to the church] unawares, who were before of old ordained to this condemnation, ungodly men,* **turning** *[like a magician's trick]* **the grace of our God** *[which was given to save us from our lost, sinful condition] into lasciviousness; [a false freedom saying that you can return to live in sin and grace will cover for you. Jude points out that this is a blatant disregard for God's justice.] And [it is] denying the only Lord God, and our Lord Jesus Christ"* (and His right to reign over us as Lord, Jude 3-4; Luke 6:46).

God's true grace gives victory over a life of sin, not an excuse to live in it. It's an ungodly, wicked teaching that says that grace means you can live in the sinful works of the flesh and still be okay with God. Beware of the serpent, twisting God's words and speaking through men. Remember, that sin has its own religions, which allows its followers to continue in its awful work, working death wherever it is given freedom to operate. Death always enters through the door of sin (Rom. 5:12). So realize, that Bible grace and sin are directly opposed to one another. They are opposing forces. It's kingdom against kingdom; grace against sin. Whenever sin holds a person captive, the grace to overcome it does much more abound if one will just wholeheartedly turn to God (1 Cor. 10:13).

Point 6: *Grace is divine ability from God* applied and imparted to the spirit of a man to enable a person to do what they could not naturally do by their own human effort. It enables us, when we believe in it, to stand strong against the enemy, the flesh and the world.

"By whom also we have access by faith into **this grace** *wherein* **we [now] stand***, and rejoice in hope of the glory of God"* (that will be ours if we remain faithful, Rom. 8:17, 5:2). *"Brethren, the grace of our Lord Jesus Christ be with your spirit. Amen"* (Gal. 6:18). Grace is supplied to the spirit of a man, to the inner man, by means of the Spirit of Grace, to make us inwardly strong in difficult situations.

"That he would grant you, according to the riches of his glory, to be strengthened with might by his Spirit [the Spirit of Grace] in the inner man" (Eph. 3:16). God said, *"And I will put my spirit [the Spirit of Grace] **within you**, and **cause you** to walk in My statutes, and ye shall keep my judgments, and **do** them"* (Ezek. 36:27).

Point 7: *Grace is God's power given to equip us* to be able to minister to others and this divine power influences and enhances every area of our Christian walk. *"As every man hath received the gift [of grace], even so minister the same one to another, as good stewards of the manifold grace of God"* (1 Pet. 4:10). Peter goes on to say that we, who have this grace, are to minister with the ability that God supplies. This grace empowers us and supplies the ability to do the will of God, and in all that He's called us to do, it will enable us to do it; For we **can do all things through Christ who strengthens** us (Phil. 4:13). *"And with **great power** gave the apostles witness of the resurrection of the Lord Jesus: and **great grace** was upon them all"* (to be apostles, Acts 4:33). *"So we, being many, are one body in Christ, and every one members one of another. Having then **gifts differing according to the grace that is given to us**, whether prophecy, let us prophesy according to the proportion of faith; Or [if we've received grace for] ministry, let us wait on our ministering: or he that teacheth, on teaching,"* and so on (Rom. 12:5-7). So again, grace is actually divine ability given so that we can live for God and function as members of the body of Christ (1 Cor. 12:18). *"For it is God which worketh in you **both to will and to do** of his good pleasure"* (Phil. 2:13). As you can see then, grace is not just an attitude of God toward us as some have mistakenly taught, but a power that influences us to do right and then gives us the ability to do it. Scripture makes it clear that people can *"resist"*; *"fall from"*; and *"frustrate the grace of God"*; or receive it *"in vain."*

Point 8: *Grace is the essence of His life* imparted to us. *"And of his fullness have all we received, and grace for grace"* (John 1:16). *"And ye are complete in him, which is the head of all principality and power"* (Col. 2:10). His grace completes us and fills up all that is lacking in us so that we can be God's peculiar people whom He's called out of a life of darkness into His marvelous light. He is the source of both our natural life and spiritual life. Therefore, He says, *"be ye holy for I am holy."* (See also Heb. 13:20-21.) *"For if the firstfruit be holy, the lump is also holy: and if the root be holy, so are the branches"* (Rom. 11:16). He is the vine and we are branches (John 15). What fruit is your branch producing? Grace is a holy power coming from a holy Savior, and we are to be holy branches.

(Point 9) *Grace is God's keeping power.* *"Who are kept by the power [grace] of God through [our] faith unto salvation ready to be revealed in the last time"* (1 Pet. 1:5; Matt. 9:29). *"For if by one man's offense [Adam's sin] death reigned [in man's flesh] by one; much more they which receive abundance of grace [in their spirits] and of the gift of righteousness shall reign in life (over sin) by one, Jesus Christ.... That as sin hath reigned [over us] unto [and resulting in] death, [moving us to break God's commandments] even so might grace (now) reign [over us] through righteousness [leading us] unto eternal life by Jesus Christ our Lord"* (Rom. 5:17, 21). Grace produces righteousness and victory over sin and Satan. It keeps us from the evil one (1 John 5:18), and enables us to reign over what had before reigned over us. *"He whom the Son sets free is free [from a life of sin] indeed"* (See John 8:34-36.) *"For the law [of God which revealed the will of God] was given by Moses, but grace [the power to carry it out] and truth came by Jesus Christ"* (John 1:17).

Point 10: *This divine grace* (free, unmerited strength) *is only available to people in Christ Jesus* (1 Tim. 1:14). No one can be saved from their life of sin without His grace and no one can stay saved from a life of sin without His grace (1 Pet. 1:5). All grace is in Christ Jesus. Jesus said, *"Abide in me, and I in you. As the branch cannot bear [righteous, holy] fruit of itself, except it abide in the vine; no more can ye, except ye abide in me. I am the vine, ye are the branches: He that abideth in me, and I in him, the same bringeth forth much [good, moral and spiritual] fruit: for without me ye can do nothing. If a man abide not [continues not] in Me, [in Christ] he is cast forth as a branch, and is withered [spiritually and morally and returns back then to a life of sin]; and men gather them [that do so], and cast them into the fire and they are burned"* (John 15:46). *"In him was life; and the life was the light of men"* (John 1:4). It's only as we abide in Him, living for God's will that we continue to draw His strength (John 15:6-14). Otherwise, you will shake yourself like Samson of old, and find that without the Spirit of Grace strengthening you, you're just as weak as any other sinful man. We abide by being willing to keep His commandments. *"If ye keep my commandments, **ye shall abide** in my love; even as I have kept my Father's commandments, **and abide** in his love"* (John 15:10). Jude said, therefore, *"**keep yourselves** in the love of God,"* and He will *"keep you from falling."* We do so by keeping ourselves willing to receive His provision and continuing on in the faith (Col. 1:21-23).

Point 11: *True grace is the essence of His life*, which produces His good fruit in us. *"Which is come unto you, as it is in all the world; and* *bringeth forth [good] fruit, as it doth also in you, since the day ye heard of it, and knew the grace of God in truth"* (Col. 1:6). *"Being filled with the fruits [the results] of [His] righteousness, which are by Jesus Christ, unto the glory and praise of God"* (Phil. 1:11). Changed lives bring glory to God. Grace enables us to walk even as He walked (1 John 2:6, 3:4-8; Gal. 2:20). God furthermore, exhorts us to grow in grace, to be strong in grace, and says that grace is only for those who sincerely love our Lord Jesus Christ. It is not for those who love sinful pleasures more than God. It is what equips us to walk down the narrow road that leads to life. *"Enter ye in at the strait gate: for wide is the gate, and broad is the way, that leadeth to destruction, and many there be which go in thereat: Because strait is the gate, and narrow is the way, which leadeth unto life, and few there be that find it"* (Matt. 7:13-14). *Grace then is given for us to serve God acceptably* and is called the manifold grace of God because it enables men to do so many different things that they, without it, could not possibly do. Both Peter and James stated that God gives this grace only to the humble, but that He resists the proud and rebellious. Scripture says that we can come to Him and obtain more grace to help in our time of need; and reveals that it gives to us what the legalistic system of the Old Covenant couldn't. They couldn't have the veil of sin removed and be grafted into Christ and draw from His grace until Christ removed, by His redemptive work, the sin barrier. Now we are grafted into His life, drawing from His grace, *"joined one spirit with the Lord."* This being grafted into Him is what saves us. The apostle said, *"Thou wilt say then, The branches were broken off, that I might be grafted in. Well; because of unbelief they were broken off, and thou standest by faith. Be not highminded, but fear:* **For if God spared not** *the natural branches,* **take heed lest He also spare not thee.** *Behold therefore the goodness and severity of God: on them which fell [away because of sin and unbelief), severity; but toward thee [who have repented of a life of sin], goodness, if thou continue in his goodness: otherwise thou also shalt be cut off. And they also, if they abide not still in unbelief [but repent and turn to the Savior], shall be grafted in: for God is able to graft them in again"* (Rom. 11:19-23). Paul taught that we must be willing to not only come to be saved by the grace of God, but we must also *"continue in the grace of God"* (Acts 13:43).

Point 12: *Grace is not irresistible* as some have erroneously taught, for the human will is always free both before and after salvation; and we can, as Paul taught, cooperate with grace or frustrate it, for God sovereignly created man's will free, and chose it to be this way (Deut. 30:19; Rev. 22:17; 2 Pet. 3:9). To say that God didn't do it this way when He revealed in His Word that He did, is to call God a liar and to try and take away from Him His sovereignty and His ability to work all things after the counsel of His own will. If grace is given for people to live holy, abound in good works, serve God, and minister to one another, which it is, as we've pointed out, it is also obvious that it is not automatically working in every Christian's life, or all would be doing all these things abundantly. Therefore, there is no such thing mentioned *in scripture* as irresistible grace. That is a manmade doctrine and human error (Matt. 15:9).

Hebrews 2:9 says, *"But we see Jesus, who was made a little lower than the angels for the suffering of death, crowned with glory and honor; that he **by the grace of God should taste death for every man**."* But not all people are saved, for not all repent and turn to God and cooperate with His grace (Titus 2:11-12; Rev. 22:17). *"Then Paul and Barnabas waxed bold, and said, It was necessary that the word of God should first have been spoken to you: but seeing ye put it from you, and judge yourselves unworthy of everlasting life, lo, we turn to the Gentiles"* (Acts 13:46).

People then must repent and use their wills to turn from Satan to God, and then God saves them by the power of His grace. *"For as many as call upon the name of the Lord shall be saved"* (Rom. 10:13). (See also John 1:12.) *"By grace [God's power] ye are saved"* (Eph. 2:5).

Paul's View

Paul, in scripture, simply told us not to *"frustrate"* this empowering grace of God (which enables us to serve God in truth from the heart) by going back to trying to be made righteous in God's sight by a legalistic, outward system of circumcision, ceremonies, and Sabbaths that are done by human efforts, and so on, which really could never inwardly change anyone. It's freedom from a life of sin and the works of the flesh that God wanted, not a religion of dead, outward works or commandments of men. Paul said not to *"receive the grace of God in vain,"* but to have faith in it and its ability in you; and further said, not to depart from grace as your source of victory. He exhorted all believers to continue on in the grace of God, and not to fall away from it or forfeit it, and he stated numerous other things concerning grace that shows we must willingly continue in it by faith in order to continue to cooperate with it.

Grace is not therefore, as some have wrongly taught, just a one time attitude of God, nor some kind of an automatic blanket for sin, nor an irresistible call, but an ongoing source of deliverance from sin and Satan, and a strength that we receive through faith (Eph. 1:19). The whole thing about true Bible faith is that it moves us to live for God and obey His will

(See Hebrews 11.), and it taps us into the grace power to be able to do it. We supply the willingness and faith in His Word, and He supplies the ability. No one can live as a Christian without His grace, but if they really have His grace in their lives, they live as a Christian. That is, they are living for God's will (Matt. 26:39). It is in this sense that it is all by grace, for none of us could save ourselves, nor deliver ourselves from sin's power on our own; nor could we wash away our own sins, but there is no scripture that says human cooperation has nothing to do with it. We must make sure we don't go beyond any boundaries of the Word and make it say something that it doesn't actually say just because of our own interpretation of things. Every scripture the New Testament says we should obey, we *should* obey. Obedience brings security (Heb. 5:9) and blessings (Rev. 22:17; James 1:22-25).

Real Faith

Let's now look at real faith.

God has created man with the ability to believe. Faith is our responsibility as Jesus clearly taught. *"Daughter **thy faith** hath made thee whole"* (Mark 5:34). And any time you obey the written Word of God, it is faith (James 1:22, 2:26). To obey the commands, instructions, and warnings then of the written Word of God is faith. To disobey is unbelief, or willful disobedience. (Read Hebrews 11.)

Like grace, it is important that you understand Bible faith and its true definition. It is never just a profession with the mouth alone. It must be accompanied by corresponding actions. Scripture says, *"What doth it profit, my brethren, **though a man say he hath faith**, and have not works? Can [that kind of professed] faith save him? Thou believest that there is one God; thou doest well [but don't you know that]: the devils also believe, and tremble. But wilt thou know, O vain man, that faith without works is dead? For as the body without the spirit is dead, so faith without works is dead also"* (James 2:14, 19 20, 26). Just saying that you believe then is not enough, for even the devils confessed that Jesus was the Christ, the Son of God (Luke 4:40-41). Your actions must correspond or it's only mental assent. James said that saying you have faith without actions is just as useless and empty as telling a starving person, be warmed and filled, and then not giving them anything to eat.

The apostle Paul said concerning some, ***They profess** [with their mouths] that they know God; **but in works** they deny him, being abominable, and disobedient, **and unto every good work reprobate"*** (Titus 1:16). Jesus said, *"Not every one that saith unto me, Lord, Lord, shall enter into the kingdom of heaven; but **he that doeth** the will of my Father which is in heaven"* (Matt. 7:21).

So, profession and actions must agree for it to be more than dead faith. Our part then, is to have the Bible-kind of faith, for real faith taps us into God's salvation and provision. We believe in the *"Word of His grace,"* and thereby tap into its power. *"For I am not ashamed of the gospel of Christ: for **it is the power of God** unto salvation to every one that believeth; to the Jew first, and also to the Greek"* (Rom. 1:16). *"By whom also we have access by faith into this grace wherein we [can now] stand, and rejoice in hope of the glory of God"* (Rom. 5:2). Only faith gives us access to the grace which empowers us to stand spiritually and morally (Eph. 6:10-17).

The willingness and faith is your responsibility. *"For if there be first a willing mind, it is accepted according to that **a man hath**, and not according to that he hath not"* (2 Cor. 8:12). *"**Whosoever will** let him come ..."* (Rev. 22:17). God tells man to "choose life" (Deut. 30:19).

Here are more scriptures that reveal man's responsibility to believe.

*"If **thou** canst believe, all things are possible to **him** that believeth"* (Mark 9:23).

*"According to **your** faith be it unto you"* (Matt. 9:29).

*"Go thy way: and as **thou** hast believed, it shall be done unto thee"* (Matt. 8:13).

*"And Jesus answering saith unto **them**, Have faith in God"* (Mark 11:22).

*"These signs shall follow **them that believe** ..."* (Mark 16:17).

*" ... and seeing **their** faith ... Jesus said ..."* (Matt. 9:2).

*"O, woman, great is **thy** faith"* (Matt. 15:28).

*"If **ye** have faith as a grain of mustard seed ..."* (Matt. 17:20).

*"And he said to the woman, **Thy faith** hath saved thee; go in peace"* (Luke 7:50).

*"Where is **your** faith?"* (Luke 8:25).

*"**Believe ye**" that I am able to do this?"* (And so on, Matt. 9:28).

Concerning the *centurion's faith*, Jesus said, *"I've not found such great faith, no not in all of Israel"* (Matt. 8:10). Jesus then clearly placed the responsibility to believe on the individual.

Paul, too, in Acts 14, preached the Gospel and then perceived that *"the man had faith to be healed"* (Acts 14:9). The man received faith from receiving God's Word (Rom. 10:17). (See also these scriptures: Rom. 1:8, 11:20; 1 Cor. 2:5; 2 Cor. 1:24; Eph. 1:15, and so on.)

And again, the Lord says, *"He that believeth shall be saved, he that believeth not shall be damned ..."* (Mark 16:16). For those who do not believe, cannot tap into the saving power of grace. If we really believe something in our hearts, our lives will be affected and changed by it. And if we really believe in Bible grace, it will empower us to serve God and obey His Word, for we are being warned as Noah was of coming judgment. Know that the scripture says, He will take vengeance on everyone who disobeys the Gospel, and therefore we seek to adjust our lives to His will. Paul wrote that Christ will come, *"In flaming fire taking vengeance on them that know not God, and [on them] that obey not the gospel of our Lord Jesus Christ"* (2 Thess. 1:8). So, like Noah, who lived righteously and prepared himself by faith for what was to come and built the ark, even so, we also adjust our lives accordingly by the aid of His grace to prepare ourselves for the coming judgment. *"Wherefore, beloved, seeing that ye look for such things, be diligent that ye may be found of him in peace, without spot, and blameless"* (2 Peter 3:14).

John the Apostle wrote, *"Beloved, now are we the sons of God, and it doth not yet appear what we shall be: but we know that, when he shall appear, we shall be like Him; for we shall see him as he is. And every man that (truly) hath this hope in him purifieth himself, even as he is pure"* (1 John 3:2-3).

God, having created man in His image and likeness, has given men the ability to believe and do what they will. All one needs to do to see man's responsibility to repent, be willing, believe, and obey, is to look up these words in the New Covenant and see with open eyes that God puts this responsibility on man. This is the whole basis for the righteous judgment of God (Rom. 2:5). Christ also rebuked people for *their* unbelief (Matt. 11:21-24). *"Afterward he appeared unto the eleven as they sat at meat, and upbraided them with their unbelief and hardness of heart, because they believed not them which had seen him after he was risen"* (Mark 16:14). He didn't believe faith was up to whether or not God would give it to an individual. So, forget all systems of manmade theology to the contrary, and let God be true concerning this and let any man who contradicts Him be a liar. The fact is that God sovereignly created man with this ability to believe and choose, and thousands of times scripture mentions this freedom of will. Extreme gracists, as we shall see, seem so frightened that their shaky definition of grace will be harmed by the words *"works"* or *"man's free will,"* that they continuously strain gnats and swallow camels, rejecting great portions of the New Covenant, its commands, its warnings, and its ways of righteousness, to protect their medieval, watered-down definition of grace taught by some man hundreds of years ago. Yet this false concept of grace that places *all* the responsibility on God for man's final salvation was not taught by Christ nor by the apostles in their doctrine (2 Pet. 1:10; 1 Tim. 6:12; Heb. 3:12-14).

It's up to us to choose to live by faith (Heb. 11:1-27), and we are commanded to obey because the grace to obey is made available to us (2 Pet. 3:14). The apostle said, *"I give thee charge [therefore] in the sight of God, who quickeneth all things, and before Christ Jesus, who before Pontius Pilate witnessed a good confession; That **thou keep this commandment** without spot, unrebukeable, until the appearing of our Lord Jesus Christ"* (1 Tim 6:13-14) As we purpose in our hearts to humbly obey God, God supplies the grace to do so.

And so it is written, *"the just shall live by faith"* (Rom. 1:17). And as we choose to live by faith in God and His Word, His grace then sustains us and enables us to walk down the narrow road that leads to life. So, John writes, *"He that doeth the will of God [enabled by grace] abideth forever"* (1 John 2:17). So then, the whole New Covenant is in perfect harmony.

True faith gives its entire self to God. Faith lives *in* God and *for* God. Faith is our loving and humble response to our Creator and His Word, and He grants grace to the humble (James 4:6). Dear Brethren, don't believe a doctrine just because it "tickles your ears." *"I charge thee therefore before God, and the Lord Jesus Christ, who shall judge the quick and the dead at his appearing and his kingdom; Preach the word; be instant in season, out of season; reprove, rebuke, exhort with all longsuffering and doctrine. For the time will come when they will not endure sound doctrine; but after their own lusts shall they heap to themselves teachers, having itching ears"* (2 Tim. 4:1-3).

By Grace Alone

We know that it's grace alone that saved us out of our spiritually dead condition, caused by the sins we've committed, and not by our human effort and works, without this grace. We know it wasn't of him that wills, nor him that runs, but of God who showed mercy and saved us by this free, unmerited power when we humbled ourselves, repented of the wickedness of our sins, and called out to Him who sits on the *"throne of grace"* to save us (Rom. 10:13). We also know that God owed salvation to no one, nor could anyone merit this glorious redemption from sin and its curse, for we had all willingly transgressed what we knew was right. We all were already guilty and worthy of death (Rom. 1:28-32, 3:19), but the truth is, if we are in the true grace of God, it now brings forth in us the fruits of righteousness (Col. 1:6), which is a life lived for God (Phil. 1:11). We are now being changed from glory to glory (2 Cor. 3:18). This is salvation from the fall. Grace has nothing to do with providing a cloak for us to live in sin, nor for us to *"fellowship with the unfruitful works of darkness"* as we did in times past (Eph. 5:11). Grace is in Christ Jesus and *"in him is no sin"* (1 John 3:4). And again, *"**whosoever abideth in him sinneth not**"* (1 John 3:6). The apostle in his doctrine further wrote, *"And ye know that He was manifested to take away our sins; and in Him is no sin"* (1 John 3:5). *"If ye know that he is righteous, ye know [then] **that every one that doeth righteousness is born of him**. Little children, let no man deceive you: he that **doeth** righteousness is righteous, even as he is righteous. **He that committeth sin is of the devil**; for the devil sinneth from the beginning. For this purpose the Son of God was manifested, that he might destroy the works of the devil"* (1 John 2:29, 3:7-8). Anyone living in sin then has sided in with the devil and is not abiding in Christ (James 4:4).

Therefore, knowing these things, John the Apostle of Christ, by the Holy Spirit taught, *"And hereby we do know that we know him [are intimately joined to Him], if we keep His commandments. He that saith, I know him, and keepeth not his commandments, is a liar, and **the truth is not in him**. [For grace and truth in operation in our lives always frees us and enables us **to do his will** once again as man was supposed to have done back in the beginning.] But whoso keepeth his word, in him verily is the love of God perfected: **hereby [by this] know we that we are [really] in Him. He that saith** [and professes] **he abideth in him** [and is grafted into Him drawing from His grace, strength and life] ought [therefore and is obliged] himself, also so to walk, even as he walked"* (that is, live as He lived, 1 John 2:3-6). And again, *"If ye know that he [Jesus] is righteous, ye know that every one **that doeth righteousness** is born of Him"* (1 John 2:29). Righteousness is not just a label, but a righteous lifestyle *"fulfilling the righteousness of the law."* (For this is what Christ and His grace truly produces in a person's life.) This too, is why Jesus said, you'll know them *"by their fruits."* Why? Because this is what New Testament grace is all about. It produces Christ's fruit in a person's life, and herein is *"**the Father glorified**"* (John 15:1-8). It enables us to live the life of Christ for the will of God, just like Jesus, the author of our faith, for Jesus was manifested to destroy the devil's work of sin in our lives and free us from the devil's power (1 John 3:4-10; John 8:34-36). He is the forerunner and He has shown us the way to heaven. It's the same way that He took, obeying the Father's will. *"Jesus saith unto him, I am the way, the truth, and the life: no man cometh unto the Father, but by me"* (John 14:6). And when His *work* was finished, He sat down on the Father's right hand. What God did through Jesus was greater than what Satan did through Adam, so now the Lord's grace brings about a walk of righteousness and a freedom from a life of sin (Rom. 8:4). To Him be all the glory. If we then are new creatures, grafted into Him, strengthened by His grace, we will produce His fruit on a consistent basis living for His will, just as He who left us an example, lived for His Father's will, and kept His commandments (John 6:38, 15:10; Matt. 7:21). And as we've shown, Jesus, the author of faith, always did those things that pleased the Father (John 8:29). So, this obeying God's will and keeping His commandments is true faith then and NOT legalism as some erroneously think (Heb. 11:6). It only looks to some like legalism if they have a false definition of grace, and their mind is, thereby, blinded by the enemy (2 Cor. 4:3-4). For to turn back to a life of sin after having come to the Lord, is to do as Adam did, and turn from God to follow Satan and self-gratification.

The true life-changing grace which enables us to take the narrow road of God's will only comes from God the Father, the God of all grace and the Lord Jesus Christ. We must never *"depart from the faith"* (1 Tim. 4:1), or *"from the living God with an evil heart of unbelief"* (Heb. 3:12); for without the grace of God that He alone can supply, we spiritually and morally will wither away and eventually die *again* just as a branch broken off from the vine dies. (See Jude 12; Rom. 8:12-13.) This is what happened to Adam back in Eden, although he didn't have access then to the cleansing power of the blood of Jesus at that time. Howbeit, he should have judged himself and confessed his sin to find mercy with God, but he didn't. He instead blamed God and the woman for his actions. Perhaps he repented later (Gen. 3:21). Oh, God's grace in us is so wonderful, supplying all that we need in every area where we are lacking. As we've shown, it is much more than just *"unmerited favor,"* it is Christ's free, unmerited power and strength imparted to us who are grafted into Him. It now enables us to live how He wants us to live and to abound in good works just as He said (Titus 2:11-15; Eph. 2:10). It saves us from a life of sin and unfruitfulness.

Continue

If we must, as the apostles taught, *"continue in grace"; "continue in the faith"; "continue in His goodness"; "grow in grace"*; determine to be *"strong in grace"*; go to the throne room to obtain more grace, trust His grace to make us strong in our weakness and give us victory over sin in our daily lives, then it is obvious that the scriptures do not teach salvation as a one time act of faith. Nor do they teach a one time receiving of some kind of irresistible grace and that's it; nor a predestination of some individuals to heaven, and other poor souls who have no choice in the matter, to hell. Let's understand that sin is Satan's work and power, so to follow a life of sin is to continue to follow Satan. Grace is God's work and power (Eph. 2:2; John 8:44; Phil. 2:13). If one continues in grace, they continue to produce the fruits of righteousness, and continue to live for God. And where sin has abounded in one's life, grace to overcome it abounds much more; so then, all can be strong in the grace that is in Christ Jesus and overcome a life of sin. *"For we are his workmanship, created in Christ Jesus unto good works, **which God hath before ordained that we should** walk in them"* (Eph. 2:10). We are not then, just sinners saved by grace; we were sinners, but now we are new creatures (in Christ), *"old things are passed away, all things are become new and all things are of God"* (2 Cor. 5:17-18). And His *"strength [grace] is made perfect in our weakness." "By the grace of God I am what I am...."* So, (therefore) it is by grace (the free, unmerited power of God) that the promise might be sure to all the seed who trust Him (Rom. 4:16; 1 Pet. 1:5). For no matter how bound a person is in sin, the grace to overcome it does much more abound. Therefore, only grace can save a person, and grace makes the victory over a life of sin sure for all, if all are willing. It makes salvation equal for all, and puts us all at an equal level (Rom. 2:11; 1 Cor. 10:13).

Grace then, is a part of our whole Christian life from beginning to end. But don't ever accept Satan's counterfeit interpretation of it that says, grace means you can continue in sin, live in the unfruitful works of darkness, follow the course of this world and the prince of the power of the air, and still remain spiritually okay. Or, don't accept that good works are contrary to grace. For Satan not only wants you to turn back and live as you did before you were saved by grace, and incur God's wrath and displeasure again (Eph. 5:5-7), but Satan also does NOT want you to work for God, nor do anything for God's Kingdom (1 Cor. 15:58). Therefore, he cleverly produces these false doctrines, which are known only by their fruit: Doctrines that okay sin and frown on good works, and anything else that will help God's Kingdom. Doctrines that say you need not really love God, obey God, nor keep His commandments, just honor Him with your lips like a hypocrite, and let your heart be far from Him. Satan knows that God will not accept that (Mark 7:6-7), but sadly, many professing Christians and even many theologians don't know. Now that we've given you just a little picture of what the grace of God truly is, and why we must continue in it, let us make it even more clear through the eyes of the apostles.

Please note, that sometimes grace means "God's saving work," revealing that it didn't originate with human effort, strength, ability, or will (Titus 2:11). The other aspect of grace is free unmerited power, ability, and strength given to us in Christ Jesus, who are grafted into Him who is the true vine. Grace, we will continue to see, is an actual power; it is something given to operate in us as we believe and willingly abide in Him (Eph. 1:19).

CHAPTER FOUR

THE APOSTLES' REVELATION ON GRACE

L et's take a closer look now at the apostles' revelation on grace.

Point 1: The apostles taught that *Grace is given* to the humble and poor in spirit who know their need of God and realize that they can't overcome sin and death by themselves. *"But **he giveth more grace**. Wherefore he saith, God resisteth the proud, but giveth grace unto the humble"* (James 4:6). *"For sin **shall not** have dominion over you: for ye are not under the law [and mere human effort], but under grace"* (God's divine power, Rom. 6:14). *"According as his divine power hath given unto us all things that pertain unto life and godliness, through the knowledge of him that hath called us to glory and virtue"* (2 Pet. 1:3). We must therefore, humble ourselves, and acknowledge to God that our dependence is on Him, and He will then give us the grace we need to overcome a life of sin. We then, by simple childlike faith, can draw strength from Jesus, the true vine, and accept the freedom He offers (Phil. 4:13), but there must first be, as we've shown, a *"willing mind"* (2 Cor. 8:12).

Point 2: The apostles revealed that *Grace teaches us* to lead holy lives in this world and that it supplies the ability to do so. *"For the grace [the saving work and power] of God that bringeth salvation [deliverance from the fall and its effects] hath appeared [and been made available] to all men, **teaching us** that, denying [and repenting of] ungodliness and worldly lusts, we should **live** soberly, righteously, and godly, in this present world [if we want to go to heaven]; looking for that blessed hope, and the glorious appearing of the great God and our Savior Jesus Christ; Who gave himself for us, that he might* *redeem us [set us free]* **from all iniquity** *[all kinds of sin], and* **purify unto Himself** *[by the power of His grace] a peculiar people,* **zealous of good works**" (Titus 2:11-14). *"For it is God which worketh in you both to will and to do of his good pleasure"* (Phil. 2:13). He both influences us to do right, and supplies the ability in this New Covenant for us to glorify Him. We only believe and supply willing submission to Him (James 4:7). We could not be saved without His grace, nor will a person stay saved if they don't continue in His grace and goodness (Rom. 11:19-22).

Point 3: *God's grace establishes* our hearts in holiness and enables us to stand strong in the faith. *"For it is a good thing that the heart be established with grace...."* (Heb. 13:9). *"Furthermore we have had fathers of our flesh, which corrected us, and we gave them reverence: shall we not much rather be in* **subjection** *unto the Father of spirits,* **and live***?"* (Heb. 12:9). *"Therefore, brethren, we are debtors, not to the flesh, to live after the flesh. For if ye [fellow Christian] live after the flesh [serving only your own wrong desires apart from God's will], ye shall die [spiritually for they all died physically regardless]: but if ye through the Spirit [of grace] do mortify [and put to death] the deeds [the sinful behavior] of the body, ye shall [continue to] live (Jude 12). For as many as are led by the Spirit of God [into paths of righteousness and a walk in the Spirit, no longer being dominated by the flesh], they are the [true] sons of God"* (Rom. 8:12-14).

Realize that the enemy has sown tares among the wheat. Tares, at first, look just like wheat but have a different nature, and you can only really see the difference at the time of harvest. Jesus said, *"Let both [those who are tares and just profess to be wheat, and those who really are] grow together until the harvest: and in the time of harvest I will say to the reapers, Gather ye together first the tares [those who are counterfeit wheat and who have lived for sin and Satan], and bind them in bundles* **to burn them***: but gather the wheat [those who have shown their true nature living for the Father's will] into my barn. As therefore the tares are gathered* **and burned in the fire***; so shall it be in the end of this world. The Son of man shall send forth his angels, and they shall* **gather out of his kingdom** *all things that offend [those who lived for sin and Satan], and them which* **do iniquity; And shall cast them into a furnace of fire: there shall be wailing and gnashing of teeth***"* (Matt. 13:30, 40-42). This is why the apostle warned, saying those *"Having a form of godliness, but denying the power [that God gave us to change] thereof: from such turn away"* (2 Tim. 3:5). Don't listen to teachers who say that there is no real need to live godly. Turn away from such people. He that has ears to hear let him hear. *"For as much then as Christ hath [strengthened by the grace of God, Heb. 2:9] suffered for us in the flesh [crucifying the flesh,*

*Gal. 5:24], arm yourselves likewise with the same mind: for he that hath suffered in the flesh hath [also strengthened by the grace of God to crucify the flesh], ceased from [a life of] sin; that he **no longer** should live the rest of his time in the flesh to the lusts of men, **but to the will of God**"* (1 Pet. 4:1-2). The truth teaches us to turn from the works of the flesh and frees us to live for the will of God. Grace strengthens and enables you to bear with and overcome temptations. *"There hath no temptation taken you but such as is common to man: but God is faithful, who will not suffer [allow] you to be tempted above that ye are able [to overcome]; but will with the temptation also make a way to escape, that ye may be able to bear it"* (1 Cor. 10:13). Grace then establishes our hearts in God, and enables us to crucify the flesh and to be good, loyal soldiers of Jesus Christ. We *can* overcome a life of sin if we will to. *"Thou therefore, my son, be strong in the grace that is in Christ Jesus.... Thou therefore, endure hardness, as a good soldier of Jesus Christ"* (2 Tim. 2:1, 3). This then, is something we must purpose to do.

Point 4: The apostle Paul also revealed that **more grace** can be obtained at the throne of grace through prayer for given situations.

"Let us therefore come boldly unto the throne of grace, that we may obtain mercy [if we have sinned], and find grace [the power] to help in time of need" (when we are going through something, Heb. 4:16). This further shows us that grace is not a one-time attitude of God, but rather an unmerited power that can help us.

Point 5: *We can grow in grace and operate in more of it as we grow in faith.* "**Grace** *and peace* **be multiplied** *unto you through the knowledge of God, and of Jesus our Lord"* (2 Pet. 1:2). "**But grow in grace,** *and in the knowledge of our Lord and Savior Jesus Christ. To him be glory both now and for ever more. Amen"* (2 Pet. 3:18). As we gain more knowledge of His will we can believe more, and thereby, tap into more of the operations of His grace. Grace is not an attitude of God, as some think. You could not grow in God's one time attitude toward you, nor receive more of it. This is what this scripture would have to say if grace were simply unmerited favor, or an attitude of God.

Point 6: *This divine ability* comes from God the Father and the Lord Jesus Christ. *"Paul, an apostle of Jesus Christ by the will of God,* **to the saints** *[separated ones] which are at Ephesus, and* **to the faithful in Christ Jesus: Grace be to you,** *and peace, from God our Father, and from the Lord Jesus Christ"* (Eph. 1:1-2). This grace is only **in Christ Jesus.** If we don't abide *in Him* we will morally and spiritually wither away and no longer live for the will of God. *"In Him is life";* outside of Him is death. Both God's Word and human experience testify of this. People that return to the pollutions of the world have fallen from grace. Only repentance can bring them back to this life saving power. Grace alone empowers us to live the Christian life, and produces the fruit of living for the will of God; therefore, *"Ye shall know them by their fruits."*

Second Corinthians 5:17 says, *"Therefore if any man **be in Christ**, he is a new creature [a new creation; a completely changed person]: old things [and sinful ways] are passed away; behold, all things are become new."* *"Knowing this, that our old man is crucified with him, that the body of sin might be destroyed, that henceforth we should not serve sin"* (Rom. 6:6). Our "old self" who was a sinner and under Satan's authority, died and was crucified with Christ, and a new man arose in Christ. *"Likewise reckon ye also your- selves to be dead indeed unto sin, but alive unto God through Jesus Christ our Lord. Let not sin therefore reign in your mortal body, that ye should obey it in the lusts thereof. Neither yield ye your members as instruments of unrighteous- ness unto sin: but yield yourselves unto God, as those that are alive from the dead, and your members as instruments of righteousness unto God"* (Rom. 6:11-13). *"For he that is dead is freed from sin"* (Rom. 6:7). By the grace of God we are who we are. The cross did away with our old sinful life. We are God's freed people (Rom. 6:1-2,7,18,22); freed once again to live in His will as was originally intended in the beginning. A new creation rec- onciled back to God! No longer the slaves of sin (John 8:34-36). *"For ye are bought with a price: therefore glorify God in your body, and in your spirit, which are God's"* (1 Cor. 6:20).

Point 7: *God's grace is His miraculous power* at work in and through man. *"And with **great power** gave the apostles witness of the resurrection of the Lord Jesus: **and great grace was upon them** all"* (Acts 4:33). The power of grace can be seen working through people. *"For he that wrought effec- tually in Peter to the apostleship of the circumcision, the same was mighty in me toward the Gentiles: And when James, Cephas, and John, who seemed to be pillars, **perceived the grace that was given unto me** [to enable me to operate as an apostle to the Gentiles], they gave to me and Barnabas the right hand of fellowship; that we should go [empowered by this grace] unto the heathen, and they unto the circumcision"* (Gal. 2:8-9).

Point 8: *People can receive it in vain* and not believe in its over-com- ing power. *"And what is the exceeding greatness of his power to usward **who believe**, according to the working of his mighty power. Which he wrought in Christ, when he raised him from the dead, and set him at his own right hand in the heavenly places"* (Eph. 1:19-20). *"We then, as workers together with* *him, beseech you **also that ye receive not the grace of God in vain**. [Not allowing it to produce its results.] For he saith, I have heard thee in a time accepted, and in the day of salvation have I succored thee [came to your aid with My grace]: behold, now is the accepted time; behold, now is the day of salvation"* (2 Cor. 6:1-2). He saved you by His grace the moment you called out to Him and behold. Now, He says, is the time to cooperate with the grace He has given you, and walk in this great salvation.

*"Therefore we ought to give the more earnest heed to the things which we have heard, lest at any time we should let them slip. **For if the word spoken by angels was steadfast**, and every transgression and disobedience received a just recompense of reward; **How shall we escape, if we neglect so great salvation;** which at the **first** began to be spoken by the Lord [Himself], and was [later] confirmed unto us by them that heard him"* (Heb. 2:1-3).

Paul revealed that people can also frustrate grace by going back to the same old dead religious works they did before they were saved to try to be made righteous, and not depending on the Holy Ghost, the Spirit of Grace to produce the true fruits of righteousness and holiness. Paul said, *"I do not **frustrate the grace of God**: for if righteousness [right living] come by [us doing the works of] the law, [apart from Christ's grace] then Christ is dead in vain"* (Gal. 2:21). Christ died to make grace available to us so we can overcome sin by grace and live truly righteously from our hearts by its effects in our lives. Grace is what really makes all the difference (2 Cor. 12:9). To go back to circumcision and Sabbath days, and manmade do's and don'ts produces nothing, but an outward show. He called it *"will worship"* (Col. 2:23). Only grace changes and establishes the heart in God. It enables us to walk in newness of life.

Point 9: *Grace then makes us truly righteous*; and, *"He that **doeth** righteousness is righteous, even as he [Christ] is righteous"* (1 John 3:7). It is the only power that can make us righteous and enable us to live this way. We are saved by grace through faith (from the power of sin and Satan, Matt. 1:21), and we are kept by grace through faith (from the power of sin and Satan, 1 Pet. 1:5; 1 John 5:18).

More Facts about Grace

Point 10: Again, *grace can be seen* working in people's lives! *"Who, when he came, and had **seen the grace of God**, was glad, and exhorted them all, that with purpose of heart they would **cleave** unto the Lord"* (Acts 11:23). (The source of this overcoming grace.) He didn't see them all living in sin and say, "Now that's grace." It's like in Acts 8 where Simon saw that the

Holy Ghost was given. He couldn't really see the Holy Ghost, but he could see the effects of the Holy Ghost in the people as they received. So in like manner, the amazing changes grace makes in people can also be seen.

Point 11: *Grace enables us* to really believe in the heart once we repent. *"And when he was disposed to pass into Achaia, the brethren wrote, exhorting the disciples to receive him: who, when he was come, helped them much which had believed through [the aid of] grace"* (Acts 18:27). *"For John came unto you in the way of righteousness, and ye believed him not: but the publicans and the harlots believed him: and ye, when ye had seen it, repented not afterward, that ye might believe him"* (Matt. 21:32). *"In that hour Jesus rejoiced in Spirit, and said, I thank thee, O Father, Lord of heaven and earth, that Thou hast hid these things from the wise and prudent, and hast revealed them unto babes: even so, Father; for so it seemed good in thy sight"* (Luke 10:21). It all depends on the heart of the individual, for God looks upon the heart (1 Sam. 16:7). And again, He resists the proud (in heart), but gives grace to the humble. The humble submit themselves to God. The proud reject God's commandments and do their own thing. Paul told the church, *"Flee also youthful lusts: but follow [after] righteousness, faith, charity [and], peace, with them that call on the Lord out of a pure [sincere], heart"* (2 Tim. 2:22). When we sincerely repented and turned to God, His grace, like a helping hand, opened our eyes and pulled us out of our old way of life. We are saved then from the pollutions of the world, and God *"delivered us from the power of darkness"* by grace. And, as Peter said, we must never go back into them again (2 Pet. 2:20-21).

Paul went about preaching the gospel about the grace of God saying that grace can enable you to overcome the law of sin in the flesh. He himself, taught people, even Christians, that if they lived their lives after the flesh or the works of the flesh, that they would spiritually die and be cut off from God's Kingdom (Rom. 8:12; Gal. 5:19-21; Jude 12). He went through much as he also, strengthened by grace, resisted sin, Satan, temptations, and persecutions, and he kept his body in subjection. Paul said, *"But none of these things move me, neither count I my life dear unto myself, so that I might finish my course with joy, and the ministry, which I have received of the Lord Jesus, to testify [about] the Gospel of the grace of God"* (Acts 20:24). He declared that God's power is available and able to save all, and that His mercy is available to forgive all, if men will repent of living their selfish, sinful, independent lives apart from the will of God. Again, Paul said, *"Whereupon, O king Agrippa, I was not disobedient unto the heavenly vision: but showed first unto them of Damascus, and at Jerusalem, and throughout all the coasts of Judaea, and then to the Gentiles, that [1] they should repent [of their lives of sin] and [2] turn to God, [in faith and He'd give them grace] and [3] do works meet for repentance"* (show God by their lives that they really are willing to cooperate with His grace and be changed, Acts 26:19-20). This turning from the power of Satan (sin) unto the power of God's grace, was Paul's message.

Point 12: *It was grace* that empowered Paul to be an apostle (Rom. 12:3; 1 Cor. 15:9-10). *"By whom **we have received grace** and apostleship, for [to preach] obedience to the faith among all nations, for his name"* (Rom. 1:5). Paul was empowered by grace to preach obedience to the faith; to make the Gentiles *"obedient by word and deed"* (Rom. 15:15-19). Various degrees of grace (the operation of God's power in us) and faith are then given to every man in Christ to function as a member of Christ's body (Eph. 4:7). By the grace of God, we are who we are, for God *"set the members in the body as it hath pleased him."* Then He gave grace to each one to give us the ability to supernaturally function there, so to God in all things be all the glory. (See Rom. 12:3-6.)

No part of salvation is of human labor alone but of God's unmerited power. *"Now to him that worketh [keeping the ceremonies and rituals of the law] is the reward not reckoned of grace [God's free unmerited, saving work], but of debt"* (human effort and labor as though God owed us salvation, Rom. 4:4). But we know that God saved us when we acknowledged we were sinners who couldn't save ourselves but needed a Savior. God again owes this to no man. He didn't have to do it and without His salvation, we couldn't be saved. God elected to save by grace those who would repent, turn to follow Him (Luke 13:3; 2 Pet. 3:9), and obey His Son (Heb. 5:9); and as long as we follow Jesus, no man or devil can pluck us out of His hand.

Point 13: *Grace alone* is what makes it sure to all people for all can repent and believe and receive grace, and thereby, all can live holy by its influence and power, for Scripture says, *"Without holiness [living a life separated to God] no man shall see the Lord."* *"Follow peace with all men, and holiness without which no man shall see the Lord: Looking diligently lest any man fail of [fall away from] the grace of God; lest any root of bitterness springing up trouble you [and hinder you from operating in faith], and thereby many be defiled"* (and become polluted again, Heb. 12:14-15). For *"faith worketh by love,"* and only faith can give access to this wonderful grace. Faith, working by love, gives access to grace. Sin and love are direct opposites just as grace and sin are opposite forces at work. Love, Paul said, fulfills the law (Rom. 13). But sin breaks it, for sin is *"transgression of the law"* (1 John 3:4). You cannot therefore, operate in Bible faith and sin at the same time, for sin is rebellion against God and His moral government. *"Beloved, if our heart condemn us not, **then have we confidence toward God"*** (1 John 3:21).

So, God does not give salvation for us to continue in sin, but He gives the gift of grace (divine ability) so that we can live godly and reign in life. Listen again to this scripture: *"According as his divine power [His grace] hath given unto us all things that pertain unto life and **godliness**, through the knowledge of him that hath **called us to** glory and virtue"* (2 Pet. 1:3). This word "virtue" means "moral uprightness"; "honesty"; "integrity"; and, "conformity to the moral law" (Webster's Dictionary). God has called us by His grace to share in His divine, holy nature and escape the moral pollution and corruption that is in the world through lust. *"Whereby are given unto us exceeding great and precious promises: that by these ye might be partakers of the divine [holy] nature, having escaped the corruption (moral pollution) that is in the world through lust"* (sinful desires, 2 Pet. 1:4; 1 John 2:15-17). God always makes a way of escape from sin, not a way to live in moral pollution.

"But not as the offense, so also is the free gift. For if through the offense [the sin] of one, many be dead, much more the grace of God, and the gift by grace, which is by one man, Jesus Christ, hath abounded unto many" (Rom. 5:15). Adam brought sin into the race, and sin in the flesh caused men to go astray from God and follow Satan and his rebellion, which thereby brought about death, for *"death spread to all men for all have sinned"* (Rom. 5:12). Jesus brought grace to the race so we can now return to God, reign over sin, live for God and thereby obtain eternal life (Matt. 7:21). The apostle Paul, in his theology wrote concerning God and His gospel, that God *"will render to every man according to his deeds: to them who **by patient continuance in well doing** [empowered by, and cooperating with, His grace] seek for glory and honor and immortality, **eternal life"*** (Rom. 2:6-7). ***"But unto them that are contentious, and do not obey the truth, but obey unrighteousness** [He will give], **indignation and wrath**, tribulation and anguish [will come], upon every soul of man that doeth [and lives for] evil, of the Jew first, and also of the Gentile; but glory, honor, and peace, to every man that worketh good, to the Jew first, and also to the Gentile: **For there is no respect of persons with God"*** (Rom. 2:8-11). Both sin and grace need the cooperation of the will of man. Only His grace can sustain us and produce the inward fruits of righteousness in us. Now, we can even more clearly see and understand what Christ meant when He said, *"Marvel not*

*at this: for the hour is coming, in the which all that are in the graves shall hear his voice, and shall come forth; they that have **done good**, unto the resurrection of life; and they that have **done evil**, unto the resurrection of damnation"* (John 5:28-29). Only those who have repented of a life of sin (Luke 13:3) and have accepted Jesus as Lord, can produce good fruit, for without Him, we can do nothing acceptable to God, and without Him, *"there is none that doeth good, no not one."* Those who refuse to obey Him are cut off from grace (Rom. 11:22). So we do owe all to the glory of His grace. Notice also that Paul said God rewards those who continue living right with *eternal life*. This is his topic.

Grace then, enables us to reign over all our enemies and do good. *"For if by one man's offense death reigned by one [because of sin gaining control]; much more they which receive abundance of grace and of the gift of righteousness shall reign in life [over sin] by one, Jesus Christ"* (Rom. 5:17). We can now reign over sin, Satan, and the pollutions of this world because of grace. *"Let not sin therefore reign [any longer] in your mortal bodies"* (Rom. 6:12), but let righteousness now reign in your life. Your old nature was sinful. Your new nature is righteousness. The Bible says, *"Be ye not unequally yoked together with unbelievers: for what fellowship hath righteousness with unrighteousness? and what communion hath light with darkness? And what concord hath Christ with Belial? or what part hath he that believeth with an infidel? And what agreement hath the temple of God with idols? for ye are the temple of the living God; as God hath said, I will dwell in them, and walk in them; and I will be their God, and they shall be my people"* (2 Cor. 6:14-16). (See Rom. 8:10.) *"And that ye put on the new man, which after God is created in righteousness and true holiness"* (Eph. 4:24). So, awake to righteousness and sin not. You changed masters the moment you were born again. Be not entangled again with the yoke of sin, bondage, and your old master (John 8:34-36).

No matter how much sin held you captive before, grace abounds over it to give you victory. Grace makes us all equal. *"Moreover the law entered, that the offense might abound [to expose sin for what it is]. But where sin abounded, grace [to overcome it] did much more abound"* (Rom. 5:20). So there is no excuse to live a life of sin any longer by anyone. Paul wrote, *"What shall we say then? Shall we continue in sin, that grace may abound? God forbid, How shall we, that are dead to sin, live any longer therein? For he that is dead is freed from sin"* (Rom. 6:1-2,7). In other words, grace doesn't keep you while you're in sin, but grace keeps you out of sin. Grace freed you from a life of sin (Heb. 2:9; Rom. 6:8-14). *"Who his own self bare our sins in his own body on the tree, **that we, being dead to sins, should live unto*** *righteousness by whose stripes ye were healed"* (1 Pet. 2:24). We are dead to a life of sin.

Sin brought about disobedience, wrath, and death. Grace produces obedience, righteousness, blessings, and eternal life. *"That as sin hath reigned unto death, even so might grace reign through righteousness unto eternal life by [obeying] Jesus Christ our Lord"* (Rom. 5:21). The apostle Paul wrote concerning Christ, *"And being made perfect, he became the author of eternal salvation **unto all them that obey him**"* (Heb. 5:9). *"Then spake Jesus again unto them, saying, I am the light of the world: he that **followeth me** [obeys Me, just as I obeyed the will of My Father] shall not walk in darkness [and sin], but shall have the light of life"* (John 8:12). For the law of the Spirit of life in Christ Jesus hath set me free of the law of sin and death. (Which before reigned in our members, Rom. 7:14, 8:2.) Believe you're free. Focus on freedom not your old master. You are now to be a slave of righteousness (Rom. 6:17-21). Righteousness is not just a label, it's a new way of life (2 Pet. 2:21; Heb. 10:20).

The Elect by Grace

So, obviously, in view of all we've said thus far, we know that election to salvation is not according to human effort nor because any man willed it to be, or by him that runs in his own strength, but it is only for those who repent of a life of sin and turn to God for this overcoming grace (Rom. 11:5). But this grace is for all men, for whosoever will can come to Christ and receive (Heb. 2:9; John 1:12; 1 John 2:2; Rev. 22:17), *"to them he gave power"* (John 1:12). Christ is called *"the elect of God."* When we repent of sin, and acknowledge our need of Him, He saves us by grace and mercy, takes us *out of Adam*, puts us *into Christ* and we become the elect *"in Him,"* and predestined *"in Him."* That is, provided that we continue to *"abide in Him"* (1 John 2:28-29; 15:6), and to no longer live a life independent of the will of God (1 John 2:17). *"And every man that hath this hope in him purifieth himself, even as he is pure ... **Whosoever abideth in him sinneth not:** whosoever sinneth [without repentance] hath not seen Him, neither known Him"* (1 John 3:3,6). When a person is born again and receives Jesus, He really does make an amazing change in one's life. This is amazing grace, the life-changing grace of our Lord Jesus Christ. The life-giving sap, so to speak, of the vine, that flows into us, the branches. *"Being filled with the fruits of righteousness, which are by Jesus Christ, unto the glory and praise of God"* (Phil 1:11).

Grace in the Epistles

Grace also enabled Paul to write and unveil God's will. *"Nevertheless, brethren, I have written the more boldly unto you in some sort, as putting you in mind, because of the grace that is given to me of God"* (Rom. 15:15).

See the many operations of grace? See how it is actually something that is given to an individual?

You received it the moment you were born again, and that's why you began to change. Continue now to walk in the light of this (Eph. 4:7).

"The grace of our Lord Jesus Christ be with you all. Amen" (Rom. 16:24).

Paul always spoke of grace as an influence and power actually given. *"I thank my God always on your behalf, for the grace of God **which is given you by** Jesus Christ"* (1 Cor. 1:4). He went on to say that by this they were enriched in everything.

Grace enabled Paul to be a wise masterbuilder even though before he had grace, he viciously destroyed the church in his religious zeal, without knowledge. *"According to the grace of God which is given unto me [to labor, 1 Cor. 3:9], as a wise masterbuilder, I have laid the foundation, and another buildeth thereon. But let every man take heed how he buildeth thereupon"* (1 Cor. 3:10).

Paul became an apostle and was amazingly changed by the grace of God and empowered and energized by this undeserved divine grace. *"And the grace of our Lord was exceeding abundant with faith and love which is in Christ Jesus"* (1 Tim. 1:14). He, because of grace's operation in his heart, had his whole disposition and life changed, and labored more abundantly than all the apostles. *"But by the grace of God I am what I am: and his grace which was bestowed upon me was not in vain; but I [cooperating with this active power] labored more abundantly than they all: **yet not I, but the grace of God which was with me**"* (1 Cor. 15:10). He said, *"Whereunto I also labor, striving according to his working [energy], which worketh in me mightily"* (Col. 1:29). Therefore grace is a mighty operation of God in us and not an attitude of God toward us. Much of the body of Christ have mercy and grace mixed up.

Our conversation too can be seasoned and empowered by this divine grace as we depend upon God. *"For our rejoicing is this, the testimony of our conscience, that in simplicity and godly sincerity, not with fleshly wisdom, but by the grace of God, we have had our [good] conversation [and our conduct] in the world, and more abundantly to you-ward"* (2 Cor. 1:12). We are to have our speech *"seasoned with grace,"* and our conduct governed by grace. *"Let no corrupt communication proceed out of your mouth, but that which is good to the use of edifying, that it may minister grace unto the hearers"* (Eph. 4:29). You can minister the grace in your heart to others.

Grace is given so that we too, can work together with God. If we don't cooperate with God's grace, we've received it in vain. *"We then, **as workers together with him**, beseech **you also** that ye receive not the grace of God in vain"* (2 Cor. 6:1). Realize there is divine grace with you to enable you to do all things through Christ who strengthens you. Believe this, and minister with the ability *"which God supplies."* Be willing to abound in the work of the Lord and He will supply the grace (2 Cor. 9:8). If you're faithful with little, you'll be faithful with more. *"But he giveth **more grace**. Wherefore he saith, God resisteth the proud, but giveth grace unto the humble"* (James 4:6).

You must see to it that you abound in grace; it is not automatic. *"Therefore, as ye abound in every thing, in faith, and utterance, and knowledge, and in all diligence, and in your love to us, **see [to it] that ye abound** in this grace also"* (2 Cor. 8:7). You tap into it by being a doer of the Word and not a hearer only (James 1:22). When you begin to act in faith on what God has said, *then* God's power steps in. It's sort of like Peter stepping out of the boat to walk on water at the word of Christ. It wasn't until he stepped out in faith on Christ's word that the other power took over and gave him the ability to do what he couldn't do before (Matt. 14:25-31).

God can give you more grace and make it abound towards you so that you have the ability to do every good work. *"And God is able to **make all grace abound toward you** [so]; that ye, always having all sufficiency in all things [by this grace], may abound to every good work"* (2 Cor. 9:8). If someone is abounding in grace then they are abounding in working for the Lord. Again the Bible reveals that grace, like faith, can be seen by people's actions. If an individual produces nothing, then they are not cooperating with the grace of God. If they are living for sinful pleasures alone, then they have left the grace of God. Grace therefore, doesn't mean that you sit like a spiritual bump on a log and do nothing, but it's an activating power.

Grace influences us and makes us generous givers. Selfishness tries to keep it all to itself. Paul wrote to one church about another, *"they glorify God for your professed subjection unto the gospel of Christ, and for your liberal distribution [of financial aid] unto them, and unto all men"*; and they thanked God *"for the exceeding grace of God in you [which moved you to give and they thank God that you obeyed its influence]. Thanks be unto God for his unspeakable gift"* (2 Cor. 9:13-15). Sinners can't understand why Christians are so influenced to give so much to the Gospel. We can! It's grace in us that moves us. We will be rewarded according to our cooperation with grace (Phil. 2:12-13). Those who don't want to tithe or give into the Gospel are not influenced by grace, but rather by the flesh and selfishness (Heb. 7:5-8).

The Gospel is all about a new life and a grace that delivers us from spiritual death, from the power of sin and Satan, and from religious dead works. Paul wrote, *"I marvel that ye are so **soon removed from him that called you into the [supernatural] grace of Christ unto another gospel"*** (Gal. 1:6). One different gospel says for people to go back to Jewish ceremonies to be justified; and another so-called gospel says that you could go back into a life of sin and that grace will provide a cloak for evil, but both of those are wrong. Scriptures reveal that nothing can save but the effectual working of God's grace. It saves us out of this world's corrupt system. *"Who is he that **overcometh the world**, but he that believeth that Jesus is the Son of God?"* (1 John 5:5). We overcome it, we don't live like it (2 Cor. 6:14-18). *"And they overcame him [the devil] by the blood of the Lamb, and by the word of their testimony; and they loved not their lives unto the death"* (Rev. 12:11). *"And the world passeth away, and the lust thereof: **but he that doeth the will of God abideth for ever"*** (1 John 2:17). Only those who do the will of God will abide with God forever.

Grace is not irresistible; it can be frustrated if it's not depended upon to enable you to live righteously. *"I do not frustrate the grace of God: for if righteousness [could] come by [us doing] the [religious works of the] law, then Christ is dead in vain"* (Gal. 2:21). Grace alone establishes the heart and produces the righteousness that God requires, but religious works such as circumcision or the lighting of candles, and so on, never could. *"For I say unto you, That except **your righteousness** shall exceed the righteousness of the scribes and Pharisees, ye shall **in no case** enter into the kingdom of heaven"* (Matt. 5:20). The Pharisees' righteousness was all just outward show and only an outward profession with the mouth, but grace changes us from the inside. They were pious in word but not in deed. You need to exceed just saying that you have faith, or just pretending to be a servant of God. The grace that saves us from a life of unrighteousness is supplied by the Spirit of Grace (Rom. 8:4). This is what enables us to fulfill the righteousness of the moral law. *"Do we then make void [invalid] the law through faith? God forbid: yea, we establish [and make firm the true righteousness of] the law"*

(Rom. 3:31). God is not looking for ornaments hung on the outside, He's looking for change on the inside (1 Pet. 3:3-4). *"For this is the covenant that I will make with the house of Israel after those days, saith the Lord; I will put my laws into their mind, and write them in their hearts: and I will be to them a God, and they shall be to Me a people"* (Heb. 8:10). He puts them in us, not so we'd disobey them, but obey, and thereby be His true followers.

Hearken to the Word

People can fall then from God's grace by going back into a religion of works thinking they'll be made righteous by this, or, on the other hand, they can do despite (insult) to the Spirit of Grace by going back into a life of sin, and face, as Paul said, a *"certain judgment." "What shall we say then? Shall we **continue in sin, that grace may abound? God forbid!"*** (Rom. 6:1) *"Christ is become of no effect unto you, whosoever of you (Galatian Christians) are justified [trying to be made righteous] by the law; **ye are fallen from grace"*** (you're no longer depending on grace, Gal. 5:4). This very statement proves that grace is not some irresistible force or attitude of God. If one can fall away from grace for doing something, so can others. So then, people can disconnect from grace. This is like a branch broken off. *"I am the vine, ye are the branches: He that abideth in me, and I in him, the same bringeth forth much fruit: for without me ye can do nothing. **If a man abide not in Me*** [in Christ], *he is cast forth as a [dead] branch, and is withered; and men gather them, and cast them into the fire, and they are burned"* (John 15:5-6). Concerning others, the apostle writes to Christians, *"Ye adulterers and adulteresses know ye not that the friendship of the world is enmity with God? **Whosoever therefore** will be a friend of the world [and its sinful ways] **is the enemy of God.**"* Jesus said, *"Ye are my friends, if ye do whatsoever I command you"* (John 15:14). Paul wrote, *"For if we sin willfully (departing from God and His will and thereby overriding God's work in our lives) after that we have received the knowledge of the truth [that we needed to repent of a life of sin and be saved out of the pollutions of the world by God's grace], there remaineth no more sacrifice for sins, but [only] a certain fearful looking for of judgment and fiery indignation, which shall devour the adversaries. He that despised Moses' **law died without mercy** under two or three witnesses: **Of how much [more] sorer punishment**, suppose ye, shall he be thought worthy, who hath trodden under foot the Son of God, and hath counted the blood of the covenant, wherewith **he was** sanctified (and by it had his past sins washed away), an unholy thing, and hath done despite unto the Spirit of Grace [who had come to free him from sin's power]? For we know Him that hath said, Vengeance belongeth unto me, I will recompense, saith the Lord. And again,*

The Lord shall judge his people. It is a fearful thing to fall into the hands of the living God" (Heb. 10:26-31). The Holy Spirit supplies grace to enable us to fulfill the righteousness of the law so that we can mortify the deeds of the body. To consistently resist His work without repentance and live after the flesh, will bring death and wrath (See Romans 8:1-13.), and *"A certain fearful looking for of judgment"* (Gal. 6:7-8). Everyone needs to heed these statements. These facts are *"forever settled in heaven"* (Ps. 119:89).

Grace changes us and makes us accepted in the beloved. *"To the praise of the glory of his grace, wherein he hath made us accepted in the beloved"* (Eph. 1:6). *"That we should be holy and without blame before him in love"* (Eph. 1:4).

This truly is a dispensation of grace, where God's grace makes us to be all He's called us to be. *"If ye have heard of the dispensation of the grace of God which is given me to you-ward"* (Eph. 3:2).

Grace enables God-called ministers to be ministers. It is the effectual working of God's power. *"Whereof I was made a minister, **according to the gift of the grace of God** given unto me [that is] by the effectual working of His power"* (Eph. 3:7). *"Whereunto [by this grace] I also labor, striving according to His working, which worketh in me mightily"* (Col. 1:29).

Grace is given to enable us to preach. *"Unto me, who am less than the least of all saints, is this **grace given, that I should preach** among the Gentiles the unsearchable riches of Christ"* (Eph. 3:8). *"And all bare him witness, and wondered **at the gracious words** which proceeded out of his mouth"* (Luke 4:22). *"And they were astonished at His doctrine: **for his word was with power**"* (Luke 4:32).

See the many operations of this unmerited power and ability? Each of us has received grace so that we can change and bring forth good fruit. *"But unto every one of us is given grace according to the measure of the gift of Christ"* (Eph. 4:7). (See also Col. 1:6.) Peter called it *"the manifold grace of God,"* and told us to minister it to one another. So, all can now obey God because of this grace. You have it right now if you're a Christian. Believe then that Satan's hold over your life is completely broken. *Never* believe those who say or teach that you can now go back and live under Satan's authority, and that Jesus' redemptive work will automatically cover for you. Remember the Bible warns you about *false teachers* that will teach such things (2 Pet. 2:1-3, 20-21).

Grace is only for the humble that love our Lord Jesus Christ in sincerity and desire to obey Him. Jesus said, *"At that day [after I'm raised from* *the dead] ye shall know that I am in my Father, and ye in me, and I in you. He [then] that hath my commandments, and keepeth them [empowered by my grace], he it is that loveth me: and he that loveth me shall be loved of my Father, and I will love him, and will manifest myself to him. Judas saith unto him, not Iscariot, Lord, how is it that thou wilt manifest thyself unto us, and not unto the world? Jesus answered and said unto him, **If a man [really] love me**, he will keep [obey] my words: and my Father will love him, and we will come unto him, and make our abode with him [that keeps My words and commandments]. **He that loveth me not keepeth not my sayings:** and the word which ye hear is not mine, but the Father's which sent me [God by this made it clear who His true people are]. These things have I spoken unto you, being yet present with you. [In other words, He will not manifest His presence to those who willingly, persistently disobey Him.] But the Comforter, which is the Holy Ghost, whom the Father will send in my name, he shall teach you all things, **and bring all things to your remembrance, whatsoever I have said unto you**"* (John 14:20-26). (This is what the Holy Ghost would do on and after the day of Pentecost in this church age for all true disciples of Jesus. He would remind us of what Jesus taught so that we would obey Jesus.) Never then, listen to anyone who says that you don't need to listen to, nor obey Jesus for they are teaching contrary to the doctrine of Christ (and they, like the serpent, do not want you to believe you have to keep His commandments, Rev. 12:17). Jesus said, *"If you love me" keep my commandments"* (John 14:15). *"Grace (then to obey) be with all them that love our Lord Jesus Christ in sincerity. Amen"* (Eph. 6:24). Paul wrote, *"If any man love not the Lord Jesus Christ, [and refuses to obey His commandments] let him be Anathema Maranatha"* (1 Cor. 16:22). This means, a branch that is cursed and cut off when the Lord comes (John 15:2).

Every real Christian has partaken of this life changing, strengthening grace of God. You can see the changes in a person who truly hooks up with the vine. It delivers and sets them free from the law of sin and death and fleshly bondages. Jesus, the author of faith, kept His Father's commandments, and abode in the truth. Satan rebelled and *"abode not in the truth"* (John 8:44). To persistently, willingly disobey is to not abide. To obey God is to abide: This is faith. To abide or not abide in Christ is up to you (1 John 2:28). You abide as you are willing to live for God, and only those who abide continue on in grace and continue in the Father and in the Son (1 John 2:24).

*We can worship and sing with grace in our hearts motivating us. "Let the word of Christ dwell in you richly in all wisdom; teaching and admonishing one another in psalms and hymns and spiritual songs, singing with **grace in*** *your hearts to the Lord"* (Col. 3:16). By this, we worship God in spirit and in truth.

This grace that God has given us to change us and to inspire hope in us assures us that if He began a good work in us by His grace, He will continue it if we will humbly continue on with Him. *"Now our Lord Jesus Christ himself, and God, even our Father, which hath loved us, and hath given us everlasting consolation and good hope through grace"* (2 Thess. 2:16). *"And you, that were at one time alienated and enemies in your mind by wicked works, yet now hath he reconciled in the body of his flesh through death, to present you holy and unblameable and unreprovable in his sight [on this condition]:* **If ye continue** *in the faith grounded and settled, and be not moved away from* **the hope of the Gospel***"* (Col. 1:21-23). First John 3:3 says, *"And every man that hath this hope in him purifieth himself, even as he is pure."* Grace saved you from the wicked one and grace will present you faultless before God, if you continue in the faith, living for the will of God. *"We know that whosoever is born of God sinneth not; but he that is begotten of God keepeth himself, and that wicked one toucheth him not"* (1 John 5:18). It's all a work of grace. Grace saves. Grace sustains.

Grace and Mercy

Grace and mercy are two different things. Mercy is His attitude of undeserved kindness to us. Grace is His undeserved power given to us to change us. *"For I will be merciful to their unrighteousness, and their sins and their iniquities will I remember no more"* (Heb. 8:12). *"He that covereth his sins shall not prosper: but whoso confesseth and forsaketh them shall have mercy"* (Prov. 28:13). *"Let us therefore come boldly unto the throne of grace, that we may obtain mercy (for sin), and find grace [the power] to help in time of need"* (Heb. 4:16). God gives mercy to the humble and repentant, and He hardens the rebellious and prideful. *"Therefore hath he mercy on whom he will have mercy, and whom he will he hardeneth"* (Rom. 9:18). Scripture says, *"Blessed are the merciful for they shall obtain mercy"* (Matt. 5:7). If He wants to be merciful to the repentant, He can be. Mercy means that He is disposed to forgive offenders. *"The Lord is not slack concerning his promise, as some men count slackness; but is longsuffering to us-ward,* **not willing that any** *should perish,* **but that all** *should come to repentance"* (2 Pet. 3:9). If they would all repent, He would have mercy on all, even though they don't deserve it, but if like Pharaoh they refuse to submit to the Lord, the Word will harden them even more. He resists the proud when they resist Him (Rom. 2:4-5). People, even so-called theologians, have many times, mixed up grace and mercy. Mercy is undeserved kindness shown to repentant sinners, and grace is the unmerited power to help repentant sinners out of sin. God commandeth **all men everywhere** to repent so He can have mercy on them all (Acts 17:30). But if they resist Him, He will resist them (Gal. 6:7).

He has provided more than enough grace to supply wherever we are lacking. *"And the grace of our Lord Jesus was exceeding abundant with faith and love which is in Christ Jesus"* (1 Tim. 1:14).

God saves us, not because of our own human efforts and what we have done, but according to His own purpose and mercy, He does it by the power of His grace. *"Who hath saved us, and called us with an holy calling, not according to our [religious ceremonial] works, [or past deeds] but according to his own purpose and grace, which was given us in Christ Jesus before the world began"* (2 Tim. 1:9; 1 Pet. 1:3,10,20). He planned to help us by His grace before the world began. No one could be saved without the saving work and power of God, for before we were born again, we were in the flesh and under the power and control of the law of sin, and therefore, *"they that are in the flesh cannot please God"* (Rom. 8:8).

So Christ is full of grace and truth. His life is grace life. *"And the Word was made flesh, and dwelt among us (and we beheld his glory, the glory as of the only begotten of the Father), full of grace and truth. John bare witness of him, and cried, saying, This was he of whom I spake, he that cometh after me is preferred before me: for he was before me. And **of his fullness have all we received, and grace for grace**"* (John 1:14-16). All we received from Him was and is, an impartation of His grace. *"I am crucified with Christ: nevertheless I live; yet not I, but Christ liveth in me: and the life which I now live in the flesh **I live by the faith of the Son of God**, who loved me, and gave himself for me."* He gave us His life and grace so we'd have the power to do as He did and live for His Father's will, obey His Father's commandments, fulfill all righteousness, resist sin and Satan, and do good works. *"He that saith he abideth in him ought himself also [therefore] so to walk, even as he walked"* (1 John 2:6).

Living holy and abounding in good works is all a product of grace. *"Jesus answered them, Verily, verily, I say unto you, Whosoever committeth sin is the servant (the slave) of sin. And the servant [the slave] abideth not in the [master's] house forever: but the Son abideth [for] ever. If the Son therefore shall make you free [by His grace from slavery to sin so that you can live as a son like He lived and not as a slave to sin], ye shall be free indeed"* (John 8:34-36). Habitual sin is always a product of the devil at work in a person's life. Sons of God are freed from Satan's slavery. *"As he is so are we in this world ..."*

(1 John 4:17). *"Let your light so shine before men, that they may see your good works, and glorify your Father which is in heaven"* (Matt. 5:16). Christ has freed us from the outward ceremonial laws of the Old Covenant, and from the power of sin also, and empowered us to do good. We are also free from all of the legalistic commandments of men.

So then, we are made righteous by His grace. *"That being justified [made righteous] by his grace, we should be made heirs according to the hope of eternal life"* (Titus 3:7). For by grace He gave us a new heart and a new spirit and enabled us to walk in righteousness. He said, *"A new heart also will I give you, and a new spirit will I put within you: and I will take away the stony heart out of your flesh, and I will give you an heart of flesh. And I will put my spirit [the Spirit of Grace] within you, and cause you to walk in my statutes, and ye shall* **keep my judgments,** *and* **do** *them"* (Ezek. 36:26-27). *"That the righteousness of the law might be fulfilled in us, who walk not after the flesh, but after the Spirit"* (Rom. 8:4). This is the *"new and living way"* of the New Covenant (Heb. 10:20).

We must never go back to a life of sin, or we do despite (insult) to the Spirit of Grace (Heb. 10:26-29). We must never go back to legalism and outward rituals to try and be made righteous, or we frustrate the grace of God (Gal. 2:21).

Grace then establishes the heart in God so that we stand steadfast in our most holy faith. Eating certain meats or not eating them, and other outward works of the law, or commandments of men, profit no one. *"Be not carried about with divers and strange doctrines [made up by the commandments of men]. For it is a good thing that the heart be established [in God] with grace; not with meats, which have not profited them that have been occupied therein"* (Heb. 13:9). For *"meat commendeth us not to God: for neither, if we eat, are we the better; neither, if we eat not, are we the worse"* (1 Cor. 8:8).

More Grace

The prophets prophesied of this supernatural grace that would come to us and change our lives. *"Of which salvation the prophets have inquired and searched diligently,* **who prophesied of the [life changing] grace that should come unto you:** *Searching what, or what manner of time the Spirit of Christ which was in them did signify, when it testified beforehand the sufferings of Christ,* **and the glory** *that should follow. Unto whom it was revealed, that not unto themselves, but unto us they did minister the things, which are now reported unto you by them that have preached the gospel unto you with* *the Holy Ghost sent down from heaven; which things the angels desire to look into. Wherefore gird up the loins of your mind, be sober, and* **hope to the end for the grace that is to be brought unto you at the revelation of Jesus Christ** *[if you've been faithful with the grace that was given to you to live for God, you'll receive more at that time to be taken up to God]; as obedient children, not fashioning yourselves according to the former lusts in your ignorance:* **but as he which hath called you is holy, so be ye holy in all manner of conversation;** *[and conduct] because it is written, Be ye holy; for I am holy. And if ye call on the Father who without respect of persons* **judgeth according to every man's work,** *pass the time of your sojourning here [on earth] in fear"* (1 Pet. 1:10-17). Praise God, more grace will be given to us and brought to us at the revelation of Jesus Christ, to make whatever changes are necessary. So, He says, *"Wherefore gird up the loins of your mind, be sober, and hope to the end* **for the grace that is to be brought unto you at the revelation of Jesus Christ"** (1 Pet. 1:13). *"Who shall change our vile body, that it may be fashioned like unto his glorious body, according to the working whereby he is able even to subdue all things unto himself"* (Phil. 3:21). *"Behold, I show you a mystery; We shall not all sleep, but we shall all be changed [by His grace]. In a moment, in the twinkling of an eye, at the last trump: for the trumpet shall sound, and the dead shall be raised incorruptible, and we shall be changed"* (1 Cor. 15:51-52). This is an act of grace (God's power).

"For I reckon that the sufferings of this present time [in ceasing from a life of sin, Gal. 5:24; 1 Pet. 4:1-2] are not worthy to be compared with the glory which shall be revealed in us" (Rom. 8:18). This suffering he is speaking of is a ceasing from a life of sin. First Peter 4:1-2 says, *"Forasmuch then as Christ hath suffered for us in the flesh [dying on he cross to sin], arm yourselves likewise with the same mind: for he that hath suffered in the flesh [crucifying the flesh] hath ceased from sin; That he no longer should live the rest of his time in the flesh [on the earth] to the lusts of men, but to the will of God."* Scripture says, *"If we suffer with him [carrying our cross daily and crucifying the flesh], we may be also glorified together"* with Him (Rom. 8:17). Christ was first crucified and then glorified. Notice also how Peter connected grace with works. He sees no contradiction in terms nor does Paul or James when it's understood correctly (2 Cor. 9:8).

Paul writes, *"Wherefore, my beloved, as ye have always* **obeyed,** *not as in my presence only, but now much more in my absence,* **work out** *your own [eternal] salvation with [a holy] fear and trembling. For it is God, which worketh in you both to will and to do of His good pleasure"* (Phil. 2:12-13). *"Wherefore, beloved, seeing that ye look for such things,* **be diligent** *that ye may be found of him in peace, without spot, and blameless"* (2 Pet. 3:13-14).

God works in us by His grace. *"Now the God of peace, that brought again from the dead our Lord Jesus, that great shepherd of the sheep, through the blood of the everlasting covenant [may He], **make you perfect in every good work to do his will, working in you that which is well pleasing in his sight**, through Jesus Christ; to whom be glory for ever and ever. Amen"* (Heb. 13:20-21). Good works then are works prompted by grace and faith; it is God's work in us. These are works produced through new creatures in Christ as we cooperate with God's grace, and are different from fleshly, defiled works done by the unregenerate, or the works of the law, for all their works are self-centered and are from some form of self-gratification or self-satisfaction, and not done to the glory of God (Eph. 2:10). And we can also see by this passage that God works in us so that we will do His will, which is holy, just, and good.

Life Is a Grace

Life is a grace. It's an operation of God. *"In him we live, and move, and have our being"* (Acts 17:28). *"Likewise, ye husbands, dwell with them [your wives] according to knowledge, giving honor unto the wife, as unto the weaker vessel, and as being heirs together of the grace of life; that your prayers be not hindered"* (1 Pet. 3:7). All life came from the God of all grace. All spiritual life does also. Life never originates with man. We only work with that which God has given us. It is important that we correctly use the life He has given us. *"So then every one of us shall give account of himself to God"* (Rom. 14:12).

Each Christian has received the grace to live as a Christian and to enable him to minister to others in one way or another. We are told to be good stewards of this grace that is given to us. *"For I say, through the grace given unto me, to every man that is among you, not to think of himself more highly than he ought to think; but to think soberly, according as God hath dealt **to every man** the measure of faith. For as we have many members in one body, and all members have not the same office: So we, being many, are one body in Christ, and every one members one of another. **Having then gifts differing according to the grace that is given to us** [by God], whether prophecy, let us prophesy according to the proportion of faith; or [if you've received grace for] ministry, let us wait on our ministering: or he that teacheth, on teaching; or he that exhorteth, on exhortation: he that giveth, let him do it with simplicity; he that ruleth, with diligence; he that showeth mercy, with cheerfulness"* (Rom. 12:3-8). So grace then, clearly is a life giving activating power working in us, and where we are weak it shows itself strong, changes us, and glorifies God.

Misapplying Grace

Listen now, to the Lord's warning in scripture about misapplying His grace. Scripture says, *"For there are certain men crept in [to the church] unawares, who were before of old ordained to this condemnation, ungodly [sinful] men, turning the grace of our God into lasciviousness [an automatic cover for immoral living and a blatant disregard for God's justice], and [by this they are] denying the only Lord God, and our Lord Jesus Christ [and all they stand for]. [Concerning this matter] I will therefore put you in remembrance, though ye once knew this, how that the Lord,* **having saved the people** *out of the land of Egypt [a type of our salvation],* **afterward destroyed them** *that believed not (and proved unfaithful). And (some of) the [holy] angels which kept not their first estate, but left their own habitation [and followed Lucifer and sinned], He [God] hath reserved [them] in everlasting chains under darkness unto the judgment of the great day. Even as Sodom and Gomorrah, and the cities about them in like manner, giving themselves over to fornication, and going after strange flesh [forcing themselves past God's proper boundaries], are set forth for an example, suffering the vengeance of eternal fire [as an example for all those who would afterwards* **live ungodly***, 2 Pet. 2:1-9). These (who teach this false concept of grace] are spots in your feasts of charity, when they feast with you, feeding themselves without [the] fear [of God] [because of believing this false concept of grace] clouds they are without water [the Holy Spirit], carried about of winds; [of doctrines made up by the cunning minds of men] trees whose [good] fruit withereth, without fruit,* **twice** *[spiritually] dead, plucked up by the roots"* (through this wrong idea about grace, Jude 4-7,12).

Jude called these people that change God's grace to mean you can disregard God's justice as *"filthy dreamers."* *"Likewise also these filthy dreamers defile the flesh, despise dominion [authorities], and [are not afraid to] speak evil of dignities"* (Jude 8). Their false concept of grace is, according to God's Word, a filthy dream with no substance.

He calls them fleshly, carnal, and says that they speak evil of things they know not, and they corrupt themselves with their false interpretation of grace. *"But these speak evil of those things which they know not: but what they know naturally, as brute beasts, in those things they corrupt themselves"* (Jude 10).

He points out that they have gone in the way of Cain, who hated his brother because his brother's works were righteous and his own works were evil. They ran greedily after the error of Balaam who loved to receive wages from unrighteous acts, and they will perish in the rebellion of Korah who rejected God's authorities that God Himself had set up.

Jude says, *"These are spots in your feasts of charity ... raging waves of the sea, foaming out their own shame [by what they teach]; [like] wandering [shooting] stars [who left their proper course and whose light went out], to whom is reserved the blackness of darkness for ever"* (Jude 12-13). (Because although they had light for awhile, they later rejected the true light, and went back into the ways of darkness.) The Bible is written in such a way that if you want to find excuses for following sin and immorality, you can twist its meaning just as some had done in Paul's day, saying, *"Let us continue in sin that grace may abound."* Paul said, *"their damnation is just."* Jesus said, *"The light of the body is the eye: if therefore thine eye be single, thy whole body shall be full of light. But if thine eye be evil, thy whole body shall be full of darkness. If therefore the light that is in thee be darkness, how great is that darkness!"* (Matt. 6:22-23). But if your heart wants to serve God, and wants righteousness and holiness, then you will clearly see what God is really is saying. (See Matt. 5:6-8; John 3:19-20, 7:16-17.)

*"And **some** of the Pharisees which were with him heard these words, and said unto him, Are we blind also? Jesus said unto them, If ye were blind, ye should have no sin: but now ye say, We see; therefore your sin remaineth"* (John 9:40-41). *"If I had not come and spoken unto them, they had not had sin: but now they have no cloak for their sin"* (John 15:22).

The apostle writes, *"But there were false prophets also among the people, even as there shall be false teachers among you [the church], who privily shall bring in damnable heresies, even [to the point of] denying the Lord that bought them and bring upon themselves swift destruction. [One so-called Christian author even wrote that once you've believed, you could even deny the Lord and still not have the slightest chance of being lost.] And **many** shall follow their pernicious [morally loose, fatal, and sinful] ways; by reason of whom the way of truth [the true way of grace] shall be evil spoken of"* (2 Pet. 2:1-2). And so it is with many who don't really want to have to take the narrow road that leads to life, but want to hear excuses so they can follow the broad way and the course of this world (1 Tim. 5:15). They follow Cain who persecuted his brother because his own works were evil and his brother's works were righteous. They want fire insurance, but they don't want to have to live for God. Remember that Satan comes as an angel of light so it is no great thing if his ministers come disguised as ministers of righteousness, whose end will be *according to their works.*

The Gospel of Grace and the Law

So, again, grace is God's energy (See Col. 1:29; 1 Cor. 15:10.) at work in us, while the works of the law means, "self-effort doing outward religious works and ceremonies apart from God's power." The law truly exposed sin and the work of Satan, while grace frees us from it. Grace then is the strength of Christ that will manifest in the midst of our human weakness and make us strong. *"But as many as received him, **to them gave he power** to become the sons of God, even to them that believe on his name: Which were born, not of blood, nor of the will of the flesh, nor of the will of man, but of God"* (John 1:12-13). Human effort trying to be righteous by itself through religious activities apart from Christ's grace is the opposite of God's grace (Gal. 2:21). These kinds of works could not cause us to become born again. And such commands as, don't watch TV; don't eat that; don't listen to that style of Christian music; dress like us; etc., frustrates the grace of God. Men cannot pull themselves up by their own boot-straps, and make themselves righteous by doing such things; and as long as they try and do so, they don't trust in God's power to truly make them right with God inwardly.

God has given us Christ, and life is in His Son. He gave us this unspeakable gift so that we could say with Paul, *"for me to live is Christ"*; and *"Follow me as I follow Christ."*

In Galatians Paul warned them not to go back to a system of human religious works such as the observance of holy days, Sabbaths, and circumcision, for it was already proven that man couldn't live a righteous or holy life on his own by these things, for Paul revealed that both Jew and Gentile were all still under the power of sin. We all need the grace and life of Christ to enable us to really live the way He wants. Grace manifests Christ's nature and life in us. The Spirit of Grace empowers us to have victory over a life of sin (Rom. 8:4, 12-13). No matter where we lack, grace has been provided to give us divine ability to live godly (2 Pet. 1:3-4). So now there is no excuse to live in sin (1 John 2:1). For the moral law of God was revealed through Moses but the grace to perform it came through Jesus Christ. *"If the Son therefore shall make you free, ye shall be free indeed."* Grace, then, is more powerful than any enticement of Satan. None of us need therefore to, *"turn aside"* and follow after Satan and this sinful world and its way of living, any longer (1 John 2:15-17).

The Gospel of Grace is the Good News that God will come back into our lives once again, and work in us both to will and do of His good pleasure. Grace is God's operation in us the way it was in man before the fall, so victory never comes through independent human effort apart from God, but because we now willingly yield to His working in us (Rom. 6:16). For independence from God and His will is what caused the fall in the first place, but we Christians have now *"returned to the Shepherd and Bishop of our souls."* Now we can be holy and, *"awake to righteousness and sin not,"* for we are *"dead to sin,"* and should now *"live unto righteousness"* (1 Pet. 2:24). Not by our own power, but His. We are to live life the way He meant for man to live in the beginning, that is, for His will and commandments, and to walk with Him. His wonderful life-changing grace now changes us, empowers us, strengthens us, gives us ability to minister, and so on. It is the effectual working of God's free, unmerited power that makes us to be what He's called us to be, so we Christians can say, *"by the grace of God I am what I am."* The power of God and the grace of God in scripture, go hand in hand. Many times they are referred to as one and the same thing. God is now working in us once again to make us perfect *to do* His will (Heb. 13:20-21); a people *"redeemed from all iniquity, zealous of good works"* (Titus 2:11-14). Christians should then press on and go from one degree of glory to another as they are changed back to the image and likeness of Christ (2 Cor. 3:18). This is the amazing purpose and effect of grace, and God gets all the glory.

I trust that this section of this book has at least revealed to you that grace is not just an attitude of God. God changes not, and still requires us to keep His moral law, but now His grace has been provided for us through Christ Jesus to enable us to live it from an inward impulse. Because of grace, we can now be holy, as He is holy. We supply the willingness and faith in His Word, and He will supply the ability. For centuries men have believed a human perspective on grace, looking at it as an attitude of God rather than God's free, unmerited power given to those who humbly look to Him. They have gotten mercy and grace mixed up. False doctrines have cropped up everywhere saying that grace means you can now live in sin because it's not by human works. They have missed the whole point. *"Do we then make void the law through faith? God forbid: yea, we establish the law"* (Rom. 3:31). True faith taps us into the power of God's grace and enables us to stand (Rom. 5:2). The only way we can fulfill the righteousness of the law in our lives is by grace. But Satan has cleverly disguised a lie and passed it off as the truth, and he goes about promoting it through many avenues. Mostly, he has done it through misled religious men and false teachers, who rather than following the Holy Spirit and all of the scriptures, have reasoned many things away with their minds and have come up with a human philosophy about these things. Using BIG words, pronouns, adjectives, and adverbs, to piece their theories together, rather than actually saying what the scriptures simply say, they fill whole, large volumes with human philosophy coming clothed as spiritual truth and lead multitudes astray. So let us believe God above any man or devil. Let God be true and anyone who contradicts Him, be a liar, and let us believe all of what the New Covenant says and teaches. If we are Christians, then let us take our stand for, and with, Jesus.

CHAPTER FIVE

GOD'S WILL, SATAN'S WILL

James, in his epistle, pointed out that *no fountain* could send forth both sweet water and bitter. (See also Isaiah 5:20-24.) Let it be known that God always *only* promotes and supplies that which is good and righteous from His own holy righteous nature (James 1:16-17), while Satan will always (in his end result) only promote sin, evil and rebellion against God's moral laws. His deceptions come disguised in many seemingly beautiful ways, teachings, and packages, but the end result is always the same: Disobey God! Live unrighteously! We need to realize that there are two kingdoms and two wills in opposition to one another. God's will is for everyone to be holy, just, and good (Eph. 4:24). Satan's will for everyone is to be unholy, unrighteous, and sinful. We pointed out earlier that Satan is a copycat and a counterfeiter. For every real doctrine of Christ, Satan has a counterfeit, and the counterfeit, although it looks on the surface like it could perhaps be true, always produces a different effect and end result. The scriptures reveal that there are true apostles and false apostles, true prophets and false prophets, true teachers and false teachers, true grace and false grace, and so on. It also reveals that there is a way that seems right to a man, but the end thereof is the way of death.

Realize that Satan, in promoting his lies through men and by other means, will always use some truth but not all of the truth; some scriptures but not all of the scriptures; and so it is with every false doctrine that's opposed to the true, complete doctrine of Christ. So, if what a person believes doesn't harmonize with all of the New Testament, it is wrong, regardless of who they are, what label they, or their organization may have, or how convincing one's argument is. *"God is not the author of* *confusion"; and "**all scripture** is given by inspiration of God and is profitable for doctrine, reproof, correction and instruction in righteousness"* (2 Tim. 3:16-17). Example: If you are going to take partial truths concerning what Paul said about grace in Romans 4 and 5 and try and prove a point, saying it means a certain thing, you must take into account all of what he said about it in his letters to the churches. He never contradicts himself. All he wrote about obedience, keeping God's commandments, and the necessity for holiness, must also harmonize with one's version of grace; for Paul, in his teaching, is talking about the same grace and Covenant throughout his letters, and we have abundantly shown what they taught about true grace.

Now every counterfeit and every tare that Satan brings and plants into the church world (Matt. 13:24-30), comes as an angel of light or a wolf in sheep's clothing, cleverly disguised as truth, for no one would ever believe in a counterfeit if it didn't even look like it could possibly be true. As we have shown, there is revealed in scripture a true overcoming Bible grace that saves us from our lost, weakened, spiritually dead condition. (Grace being God's divine influence on the heart to do right and the power to carry it out.) Real grace, as we've stated, gives to the New Testament believer, victory over a life of sin and Satan, enabling us to walk victoriously down the narrow road that leads to life. (See 1 John 2:3-6; 1 Cor. 7:19; Rom. 5:17; Rev. 22:14; Matt. 7:13-14; 1 Pet. 1:5.)

There is also revealed in God's Word, an opposing, false, ungodly teaching about grace that's filled with devilish presumptions and human reasoning, which turns the grace of our God into lasciviousness (rebellion against God's holy will) (Jude 4). This counterfeit grace sounds wonderful to those who want to continue in sin, and says or implies that grace means, if you merely confess that you believe in Christ with your mouth (Matt. 7:21), you are therefore the elect. It teaches that you could then live in sin, willingly live contrary to God's will and commandments, taking the broad road once again, and that God's own grace would automatically cover and provide a cloak for you, making you eternally safe and secure as you live the way you want regardless of whether you live for His will or not (James 2:14-26). But this is just another trick of the adversary to get people to submit to him once again, and to come under his power (2 Tim. 2:24-26). The false concept of grace also implies in some circles that blessings too will come without *"obedience to the faith,"* as Paul preached it (Rom. 1:5; 1 John 3:22). Now we know that God's goodness and influence will work to lead a person to repentance (Rom. 2:4-5), and that there is great mercy, especially for new believers and the ignorant, but with light also comes responsibility (1 John 1:7). To whom much is given, of him is much required. This false grace, though, totally dishonors God and will accept only some scriptures but not all of them. It's really contrary to Bible grace and it removes from man the responsibility to cooperate with the grace, influence, and power of God, which the scriptures reveal, must be done if men are to receive the blessings and benefits of grace (2 Cor. 6:1; 1 Cor. 15:10).

As we've stated, the very grace, influence, and power of God that God has given to us as His children, to overcome a life of sin and Satan, and to labor for the Lord, has been changed by some to say that grace means you could now, as a Christian, draw back again, walk down the broad road as before, and live a life of sin following Satan and his rebellion once again, and still remain spiritually okay and secure with God. This, my friend, is not Bible grace at all (Rom. 6:1-2). It is a cleverly disguised lie of Satan, and Satan can save no one. This teaching is opposed to the will of God. Jesus clearly said, *"Not every one that saith unto me, Lord, Lord, shall enter into the kingdom of heaven; but he that doeth the will of my Father which is in heaven"* (Matt. 7:21). And it is *not* God's will that you return to the will and lusts of the devil (John 8:44; Eph. 2:2-3).

Satan's Teaching

Satan, the first teacher of unconditional eternal security, has taught this false concept of grace from the beginning. For when God, the God of all grace, told Adam not to break His commandment or he would surely die, the serpent came along and said to Eve, go ahead, eat, break the commandment, *"ye shall not surely die."* (You're secure!) But they did die and forfeited the grace of God and became weak and sinful, and came under the authority and power of the devil (Rom. 5:12). Let us not believe any of the serpent's teachings, which began in seed form way back in the book of Genesis and are presently scattered deceptively throughout the religions of the world, and even more cleverly in the church. His end result is always the same, "Disobey the true God, it's okay." God's warnings concerning these things are many. God says in scripture, *"He that keepeth the commandment keepeth his own soul; but he that despiseth the Lord's ways shall die"* (Prov. 19:16). *"He taught me also, and said unto me, Let thine heart retain my words: keep my commandments, and live"* (Prov. 4:4). And again, ***"Blessed are they that do his commandments, that they may have right to the tree of life, and may enter in*** *through the gates into the city"* (Rev. 22:14).

Jesus said in Revelation 2:7, *"He that hath an ear, let him hear what the Spirit saith **unto the churches**; to him [in the church] that overcometh [Satan and the pollutions of this world] will I give to eat of the tree of life, which is in the midst of the paradise of God."* (See 1 John 2:14-17, 5:4; 2 Pet. 2:20-21.) The true Gospel of grace restores to us the one true religion of reverence, worship, and obedience to the one true God, the way it should have been back in the Garden of Eden. The false teaching on grace continues the teaching of the serpent, "Ye shall not surely die just because of willful disobedience to God. Go ahead, eat of the tree of disobedience." He says, "Resist and frustrate grace in your life, live the way you want, regardless of God's will, and all is still well with your soul. Isn't grace wonderful? SSSSSSS!" Everything still falls under the category of either God's will or Satan's will, good or evil, darkness or light. God says in scripture, *"Be ye not unequally yoked together with unbelievers: for **what fellowship** hath righteousness with unrighteousness? and **what communion** hath light with darkness? And **what concord** hath Christ **with Belial?** [that is, the devil], or **what part** hath he that believeth with an infidel?"* (2 Cor. 6:14-15).

We will see in this section of this treatise that it is the same for us today as it was for Adam in the garden. The serpent is still saying through his many deceptions, the same things to us today about God's Word and God's commandments, just as he did to Adam and Eve. (See 2 Cor. 11:3; Rom. 8:12-13.) But as with Adam, God's Word is certain, the judgment is sure, and it cannot be changed! The Word alone and what it actually says will *"judge us in the last day"* (John 12:47-49; Rom. 3:3-4). Keep the commandments and live. We are then to keep the commandments as they are recorded in the New Covenant. For grace, which is God's divine influence and power, is restored to us once again for this very purpose, to lead us to repentance, steer us in the right direction, and then to give us power to obey His commandments and live for His will (1 Cor. 7:19). Therefore, we repeat, it is by grace, but not a grace to disobey God, but an enablement to obey Him and to keep His commandments and live (2 Cor. 12:9). The test under this dispensation is: Will we who have been delivered from our spiritually old, dead, sinful way of life by God's grace (Eph. 2:5) now live for Him, seeing He has provided both the influence and the power to do so by it? *"For it is God which worketh in you both to will and to do of his good pleasure"* (Phil. 2:13). The writer of Hebrews said, May God *"make you perfect in every good work **to do his will**, working in you that which is well pleasing in his sight, through Jesus Christ; to whom be glory for ever and ever. Amen"* (Heb. 13:21). And as Peter the Apostle taught in 2 Peter 1:3, *"According as **his divine power hath given*** *unto us all things that pertain unto life and godliness*, *through the knowledge of him that hath called us to glory and virtue"* (moral uprightness). God commands us to obey because He has given us the grace to obey. Hence, the true New Covenant. We are freed from slavery to sin. This is it, just as Paul preached it. The true Gospel brings about an obedience to God that springs from real genuine faith from the heart (1 John 3:3; Rom. 1:5, 6:17,16:26).

Good Trees, Bad Trees

Now Jesus said, *"A good tree [God] cannot bring forth evil fruit, neither can a corrupt tree [Satan] bring forth good fruit"* (Matt. 7:18). Paul wrote, *"If the root [the source] be holy, so are the branches"* (Rom. 11:16) (whatever comes forth out of it). *"Wherefore by their fruits ye shall know them."* The Bible says, *"The fruit of the wicked is sin."* You'll know the difference then between a true and a counterfeit doctrine' whether it comes from God or from Satan, by what fruit it finally produces. (See 1 John 1:5.) Are the results leading people to be holy or unholy, moral or immoral? What does it imply? Does it teach that you could walk down the broad road living contrary to God's commandments and yet be blessed by Him and go to heaven just because you professed to believe something? That you don't need to obey Jesus, the very author of our faith? (Heb. 5:9) Does it imply that you could toss aside the apostles' commands, doctrines, and warnings? Does it say, let us do evil that God's grace may be magnified? Paul knowing the outcome of such self-deceived people said concerning those who do (and teach) such things that *"their damnation is just"* (Rom. 3:8). Or does it teach the true doctrine of grace as Paul taught it that, " *... **The grace of God** that bringeth salvation [and deliverance from the fall] hath appeared [and been made available] to **all** men, teaching [instructing and empowering] **us** that, denying [and turning away from all] ungodliness and worldly lusts, we should live soberly, righteously, and godly, in this present world,"* looking forward to eternal life in the world to come? (Titus 1:12-14; Heb. 12:1-3). *"Nevertheless we, according to his promise, look for new heavens and a new earth, wherein dwelleth righteousness. Wherefore, beloved, seeing that ye look for such things, be diligent that ye may be found of him in peace, without spot, and blameless"* (2 Pet. 3:13-14). Realize that Satan will never work to get people to obey, love, serve, or follow Jesus in paths of righteousness, and God will never provide for, nor cover for, a person to walk in unrighteousness and rebellion contrary to His will, for God says that the Lord *"hates iniquity and loves righteousness"* and *"the face of the Lord is against them that do evil"* (1 Pet. 3:12). God has made no *"provision for the flesh,"* or for us to continue on in an evil course, but He will be abundantly merciful if one falls into sin and then repents, as we shall see (Rom. 13:14).

I want to encourage you to continue to journey with me through God's Word. Please go through these many scriptures that follow in the rest of this book with an open and honest heart (Luke 8:15). And let the Word of God speak for itself to you concerning this subject, for many people's eternities are hanging in the balance. If you really want the truth and are open to *all* of God's Word, I believe you'll see the real truth more and more clearly and the distinct differences between true Bible grace as it's revealed in the scriptures, and the counterfeit grace, which over emphasizes some scriptures while rejecting, or completely ignoring others, and was cleverly introduced into the church by Satan. Although his doctrines come in many seemingly spiritual packages and through many seemingly spiritual people promising life and blessing, and pretending to magnify God's grace and goodness, his real goal is only to kill, steal, and destroy. Sadly, because of His deceptions, there are many taking the broad road, thinking it leads them to eternal life and blessing, when in reality it leads only to death and cursings (Deut. 30:19). For the whole New Covenant in its entirety is the faith of Jesus, and *"the faith that was once delivered to the saints,"* and to be safe, we must live according to all His words. As we before stated, you cannot just take the part of the contract that seems good to you, nor can you be safe and secure by accepting a false interpretation of grace. (See Ps. 50:16-22.) For no man can deliver you from the consequences of living contrary to God (Heb. 10:31).

Jude's Warning Concerning the Teaching of False Grace

Let's look again in the epistle of Jude, Verses 3–4, Jude writes, *"Beloved, when I gave all diligence to write unto you of the common salvation, it was needful for me to write unto you, and exhort you that ye should earnestly contend for [and fight in defense of] the [real] faith which was once delivered unto the saints. [A faith which Jude called "our most holy faith," for he knew what true grace produced.] For there are certain men crept in (among the church) unawares [unnoticed], who were before of old ordained to this condemnation [God foresaw that some false teachers would sneak into the church and would willingly misapply His grace and teach this false concept to others], ungodly men [impious], turning [like a magician's trick]* **the grace of our God** *[which He gave to us to enable us to live right]* **into** *lasciviousness [an automatic cover for sinful and immoral living and a disregard for God's justice], and [by this they are] denying the only Lord God, and our Lord Jesus Christ."* (See also

Titus 1:16.) To teach that it is now possible for Christians to rebel and no longer really have to obey what Jesus, the author of our faith, and the apostles taught, and that one could take the broad road and follow after Satan once again and still be okay with God, is to outright deny the Lord and His salvation which frees us from Satan and a life of sin (John 8:34-36). How in the world can people living in sin and rebellion against God glorify God's grace or Christ's finished work? This is what the false concept of grace says or implies. The true grace of God never has provided any such thing as an automatic cover (or cloak) for sinful living, only the counterfeit one does. But it's an empty promise void of fulfillment, as we will clearly show you beyond any shadow of a doubt, if you will believe the Word over men's reasonings and doctrines. Jesus said, *"If I had not come and spoken unto them, they had not had sin: but now they have **no cloak** for their sin"* (John 15:22). (See also Rom. 6:1-2,14.)

In Jude's day there was a doctrine about grace being promoted by some that said grace, instead of delivering men from a life of sin, would automatically provide a cloak for them even if they willingly followed after sin, Satan, and evil, and that grace would automatically impute to them, a righteousness without repentance or confession of sin, because Jesus did it all. (See 1 John 1:9; Rev. 2:1,5,11,16,21-22,26,29.) Things that the apostles' taught were being twisted (2 Pet. 3:16). These false teachings literally turned God's wonderful grace (which God gave to us to serve and obey Him) into an open door and license to commit sin and rebellion against God, implying that people, once they had just professed faith in Christ with their mouth, could now live contrary to God and follow Satan in their lives (Eph. 2:2) without fearing any eternal consequences or displeasure from God. Please realize that sin is going astray from God's will and is rebellion against God's moral government. Sin is always revealed in scripture as a work of the devil (1 John 3:8), and God is never pleased with it. Would God then ever provide something that would condone a work of the devil, or automatically cover for it while His people lived in it? God forbid! Who then would? The devil himself! For he wants people who had once repented of sin and turned from him to follow Christ, to return and follow him once again (Acts 26:16-18). So he constantly works through his deceptions to seduce people away from God with cleverly disguised false teachings, just as he did back in the beginning in the garden. Only now, most of his works are done through men (usually naturally, highly intelligent, but spiritually undiscerning men) who he can use to convince other people's minds with great intellectual and seemingly spiritual arguments. And so, with many good words and fair speeches they deceive the hearts of the unsuspecting (Rom. 16:17-20,26; 2 Cor. 11:3,13-15), and the people unknowingly become followers of blind guides, just as in days gone bye.

The word "lasciviousness" used by Jude in his warning to the church concerning this false grace, is the Greek word *aselegeis*, and it has to do with a wide range of unbridled passions and lusts of the flesh. Those who have given themselves over to this false idea of grace according to this word, are even "proud of their emancipation from the restraints of personal conscience or public opinion," thinking freedom to sin or not sin is the freedom God gave us. So, some who yield to this false concept of grace begin to stop listening to their conscience and stop listening to the true authorities that God has sent to help them live right (Rom. 8:4; Heb. 13:17), thinking that they are still the righteous no matter how they live. They, many times, follow Satan and the flesh, and go back into slavery to sin and back into the same evil bondages they were in before they were saved. By this they actually "frustrate," "fall from," and "forfeit" the grace of God mistakenly thinking that because of the false doctrine they were taught, they are still in grace (Gal. 2:21, 5:4; Heb. 12:12-17). The light they have is really darkness. This is what the word lasciviousness means, and this is the effect that this false doctrine has on many of the people who embrace it. It numbs the conscience and gives a false sense of security while living in unbridled lusts. Here false grace comes disguised as love and a wonderful, beautiful, righteous cloak for evil, teaching or implying that evil for the Christian is now acceptable, or permissible, because of grace. And so they believe that they won't displease or be judged by God even if they were to persist in sin without repentance; but that when they were a sinner they would go to hell for living in these very same things. But the apostle says concerning those who do these things, ***"Who knowing** [and understanding clearly] the **judgment of God, that they which commit such things are worthy of death, not only do the same, but have pleasure in them that do them"*** (Rom. 1:32). He goes on to say that such people are *"without excuse"* when they knowingly and persistently live wrong, and that God's judgment is sure for all who live this way (Rom. 2:1-11). So again, it is not freedom to sin, but freedom from a life of sin and its controlling power that the scriptures reveal is ours by grace in this New Covenant (John 8:34-36; Rom. 6). This is what brings life and blessing, and with this, *all* the New Testament scriptures harmonize.

What Does It Mean to Live by Faith?

Satan has worked to get people to believe that if they just profess they believe, that this is enough, but it is not. The apostle Paul wrote, *"They profess that they know God; but in works they deny him, being abominable, and disobedient, and unto every good work reprobate"* (Titus 1:16). They shout by *"grace and faith alone"* not knowing God's definition of either of these words. This false concept of Bible faith is just another one of the devil's tactics to get people to *disobey* God. Christ's true doctrine in the Bible says, *"the just shall **live** by faith"* (Rom. 1:17). What does this mean? Does this mean just a profession with the mouth, or does it mean action? Let's let scripture interpret scripture and see what the apostles said about living our faith.

In Romans 6:2, it means to NOT *live* in sin any longer.

In Romans 6:8, it means to be *dead to a life of sin,* and to *live* unto God.

In Romans 8:12-13, it reveals that we are to *no longer live after the-flesh and its lusts*.

In Romans 10:5, to not *live for* the Mosaic Law and its carnal ordinances any longer.

In Romans 14:8, it is to *live for the Lord*.

In 1 Corinthians 5:15, it means to *no longer live for* ourselves, but for Him who rose from the dead.

In Galatians 2:19, to *live* unto God.

In Galatians 2:20, to *live* the life of Christ (Phil. 1:21).

In Galatians 5:25, to *live* and walk in the Spirit, and "not fulfill the lusts of the flesh."

In 1 Thessalonians 3:8, it means to stand fast in the Lord and thereby *live*.

In 2 Timothy 3:12, to *live* godly in Christ Jesus.

In Titus 2:12, to *live* soberly, righteously, and godly in this present world as you wait for His appearing.

In Hebrews 12:9, it is to be in subjection to the Father of spirits and *live*.

In Hebrews 13:18, to have a good (clear) conscience and *live* honestly.

In 1 Peter 2:24, to be dead to sin and *live **unto righteousness***.

In 1 Peter 4:2, to *no longer live* in the flesh to the lusts of men, but for the will of God.

In 2 Peter 2:6, to not *live* ungodly.

In 2 Peter 2:18, to no longer *live* like those who live in error.

This is living by faith. No wonder He said that those who do so are the "just."

"For whatsoever is born of God overcometh the world: and this is the victory that overcometh the world, even our faith" (1 John 5:4).

Jesus said, *"It is written, Man shall not **live** by bread alone, **but by every word that proceedeth out of the mouth of God**"* (Matt. 4:4).

*"By faith Noah, being warned of God of things not seen as yet, moved with fear, **prepared an ark** to the saving of his house; by the which he condemned the world, and became heir of the righteousness which is by faith"* (Heb. 11:7). By faith he prepared himself. And all one needs to do is to go through the book of Hebrews, chapter eleven to see that Bible faith is obedience and action and not mere profession alone.

*"Beloved, now are we the sons of God, and it doth not yet appear what we shall be: but we know that, when he shall appear, we shall be like him; for we shall see him as he is. And every man that hath this hope in Him **purifieth himself**, even as he is pure"* (1 John 3:2-3). But a false concept of grace and faith says that there is no real vital need to purify oneself. Yet, the scriptures clearly teach otherwise.

So here is a picture of the faith that the just are to live by. And faith, as we shall see, always shows itself in what it does. If it doesn't do anything, it's not Bible faith at all, it's only mental assent. "Ultra gracists" may use the right words, but they have the wrong definition. And if their definition of faith and grace are wrong, then everything they say about these two subjects are wrong. *"Unless the Lord build the house, they labor in vain that build it."*

God's Word says, *"But wilt thou know, O vain man, that faith without works is dead? For as the body without the spirit is dead, so faith without works [corresponding actions] is dead also"* (James 2:20,26). Remember, Paul said, *"They profess that they know God; **but in works they deny him**, being abominable, and disobedient, and unto every good work reprobate"* (Titus 1:16). So, when people say it's all by faith and grace, ask them what they mean. Do they mean a living faith that obeys the Lord, and do they believe in God's life-changing grace which produces the fruits of righteousness in us? Or do they mean a dead, hypocritical faith that only professes with the mouth, and a counterfeit grace which says that you can live in unconfessed sin and all is well? A person's definition is most important. Let's stay right with the Word.

Jude spoke of *"the faith"* that was once delivered to the saints and called it our *"most holy faith."* The faith is all of the teachings, commands, and instructions of Jesus Christ (the author and finisher of our faith). Jesus told His disciples *after His resurrection, and **at the beginning of this New Covenant*** to go teach all nations, *"Teaching them to observe all things whatsoever I have commanded you: and, lo, I am with you alway, even unto the end of the world"* (Matt. 28:20). Notice, we are to observe *"all things;"* He commanded them, even *"unto the end of the age."* That is, the Church Age. This is *"the faith of Jesus Christ."* This is the will of God. This includes all of His teachings and His commandments in the Gospels (Matt. 24:3,14), and also through the apostles (1 Cor. 14:37). No word of God can be nullified. Jesus said, *"He that rejecteth me, and receiveth not my words [my teachings], hath one that judgeth him, **the word that I have spoken [when I was here in the flesh], the same shall judge him in the last day"*** (John 12:48). The apostle John said, *"Whosoever transgresseth, and abideth not in the doctrine [the teaching and instructions] of Christ, hath not God. He that abideth in the doctrine [the teaching and instructions] of Christ he hath both the Father and the Son"* (2 John 9). Satan's problem was *"he abode not in the truth"* (John 8:44); and all who follow him willingly or ignorantly, also, do not abide in all of the truth of Christ.

He That Hath Ears to Hear

Dare anyone say that we need not obey the faith of Jesus Christ? He, the author and finisher of our faith, said we should strive to enter at the straight gate. He taught that we should obey Him, take the narrow road, keep His commandments, and that if we act according to His sayings, we are wise people. He told us to follow His example, pick up our cross daily, and deny ourselves, or we *would not* be His disciples. He said that if you tried to save your sinful life in this world, you'd lose your soul. Dare anyone do as the Pharisees of old did and make His words of none effect through their philosophies induced by the serpent? Dare anyone say that there really is no need to follow the faith and example of Christ at all? Grace is given to us to obey Him, not disobey Him. So how could our obedience possibly take away from His grace, as some ignorantly say, when it's a product of His grace? (Heb. 12:28; 2 Cor. 9:8). People living righteously by His grace is what glorifies Him. Woe be to the man that takes away from, or adds to, the words of Christ. *"For I testify **unto every man** that heareth the words of the prophecy of this book, If any man shall add unto these things, God shall add unto him the plagues that are written in this book: and if any man shall take away from the words of the book of the prophecy, **God shall take away his part out of the book of life, and out of the holy city,** and from the things which are written in this book. He [Jesus] which* *testifieth these things saith, Surely I come quickly. Amen. Even so, come, Lord Jesus"* (Rev. 22:18-20). This passage alone shows that predestination, election, and irresistible grace, as some interpret it, are folly; and that once saved, always saved, or once in grace, always in grace, regardless of how one lives, is just a theory of men. Reread it and see! Let no man deceive you. He couldn't threaten to take people's names *out* of the Book of Life if He Himself, automatically predestined whose names would be in it. This also makes it clear that no one's name automatically stays in it unless they live as He says. You must, the Bible says, *"fight the good fight of faith,"* to lay hold on eternal life. In other words, keep living for God (Heb. 3:14).

The apostles taught that we must *"continue in the grace of God"*; *"continue in His goodness"*; *"continue in the doctrine and teachings of Christ"*; and *"continue in the faith."* Otherwise, we have not God, but are trusting in a human philosophy and the *"cunning craftiness of men,"* in inventing errors and making it look like truth. Over and over again scripture states, *"Let no man deceive you."*

Faith, Real Faith

Don't be duped by Satan's counterfeit definitions of Bible words. According to Hebrews chapter eleven, real faith gives to God, walks with God, obeys God, works for God, confesses God's truth, keeps God's ordinances, and refuses the pleasures of sin in order to follow Christ. Real faith works righteousness, forsakes Egypt (the world), in order to obtain a better city, and so on. Faith always has these kinds of works. Faith without these kinds of works is not living faith at all, but is a dead faith with an empty profession. It is being no more than a hypocrite honoring Him with our lips while our heart is far from Him.

If Abel had said that he believed God, but didn't give his best to God, he wouldn't have been accepted any more than Cain.

If Abraham had said that he believed, but didn't obey God and leave Ur of the Chaldees, offer up his son, keep God's statutes, and so on, he wouldn't have been justified, nor been called *"the friend of God"* (Gen. 22:18, 18:18-19; James 2:21-26).

If Noah had just said that he believed, but didn't work and build the ark, he would have drowned just like the rest of the world.

If Moses had said that he believed, but didn't forsake the pleasures of sin and Egypt, he would never have been accepted nor been used as a deliverer by God.

If David, Samuel, Ezekiel, Elijah, or any other Old Testament men or women of faith said that they believed, but didn't have corresponding actions, their professing it would have meant nothing to God. The same is true of the New Testament men of faith, and so it is today.

"What doth it profit [then], my brethren, though a man say he hath faith, and have not works? can [that kind of] faith save him? For as the body without the spirit is dead, so faith without works is dead also" (James 2:14,26).

Jesus said, *"Not every one that **saith** unto me, Lord, Lord, shall enter into the kingdom of heaven; but he that doeth the will of my Father which is in heaven"* (Matt. 7:21).

*"And **why call ye Me, Lord, Lord, and do not** the things which I say?"* (Luke 6:46).

A person just saying that they believe, means no more to God than the Pharisees saying, "We are Abraham's children," by virtue of the outward flesh and circumcision, yet, failing to *"do the works of Abraham"* (John 8:39). Paul showed them that it wasn't outward circumcision or outward profession that made one a real Jew (or a real Christian for that matter), but a heart living for the praise and will of God (Rom. 2:28-29, 6:17; 1 Cor. 7:19).

God's Conditional Covenant

"Know therefore that the Lord thy God, he is God, the faithful God, which keepeth covenant and mercy with them that love him and keep his commandments to a thousand generations" (Deut. 7:91). (See also Rom. 8:28 and John 14:21-24.)

We cannot bargain with God. To be secure we must obey Him and be *"obedient to the faith,"* as the apostles taught. Forget the philosophies of men concerning this (Rom. 1:5; Heb. 5:9). Forget Calvinistic theories and great volumes of theological nonsense and human reasoning by others, and let's get back to the Bible. We know that God didn't have to give us this Covenant. We deserved death. We didn't merit it. But since God provided this narrow way by His grace, this is the *only* way (Ps. 23:3). As with Adam, God said that it's conditional regardless of anyone's philosophy about grace. The only way grace provided was a narrow way of escape. It provided the way of repentance if one does sin, the way of obeying Jesus, and the way of following the Good Shepherd down paths of righteousness (John 10:4). God provided the way of taking up our cross daily, denying self, and following Him. Jesus saith, *"I am **the way, the truth, and the life**, and no **man** cometh unto the Father except by me."* In other words, you'll do it Jesus' way, or you'll not get to the Father. *He, and His life's example, is the way.*

Do you understand? Paul preached *"obedience to the faith."* That is, obedience to the faith and teachings of Jesus, and said, *"If any man teach otherwise, and consent not to wholesome words, even the words of our Lord Jesus Christ, and to the doctrine which is according to godliness; he is proud, knowing nothing ..."* (1 Tim. 6:3-4). (See also Acts 6:7.) For remember, Christianity restores to us the one true religion as it was to be in the garden before the fall. Anyone who tells you that you can live a life disobedient to God, disobeying His commandments: that repenting is not necessary; and saying you will still be able to partake of the tree of life; is speaking to you the serpent's same lie. They are teaching one of the worst and most deceptive forms of Satanism ever taught. They are telling you that you can live by the tree of knowledge of good and evil, and saying, "Be your own god, no one owns you" (1 Cor. 6:20); "You shall not surely die." Listen to the Lord, *"And unto the angel of the church in Sardis write; These things saith he that hath the seven Spirits of God, and the seven stars; I know thy works, that **thou hast a name that thou livest, and art dead.... He that overcometh**, [the world and its pollutions] the same shall be clothed in white raiment; and **I will not blot out his name out of the book of life**, but I will confess his name before my Father, and before his angels.... **To him that overcometh** will I grant to sit with me in my throne, **even as I also overcame**, and am set down with my Father in His throne"* (Rev. 3:1,5,21). Overcoming the fallen world and its ways is of utmost importance, or Christ wouldn't have placed such emphasis on it when speaking His message to *all of* the *churches* (1 John 2:14; Rev. 12:11; 1 Pet. 2:20-21). Repentance of sin committed was the first word Jesus preached, and the last message He gave to the churches in Revelation. If people humble themselves and repent, God can be merciful. If they do not, they will be judged and eventually suffer the consequences (Rev. 2:18-29). We need to listen to *all* the Lord Jesus has taught.

Paul said that the Gospel first began to be *preached by the Lord,* and afterwards, by them that heard Him (Heb. 2:3). *"The law and the prophets were **until** John ..."* (Luke 16:16). What Jesus taught them was the Gospel of the Kingdom and said, *"And this gospel of the kingdom shall be preached in all the world for a witness unto all nations; and then shall the end come"* (Matt. 24:14). It is all *"the whole faith"* we need then, whether in the Gospels, epistles, or the book of Revelation. So again, do not do what the Pharisees under the influence of the powers of darkness did and nullify His words through tradition or *"doctrines of men."* *"Let no man deceive* *you,"* saying you need not obey the Lord. Whether they try to nullify what He said in the Gospels or the Epistles, or anywhere, such a man is either self-deceived or a false teacher (2 Pet. 2:1-22).

This deceptive teaching of false grace sown into the church by the adversary implies that God's grace will now, somehow, automatically, mysteriously, cover for sin and keep God from seeing rebellion against Him when the believer willingly commits it, but not when the sinner does. It says that we really need not obey Jesus, for they say that *"it's all by grace."* Yes, it is all by grace, if you have the right definition of Bible grace. Paul taught that we are saved out of a life of bondage to Satan, sin, and spiritual death by grace (God's power) through faith, and that not of ourselves (not of our own strength), nor of works so no one can boast. The apostles also taught that we are now kept from a life of sin by grace (God's power) and faith (Rom. 6:14-22). So it is not a one-time saving but a continual keeping from a life of sin (Satan's operations), if the grace which was once received is truly continued. (See Rom. 6:14; 1 John 5:18; 2 Tim. 4:2-5.) Grace, as we've shown, is God's power and ability given to us as believers and sons of God, to deliver us from sin's controlling power that man came in bondage to at the fall (2 Cor. 12:9). It is given (as we shall see) to make us overcomers, for the same grace that saved us out of a life of sin and provided justification for us by the blood of Christ, also sanctifies us. Grace takes care of everything. It doesn't leave us (the redeemed) under the power of sin and Satan; and no one who cooperates with the grace of God by faith will live as they did before when they were following Satan (Col. 1:6). *"Take heed, **brethren**, lest there be in any of you an evil heart of unbelief, in departing from the living God"* (Heb. 3:12). For if we get back into sin, we can return to a life of unbelief and lose our hold on grace (Rom. 5:2): *"Holding faith, and a good conscience; which some having put away concerning faith have made shipwreck"* (1 Tim. 1:19).

Now we know quite well that we can neither be saved nor stay saved without God and His power (2 Pet. 1:3-4). But neither will God save a person nor keep them saved without their own willingness to *be* saved, and to continue in it (Rev. 22:17; Rom. 11:22; Eph. 2:8-9; 1 Pet. 1:5; Heb. 3:12-14). But, as we've said, some have misinterpreted what grace is and what it's given for, just as they have not understood the Bible definition of faith, thinking that faith means merely a profession with the mouth or mentally believing, not realizing, as we've shown, that the *"just shall live by faith"* (Acts 8:9,13,18-23). Faith then is a lifestyle, a living for the will of God by a conviction in the heart that God means what He says. We are to heed His warning to flee from the wrath to come (Matt. 3:7). (See Heb. 11:7; Rom. 6:17-18.) This then taps into the strength that grace provides (2 Cor. 12:9). There were the same kind of misinterpretations and twisting of the Apostles' Doctrines even in the apostles' day (2 Pet. 3:14-17). This comes from undiscerning people adding to, or taking away from, what the apostles of Christ taught.

The Work of Faith

The Lord can be denied by a person's works (lifestyle) just as well as by what they say. Again, Paul, in his theology said, *"They profess that they know God [with their mouths]; **but in works they deny** [disown] him, being abominable, and disobedient, and unto every good work reprobate"* (Titus 1:16). Paul believed then that actions speak louder than words. Jesus said, *"If you deny me, I will deny you."* *"He [Jesus] answered and said unto them, Well hath Esaias prophesied of **you hypocrites** as it is written, this people honoreth me with their lips, but their heart is far from me"* (Mark 7:6). Here we see that Christ will not honor nor accept, empty professions from the mouth, while the heart and life is lived contrary to the profession. Saying that you have faith in Jesus without having corresponding actions then is dead faith (James 2:14-26), and it is not acceptable to God (Luke 6:46).

A person just saying that they have faith in the Lord means nothing to God if the life is lived contrary to God, or contrary to the faith they say they have. For according to the Bible, to love God and have faith is to keep His commandments (1 John 2:3-6; 2 John 6; 1 Cor. 7:19; John 14:20-26).

If a person has real faith that saves, it also saves them from living after the works of the flesh and from walking with the devil. Real faith produces the work of righteousness and *"purifies the heart."* Abraham didn't just say he believed God, Abraham by faith obeyed God (Heb. 11:8; Acts 15:8-9).

God's Word says, *"Was not Abraham our father justified [then] by works, when he had offered Isaac his son upon the altar? Seest thou how faith wrought with his works, and by works was faith made perfect? And the scripture was [then] fulfilled which saith, Abraham believed God, and [because he had the kind of faith that obeyed] it was imputed unto him for righteousness: and he was called the Friend of God"* (James 2:21-24). In other words, the doctrine and faith of Christ says that faith must have corresponding actions or it's dead. Abraham's faith caused him to obey and keep God's commands

(Gen. 18:19). And he was *therefore* called the friend of God. (See John 15:14.) This was then, what is meant by believing God. Believing caused repentance, forsaking his old way of life, and the keeping of God's commands. This kind of faith in God's Word made him the friend of God (Gen. 26:5).

Both Paul and Christ taught that to keep the faith is to keep the commandments. In John 15:10, Jesus, the author of faith said, *"If ye keep my commandments, ye shall abide in my love; even as I have kept my Father's commandments, and abide in His love."*

Paul, who was sent by Christ to preach the Gospel and obedience to the faith wrote, *"Circumcision is nothing, and uncircumcision is nothing, but [what matters is] the keeping of the commandments of God"* (1 Cor. 7:19). John the Apostle wrote in 1 John 2:2-6, *"And he is the propitiation for our sins: and not for ours only, **but also for the sins of the whole world. And hereby we do know that we know him, if we keep his commandments.** He that **saith,** I know him, and keepeth not his commandments, **is a liar,** and the truth is not in him. But whoso keepeth his word, in him verily is the love of God perfected: hereby know we that we are in him. He that saith he abideth in Him ought himself also so to walk, even as he walked"* (1 John 2:2-6).

This, then, is the kind of faith that justifies, just as Abraham's faith justified him. Paul and Christ also taught that God rewards and punishes people according to their works. (See Eph. 6:8; Col. 3:25; Matt. 25:34-46.)

According to Paul, if you follow and live after the works of the flesh, you will be condemned and spiritually die again. (See Gal. 5:19-21; Rom. 8:12-13, 1:28-32.)

In Romans 8:1 he says, *"There is therefore now no condemnation to them, which are in Christ Jesus, **who walk not after the flesh, but after the Spirit.**"* But there is still condemnation to those who live their lives after the flesh.

We are called and freed by grace from a life of sin to now walk after the Spirit. And sowing our lives to the Spirit will cause us to reap eternal life, but a life sown to the flesh, He said, will still reap condemnation, corruption, and ruin (Gal. 6:7-9). Realize that if you're a Christian, you've been delivered from your old bondages and your old way of life, for salvation from the fall has come to you.

Christ, the author of faith, obeyed His Father's commandments, submitted to His Father's will, did good works, prayed, fasted, obeyed, fulfilled all righteousness, denied Himself, and so on. He is *the way.* And remember, *"grace and truth"* came by Jesus Christ. He is also the author of faith and grace, so all of these things, then, are the actions of faith and are not legalism in the least. If it doesn't line up with the life, teaching, and ministry of Jesus Christ *it is wrong!* It is neither faith, nor grace.

Paul himself never, ever taught a lifeless faith or a faith that would nullify any of the instructions or commands of Christ. If anyone does, they *are not* following the doctrine of grace as taught by Paul, but are caught up in the false philosophy of grace that Jude warned of (1 Tim. 6:3-4). Know this too, the only works Paul rejected were Jewish legalistic works, heathenish works, and any works of the unregenerate. *"Because the carnal mind is enmity against God: for it is not subject to the law of God, neither indeed can be. So then they that are in the flesh cannot please God"* (Rom. 8:7-8). But as Christians he said we are to *"be careful to maintain good works"* (Titus 3:8); to be *"zealous of good works"* (Titus 2:14-15); and to *"provoke one another to good works."* He further taught that grace empowers you to work (2 Cor. 9:8; Heb. 12:28). Now, we know that we are not saved by good works, but are rewarded for them, and yet we stay in right relationship with God by obeying His moral law (1 John 1:5-7; James 4:4).

Paul taught that as an unregenerate, you couldn't be saved by your works, but only by faith in God's redemption. But once you've repented of a life of sin and are saved, you must then continue living right, showing forth your faith by your changed life and works, and never go back to the world and live like them, or you will die again spiritually (Rom. 8:12-13; Jude 12). *"For we are made partakers of Christ [eternal life, 1 John 1:1-3], if we hold the beginning of our confidence steadfast unto the end"* (Heb. 3:14). The way the world lives, and their refusal to return and live for God's will, is what is sending them to hell (Eph. 2:2-3; Acts 17:30; 1 John 2:15-17; Matt. 7:21).

God Will Not Spare the Rebellious

Because of its importance, let's go over in a little more detail, a few more things concerning what the scriptures teach about false grace in the book of Jude. His passage deals specifically with false teachers teaching a false concept of grace.

Jude reminds the Christians he was writing to of the teaching of the scriptures and points out that God's warnings to rebels concerning judgment still stand true even in this dispensation of grace. So, he says in his warning to the church against this false, deceptive teaching on grace, *"I* *will therefore put you in remembrance [fellow Christian], though ye once knew this, how that **the Lord, having saved the people** [who were called His people] out of the land of Egypt, **afterward destroyed them** that believed not. [And proved unfaithful and He blotted them out of His book, Ex. 32:33; Rev. 3:5.] And the angels [of God once called sons of God] which kept not their first estate, but left their own habitation [their own proper boundaries], He [God] **hath reserved** them in everlasting chains under darkness unto the judgment of the great day."* Jude is telling these Christians not to leave a life of obedience to God and His moral government, but to stay following Christ in their daily lives. In other words, Jude was saying, don't let anyone persuade you with a false (twisted) teaching about grace, saying that grace will automatically cover for a life of sin, unfaithfulness, and rebellion against God's will; or what's written in these scriptures about those Israelites, Sodom, and the fallen angels, will eventually be the final outcome of your life as well. Nowhere in scripture is there an unconditional grace or love that will protect you or bless you if you live a life of willful rebellion (1 Pet. 3:12). There is no such example in the Bible. For to live a life of rebellion is to live a life of unbelief and not faith.

Peter, in writing concerning this same thing, said that God *spared not* the angels that sinned; that God *spared not* the old world with millions of people in it, and He *spared not* Sodom (2 Pet. 2). Nor did He spare the Egyptians who hardened their hearts against Him; nor the Canaanites; nor the Amorites; nor anyone else who persistently rebelled against Him (Ps. 78:50). Peter's warning is clear. Paul, too, wrote in Romans 11:21-22, *"For if God spared not the natural branches, take heed lest he also spare not thee. Behold therefore the goodness and severity of God: on them which fell, severity; but toward thee, goodness, if thou continue in his goodness: otherwise thou also shalt be cut off."* (And experience His severity towards unrepentant evildoers.) There is no automatic imputed righteousness, imputed outwardly, which doesn't change one inwardly (1 John 2:29). People that have Bible faith *live* by faith, and those who don't continue in the faith will be *"cut off."*

False Prophets and Teachers

In Deuteronomy 29:19-20 God says, *"And [if] it come to pass, when he [such a man] heareth the words of this curse [about what will fall on all those who rebel and walk after other gods], that he bless himself in his heart, saying, I shall have peace [even], though I walk in the imagination of mine heart [not obeying the Lord but following my own desires], to add drunkenness to thirst:* **the LORD will not spare him,** *but then the anger of the Lord and his jealousy* *shall smoke against that man [who thinks the curse cannot touch him], and, [1] all the curses that are written in this book shall lie upon him, and, [2] the* Lord *shall blot out his name from under heaven."* See Revelation 22:18-19, where the same kind of warning is given to believers in the New Covenant who are to hear and heed what the Spirit is saying to the churches (Rev. 1–3).

The Lord further warns about false prophets and teachers who teach that we need not really obey the Lord, and says in Jeremiah 23:16-24, *"Thus saith the* Lord *of hosts, Hearken not unto the words of the prophets that prophesy unto you: they make you vain: they speak a vision of their own heart, and not out of the mouth of the* Lord. *They say still unto them that despise me [by not obeying Me], The* Lord *hath said, Ye shall have peace;* **and they say** *unto every one that walketh after the imagination of his own heart,* **No evil shall come upon you.** *For who hath stood in the counsel of the* Lord *[they say], and hath perceived and heard His Word? Who hath marked his word, and heard it? Behold, a whirlwind of the* Lord *is gone forth in fury, even a grievous whirlwind: it shall fall grievously upon the head of the wicked [on the evildoers and the lawless]. The anger of the* Lord *shall not return, until he have executed [it], and till He have performed the thoughts of His heart:* **in the latter days ye shall consider it perfectly.** *I have not sent these prophets [these teachers, these men with their message which tell people they can do evil and yet still be blessed and be at peace with God], yet they ran: I have not spoken to them, yet they prophesied. But if they had [really] stood in my counsel,* **and had** *[truly] caused* **my people to hear my words, then [this would be the true result] they should have turned them from their evil way, and from the evil of their doings.** *Am I a God at hand, saith the Lord, and not a God afar off? Can any hide himself in secret places that I shall not see him? Saith the* Lord." The Word says, *"All the paths of the* Lord *are mercy and truth (only)* **unto such** *as keep his Covenant and his testimonies"* (Ps. 25:10). *"Know therefore that the* Lord *thy God, he is God, the faithful God, which keepeth covenant and mercy* **with them that love him and keep his commandments** *to a thousand generations"* (Deut. 7:9). So, take heed then My brethren, let no man deceive you, regardless of how many people may follow someone, for Peter wrote that "many" in the professing church would follow false teachers and their lawless ways, just as many followed false prophets in the Old Testament. God's Covenant is conditional regardless of what any man says. Don't believe a person, no matter what label he may have attached to his name, or how nice he sounds, if he tells you that you could willingly take an evil course and still be accepted with the Lord or blessed by Him. Nor should you believe him if he tells you that you could live this way and grace will cover for you. He may teach dozens of things right, but if he's wrong here, that person is speaking not for the Lord, but is speaking the imagination of their own heart, and is under the influence of deceiving spirits (1 Tim. 4:1). For to teach such a thing is to teach a damnable heresy which can lead those who follow it, to hell. That person is, perhaps, only allowed to continue as a test to the people of God (Deut. 13:1-5) to see whether or not they will be faithful to God, or choose an evil route, and thereby, have the true thoughts and nature of their hearts revealed (Luke 2:34-35).

Peter said in 1 Peter 3:12, *"For the eyes of the Lord are over the righteous, and his ears are open unto their prayers: **but the face of the Lord is against them that do evil.**"* They who say and teach contrary things are speaking for the serpent and not for the Lord.

*"Then said Jesus (the true light) unto his disciples, If any man will come after me [and be a follower of mine], **let him deny himself** [no longer following Satan and the course of this world, Eph. 2:2], and **take up his cross** [crucifying whatever is contrary to the will of God, Gal. 5:24], **and follow** Me [down the narrow road]. For whosoever will save his [sinful] life [in this world] shall lose it: and whosoever will [choose to] lose his life for My sake shall find it"* (Matt. 16:24-25). (The other gospel says that they will then *"save it unto life eternal."*) Hebrews 5:9 says that Christ is *"the **author of eternal salvation** unto all them that obey him."* True eternal security then rests in obedience to the Lord and repenting of sin, when and if, it's committed. But "these" (people and teachers that have given themselves over to *aselegeis*, and a false concept of grace are as Jude said) *"spots [blemishes] in your feasts of charity [Christian gatherings], when they feast with you, feeding themselves without [the] fear [of God], clouds they are without water [empty clouds promising refreshing rain but producing nothing], carried about of winds [of doctrines];trees [people] whose fruit [they once had] withereth [now]; without fruit, twice dead [spiritually], plucked up by the roots"* (by this teaching). Those who get caught up in and follow this wrong belief about grace and who live ungodly, may profess and speak many things, but nothing of any spiritual value is really produced by them any longer (vs. 11-12). Jude revealed that they have been led astray once again and gone now in the way of Cain, Balaam, and Korah. Again, Cain killed his brother because his own works were evil and his brother's works were righteous (1 John 3:12). Balaam *forsook* the right way and chose the wages of unrighteousness. And Korah, who also was delivered out of Egypt, rebelled against God-ordained authorities, and tried to lead the other people of God astray also in his rebellion, professing he could hear from God as well as

Moses; but the earth opened up and swallowed him and his family, and they went down alive into hell. All of these actions and responses from people can be caused, as Jude pointed out, by a false concept of grace and thinking wrong about God's attitude concerning these things. So it is not what people think that counts, but what God has said. After all is said and done, God will have the final word. All that is written will be proved to be true.

Jude's description is clear. Some have presumed so much on God's grace and have misinterpreted it to such a degree that they have, because of believing in this counterfeit grace, been led astray, and lost the good fruit of a changed life they once had. They have lost the fear of the Lord, their living faith also was uprooted, and they eventually became people (spiritually) twice dead, no longer really living for the Lord, broken off from the vine. But Jude said, they, like the fallen angels before them, and many in Israel who were judged in old times for going astray, are *"wandering stars"* gone out of orbit (the proper course set for them by God). Yet they continued, at times, to attend Christian events and feasts but they no longer willingly followed the *"paths of righteousness"* laid down for them in the Word (Ps. 23:1-3; 1 Pet. 2:25), thinking their version of grace would automatically cover for their wickedness. But they only deceive themselves and now believe a lie (2 Thess. 2:10-12).

Be assured that real faith and grace will always cause a person *to go on* from glory to glory, being more and more changed into Christ's moral image and likeness (Col. 3:10; Eph. 4:24; 2 Cor. 3:18), bearing more and more good fruit. We are to go on from glory to glory and put on the new man, which is created in righteousness and true holiness. Never will the true Gospel cause a person to go from godliness to sin if it's continued in. (Howbeit those who follow the counterfeit teaching may.) And *if a man abides not in Christ*, his good fruit *will* wither away (John 15:6).

The true Gospel will never tell you that you need not obey the Gospel (Rom. 10:16). The true faith will never tell you that you need not follow the author of faith. The true *Word* of God will never tell you that there is no need to obey the *Word*. Paul warns and says, *"And to you who are troubled, rest with us, when the Lord Jesus shall be revealed from heaven with his mighty angels, in flaming fire taking vengeance on them that know not God, and [on those]* **that obey not** *the Gospel of our Lord Jesus Christ"* (2 Thess. 1:7-8).

Produce Good Fruit

Paul also said concerning those that lose or produce no good fruit because of not continuing in God's goodness and provision, *"For the earth [those people] which drinketh in the rain [the blessings of God] that repeatedly [have cometh] oft upon it, and bringeth forth herbs meet [and profitable] for them by whom it is dressed [if it produces good fruit for the husbandman who cultivates it],* **receiveth blessing from God***: But that which beareth thorns and briers is rejected [if it continues to yield thorns and briars, and a sin filled life], and is nigh unto cursing [it has lost its value];* **whose [final] end is to be burned"** (Heb. 6:7-8).

"Ye are the salt of the earth: but if the salt have lost his savor [its effectiveness to do what it was created for], wherewith shall it be salted? **it is thenceforth good for nothing***, but to be cast out, and to be trodden under foot of men"* (Matt. 5:13). Here is the point: God's blessing of grace now gives us the ability to live the way God wants us to live and to produce good fruit. This is what He is cultivating us for. Jesus said, *"I am the true vine, and my Father is the husbandman. Every branch in me that* **beareth not fruit he taketh away** *[prunes off]: and every branch that beareth [some] fruit, he purgeth it, that it may bring forth more fruit"* (John 15:1-2).

"And [even] now also the ax is laid unto the root of the trees: therefore every tree [every person] which bringeth not forth good fruit is hewn down, and cast into the fire" (Matt. 3:10). Now we understand that a corrupt tree (us before we were saved) could not bring forth the kind of good fruit God desired, for we were children of wrath by nature. So none of us could have saved ourselves by our dead and defiled works out of the pollutions of the world, for we were then *"without strength"* walking after, and controlled by, the flesh, and ruled over by the devil. We were, at that time, slaves of sin without Christ, without God, and without hope in this world (Eph. 2:12). But now by grace we have been saved from our ties with Satan; grafted into Christ, the true vine; are drawing from His strength, and are partakers of His righteous nature. We are now to be trees of righteousness, the planting of the Lord, that He might be glorified in the earth (Eph. 2:10; Isa. 61:3).

By His grace and power we can now bring forth that which is good and bear good fruit, and so God (the husbandman) expects this from us, as pointed out. Jesus said, *"Every branch* **IN ME that beareth not** *[any] fruit He taketh away [He cuts if off]: and every branch that beareth [some] fruit, he purgeth it [He continues to prune from it all that is dead and still clinging on from the old life], that it may bring forth more fruit"* (John 15:2). He will perfect that which concerns you if you continue on with Him. So, Jude's epistle was written to warn the church about people having all of their fruit wither away and becoming trees twice dead, plucked up by the roots, because of believing in a counterfeit grace. The picture is graphically clear. So be aware that there are such false teachings on grace out there which removes the need to live right, for the Bible addresses this issue (Matt. 5:6; 2 Thess. 2:11-12).

God Hates Sin

So then, Jude's epistle was written to stop Christians from being misled by ungodly teachers who presume too much about the grace of God and misinterpret it as though, because of grace, God wouldn't deal with sin that's persisted in. The truth of the matter is that God has to, according to His own righteous nature. Hear the Word of the Lord, *"And I sought for a man among them, that should make up the hedge, and stand in the gap before me for the land, that I should not destroy it: but I found none.* **Therefore** *have I poured out mine indignation upon them; I have consumed them with the fire of my wrath:* **their own way have I recompensed upon their heads, saith the Lord G**ᴏᴅ*"* (Ezek. 22:30-31). God's righteous indignation against sin must eventually strike at sin if it's not repented of. He desires to be merciful, but men must repent in order to receive His mercy.

The apostle wrote, *"The Lord is not slack concerning his promise, as some men count slackness; but is longsuffering to us-ward,* **not willing that any** *should perish [and suffer His wrath against evil] but that all should come to repentance,"* and repent of their evil deeds before it's too late (2 Pet. 3:9). Jesus said, *"For God so loved the world, that he gave his only begotten Son, that whosoever believeth in him should not perish, but have everlasting life"* (John 3:16). But Jesus also said in Luke 13:3, *" ... except ye repent,* **ye shall all likewise perish**.*"* (And suffer God's wrath against evil.) Paul wrote to Christians in Ephesians 5:6-7, *"Let no man deceive you [Christians] with vain words[or empty promises]: for because of these things cometh the wrath of God upon the children of disobedience.* **Be not ye therefore partakers with them**.*"* You can obviously see that this is so in numerous places throughout scripture in both Covenants, as also in the case of Nineveh in the book of Jonah. The time came for the judgment of God to fall on their wicked-ness, but God wanted to be merciful to them so He sent Jonah to preach to them, that perhaps they would repent. If they would repent He could then have mercy on them, if not, they, too, would have to fall under the wrath of God towards evil. It was repent of the evil, judge themselves, and thereby receive mercy, or be judged by God for the evil, once the longsuffering of God had run its course. Thank God they repented before it was too late. It's the same for us today (Rev. 2:18-21).

The apostle Paul said that *if* we'd judge ourselves, then we'd not be judged (1 Cor. 11); then the blood of Jesus would cleanse us from all unrighteousness (1 John 1:9). Jude's warnings with scriptural accounts of God's dealing with persistent rebels in times past is abundantly clear. His meaning and implication in his letter to the church about this counterfeit concept of grace is also abundantly clear, if you'll just believe what it says. Realize this, Adam, too, was created as a son of God by the grace and love of God, but when he committed treason and withdrew his allegiance from God, he died spiritually regardless (Luke 3:38). God still loved Adam, but *Adam's decision* to sin and follow Satan, separated them (Isa. 59:2). He forfeited grace and fell under the power of sin. The inevitable result was death (Rom. 5:12). He, like Lucifer, had rejected God and His will out of his life, and chose independent self-life and action apart from the will of God. This is the false way of life and alienates anyone who chooses that route *"from the life of God"* (Eph. 4:18). They then are *"without God and without hope in this world"* (Eph. 2:12). If we reject living for His will on the earth, we cannot have heaven (which is His will). However, we do believe Adam later repented and believed God's promise which was spoken about a coming redeemer (Gen. 3:15-21).

The angels, too, are called sons of God (Job 1:6), but some of them, because of their rebellion and following after Satan, are now called devils (adversaries). They are no longer holy, nor do they have the ability in themselves to be holy apart from God. All of mankind, too, was originally intended to be sons of God, but became children of wrath for following after sin and Satan (Eph. 2:2-3). Satan is revealed in scripture as another "god," and should never be followed (Eph. 2:2), for he always leads only in the way of death (2 Cor. 4:3-4). He is, right now, at work in all disobedient people whomever they may be (Eph. 2:2). Now we know that he is not really a god by nature, but, rather, only a fallen angel, yet people can follow false gods if they will to. *"For all the gods of the nations are idols: but the Lord made the heavens"* (Ps. 96:5). Of course, we do know that there is only one true God, but if you follow one as your course in life you reject the other (Matt. 12:30). You cannot serve two masters, and God, as we shall see, *must* judge all unrepentant rebels who follow Lucifer's rebellion no matter who they claim to be with their mouth (Matt. 3:9). You cannot, with your mouth, say that you're a believer, and with your life, follow Satan and the course of this world, and expect to be accepted (2 Thess. 2:10-12). *Note*: God being totally good is *always* naturally against evil; but God being totally good is also merciful. So, He worked out a plan to satisfy His own justice and to open up a door of mercy for us. He sent His Son to be the Savior of the world. His Son, then, came here by the will of God as a man, to bare the wrath due our evil behavior and provide for us the Spirit of Grace. (The Holy Spirit Baptism, Ezek. 36:26-27; Acts 1:4-5.) Now, because Jesus bore the wrath to deliver us from the wrath to come that must fall on evil, God can now have mercy on all who use their wills and repent and turn to Him for mercy. (Jesus said *repentance* and remission of sins should be preached to all nations, Luke 24:46-47.) A person now can have all their *past* evil washed away by the blood of Jesus in a moment of time (Rev. 1:5-6); and if they have repented of it, and their old self has passed away, they become a new creature and can now walk in *"newness of life."*

We all, like prodigal sons, had gone astray and died spiritually. The picture of the prodigal son is a perfect picture for us. He had gone astray, his life had become a mess, he had ended up in the pigpen of this world, he wasted his life on harlots and riotous living, but then he came to himself, used his will, repented, and turned back to his father. He confessed his life of sin and renounced it. He was willing to be a servant. His Father, then, joyously and graciously received him and blessed him after he had so done and said, *"My son who was dead is alive again."* God, in this story, didn't save him and accept him in his evil, but when he willingly wanted to come out of it. Hear what Jesus taught. I've come to *"call sinners to repentance,"* to come out of the vomit and pigpen of the world and to never turn back. (Remember Lot's wife.) If they do turn back, God says, *"after they have escaped the pollutions of the world through the knowledge of the Lord and Savior Jesus Christ [and], they are **again** entangled therein, and overcome, the latter end is **worse with them** than the beginning. **For it had been better for them not to have known the way** of righteousness, than, after they have known it, to turn from the holy commandment delivered unto them. But it is happened unto them [who go back to live in the pollutions of the world after being washed] according to the true proverb. The dog is turned to his own vomit again; and the sow that was washed to her wallowing in the mire"* (2 Pet. 2:20-22).

So, God never provided that His love or grace would automatically cover for us and bless us if we turned back to a life of disobedience. But rather, He provided that His grace would deliver us from a life of disobedience, and thereby, we'd be in a position to be blessed. *"Unto you first God, having raised up his Son Jesus, sent him **to bless you, in turning away every one of you from his iniquities"*** (Acts 3:26). *"And whatsoever we ask, we* *receive of him, because **we keep his commandments, and do those things that are pleasing in his sight*** (1 John 3:22). Thank God, He also provided the blood of Jesus that if a Christian did sin, he could go to the great High Priest, Jesus Christ, confess his sin and be completely and instantaneously cleansed by the blood of the Covenant. God, who is abundant in mercy, doesn't want to judge anyone but desires for all ***to come to repentance*** so He can be merciful to them. So let us never put Him in the position where He has to judge us.

The Law Was Given to lead Us to Grace

The law was given to lead us as sinners to this grace, showing us that we were under Satan and sin's control, and without God in this world, and therefore could not save ourselves from judgment, nor could we keep God's moral law on our own (Rev. 7:12-25). God's grace, as we've shown, was given to free us from Satan and a life of sin so that we would have the ability to keep the moral law, produce good fruit and good works, and be truly able to follow Jesus in paths of righteousness. It is God who supplies all the ability in this New Covenant (2 Pet. 1:3-4). And the moral law is still a part of the New Covenant, as you will also clearly see, only it is now God's grace that influences and empowers us to keep it, as we willingly cooperate with it.

Here is Paul's message of grace. *"For sin [Satan and the pollutions of this world] **shall not** [no longer] **have dominion** [or control] **over you:** for ye are not under the law [of Moses], (where unregenerate people still controlled by the spirit of disobedience had to try and keep God's moral law, Eph. 2:2-3) but under grace. [The dispensation where you are freed from the authority of darkness and delivered from sin's power by grace, the new birth, and the indwelling Holy Ghost.] "What then? [Someone may say] Shall we sin [and take the broad road], because we are not under the law [of Moses and the law's condemnation], but under [the dispensation of] grace? God forbid. [Don't even think such a thing]. **Know ye** not [that this still stands true], that to whom ye yield yourselves servants to obey, **his servants ye are to whom ye obey;** whether of sin [and Satan, a false god] unto [spiritual and eternal] death [Wrath, naturally, must still strike at all who live in sin and don't repent.], or of obedience unto righteousness? But God be thanked, that ye were the servants [and slaves] of sin, **but ye have obeyed from the heart** that form of doctrine, which was delivered you. **Being then made free from** [serving] **sin** [and Satan, and by this, freed from the coming judgment which must fall on all sinners and rebels], ye became the servants [and followers] of righteousness [and of God]. But now **being made free from sin** [by God's grace and the power of the Holy Spirit],* *and [having] become servants to [and of] God,* **ye have your fruit unto [and are producing] holiness and the end** *[of a life of serving God in this way is] everlasting life"* (Rom. 6:14-18,22). For *"without holiness no man shall see the Lord"* (Heb. 12:14). Do you not see it? Free from a life of sin, and free from following after Satan by grace and the Holy Spirit, so that you can now produce the fruits of holiness and the end result of this way of living and taking the narrow road, just as Jesus said, is eternal life. (See Rom. 2:3-11.) You are under the same test as Adam and the angels were, to see whether or not you'll prove faithful to live for God and obey His Son so that you might be trusted with eternal positions in God's Kingdom; or whether you'll choose to follow the adversary and his lies and rebellion against God's moral government as other rebels have, in times past. So, do not be led astray by the enemy's counterfeit, cleverly disguised teaching on grace in which he deceptively gives out that people can follow his rebellion telling them "all is well" in their relationship with God, while they are living contrary to God and following him. Most of the world who seem to be living just nice, natural lives are really following Satan's rebellion.

Their sin is that they don't want to submit to God and His will as a part of their daily lives (1 John 2:15-17).

The apostle Peter said, *"Ye therefore, beloved, seeing ye know these things before, beware lest ye also, being led away [off the right path] with the error [and misguided ways] of the wicked [that is, false teachers, 2:1-2], [you] fall from your own steadfastness"* (2 Pet. 3:17, and safe foothold).

Romans Seven and Eight

Romans chapter seven reveals our condition as sinners under the control of the law of sin and death. But Romans chapter eight reveals that Christ dealt with the sin problem and set another law in motion, which sets us free from sin's control. *"For the law of the Spirit of life in Christ Jesus hath made me free from the law of sin and death"* (Rom. 8:2). We are no longer under sin's control and therefore freed from the (control of the) law of sin and death that once held us captive and led us like slaves in shackles down the broad road to destruction. But the wages of living after a life of sin without repentance is still death for anyone. In other words, the broad road still *always* leads only to destruction. There is no grace revealed in the New Covenant, which will automatically cover for anyone and make them acceptable in God's sight, if a person *chooses* an evil course of life. God sent us the Spirit of Grace. *"That the righteousness of the law might be fulfilled in us, who walk not after the flesh, but after the Spirit"* (Rom. 8:4). To God then be all the glory. And if we continue on in His grace (His goodness), we will continue to bring forth more and more good fruit as time goes on. (See Phil. 1:11.) God continues to prune us and deal with us, so that we continue to grow and change. *"And ye have forgotten the exhortation which speaketh unto you as unto children, My son, despise not thou the chastening of the Lord, nor faint when thou art rebuked of him: For whom the Lord loveth he chasteneth, and scourgeth every son whom he receiveth. **If ye endure** chastening, God dealeth with you as with sons; for what son is he whom the father chasteneth not? But if ye be without chastisement, whereof all are partakers, then are ye bastards, and not sons. Furthermore, we have had fathers of our flesh, which corrected us, and we gave them reverence: shall we not much rather **be in subjection unto the Father of spirits**, and live? For they verily for a few days chastened us after their own pleasure; but he for our profit, that we might be partakers of his holiness. Now no chastening for the present seemeth to be joyous, but grievous: nevertheless, afterward it yieldeth the peaceable fruit of righteousness unto them, which are exercised thereby. Wherefore lift up the hands, which hang down, and the feeble knees; and **make straight paths for your feet**, lest that which is lame [cause you to] be turned out of the way; but let it rather be healed. Follow peace with all men, and holiness, without which no man shall see the Lord: Looking diligently lest any man [among you Christians] **fail of the grace of God**; lest any root of bitterness springing up trouble you, and thereby many be defiled"* (Heb. 12:5-15).

So, we who are released from sin's control are now heading down the narrow road which leads to life eternal, and experience His guidance, dealings, and chastening, but those still controlled by sinful flesh cannot please God. So again, *"By their fruits ye shall know them."* Anyone then who continues in Christ and in the grace of God will go from glory to glory, never in reverse, back into a life of habitual sin, or back to live in the things they were once already delivered from. If they go backward and remain there, it only shows that they are not continuing in the grace of God, which enables us to live righteously, but have turned back to follow Satan down the broad road that leads to destruction. Paul said, *"For some are already turned aside after Satan."* Grace then is not something that will automatically cover for willful rebellion against light once it's received. *But all sin will be forgiven* because of the blood of Jesus and God's great mercy if it's repented of, and confessed to God (1 John 1:9). This is His wonderful provision in this Covenant and His simple requirement. Any idea of grace must line up with all of these scriptures or it is wrong.

Satan Comes as an Angel of Light

Sad to say, but many in our day have also slipped into the same deceptive teaching concerning grace and righteousness as those in Jude's day, as though grace will somehow automatically impute righteousness and cover over all unconfessed sins and future sins without repentance or confession, or partaking of our High Priest's ministry. Sadly, some of them like those in Jude's day, say and teach that God, because of grace, will continue to respond to a person that's professed faith in Christ with their mouth, in the same way all the time, regardless of how they live or act. They ignorantly say that a person's behavior, or sin (which is living contrary to God's known will), doesn't change God's response to that individual. Some even go so far as to say that repentance from following Satan and his enticements is not necessary at all once one has received Christ, for they consider that if it was necessary, it would be legalistic works to have to obey God and follow Jesus' example. They believe it's wrong if you say you have to stop following Satan and the course of this world, revealing that they don't even know what faith, repentance, or legalism is. It is not legalism to follow the example of Jesus, the author and finisher of our Christian faith, who kept His Father's Word and commandments. And Jesus said, *"The prince of this world cometh and hath nothing in me...."* They presumptuously also think that all of your future sins and following after Satan are already forgiven without ever having to do what the Word says to do concerning sin. This, too, is a trick of the adversary to get people to disobey God, harden their hearts against God's ways, and eventually incur the death penalty once again, just as He did with Adam. *"And no marvel; for Satan himself is transformed into an angel of light. **Therefore it is no great thing if his ministers** also be transformed as [and pretending to be] the ministers of righteousness; whose end shall be **according to their works**"* (what they have done and how they have lived), (2 Cor. 11:14-15), just like everybody else.

Certainly, the blood has the power to cleanse away every sin if the sin is confessed and the blood's power is partaken of. But don't be fooled by men's titles and outward show. *"Prove all things"* only by looking at all scriptures on the subject. The question is, what are they implying or saying?

Remember, Jesus said that the enemy sowed tares among the wheat. They both look similar until the time of the harvest and then their true natures are seen. (See Matthew 13:24-30,36-43.) Christ's final messages to the churches in the book of Revelation on repentance, clearly show that His command for Christians and church members who do wrong is to repent, or else suffer the consequences of their sin. See for yourself that He spoke clearly His responses to the unrepentant people in the churches (Rev. 2–3). So, this false concept of grace is just another tactic of the enemy to persuade people not to obey God or His Word, and to get people to side in with him and his rebellion against God's moral government. All who are deceived by this counterfeit grace and live for the will of Satan will be judged with him. Jesus will say, *"Depart from me all ye workers of iniquity"*; and *"Then shall he say also unto them on the left hand, Depart from me, ye cursed, into everlasting fire, prepared for the devil and his angels"* (Matt. 25:41).

God Doesn't Change

Some say, "our behavior can't change God." Well, certainly we know people's actions don't change God " … *with whom is no variableness, neither shadow of turning,"* for God always works only according to what's written, for His Word is His integrity. Once He says it, He will not alter it; it is forever settled in heaven (Ps. 89:34; James 1:17). It comes from His perfect nature, and because God doesn't change, Paul used many examples of how God dealt with people in times past to teach Christians, and wrote warnings to Christians showing that God still deals with people today just as He did in times past, *"Now all these things [that] happened unto them [Israel] for ensamples [for us]: and they are written for our admonition [and learning], upon whom the ends of the world are come. Wherefore let him that thinketh he standeth take heed lest he fall"* (1 Cor. 10:11-12). But coming *disguised* as Bible love and grace (while their message implies you could really live contrary to both), some of these teachers really promote, or excuse unrighteousness and the devil's work, and try to change God and His grace to fit their own imagination. These misled teachers try to make God in the image they desire, telling God how He must respond if He is grace-full, giving out their own private interpretation of what grace is, rather than accepting all of what God's Holy written Word says and teaches about it. Some of them imply that if He's grace-full and loving He should excuse their rebellion against Him without their repentance or confession of it. They think *contrary* to what the apostle Paul wrote in God's Holy Word, believing that grace means that they don't have to judge themselves or obey God. Paul never taught that (1 Cor. 11:31; 2 Thess. 1:8-9). Please realize that God will always respond to people just as His written Word says He will. He is no respecter of persons, but still judges according to every man's actions (Rom. 2:6-11). If

He says in scripture to repent of sin committed, *we need to do so* in order to receive what His love, mercy, and grace have truly provided for us, or He never would have said it. Not a jot or tittle of this Covenant has passed away. Don't let the *"angel of light"* persuade you otherwise. God must respond according to what's written for He is unchangeable and cannot lie about these things. So, live accordingly.

To Christians Peter writes, *"And if ye call on the Father, who **without respect of persons judgeth according to every man's work** [behavior], pass the time of your sojourning here [in the earth] in [reverent] fear"* (1 Pet. 1:17). (See also Phil. 2:12-13.)

Take the time, if necessary, to read or look up all of the scriptures written in this book, and you will see as we continue on, that God does respond to us according to our wills and actions. This too, then, will clearly reveal to you that this other concept of grace is really false. Those who don't believe that they *really* need to obey God, nor continue on in His Covenant and its conditions to receive His continued blessings or eternal life, say, "only believe." They think presumptuously, that if you just verbally profess with your mouth that you believe that you are operating in Bible faith and meeting all the conditions that God gave us in His Word, that you will, therefore, be saved and blessed regardless of how you live. And they say or imply by this, that these many scriptures and commandments God has given to us in the New Covenant (this new contract with the human race) to obey by faith and stay on the narrow path, are unnecessary and legalistic. And they say or imply that anyone who teaches that obedience to God and His Word and staying on the narrow path is necessary, is either legalistic or self-righteous. Can you not hear the hiss of the serpent in all of that? It's the same hiss that was hissed by the serpent back in Genesis, chapter three. Know ye not that Jesus, the author and finisher of our faith, always obeyed and kept His Father's commandments (John 15:10), and always did things that pleased the Father (John 8:29), and that without faith, it's impossible to please God? (Heb. 11:6). So then, this *is faith!* Let no one persuade you otherwise. And Christ told us to follow His example and to keep His commandments (John 15:10) and said, *"Ye are my friend [on this condition] IF ye do whatsoever I command you"* (John 15:14).

Realize there is always the narrow path that leads to life and the wide path of self-will that always leads only to destruction. To walk the narrow path is to walk the way of God's will and commandments (1 John 2:3-6). The wide path is to live your own way, doing your own thing with no regard for God's commandments or His will. So what saith the Word, the *whole* Word, and nothing but the Word? For it alone reveals the mind and will of the heavenly Father. It alone reveals both the privileges and the conditions of the Covenant. We will continue to clearly show you from the scriptures that Bible faith is more than just a verbal profession. It is a way of life. *"The just shall live by faith"* (Rom. 1:17). It is a commitment of the heart and soul to live for the will of God. (See 1 Pet. 4:2.) Sons of God will live for the will of God. Jesus said, *"For whosoever shall do the will of my Father which is in heaven, **the same** is my brother, and sister, and mother"* (Matt. 12:50). Jesus will not identify Himself with those who are living in rebellion against His Father. *"In this the children of God are manifest, and the children of the devil: whosoever **doeth not** righteousness **is not of God** [they are not on God's side, nor do they have Christ, the righteous one, living in them, Phil. 1:11], neither he that loveth not his brother"* (1 John 3:10).

CHAPTER SIX

ADAM AND GOD'S UNIVERSAL LAW: GOD'S LAW IN OUR HEARTS

Now, we will see that God has freed us and saved us from our old sinful way of life by His grace, and has given us a new start and the privilege, once again, to be His sons and daughters. Also that He has given to us the power to live a holy (separated) life (2 Cor. 5:17-18). The moral law is not done away; it is now clearly within our hearts once again. *"**For this is the covenant** that I will make with the house of Israel after those days, saith the Lord; **I will put my laws into their mind, and write them in their hearts:** and I will be to them a God, and they shall be to me a people"* (Heb. 8:10). Whatever is written in the New Testament is our Covenant (John 14:26). And if God included in this new contract some things from the Old Covenant, then even though the old has passed away, those specific things, which are taken from the Old Covenant and written in the new, are now a part of our Covenant. Realize this, and it will greatly help you to rightly divide the Word of Truth. For example, Paul included nine of the Ten Commandments in the New Covenant. So these moral commandments are now part of the new contract and every one of them has binding results (Eph. 6:1-3). We then exclude what was excluded and keep what has been brought into the New Covenant from the Old Covenant. The New Covenant reveals the conditions, the responsibilities, and the privileges of the Covenant. This Covenant stands as is, in its entirety, and cannot be altered or broken without suffering the consequences of the warnings stated herein. Be careful then that *no man* deceive you, implying that you need not keep, nor fulfill your part of this written contract (Heb. 2:1-3); or by teaching you that you could obtain the blessings of the contract while rejecting the parts which show your responsibility to live as God said, and to repent when necessary. This New Covenant reveals that if you live contrary to God, you will eventually obtain wrath, not blessings (Rom. 1:17; Eph. 5:5-7). Thus saith the Word!

Let's continue. Adam, who was originally created to be a son of God (Luke 3:38), had eternal life (John 17:3), and God's law clearly written in his heart by the Spirit of God. But Adam sinned and fell short of the glory of God (Ps. 8:4-5; Rom. 3:23, 5:12; 1 Pet. 4:14). Through sin (Adam's willing act of high treason against God and his choice to act independently of God), God and man were separated. The Holy Spirit of grace then departed (Gen. 6:3), and Satan entered this world and became its god (2 Cor. 4:3-4; Luke 4:6-7; John 14:30); and death, too (spiritual and physical), came in through sin (Eph. 4:18). The Bible clearly shows that whichever God men choose to obey, serve and live for is considered their God, for no man can give allegiance to and serve two opposite masters. God further reveals that His universal law was originally written in the hearts of all men. The apostle Paul wrote, *"For when the Gentiles [of the nations] which have not the [written] law, **do by nature** the things contained in the [moral] law these, having not the [written moral] law, are a law unto themselves: **Which show the work of the law written in their hearts**, their conscience also bearing witness, and their thoughts the meanwhile accusing, or else excusing, one another"* (Rom. 2:14-15).

But men have suppressed the truth of this universal law of conscience by their unrighteousness. *"For the wrath of God is revealed [in the Gospel] from heaven against all ungodliness and unrighteousness of men, who suppress the truth [of what they know in their hearts is right] by their unrighteousness"* (Rom. 1:18).

"For all have sinned, and come short of the glory of God" (Rom. 3:23). For *"him that knoweth to do good and doeth it not, to him it's sin"* (James 4:17). If they all sinned, then they all must have knowingly crossed the boundaries of right and wrong (and this universal law of conscience) in their own hearts. The apostle John wrote, *"For sin is the transgression of the law"* (1 John 3:4).

*"Wherefore, as by one man sin entered into the world, and death by sin; and so death passed upon all men, **for that all have sinned**"* (Rom. 5:12). But sin is not imputed where there is no law. *"The soul that sinneth, it shall die. The son shall not bear the iniquity of the father, neither shall the father bear*

the iniquity of the son: the righteousness of the righteous shall be upon him, and the wickedness of the wicked shall be upon him" (Ezek. 18:20). So if they all died spiritually at some point (Eph. 2:1; Rom. 7:9), they must have knowingly transgressed the law of God originally written in their hearts. For all over the world, people intuitively know that they shouldn't curse God, steal, kill, hate, commit adultery, lie, or covet their neighbor's wife or goods, and so on (John 1:9; Rom. 7:9). This is why a criminal runs when he knows the law is coming. His conscience testifies against him.

As time passed men became more and more hardened in their hearts because of sin and went more and more into moral and spiritual darkness, and God said, *"My Spirit shall not always strive with man."* God later wrote *the same* eternal, moral law on tables of stone with the finger of God (that is, by the Spirit of God), and revealed it to Israel (Luke 11:20; Matt. 12:28). That is a picture that He would later write His laws again on our stony hearts. (See Ezek. 36:25-27; 2 Cor. 3:2-3.)

Now He did this to clearly reveal His will once again to mankind. *"Now we know that what things soever the law saith, it saith to them who are under the law: that every mouth may be stopped, and **all the world** may become guilty before God"* (Rom. 3:19). Paul said that both Jew and Gentile were all under sin.

This is not speaking of the numerous Jewish ceremonial laws which were added later because of their rebellion and only as pictures of coming realities, but of the universal law of God, originally written in men's hearts. For all the world was never under the Jewish Mosaic ceremonial laws.

*"Therefore all things whatsoever ye would that men should do to you, do ye even so to them: **for this is the law and the prophets**"* (Matt. 7:12). This summarizes it. For all know what they do and don't want to have happen to them. All therefore know this royal law in their hearts (James 2:8-9), and are responsible when they knowingly break it. Paul said that men's thoughts will accuse or excuse them in the day when God judges the secrets of men, and there will then be a revelation of *"the righteous judgment of God."*

Because of sin then, and men constantly following after Satan and the flesh, the Holy Spirit withdrew and men were left on their own, to follow their own ways *"and be filled with their own devices."* (See Prov. 1:24-33.) They then came more and more under the authority and control of darkness and the law of sin and death, *"holden with the cords"* of their own sins, and were seduced and moved by the prince of the powers of the air into all forms of sin, rebellion, unbelief, unrighteousness, and idolatry. *"Wherein in time past ye walked according to the course of this world, according to the prince of the power of the air, the spirit that now worketh in the children of disobedience." "Among whom also we all had our conversation [and conduct] in times past in the lusts of our flesh, fulfilling the desires of the flesh and of the mind; and were by nature the children of wrath, [because of this] even as others"* (Eph. 2:2-3). For we all, to various degrees, lived contrary to this universal, moral law, and followed the prince of the powers of the air, the spirit of rebellion that is now at work in disobedient people (Eph. 2:2). (See also Eph. 4:17-19.) Paul wrote, *"For we ourselves also were sometimes [at one time in our past] foolish, disobedient, deceived, serving divers lusts and pleasures, living in malice and envy, hateful, and hating one another"* (Titus 3:3).

But God sent His wonderful Son to save us *from* our sins and this spiritually dead and lost condition, which came about at the fall of Adam, and by our own transgressions as well. He also came to free us from the domain of Satan (1 John 3:8). Christ came and fulfilled God's holy, moral law, and the Law of Moses with all its shadows and types for us, and then went to the cross to bear the penalty for our sins and to release us from the authority of darkness and cancel the devil's operation in us. And now, because of Christ's work, we can once again be born again and be reinstated back as sons of God, back into the family of God *just like Adam was before the fall* (Rom. 6:6-7). When we now repent of our ties with Satan (Acts 26:18), accept Christ, and choose to follow Him, our sins are washed away by His blood and mercy (Rom. 3:25), and we are also freed from sin's controlling power and delivered from the authority of darkness (Col. 1:13). Through Christ's blood cleansing us and after regeneration, the Holy Spirit then comes back into our hearts to live and to empower us as He was originally with Adam. *"That the righteousness of the [moral] law might be fulfilled in us, who walk not after the flesh, but after the Spirit"* (Rom. 8:4). *"For this is the covenant that I will make with the house of Israel after those days, saith the Lord; I will put my laws [once again back] into their mind, and write them in their hearts: and I will be to them a God, and they shall be to me a people"* (Heb. 8:10). Not the numerous ceremonial laws of the Mosaic law, but the moral laws of God. Paul said, *"To them that are without law, [I became] as without law [being not without law to God, but under the law to Christ], that I might gain them that are without law"* (1 Cor. 9:21). Paul realized he was still under God's moral law, the law of love.

"Jesus said unto him, Thou shalt love the Lord thy God with all thy heart, and with all thy soul, and with all thy mind. This is the first and great commandment. And the second is like unto it, Thou shalt love thy neighbor as thyself. On these two commandments hang all the law and the prophets" (Matt. 22:37-40). Do these and live.

God's law of love is not now written on tables of stone but, once again, it's clearly written on the fleshly tables of the heart by the Spirit of the living God, that we might obey it as God originally intended. The aim of the commandments, Paul stated, is love that comes from *a pure heart, a good conscience, and a sincere faith* (1 Tim. 1:5). God now commands us to obey it because He's given us grace to obey it. Love works no ill towards God or man. *"And hope maketh not ashamed; because the love of God is shed abroad in our hearts by the Holy Ghost which is given unto us"* (Rom. 5:5). *"But as touching brotherly love ye need not that I write unto you: for ye yourselves are taught of God to love one another"* (1 Thess. 4:9). But the devil continues to try and get people to believe that they can live contrary to this law, and he is still saying to the sons of God and sons of Adam in his doctrines and deceptions, "go ahead, live contrary to God's law, ye shall not surely die." He said this to Adam, a son of God, and evidently also to the angels also called sons of God, and caused them both to commit treason against God, and incur God's wrath towards evil. *"All we like sheep have gone astray; we have turned every one to his own way"* (Isa. 53:6). Men, then, became children of the devil and children of wrath with Satan as their spiritual stepfather because of this (1 John 3:10; John 8:44). So, Paul warns his Christian brothers, *"Therefore **brethren**, we [also] are debtors, not to the flesh, to live after the [sinful ways of the] flesh. For if ye **live after** the flesh [breaking God's law without repenting and availing yourself to the blood of Jesus], **ye shall die** [that is, you will again die spiritually for all died physically regardless]: but if ye through the Spirit do **mortify the [selfish] and sinful deeds of the body, ye shall live.** For as many as are led by the Spirit of God [out of a walk of being dominated by the flesh] **they** are the [true] sons of God"* (Rom. 8:13-14). Verse 17: *"And if children, then heirs; heirs of God, and joint-heirs with Christ; **if so be** that we suffer with Him (resisting sin, Gal. 5:24; 1 Pet. 4:1-2; Heb. 12:4), that we may be also glorified together." "Nevertheless the foundation of God standeth sure, **having this seal.**The Lord knoweth them that are [really] his. And, let every one that nameth the name of Christ **depart from iniquity"*** (2 Tim. 2:19). *"They that [truly] are Christ's have crucified the flesh with its passions and lusts"* (Gal. 5:24). Others that only have the *"form of godliness"* are tares, which outwardly look like wheat, but inwardly are not living for God (Rom. 2:28-29).

James wrote a similar thing in James 5:19-20: *"Brethren, if any of you do err [are seduced away] from the truth, and one convert him [turn him back to follow the Lord]; let him know that he which converteth the sinner [the brother that's gone astray] from the error of his way [from his evil course and misguided ways] shall save a [man's] soul from death, and shall hide a multitude of sins."* For God teaches, the *"soul that sinneth"* (following after Satan), without repentance still *"shall die."* This law is still in force unless we avail ourselves to the blood of Jesus. *"If we confess our sins, he is faithful and just to forgive us our sins, and to cleanse us from all unrighteousness"* (1 John 1:9). *"If we would judge ourselves, [then] we'll not [have to] be judged"* [by God]. Then the blood is applied by Jesus Christ, the righteous, the great High Priest of our confession, and we are thereby cleansed (Heb. 3:1; 1 John 2:1). Paul said, *"IF ye be led of the Spirit (then) ye are not under the law"* (or its curse, Gal. 5:18-24). And, of course, the Spirit will lead you out of a walk of being dominated by the flesh into the fruit of the Spirit. *"But the fruit of the Spirit is love, joy, peace, longsuffering, gentleness, goodness, faith, meekness, temperance: against such there is no law"* (Gal. 5:22-23).

Love and the Law

As we've stated, nine out of the ten commandments of the Old Covenant that God had gave to Moses and wrote on tables of stone, are now written in the epistles and Gospels in the New Covenant, and are therefore still in force. These are directly connected with the love law, which is the moral law. The only commandment left out is the Sabbath Day (Col. 2:16), for now every day is a day lived for the Lord (2 Cor. 5:15). Howbeit the New Covenant mentions *"the Lord's Day"* (Sunday), and exhorts us to assemble together on it (Rev. 1:10; Heb. 10:25). Paul said we are to enter into His rest by yielding up our selfish self-life, which was lived independently and contrary to His will (Heb. 4:1-10; 1 Pet. 4:2). This selfish, independent way of life, is the original sin, both of angels and men; and this denying of one's self and picking up the cross daily, to live for God is the true way of Christianity. So then, all these moral commandments still are a part of our Covenant that we have with God. Who can deny this? They are clearly written right in the contract.

People who teach that grace now allows or permits lawlessness really do not understand what has taken place in God's plan, nor do they grasp the enemy's wiles. Neither grace, nor love, ever excuses lawlessness; love fulfills the law and grace empowers us to keep it. The apostle Paul therefore writes, *"For this, Thou shalt not commit adultery, Thou shalt* *not kill, Thou shalt not steal, Thou shalt not bear false witness, Thou shalt not covet; and **if there be any other commandment**, it is briefly comprehended in this saying, namely, Thou shalt love thy neighbor as thyself. Love worketh no ill to his neighbor: therefore love is **the fulfilling of the law**.... The night is far spent, the day is at hand: let us therefore cast off the works of darkness, and let us put on the armor of light"* (Rom. 13:9-10,12). Because of partaking of God's divine, righteous nature and being grafted into Christ, we can now keep this love law and escape the corruption that is in this world because of people breaking this law. We are commanded in our Covenant to do so (John 13:34, 15:2), in order to make our calling and election sure (2 Pet. 1:10-11). *"For the love of God is shed abroad in our hearts by the Holy Ghost"* (Rom. 5:5). John, in his epistle, went on to say that this really isn't a new commandment but it is the one which was *from the beginning*. As long as we were under the power of Satan and sin, we couldn't keep God's love law, but now we who are new creatures, a part of the New Covenant, have love shed abroad in our hearts by the Holy Ghost and His grace within; we are commanded to do so (John 13:34), and we are commanded to confess any willing transgressions of it to God. This is stated in our contract. *"If ye fulfil the royal law according to the scripture, Thou shalt love thy neighbor as thyself, ye do well"* (James 2:8).

Love and the law (faith and the commandments) then go hand in hand. (See Rev. 14:12.) Not the works of the law which are the Jewish ceremonial laws (they were only shadows, types, and pictures, and are passed away because they were fulfilled), but we are emphasizing the eternal law of God's nature. (His nature is love.) Beware of any teacher who tells you that you need not keep this royal law (James 2:8-12). Beware of the hiss of the serpent. For grace and the Spirit now empower us to keep God's moral love law. Paul said, *"Do we then make void the law through faith? **God forbid: yea, we establish the law**"* (Rom. 3:31). It's just that it's established now through faith, which taps us into the power of grace, and not by ceremonial, legalistic works, for that type of a legalistic setup was "not of faith." It is now a new and living way. Would God ever then supply a grace that would give you, who are now His sons, freedom to go against this law of truth and love, against the work and teachings of Christ, against the Holy Spirit and the apostles' writings, and against the well being of others, or against His own moral government? Of course not! God is light and what fellowship has light with darkness, or righteousness with unrighteousness? God has not provided any means of continuance in darkness, but His great mercy will forgive all of the works of darkness and the sins people have committed, if they repent as

He said. They then turn from darkness to light and humble themselves before Him, and when they do, He has abundant mercy on them and can respond this way without going contrary to His own holy nature, and they are then cleansed by the precious blood of Jesus. Being cleansed, they then stand pure and holy before Him. This is His glorious, undeserved provision and kindness. But He does not automatically impute light to darkness, and then fellowship with darkness. He expects us to walk in the light we have received and accepts us as we walk accordingly (Phil. 3:16; Luke 12:47-48). (See also Ezek. 18:21-28.)

God has further commanded us in this new contract that we who have accepted Christ are now to *"continue in the faith."* That we are (and will be) made partakers of Christ (and share in His life), *"If we hold the beginning of our confidence steadfast unto the end"* (of our lives, Heb. 3:14), and if we don't forsake our cross and turn back to follow Satan and the course of this world again (Matt. 16:23-25). This is the real provision and design of faith and grace. This is the real Covenant. And this is the fight of faith that we are engaged in, for the serpent is still trying to get us once again, to rebel against God, just like he did with Adam and Eve of old.

The same trial of our faith is now also taking place. *"That the trial of your faith, being much more precious than of gold that perisheth, though it be tried with fire [that genuine faith, like genuine gold], might be found unto praise and honor and glory at the appearing of Jesus Christ ... Receiving the end [result] of your [genuine] faith [which continues to live for God and His will even through fiery trials], even the salvation of your souls"* (1 Pet. 1:7,9). *"Wherefore gird up the loins of your mind, be sober,* **and hope to the end** *for the grace that is to be brought unto you at the revelation of Jesus Christ; as obedient children, not fashioning yourselves according to the former lusts in your ignorance: but as He which hath called you is holy, so be ye holy in all manner of conversation; because it is written, Be ye holy; for I am holy. And if ye call on the Father, who without respect of persons judgeth [not according to some kind of automatic grace or automatic righteousness but) according to every man's work (their actions and responses to God's Word], pass the time of your sojourning here [in the earth] in (reverential) fear"* (1 Pet. 1:13-17). So, we see that through faith and God's grace we can now live lives pleasing to God and keep the law written in our hearts by the power of the Holy Spirit. We repeat, *"That the righteousness of the law might be fulfilled in us,* **who walk not after the flesh,** *but after the Spirit"* (Rom. 8:4). *"There is therefore now no condemnation (no coming judgment) to them which are in Christ Jesus, who walk not after the flesh, but after the Spirit"* (Rom. 8:1). But there is a coming condemnation for all those who live after the flesh. *"Wherefore we receiving a kingdom which cannot be moved, **let us have grace, whereby we may serve God acceptably** [in a way He is pleased with] with reverence and godly fear"* (Heb. 12:28-29).

God's Great Mercy

Now we know that God is longsuffering and gives people space to repent and is very merciful to all who ask His forgiveness. He will cast their sins into the sea of His forgetfulness if they repent and confess it. *"He that covereth his sins shall not prosper: but whoso confesseth and forsaketh them shall have mercy"* (Prov. 28:13). We further know of His great mercy towards new babes in Christ who ignorantly sin, and of the struggle people may have as they strive against sin (Heb. 12:4). Surely, He will also instantly welcome back every prodigal son and backslider who repents of following Satan, because of God's wonderful mercy and grace, and He rejoices over all those who do so. This gracious forgiveness through the blood of Jesus, when sins are confessed along with victory over a life of sin, is what His true grace and mercy have really provided (Heb. 4:16). God cannot vary from His own nature, so there will be multitudes in heaven who were repentant sinners, but there will be no rebels who have refused to repent.

In the Old Covenant people would, many times, have been stoned to death instantly for the things we can now repent of and receive mercy and grace for. This is because the blood of Jesus can purge away sin and its effects in us. Truly, this is a dispensation of great mercy and grace, but it is not a dispensation where you can live as you please, at least not if you want to go to heaven. So let's make sure we all look to His Word to see the whole counsel of God, for it is only *"the counsel of the Lord that shall stand."* His Word will *"judge us in the last day."* There will be no excuses on that day for *"the scriptures cannot be broken."* And remember, the Word is God talking and He gave us *"all scripture"* (2 Tim. 3:16-17); and in it He's made known to us the mystery of His will. All judgment will be according to exactly what's written. Not even a dotting of an "i" or the crossing of a "t" will be left out (Matt. 5:18). Make sure then that no man deceive you into thinking you can automatically escape the consequences of living contrary to great sections of this Covenant (Heb. 2:1-3) by their theories about grace. Let no man convince you to nullify or not obey, anything at all that Jesus or the apostles taught. They do to the Christian world with all their theories, what Darwin did to the secular world. They get great multitudes of people believing the wrong things, believing human speculations, and believing that darkness is light, and so a vast majority of people follow the theories of men rather than God's Word of Truth.

Continual Endurance Is Needed

Revelation 14:12 says, *"Here is the patience [the endurance] of the saints: here **are they that keep** [obey] the commandments of God, and [keep] the faith of Jesus."* Here God says the saints **are those that keep** (obey) the commandments of God and keep the faith of Jesus. The first and great commandment is still to *"love the Lord your God with all your heart, and your soul, and all your mind"*; and He said, *"If ye love me, keep my commandments."* Adam disobeyed God's commandment, and withdrew his allegiance to God and sided in with God's enemy. We, the redeemed (those delivered from the enemy), are to keep God's commandments. For Revelation 22:14 says, *"Blessed are they that do His commandments, that they may have right to the tree of life, and may enter in through the gates into the city."* Are we not then, in a similar position as Adam? The very word "saint" means "separated one." Paul himself taught *"obedience to the faith"*; or, an obedience to God that springs from faith in the heart, which also purifies the heart from evil. It is not just *saying* you have faith (Rom. 1:5,6:17,15:18). Words by themselves (if not really motivated by the heart) are cheap. Anyone can say, "the good Lord." Real faith taps you into grace that empowers you to turn from Satan and to live in continual obedience to God. Remember, there is the power of sin, and the re is the power of grace, which frees you from sin. The apostle says, *"But God be thanked, that ye were (in times past) the servants of sin [wrong-doing and Satan] but **ye have obeyed** from the heart that form of doctrine which was delivered you. Being **then made free from sin**, [free from the power of lawlessness] **ye became the servants of righteousness"*** (living for God's moral will and law, Rom. 6:17-18,8:4).

A faith that doesn't continue to work to purify the heart or move you to continue to serve righteousness, is not Bible faith at all (Acts 15:9; 1 John 5:4). Paul wrote in 2 Timothy 4:7-8, *"**I have fought a good fight, I have finished my course, I have kept the faith** [the faith of Jesus being His teachings and instructions]: Henceforth [because of this] there is laid up for me a crown of righteousness, which the Lord, **the righteous judge**, shall give [and award] me at that day: and not to me only, but unto all them also that love [and look forward to] His appearing."* Anyone willingly living a life of sin will not love (and look forward to) His appearing (1 John 2:28). What does it mean to *"keep"* the faith, or to *"continue in the faith"*? Does it just mean a verbal profession, or mentally assenting to it while living contrary? No, for as we've seen, the scripture says that the *just shall 'live' by faith.*" And, "*Man shall not live by bread alone, but by every word that proceedeth out of the mouth of God*" (Matt. 4:4). Even demons confess and believe that Christ is the Son of God; the Holy One; the Lord from heaven; but they don't have living faith (James 2:18; Luke 4:41). Bible faith is a commitment of faith *to live* for God, His will, and His Kingdom, and not for Satan or the world and its pollutions any longer (Heb. 11:7). Paul said that God will reward every man according to their actions. "*To them who by **patient continuance in well doing** seek for glory, honor and immortality [He will award] **eternal** life.*" But for those that don't continue on in His goodness, He will give indignations and wrath (Rom. 2:6-8). Sin wages war on this faith commitment. This is the trial of our faith and the fight of faith we are engaged in. Peter said, "*Dearly beloved, I beseech you as strangers and pilgrims [in the earth], abstain from fleshly lusts, which war [and battle] against the soul*" (1 Pet. 2:11), trying to take it captive once again. Satan used this world to seduce Adam and Eve and he still uses this world to try and seduce you away from God (James 4:4). Regardless of any disguise, anything that would lead you into any form of rebellion or action of unrighteousness, or into anything that is contrary to truth or God's holy nature, saying it's now okay, is of Satan. It is known by its own fruit. "*A good tree cannot produce corrupt [immoral] fruit.*"

Paul wrote, "*Take heed [then], **brethren** [you redeemed of Adam's seed), lest there be in any of you an evil heart of unbelief, in departing (once again) from the living God (and turning back to follow Satan]. But exhort one another daily, while it is called today; **lest any of you** be hardened [into persistent rebellion] through the deceitfulness of sin*" (Heb. 3:12-13). (To depart from God is to return back to a life of sin without repentance.) There are numerous other scriptures that we will point out that prove this point, which we will share with you as we go on. But we want you to see that the scriptures reveal that when the conscience becomes seared (and stops feeling sorrow for sin), and the heart becomes hardened through unconfessed and unrepented-of sin, it eventually, over time, will release its commitment of faith to live for God and His Kingdom, being self deceived and even, perhaps, still thinking all is well, while it lives a contrary life. When the heart releases the commitment it once had to live by faith and turns back to live in unbelief for Satan, self-will, and the world, it is then disconnected and has committed treason against God, just as Adam and other free moral agents have done in times past (Eph. 4:18-19). It has once again joined Satan's rebellion and that soul has departed from God. *"Ye adulterers and adulteresses, know ye not that the friendship of the world is enmity with God?* **whosoever therefore** *will be a friend of the world [and its lusts, 1 John 2:15-17]* **is the enemy of God"** (James 4:4). Only repentance then can open the way for that person's restoration. The person must once again turn from darkness to light and get on the right path, or he is headed once again, down the broad road of eternal ruin and punishment just as he was before (2 Thess. 1:8; James 5:19-20).

As we've stated before, the scripture says, ***"For if after they have escaped*** *the pollutions of the world through the knowledge of the Lord and Savior Jesus Christ [which had instructed them that to be saved, they had to turn from a life of sin, and pick up their cross and follow Him if], they are* ***again entangled therein, and overcome*** *[conquered by them], the latter end is worse with them than the beginning. For it had been better for them not to have known the [Lord's] way of righteousness, than, after they have known it, to turn from [turn their backs on and walk away from] the* **holy commandment** *[that was once] delivered unto them (returning back to their former way of life]. But it is happened* **unto them** *according to the true proverb, The dog is turned to his own vomit* **again***; and the sow that* **was washed** *[back] to her wallowing in the mire"* (2 Pet. 2:20-22). The only way someone could have escaped the pollutions of the world is not by human strength, will power, or works, but by God's power and grace. So this definitely is talking about people who went back to willful sinning as a decision after they had once been cleansed from a life of sin, choosing the temporal pleasures of sin and this world over God once again. Go back and carefully read that passage of scripture again. (See also Hebrews 10:19-31, which proves this also.)

This is the reason why we must stay away from sin, or confess it right away if it's fallen into, because sin causes spiritual darkness, hardening of the heart, and self deception, and it works to destroy this commitment of faith, and to get the person to where they may verbally profess the same things but they no longer *"keep the faith"* (1 Pet. 1:9). This is the fight of faith we are engaged in. Remember, God said the just are those that *"live by faith,"* not just "say" they have faith (James 2:14; 1 Pet. 4:19). And, as shown, faith without corresponding actions is dead as far as God is concerned (James 2:14-26).

We will continue to clearly see as we go on, that the scriptures reveal that the saints need to have patient endurance in this race to the finish line. Grace will abundantly sustain them and keep them living for God if they will believe and continue in *"His goodness,"* and *"continue in the faith."* He can certainly keep us from falling away if we want Him to

(1 Pet. 1:5). Otherwise, Paul said, if they don't continue in the faith and in God's goodness, but rebel and go back to the world, they also, like many in Israel of old who were once God's elect, would also be cut off (Rom. 11:22; 2 Pet. 1:10). *"He that endureth to the end shall be saved"* (Matt. 10:22). Jesus said some *"endure but for a time: afterward, when affliction or persecution ariseth for the word's sake, immediately they are offended"* (Mark 4:17). Blessed are they that continue to go on from faith to faith and glory to glory, walking in paths of righteousness, rather than the ways of darkness (Prov. 4:18-19).

Christians Not Yet Perfect

Now we know that Christians are not yet perfect for no one is yet perfect in knowledge. We all need His mercy where we are ignorant, but still we are to continue in the faith, living for God's will and pressing on to perfection (Phil. 3:13-19). We are to continue to yield ourselves to God to be pruned in order that we might bring forth more and more good fruit (John 15:1-3). (Though at times we understand that people can go through struggles with the tempter and this world and fall into sin for a short time, 1 John 2:1.) And if they do sin, they need to confess it to God in order to be cleansed of that sin and then instantly they are cleansed (1 John 1:9). But never should we allow sin and its deceitful effects cause in us a willingness to turn away from God or from the way of righteousness (Eph. 4:22). For whereas sin is destructive to faith, the way of righteousness protects your faith. Paul wrote, *"But thou, O man of God, flee these things; and **follow after righteousness**, godliness, faith, love, patience, meekness. Fight the good fight of faith, lay hold on eternal life, where-unto thou art also called, and hast professed a good profession before many witnesses"* (1 Tim. 6:12-13).

So, we are to always turn from darkness to light; from the power of Satan to God. If you're willingly living in, or going back to live a life of sin, then you're turning away from light to darkness, from God to Satan, and any person who does this can neither continue to receive God's blessings nor eternal life from the Lord (James 1:7-8). They have then elected not to be the elect. (Election is only in Christ, the elect of God.) Only then when you use your will to repent of sin do you turn from Satan to God who *then* freely gives mercy and grace to all who turn to Him in humility, acknowledging their need (James 4:6). And only then are your sins blotted out. All grace must be willingly received and continued in, including the grace of forgiveness (1 John 1:9; Rev. 22:13). To receive it we must turn *to* God as our source to obtain it (Heb. 4:16). So let us all continue to fight the good fight of faith in order to lay hold on eternal life as our eternal possession, as the apostle said (1 Pet. 1:5; Rev. 22:14): *"In hope of eternal life, which God, that cannot lie, promised before the world began"* (Titus 1:2).

Hebrews 12:1-2 *"Wherefore seeing we also are compassed about with so great a cloud of witnesses [the faithful saints that have finished the race and made it into heaven before us], let us also lay aside every weight, and the [life of] sin which so easily besets us [and trips us up and causing some to stumble off the right path, Heb. 12:13-14], and let us run with patience [and endurance]* **the race** *[to heaven]* **that is set before us.** *Looking unto Jesus the author and finisher of our faith;* **who for the joy that was set before him** *endured the cross, thinking nothing of the shame, and is [now] set down at the right hand of the throne of God."* You are to also put your focus on the joy of heaven set before you. This will help you to endure in this race to the end of your earthly life if you are willing to do so. Jesus finished His course and so can you. Paul then went on to say, *"ye have not yet resisted unto blood striving against sin."* (As sin once again tries to get mastery over you to get you to quit the race.)

Why would the apostle encourage us to strive against sin if it cannot have any effect on us, or on this race we are in? Unconfessed sin is faith's worst enemy causing spiritual blindness, spiritual weakness, hardness of heart, and is a hindrance to victory (Isa. 59:2). It wars against the soul (Heb. 3:12-14), and brings many troubles. And why would the apostle Paul say, *"fight the good fight"* to lay hold of eternal life if they, or we, permanently, had it already? (1 Tim. 6:12) The truth is, we must continue to keep our faith's commitment to live for God until the end of our lives, however long that may be, then it will be granted to us to partake of the tree of life, which will then lock us into eternal life forever (Titus 1:2; Rev. 2:7; Gen. 3:22-24). But, for now, Paul said, it's the *"hope of eternal life."* God wants to see our faith. He doesn't accept it if it's hypocritical faith that merely professes it, but doesn't live it. He says, *"Be thou* **faithful** *unto death and [then] I will give thee a crown of life"* (Rev. 2:10). *"Blessed is the man that endureth temptation: for when he is tried, he shall receive the crown of life, which the Lord hath promised to them that love him"* (James 1:12).

Blessed Are They That Keep God's Commandments

Listen to these words of God, In Revelation 22:14 He says, ***"Blessed [favored] are they that do his commandments, that they may have [the] right to the tree of life, and may enter in through the gates into the city."*** (See also

Rev. 1:3.) Note: That they may have the right, the privilege, to enter the city of God and partake of the tree of life. Adam was God's son but disobeyed God's commandment and couldn't partake of the tree of life BECAUSE he obeyed the devil and sin instead of God. The Lord said, *"He that hath my commandments, and keepeth them, he it is that loveth me: and he that loveth me shall be loved of my Father, and I will love him, and will manifest myself to him … He that loveth me not keepeth not my sayings: and the word which ye hear is not mine, but the Father's which sent me"* (John 14:21,24). The Father has made it clear who loves Him and who doesn't. As it was in the beginning, so it is now. So a person cannot be willingly living a life of sin, which is contrary to God, and still love God. They might say it with their lips, but it's not from their heart (Matt. 6:21). Can you not see the pattern then how we also are to keep God's commandments that we may have the right to eat of the tree of life? Which commandments? Whatever is written in our New Covenant. They are all simply fulfilled by love. God Himself gave us a new heart and the grace to live it. But the same serpent who deceived Adam and Eve away from the tree of life by getting them to disobey God's commandments, is at work now to try and deceive us also away from God and this tree, by the same lie and temptation (2 Cor. 11:3). Extreme gracists would say that these scriptures cannot be so, because they don't agree with their doctrine and concept of grace, which states that you could go back and live in sin and still have God's favor and eternal life. They say that if you merely profess faith in Christ it is a one-time thing and that's enough, and you're therefore righteous regardless of how you live. And they say that it's not *really* necessary to *continue to* obey Him, live righteously, nor do His commandments, yet this scripture from the book of Revelation is not from the Old Testament but from the New, which reveals to us God's present will and conditions for entering heaven. This agrees with Christ's teaching also in the New Covenant in Matthew 7:21 which says, *"Not every one **that saith** unto me, Lord, Lord, shall enter into the kingdom of heaven; but he that doeth the will of my Father which is in heaven;"* and Paul's teaching which says, *"Circumcision is nothing, and uncircumcision is nothing, but [what matters is] the keeping of the commandments of God"* (1 Cor. 7:19). And *"Know ye not that the unrighteous **[those who follow the devil and his ways]** shall not inherit the kingdom of God? Be not deceived [or misled by any man]: neither fornicators, nor idolaters, nor adulterers, nor effeminate, nor abusers of themselves with mankind, nor thieves, nor covetous, nor drunkards, nor revilers, nor extortioners, shall inherit the kingdom of God"* (1 Cor. 6:9-10).

Here then is God's revelation for all those who are under the New Covenant. For those things are all still of Satan's kingdom, and if people live for those things, they live not for God but for Satan and are on the road to destruction. Again, we are not speaking of a Christian who is living for God but falls into a sin or sins for a short while, because of weakness of the flesh, and then soon afterwards, repents. That person still wants to live for God but just had a struggle with temptation and the flesh. And God accepts us according to our willingness. He who confesses his sin is thereby thoroughly cleansed. The weakest Christian who wants to live for God will make it into heaven. These things are written to warn those who may become hardened by unconfessed sin or deceived by false teachings, and choose to turn back and live in those things and *walk with Christ no longer,* thinking they will still go to heaven just because they *say* they still believe in Him (James 2:14; Luke 6:46; Matt. 7:21; John 6:66). We are trying to awaken such individuals now before it's too late. Otherwise they will wake up to the truth when they stand before God and give an account of their lives upon the earth (Rom. 14:12). *"Awake to righteousness, and sin not; for some have not the knowledge of God: I speak this to your shame"* (1 Cor. 15:34).

Paul emphasized that the unrighteous are those who live unrighteously. John wrote, *"Everyone that **doeth** righteousness is righteous,"* even as He (Christ) is righteous. A label one thinks he has is not good enough if he's not *"obedient to the faith,"* which includes repentance and confession of known sins committed. It greatly helps us to see that Bible faith is a soul's commitment to live for and obey God, not by our own strength but by God's (2 Pet. 1:3). This is what's different in the New Covenant. In the Old Covenant they couldn't be sons yet, but after Christ's redemptive work, He is now the first born among *many brethren. His life* has been birthed into us (1 John 5:11-12; John 1:12). *"I have been crucified with Christ [My old sinful life has died. Paul said that we are dead to sin.]: **nevertheless I live; yet not I, but Christ liveth in me** [His life]: and the life which I now live in the flesh **I live by the faith of the Son of God**, who loved me, and gave himself for me"* (Gal. 2:20). Would Christ in us ever follow Satan? Never! And if we really are His sheep, we follow Jesus. He is our righteousness and lives His life out through us when we yield to His Lordship. Jesus in us will move us to obey His Word just as He obeyed His Father's commandments when He was here full of grace and truth as the Son of Man. He must increase and we must decrease, as far as our old way of life is concerned. Anyone full of grace and truth will do the same as Jesus.

Listen to the written Word speak: *"For if that first covenant had been faultless, then should no place have been sought for the second, for finding fault* **with them** *[who were still bound and under the control of the law of sin and death], he saith, Behold, the days come, saith the Lord, when I will make a new covenant with the house of Israel and with the house of Judah: not according to the covenant that I made with their fathers in the day when I took them by the hand to lead them out of the land of Egypt;* **because they continued not in my covenant, and I regarded them not, saith the Lord.** *For this is the Covenant, that I will make with the house of Israel after those days, saith the Lord; I will put my laws into their mind, and write them in their hearts [by My Spirit in them once again]: and I will be to them a God, and they shall be to me a people"* (Heb. 8:7-10). His eternal law of love is once again clearly written in our hearts (1 Thess. 4:7-9). If we love Him, we'll keep His commandments, and continue in them. If we will love our neighbor, we will work no ill towards them; these are His simple requirements. We are to obey the law of love (Rom. 13:9-10). If you do so, the Bible says, *"ye do well."*

Bible Faith and Grace

Now, knowing that Bible faith is responding to and obeying God's Word, and it is a willing commitment to live for God by faith, and that God gives the grace and the ability by His Spirit to do it, will help you to understand why Jesus and the apostles said what they said about the necessity of doing God's will and obeying His commandments, and yet they spoke of grace. Therefore, it all harmonizes and there are no discrepancies. All will be judged according to their works. This is what the grace of the New Covenant is given for and why James said, professing you have faith while there are no actions and not living by faith is dead faith, not genuine faith (James 2:20). For God-imparted faith and grace always produces actions that conform one to God's will (Rom. 12:2-3). There is no such thing as a grace given to live contrary to God's will, or a faith that does nothing.

For the most part, extreme gracists do not understand what real faith or grace is. They think you could say one thing and live another and it would still be faith, but it's not. At least according to the scripture definition of faith, it's not.

Anyone who turns back to live like the world, James said, *"makes himself the enemy of God"* (James 4:4). And God said that there is *"a certain fearful judgment"* for all that do so (Heb. 10:26-27). Why? Because the world is following *the prince of the power of the air,* **the spirit that is now at**

work in all people who are disobedient (Eph. 2:2). Satan, after all, is God's adversary. And if you submit to him, he becomes your master and his destiny will be your destiny. If you then follow him, this would make you an enemy of God (Matt. 25:41).

People who once lived as a Christian but who now have turned back, have lost their faith's commitment to live by faith and follow Christ, and have turned back to follow Satan once again. They have repented in reverse and made another choice. They are no longer called "the just," but, a "sinner" (James 5:19-20). They may profess one thing with their mouths, still hoping to go to heaven, but their actions declare something else (Titus 1:16). Their actions are speaking so loud that God can't hear what they are saying. Now we know that no devil nor certain sin can get you out of the body of Christ. Satan must work on your will, warring against you with sin to try and get you to make the decision yourself to not repent, and to walk with Christ no longer down the narrow road that leads to life. *"Because strait is the gate, and narrow is the way, which leadeth unto life, and [there are] few there be that find it"* (Matt. 7:14). *"Beware [then] of false prophets, which come to you in sheep's clothing [professing to be the righteous], but inwardly they are ravening wolves. Ye shall know them **by their fruit**. Do men gather grapes of thorns, or figs of thistles?"* (Matt. 7:15-16). If they, like the false prophets in the Old Testament, teach that you could willingly walk in evil ways and still be secure with God, they are wolves in sheep's clothing trying to devour your real faith. You'll know them (these false teachers and false prophets) by what they tell you that you can do. This is what the apostles warned us about. Paul said concerning these so-called *"ministers of righteousness,"* that *their* end will be according to the works just like everyone else. Jesus said in Luke 6:46, *"And why call ye me, Lord, Lord, and do not the things which I say?"* He will either be Lord of all, or not your Lord at all (Rom. 14:7-9).

THE DOCTRINE OF CHRIST

So now, let's look at the doctrine of Christ in the Gospels, the Acts of the Apostles, and the epistles and let's see God's responses to people revealed. We will see that what the author of our faith taught is *the faith* we are to keep. *"Here is the patience of the saints: here are they that keep the commandments of God, **and the faith of Jesus**"* (Rev. 14:12). After His resurrection and at the beginning of the New Covenant, He commanded His disciples to go forth to all nations, *"Teaching them to observe **all things whatsoever I have commanded you**: and, lo, I am with you alway, even unto the end of the world. Amen"* (Matt. 28:20). So, never dissect or disregard any of the words or teachings of Christ in the Gospels or epistles as if they weren't for us. Paul said that Jesus is both the author and finisher of our faith (Heb. 12:2). It is all the faith of Jesus, for there is only *"one Lord, and one faith,"* and the law and the prophets were only until John. Since then, Jesus preached the Gospel of the Kingdom, and said, *"And **this gospel** of the kingdom shall be preached in all the world for a witness unto all nations; **and then shall the end come**"* (Matt. 24:14; Heb. 2:1-4).

Let's take a good, clear look into the teaching of Christ in the New Covenant. If all blessings and eternal life were automatically by a grace which requires no commitment of faith or actions from the person, then we'd have to do nothing and all would be blessed equally and automatically, for Jesus *"by the grace of God, tasted death **for every man**"* (Heb. 2:9).

The Gospel, the Bible says, is for *"all the world"*; and, *"every creature"*; and God is *"not willing that **any** perish,"* even though multitudes do perish every day contrary to God's will for them because they are not willing to turn to God. But, as we will see, every part of this Covenant operates by a living faith, which taps us into grace's power, which then produces a change of life. This change produced by real grace then moves us into position to receive God's blessings. *"Unto you first God, having raised up his Son Jesus, sent Him to bless you, in turning away every one of you from his iniquities"* (Acts 3:26). (See also 1 John 3:22.) *"Who his own self bare our sins in His own body on the tree [so] that we, being dead to sins, should live unto righteousness; [because of His grace] by whose stripes ye were healed"* (1 Pet. 2:24).

In the beginning of the Gospel message Jesus preached, *"Repent and believe the Gospel"* (Mark 1:14-15). Paul made it clear that the Gospel he preached *first* began to be preached by the Lord (Heb. 2:1-4). Before real faith, the Bible reveals there must be "repentance" (a turning away from sin and Satan), and getting off of the road that leads to destruction (Luke 13:3). And, as we will further show, with faith there must also be action (Hebrews 11). Real faith is walking down the narrow way as Christ taught. You cannot operate in faith towards God and live a life of unconfessed sin following Satan at the same time; or, as Paul said, you cannot sit at the Lord's table and the table of demons. These are of two opposite kingdoms and anything divided against itself, cannot stand (John 5:44).

Abide in Christ's Teachings

In 2 John 8-9 the apostle writes:

"Look to yourselves (then), that we lose not those things which we have wrought, but that we receive a full reward. Whosoever transgresseth, and abideth not in the doctrine [the teachings] of Christ, hath not God. He that abideth in the doctrine [the teachings and instructions] of Christ, he hath both the Father and the Son." Many extreme gracists try to do away with Christ's teachings in the Gospels, as though they really need not be heeded. By doing so, they are denying the faith of Jesus. Jesus told His true disciples after His resurrection concerning this New Covenant to go teach all nations, *"teaching them to observe all things **whatsoever I have commanded you**: and, lo, I am with you alway, **even unto the end of the world**"* (Matt. 28:20). And, again, Christ said to those Jews which believed on Him, *"If ye continue in **my word**, then are ye my disciples indeed; and ye shall know the truth, and the truth shall make you free"* (John 8:31-32). He also said that the word that He spoke while He was here in the flesh would judge us in the last day (John 12:48; Heb. 2:2-3).

We must then abide in Christ's teachings as is found in the Gospels, the book of Acts, the epistles, and the book of Revelation. Anything at all that is contrary to what's clearly written in any of them does not come from Christ but from the adversary, for he works to twist the scriptures and produce many false, unrighteous doctrines.

If you can find two or three clear scriptures in the New Testament that contradict what someone believes, or that shows they've only taken partial truths, then what they are believing is wrong. All scriptures must harmonize into one picture. As we go on, we will literally give you dozens and dozens of other clear scriptures from the teaching of Christ that will show you that the false idea of extreme grace believed by some, is wrong and way out of balance, and it contradicts much of the New Covenant. Many people believing something doesn't necessarily mean it's right. Many people also believe in the false theory of evolution or Hinduism. Even the vast majority of the people of Israel wanted to return to Egypt. We must *"prove all things"* by the Word, for the Word, rightly divided, is always right. So then, if some group or denomination teaches one thing and the Word of the Lord another, always remember that the Word is always right and it is the only thing that will *"judge us in the last day"* (John 12:48). You are responsible to *"prove all things and hold fast to that which is good"* (1 Thess. 5:21).

Christ's Teaching in Matthew's Gospel

Here Christ reveals the law of truth. For the law of the Old Covenant was until John the Baptist, but grace and truth came by Jesus Christ. And remember, John the Apostle said that anyone who doesn't continue in the teachings and instructions of Christ, *"hath not God;"* for God commanded Him what to say (John 12:48-49); and, Jesus said, we are *"to observe all things"* He commanded them *"even unto the end of the [Church] age"* (Matt. 28:20). It's important to side in then with God rather than man (Rom. 3:3-4).

"For the LORD *giveth wisdom: out of his mouth cometh knowledge and understanding. He layeth up sound wisdom for the righteous: he is a buckler to them that walk uprightly"* (Prov. 2:6-7).

Let's listen then to Christ's teachings for it is grace talking; and also, to the apostles' doctrine concerning these things, and let us notice God's instructions and responses to people. Notice, in these next passages the words "for they."

Matthew 5:1-12

"And seeing the multitudes, he went up into a mountain: and when he was set, his disciples came unto him: and he (the Lord of Grace) opened his mouth

*and taught [and instructed] them, saying, Blessed are the poor in spirit [the humble who see their spiritual need of God]: for **theirs** is the kingdom of heaven. Blessed are they that mourn [because of sin, 1 Cor. 5:2; 2 Pet. 2:8]: **for they** shall be comforted. Blessed are the meek [those of a gentle spirit]: **for they** shall inherit the earth. Blessed are they which do hunger and thirst after righteousness [for being and doing what's right]: for they shall be filled [by God with goodness].* **Blessed are the merciful [those who show mercy]: for they shall obtain mercy,** *Blessed are the pure [the sincere] in heart: for they shall see God. Blessed are the peacemakers [those who make peace]:* **for they** *shall be called the children of God. Blessed are they which are persecuted for righteousness' sake [for being and doing what is right in the sight of God]: for **theirs is** the kingdom of heaven (2 Tim. 3:12). Blessed are ye, when men shall revile you, and persecute you, and shall say all manner of evil against you falsely, for my sake. Rejoice, and be exceeding glad: for great is your reward in heaven: for so persecuted they the (holy) prophets which were before you."*

Do you see whom the blessings are promised to? *Only to those* who are doing something for God, or living as God wills; those whose faith is alive and whose heart is right (Luke 8:14-15). The blessings are for those who live the way God wants them to live who willingly cooperate with the grace of God (1 Cor. 6:1; James 1:22). The *"Word of His grace"* has the faith and grace in it to obey if we are willing (Acts 20:32). *"For the Lord God is a sun and shield: the Lord will give grace and glory: no good thing will he withhold **from them that walk uprightly"*** (Ps. 84:11).

Verse 7

Notice: *"Blessed are the merciful:* **for they** *shall obtain mercy." "Blessed are the pure in heart* **for they** *shall see God"* and so on. But our Covenant also says that *"He will have judgment without mercy"* on those who show no mercy (James 2:13). See, there is no automatic cover or protection by an outward label of righteousness if we inwardly are choosing to live unrighteously. God's design in setting up this Covenant was not to produce hypocrites. Throughout His teaching, we can see that there is a response given from heaven depending on the actions and heart attitudes of men upon the earth (Heb. 2:1-3; Col. 3:25). God's response is not just on the basis of some kind of unconditional grace, unconditional love, nor imputed positional righteousness; nor will He bless a verbal profession without actions (James 1:22; Mark 7:6; Matt. 6:1-8). The scriptures reveal that if we deny Him, He will deny us; If we return to Him, He will return to us; if we forsake Him, He will forsake us; if we show others mercy, He will show us mercy. If we don't forgive others, He won't forgive us; if we walk contrary to Him, He will walk contrary to us; if we draw nigh to Him, He will draw nigh to us; if we forsake Him, He will forsake us. These, and dozens more scriptural truths like them, reveal that we regulate God's response to us by our response to Him and the truth.

"Be not deceived; God is not mocked: for whatsoever a man soweth, that shall he also reap" (Gal. 6:7). (You can find out more concerning the law of God's response by obtaining our book, *Activating God's Response in Your Life*. This book clearly shows that Galatians 6:7 is an irrefutable law of God's response to us). (See 2 Sam. 22:25-27.) Remember, the Lord always *"looketh on the heart;"* and what's in people's hearts their mouth will speak or their actions will declare. For where a man's treasure is *"there will his heart be also."* These teachings of Christ, who is the author and finisher of our faith, and the one who is full of grace and truth, are confirmed many times throughout the epistles. And know this, that the law and the prophets were *until* John the Baptist, but since then, Jesus preached the Gospel of the Kingdom of God and *"grace [to obey] and truth came by Jesus Christ"* (Heb. 2:3). He *is* the *truth,* so if any man does not continue in the doctrine and teachings of Christ, John said that they are not of God, and do not speak the truth, or, perhaps, they are sincere but greatly deceived by the adversary or by a seminary. Similar to Saul of Tarsus who was trained under the Pharisees and was destroying the church *thinking* he was doing God a service. Extreme gracists, as we will see, do the same thing, shouting grace while ignorantly saying all the time in their doctrine that you could live contrary to grace's effects in our lives, and that you really need not abide in the teachings of Christ. To abide means to "live in"; "to obey."

Paul later wrote in 1 Timothy 6:3-4: *"If any man teach otherwise, and consent not to wholesome words, **even the words of our Lord Jesus Christ, and to the doctrine which is according to godliness**; he is proud, knowing nothing, but doting about questions and strifes of words, whereof cometh envy, strife, railings, evil surmisings."* The true Gospel will always agree with Christ's teachings in the Gospels (Heb. 2:3), and produce more godliness (Titus 1:1) as a person continues on in it (John 17:17). If they don't continue in it, then the good fruit of the changed life they once had will wither away. Christ's doctrine is always according to godliness. It is designed to keep people away from the evil one who is always seeking to destroy their faith and get them, once again, to walk down the broad road to destruction. Jesus prayed that the Father would keep us from evil. (See John 17:14-17.) Remember, all that is good is from God while anything that condones, excuses, promotes, or automatically covers for known evil is from the evil one. Every teaching is *"known by **its own fruit**,"* not by *"good* *words and fair speeches"* (Rom. 16:17-18). Paul said that the Kingdom of God is righteousness, joy, and peace in the Holy Ghost. If the Kingdom of God is righteousness, then anything contrary to righteousness *is not* of God's Kingdom. And if God's Kingdom is righteousness, to say He, Himself permits unrighteousness is to say that His kingdom is divided against itself, for it then is permitting what Satan's kingdom desires. Remember, Jesus said, any kingdom divided against itself cannot stand. So again, what is the bottom line? What is the end result of what's said? Real grace is given to us to enable us to keep God's moral law while a false grace says you need not keep it, but can live the same as you did when you were classified as a sinner and an enemy (of God) in your mind by wicked works (Col. 1:21-23).

James, in writing to Christians (James 1:2) in this Church Age writes and reinforces what Christ taught and says, *"So speak ye, and so do, **as they that shall be judged by the law of liberty**. For he shall have judgment without mercy, that hath showed no mercy; and mercy rejoiceth against judgment"* (James 2:12-13). The Son of God has set us free from our old, sinful lives and has given us the privilege to be called sons of God once again (1 John 3:2), so James admonishes us to speak and do accordingly. So then, he reveals that God will have judgment without mercy *on them* that show no mercy and that the merciful shall obtain mercy from God. This is so, as James pointed out, for anyone, Christian or not, for there is *"no respect of persons with God."* The advantage we have as Christians is that we have His grace and His Spirit to empower us to live right. We have a new and tender heart, which is given to us in the new birth, and the blood of Jesus to cleanse us if we do sin, providing that we repent; and we also have the knowledge of the scriptures that reveal these things to us. We do not deserve any of this, but His grace and mercy have provided it all. Our willingness and faith simply partakes of it and walks it out (2 Cor. 5:7-11). Without this provision of grace, none of us would be, nor ever could be, saved. But without a person's willing, continual cooperation with His grace, no man will be saved, nor will he stay saved. Jesus said, *"If a man abide not in me [in Christ], he is cast forth as a branch, and is withered; and men gather them, and cast them into the fire, and they are burned"* (John 15:6). The choice, then, is theirs (Rev. 22:17).

Paul, in writing for Christ wrote to the Galatian Christians, *"Be not deceived [don't be under any illusion], God is not mocked [made a fool of], **for whatsoever a man soweth** that shall he also reap"* (Gal. 6:7). You will reap from the actions of your life. *"For he that soweth to his flesh shall of the flesh reap corruption [ruin and decay]; but he that soweth to the Spirit shall of the*

*Spirit reap **life everlasting**. And let us not be weary in well doing: for in due season we shall reap [life everlasting], if we faint not"* (if we don't give up, Gal. 6:8-9). A person's harvest in life then depends entirely on what he sows. A life sown to follow after the flesh will reap destruction, not blessings, from God (Ps. 84:11; 1 John 3:22). A life sown to follow after the Spirit will reap life eternal and the blessings, so keep doing well and keep following the Spirit (See 1 Peter 4:19.), and you'll be blessed both now, in this life, and in the world to come. The Bible says, *"A faithful man shall abound with blessings."*

Back to Matthew's Gospel

In Matthew 6:1-4 Jesus said,

"Take heed [then] that ye do not your alms before men, to be seen of them [just to attract other people's attention]: otherwise ye have no reward of your Father which is in heaven. Therefore when thou doest thine alms, do not sound a trumpet before thee, as the hypocrites do in the synagogues and in the streets, that they may have glory of men.

"Verily I say unto you, they have their reward. But when thou doest alms, let not thy left hand know what thy right hand doeth: That thine alms may be in secret: and [then] thy Father which seeth in secret himself shall reward thee openly."

Here we see in Christ's doctrine of truth, that if your giving is not to the Lord, but is done to be seen of men, God, who knows every heart, will not reward you (the same is true with prayer and fasting). This shows us that God sees and responds to all people according to their motives. It's the heart that God sees (1 Sam. 16:7). He resists the proud but gives grace to the humble (1 Pet. 3:4). He won't vary from these things that are written in His Word, nor from Christ's teachings regardless of anyone's contrary idea of grace (1 Pet. 5:6), for Jesus said that He did not speak of Himself, but spoke what the unchangeable Father had commanded Him to speak (John 12:46-50). Not one jot or tittle can change. He is the same yesterday, today, and forever, and there is no variation with God, but people vary and He responds to them accordingly. However, He responded to people in the Bible, He responds to them today (1 Cor. 10:5-11). He says, *"I am the Lord, I change not."* So, let us heed the Lord's teachings or He is not our Lord (Luke 6:46). Real faith then purifies the heart and moves us willingly to do what's right in His sight with the right motives, and thereby puts us in the position to receive God's blessing by faith (Deut. 28:1-2; 1 John 3:22). And faith will move a person to repent of, and confess their sin if they do stumble and sin.

Verses 5-6

*"And when thou prayest, **thou shalt not be as the hypocrites are** [like actors to be seen by an audience]: for they love to pray standing in the synagogues and in the corners of the streets, that they may be seen of men. Verily I say unto you, they [these prideful people] have their reward. But thou, when thou prayest enter into thy closet, and when thou hast shut thy door, pray to thy Father which is in secret; and [then] thy Father which seeth in secret shall reward thee openly."*

Real faith is lived unto the Lord. He'll never bless hypocrisy, or those who seek glory from men. He gives *grace* to the humble, not to the rebellious or to hypocrites, and He never promised He would. Hypocrites are ones who honor Jesus with their lips only, but they habitually live their lives contrary to the will of the Lord. A hypocrite will try and get the blessings of God without the obedience of faith (Isa. 1:19-20).

In Matthew 6:14-15, Jesus said in His teaching:

*"For if ye forgive men their trespasses, your heavenly Father will also forgive you: **But if ye forgive not men** their trespasses, **neither will your Father forgive your trespasses**."* If you don't forgive others, neither will *your* Heavenly Father forgive you. This is God responding to us according to what we have sown. This is what is "written," and God will always respond according to what's written (Jer. 1:12) for it is His Word, forever settled in heaven. Faith would move us to forgive because this is what God's Word declares we should do. If you will really study the Word, you will see that God *always, always* deals with people depending on their actions and their conformity to what He said in His Gospel (Rom. 2:6-11). As we have shown, the scriptures reveal that if we draw near to Him, then He will draw near to us; if we walk contrary to Him, He will walk contrary to us; if we forsake Him, He will forsake us; if we confess Him, He will confess us; if we deny Him, He will deny us. *"With the merciful thou wilt shew thyself merciful, and with the upright man thou wilt shew thyself upright. With the pure thou wilt shewthyself pure; and with the froward thou wilt shew thyself unsavory"* (2 Sam. 22:26-27). So, you determine His response to you. Grace simply gives you the power to do right if you so choose. It is not irresistible. And grace certainly doesn't mean that you can live any way you want and God will always respond to you the same.

Verses 16-18

*"Moreover when ye fast, **be not, as the hypocrites,** of a sad countenance: for they disfigure their faces that they may appear unto men to fast. Verily I say unto you, They have their reward. But thou, when thou fastest, anoint thine head, and wash thy face; that thou appear not unto men to fast, but unto thy Father which is **in secret: and thy Father, which seeth in secret, shall reward thee openly."*** Think about it: would Christ say, "But shortly I'm going to die for your sins and then you, My followers, can rebel, follow Satan, and live as hypocrites, and grace will cause Me to see you as righteous regardless of whatever you do." If He would have taught some false idea of grace as some do, He would have lost all His influence as a holy leader.

Again, these along with many other things prove that God responds to people differently depending on their heart, their faith, and their actions whether they are Christians or not. (See James 1:22,25.) God sees all things. God changes not, and will not change nor vary from what's written in His Word regardless of anyone's private interpretation of grace, which says that God sees all Christians through the eyes of grace and an imputed righteousness, regardless of what they do or what their motives are. It sounds real nice and it is easy on the flesh, but is biblically unsound and contrary to Christ's own teaching (1 Pet. 3:10-12). Satan knows this and that's why he's planted such a corrupt teaching (tares) into the church. True mercy and grace enables us to stand in Christ's perfect righteousness when sin is repented of and confessed, and then when sin is washed away by the precious blood of Christ, all that's left is Christ's beautiful righteousness. With sin washed away, God then deals with us just as if we'd never sinned. This is the true provision of mercy and grace. (See 1 John 3:3-8.) But God still desires *"truth in the inward parts,"* and that we follow after Jesus, the captain of our salvation, walking in *"paths of righteousness"* (1 Pet. 2:24-25). And He still rewards those who *diligently* seek Him. If you call this works or legalism, you are ignorant. Paul wrote, *"If any man [wills to] be ignorant, let him be ignorant"* (1 Cor. 14:38). Do a word study in the Bible on "rewards" and "works" and you will see all are dealt with accordingly.

Matthew 6:33

"But seek ye first [continue to pursue] the Kingdom of God, and his righteousness [uprightness before Him as your goal] and all these things shall be added unto you" (as a result of this). Things we do can please or displease God. (See John 8:29; 1 Cor. 10:5-11.)

God has only promised to add things to those who seek first His kingdom and His righteousness. He will not change. Those who don't *seek first* His Kingdom and purpose to walk in His righteousness by faith cannot expect these things to be added to them. God says, *"the faithful man shall abound with blessings."* (Not the unfaithful.) *"Awake to righteousness and sin not."* Again, *"And whatsoever we ask, we receive of him [He will grant all our requests], because [for this reason]* **we keep his commandments, and do those things that are pleasing in His sight"** (1 John 3:22). Why do we receive? Because why? It's when we seek first His Kingdom that He adds things to us; and it's when we delight ourselves in the Lord that He gives us the desires of our heart. Now we also know there are many operations of mercy and grace for the ignorant who are not willfully, but ignorantly, transgressing, yet, *"to whom much is given, of them is much required."* And *"Without faith [this faith that moves a person to act] it is impossible to please him: for he that cometh to God must believe that he is, and that* **he is a rewarder of them that diligently seek him"** (Heb. 11:6).

Here again, it's revealed that He rewards those who keep His commandments and diligently seek Him. Those that don't diligently seek Him, nor obey Him, then, aren't rewarded the same as those who do. Those who do obey God are operating in faith and living by faith following after the Spirit, while those who don't obey God are in unbelief following after the flesh (Rom. 8:6). Real faith always moves a person into action to obey God. Just read Hebrews chapter eleven to see God's definition of faith. Grace, then, doesn't mean He responds to all alike regardless of how they live, but He will have mercy on all who repent of their sins committed, regardless of what they have done. Then once cleansed, they can all, empowered by His grace, act on and obey His Word and be blessed equally. (See James 1:22-25.) This is what He has truly provided. So, the blood of Jesus, when partaken of, puts us all on equal ground (Heb. 10:19), and provides for us all the same righteousness. So what the Mosaic law couldn't provide, Christ did. Furthermore, it's everywhere seen that He does respond to people according to their faith (Matt. 9:29) and actions (Matt. 7:24-27). According to the Bible, certain things you do can hinder or increase your faith (2 Thess. 1:3; 1 John 3:18-21; Jude 20), proving once again that He responds to us all according to our behavior, our diligence, our prayer life, and our faith (Matt. 6). That is, our response to His Gospel and His grace. Faith makes one a doer of the Word and taps us into the power of the Word (Rom. 1:16). Those who don't live and walk by faith doing the Word, deceive themselves out of the blessings (James 1:22). (See also, Eph. 6:8; Col. 3:25; 1 Pet. 2:8.)

As a matter of fact, just read Christ's teachings out loud to yourself and you will hear the conditions of the faith of Jesus, *from* Jesus, *for* yourself.

Be Not Deceived

Galatians 6:7 states:

"Be not deceived; God is not mocked: **for whatsoever a man soweth, that shall he also reap."**

This is still the Doctrine of Christ (1 Cor. 14:37).

A person cannot sow to the flesh and sin, and continually reap the blessings from God. You cannot sow evil and reap good. This would be contrary to God's own Word. God never has and never will bless disobedience (1 Pet. 3:12). Believe not anyone who contradicts God's Word here. Remember, only Satan will promote evil and sin and condone, or okay, evil behavior in any form, but he's a master of disguise and brings forth many counterfeit doctrines. His evil work is to get Christians to think that living in unconfessed sin won't bring God's displeasure nor eventually cause death. He still says, *"Ye shall not surely die."* "Bible grace will cover for you." "God's love is unconditional you know." But God's own Word says that He is against evil, and will judge accordingly, except people repent. The true Word and love of God has provided us a way to escape a life of sin and therefore a way to escape the wrath to come (1 Cor. 6:9-10); and we are exhorted to *"Flee from the wrath to come."* But unconditional love did not save Lucifer or the fallen angels, or Sodom, or Israel, or Judas, or Ananias and Sapphira, or anyone else who lived in rebellion against God, and God never promised it would. No other creature can separate you from God's love, but God says, *"your sins and iniquities have separated you and your God"* (Isa. 59:2). The whole world is separated from God because of their sins and yet, *"God so loved the world"* (John 3:16). There is not one scripture that says that unconditional love will protect a person while they are in willful disobedience and persisting in living the wrong way. His love may be unconditional, but His salvation is not. He will not force His salvation on anyone.

Who then will you believe, God or Satan? Let us never believe the original lie of the serpent (Gen. 3:4), that we need not keep God's Word or His commandments. The unchangeable God was a God of love and the God of all grace way back in Eden, but Adam died anyway when he withdrew his allegiance to God and broke God's commandment and followed Satan. God's righteousness has to deal with all things righteously, for there is coming a *"revelation of the righteous judgment of God."*

In Matthew 7:1-2 Jesus said,

"Judge not, that ye be not judged. For with what judgment ye judge, ye shall be judged: and with what measure ye mete, it shall be measured to you again." (See James 4:11-12.) He didn't say that you could critically judge others, but that grace would then protect you from being judged. This would be a strange doctrine indeed, if it did.

God will judge you with the same measure you use to critically judge others. This is His statement of fact. God is consistent in His dealings with all and will always respond to all just as He has revealed He would in His Word. By faith we realize this is true and therefore adjust ourselves accordingly. This is what is meant by living by faith (Heb. 11:7). By obeying God's Word, then, we are thereby more blessed (James 1:25). Don't misinterpret His longsuffering and giving space to repent as overlooking evil. (See Rev. 2:21; Rom. 2:4-6.)

Ecclesiastes 8:11 says, *"Because sentence against an evil work is not executed speedily, therefore the heart of the sons of men is fully set in them to do evil."* Unless evil works are repented of during the space given to repent, they will be judged. *"And there is no respect of persons with God."* Hear Solomon speaking by the wisdom of God: *"Let us hear the conclusion of the whole matter: Fear God, and keep his commandments: for this is the whole duty of man. For God shall bring every work into judgment, with every secret thing, whether it be good, or whether it be evil"* (Eccles. 12:13-14). This is the truth. We must do as Paul said and *"judge ourselves,"* or be eventually judged by God.

In Matthew 7:19-23: The true doctrine of Christ states:

"Every tree that bringeth not forth good fruit is hewn down, and cast into the fire. Wherefore by their fruits ye shall know them. **Not every one that saith unto me, Lord, Lord**, *shall enter into the kingdom of Heaven; but he that doeth the will of my Father which is in heaven." [This is the fruit He is looking for.]* **"Man***y will say to me* **in that day** *[that stand before Him], Lord, Lord, have we not prophesied in thy name? and in thy name have cast out devils? And in thy name done many wonderful works? And then will I profess unto them, I never knew you]One translation says, "you were never (close) friends of mine," John 15:14]:* **depart from me, ye that work iniquity."**

He will respond to them according to their unrepented of iniquity, according to their evil behavior, evil works, and evil fruit. Gifts such as power to cast out devils, prophesying, and healing the sick are one thing; fruit produced by the life of an individual, is another. It's not what gifts someone may have operated in at one time (as wonderful as the gifts of the Holy Spirit are), nor is it what you've done in the past. The question is, have you continued in the race? It's not how you start the marathon that counts, but how you finish. So then, saying with the mouth, He is Lord, is not enough if the life is, at some point, willingly lived contrary and has lost its commitment to live by faith. Christ's warning is both clear and steadfast. His Word will *"judge us in the last day."* Don't *ever* let any man's teaching carry the same weight as Christ's! *"Let God be true and every man [who contradicts Him]* **be a liar**" (Rom. 3:3-4). Anyone who contradicts the teaching of Christ is teaching wrong, and scripture says that they should be "avoided."

Verse 21

Notice again Christ's teachings: *"Not every one that saith unto me,Lord, Lord, shall enter into the kingdom of Heaven;* **but he that doeth [is obedient to] the will of my Father** *which is in heaven."*

Is this self-righteousness or an obedience that springs from faith? The only ones the Lord will permit into heaven are those who have lived for the will of His Father in heaven. If they don't want His will on earth, they can't have His will for them concerning heaven. He told us to *"choose life."* This obedience obviously pleases God and it, therefore, must be faith. (See Heb. 12:2; John 8:29, 6:38,15:10.) Imperfect though Christians may be at times as they are learning to cooperate with God's grace and Spirit, there must be a willingness of heart to continue to live for God's will. What Christ, the author of faith, taught, is *the faith! "For if there be first a willing mind, it is accepted according to that a man hath, and not according to that he hath not"* (2 Cor. 8:12). Paul said, *"Nevertheless, whereto we have already attained, let us walk by the same rule, let us mind the same thing. Brethren, be followers together of me, and mark them which walk [live] so as ye have us for an ensample. For many walk [live their lives in such a way], of whom I have told you often, and now tell you even weeping, that they are the enemies of the cross of Christ: Whose end is destruction, whose God is their belly [their own selfishness], and whose glory is in their shame, who mind earthly things"* (Phil. 3:16-19). Only *"obedience to the faith"* is living faith. This is true believing (Rom. 1:5, 10:16; Acts 6:7). These are those who are willing to go on with God and confess their sins and repent of them when they do stumble and do something contrary to God's will. And this is the wonderful grace of repentance, that God is willing to blot out any sin that's repented of and treat the person as though they had never sinned. All sin is erased and washed away by the blood of Jesus as soon as sincere confession of it is made (1 John 1:9). Then with sin blotted out, a person instantly stands in Christ's perfect righteousness. This is the mercy and grace of God in truth. But grace is not, nor ever will be, *an automatic cloak* for wickedness without repentance and confession of it to God. God has made no provision for the lusts of the flesh or a continuance in evil. Grace does not cause Him to close His eyes when a Christian does evil. The Bible says, *"And God saw the wickedness of man …"* (Gen. 6:5). Paul wrote to Christians, *"Neither is there any creature that is not manifest in his sight: but all things are naked and opened unto the eyes of Him with whom we [Christians] have to do"* (Heb. 4:13). And Paul warned Christians, *"He that doeth wrong shall receive for the wrong which he hath done: and there is no respect of persons"* (with God, Col. 3:25). So then, God still sees the evil regardless of who does it (1 Pet. 3:12), and deals with all accordingly.

Matthew 9:29

*"Then touched he their eyes, saying, **According to your faith** be it unto you."* Do you see? It's according to your faith, your forgiveness, your actions. This is the Gospel of God. Not the "hearers" will be blessed but only the "doers." Only those who *"live by faith,"* and, *"keep the faith,"* will find life and blessings. God said in Proverbs, *"Keep my commandments and live."*

Your faith and your receiving of God's provisions then, depends on your obedience, your study, your prayer, and so on. To say it doesn't, is to deny what the Word teaches (Rom. 10:17). For real faith always responds to the Word of His grace and obeys it (Heb. 11). Again, any time you obey the teaching of Christ in the written Word, it is faith.

You don't need any special revelation. To obey anything the author of faith taught is never legalism or fleshly works, but faith! If He says, give, and you give, it is faith. If He says, men ought always pray, and you pray, it is faith. If He says, blessed are the merciful, and you act mercifully towards others, it's faith.

James 1:22,25

*"But be ye doers of the word, and not hearers only, **deceiving your own selves** … But whoso looketh into the perfect law of liberty and continueth therein, he being not a forgetful hearer, but a **doer** of **the work, this man** shall be blessed in his deed."* God blesses doers, not hearers. *"If ye **be willing and**

obedient ye shall eat the good of the land: but if ye refuse and rebel, ye shall be devoured with the sword: for the mouth of the Lord hath spoken it" (Isa. 1:19-20). The word "works," in the Bible, basically means in most cases, "actions and deeds;" or carrying out something. There is, Paul said, *"the work of faith and labor of love."* Good works are works of faith (Matt. 5:16, 10:32; Acts 9:36; Eph. 2:10; 1 Tim. 2:10, 6:17-18; 2 Tim. 3:16-17). To live wrong is called the *"unfruitful **works** of darkness."* Jesus Himself, the very author of faith, did good works and told us to do the same (Matt. 5:16). These works motivated by faith and done to the glory of God fully please the Father (Eph. 2:10). So the word "works," as we will later see, is not always something legalistic but many times the expression in scripture of a person's faith and grace operating in their lives (2 Cor. 9:8).

Matthew 12:36-37

Jesus said, *"But I say unto you, That every idle word that men shall speak they shall give account thereof in the day of judgment. For by thy words thou shalt be justified, and by thy words thou shalt be condemned."* Men will give an account of every idle word in the Day of Judgment. Just as He knows every hair on your head and every star by name, God keeps track of every evil word spoken that hasn't been repented of, or that have influenced others negatively. For words influence other people's wills and actions and those who use their words unwisely are responsible (James 3:1). Especially those who desire to stand in the office of a teacher. Some Christians will lose much reward because of their mouths and what they've taught (Matt. 5:19). Misled teachers who teach damnable heresies and follow a false way will lose their own soul, and continue to mislead others except they repent. Sometimes I wonder if some of these professed teachers really read their Bibles or just read each other's books, listen to each other's tapes, and just teach what some man taught them at a seminary or somewhere else. So many of the books I've seen on so-called "grace" have so little scripture and so much human reasoning in them. Paul told Timothy, *"Take heed unto thyself, and unto the doctrine; continue in them: for in doing this thou shalt both save thyself, and them that hear thee"* (1 Tim. 4:16). And again, *"As ye have therefore received Christ Jesus the Lord, so walk ye in him: Rooted and built up in him, and stablished in the faith, as ye have been taught, abounding therein with thanksgiving. Beware lest any man spoil you through philosophy and vain deceit, after the tradition of men, after the rudiments of the world, and not after Christ"* (Col. 2:6-8).

Matthew 12:49-50

*"And he stretched forth his hand toward his disciples, and said, Behold my mother and my brethren! **For whosoever shall do the will of my Father** which*

*is in heaven, **the same** is my brother, and sister, and mother."* Those who don't do the will of His Father are not included in His statement. Certainly not those who knowingly live their lives contrary to God's known will and commandments without repenting. If anyone lives that way, their course of life shows that they are not living by faith but are in unbelief and disobedience and therefore are not considered "the just" (Rom. 1:17). They are then a child of unbelief, or what is sometimes called, backslidden (or a fallen away condition).

Matthew 15:1-5

*"Then came to Jesus scribes and Pharisees, which were of Jerusalem saying, Why do thy disciples transgress the tradition of the elders? for they wash not their hands when they eat bread. But he answered and said unto them, **Why do ye also transgress the commandment of God by your tradition? For God commanded, saying,** honor thy father and mother, and, he that curseth father or mother, let him die the death. **But ye say,** Whosoever shall say to his father or his mother, It is a gift, by whatsoever thou mightest be profited by me; And honor not his father or his mother, he shall be free. Thus have ye made the commandment of God of none effect by your tradition."* Notice: "God commanded saying, **but ye say.**"

Those who have changed *God's commandments* by their tradition saying we need not really keep them, are those who put what they say in place of the Word and commandment of God. They do exactly the same thing as the Pharisees of old did, and they stop multitudes of people from actually reverencing and obeying God's Word. Oh, that God's people would just obey God's written Word rather than men's strong opinions, or "taken out of context" doctrines, or intellectual philosophies. God says one thing and ultra gracists another. We will stay with God. *"**Whosoever therefore** shall break one of these least commandments, and shall teach men so, he shall be called the least in the kingdom of heaven: but whosoever shall do and teach them, the same shall be called great in the kingdom of heaven"* (Matt. 5:19). Christ's words abide forever (Heb. 2:1-3,13:8). This is the doctrine and teaching of Christ.

In verse 8 Jesus said:

"This people draweth nigh unto me with their mouth, and honoreth me with their lips; but their heart is far from me." Some use the word "grace" like a magic wand, as though it means whatever they say it means. But God is only responsible for what He has actually said about it in His Word, and all the scriptures we are giving in the doctrine of Christ are perfectly clear. *"Ye shall not add unto the word which I command you, neither shall ye diminish ought from it, **that ye may keep the commandments of the***

Lord your God which I command you" (Deut. 4:2). (See also the strong warning of Revelation 22:18-19, concerning intentionally adding to, or taking away, from His Word. He said He'd **take their name out** of the Book of Life.) And remember, it is the real grace of the Lord Jesus Christ that we need, and not a humanistic philosophy about it. And real grace is all in harmony with what Christ has said and revealed in this New Covenant (Gal. 1:6-12). A person must be willing to turn to Him to freely receive it. If they turn to Him, they then turn away from Satan. If they later turn to follow Satan and this world, they then turn away from the Lord. If they become unwilling to continue to receive from God and to walk by faith through being hardened by sin, that is their choice and God respects man's choice. Paul showed that it is possible for a person to once again *"depart from the living God"* because of their heart becoming hardened once again by sin (Heb. 12:15,3:12-14). The free will is always involved both in receiving salvation and in continuing in it (Rev. 22:17). Therefore, *"Keep thy heart with all diligence; for out of it are the issues of life"* (Prov. 4:23). And, *"keep yourselves in the love of God"* (Jude 21).

This departing from God means that they let go of their commitment to live by faith and live for God (Titus 1:16). Sin's deception will cause them to still think all is well while they follow Satan. *"And for this cause God shall send them strong delusion, that they should believe a lie: that they all might be damned who believed not the truth,* **but had pleasure in unrighteousness"** (2 Thess. 2:11-12). Unrighteousness is what they wanted, so He sent them what their hearts demanded. As in Romans, chapter one, He will give people up to sinful passions and vices if they persist in rejecting the true knowledge of God (Rom. 1:28).

Paul Preached the Same Gospel as Christ

Paul said what he wrote were *"the commandments of the Lord."* And in the doctrine and Gospel of Christ inspired by God, he writes in Romans 2:6-11, God *"will render to every man* **according to his deeds [behavior]**, *[what his life's actions deserve]; To* **them who by patient continuance in well doing seek for glory** *and honor and immortality [He will give], eternal life [these are people who continue to live by faith drawing strength from the grace of God]: But unto them that are contentious,* **and do not obey the truth, but obey unrighteousness** *[and rebel against God's plan because they want to go back to live in the world and seek selfish ends], [He will give to them] indignation and wrath.* **Tribulation and anguish (will come), upon every soul of man that doeth evil, of the Jew first, and also of the Gentile,** *but glory, honor, and peace to every man* **that worketh good,** *to the Jew first and also to the Gentile:*

For there is no respect of persons with God." (See also verse 16.) This is a part of the Gospel of Christ that Paul preached. Its message is clear. He was speaking of eternal life and eternal damnation. *"But I certify you, brethren, that the gospel which was preached of me is not after man. For I neither received it of man, neither was I taught it, but by the revelation of Jesus Christ"* (Gal. 1:11-12). Jesus revealed these things to Paul (Rom. 1:16-18). It's all a part of Christ's same Gospel; the Gospel of the Kingdom (Matt. 24:14).

Notice, God is still concerned with good and evil. He still commands us to obey His commandments as His sons, just as He did with Adam, who was called a son of God. Jesus in His doctrine said, *"Marvel not at this: for the hour is coming, in the which all that are in the graves shall hear his voice, and shall come forth;* **they that have done good, unto the resurrection of life; and they that have done evil, unto the resurrection of damnation"** (John 5:28-29). This speaks of how people lived in the earth. God who is perfect justice must judge evil and anyone involved in it, if it's not repented of. But He wills that they all would come to repentance so that He could have mercy on them and bless them. But for those who persist in evil and do not walk in the ways of faith (2 Cor. 5:7), He will reward them, Paul said, with indignation and wrath. And for those who come to Christ and then patiently continue in that which is good (though at times they may struggle with sin and then repent), He will give glory, honor and *eternal life*. We, brethren, are freed by His grace to continue in that which is good, and keeping His commandments; and God ordained before the foundation of the world that *we should* walk in His ways (Eph. 2:10; Luke 1:75; Eph. 1:4). Always remember that *real* faith is the victory that *overcomes* the world (1 John 2:14; 5:4)! It is not a cloak that excuses us to live like the world. We are in the world, but we (Christians) are not of the world. We are sanctified by the real truth. That is, separated from the fallen world and the evil one (John 17).

God Is No Respecter of Persons

A false perception of grace tries to make God a respecter of persons saying that a Christian who knows God's good will and commandments can, willingly, live in all manner of evil following Satan without repenting and still be covered by grace, while another person who doesn't even know God's will and is ignorant will be judged by God and condemned for those very same things. But go back and see that He says *"every man"* will be judged as to whether or not they repented of, and turned from, evil. He doesn't say peace, grace, and blessing to those who do evil, but rather, tribulation and anguish (2 Pet. 3:9). And be assured, *"There is no respect of persons with God." "Therefore thou art inexcusable [you'll have nothing to say in your own defense], O man, whosoever thou art that judgest: for wherein thou judgest another [saying they need to repent of sin and turn to God], thou condemnest thyself;* **for thou that judgest doest the same things** [as the sinners do]. **But we are sure that the judgment of God is according to truth against them, which commit such things. And thinkest thou this, O man, that judgest them which do such things [saying that they need to be saved], and [yet thou] doest the same, that thou [above others] shalt escape the judgment of God?"** God's judgment, in other words, is impartial (Rom. 2:1-3). God will not vary from this. You cannot just call yourself a Christian and then do the same things the sinner does and escape the judgment of God: Not unless you repent (Luke 13:3).

Now we know He is longsuffering and gives space to repent, but please read that passage again. *"And think not to say within yourselves, We have Abraham to our father: for I say unto you, that God is able of these stones to raise up children unto Abraham"* (Matt. 3:9). And think not to say, "I professed Christ ten years ago, therefore I'm fine even if I live contrary to God." For God loves all people, but yet billions will go to hell because of their unrepented of sins and not living by faith for His will, regardless of His love or His grace, for He has promised only to save those who repent of their lives of sin and rebellion, and live for His will (Heb. 5:9; Matt. 7:21). His righteous nature allows Him to be merciful to the repentant sinner, but wrath will fall on the rebellious and those who persist in wrongdoing, for this too is His righteousness (Rom. 1:18). Some extreme gracists have a false concept of God and His dealings with man. They only see the side of God which is love, but the other side, which they don't perceive, is the side of God's wrath towards rebels and evildoers. If He's for one thing, then He is naturally against its opposite. Paul understood both aspects of this. *"Behold therefore the **goodness and severity of God:** on them which fell, severity; but toward thee, [who have repented] goodness, if thou continue in his goodness, otherwise thou also shalt be cut off"* (and experience His severity if you choose to rebel against Him, Rom. 11:22). *"It is a fearful thing to fall into the hands of the living God."* The same God who prepared heaven for His good and faithful servants, also prepared a place of eternal torment void of all that is good, for all rebels and unrepentant evildoers (Heb. 10:31). If they want to reject God's goodness, they must face His wrath. *"Wherefore we receiving a kingdom which cannot be moved, let us have grace, whereby we may serve God acceptably with reverence and godly fear: For our God is a consuming fire"* (Heb. 12:28-29).

Paul said, *"Knowing therefore the terror of the Lord [towards evildoers]we persuade men"* (2 Cor. 5:11), to repent, turn to God, and prove your faith by how you live (Acts 26:18-24).

Listen to the Lord's warning: *"And it shall come to pass, that from one new moon to another, and from one Sabbath to another, shall all flesh come to worship before me, saith the Lord. And they shall go forth, and look upon the carcasses of the men that have transgressed against me [and have not repented]: for their worm shall not die, neither shall their fire be quenched; and they shall be an abhorring unto all flesh"* (Isa. 66:23-24). This is what the Lord has prepared for all rebels who refuse to repent. They will be a visible example for all ages to come to see what happens to those who choose to live their lives in persistent rebellion against God. If they reject God's goodness, they must face His wrath. If you don't want to obey God, then neither will you get His blessings. No one will make it into heaven following sin, Satan, and unrighteousness.

So let us not presume anything that is not clearly written in the scriptures. God Himself prepared the lake of fire for the devil and anyone that follows him, so there is this aspect of God's nature that must be noted. If they choose what is opposite of God's goodness, God will let them have His severity. (See our mini-book on *What Hell is Like, Who Must Go There and Why.*) But if you live for God and repent when you do sin, you'll never have to experience this side of God, but only His goodness. But never tell anyone they can live in rebellion against God and be covered by an unconditional love or imputed righteousness. Never tell anyone that there is no need for repentance or confession of their sins. Scriptures never, ever teach any such thing, but Satan does! For a person to live contrary to God shows that they don't have the kind of faith that justifies (James 2:14-26), and anyone who teaches such things as a "sinning saint religion," reveals they are a teacher who is either ignorant of the ways of God, or a deceiver. It makes no difference how many people follow them, or how respected they are among men. Multitudes of Christians are ignorant of what to believe and so follow almost anything. In the natural realm many times, a goat is used to lead sheep to the slaughter. Take heed then that you're not following a goat, or a wolf in sheep's clothing.

In 1 Peter 4:1-5 Peter writes:

*"Forasmuch then as Christ hath suffered for us in the flesh [dying on the cross for our sins], arm yourselves likewise with the same mind: for he that hath suffered in the flesh [has crucified his flesh, Gal. 5:24], hath **ceased from sin;***

that he no longer should live the rest of his time [on earth] in the flesh to the lusts of men, but to the will of God. For the time past of our life may suffice us to have wrought the will of the Gentiles [those who are outside of the Covenant], when we walked in lasciviousness, lusts, excess of wine, revellings, banquetings, and abominable idolatries: Wherein they think it strange that ye run **not with them** to the same excess of riot, speaking evil of you: Who shall give account to him that is ready to judge the quick and the dead." A false concept of grace will tell you that you could still run with them, no longer keeping the faith but breaking God's moral commandments, hurting others, and grieving the Holy Spirit, and still be in God's favor receiving His blessings; but Bible grace says no such thing. Being under the dispensation of grace means being in the dispensation where we are freed from sin's controlling power; so James says, therefore live accordingly or face the consequences (James 2:12).

People (even some professing Christians) will speak evil of you when you proclaim that you need to live right and obey God, or that you need to do as Paul and the other apostles said and keep the faith. Under the influence of a deceiving spirit and their false philosophy about grace, they will call you legalistic, self-righteous, and other things, and no marvel, for Paul wrote in 2 Timothy 3:12, *"Yea, and **all that will live godly**, in Christ Jesus shall suffer persecution."* This persecution comes from the devil himself, for he gets upset with anyone who exposes his false doctrines and the tares that he has sown into the church. If you walk in the light, you expose those who live in darkness. God says, *"And the dragon was wroth with the woman, and went to make war with the remnant of her seed, **which keep the commandments of God, and have the testimony of Jesus Christ**"* (Rev. 12:17). Here we see two things: those who really have the testimony of Jesus also keep God's commandments, and these are the ones Satan is upset with; the other people he already has. But, sadly, some of the persecution and ridicule comes through extreme gracists which, being used as the devil's tool say you don't really need to live godly nor obey God or the faith that was once delivered to the saints, and they mock or ridicule those who say you do need to live for God's will. The aggressive ones like Cain who slew Abel are those who listen to the wicked one. Cain slew Abel because his own works were evil and his brother's works were righteous (1 John 3:12). They, like those whom Jude in his epistle, dealt with and condemned, think a dead hypocritical faith is all that's necessary.

Contrary to Paul and his message about holiness and grace, they imply that profession with the mouth is all that's needed (Titus 1:16). It is they who are not continuing in the grace of God that would enable them to live right if they truly continued in it. They are living in a religious dream world. Satan has captured their imagination with this wrong concept of grace and a wrong perspective of this New Covenant. They are in the devil's snare and know it not, thinking a mere profession will save them. James 2:19 says, *"Thou believest that there is one God; thou doest well [that's all fine and good, but]: **the devils also believe**, and tremble."* They, too, confessed Christ as the Son of God and knew that He was the Lord. To know He is the Lord benefits you nothing unless you obey Him. Jesus, Himself said, *"And why call ye me, Lord, Lord, and do not the things which I say?"* (Luke 6:46). (See also James 2:14.) If you only say that you believe, you do no more than the demons do. And for anyone who teaches others this counterfeit grace, they are responsible for their spiritual well-being and will receive a more strict judgment for standing in, or putting yourself in, the office of a teacher (James 3:1), and instructing people that they need not really keep the faith of Jesus. Although there is forgiveness if repented of, there can come much loss of rewards because of it (1 Cor. 3:11-15).

Love Not the World

In 1 John 2:15-17 John the apostle wrote to Christians:

*"Love not the world, neither the things that are in the world. [Nor what the ungodly world has to offer.] **If any man love the world, the love of the Father is not in him** [they have no love for the Father], for all that is in the world, the lust of the flesh, and the lust of the eyes, and the pride of life, is not of [and did not come from] the Father, but is of the world. [It's a work of the devil, Eph. 2:2.] And the world [and everyone in it following Satan's system, John 3:16] passeth away, and [those involved in] the lust thereof: **but he that doeth [perseveres in doing] the will of God abideth forever."** (This is the Apostles' Doctrine.) You will notice *they all* spoke of doing God's will, and that it is this that would bring the blessing of eternal life from God. It's God's grace and faith that enables you to do it (Heb. 13:20-21), but you're either doing Satan's will or God's will (2 Tim. 2:24-26); living in grace or living in sin. Again, it's the heart and soul's commitment of faith to live for the will of God that will bring the blessings of God and eternal life. This is "faith." Faith and grace alone saves us out of a world drowning in moral pollution. None of us could do it ourselves in our own strength. (See Rom. 8:3-4.) If you don't follow the Spirit you'll find you're as weak as any other man; *"but if you through the Spirit mortify the deeds of the body ye shall live"* (Rom. 8:13). So, once you're saved out of the

world's polluted system, don't cast yourself back into it again. God said that if you do, it's like a dog returning to eat its own vomit. A drowning man who's pulled out of the water by another, would be foolish to throw himself back in again.

Love Not the World But Love the Lord

Verse 15

Again, *"Love not the world, neither the things that are in the world. **If any man** loves the world, the love of the Father **is not in him**."* God has only promised His Kingdom to those who love Him. If any man love *the world and its pollutions*, they don't love the Father. To love the world is to live for the world and obey its lusts without repentance and godly sorrow. *"Where your treasure is there will your heart be also."* Christ's doctrine always says *"he that **doeth** the will of God abideth forever."* *"Again, the devil taketh him up into an exceeding high mountain, and showeth him all the kingdoms of the world, and the glory of them; and saith unto Him, **All these things will I give thee, if thou wilt fall down and worship me**."* (He still says the same thing today to other sons and daughters of God.) Then saith Jesus unto him, *"Get thee hence, Satan: for it is written, Thou shalt worship the Lord thy God, and him only shalt thou serve"* (Matt. 4:8-10). Has God now provided that we could forsake Christ's example, obey Satan, and follow his tempting lusts and promises, and worship him by doing so? And that God now okays this because of grace, or an imputed righteousness? Or is faith the victory that overcometh the world (1 John 5:4) and the evil one (1 John 2:14)? Is not Jesus, our example? If so, then let us also say to Satan, *"Get thee hence,"* *"for it is written,"* "we shall worship only the Lord our God and Him alone will we serve, and we will not yield ourselves to follow after your evil ways and worldly enticements."

If those who do the will of God will abide with Him forever, what then will happen to those people that don't do God's will; who instead live only for self will and for this world? They obviously won't abide with God forever! As we've said before, there is no promise stated for them. Give one if you can. Again, God's mercy is great to all who repent. His mercies are new every morning, so go to Him, yea, run to Him to obtain it if you do sin.

James 4:4

James, in writing to brethren says, *"Ye adulterers and adulteresses [unfaithful people], **know ye not** that the friendship of the world is enmity with God? **Whosoever** therefore will be a friend of the world is the enemy of God."*

(He takes his stand as one of God's enemies.) Evidently, some of those Christians didn't know this, just as the extreme gracists of today don't realize it. Let them also heed James' warning. James' letter was written to Christians. God certainly responds to us depending on our response to His Gospel, to whether or not we obey it (Gal. 6:7). Paul wrote, *"But they have not all **obeyed the Gospel"*** (Rom. 10:16). But extreme gracists think they could be a friend of God and Satan at the same time. Not so: No man can serve two masters. Jesus said in John 15:14, *"Ye are my friends, **if ye do whatsoever I command you.***" Abraham too, obeyed God and kept His statutes and His judgments, and was thereby called God's friend (Gen. 18:19; Heb. 11:8). If you hang around, obey, and follow the devil, then you're his friend (if he has any), not God's.

Romans 6:16

To the Roman Christians Paul writes, *"**Know ye not**, that to whom ye yield yourselves servants to obey, **his servants ye are to whom ye obe**y; whether of sin [this fallen world's system set up by Satan and its lusts] unto [resulting in] death, or of obedience unto [resulting in] righteousness?"* Following Satan will always eventually cause death. Paul said concerning some former Christians, *"Having damnation, because they have cast off their first faith ... For some are already turned aside after Satan"* (1 Tim. 5:12,15). God will not bless Satan's servants. Jesus said in John 12:25-26, *"He that loveth his life shall lose it; and he that hateth his [sinful] life in this world shall keep it unto life eternal. If any man serve me, **let him follow me** [and live after His example]; and [then] where I am, **there shall also my servant be**: if any man **serve me**, him will my Father honor."* If we truly belong to Christ, we then will follow His example doing as He did, living for the will of God (John 6:38). These are the ones the Father honors, but those who don't obey and serve Christ, dishonor Him.

Second Timothy 4:10

Paul wrote, *"For Demas hath forsaken [and deserted] me, **having loved** [his heart was set on living for] **this present world**, and is departed unto Thessalonica; Crescents to Galatia, Titus unto Dalmatia."*

Here, Paul's fellow minister chose to go back to the world. The will is always free whether one is a Christian or not, and those who choose to go back and live in the world and its pollutions and rebel against God's commands at the same time, cannot be choosing the path of faith and grace which gives victory over the world. Sin and faith don't mix. One is following the devil, and the other one is following God. Each is a choice. They are contrary to each other. They are the two different roads; one narrow, and one broad. *"Whatsoever is not of faith is sin";* and whatsoever is sin is not of faith, it's unbelief. You do not gain access by sin into grace, but by faith (Rom. 5:2). And remember, the only kind of faith that Paul spoke of was a faith that brought about obedience. So faith and obedience are in harmony with one another, and obedience to God then is not legalism but faith (1 John 2:2-6, 5:3). Any disobedience is either rebellion or unbelief. Now we can also understand that grace and keeping God's commandments also perfectly harmonize, but sin and disobeying God's commandments are opposed to grace. Grace and works when understood properly, also harmonize (1 Cor. 15:10; 2 Cor. 9:8).

CHAPTER EIGHT

LOVING GOD—THE WAY TO LIFE

Jesus said, *"Thou shalt love the Lord thy God with all thy heart"; this is* the first and great commandment (Matt. 22:37-40).

James 1:12

*"Blessed is the man that endureth temptation [he continues on living for the Lord]: for when he is tried, he shall receive the crown of life, **which the Lord hath promised to them that love him.**"*

Again, we see it's promised only to those that love Him and continue on with Him. In scripture, God says, *"I love them that love Me."* In Exodus 20:6 God says, *"And showing mercy unto thousands of them **that love me,** and **keep my commandments.**"* In Deuteronomy 7:9, He says, *"Know therefore that the Lord thy God, he is God, the faithful God, **which keepeth covenant and mercy with them that love him and keep His commandments to a thousand generations.**"*

*"Hearken, my beloved brethren, Hath not God chosen the poor of this world rich in faith, and heirs of the kingdom which he hath promised **to them that love him?**"* (James 2:5). *"Therefore thou shalt love the Lord thy God, and keep his charge, and his statutes, and his judgments, and his commandments, alway"* (Deut. 11:1). (See Josh. 23:11-13.)

1 Corinthians 2:9

*"But as it is written, Eye hath not seen, nor ear heard, neither have entered into the heart of man, the things which God hath prepared **for them that love him.**"* Notice again, everything is promised only to them that love Him. Can we be lovers of pleasures more than lovers of God and it not affect

our relationship with God? Not according to Christ's doctrine and the teaching of the New Testament.

*"**This know also, that in the last days perilous times shall come.**"* (One translation says, *"In the last days it is going to be very difficult to be a Christian."*) *"**For men shall be lovers of their own selves** [totally self-centered] covetous, boasters, proud, blasphemers, disobedient to parents, unthankful, unholy, without natural affection, truce breakers, false accusers, incontinent, fierce, despisers of those that are good, traitors, heady, high-minded, **lovers of pleasures more than lovers of God** [they will put living for selfish pleasures before the love of God]; having a form of godliness [maintaining an outward show and profession of righteousness and piety], but denying the power thereof [they are by their lives denying its reality]: from such turn away"* (avoid such people as these, 2 Tim. 3:1-5). Therefore let *no man* deceive you, no matter how wonderful and bubbly their message sounds.

I fully understand that the false grace message sounds so nice, so fluffy and easy, and it makes it look like everyone's okay, even if in reality they are on the broad road to destruction. And I know that it comes disguised as love, and some people are taken in by this, but if it's not truth, which it's not, it's a vain imagination and it is not love at all, but a deception from the adversary. God warns, *"And it shall be, if thou do at all forget the LORD thy God, **and walk after other gods** [Satan and the course of this world], **and serve them**, and worship them, **I testify against you this day that ye shall surely perish.** As the nations which the LORD destroyeth before your face [because they served other gods], so shall ye perish; **because ye would not be obedient unto the voice of the LORD your God"*** (Deut. 8:19-20). And, *"**If there arise among you** a prophet [a teacher, 2 Pet. 2:1-4], or a dreamer of dreams, and giveth thee a sign or a wonder [offering you some supernatural proof], and the sign or the wonder come to pass, whereof he [then] spake unto thee, saying, Let us go after other gods [or let us follow the course of this world and the spirits of disobedience], which thou hast not known, **and let us serve them; Thou shall not hearken unto the words of that prophet**, or that dreamer of dreams [or that teacher, 2 Pet. 2:1]: for the LORD your God proveth you [is testing you], **to know whether ye [really] love the LORD your God with all your heart and with all your soul. Ye shall walk after the LORD your God, and fear him, and keep his commandments, and obey his voice, and ye shall serve him,** and cleave unto Him. And that prophet, or that dreamer of dreams, shall be put to death; **because he hath spoken to turn you away from [and rebel against] the Lord your God, which brought you out of the land of Egypt [a type of the world], and redeemed you out of the house of bondage** [out of slavery to sin], to thrust thee out of the [good] way [of righteousness] which the LORD thy God* *commanded thee to walk in. So shalt thou put the evil [person] away from the midst of thee"* (Deut. 13:1-5). Evidently then, sometimes false teachers are allowed to continue their false teachings for awhile, to test God's people to see whether or not they will follow the truth and continue to obey and love God, or choose to believe cleverly disguised lies, desire sin, and follow Satan (John 3:19-21).

If your heart is right, you'll stay right with the truth, which, as Paul said, is always according to godliness. The apostle Peter warned, *"But there were false prophets also among the people [in the Old Covenant], even as there shall be false teachers among you [in this New Covenant], who privily shall bring in damnable heresies, even [to the point of] denying the Lord that bought them [in their teachings], and bring upon themselves swift destruction. These are wells without water, clouds that are carried with a tempest; to whom the mist of darkness is reserved forever. For when they speak great swelling worlds of vanity, they allure through the lusts of the flesh, through much wantonness, those that were clean [and had just] escaped from them who live in error. While they promise them (who listen to them) liberty, they themselves are [inwardly] the servants of corruption: for of whom a man is overcome, of the same is he brought in bondage"* (2 Pet. 2:1, 17-19). And, *"out of the abundance of the heart the [man's] mouth speaketh."*

Did God provide a way for us now in this new and better Covenant to go back into Egypt and live there with its idolatry and slavery? God forbid! Has God built again by grace what He sent Christ to destroy? (1 John 3:8). Does the faith of Christ say that you need not obey Christ? No! The truth is that He set us free to serve Him and walk in His ways and told us not to listen to anyone who teaches you that you can turn from the ways of the Lord and still be in God's favor. Only a false prophet or false teacher would say such a thing, or perhaps, a sincere but extremely deceived and misled one. Remember God's displeasure with Israel when they made the golden calf and desired to return to Egypt (a type of the polluted world's system). He said He would blot them out of His book which He had written. God is the same person today. If you, as a person, were to provide something that would automatically cover for robbers, rapists, liars, murderers, and so on, you would be guilty of the crimes yourself.

How then could anyone dare say God provided such a thing? God hasn't, but warns that these such like things, and all of the works of the flesh mentioned in Galatians 5:17-22, will bring death and eternal ruin if not repented of, and that those who do such things without repentance, *"shall not inherit the Kingdom of God."* Sure, God greatly loves you and has provided mercy through the blood of Christ, but He being God, must judge evil. But, if we'd judge ourselves, we'd not be judged. So God wants us to repent of any wrongdoing, that He might do us good in the latter end. Grace has provided all we'd need to walk down the narrow road that leads to life. Let us therefore stay on it.

Exodus 20:1-6

"And God spake all these words, saying, I am the Lord *thy God, which have brought thee out of the land of Egypt, out of the house of bondage. Thou shalt have no other gods before me. Thou shalt not make unto thee any graven image, or any likeness of any thing that is in heaven above or that is in the earth beneath, or that is in the water under the earth: Thou shalt not bow down thyself to them, nor serve them [for Satan is behind them all]: for **I the** Lord **thy God am a jealous God, visiting the iniquity of the fathers upon the children unto the third and fourth generation of them that hate me; And showing mercy unto thousands of them that love me, and keep my commandments.** Thou shalt not take the name of the* Lord *thy God in vain; for the Lord will not hold him guiltless that taketh his name in vain."* Your children may suffer if you forsake the right ways of the Lord. *"O that there were such an heart in them, that they would fear me, and keep all my commandments always, that it might be well with them, and with their children for ever!"* (Deut. 5:29).

What Is Love?

"For this is the love of God, that we keep his commandments: and his commandments are not grievous" (1 John 5:3).

Who are the ones that love Him? They are not the ones who just profess to, but those who keep His commandments. Who does He show mercy to? To those who endeavor to keep His commandments. Some not wanting to obey God, try and say, "but this is Old Testament." Well then, if that's their excuse, let's see the doctrine of Christ in the New and see if it's any different.

John 14:20

"At that day ye shall know that I am in my Father, and ye in me, and I in you." He's speaking of after His resurrection when you're in Christ and Christ is in you. Listen now to what He says in verses 21-26: *"**He that hath my commandments, and keepeth them [obeys them], he it is that loveth me: and he that loveth me shall be loved of my Father, and I will love him,** and will manifest [reveal] myself **to him** [that obeys me]. Judas saith unto him, not*

Iscariot, Lord, how is it that thou wilt manifest thyself unto us and not unto the world? [To sinners] Jesus answered and said unto him, **If a man [or anyone really] love me, he will keep my words** *[obey Me]:* **and my Father will love him and we will come unto him, and make our abode with him.** **He that loveth me not, keepeth not my sayings: and the word which ye hear is not mine, but the Father's which sent me.** *These things have I spoken unto you, being yet present with you. But the Comforter which is the Holy Ghost, whom the Father will send in my name [after My resurrection], he shall teach you all things,* **and bring all things to your remembrance** *[all of these things], whatsoever I have said unto you."* In other words, when you're filled with the Holy Ghost in the New Covenant, He will remind you of the things that *Jesus said*, so that you'll keep and obey His words and commandments. But God has not promised through His grace, nor by any other means, anything to those who love this world and its pollutions more than God. And He definitely declared He'd respond differently to those who kept His Word and those who didn't. He will not change from the way He said He'd respond. There is no other God (Gal. 6:7). He's very merciful to the repentant, but resistant to the rebellious. This is the teaching of Christ. Real faith though, responds to the Gospel by obeying it and thereby it can receive from the Covenant. A person that hears the Gospel but doesn't obey it, only deceives himself (James 1:22), and is a foolish person (Matt. 7:24-27).

Certainly neither man's behavior nor what they believe changes God, for His word is *"forever settled in heaven"* (Ps. 119:89). What is written will never change regardless of some modern interpretations of what grace is. Christ said, *"Heaven and earth shall pass away but* **my words** *shall not pass away"* (Matt. 24:35).

Although some try and change God's definition of grace to fit their immoral doctrine rather than Christ's true teaching, which is always according to godliness, it will not stand on the day of judgment. To nullify His words is to deny Christ. This too will be forgiven them if it's repented of.

Sin

Sin must be confessed as sin, then it's washed away completely. This is an action of faith based on what God has said in the Word (1 John 1:9). There is mercy for the repentant, but there is no cloak for sin provided for anyone to go back into a life of sin. The Holy Ghost is here to convict of sin and to lead us into a walk of righteousness. He is here to help us mortify the deeds of the body (Rom. 8:13). Unconfessed known sin though, destroys faith, hardens the heart, sears the conscience, wars against the soul, grieves the Holy Spirit and gets people back to where they are no longer willing to repent and receive what grace offers; or it deceives them into thinking they don't need to repent, and thereby, sadly, they never partake of the cleansing power of the blood of Jesus, but become harder and harder, and more and more blinded. Sin is like playing with fire in a field of dry grass. You never know when it might get out of control. Or, it's like swimming in a lake that has a lot of strong, unseen undercurrents ever seeking to pull a victim under for the last time.

No wonder Solomon wrote, *"Fools make a mock of sin."* So taking the broad road will always lead to eternal destruction.

1 John 2:1

"My little children, these things write I unto you, that ye sin not. And if any man sin, we have an advocate with the Father, Jesus Christ the righteous." If you do sin, go to Him, acknowledge you're wrong and then He will plead your case to the Father and abundantly pardon. It is an honor to be man or woman enough to acknowledge it to the Lord, but it's a disgrace to willingly live in the pollutions of the world, saying that grace will cover for you.

Confessing and Judging Our Sins

1 John 1:9

*"If we confess our sins, he is faithful and just to forgive us our sins, and to cleanse us **from all unrighteousness**."* Notice John said,*"IF."* This means *"upon this condition"* He will cleanse you. You confess it; then He cleanses you. Satan doesn't want a Christian (a son of God) to obey this so he makes up false doctrines to keep people held by the cords of their own sins. He knows that sin deceives, hardens and blinds a person, and makes them dull of hearing. Satan is also aware of the power of the blood of Jesus more than some Christians, and so seeks to keep people away from partaking of its cleansing power by giving out wrong doctrines, by telling some they don't need to repent of, or confess, their sins to God when God *and* the Apostles Doctrine *says they do* need to in order to partake of it (1 Tim. 4:1). Satan knows full well that we overcome him by the blood of the Lamb. Scripture also says, *"His own iniquities shall take the wicked [the evil doer] himself and he shall be holden with the cords of his sins. He shall die without instruction; and in the greatness of his folly he shall go astray"* (Prov. 5:22-23). Even back in Eden God looked for a confession

from Adam and Eve, the first created son and daughter of God, but they passed the blame on to others (Gen. 3:8-13). And John revealed that a Christian (called a son of God) who sins, needs to be cleansed of the "unrighteousness." Some extreme ultra gracists teach that confession and repentance is a work, so it's therefore contrary to grace, and not necessary. Their ignorance is almost beyond what I can imagine. For anytime we obey the Word, it is faith; and the Lord commanded the churches in Revelation chapters two and three, to repent, or suffer the consequences.

How are we cleansed? By repentance and confession (1 John 1:9). Then God cleanses us with the blood of His Son. This then, is an act of faith. If a person goes astray, they need to turn back to God and receive by faith the wonderful provision of mercy and grace that is given to us in the New Covenant. Then sin's effect in the soul is removed and the heart stays sensitive to God. All of this is an operation of grace. Adam though, didn't have the blood of Jesus available to him to cleanse him like we do. All we need to do is to partake of it through confession of it and we're cleansed. That's one of the major differences between him as a son of God, and us as sons of God. Every good thing and provision of this New Covenant is by the operation of grace, and is received by faith. We didn't deserve any of it. Our deliverance from Satan, his pollutions, and his kingdom is all by grace.

In all that the Lord commands us to do, He will enable us to do; only harden not your hearts against Him as Israel did in the wilderness of sin (Heb. 3:7-12).

1 Corinthians 11:27-32 In speaking to Christians Paul wrote:

*"Wherefore whosoever shall eat this bread, and drink this cup of the Lord, unworthily, **shall be guilty** of the body and blood of the Lord. But let a man examine himself, and so let him eat of that bread, and drink of that cup. For he that eateth and drinketh unworthily, eateth and drinketh damnation to himself, not discerning the Lord's body [not walking in love]. For this cause many are weak and sickly among you, and many sleep. For if we would judge ourselves, we should not be judged. **But when we are judged, we are chastened of the Lord, that we should not be condemned with the world."***

Here we see that if we judge ourselves and repent when we do wrong, we will not be judged. But if we don't, the Lord Himself will judge us and permit temporal chastening in order that we might repent and change our mind so that we not be condemned with the world. If you're going to willingly yield to the wicked one in your soul, God may let you get a taste of suffering at the hands of the wicked one. This is intended to cause the person to *"awake to righteousness and sin not,"* for continual sin can eventually destroy the person, their faith, and finally their soul (1 Cor. 5:1-12; James 5:19-20). Does it sound like He continues then to treat them all the same by an automatic grace or imputed righteousness? NO! Didn't Paul say that they were *guilty* if they had done wrong and needed therefore to judge themselves? Yes! Sin is always, as we've stated, faith's worst enemy. Faith is from God; sin is from the devil. Sin is still sin for Christians or the unregenerate. There are two different kingdoms at work here. Remember, sin is working to get a person to no longer live for God. It wages war, Peter said, against the soul. Would God then provide for us to live in that which destroys our relationship with Him and destroys faith when without faith it is impossible to please Him? We live by faith. Jesus said, *"Every kingdom divided against itself shall not stand."* It is unbelief that causes a person to depart from the life of faith. So grace would never work to cover over unrepented of sin, which destroys faith and causes unbelief. Like oil and water, good and evil do not mix, nor do grace and sin. So again, God does respond differently to those Christians who judge themselves and to those who don't, as can be clearly seen by this passage and many others (1 Thess. 4:6). On one He has mercy; the other He judges. So He will always respond exactly as He has revealed in His written Word. In this way He changes not (1 Cor. 5:5). He judges according to every man's work (actions and deeds). For all have free wills to do as they choose, and are responsible for their choices.

Showing God We Love Him

Deuteronomy 7:9

"Know therefore that the Lord thy God, he is God, the faithful God, which keepeth covenant and mercy **with them that love him and keep his commandments** *to a thousand generations."*

Unto how many generations is this so? Then this scriptural condition is so, even in our day.

God keeps Covenant with *them that love Him* and keep His commandments. These are people who live for God and His will. Adam was to show his love for God by keeping His commandment and so are we. *"And we know that all things work together for good to them that love God, to them who are the called according to his purpose"* (Rom. 8:28).

Notice, that He only works on behalf of those who love Him and endeavor to keep His commandments. These He foreknew and they who do God's will are predestinated to be conformed to the image of His Son (vs. 29). For this is their desire now (Matt. 12:50). Those who won't obey are not included.

Friend, this is far more serious than many people think. It's a matter of eternal life and eternal damnation. Again, what is this love for God? Is this still so in the New Covenant? Let's see a little more on this.

1 John 2:5

"But **whoso keepeth his word**, *in him verily is the love of God perfected:* **hereby know we that we are in him.**" (This is the way we can be sure we are in Him and are in union with Him.) *"He that saith, I know him, and keepeth not his commandments, is a liar, and the truth is not in him"* (1 John 2:4). Anyone who lives like the world doesn't know Him, or love Him, or they are a prodigal son who's willingly gone astray from the pathway of life.

1 John 5:2-3

"By this we know that we love the children of God, when we love God, and keep his commandments. **For this is the love of God, that we keep his commandments**: *and his commandments are not grievous."* Do you see what love for God is? It's willingly wanting to obey His commandments. His commandments represent Him and what He is like. And remember, all His promises are to those that love Him. This is New Testament Christianity. His commandments are still important and still in operation. The apostles didn't throw out these truths about God or His moral law that they had learned from the Old Testament scriptures, but rather, expounded on them and showed that they were now also a part of this New Covenant.

Paul wrote to Christians, *"Honor thy father and mother; which is the first commandment with promise; That it may be well with thee, and thou mayest live long on the earth"* (Eph. 6:2-3). He fully knew it was still operational for New Testament believers and was still God's will. God had him write it into our Covenant.

They knew how then to differentiate between God's eternal, moral law and the legalistic system of the Mosaic law put on the Jews to control, to a degree, their unrighteousness, and to keep them occupied until true deliverance came, but many today do not. Paul wrote, *"Awake to righteousness, and sin not; for some have not the knowledge of God: I speak this to your shame"* (1 Cor. 15:34). Ultra gracists do not have the true knowledge of God in this area.

In 1 Corinthians 7:19 Paul wrote:

"Circumcision is nothing, and uncircumcision is nothing, **but [what is important is] the keeping of the commandments of God."**

Paul loved God. He believed in keeping God's moral commandments. He did not look at this as legalistic, or self-righteous, or contrary to grace, as some ultra gracists believe. He looked at it as the whole reason grace was given. He saw that faith taps us into grace's supernatural power, which was provided for us by Christ's redemptive work. By this then, we establish the righteousness of the law as we walk by faith (Rom. 3:31). Grace, in other words, enables us to live holy, if we are willing to. The ultra gracists have not rightly divided the Word here. They really have made up their own little religion with their own little interpretation of what grace is, and it's the only thing they will see, hear, or receive. It is merely another tradition of men and doctrine of devils, which has made the *"Word of God of none effect"* in the lives of those who embrace it, yet they know it not. Jesus said, *"If therefore the light that is in thee be [really] darkness, how great is that darkness!"* (Matt. 6:23). Grace simply has freed us from Satan so that we can now serve God and keep His commandments as recorded in the New Covenant. It saved us from our lost, spiritually dead, and weakened condition. *"How much more shall the blood of Christ, who through the eternal Spirit offered himself without spot to God, purge your conscience from dead [sinful] works to serve the living God?"* (Heb. 9:14; Eph. 5:10-11) We were then reinstated back into God's family. It is God who works in us (Phil. 2:13). Let us not grieve His Holy Spirit and go our own way as Israel did in the wilderness. Should we listen to those who say we can go back to Egypt and still be pleasing to the Lord? Name one person in the Bible that was rebellious and received God's blessing, or went to heaven without repenting. There's no such example, so take heed. There are countless examples of God judging people when they continued in evil in the sight of the Lord, or turned away from the right path (Num. 32:13; Judges 3:7-10; 2 Chron. 33:2). *"Ye have wearied the Lord with your words. Yet ye say, Wherein have we wearied him? When ye say, Every one that doeth evil is good in the sight of the Lord, and he delighteth in them; or, Where is the God of judgment?"* (Mal. 2:17) ***"For he that will love life, and see good days***, *let him refrain his tongue from evil, and his lips that they speak no guile: Let him eschew evil, and do good; let him seek peace, and ensue it. For the eyes of the Lord are over the righteous, and his ears are open unto their prayers: but the face of the Lord is against them that do evil"* (1 Pet. 3:10-12).

Are There New Testament Commandments?

Listen once again to Paul. *"If any man think himself to be a prophet, or spiritual, let him acknowledge that **the things that I write unto you are the commandments of the Lord**. But if any man be ignorant, let him be ignorant"*

(1 Cor. 14:37-38). Extreme gracists are evidently ignorant of this. He didn't say that it was the Lord's advice, but His commandments.

Jesus said if you love Him you will keep His commandments, and then He will manifest Himself to you. Again, wasn't this the same test that Adam faced? The epistles also contain and are filled with His commandments, which we are to keep. They were given to Paul by Jesus to instruct the church (Gal. 1:11-12). So we see there are commandments for New Testament believers just as there were for people in the Old Testament. (Although all of these things are moral commandments, which are fulfilled by love and the fruit of the Spirit and not by legalistic things such as observance of days, Sabbaths, circumcision, and carnal ordinances.) We understand and know that we are not under that legalistic system, nor under Jewish ceremonial laws. And we also know that He said He'd manifest Himself more and more only to those that love Him and keep His commandments. Actually, "love" fulfills the moral law for it works no ill towards God or others. This is what God has always wanted. This love is not a love that excuses sin or evil behavior while a person goes about harming others, but a love that fulfills the moral law. God who is love, will cast Satan and all who follow him in evil behavior into the lake of fire. For God is against evil. If they want that which is contrary to God, He has prepared a place for them void of the good things of God.

So, if you willingly don't follow the love of God shed abroad in your heart and walk in love and keep His commandments of love, it shows that you don't love Him (John 14:21,24). We understand that there are new Christians, old folks, and babes in Christ that struggle and don't comprehend things; and we understand that people, for awhile, have struggles with the flesh as they learn to overcome. God too, understands this but let us walk according to how far we have attained. The apostle wrote, *"Nevertheless, whereto we have already attained, let us walk by the same rule, let us mind the same thing, For many walk [live their lives in such a way], of whom I have told you often, and now tell you even weeping, that they are the enemies of the cross of Christ: Whose end is destruction, whose God is their belly [their own selfishness], and whose glory is in their shame, who mind earthly things"* (Phil. 3:16,18-19). Let us then set *our affections* on things above, as the scriptures admonish us, and not on any sinful thing in the earth (Col. 3:1-2).

In Psalm 91:14 the Lord says:

"Because he set his love upon me, therefore *will I deliver him: I will set him on high,* ***because*** *he hath known my name."* Notice: *"because," "therefore."*

Again, God responds according to a person's response and their love for Him. The whole Bible, Old and New Testament, declares this. God declared that this is the way He operates (Rev. 3:10). If your life is focused on living for God but you slip and sin, God says to go to Him, repent, and then He will abundantly pardon for He is of great mercy. His mercies are new every morning. No matter who you are or what you've done you can go to God and find complete and instant forgiveness. God is always willing, but the question is, are you? Don't ever be misled by a false concept of grace saying that you need not go to Him and ask. God's Word says, *"You have not because you ask not."* It is Satan who doesn't want you to ask. God's question is to us as it was to one in the Bible, *"Wilt thou be made whole?"* Are you willing to let Him work in your life?

Psalm 89:34

"My covenant will I not break, nor alter the thing that is gone out of my lips." "All scripture [Old and New Testament] is given by inspiration of God...." It all came from the same unchangeable person (James 1:17).

Deuteronomy 11:16-28

Now listen to the Lord and heed His eternal Word. Paul said that what was written before time, was written for our admonition and learning that we might, in this church age, understand the ways of the Lord (1 Cor. 10:5-12).

*"**Take heed [then] to yourselves, that your heart be not deceived** [misled by men's or devils teachings or opinions], and, '**ye turn aside**' [off the narrow road of life], **and serve other** gods, and worship them [which is synonomus with this world and its sinful ways, Eph. 2:2-3]; **and then the** Lord's **wrath be kindled against you**, and He shut up the heaven, that there be no rain, and that the land yield not her fruit; and lest ye perish quickly from off the good land which the* Lord *giveth you. [And all the blessings stop.]Therefore shall ye lay up these, My words, in your heart and in your soul, and bind them for a sign upon your hand, that they may be as frontlets between your eyes. And ye shall teach them to your children, speaking of them when thou sittest in thine house, and when thou walkest by the way, when thou liest down, and when thou risest up. And thou shalt write them upon the door posts of thine house, and upon thy gates: That your days may be multiplied, and the days of your children, in the land which the* Lord *sware unto your fathers to give them as the days of heaven upon the earth. **For if ye shall diligently keep all these commandments which I command you, to do them, to love the** Lord **your God, to walk in all his ways,** and to cleave unto him; Then will the Lord drive out all these nations from before you, and ye shall possess greater nations and mightier than yourselves. Every place whereon the soles of your feet shall tread shall be yours: from*

the wilderness and Lebanon, from the river, the river Euphrates, even unto the uttermost sea shall your coast be. There shall no man be able to stand before you: for the LORD *your God shall lay the fear of you and the dread of you upon all the land that ye shall tread upon, as he that said unto you,* **Behold, I set before you this day a blessing and a curse; a blessing if ye obey the commandments of the** LORD **your God, which I command you this day: And a curse, if ye will not obey the commandments of the** LORD **your God,** *which I command you this day:* **but turn aside out of the way** *which I command you this day, to go after other gods, which ye have not known."*

Blessings if we obey; curses if we don't. This is still true today regardless of what any man may teach to the contrary. Paul said, *"Give no place to the devil."* There still is the law of sowing and reaping (Gal. 6:7), and this law is still in effect. The difference under the New Covenant is, if you confess your sin when, and if, you sin, the blood of Jesus washes it completely away and then the curse and Satan cannot legally overcome you; IF you then stand in faith against it. We overcome the devil by the blood of the Lamb and by the Word of our testimony (Rev. 12:11). Christ's blood totally breaks Satan's legal hold on us when we run under its protection. If you sin, you are to go back to the blood and get cleansed, confessing your sin as the Lord has said. It is obvious the curse and Satan overcome many Christians, so the blessings cannot all be automatic. So, if you sin and give place to the devil, you can confess it to the Lord, judge yourself, and His blood will cleanse you and legally close the door on the devil. Then the heart is sprinkled from an evil conscience (Heb. 10:22) and then you can stand in faith. *"Beloved, if our heart condemn us not,* **then** *have we confidence toward God"* (1 John 3:21).

Now again, Paul wrote in his letter to the church, *"For whatsoever things were written before time were written for our learning."* Listen now as the apostle speaks. *"But* **with many of them** *[in the Old Covenant]* **God was not well pleased** *[they were not accepted by God]: for they were overthrown [and then died] in the wilderness [of sin]. Now these things* **were our examples** *[and warnings to us to teach us],* **to the intent we [Christians] should not** *lust after evil [forbidden] things, as they also lusted.* **Neither be ye** *idolaters [and follow false gods],* **as were some of them;** *as it is written, The people sat down to eat and drink, and rose up to play.* **Neither let us** *commit fornication, as some of them committed, and fell in one day three and twenty thousand.* **Neither murmur 'ye' as some of them murmured** *[against God and His leaders], and were destroyed of the destroyer. Now all these things happened unto them for ensamples [as examples]: [of the way God always works] and they are written* *for our admonition [our instructions and warning] upon whom the ends of the world are come"* (1 Cor. 10:5-11).

God expects us to learn by His response to them that He won't tolerate, nor put up with, sin and rebellion if it's continued in. God had this written for our learning. Paul, like Jude, was saying, don't let what happened to them happen to you, but rather, obey and please God. Paul wrote, *"Furthermore then we beseech you, brethren, and exhort you by the Lord Jesus, that as ye have received of us how ye ought to walk and to please God, so ye would abound more and more,* **for ye know what commandments we gave you by the Lord Jesus"** (1 Thess. 4:1-2). You will only abound more and more as you live to please God and keep His commandments.

James 1:22

"But be ye doers of the word, and not hearers only, deceiving your own selves." (If a person doesn't obey the Word and do what it says, God promises them nothing, but declares they deceive themselves.) Only those who do and obey the Word of God are blessed (vs. 25).

Ephesians 4:27

"Neither give place to the devil." Sin brings a different response from people, from the devil, and from God.

Obedience Brings Life

Hebrews 5:9

"And being made perfect, he [Jesus] became the author of **eternal salvation unto all them that obey Him."** To whom? To all that **obey** Him, which means, to all who comply with His commands. There is no good promise made to those who refuse to obey Him or His commandments; nor has God promised eternal life to those who choose to rebel against His Son or merely profess that they are a Christian. (See Luke 6:46.) Yes, we have eternal life now as Christians, but Paul said to Christians, *"fight the good fight of faith, lay hold on eternal life,"* for it only becomes our permanent possession after we've fought the good fight, finished our course, and kept the faith. *"He that hath an ear, let him hear what the Spirit saith* **unto the churches; to him that** *overcometh [Satan, the world and its pollutions] will I give to eat of the tree of life, which is in the midst of the paradise of God"* (Rev. 2:7). *"Blessed are they* **that do** *his commandments, that they may have right to the tree of life, and may enter in through the gates into the city"* (Rev. 22:14). Partaking of this tree of life is what will then lock us into the blessed condition forever (Gen. 3:22). Eternal life is something separate

from us. It is not something we have permanently received right now, nor is it a part of us. Paul spoke of the hope of eternal life (Titus 1:1-2). It is *God's uncreated life* imparted to our spirits (Eph. 4:17-18). Adam, too, was a *"living soul."* He had eternal life and by this life knew God (John 17:3), but *"the soul that sinneth shall die."* That is, be disconnected from life (Eph. 4:18). Adam disconnected from Jesus. He became a branch broken off the vine, and became spiritually withered.

Christ is called *"eternal life"* in 1 John 1:2, 5:11-12. And Hebrews 3:14 states, *"For we are made partakers of Christ [eternal life], if we hold the beginning of our confidence* **steadfast unto the end*** "* (of our lives). *"If,"* He said. (This means, on this condition.) It's stated this way because it's possible for us to abide or not abide *"in Him."* And, *"in Him is life."* But Jesus said, *"If a man abide not in me [that is, in Christ], he is cast forth as a branch [that once was grafted in but now is broken off from the vine], and is withered; and men gather them, and cast them [dead branches] into the fire, and they are burned"* (John 15:6). This life we've received is eternal, it's true, but not yet eternally ours. Christ has freed us by His life from sin's controlling power and has given us the grace to do what He's required of us so that we can now take the narrow road that leads to eternal life being permanently ours (Rom. 5:10; Phil. 1:21). It will become our eternal possession after we have lived our lives for the will of God. So after we have overcome, we'll be granted to eat of the Tree of Life and live with God forever (Rev. 2:7,22:14). This then shows Him that we love Him. All He needs is our willing (loving) cooperation and He'll provide the rest. So yes, it is all by grace (by His power), and by our willing cooperation with His power; and for the extreme gracists, a proper scriptural knowledge of what He's saying. That is simply to "continue" on in the faith, empowered by His grace. Paul told Timothy, *"Take heed unto thyself, and unto the doctrine; continue in them: for in doing this thou shalt both save thyself, and them that hear thee"* (1 Tim. 4:16).

So, it makes all the difference whether we love God or not; and if we love Him, the only way we can show it is if we love, keep, and side in with His Word (1 John 2:3-6, 2:15-17, 5:2-3; James 1:12, 2:5; 1 Cor. 2:9; Eph. 6:24; John 14:20-26; 2 Tim. 3:4-5; Gal. 5:6). And He has only promised as these scriptures declare, *His kingdom* to them that love Him. Paul wrote, *"If any man love not the Lord Jesus Christ, let him be Anathema Maranatha"* (1 Cor. 16:22). (That is, let him be accursed when the Lord comes.) *"Beloved, if God so loved us, we ought also to love one another"* (1 John 4:11).

CHAPTER NINE

THE IMPORTANCE OF OBEYING THE GOSPEL

P aul wrote, *"Wherefore we labor, that, whether present or absent, we may be accepted of him"* (2 Cor. 5:9).

2 Thessalonians 1:7-9 *"And to you who are troubled rest with us, when the Lord Jesus shall be revealed from heaven with his mighty angels, in flaming fire taking vengeance on them that: [1] know not God, and [2] that obey not [refuse to obey] the gospel of our Lord Jesus Christ."*

Two groups will suffer the Lord's vengeance. It is really His vengeance on evil.

Paul went on to say that these two groups will be punished with *"everlasting destruction,"* and not just be cast to the outer skirts of heaven, as I've heard one extreme gracist ridiculously teach. See how much importance Paul put on obeying the Gospel? So obviously, his teaching on grace was never that you could be disobedient to the Gospel and still be covered by grace or have an imputed righteousness.

Paul tells Christians in Romans 6:16:

*"Know ye not, that to whom ye yield yourselves servants to obey, **his servants ye are to whom ye obey; whether of sin** unto death [spiritual and eternal], or of obedience **unto righteousness**?" The life and death he is speaking of in Romans 6 are both eternal.* (See also Rom. 2:7.)

Sin still works to destroy faith and lead a person to follow Satan down the broad road towards eventual spiritual death. The true righteousness of Christ, on the other hand, keeps a person on the pathway of life. You are a servant of the one you obey. Both pay wages and both have end results. *"He leadeth me in paths of righteousness for His name's sake."* And Paul on a number of occasions wrote, follow after righteousness and godliness, and *"awake to righteousness and sin not."*

In Galatians 5:7 he says,

*"Ye did run well; who did hinder you that ye should **not obey the truth**?"* It's either those who teach legalism, or those who turn the grace of God into lasciviousness who do so. One teaches an outward religion; the other, a false way of grace. Both hinder people from obeying the truth.

Then in Ephesians 6:1-3 he writes:

*"Children **obey your parents** in the Lord: for this is right. Honor thy father and mother; **which is the first commandment** with promise; that it may be well with thee, and thou mayest live long on the earth."*

So again, Paul taught that these moral commandments were still fully functional under the New Covenant and that people would still be blessed for keeping them, or reap the consequences of disobeying them (Col. 3:25). Only the civil and Jewish ceremonial laws which were added later after Israel's disobedience have ceased with its legalistic outward ordinances such as circumcision, Sabbaths, dietary laws, and so on. These couldn't possibly inwardly change a person nor enable a man to overcome Satan and sin, but were mostly only pictures, shadows, and types of good things to come. But now that the reality has come, we need not keep this legalistic Mosaic system of Jewish law. God's moral law however, is eternal and will always exist. It is His divine will and nature expressed and will last as long as God does; that is, forever. That's why God still includes it in the New Covenant and why Peter the Apostle wrote, *"Nevertheless we, according to his promise, look for new heavens and a new earth, wherein dwelleth righteousness"* (2 Pet. 3:13).

There will be no sinful free-for-all in the time to come. Grace never has, nor never will, provide such a thing. True, Christ was the end of the civil and Jewish ceremonial laws such as Sabbaths, circumcision, dietary laws, and so on. These, we know, were secondary, and only shadows, types, and pictures destined to pass away. These are the *"works of the law,"* that Paul expressed we don't have to keep, and by which no one could be saved. In many of his writings, Paul was speaking to Jews who were under the law with all of its outward ordinances. But, Paul taught that we can now walk in the spiritual reality of these things and obey God's moral government by the life and grace of Christ within, without these outward ordinances. So then, these outward works of the Jewish law have ceased, for Christ put an end to those things by fulfilling their shadows and types. But God's moral law has not ceased (See 1 Cor. 7:19.), which law God included in both Covenants. This is the Covenant test we are under. We, who have received His grace, have no excuse now to return to the world and its pollutions *for He gave us* all we'd need in order to overcome it (2 Pet. 1:3). If we continue to love God, we will continue to live for Him, and continue (1 Cor. 10:13) by His grace, to be able to walk down the narrow road that leads to life.

God's Eternal Law

All through Genesis and Exodus, God dealt with people who broke His moral commandments *even before* His moral law was written in stone and given to Moses. (Examples: Gen. 20:3; Exod. 12:11.) The same is true with His dealings with Lucifer and the fallen angels, for God's moral law and government is eternal. It's the same yesterday, today, and forever. It really is the law of love, and His Kingdom is a kingdom of righteousness. Do not think we are under some unusual dispensation where God will now close His eyes and ears to what's going on, for this is not the case. In the New Covenant He has written His laws in our hearts and minds for us to obey, and He's done it by the Spirit of God, and empowered us by His Spirit to walk in His ways. Do you not see the test we are under? Will we be faithful or unfaithful to our Creator? The Lord says in Revelation 2:10, *"Be thou faithful unto death and I will give thee a crown of life." "He that hath an ear, let him hear what the Spirit saith **unto the churches**; to him that overcometh [this sinful world] will I give to eat of the Tree of Life, which is in the midst of the paradise of God"* (Rev. 2:7). To whom? Overcomes what? The Bible interprets itself and speaks of overcoming sin, overcoming the wicked one, and overcoming the world and its moral pollutions (2 Pet. 2:20; 1 John 2:14,5:4).

In Ezekiel 36:27 concerning the New Covenant He says:

*"And I will put my spirit within you, **and cause you** to walk in my statutes, **and ye shall keep** my judgments, and do them."*

"That the righteousness of the law might be fulfilled in us, who walk not after the flesh, but after the Spirit" (Rom. 8:4).

"Do we then make void the law through faith? God forbid: yea, we establish the law" (Rom. 3:31). We must always rightly divide the Word and determine how the word "law" is used in order to determine what He's speaking of. Just as we have to see how the words "baptism" and, "works" are used in scripture in order to know which baptism, or type

of works He speaks of. We should also realize that although the Old Covenant Mosaic law has passed away, nevertheless, anything from the Old Covenant that is now included in the New, is still then for us today and should be obeyed, for it's now a part of the New Covenant.

2 Thessalonians 3:14-15

*"**And if any man obey not our word by this epistle, note that man, and have no company** with him, that he may be ashamed. Yet count him not as an enemy, but admonish him as a brother."*

It does not say, treat him as though he hasn't sinned, but admonish him as a brother and work to restore him in a spirit of meekness to come back into obedience to the Lord, lest the world and Satan gain a hold on Him once again (Gal. 6:1). Read the epistle. Paul said, if anyone does not *obey it*, have no company with that person. Should we then listen to those who teach others that you don't *really* need to obey it? You should then, have no company (fellowship) with them, that they may be ashamed for teaching such things, and perhaps come to repentance.

1 Peter 2:7-8

*"Unto you therefore which believe [and obey Him] He is precious: but unto them which **be disobedient**, the stone which the builders disallowed, the same is made the head of the corner, and a stone of stumbling, and a rock of offense, **even to them which stumble at the word, being disobedient:** where unto also they were appointed."* (It was foreseen that some would fall into this category.)

Disobedience to the Word causes people to stumble into false beliefs and Satan's snares, and can cause a false security. You cannot purposely live a disobedient life and be blessed by God. God's grace and love never promised any such thing. God's Word only shows that you will suffer the consequences of unconfessed sin and *"he that doeth wrong shall receive for the wrong he hath done"* and *"there is no respect of persons with God"* (Col. 3:25).

1 Peter 4:17

*"For the time is come **that judgment must begin at the house of God**: and if it first begin at us, **what shall the end be of them that obey not the gospel of God?"***

A false view and concept of grace will imply that you really don't have to live for God, nor obey the Gospel to be saved or blessed, and that God would never judge the House of God. They teach that this would be works, as if obeying the Lord or the faith of Christ was a dead ceremony or carnal ordinance. Yes, they ridiculously say that they could sin and do evil and not repent, and that grace would still cover for them; and that to have to obey God is legalistic works. But none of the early church fathers believed this way in their writings, nor did the apostles, nor does the scripture teach such things. Therefore, *"Let no man deceive you,"* with carefully disguised deceptions that he himself has been deceived by. *"That we henceforth be no more children, tossed to and fro, and carried about with every wind of doctrine, by the sleight of men, and cunning craftiness, whereby they lie in wait to deceive"* (Eph. 4:14). For we have already shown that grace is given so that we are able to keep God's moral law, and that faith is more than just a verbal profession of a belief, but rather, actions, and profession agreeing with one another.

Again, the works of the law have to do with the outward ordinances and Jewish ceremonies. They were not a part of God's original eternal law, and they are secondary and done away with in Christ. They were not added into our new contract, so we don't have to keep them. But obeying God's moral law by faith is not included in the term, *"works of the law,"* but it is rather, obedience, and true righteousness. It is a product of living faith in the heart and is a part of the New Covenant (James 2:14-26). There is no faith if there are no works or actions. You'll notice that where Paul mentions the word "works," in a negative way as contrary to grace, he is always talking about Jewish or religious, outward ceremonies and routines which people think will justify them and make them righteous if they do them without really obeying God from the heart. You'll see the word "circumcision" or "Sabbath days," close by the word "works," when it's used in such a way. We know that we weren't saved by these kinds of works, nor any dead, religious, outward ordinances that we ourselves could do, or keep on our own, for we were then dead in sin and a *"corrupt tree could not bring forth good fruit"* from the heart (Eph. 2:10). God has saved us from the dead works of our old way of life and grafted us into Christ, so that we would serve Him *"in newness of spirit,"* and He has given us ability to do so. So now He expects our cooperation, and He planned that we should walk in good works and produce good fruit in our lives by grace (Eph. 2:10). By this we were to be a light unto the world. *"Do all things without murmurings and disputings: That ye may be blameless and harmless, the sons of God, without rebuke, in the midst of a crooked and perverse nation, among whom ye shine as lights in the world"* (Phil. 2:14-15). (See also Heb. 9:14.) *"That he would grant unto us, that we being delivered out of the hand of our enemies might serve him without fear, in holiness and righteousness before him, all the days of our life"* (Luke 1:74-75).

Rightly Dividing the Word

Here is one area the ultra gracists don't perceive. They haven't distinguished between God's eternal moral law and the outward carnal works of the law, which were added later to teach Israel certain things, and to keep them occupied until true deliverance came. So they think obedience to God's moral law and government, as it is revealed in the New Testament, is legalistic works, or works of the law that they need not really obey, but it's not. It actually is living by faith. Some of them ridiculously think that you put yourself under the curse if you say you have to obey God, keep His commandments, or keep the faith as it's revealed in the New Covenant. Can anyone be more deluded than this? Even common sense should tell them their theology is messed up. What does the Word say?

Revelation 22:14

"Blessed *[holy and blessed with divine favor]* **are they that do his commandments** *[His moral law],* **that they may have right** *[the privilege] to the Tree of Life, and may enter in through the gates into the city."* So it is obvious their perception of things is way off. God says, those who do His commandments are "blessed," not cursed. The opposite is also true. (See Psalm 1 also.)

Those, then, that don't do them because they are not willing to, will not be blessed, nor have the right to the Tree of Life. This is God's decree. It was the same with Adam. God expects people to walk in the light they have, and to keep their allegiance to Him. He expects the just to *live by faith* (Rom. 12:3). He expects us to *"follow after holiness"* (Heb. 12:13-14). To whom much is given, of him is much required. He doesn't expect less from us; He expects more. *"For I say unto you, that except **your** righteousness shall exceed the righteousness of the scribes and Pharisees, ye shall **in no case** enter into the kingdom of heaven."* They honored Him with their lips, but their hearts were far from Him. They said the right things but didn't do them. He called them whitewashed sepulchers clean on the outside before men, but full of dead men's bones inside. He said that they "say, and do not." Ultra gracists, too, shout an outward imputed righteousness that needs no inward change of heart, and some of them then have the form of godliness, but deny the life-changing power. (See Rom. 2:28-29.) But the apostles never thought of righteousness as just outwardly imputed. Paul said, *"awake unto righteousness and sin not."* He spoke of righteousness as freedom from a life of sin, so, yes, God is merciful to the repentant, the ignorant, and to babes in Christ, but not towards the willfully rebellious (1 Tim. 1:13). This too, is His righteousness. His nature cannot vary from this. So He commands men everywhere to repent so that He can have mercy on them (2 Pet. 3:9; Acts 17:30).

Remember Lot's Wife

To love God then is to keep His commandments, which is His Word. This means to walk in His ways. This doesn't mean a person has reached perfection (who has?), but he is living his life for God and not for the pleasures of sin, and he let's the Lord perfect that which concerns him. If he sins, he repents and confesses it, and it is washed away. *So through repentance and faith, his spiritual walk and life is maintained.* And Jesus said in His doctrine, *"all manner of sins will be forgiven to the sons of men,"* because His love and mercy is great. Remember, to continue in the Gospel is to go on from glory to glory, to set our hand to the plow and not turn back to a worldly system under judgment. Jesus said, *"Remember Lot's wife,"* who because her heart was still in Sodom, she received the same judgment as Sodom when she turned back. Her receiving judgment was not God's fault, then, but hers. God *had called her out* of that ungodly system, *but she turned back in her heart.* One person who exaggerates grace says, "see, she's still the salt of the earth"; but fails to mention that the salt sea in that area which was judged by God has also become known as the Dead Sea, and is void of any vegetation to this day, a visible example of God's judgment. Jesus revealed that there is salt that has lost its savor and is good for nothing, but to be cast out and trodden under feet of men.

As Christians we are *"in this world but not of this world."* This world is under the judgment of God because of its evil (1 Cor. 11:32). We also are warned not to turn back. *"But and if that evil servant shall say in his heart, My lord delayeth his coming; and shall begin to smite his fellow servants, and [goes back] to eat and drink with the drunken; The lord of that servant shall come in a day when he looketh not for him, and in an hour that he is not aware of, and shall cut him asunder,* **and appoint him his portion with the hypocrites:** *there shall be weeping and gnashing of teeth"* (and bitter regret, Matt. 24:48-51). There will be no weeping nor gnashing of teeth in heaven. So this unfaithful servant didn't make it (Rev. 21:4-8). The Gospel message is not just saying, mentally believe, but repent (turn from all evil), and believe the Gospel with all your heart, and obey it. *"And [Jesus] said unto them, Thus it is written, and thus it behooved Christ to suffer, and to rise from the dead the third day: And that* **repentance and remission of sins***

should be preached in his name among all nations, beginning at Jerusalem" (Luke 24:46-47). We are always to turn people from darkness to light; from the power of Satan to the power of God. Never tell anyone that God has provided that they can now go back and live under the power of Satan (Acts 26:18), nor that they don't have to turn from Satan to be saved (Luke 13:3). We are to *"flee from the wrath to come."* Paul said, like Noah, we have *"fled for refuge to lay hold upon the hope set before us"* (Heb. 6:18).

The will of man always turns from one to receive from the other. Jesus said, *"He that is not with me **is against me**; and he that gathereth not with me [people to follow Me] scattereth abroad,"* (is driving them away, Matt. 12:30). If we don't pick up our cross and follow Jesus, we are following Satan and are against Jesus. If we tell others in our doctrines that they can follow Satan or unrighteousness and it will be okay with God, we are against Jesus (Matt. 18:6).

Matthew 22:37-40

"Jesus said unto him, Thou shalt love the Lord thy God with all thy heart, and with all thy soul, and with all thy mind. This is the first and great commandment. And the second is like unto it, Thou shalt love thy neighbor as thyself. On these two commandments hang all the law and the prophets." This has always been the case since the time of Adam, and before.

If we love God, then we are not living our lives for selfish lusts and sin which grieves God and are contrary to God's known will. The first and greatest commandment is to love God, and if we love God, we desire to keep His commandments. (Again, this doesn't mean the legal, ceremonial system of the Old Covenant, but rather, what is written in the New Covenant.)

A person's will and heart will not suddenly change just because his body dies. (Unless he truly repents and allows Christ's blood to cleanse him of the evil before he dies.) Scripture says, *"He that is unjust, let him be unjust still: and he which is filthy, let him be filthy still: and he that is righteous, let him be righteous still: and he that is holy, let him be holy still"* (Rev. 22:11).

Remember Jesus said, *"He that loveth me not keepeth not my sayings: and the word which ye hear is not mine, but the Father's which sent me"* (John 14:24). No one who lives a life of sin persistently, willingly committing evil contrary to God's good Word without repentance, loves God, nor are they in the faith. Every tree is known by its own fruit. If they once had the good fruit of a changed life by the grace of God and were once living for God, but now that fruit is gone, it simply shows they are not abiding in Christ (John 15:6; 1 John 2:4-6), nor are they continuing in grace. To continue *"in the faith,"* is more than just saying you "still" believe. It is a continual obedience to it (1 John 3:3). *"And hereby we do know that we know him, if we keep his commandments"* (1 John 2:3). (To know means to be intimately joined to Him at the present time.) *"He that saith, I know him, and keepeth not his commandments, **is a liar, and the truth is not in him"*** (1 John 2:4). Notice, anyone who says that they know Him (and are in present union with Him), but then says that we don't need to keep God's commandments *IS A LIAR and the truth is not in him!* Will you believe a liar then over the apostles? A person may *have* known Him, but now *not* know Him. It's like a man and woman divorced from one another. They knew each other once, but are now estranged from one another. To continue in the faith is to continue to live by faith and keep His commandments, strengthened by His grace to do so. To live by faith is to live by the law of the Spirit of Life, which sets you free from the law of sin and death that once controlled you. This is how you continue in the New Covenant. So if someone is living by faith, they are living for God and His will and are free from sin's dominating control. They no longer serve sin as their master but have obeyed from the heart the doctrine of God (Rom. 6:17-18,21). They are partaking of Christ's righteous nature and the results are seen. They are freed from a lifestyle of sin (Phil. 1:11). The just shall live by faith; and whom the Son sets free from being sin's slave and servant, is free indeed. This is a picture of a Christian.

Romans 8:28

*"And we know that all things work together for good **to them that love God**, to them who are the called according to his purpose."*

To whom? Not to everyone, but to them that love God and keep His commandments (John 15:7).

Faith will not work without this love for God. If you have not love for God, you are nothing (1 Cor. 13). If you claimed to have faith to move mountains but had not love, if profits you nothing, for faith worketh by love and this is love, that we keep God's commandments (Gal. 5:6; 1 John 5:3).

First John 3:22

*"And whatsoever we ask, we receive of him, **because we keep his commandments, and do those things that are pleasing in his sight.**"* Again, this keeping of His commandments is what walking by faith and love is all

about. It is faith because it pleases God and *"without faith it is impossible to please him"* (Heb. 11:6). Faith enables us to be a partaker of His divine righteous nature and overcome sin, and the law of sin and death, which before had control over us. Adam should have by faith, kept the command given to him, but he didn't. He could have said, God understands my heart; and he could have professed that he still believed in God, and professed that they were loving and graceful, but that wouldn't have helped him. God looked for a confession and for repentance, and because Adam didn't do it, but rather passed the blame on to God, he was driven from paradise and from the Tree of Life. God's righteous nature couldn't automatically release Adam. Some extreme gracists, along with the serpent, also say that you can sin and that God Himself has provided the grace to cover for you while you do it. They also pass responsibility on to God. If they persistently live this way, they too will be driven from paradise and from the Tree of Life.

1 Corinthians 8:3

"But if any man love God, the same is known of Him."

1 Corinthians 16:22

"If any man love not the Lord Jesus Christ, let him be Anathema Maranatha." (Greek: excommunicated and cursed) Paul said, let him be cut off. You only love Him if you keep His commandments (John 14).

Ephesians 6:24 says:

"Grace be with all them that love our Lord Jesus Christ in sincerity. Amen." Grace, then, is for those who love our Lord Jesus Christ in sincerity. Sincerity means *"with an honest and true heart; with unmixed dedication; being really what one appears to be."*

Those who say that they love God and are constantly living contrary to God's ways and God's will don't really love Him in sincerity. Is grace then for them? Only if they repent and have a change of heart.

Titus 1:16

Paul said, *"They profess that they know God; but in works [behavior] they deny him, being abominable, and disobedient, and unto every good work reprobate."* Paul knew that grace changes us and enables us to do good. He knew grace causes obedience.

One who is truly a Christian may slip, be tempted and sin, but he is soon afterward sorry and repents of sin. This is godly sorrow. But it is spiritually dangerous for one to think they can live in sin and be okay without repentance, thinking grace makes it so he could never be lost again. The serpent is still saying, "*ye shall not surely die.*" He tricked Eve by this lie and he is still deceiving Eve's offspring to this very day. The extreme gracists are simply believing the exact same lie, said to them in another way. Hopefully they are not living what they say they believe in this area.

Jude 21

Jude wrote, "**Keep yourselves in the love of God, looking for the mercy** *of our Lord Jesus Christ unto eternal life.*" *Keep yourselves* in the love of God, looking for eternal life. How?

John 15:10

"*If ye keep my commandments,* **ye shall abide in my love;** *even as I have kept my Father's commandments, and abide in his love.*" Jesus always pleased the Father (John 8:29). "*But [again] without faith it's impossible to please God*" (Heb. 11:6). So, if Jesus kept His Father's commandments and always pleased God, it was faith that moved Him to do so and not dead works, or legalism as some call it. Real faith then that pleases God moves us to keep (and obey) God's commandments, following the examples of Jesus (the author and finisher of our faiths). Here then is what faith is all about.

If you don't keep His commandments then *you don't abide* in His love and you don't keep yourself in the love of God. And remember that God's promises are only to them that love Him. Jesus said it and all is exactly as He said it; it's impossible for His Word to change. This is the true Doctrine of Christ. This is not self-righteousness, but is rather, faith, which is pleasing in the Lord's sight. It is walking in righteousness by His empowerment and grace. Again faith really frees us from sin's control and taps us into Christ's righteous nature so that we can live right and do all things through Christ who strengthens us. *Faith*, then, is the victory that *overcomes* the world and its pollutions (1 John 5:4). Faith taps us into grace (God's power), which gives us victory and the ability to *live a life* that pleases God. "*Furthermore then we beseech you, brethren, and exhort you by the Lord Jesus, that as ye have received of us how ye ought to walk and to please God, so ye would abound more and more.* **For ye know what commandments we gave you by the Lord Jesus**" (1 Thess. 4:1-2).

The apostles gave us commandments *by the Lord Jesus,* and then commanded us to obey them. Who, then, has the authority to say we don't really need to? Beware that you don't twist the Lord's words!

"*Ye shall not add unto the word which I command you, neither shall ye diminish ought from it,* **that ye may keep the commandments of the Lord your God which I command you**" (Deut. 4:2; Rev. 22:19). Jesus said, if we reject His words, we reject Him (John 12:48).

Acts 5:1-11

*"But a certain man named Ananias with Sapphira his wife, [in the church] sold a possession, and [deceptively] kept back part of the price, his wife also being privy to it, and brought a certain part, and laid it at the apostles' feet [pretending to give it all]. But Peter said, Ananias, why hath Satan filled thine heart to lie to the Holy Ghost, and to keep back part of the price of the land? Whiles it remained, was it not thine own? And after it was sold, was it not in thine own power? Why hast thou conceived this thing in thine heart? **Thou hast not lied unto men, but unto God. And Ananias hearing these words fell down and gave up the ghost:** and great fear came on all them that heard these things. And the young men arose, wound him up, and carried him out, and buried him. And it was about the space of three hours after, when his wife, not knowing what was done, came in. **And Peter answered unto her,** Tell me whether ye sold the land for so much? And she said, Yea, for so much. Then Peter said unto her, How is it that ye have agreed together to tempt the Spirit of the Lord? behold, the feet of them which have buried thy husband are at the door, and shall carry thee out. Then fell she down straightway at his feet, and yielded up the ghost: and the young men came in and found her dead, and, carrying her forth, buried her by her husband. **And great fear came upon all the church,** and upon as many as heard these things."*

The counterfeit idea of grace based on old, medieval errors and a false, erroneous concept of love and imputed righteousness, would say that God would never respond that way to a Christian. They would say, His grace and unconditional love would just cover their sin and He'd respond to them as though it never happened even if it wasn't repented of. They'd say Peter was too hard on them, too legalistic. They would try and paint a picture that Peter was wrong and they are right: That they are more graceful, righteous, and loving than God and His chosen apostles. It is really they who are self-righteous and self-exalting, and they comprehend it not, for they constantly exalt their beliefs like the Pharisees of old over God's Word, the apostles, and even over the Lord Jesus Christ Himself. Is there anything more self-righteous as this?

Their brand of love excuses the works of the devil, tolerates evil, nullifies true grace, and does away with obeying God. I will choose God's version.

But these scriptures reveal how God Himself, in this Church Age responded to these Christians who had acted deceptively towards the church. They had every opportunity to repent but didn't take it. They were then *judged by* God Himself, and died. This one passage alone shows that this false concept of grace is wrong and way off balance, for why, then, didn't imputed righteousness or unconditional favor automatically work for them?

First Thessalonians 4:6-7

Listen to what Paul said. He warned: *"That no man go beyond and defraud [deliberately cheat] his brother [in Christ] in any matter: because that **the Lord is the avenger of all such,** [He will pay you back terribly for this] as we also have forewarned you and testified. For God hath not called us unto uncleanness, but unto holiness."*

Notice, the Lord will punish any Christian who defrauds his brother in Christ. This shows also, that God doesn't continue to respond to all alike just because of grace or imputed righteousness. Grace and mercy are always there and available IF the person repents and receives it. The will though, must turn (repent) and receive what grace and mercy have provided and offers (forgiveness through the blood of Jesus when it's confessed). In order for a person to receive it, they have to turn from Satan and sin, and turn to God. (Repent and believe is always the key.) So you cannot receive from grace as long as you're persistently going contrary to it. If you turn from one, you turn to the other. No man can walk down the paths of righteousness and unrighteousness at the same time. God says, false teachers *"have forsaken the right way [leaving the straight road], and are gone astray, following the way of Balaam the son of Bosor, who loved the wages of unrighteousness"* (and to profit from wrong doing), *"but he was rebuked for his iniquity"* (2 Pet. 2:15). He needed a dumb donkey to rebuke him for his sinful ways, for he thought he was getting away with it. The donkey saw the danger more clearly than he did. Sin blinds, and any attitude that agrees with it, blinds the mind of the person that has that attitude. Paul spoke of *"the deceivableness of unrighteousness."*

In 1 Corinthians 5:1-5 Paul wrote to believers in the church:

*"It is reported commonly that there is fornication **among you,** and such fornication as is not so much as named among the Gentiles, that one should have his father's wife. And ye are puffed up [thinking you're so loving in tolerating this], and have not rather mourned [and been deeply grieved], that he that hath done this deed might be taken away from among you. For I verily, as absent in body, but present in spirit, **have already judged,** as though I were present, **concerning him that hath so done this deed,** in the name of our Lord Jesus Christ, when ye are gathered together, and my spirit, with the power of our Lord Jesus Christ. **To deliver such an one unto Satan** for the destruction of*

the flesh, that the spirit may [perhaps] be saved in the day of the Lord Jesus." Here the church is ordered *by the Lord* through Paul *to deliver* this man to Satan in order that his flesh may be destroyed. Why? So that he would repent, use his will, and turn back to God, and his spirit would thereby, not be lost forever. Does it sound as though God just continued to respond to him as though he were holy or righteous, or that he was in some positional standing and therefore was automatically blessed by him? No! God is realistic about these things. This is not pretend Christianity, where one just pretends like a person's not really doing what they are doing. God dealt with his sin lest perhaps his living in sin completely destroy his faith and send him to hell, and influence others also to do the same. *"There is [still] no respect of persons with God."*

Included in God's gift of righteousness is the ability to live righteously by faith, so Paul boldly says, *"Awake to righteousness and sin not."* (See also 1 Pet. 2:24.) This command means that we can obey it. The law of the Spirit of life in Christ Jesus has set us free from the law of sin and death, which before controlled us (Rom. 8:2-4).The man could not be abiding with his father's wife in unrighteousness and abiding in Christ's righteousness at the same time (1 John 3:5-6). He had to turn from one to live and abide in the other. There is no positional standing, label, or nametag that could protect him from God's judgment unless he repented, even though he once had accepted Christ.

Colossians 1:13

*"Who **hath delivered us from the power of darkness**, and hath translated us into the kingdom of his dear Son."*

Romans 8:4

"That the righteousness of the law might be fulfilled in us, who walk not after the flesh, but after the Spirit."

1 John 3:6

"Whosoever [continually] abideth in him [Christ] sinneth not." (Doesn't continue in sin. No one who maintains union with Christ lives in sin.) Our righteousness is *"in Him."* *"**He that saith** he abideth in him ought himself also so to walk, even as he walked"* (1 John 2:6). Why? Because as we abide in Him we live out His life by His life within us (Phil. 1:21). He's saying you can't just talk the talk, you have to walk the walk. Faith isn't merely a profession, it's a lifestyle produced by the vine life. *We can't* habitually sin if we maintain union with Him, and anyone who willingly does is not abiding in Christ. They neither have grace or redemption, which is only for those who abide *in Christ Jesus!* (1 Cor. 1:30; Eph. 1:7).

1 Corinthians 5:11-13

"But now I have written unto you not to keep company, if any man that is called a brother be a fornicator, or covetous, or an idolater, or a railer, or a drunkard, or an extortioner; **with such an one no not to eat.** *For what have I to do to judge them also that are without? Do not ye judge them that are within? But them that are without God judgeth.* **Therefore put away from among yourselves that wicked person"** (who is willingly breaking God's moral law).

Paul didn't say the person is righteous, but just has a little behavior problem, so just show him love while he lives in his sin and yields his life over to the devil. No, he said, *"not to be puffed up"* and be so accepting of someone who is living willingly like this, contrary to God and following Satan and his ways. Paul the Apostle who gave us the revelation of true grace said, *"put away from among yourselves that WICKED PERSON"* (who thinks he can just wear the label of being a Christian and call himself a brother). Paul showed that we are still not to tolerate continuance of known evil in our midst.

A Little Leaven

That is, until he repents. *"A little leaven leaveneth the whole lump."* Certainly, we know we should try and restore a fallen brother so that they come back and continue to walk in the *"way of righteousness"* (Gal. 6:1). But his known actions, if accepted, would have had an effect on others and would have encouraged others to sin if tolerated, which then would have had a destructive effect on faith and the Lord's church. The Lord constantly works for the highest good of all to keep all away from sin. Remember, sin and grace are direct opposites. One will never cover for the other, but grace does deliver us from sin's power. Always remember, sin is Satan's power trying to draw people away from God. Those who teach a promiscuous grace in their churches have churches full of worldly people, and why not? It's what they are promoting. "As is the priest, so are the people." God said, *"My people are destroyed for lack of knowledge: because thou hast rejected knowledge, I will also reject thee, that thou shalt be no priest to me: seeing thou hast forgotten the law of thy God, I will also forget thy children"* (Hosea 4:6). If a minister won't properly take care of God's children by giving them the truth, then God will forget *their* children. We are to feed His lambs and sheep (John 21:15-17).

Humanistic Grace

This humanistic grace (similar to some psychiatrists' view) promoted by some (who profess to be a part of the church) in *their* doctrine, implies that there is no need for repentance in the church. They say that there is no need of availing themselves to what the Lord said in 1 John 1:9, for they, contrary to what the Word of the Lord says with no scripture to verify it, say that all sins, past, present, and future, are already forgiven automatically. Howbeit, the Bible never states that, nor does it ever once say, "once saved, always saved"; nor does it say that people *couldn't* forfeit eternal life; nor that any form of unconditional love will save you while you live a life of habitual sin; or "once a son, always a son." IF that were so, then we who were all children of wrath by nature (Eph. 2:3) could have never become sons of God, nor could Adam and his offspring who were originally created to be sons of God, have become children of the devil. *Some* (not all) psychiatrists, like the extreme gracists, similarly just try to convince the patient that there is no sin, or no need for remorse. The effect is similar. They both say, "Your problem is your religion." They both seek to get rid of a sensitive conscience and the need for godly sorrow. Christian Science also promotes a similar view and effect, for they deny the reality of sin and of a judgment. If there's no such thing as sin, then there is no need for a guilty conscience. Secular psychiatrists, many times, don't tell people their problem is their sin and the evil they or others have done, but their religion, and that it's their beliefs which makes them feel bad when they act certain ways. Their kind of peace all comes through deadening the conscience and making it insensitive to the shame of sin. Extreme gracism produces the same effect as the cults and humanistic psychiatry, and yet they think it's godly peace; but it's not peace, but deception (1 Thess. 5:3). God, on the other hand, always says to turn from sin, *"that iniquity be not your ruin;"* and that, *"to be spiritually minded is life and peace,"* but to be *"carnally minded **is death**."*

WHAT SAITH THE

LORD TO THE CHURCHES?

Revelation 2:7

*"He that hath an ear, let him hear what the Spirit saith **unto the church-es; to him that overcometh** (and conquers Satan and the world because of their love for God) **will I give to eat of the tree of life**, which is in the midst of the paradise of God."*

Overcomes what? Overcomes *the pollutions* of the world and he who's behind them. Read Christ's messages to the churches in the book of Revelation. You will see that *all of His promises are to those in the church who overcome the world's evil ways and none are given to those who let the world overcome them by going back into the world's pollutions they were once delivered from* (1 John 5:4). We must all fight the good *"fight of faith,"* to lay hold on eternal life as our eternal possession (1 Tim. 6:12). It is a fight to the finish, choosing the next world over the present one. *"Receiving the end [the final outcome or the final harvest] of your faith, even the salvation of your souls"* (1 Pet. 1:9; 1 John 2:14, 5:4; 2 Pet. 2:20-21).

Revelation 2:12,16

*"And to the angel **of the church** in Pergamos write; These things saith He which hath the sharp sword with two edges; ...**Repent** [let the blood cleanse you]; or else I will come unto thee quickly, and will fight **against** them [that don't repent] with the sword of my mouth."*

Here he told this church to repent or he'd fight against them. God fought against Israel at times in the Old Covenant when they persisted in an evil course. It's revealed here that He is the same yesterday, today, and forever. *"But they rebelled, and vexed his holy Spirit: therefore he was turned to be their enemy, and he fought against them"* (Isa. 63:10.) And again, all of his dealings with them are based on their heart, their actions, and their works. *"The face of the Lord is [still] against them that do evil."* Why? Because He's against wrongdoing (1 Pet. 3:12). But He's also very merciful to those who repent and He will, in His goodness, work to lead people to repentance, for His perfect will is to always bless them when they turn to what's right.

Revelation 2:18-23,26

*"And unto the angel **of the church** in Thyatira write; These things saith the Son of God, who hath his eyes like unto a flame of fire [who sees through all things], and his feet are like fine brass [brass speaks of judgment]; **I know thy works**, and charity, and service, and faith, and thy patience, **and thy works**; and the last to be more than the first. [These He commended.] Notwithstanding I have a few things against thee, because thou sufferest that woman Jezebel, which calleth herself a prophetess [one who says she speaks for God and claims to be inspired but is not], to teach and to seduce my servants **to commit** fornication [by her wrong teachings she seduces My servants to commit immorality], and to eat things sacrificed unto idols. And I **gave her space to repent of her fornication [and immorality]; and she repented not. Behold, I will cast her into a bed, and them that commit adultery** [with the world along] with her [fellowshipping with the world and its pollutions, James 4:4] **into great tribulation** [in their lives], except they repent of their deeds. **And I will kill her children with death; and all the churches shall know that I am He which searcheth the reins and hearts: and I will give unto every one of you according to your works** [behavior]....And he that overcometh, and keepeth **my works [and perseveres in them] unto the end [of this life], to him** will I give power over the nations."* This one passage alone disproves the false grace theory that Satan has sown into the church world.

Here this woman teacher *in the church* told the Lord's real servants that God would not judge fornication and other evils. It caused worldliness and sinful lifestyles, but the Lord clearly gave His response to this teaching saying that if they would not repent of *their deeds* they would be judged by God and be cast into a time of great tribulation. So then, Jesus does look at deeds done and tries to lead people, even in the church, back to repentance so that He can have mercy on them rather than have to judge them. It's repent of the evil and the sin and receive mercy, or be judged by the Lord for the evil. He gives space to repent and is longsuffering, but the clock is ticking and He promises to deal with, and judge, those in the church who don't repent of their evil deeds. If the person doesn't respond to His goodness, Paul said that their "*impenitent [unrepentant] heart stores up wrath for itself.*" Christ *never,* ever mentions a grace that will cause Him to always respond to us the same way regardless of our actions and works, in any of His statements or warnings *to the churches.* He never, ever speaks of a grace that has forgiven all future sins of people irregardless of their repentance. So the ultra gracist's grace is fictional and their thinking that God's only condition for eternal life is to profess that they believe with their mouth, is wrong. Yes, we know all about John 3:16, Romans 6:23, and other scriptures along this line, and they are fully true as long as they are kept in context and placed in the whole picture of all the New Testament. For He also said in the same Gospel, "*Except ye repent,* **ye shall all** *likewise perish.*" And in Romans He told brethren, "*If ye live after the flesh, ye shall [spiritually] die.*" Notice also He said, "*I will give unto every one of you* **according to your works!**" And it's impossible for Him to lie. These works mean, according to how they live, for your life is made up of decisions of your own will.

Revelation 3:1-6

"*And unto the angel* **of the church** *in Sardis write; These things saith he that hath the seven Spirits of God, and the seven stars;* **I know thy works** *[actions and deeds], that thou hast a name that thou livest, and art dead. Be watchful, and strengthen the things which remain, that are ready to die:* **for I have not found thy works perfect before God.** *Remember therefore how thou hast received and heard, and hold fast,* **and repent. If therefore thou shalt not watch, I will come on thee as a thief,** ["* ... and cut you asunder and give you your portion with the hypocrites"; see Matt. 24:42-51.] and thou shalt not know what hour I will come upon thee. Thou hast a few names even in Sardis, which* **have not defiled their garments** *[by living in the sinful activities of the flesh; Jude 23]; and* **they shall walk with me in white: for they are worthy.** *He that overcometh [Satan and the world], the same shall be clothed in white raiment; and I will not blot out his name out of the book of life, but I will confess his name before my Father and before his angels. [Why? because they didn't deny Him either by words or actions; Matt. 10:32-33; Titus 1:16.] He that hath an ear, let him hear what the Spirit* **saith unto the churches.**"

Notice, He said there are some who would walk with Him in white for *they are worthy*, for they didn't defile their garments. Grace, then, doesn't mean He will treat all the same, regardless of how they live, but thank God, mercy provides forgiveness for everyone if everyone repents of evil. They are all, then, on equal ground because of repentance and willingly receiving what mercy truly offers (the cleansing power of the blood of Jesus to all who repent, Heb. 4:16). But all will be rewarded differently in heaven by their lives on earth and what they have done for the Lord (2 Cor. 5:9-10). So, Christ said that if we overcome the devil by not going back to the world and its ways, He, then, would not blot our name out of the Book of Life, which was written in when we repented and believed. Everyone's name was originally in it, but was blotted out when they knowingly sinned, as we shall later point out. It gets written in again through *repentance* and faith and stays in as long as we continue to live for the will of God and abide in Christ (John 15:6). Note: He carefully watched everyone's "works." These are works and actions produced by grace in the heart and the person's willing cooperation with it (1 Cor. 15:10,58); or they are the actions of yielding to Satan and the fallen world's influences.

Revelation 3:7-8, 10

*"And to the angel **of the church** in Philadelphia write; These things saith he that is holy, he that is true, he that hath the key of David, he that openeth, and no man shutteth; and shutteth, and no man openeth; **I know thy works** [labors, actions, and deeds motivated by faith]: behold, I have set before thee an open door, and no man can shut it: for thou hast a little strength, and hast kept my words, and hast not denied my name…. **Because thou hast kept** the word of my patience, **I also will keep thee** from the hour of temptation, which shall come upon all the world, to try them that dwell upon the earth."* Note: Because you keep God's Word, He also will keep you from the hour of tribulation. They reaped what they sowed (Gal. 6:7).

Notice His response to them *because of their* faithfulness (their behavior). I use the word "behavior," because many ultra gracists sometimes excessively do so in their writings and teachings saying such things as, "Can our behavior stop the grace of God?" All through the Bible, scriptures reveal that God's response to us is according to our response to truth (James 1:22; Matt. 6:33; Heb. 2:1-3,11:6; Col. 3:25; Eph. 6:8; 1 Thess. 4:1). No, evil behavior cannot stop the grace of God when evil behavior is repented of. Each living soul must willingly turn from sin and turn to God to receive anything (Rev. 22:17). First of all, we've already clearly shown that some don't grasp that grace was given to us to change our behavior. Secondly, our behavior reveals our willingness, or unwillingness, to do, or not do something; and being unwilling to walk in this victorious faith can hinder God's grace in our own lives, for He resists the proud, but gives grace only to the humble. For everything is either received or rejected by the human will. We cannot be willing to receive grace from God and be willing to follow Satan at the same time. One is a road of faith; the other of unbelief. *"No man can serve (nor follow) two masters"* at the same time (2 Cor. 6:1; Gal. 2:21).

Romans 6:16 says:

Paul, in his theology, wrote to the church, *"Know ye not, that to whom ye yield yourselves servants to obey,* **his servants** *ye are to whom yeobey; whether of sin unto death, or of obedience unto righteousness?"* (Rev. 22:17; John 5:6) This was written to believers.

To go back then into *a life* of sin is to follow Satan and is unbelief (1 John 3:8; Eph. 2:2). The warnings in scripture against doing so are many. When God told Israel in the Old Covenant not to turn aside and follow other gods, it was a picture also for us not to turn aside and follow Satan and his ways. Paul said in 1 Timothy 5:15, *"For some are already turned aside after Satan."* And *"She that liveth in [sinful] pleasure is [spiritually] dead while she liveth"* (physically). Death was the result then for choosing to follow Satan and so it is now. And notice too, that He dealt with all churches and church members differently, depending on their works and their keeping, or not keeping His words (Eph. 6:8; Col. 3:25).

In Revelation 3:19 Christ says to His church:

"As many as I love, I rebuke and chasten: be zealous therefore, **and repent.***"* ("Turn from evil and return to Me.") Love rebukes and chastens when people persist in doing wrong. It never tells them they are okay in their sin. It is a false love and false righteousness that comforts people while they live in sin. True love would seek to show them the error and danger of their ways and seek to restore them. *"For whom the Lord loveth he chasteneth, and scourgeth every son whom he receiveth"* (Heb. 12:6; 2 Cor. 7:10).

Those in the Church Who Sin Need to Repent

To teach that there is no need for repentance because one is now in the church is to be deluded by the adversary, and it contradicts Christ's clear message to the churches and all of the teaching of the apostles and prophets. You partake of the cleansing power of the blood of Jesus by repentance and confession of sin to the great High Priest. Satan wants to stop people from doing this, for he wants sin to eventually harden their hearts against the ways of God. He wants them to be deceived by sin, and in the process of time, to use their will to return to a rebellious life once again and incur the death penalty a second time. (See Rom. 1:28,32, 8:12-13; Jude 12.)

If a Christian sins, he needs to repent or he will be dealt with by God. If he continues in sin without repenting, he is heading once again towards spiritual death and will eventually make shipwreck of his faith (1 Tim. 1:19). Although God doesn't desire it, God will allow that person eventually to eat the fruit of their own ways. The Lord said, "*My Spirit shall not always strive with man....*"

So, you cannot be willfully rebelling and living in sin, and receiving grace at the same time. Just as in the beginning of your life of faith, you must turn from sin and reach out to God for forgiveness, then grace restores, cleanses, and sustains. Not because you deserve it or merit it, but because God is merciful and graceful to the repentant soul (2 Pet. 3:9). He owes it to no man, therefore we must let Him set the rules.

In writing to the church in James 5:19-20, James says,

"*Brethren, if **any of you** do err [are misled] from the truth [John 17:17], [stop living by faith and obeying God's moral commandments] and one convert him; let him know, that he which converteth the sinner [the brother that has gone astray into a life of sinning without repenting] from the error of his way shall save **a soul** [that person's soul] from death, and shall hide a multitude of sins.*" Save what from death? A body? No, a soul."*The soul that sinneth, it shall die*" unless it repents and confesses its transgressions and thereby partakes of God's grace and mercy. This doesn't happen every time a person slips and sins, but after time, unconfessed, repeated sinning will harden the heart, sear the conscience, and move the soul back step-by-step into unbelief, and it will finally influence the will to depart from God back to its old ways. It may still maintain its outward show and profession to others when around them, but inwardly the heart has departed from God. This is drawing back from the narrow way to return to the broad road of perdition (2 Pet. 3:7). When the person stops living for God and stops doing the will of God from the heart, and lives only for Satan and self, they have then departed from the living God with an evil heart of unbelief, and they will die again.

Read this next passage carefully and realize it's God's unchanging Word, for in the New Testament there are a number of similar things stated (James 5:19-20), and what was written before was written for our admonition and learning.

The unchangeable Lord says:

*"But if the wicked will turn from all his sins that he hath committed, and keep all my statutes, and do that which is lawful and right, he shall surely live, he shall not die. All his transgressions that he hath committed, **they shall not be mentioned unto him:** in his righteousness that he hath done he shall live. Have I any pleasure at all that the wicked should die? Saith the Lord GOD: and not that he should return from his [sinful] ways, and live? **But when the righteous turneth away from his righteousness, and committeth iniquity, and doeth according to all the abominations that the wicked man doeth, shall he live?** All his righteousness that he hath done shall not be mentioned: in his trespass that he hath trespassed, and in his sin that he hath sinned, in them shall he die. Yet ye say, The way of the Lord is not equal. [Ultra gracists would say the same thing to the Lord.] Hear now, O house of Israel; Is not my way equal? Are not your ways unequal? When a righteous man turneth away from his righteousness, and committeth iniquity, and dieth in them; for his iniquity that he hath done shall he die. Again, when the wicked man turneth away from his wickedness that he hath committed, and doeth that which is lawful and right, he shall save his soul alive. **Because he considereth, and turneth away** from all his transgressions that he hath committed, he shall surely live, he shall not die. [For God can be merciful to all who repent and turn from their evil ways.] Yet saith the house of Israel, The way of the Lord is not equal, O house of Israel, are not my ways equal; **are not your ways unequal? Therefore I will** judge you, O house of Israel, every one according to his ways, saith the Lord God. **Repent, and turn yourselves** from all your transgressions; so iniquity shall not be your ruin"* (your destruction, Ezek. 18:21-30). (See also Acts 3:19,26.) It's obvious by this that no one is predestined as an individual, one way or the other, only God's eternal plan is, but not who's a part of it (Rev. 22:17; Heb. 2:9).

Whoever enters *"into Christ"* by repentance and faith (John 10:9), and continues to abide *"in Him"* (John 15:1-6), is predestined *in Him* as long as they continue in the faith (Col. 1:21-23). Even scriptures such as Romans 8:28-30 say that God foresees those who will willingly choose with their own free will to accept and continue to follow Christ. The promise is to those who love Him and keep His words and commandments. Those whom He sees doing this by foreknowledge He also predestinated to receive glorified bodies, which is part of His predetermined plan to have glorified sons and daughters in the image of His Son. But by foreknowledge He only sees the decisions that free moral agents make. He foreknew some would repent, believe, and obey, but He doesn't make their decisions for them. It can also be saying that He foresaw that some would accept Christ and follow Him, and He predestinated that all who do this would be glorified. But who He sees doing this is left up to the individual (Rev. 22:17). Each must turn from wickedness to righteousness and then their sins won't be mentioned to them again. Then they are in Christ.

Ultra gracists, like Israel, would argue with the Lord and say, it's not fair. Why should we die if we go back to iniquity? They look down at God's righteous decree and judgment. David said, *"The fear of the Lord is clean, enduring forever: the judgments of the Lord are true and righteous altogether"* (Ps. 19:9). There will come, as Paul said, a *"revelation of the righteous judgment of God"* (Rom. 2:5). If they would think for a moment about their stand, they would realize that there could never be a revelation of a righteous judgment of God if all was happening as they suppose. We say with Abraham, "Shall not the judge of all the earth do right?" Certainly He will.

Let's see more of this in the New Covenant. First, Paul said what was written aforetime was written for our admonition and learning. Then second, he also wrote instructions after he strongly rebuked the Corinthian church for their behavior.

In 2 Corinthians 7:9-10 in his letter to the church, Paul writes:

*"Now I rejoice, not that ye were made sorry, but that ye sorrowed **to repentance:** for ye were made sorry after a godly manner, that ye might receive damage by us in nothing. For godly sorrow worketh **repentance that leads to salvation** not to be regretted: but the sorrow of the world worketh death."* Godly sorrow causes people to repent of sin, which then keeps them on the pathway of salvation. It moves them to turn from wickedness and live. All through the New Covenant, this principle of the Lord is shown to be the same. If you turn from evil to righteousness, your sins won't be mentioned to you again. But if you turn from the way of righteousness to evil, your righteousness won't be mentioned to you and your judgment will be worse. Jesus said to one man who was forgiven and healed, *"sin no more lest a worse thing come upon you."* You'll eventually die in your sin except you repent of living in sin. Again, God is merciful to the repentant

soul, but judges any who continues in a course of evil. God *never, ever* said that grace would cover for a person who turns from *"the way of righteousness,"* back to a life of sin. He only promises them a *certain fearful looking for of judgment*, which will devour all adversaries (Heb. 10:26-31). His warnings are given to reveal to us *how He must deal with these things* that we might prepare ourselves and *"flee from the wrath to come"* (Heb. 11:7). *"And every man that hath this hope in him purifieth himself, even as he is pure"* (1 John 3:3).

Acts 3:26

"Unto you first God, having raised up his Son Jesus, **sent him to bless you, in turning away every one of you from his iniquities."** We are only blessed as we turn away from iniquity. (See also Deut. 28:1-14; Psa. 1, 106:3, 119:1-2; Rev. 1:3, 22:14.) The Word teaches us that if we regard iniquity in our hearts, the Lord will not hear us (Ps. 66:18). Blessings are laid out for the obedient, although the goodness of God will bless at times, the ignorant, or those sincere but struggling, in order to lead them to repentance (Rom. 2:4), for He knows every heart. He works at times in this way to show them that it is a good thing to serve Him, and that the *"way of the transgressor is hard."* Always remember that grace is given to change you and enable you to live the way He wants you to live. Then you are blessed (James 1:25). God *only* responds to us the way we respond to Him (2 Sam. 22:26-27; Hosea 4:6; James 4:8; Deut. 31:16-17; Lev. 26:23-24; Mal. 3:7; Matt. 5:7, 10:33; Rev. 3:10; Gal. 6:7; etc.).

2 Timothy 2:25-26

"In meekness instructing those that oppose themselves; **if God peradventure will give them repentance** *to the acknowledging of the truth [which is after godliness, Titus 1:1]; and that they may recover themselves [and come to their senses] out of the snare of the devil [the devil's trap], who are taken captive by him at his will"* (who has caught them by his wiles and are following what he wills).

Repentance and acknowledging of the truth is a necessary part of the doctrine of Christ; a foundational teaching of the church (Heb. 6:1-3). It's the only way for people to recover themselves out of Satan's snare. Don't ever think that you can live contrary to truth and not be in Satan's snare. It's truth or a lie, light or darkness, righteousness or unrighteousness (1 John 2:21). If you try and remove repentance and judgment from the church and Apostolic Doctrine, you remove two of the foundational stones in the doctrine of Christ. Paul said, *"According to the grace of God which is given unto me, as a wise master builder,* **I have laid the foundation, and another buildeth thereon. But let every man take heed how he buildeth thereupon**" (1 Cor. 3:10). We are warned to leave all things as they are written. If you remove repentance, you are trying to build on a partial, crumbling foundation. If you don't leave *all* things as they are written, then you are not teaching what Christ taught, but what *you* think (Deut. 4:2). (See also Prov. 25:19; 2 Tim. 2:2.) Remember that Satan will use some scripture, but never all the scriptures. The only way out of Satan's snares of death then, once you've entered into them, is by repentance and acknowledging of the truth. When the will then turns to God for help, He is *always* there to help and give light (Rom. 10:13).

In 2 Corinthians 12:20-21 Paul wrote to the church at Corinth and said, *"For I fear [for your safety], lest, when I come, I shall not find you such as I would, and that I shall be found unto you such as ye would not: lest there be debates, envyings, wraths, strifes, backbitings, whisperings, swellings, tumults: And lest, when I come again, my God will humble me among you,* **and that I shall bewail [and cry over] many which have sinned already, and have not repented of the uncleanness and fornication and lasciviousness which they have committed.**" *"For many walk, of whom I have told you often, and now tell you even weeping, that they are the enemies of the cross of Christ:* **Whose end is destruction,** *whose God is their belly, and whose glory is in their shame, who mind earthly things"* (Phil. 3:18-19).

Why was Paul so concerned about them repenting if grace would have automatically covered for them, if there were no need for repentance, and if they were all still righteous or predestined to heaven? Did Paul think that all of their future sins were already forgiven? No, he knew for them that to be cleansed they had to repent and confess their sins. He himself, told them only if they judged themselves, they would not be judged.

The false concept of grace taught by some in so many books and in so many places actually goes so far as to turn grace into an open license to sin and to yield to Satan, although, perhaps they would never put it in those words, for then their deceptive doctrine would be too obvious. Yet, in essence, what they are implying is that very same thing, and this is what Satan wants them to believe; that God gives grace so you can now disobey His moral commandments. Is there anything more unscriptural? Is this the solution God came up with? Or, they pridefully believe that others are predestined to be lost, and they themselves, saved? (2 Pet. 3:9; 1 Tim. 2:4). I have never heard anyone who says they believe in predestination of individuals say that they are one of the ones predestined for hell. Well, of course not. Human pride can't have that.

Some of them say that God only sees you through grace no matter what you do or how you behave, and that God has to accept them. Paul didn't think so, nor did any of the other New Testament men of God, nor did the early church fathers of the first centuries. By what authority then, do some men now say or teach such things? By their own authority. No wonder Paul wrote, *"Beware that 'no man' deceive you."* Adam could have said the same thing about grace but it wouldn't have changed anything. It's not a matter of love; it's a legal matter and a matter of God's perfect righteousness and justice. Sin must be judged. If we judge it ourselves, we won't be judged. But if we persist in it without repentance, Paul said there is *a certain fearful looking for of judgment*. So, again, we must always ask ourselves, what saith the Word, for there are no contradictions in it, and it all means exactly what it says. And if your Bible teacher cannot tell you to believe everything in the New Covenant, he is wrong. If a judge has mercy on one for his past driving record and lets him go, can he automatically escape the next time? Is it, "once released, always released"? There is no such thing anywhere in any system of justice, and there is no such thing in the Bible.

CHAPTER ELEVEN

FALSE TEACHERS AND FALSE TEACHINGS IN THE CHURCH

Second Peter 2:1-2

*"But there were false prophets also among the people [in the Old Testament], even as there shall be **false teachers** among you [in the New Covenant], who privily [and secretly] shall bring in [to the church] damnable heresies, even [to the point of] **denying the Lord that bought them**, and bring upon themselves swift destruction. **And many shall follow their pernicious [morally loose and fatal] ways;** by reason of whom the [real] way of truth shall be evil spoken of."*

Pernicious means "lawless; hurtful; deadly ways of going back to unbridled lusts." It means that it brings great ruin to those who follow it. Notice, God said that *many* would follow false teachers. God foresaw the vast impact this false grace teaching would have. One person in our country who has a fundamentalist church of about ten thousand people, even says in one of his books that you could *deny* the Lord and you would still not have the slightest chance of being lost, for says he, "faith is a one time act." He does the very thing Peter warns against. Peter calls it a damnable heresy, for our God never said nor promised any such thing; nor is there any scripture that says faith is a one-time act, but that the *"just shall live by faith."* But again, Peter said that *"many"* would follow these pernicious ways, listening to these teachers. And some ignorant Christians think, "how nice that it's this way," for they erroneously think that they too, can do their thing, and

God is obligated to accept them because of Christ. But God said that eternal salvation is only for those who obey His Son (Heb. 5:9), and that some *"stumble at the Word being disobedient"* (1 Pet. 2:8,11). Notice, Peter said some would even go so far as to teach in their false doctrines that you could "deny" the Lord and still be saved. The swift destruction is not necessarily something seen by others right now in this life, but it can cause instant spiritual blindness as to the real truth and lead to destruction. (See Acts 13:11.)

The Lord would also deny (disown) a person when He comes in His glory if they did so to Him now before men, *"But whosoever shall deny me before men, **him will I also deny before my Father which is in heaven**"* (Matt. 10:33). "Deny" means to "disown." *"Whosoever therefore shall be ashamed of me and of my words in this adulterous and sinful generation; **of him also** shall the Son of man be ashamed, **when he cometh** in the glory of his Father with the holy angels"* (Mark 8:38). Evidently, then, that person who teaches contrary to the Lord here is ignorant of these scriptures, and so are the thousands that listen to him. They follow the deceptive teaching about grace that both Jude and Peter warned against, and have let a sweet talking, but ignorant, man deceive them. Again, we don't question his sincerity or his motivation, God is his judge, but rather, his knowledge of the scriptures. But even this will be forgiven him if the person repents of his damnable heresies. Oh, the mercy of God is great! Every teacher had better make sure he is rightly dividing the Word of Truth. *"My people are destroyed for lack of knowledge: because thou hast rejected knowledge, I will also reject thee, that thou shalt be no priest to me: seeing thou hast forgotten the law of thy God, I will also forget thy children"* (Hosea 4:6).

Here, then, is Peter's teaching concerning the false teaching that says God will allow lawless ways without repentance, and that His grace would cover for them. Notice the similarity between Peter's teaching and Jude's teaching. Both are basically teaching against a false counterfeit concept of grace and the teachers that teach it.

2 Peter 2:4-6

Peter the Apostle says concerning this, *"**If God spared not** the [numerous] angels **that sinned**, but cast them down to hell, and delivered them into chains [and dungeons] of darkness, to be reserved [and kept there] unto judgment; and [God] **spared not** the old world [with millions of human souls in it], but saved Noah the eighth person, a preacher of righteousness [who preached that people must turn to God and live right], bringing in the flood upon the* *world of the ungodly [who lived in sinful ways]; And [God] turning the cities of Sodom and Gomorrah into ashes condemned them [and terminated them]* **making them [thousands and thousands of people] an ensample unto those that after should live ungodly....**" (To live ungodly is to live a life of sin after the flesh without repentance.) God then set their destruction forth as a clear warning and an object lesson for anyone afterwards, in any age, who would live ungodly. Peter implies if he didn't spare others, why would he spare anyone else that chooses to live contrary to His will? His point is clear. The God of the Old Testament is still the God of the New Testament, and He will still deal with all rebels the same. There is no variableness or respect of persons with God.

Don't listen to false teachers or teachings that say God will spare a person while they choose to go back to the world and live ungodly. His longsuffering may, for a while, wait. His goodness will try and lead a person back to repentance. He will give the person space to repent because He's slow to anger, but the outcome of living contrary to Him is always eventually corruption (Gal. 6:7-8), judgment, and finally death if they don't turn back (James 1:14-15). Do not think God loves you more than He did Saul, Korah, Judas, the Egyptians, nor anyone else He's ever judged and cast down to hell. He loves and deals with all people equally. His wrath will judge sin. It's either repent of sin and judge yourself, or you put yourself in a position to receive His wrath against evil. (See Eph. 5:5-7.) Paul wrote in Romans 11:22, *"Behold therefore the goodness and severity of God: on them which fell [away from God], severity; but toward thee, goodness, if thou continue in his goodness: otherwise thou also shalt be cut off."* If you continue with Him, He will continue with you. If you walk contrary to Him, He will walk contrary to you (Lev. 26:23-24).

The Lord had Paul write to the brethren in Romans 8:12-13 and said:

"Therefore **brethren** *[fellow Christians], we are debtors, not to the flesh, to live after the flesh. For if ye live after the flesh [in sinful pleasures rather than living by faith], ye shall die [spiritually, for all died physically regardless]: but if ye through the Spirit do mortify the deeds of the body, ye shall live"* (forever). As stated, sin, if unconfessed and not repented of, will eventually destroy the faith life (1 Tim. 1:19), then grace can no longer be received (Rom. 5:2); for it must be willingly received, and it must be continued in by faith (Rev. 22:13; Acts 13:43). Jude spoke in his epistle of people losing their fruit, being uprooted, and becoming *twice* dead (vs. 12). There is therefore, no such thing as irresistible grace, nor respect of persons with God. He judges all according to their own actions (Rom. 14:12).

Let the extreme gracists come forth with as many clear *scriptures* concerning their perspective, without contradicting any of these passages; they cannot. For they only have human reasoning based on a few twisted texts and their own big drawn-out philosophical view on this subject. They neither have Bible love, faith, nor grace as a foundation for their doctrines, but, rather, are ignorantly promoting a counterfeit doctrine of devils (1 Tim. 4:1). And you will notice that they constantly use human rationalization, reasoning, and great intellectual arguments in their teachings, yet very few scriptures, except for their carefully hand-picked texts. And they ignore all else that Christ and His apostles taught which contradict them. For some of them, their false doctrine just makes them special, favored sinners who can never be lost no matter what evil they do and refuse to repent of. But there will come a great eye-opening at the judgment seat when there is a revelation of the righteous judgment of God. There is no security in the false concept of grace.

Second Peter 2:18 Listen to what else Peter says about these teachers:

"For when they [these misguided teachers who teach grace will automatically cover over a life of disobedience] speak great swelling words of **vanity** *[big empty words and promises in their doctrines to their listeners], they allure [to themselves] through the lusts of the flesh [using lust and sinful desires as the bait], through much wantonness, those that were just escaping from them who live in error."* (With their phrases that really have no scriptural meaning and their teaching that says you don't need to live righteously, but God will still respond as though you do, they lead people back to their former lusts and errors they had once repented of; and by this, they lure people to listen to them, but they don't speak for God. They only speak empty promises saying things God never said, and promising things God never promised.) Peter said there were *many* false prophets in the Old Testament, which led the people astray from God and His ways with similar sayings and promises. Here he has shown that there would also be many false teachers and ministers among Christians who do and teach similar things (James 3:1). So it is definitely happening among us, yea, all around us! Again, all you need do is read 2 Peter 2 and then the book of Jude's teaching concerning false grace, and you'll see their emphasis is the same. Let's continue. (See 1 John 4:1; Matt. 7:15-21.)

Verse 19

"While they [these teachers] promise them [unstable Christians] liberty [and freedom] they themselves are the servants of [moral] corruption: for whatever

overcomes a man, of the same is he brought in bondage" (and becomes a slave of). A man is a slave and a servant to whatever overcomes him.

These false teachers promise liberty but cannot produce real liberty by their teaching. For real freedom is freedom from sin, not freedom from the condemnation of it while you live in it. There is no such thing as that which they promise (Rom. 8:1). You'll notice that false teachers in our day teach the exact same false doctrines as those that Peter and Jude dealt with, for the devil and his wiles are also the same. How cleverly Satan disguises his doctrines and by it *"the way of truth is evil spoken of."* Peter called them *"wells without water."* Jude called them *"clouds without rain"* implying that the promises of their doctrine being a refreshing, are really empty promises void of the Spirit, for the Spirit will always only lead us into a holy walk (Rom. 8:4). The people who listen to these teachers may be enthusiastic at first, thinking they found some new kind of freedom, but will eventually dry up spiritually if they think they can live contrary to God and still be blessed and produce good fruit (Isa. 1:19-20). They will end up with the form of godliness, but deny its power and will be known by their fruit (Heb. 6:7-8).

In John 8:34-36

"Jesus answered them, Verily, verily, I say unto you, Whosoever committeth sin is the servant [and slave] of sin. And the servant [the slave] abideth not in the [master's] house [of God] forever: but the Son abideth ever. If the Son therefore shall make you free [from sin's power], ye shall be free indeed." This means, freedom from being sin's servant (Rom. 6:18). This is real liberty. We are now free to serve God once again.

2 Peter 2:20-21

*"For if after they [these teachers in the church who teach a counterfeit grace and lawless ways, or those who have followed them] have escaped the [moral] pollutions of the world through the knowledge of the Lord and Savior Jesus Christ, they are **again** [a second time] entangled therein, **and overcome** [to where they would no longer repent and turn back to God for mercy], the latter end is worse with them than the beginning. **For it had been better for them not to have known the [Lord's] way of righteousness, than, after they have known it, to turn from the holy commandment [that was] delivered unto them."***

For one who is a Christian to knowingly turn from the way of righteousness and go back to the way of unrighteousness to live in the pollutions of the world (which is run by Satan), thinking they are still in grace, is to be greatly deluded by the adversary. For their actions show they are not willing to abide in the grace of God, nor continue to receive this overcoming grace (Eph. 2:2). God certainly will respond according to people's choices, actions, and lives whether they be Christian or not, because He has made man a free moral agent, and man always retains his free moral agency even after salvation; and God sovereignly chose it to be this way, for it is the only, truly just way. We could probably give you a hundred New Testament scriptures to prove this. God *always* responds to us depending on how we respond to the law of love which fulfills His commandments and our individual responses to His Gospel (Gal. 6:7-9; Rom. 13:8-10). Besides this, a gift once received can later be rejected. Most of the world is rejecting the gift of eternal life, but yet, God's grace is offering it to them. Jesus *"by the grace of God tasted death for every man"* (Heb. 2:9). Jesus said, *"Preach the gospel to **every** creature"* (Mark 16:15). Yet, if they don't repent, turn from Satan, and turn to God, and use their will to receive what He offers, they will be lost forever regardless of His love, His will, or His grace. The same is true if one receives, but later turns from God, uses his will to go back to the world and back to Satan once again, and to the things they were formerly saved out of (James 4:4). Paul said they then, *"forfeit the grace of God"* (Heb. 12:14-15, literal). (See also Heb. 3:12-14; Rom. 11:22; John 15:6.)

1 Timothy 4:1

*"Now the Spirit speaketh expressly, that in the latter times **some shall depart from the faith**, giving heed to seducing spirits, and doctrines of devils."* (This has to be speaking of Christians who once heard and lived according to the Christian faith.) You cannot depart from somewhere you have never been.

Some will depart from the real faith (our most holy faith as Jude said), because of believing other doctrines and teachings made up by demons and promoted by men (1 John 4:1, 21). Remember that God will always only promote good and an increase in godliness. Satan craftily promotes unrighteousness and excuses for it even using Bible words and phrases, which he has twisted the meaning of to suit his own purposes. Then he attacks the real with the counterfeit, labeling true grace as legalistic because it's not morally loose. *"And no marvel; for Satan himself is transformed into an angel of light. Therefore it is no great thing if his ministers also be transformed as the ministers of righteousness; whose end shall be according to their works"* (2 Cor. 11:14-15). According to what? True grace empowers us to live righteously. *"Grace be to you and peace from God the*

*Father, and from our Lord Jesus Christ, who gave himself for our sins, **that he might deliver us from this present world**, according to the will of God and our Father"* (Gal. 1:3-4).

1 Timothy 6:3-4 the apostle Paul clearly states,

*"If any man teach otherwise, and consent not to wholesome words, even the words of our Lord Jesus Christ, **and to the doctrine which is according to godliness**; he is proud, knowing nothing, but doting about questions and strifes of words, whereof cometh envy, strife, railings, evil surmisings."*

Christ's doctrine always shows that you must live godly. *If any teach otherwise, …he is proud, knowing nothing…"* Notice, those who don't stay with what Jesus taught and the doctrine of godliness, stir up strife and suspicion of those who preach the real Gospel. They think grace okays godlessness and evil behavior but the Bible teaches just the opposite. Grace, in truth, frees us from those things. Paul said that a person that teaches such contrary things is *"proud, knowing nothing,"* and *"their damnation is just."* So if they don't know this basic fundamental teaching, do they really know other important things? Think about it! You are responsible for who you listen to. You, dear Reader, are to *"prove all things and hold fast to that which is good."*

Titus 1:1

*"Paul, a servant of God, and an apostle of Jesus Christ, according to the faith of God's elect, **and the acknowledging of the truth which is after godliness."***

Paul knew that sin was faith's worst enemy, for all sin originates with the influence of the devil (Eph. 4:27). He said, *"You have not yet resisted unto blood striving against sin."* Will you acknowledge too that the truth teaches godliness, not godlessness? This too, is the Apostles' Doctrine.

So then, grace must be continued in and received by faith, and grace is always in agreement with the doctrine which is according to godliness (Acts 13:43). You cannot turn to God for grace and mercy until you've turned from the evil one and sin. So the solution is always repentance and faith (Acts 20:21) for any permanent blessings, and by repentance and faith, you obtain mercy and grace (Heb. 4:16).

Sure, we know *"by grace we are saved **through faith**,"* and that's just the point. We didn't deserve any of this salvation, but the way grace provided was a *"narrow way,"* which is the way of forgiveness, obedience, righteousness, and so on, plus the ability to walk in it. You have to turn from sin in order to receive and you must operate in faith to receive grace. For whatsoever *is not of faith* is sin. Sin and faith cannot mix. So repent of sin and then you can operate in faith and partake of grace, which gives you the ability to serve God. Paul said, *"faith worketh by love"*; and John wrote, *"And this is love that we walk [and live] after his commandments"* (2 John 6). Remember, love fulfills the law. As we walk in real love, then our faith works, but if we walk in sin, it's like a car without gasoline; it won't run. You're missing a key ingredient. You can profess that it will run without gasoline all you want, but it won't (James 2:20, 26). So God says that *"faith without works is dead also."*

Romans 11:22

Paul wrote in his doctrine, *"Behold therefore the goodness and severity of God: on them, which fell, severity; but toward thee, goodness, **if thou continue in his goodness: otherwise thou also shalt be cut off."***

A person who has once begun in the goodness of God by accepting Jesus as Lord must continue in it, or else they will suffer the consequences of their own actions (Rom. 11:22). If they persist in rebellion to the end of their life, they also will be cut off just as multitudes were in days gone by. *"For Moses truly said unto the fathers, a prophet shall the Lord your God raise up unto you of your brethren, like unto me; **him shall ye hear in all things** whatsoever he shall say unto you. And it shall come to pass, that every soul, which will not hear [and heed, Matt. 7:24-27] that prophet, **shall be destroyed** from among the people [Luke 6:46]. Yea, and all the prophets from Samuel and those that follow after, as many as have spoken, have likewise foretold of these days"* (Acts 3:22-24). Any teacher who teaches you that you need not listen to the teachings of Christ in the Gospels, is a false teacher. Moses and Peter both said that *"every soul"* which would not listen to Christ *"in all things"* **shall be destroyed**. (See also Matt. 28:20; Heb. 2:3; John 12:48-49; Luke 16:16.)

Hebrews 12:28-29

*"Wherefore we receiving a kingdom which cannot be moved, **let us have grace, whereby we may serve God acceptably** with reverence and godly fear: For our God is a consuming fire."* To "serve" means "to work for and obey the duties and orders given"; "To work for one as a servant"; "To give obedience and reverent honor to God." Now we can see what Bible grace really is and what it's given for. Men may have their own private interpretation, but this is God's definition.

Titus 2:11-12

Paul, in his theology, wrote, *"For the [real] **grace of God** that bringeth salvation [deliverance from the fall] hath appeared to all men. **Teaching us*** *that, denying ungodliness and worldly lusts, we should live soberly, righteously, and godly, in this present world"* (if we want to go to heaven, Rev. 22:14). Paul went on to say that Christ came to *"redeem us from all iniquity"* (evil behavior). This is redemption.

This is the real grace that brings salvation. A grace that says a person can live in sin and evil and doesn't have to repent, obey God, love God, confess their sins, or that you are one of the predestined ones, so do as you please, doesn't bring salvation, but eternal death. It is a deception of Satan; it is the old deceiver's counterfeit. Don't listen to anyone who teaches such a doctrine for they have become a mouthpiece for the serpent in this area, but pray for them that their eyes may be opened, that they might repent of promoting the serpent's teaching before it's too late. Real faith always produces living according to God's Word (Rom. 1:17-18).

Don't be lifted up with pride thinking you couldn't possibly be deceived (1 Cor. 3:18). Only the word of Christ can enable us to overcome the father of lies. *"Let the Word of Christ dwell in you richly in all wisdom; teaching and admonishing one another in psalms and hymns and spiritual songs, singing with grace in your hearts to the Lord"* (Col. 3:16). A thing is not so, just because a person believes it is so. *"If therefore the light that is in thee be darkness, how great is that darkness!"* (Matt. 6:23)

Matthew 1:21

"And she shall bring forth a son, and thou shalt call his name Jesus: for He shall save his people from their sins." (Not IN their sins.) He came to release us from the law of sin and death, which before controlled us (Rom. 7–8).

Romans 6:14

Paul, in his instructions to the church wrote, *"For sin shall not have dominion over you: for ye are not under the law, but under grace."* Sin's dominion over us, He said, is broken by grace.

Again in 2 Corinthians 12:9 the Lord says,

*"**My grace** is sufficient for thee: for **my strength** is made perfect in weakness. Most gladly therefore will I rather glory in my infirmities, **that the power of Christ** may rest upon me."*

Therefore, again we state that the interpretation of some concerning what grace is, is totally wrong. But believing it the way they do as just unmerited favor, creates a false peace, a false faith, and a false security just like those involved in Christian Science who deny the reality of sin and Satan. As Peter put it, it's "vanity." But it will not bring the true blessing of God, nor will it help people to overcome when they are judged. Yes, we have liberty but it's a freedom from the power of sin as we walk by faith, and a freedom from the legalistic works of the law. But God says, use not your liberty as an occasion to (follow) the flesh and, *"make no provision [Paul said] for the flesh"* (Gal. 5:13-21). Did Paul then by his teaching on grace make any provision for the flesh? Certainly not! He said, *"And have no fellowship with the unfruitful works of darkness, but rather reprove them. For it is a shame even to speak of those things which are done of them in secret"* (Eph. 5:11-12).

These misguided teachers and this wrong teaching on grace is a corrupt doctrine, an empty well, a false perception, a lawless way that fights the conviction of the Holy Ghost labeling the sanctifying work of the Holy Spirit, "condemnation." It actually makes a provision for the flesh, and those who are deceived by it will have a real problem hearing the true Gospel, which is always according to godliness, except they repent (2 Tim. 2:25-26).

God *never, ever* said, nor ever implied, that grace or imputed righteousness covers over all sin automatically, as some teach. There is not one scripture that says He does, but all show He responds to us according to our faith, our actions, our behavior, repentance, and confession (Eph. 6:7-8; Col. 3:25; Gal. 6:7-8). Even initial salvation comes when *we repent and believe*, even though we are saved by grace.

Confess Your Sins

John wrote to Christians in First John 1:9:

"If we confess our sins, He is [then] faithful and just to forgive us our sins and to cleanse us from all unrighteousness." (See 1 John 2:1.)

God *never, ever* said that His grace would cause Him to see a person one way regardless of how that person lives or acts. But His Word does teach that if we confess our sins and are cleansed by the blood, then He sees us with a robe of perfect righteousness on (Jude 23). We must though, as Jude said, hate even *"the garment spotted [stained] by the flesh."* When sin is confessed, instantly, perfect righteousness is yours. The blood washes away all stains and purges the conscience. This is what grace has provided. When you have done this, then, you can operate in faith. The human will is always free, so it must willingly, freely receive. Jesus *"by the grace of God tasted death for every man"*; but, as we've stated before, it is only those who are willing to turn from Satan and turn to God to receive the grace provided who will be saved. Once received, the person continues to receive and walk in it if they continue to willingly live for God by faith, even though they may have some struggles with the flesh. *"Who are kept by the power of God through faith unto salvation ready to be revealed in the last time"* (1 Pet. 1:5). So we are kept by God's power only as we walk by faith, but faith and sin do not mix, and *"faith worketh by love."*

Let us never teach our children, or our youth, nor anyone else that they can go out and live like the world, and that grace will automatically cover for them. To do so would be to open a large door for the devil to work on them and try and convince them to turn against the ways of God (Eph. 6:1-3). To teach this would be to mislead the children and possibly send them to hell. Jesus said, *"But whoso shall offend [and put a rock of stumbling in the path of] one of these little ones which believe in me, it were better for him that a millstone were hanged about his neck, and that he were drowned in the depth of the sea"* (Matt. 18:6). "Offend" here means *"to cause them to stumble away from Him."*

1 John 3:18-22

"My little children, let us not love in word, neither in tongue; but in deed and in truth, and hereby we [will] **know that we are [really] of the truth**, *and shall assure our hearts before him. For if our heart condemn us, God is greater than our heart, and knoweth all things. [He knows what's going on in every person.]* **Beloved, if our heart condemn us not, then have we confidence toward God. And whatsoever we ask, we receive of him, because we keep his commandments, and do those things that are pleasing in his sight."** *Because why?* This false teaching about grace says your heart can be assured before Him, regardless of how you live. Nevertheless, it is obvious that God does respond to us all in agreement with our lives and actions as we shall further abundantly, clearly point out.

Now we know He blots out every sin that's confessed and repented of, and instantly a person is on holy ground because of His great mercy, and that his sin (that person's) will not be remembered any more. But answered prayer also is seen to be in response to obedience to His commands and by doing what's pleasing in His sight. *"For the eyes of the Lord are over the righteous, and his ears are open unto their prayers: but the face of the Lord is against them that do evil"* (1 Pet. 3:12). *"And when ye stand praying, forgive, if ye have ought against any: that your Father also which is in heaven may forgive you your trespasses"* (Mark 11:25). And remember, as we've shown, obeying His commands and doing what's pleasing in His sight is faith (Heb. 11). Jesus kept His Father's commandments, prayed, fasted, attended the synagogue, and always pleased the Father so this *must be* faith, for *"whatsoever isn't of faith is sin,"* and Jesus never sinned. (See John 8:29, 15:10; Heb. 11:6.) So, some things we do can grieve God and some things can please God (Gen. 6:5-6; Heb. 13:16). This has been so in every generation and really is the only way it could be (Ps. 100:5). And God has always blessed and rewarded those that please Him. *"And he that sent me is with me: the Father hath not left me alone; **for I do** always those things that please him"* (John 8:29). *"Behold, I set before you this day a blessing and a curse; A blessing, if ye obey the commandments of the Lord your God, which I command you this day: And a curse, if ye will not obey the commandments of the Lord your God, but turn aside out of the way which I command you this day, to go after other gods, which ye have not known"* (Deut. 11:26-28). And as we've already shown, Jesus, the author of our faith, obeyed the Father's commandments and did His will (John 15:10). And there is only *"one faith,"* and one true example, and that is Christ (1 Cor. 11:1). And anytime you obey His Word, it's faith. *"Then spake Jesus again unto them, saying, I am the light of the world: he that followeth me shall not walk in darkness, but shall have the light of life"* (John 8:12).

Jude's and Peter's Teaching Concerning False Grace

Because of their importance, here again, we will re-emphasize a few of the things that the Lord has revealed about misapplying His grace.

Jude 3-6, 12-13, 22-23

*"Beloved, when I gave all diligence to write unto you of the common salvation, it was needful for me to write unto you, and exhort you that ye should earnestly contend for [and vigorously defend] the faith which was once delivered unto the saints. For there are certain men crept in unawares [among us], who were before of old ordained to this condemnation [God revealed that they would be here], ungodly [immoral] **men, turning the grace of our God** [which God gave us to overcome a life of sin] into lasciviousness [an excuse to live in sin] and [thereby] denying the only Lord God, and our Lord Jesus Christ."* They deny Christ by denying what He said and taught (Titus 1:16).

In John 12:48

Jesus said, *"He that **rejecteth me, and receiveth not my words,** hath One that judgeth him: **the word that I have spoken, the same shall judge him in the last day.**"* In other words, the judgment will be according to what's written. It will be according to Christ's doctrine even if people don't believe it that way. Christ said, *"The scriptures CANNOT be broken"*; they can't be changed. It all has to be as it is written, and so it shall be.

Jude continues to warn his readers not to yield to the false concept of grace that some have sown as tares into the church. He said, *"I will therefore put you in remembrance, though ye once knew this [by the scriptures], how that the Lord, having saved the people [who had put faith in the Passover, a type of Christ's sacrifice] out of the land of Egypt [a type of the world], afterward destroyed them that believed not. [They no longer lived for Him and walked by faith, but in all probability they confessed that they still believed that He was God, James 2:19.] And the angels [once in God's grace and favor] which kept not their first estate, but left [and departed from] their own habitation [the proper boundaries set for them by God because of believing Satan's lies and yielding to his influence instead of God's], He hath reserved in everlasting chains under darkness unto the judgment of the great day."*

God then, through Jude, reveals that He deals with things the same today as in times past if people don't repent. Jude said that these false teachers which teach such things about grace and teach that you could live wrong, *"are spots (blemishes) in your feasts of charity [Christian gatherings], when they feast with you, feeding themselves without fear [the fear of God]: clouds they are without water [the Spirit], [promising refreshing rain but they are empty clouds], carried about of winds [of doctrines, Eph. 4:14]; trees whose fruit [they once had] withereth, without fruit, twice [spiritually] dead, [their faith] plucked up by the roots; raging [restless] waves of the sea [out of their own mouths they are], foaming out their own shame [as they teach such things]; wandering stars [they too like shooting stars, who burn bright for a while but then go out and have gone back into darkness leaving the paths of righteousness], to whom is reserved the blackness of darkness forever"* (because they rejected the light they had once received). Jude says in verse 10, that they (these people who've chosen this route) malign whatever they do not understand; and like irrational animals they follow Cain's path who listened to the wicked one and left what is right. Like Balaam, they turned from doing right in God's sight to selfish gain; and they are also like Korah, who rebelled against Moses (God's chosen leader); these also rebel against God-ordained authorities and they'll now share Korah's doom. *This,* dear Reader, is serious business.

Swept along by winds of teachings, they are trees that no longer bear fruit, doubly dead, with their faith torn up by the roots; wild waves foaming out shameful deeds of disgrace, teaching an unholy faith; stars which have wandered from their course. He said these people that choose that course are forever doomed to utter darkness. *"And this is the condemnation [the basis for the judgment], that light is come into the world, and **men loved darkness rather than light, because their deeds** [Greek:*

*'works'; and, 'behavior'] were evil. For every one that doeth evil hateth the light, neither cometh to the light, **lest his deeds** [works and behavoir] should be reproved"* (John 3:19-20). Can we love evil then and love God at the same time?

Why do extreme gracists, if they are Christian (which I'm sure some of them are), even want to continue in sin or fight for their right to continue in it? Something is wrong with that attitude (Phil. 4:8); seriously wrong. *"And of some have compassion, making a difference: And others save with fear, pulling them out of the fire [of hell]; hating even the [holy] garment spotted [and stained] by the flesh."*

The Lord had Jude and Peter write about people and teachers creeping into the church with a false doctrine about grace. He knew there would be misinterpretations of it and that some people would abuse it. Even in Jude's day there had already come a false doctrine, which turned grace into a cloak for lawlessness as though grace would somehow cover for sin automatically, as long as you said you were a Christian, or said you were a part of the church. Jude's whole point in his letter was that God judged Israel after He saved them when they crossed certain boundaries and refused to repent. And God judged the angels when they left their proper estate and followed Satan's rebellion, and He set the destruction of Sodom as an example to all those who would leave certain natural boundaries and afterwards *live ungodly*. His obvious point is this, that He will do the same today with anyone else regardless of their profession. This warning was written to Christians. *This same false, cunningly crafted doctrine cropped up again right after the Reformation.* Large volumes of books filled with devilish and human philosophy have been written to persuade people not to believe all of the New Covenant, but rather, a false concept of grace.

It is a dangerous doctrine clothed in beautiful language promoted as magnifying the grace of God, but it really substitutes a human view of grace and a doctrine of devils in place of Bible grace, and it totally dishonors Bible grace and God's righteousness. It is so dangerous because it can actually deceive people and lead them straight to hell even when they think all is well. This is why Peter called it a damnable heresy. And besides all this, if one believed in such "irresistible grace," or "predestination," as some ultra gracists do, regardless of how one lives, he would never really know he was one of the predestined ones until he was actually in heaven. What if he was predestined to be a Judas at the last hours of his life and wasn't one of the chosen ones after all? What kind of comfort and security is there in that?

Paul also said that there would be false apostles who are not really apostles but counterfeits masquerading as ministers who taught righteousness, proclaiming themselves as those who bring truth.

2 Corinthians 11:14

*"And no marvel; for Satan himself is transformed into an angel of light. Therefore it is no great thing [no surprise] if **his ministers** also be transformed [and masquerade] as the ministers of righteousness; whose end shall be according to their works"* (vs. 15). (They will one day get what their deeds deserve.) Look at it this way, if we were wrong about this (which we are not, as is obvious by these numerous scriptures), but for sake of argument, we'd have nothing to lose but just be blessed for doing what's right as the Word so clearly promises (for we too, know that we have been born again and according to the ultra gracists, couldn't lose our salvation regardless of what we did or how we lived); but if the ultra gracists are wrong (which they are), they could lose out on eternal salvation if they didn't live for God, and the teachers of it would face strong and severe judgment (James 3:1) for leading others astray. (See Matt. 18:6-7.) An ultra gracist, who says that no believer could lose salvation, couldn't then make us lose it no matter how upset they got with us for exposing their false concept of grace. We know that no man can pluck us out of God's hand. The only way out is to walk out and walk no more with Him, which we will never do. There is eternal security as long as you keep the faith and keep following the Lord by obeying Him (Heb. 5:9). These are His conditions. The conditions grace has laid down. Don't substitute man's definition of grace for God's definition. When a person willingly chooses to depart back again to live in the pollutions of the world, he has then made a reverse choice and God respects man's right to choose (Josh. 24:14-15; Prov. 1:23-33).

Now, Paul said concerning false apostles, they come giving their view of imputed or positional righteousness saying, *no matter how you live,* you're still righteous. But Paul, in his true doctrine, said, *"Awake to righteousness and sin not, for some have not the knowledge of God."* Those who don't understand that God gave us the gift of being able to live righteously by grace and the gift of His Holy Spirit have misinterpreted God's Word, and thought imputed righteousness means you can sin *a lot.* (See Rom. 8:4; Ezek. 36:27.) Of course, we believe in our positional standing and righteousness in Christ as long as we abide in Him and not follow after a life of sin (1 John 3:4-8). And we do believe in the tremendous miracle-working power of the blood of Jesus, which cleanses away all confessed sin instantly. And that because of the blood, God deals with us just as if we'd never sinned, but this is all partaken of by repentance when necessary and by faith, just as the scriptures teach. And, again, we don't believe that if one sins, he's automatically lost until he confesses, but rather, if he continues in sin without repentance, he will eventually harden his heart and sear his conscience and shipwreck his faith. He then may willfully depart from the living God with an evil heart of unbelief and no longer live for God. As with Lucifer, when self-will replaces God's will, then the person will eat the fruit of their own ways. Lucifer too, fell by his own will (Isa. 14:12-14; Ezek. 28:11-19; John 8:44).

1 Peter 1:14-17 Listen again to the Lord's doctrine.

*"**As obedient children**, not fashioning yourselves according to the former lusts in your ignorance: but as he which hath called you is holy, so be ye holy in all manner of conversation [behavior]; because it is written, Be ye holy; for I am holy. **And if ye call on the Father, who without respect of persons judgeth according to every man's work, pass the time of your sojourning here [in the earth] in fear**"* (a real reverence for God). For you have numerous examples in the Bible of how He dealt with all unrepentant rebels in times past.

Many who promote an extreme view on grace are critical and resistant to any who don't see it their way. Thinking they have a special insight or revelation on some super grace, they become unreceptive to any teaching of the Word that doesn't agree with their doctrine regardless of how many scriptures contradict them. This is the effect that deception has over a person's soul, no matter who that person is. Jesus said, *"IF therefore the light that is in thee be [really] darkness, how great is that darkness!"* Some have come to the place where they cannot endure the sound doctrine of Christ which is always according to godliness, but search for seeming proof texts they can twist to fit their views. Peter the Apostle wrote, *"And account that the longsuffering of our Lord is salvation; even as our beloved brother Paul also according to the wisdom given unto him hath written unto you; As also in all his epistles, speaking in them of these things; in which are some things hard to be understood, **which they that are unlearned and unstable wrest [twist], as they do also the other scriptures, unto their own destruction.**Ye therefore, beloved, seeing ye know these things before, beware lest ye also, being led away with the error of the wicked [who twist the scriptures in their teachings], fall from your own steadfastness"* (2 Pet.

3:15-17). The light of the truth will always make the darkness of error flee, and those who don't want the true Word will be driven from the light and the presence of it if it is preached.

Second Timothy 4:1-4

Paul wrote, *"I charge thee therefore before God, and the Lord Jesus Christ, who shall judge the quick and the dead at his appearing and his kingdom; Preach the word; be instant in season, out of season;* **reprove, rebuke, exhort with all longsuffering and doctrine. For the time will come when they will not endure sound doctrine** *[many people won't want to listen to the truth];* **but after their own lusts** *[to gratify their own evil desires and inclinations] shall* **they heap** *[search out and gather] to* **themselves teachers** *[who teach them what they want to hear], having itching ears [they'll want their ears tickled]; And* **they shall turn away their ears from the truth** *[and they will refuse to listen to the truth which is always according to godliness any longer], and shall be turned unto fables"* (stories and fictitious doctrines made up by men).

Brethren, we must stay right with the Apostles' Doctrine. Paul said that people will want to hear doctrines which say they can continue in their own lusts, and they will then *turn away their ears* from the truth which is always after godliness. If the Bible speaks of this category of people, then be assured there must be some who do fall into this category. Be not ignorantly among them. But rather, be like the early disciples in Acts 2:42: *"And they continued steadfastly* **in the apostles' doctrine** *and fellowship, and in breaking of bread, and in prayers."*

Extreme Grace

Some, having an extreme view of grace pulling some scriptures out of Romans, presume their version is so because they pull a few scriptures out of context and they think it is so. But it will not be our presumptions which will judge us in the last day, but what Christ has actually said in His complete doctrine. Whose doctrine are you continuing in? Whose disciple are you? What sect in Christendom do you say you belong to? This is written so that you continue in the "Apostles' Doctrine," and contend for the real faith, our *"most holy faith,"* and not some human made doctrine. Just read out loud to yourself everything Jesus and the apostles taught, and say after each statement, "I believe that, and I believe it's true today." *Ultra gracists and others in heresy can't do this.* But if you rightly divide the Word of Truth, *you can,* for it *never* contradicts itself.

Again, let us repeat what Jesus said in John 12:47-48, Jesus said:

*"And if any man hear my words, and believe not, I judge him not: for I came not to judge the world, but to save the world. He that rejecteth me, and receiveth not my words [My teachings and instructions], hath one that judgeth him: the word [the teaching] that **I have spoken, the same shall judge him in the last day**."* So, don't listen to those who say we need not heed Christ's teaching in the Gospels. Jesus is the truth, and truth never changes. It was Jesus speaking both in the Gospels and in the Epistles. There is only one Lord, and only one faith, and Jesus is the author and finisher of it all. And remember, *"Grace and truth came by Jesus Christ,"* and after all is said and done, He will have the final word (John 1:1). The judgment *will* be according to what Christ taught. Paul said, *the Gospel first* began to be spoken by the Lord *and then* by the apostles (Heb. 2:3). Paul said what he wrote were the *"commandments of the Lord"* (Jesus Christ). It's all *one Gospel* message. (See Gal. 1:6-11 and Luke 16:16.) Preach no other Gospel!

Listen to Jesus, the Teacher of Truth

Matthew 13:36-43

"Then Jesus sent the multitude away, and went into the house: and his disciples came unto him, saying, Declare unto us the parable of the tares of the field. He answered and said unto them, He that soweth the good seed is the Son of man: the field is the world; the good seed are the children of the kingdom; but the tares [who look just like the wheat] are the children of the wicked one; The enemy that sowed them [in among the church] is the devil; the harvest is the end of the world; and the reapers are the angels. As therefore the tares are gathered and burned in the fire; so shall it be in the end of this world." (Here's His revelation.) ***"The Son of man shall send** forth his angels, and they shall gather out of his kingdom [all who profess that they are a part of His Kingdom] all that offend [and all who lead others to do wrong] and them which 'do' iniquity [and live in sin]; And shall cast them into a furnace of fire: there shall be wailing and gnashing of teeth [and bitter regret]. Then shall the righteous (who do not live for iniquity but live for the will of God) shine forth as the sun in the kingdom of their Father. Who hath ears to hear, let him hear."* Do you have ears to hear (John 5:28-29)?

First John 2:29

John wrote, *"If ye know that he is righteous, ye know that every one that doeth righteousness is born of him."* For being grafted into Him we produce His fruit (Phil. 1:11).

Some think that as long as they *call* themselves Christians and profess an imputed righteousness, they are okay. They presume, just as the Pharisees of old did, *saying, "We are Abraham's children,"* as though by virtue of their *saying* they were connected to Abraham, they were saved. John the Baptist said, *"And think not **to say within yourselves**, We have Abraham to our father, for I say unto you, that God is able of these stones to raise up children unto Abraham: And now also **the ax is laid unto the root of the trees: therefore every tree [every individual] which bringeth not forth good fruit is hewn down, and cast into the fire.**"* John said, a person saying something is not enough. There must come forth good fruit (Matt. 3:9-10). Jesus said if they were (really) Abraham's children and had his kind of faith, *"they would **do the works** of Abraham."* That is, their lives would be changed by the Abraham kind of faith just as his was, for Abraham obeyed God, kept His commands and His statutes (Gen. 18:17-19; James 2:20-26). He is the father of those who have this kind of faith (Gal. 3:7)."*Because that Abraham obeyed my voice, and kept my charge, my commandments, my statutes, and my laws"* (Gen. 26:5). God said He'd bless Abraham.

Grace clauses in any document only go so far as what's written in the contract. Presumptions concerning them won't stand up in any court of law. (Read Romans 1:28-32.) We must believe in all that God revealed about grace and why it's given.

It's true that we don't obtain salvation by our merits, but by Christ, His provision, and His power, *when we repent* of sin and believe. This is the beginning of the life of faith (John 1:12). He saved us from our lost, spiritually dead, and polluted condition, and broke Satan's and sin's legal hold on us when we turned from Satan and turned to Him. We did not earn this or deserve this. We were saved by the power of His grace. Then we must let Christ set the rules. He said if you repent and confess your sins (you're yielding to Satan and the world's enticements) after this, they will then be cleansed away and blotted out.You then keep yourself in position to continue to receive of His grace through your faith and your willingness to follow Him; but beware, lest as Paul wrote, *"any man forfeit the grace of God"* (Heb. 12:14-17). (So we continue on with Him by repentance when necessary, and by faith.) We were as sheep gone astray, but now we have returned to follow the Good Shepherd in paths of righteousness. He said that His true sheep *"follow Him,"* and He never leads one to sin. If we turn from this *"way of righteousness"* as Peter said, we turn away from Him who is *the way* to heaven; and we also, then, turn away from the truth and the life (John 14:6).

Hebrews 5:9

*"And being made perfect, he became the author of eternal salvation **unto all that obey him.**"* Once we've been saved by grace out of the world's polluted system, God expects us to stay out of it and obey His Son. He's given us grace to do so. We only provide the willingness and the faith to obey.

Jesus, the teacher of truth said in Matthew 7:21,

*"Not every one **that saith** unto me, Lord, Lord, **shall enter into the kingdom of heaven**; but he that doeth the will of my Father which is in heaven."* ("Doing" is behavior; it's action, and it's living the life of faith.) This statement is absolutely clear and just means what it says (1 John 2:15-17).

Luke 6:46

*"And **why call** ye me, Lord, Lord, **and do not** the things which I say?"*

There is no sense in saying Jesus is your Lord unless you live under His Lordship, obeying His commands. To honor Him with our lips only is to be a hypocrite, and as shown, He will not accept hypocrites (Heb. 5:9). Grace may be contrary to Old Testament ceremonies, and the lifeless works of the unregenerate, and human ordinances, but it is not contrary to obedience and living right, nor is it contrary to God's moral law.

In Matthew 24:42-51 Jesus said to His disciples in His doctrine of truth, *"Watch therefore: for ye know not what hour **your Lord** doth come. But know this that if the good man of the house had known in what watch the thief would come, he would have watched, and would not have suffered his house to be broken up. Therefore **be ye also ready** [be a good man]: for in such an hour as ye think not the Son of man cometh. **Who then is a faithful and wise servant**, whom his lord hath made ruler over his household, to give them meat in due season? Blessed is that servant, **whom his lord when he cometh shall find so doing**. Verily I say unto you, That he shall make him ruler over all his goods. **But and if that evil servant shall say in his heart, My lord delayeth** his coming; and shall begin to smite his fellow servants, and to eat and drink with the drunken; The lord of that servant shall come in a day when he looketh not for him, and in an hour that he is not aware of, and **shall cut him asunder, and appoint him his portion with the hypocrites: there shall be weeping and gnashing of teeth**"* (and bitter regret).

Here again is the Lord's response to those who turn *in their hearts* from Him and begin to fellowship with the world and its pollutions (James 4:4). The others we've read about who were weeping and gnashing their teeth, were that way because they were cast into a *"furnace of fire."* So, it's obvious if we let scripture interpret scripture, that this is where these unfaithful ones will also end up. (Scripture interprets scripture.)

2 Peter 1:20-21

"Knowing this first, that no prophecy of the scripture is of any private interpretation. For the prophecy came not in old time by the will of man: but holy men of God spake as they were moved by the Holy Ghost." Only scripture can interpret scripture and this being the case, we must accept all the scriptures on any subject to get the whole truth.

Will He respond to us according to our lives then? Most assuredly, yes. But thank God, if we confess our sins and judge ourselves, He will cast those sins into the sea of His forgetfulness and will not remember any sin against us that we've repented of. This is mercy and grace…. We don't deserve this but He's abundantly merciful. If He didn't offer this to us, where would any of us be?

What About Secret Sins?

You know when you've sinned, for it is a decision to knowingly, in your heart, go contrary to what is right (James 4:17). You confess it when *you know* you've crossed certain boundaries in your heart and God will cleanse you of *all* unrighteousness. Don't worry about secret sins that you don't even know about. And as we've shown, an individual sin doesn't cause you to lose out on salvation, but if you continue in unconfessed known sin it wars against the soul, works to destroy the faith life, and tries to take you captive again. And it eventually will, except ye repent. If you then *decide* in your heart to go back into the pollutions (you once were delivered from) and live in them, *then* you depart from the faith. You are not abiding in Christ then, but have made your stand against God (James 4:4).

His Disciples

Matthew 16:24-26

*"Then said Jesus unto his disciples, IF any man will come after me, let him deny himself, and take up his cross and follow me. **For whosoever will save his [sinful] life shall lose it:** and whosoever will lose his life for my sake shall find it. For what is a man profited, if he shall gain the whole world, and lose his own soul? Or what shall a man give in exchange for his soul?"*

Who ever holds on to his worldly life of living for self and the pollutions of this world contrary to the will of God, will lose eternal life; but the scripture says, *"he that **doeth** the will of God abideth forever."* Paul wrote, *"Brethren, be followers together of me, and mark them which walk* *[live] so as ye have us for an ensample. For many walk [conduct their lives in such a way], **of whom** [about these people] I have told you often [over and over again], and now tell you even weeping [with great sorrow in My heart], that they are the enemies of the cross of Christ [they have come to reject picking up their cross daily and crucifying those things which are contrary to God's will]: **Whose end is destruction** [eternal ruin], whose God is their belly [living for their own sinful desires], and whose glory is in their shame, who mind earthly things"* (Phil. 3:17-19). God says to Christians (James 1:1-2) through James, *"Ye adulterers and adulteresses know ye not that the friendship of the world is enmity with God? **Whosoever** therefore will be a friend of the world [and its polluted system] is **the enemy** of God"* (James 4:14). Whosoever means "whosoever." *"Brethren, if **any of you** do err from the truth, and one convert him; let him know, that he which converteth the sinner from the error of his way shall save a soul from death, and shall hide a multitude of sins"* (James 5:19-20). James and Paul were both talking concerning brethren who once were saved, but chose to live again for this world. Paul wept over them and we feel sorrow too, for those who have gone back to living in sin with no repentance thinking that all is well with their soul, while at the same time, they are heading for eternal ruin.

Kingdom of Heaven – Kingdom of God

*"Then said one unto him, Lord, are there few that be saved? And He said unto them, strive to enter in at the strait gate: **for many, I say unto you, will seek to enter in [thinking they will be permitted], and shall not be able.** When once the master of the house is risen up, and hath shut the door, and ye begin to stand without, and to knock at the door, **saying, Lord, Lord,** open unto us, and he shall answer and say unto you, I know you not whence ye are: Then shall ye begin to say, We have eaten and drunk in thy presence, and thou hast taught in our streets. But he shall say, I tell you, I know you not whence ye are; depart from me **all** ye workers of **iniquity.** [All you who live for sin.] There shall be weeping and gnashing of teeth, when ye shall see Abraham, and Isaac, and Jacob, and all the prophets, in the kingdom of God, and **you yourselves thrust out"** (Luke 13:23-28). In Matthew's Gospel he said, *"the kingdom of heaven."* The Kingdom of God and the Kingdom of Heaven are the same thing. All of those who, because of disobedience and unbelief, go back to live in iniquity He said, will be cast out of the Kingdom, whether they be Jew or Gentile, it makes no difference.

For further proof that the Kingdom of Heaven and the Kingdom of God are the same, compare:

1) Matt. 4:17 with Mark 1:14-15

2) Matt. 10:7 with Luke 9:2

3) Matt. 13:11 with Luke 8:10

4) Matt. 13:31 with Mark 4:30 & Luke 13:18

5) Matt. 18:4 with Luke 18:17

6) Matt. 19:23 with Mark 10:23-24

7) Matt. 5:3 with Luke 6:20

8) Matt. 11:11 with Luke 7:28

9) Matt. 13:24 with Mark 4:26

10) Matt. 13:33 with Luke 13:20-21

11) Matt. 19:14 with Mark 10:14

These and other such scriptures prove that Jesus referred to the Kingdom of Heaven and the Kingdom of God as the same thing (Matt. 7:21).

Matthew 18:21-35

"Then came Peter to him, and said, Lord, how oft shall my brother sin against me, and I forgive him? Till seven times? Jesus saith unto him, I say not unto thee, Until seven times; but until seventy times seven. Therefore is the kingdom of heaven likened unto a certain king, which would take account of his servants. And when he had begun to reckon, one was brought unto him, which owed him ten thousand talents. But for as much as he had not to pay, his lord commanded him to be sold, and his wife, and children, and all that he had, and payment to be made. The servant therefore fell down, and worshipped him, saying, Lord, have patience with me, and I will pay thee all. **Then the lord of that servant was moved with compassion, and loosed him, and forgave him the debt.** *[This is what the Lord had done for us when we besought Him.] But the same servant went out, and found one of his fellow servants, which owed him an hundred pence: and he laid hands on him, and took him by the throat, saying, Pay me that thou owest. And his fellow servant fell down at his feet, and besought him, saying, have patience with me, and I will pay thee all. And he would not: but went and cast him into prison, till he should pay the debt. So when his fellow servants [the angels, Rev. 22:8-9] saw what was done, they were very sorry, and came and told (reported) unto their lord all that was done.* **Then his lord, after that he had called him, said unto him, O thou wicked servant,** *I forgave thee all that debt, because thou desiredst me: Shouldest not thou also have had compassion on thy fellow servant, even as I had pity on thee?* **And his lord was wroth, and delivered him to the tormentors, till he should pay all that was due unto him. So likewise shall my heavenly Father**

do also unto you, if ye from your hearts forgive not every one his brother their trespasses."

Again, Jesus clearly reveals that God will respond to us according to what we have sown and how we have acted and responded to *"the royal law"* of love unless we repent and do right. He'll treat us like we treat others. *"Therefore all things whatsoever ye would that men should do to you, do ye even so to them: for this is the law and the prophets"* (Matt. 7:12).

Hebrews 2:1-3 Paul, in writing to Hebrew Christians wrote,

*"Therefore we ought to give the more earnest heed to the things which we have heard, lest at any time we should let them slip. For **if the word spoken by angels was steadfast, and every transgression and disobedience received a just recompense of reward; How shall we [Christians] escape, if we neglect so great salvation;** which at the first began to be spoken by the Lord, and was confirmed by them that heard him."* The real Gospel *first began to be spoken by the Lord and **then*** by the apostles. It's all the same Gospel and never contradicts itself. All warnings are intact and are abundantly clear. How shall we escape if we neglect His warnings? Every transgression and disobedience not repented of will receive a just recompense of reward in due time. Paul never implied that there was any kind of grace or an imputed righteousness that would automatically protect a person who lives contrary to God's Word. But He did tell Christians not to do what the world does or they, too, would be partakers of the wrath of God (Eph. 5:5-7).

Matthew 25:31-46

*"When the Son of man shall come in his glory, and all the holy angels with him, then shall He sit upon the throne of his glory: and before Him shall be gathered all nations: and He shall separate them one from another, as a shepherd divideth his sheep from the goats. And he shall set the sheep on his right hand, but the goats on the left. Then shall the King say unto them on His right hand, Come, ye blessed of my Father, **inherit the kingdom** prepared for you from [before] the foundation of the world: **for I was an hungered, and ye gave me meat: I was thirsty, and ye gave me drink: I was a stranger, and ye took me in: Naked, and ye clothed me: I was sick, and ye visited me: I was in prison, and ye came unto me. Then the righteous shall answer him,** saying, Lord, when saw we thee an hungered, and fed thee? Or thirsty, and gave thee drink? When saw we thee a stranger, and took thee in? Or naked, and clothed thee? Or when saw we thee sick, or in prison, and came unto thee? And the King shall answer and say unto them, Verily I say unto you, **In as much as ye have done it** unto one of the least of these my brethren, ye have done it unto me. Then shall he say also unto them on the left hand, Depart from me, ye cursed,*

into everlasting fire, prepared for the devil and his angels: for I was an hungered, and ye gave me no meat: I was thirsty, and ye gave me no drink: I was a stranger, and ye took me not in: naked, and ye clothed me not: sick, and in prison, and ye visited me not. Then shall they also answer him, saying, Lord, when saw we thee an hungered, or athirst, or a stranger, or naked, or sick, or in prison, and did not minister unto thee? Then shall he answer them, saying, Verily I say unto you, **In as much** *as ye did it not to one of the least of these, ye did it not to me.* **And these shall go away into everlasting punishment: but the righteous [who have done good] into life eternal.**" (Also see James 2:14-17.) *"Marvel not at this: for the hour is coming, in the which all that are in the graves shall hear his voice, and shall come forth;* **they that have done good**, *unto the resurrection of life;* **and they that have done evil**, *unto the resurrection of damnation"* (John 5:28-29).

Is the Lord concerned about our actions? Our lives? Our behavior? About good and evil? Certainly, for He pointed out that the righteous are those who live righteously. (See also 1 John 3:6-10, 2:28-29.) To not obey Jesus is to dishonor Him. This false teaching on grace though, does away with the need of holiness or right living, or doing good, or putting God first, labeling real Bible faith as legalistic works when really it's true grace and faith in action; and people ignoring hundreds of scriptures about God's commands to live right and do good works ignorantly follow these unscriptural theories just as multitudes followed the Pharisees in times past. The Lord's doctrine doesn't do away with doing God's will, but it commands it. We live it out by faith, and grace gives us the power to fulfill it (Heb. 12:12-15; 1 Pet. 1:14-17; 1 John 3:2-8). As a matter of fact, it's even more strict than the Old Covenant (Matt. 5:27-29). But He's given us the ability to do it in this New Covenant. *"So speak ye, and so do, as they that shall be judged by the law of liberty"* (James 2:12; Gal. 5:1, 13; Ezek. 36:26-28).

His supernatural grace is given to us so that we may abound in good works and live right, not to free us to do evil works and live wrong. You were not saved from spiritual death and the pollutions of this world by any works without grace, but once grace is received, it empowers you to work and live right. The time to start working is after you've received grace. *"But by the grace of God I am what I am: and his grace which was bestowed upon me was not in vain; but I labored more abundantly than they all: yet not I, but the grace of God which was with me"* (1 Cor. 15:10). *"And God is able to make all grace abound toward you; that ye, always having all sufficiency in all things, may abound to every good work"* (2 Cor. 9:8).

To whom much is given, of him is much required! Faith and grace in one's heart always reveals itself in people's behavior and works; so does sin, unbelief, and disobedience. For each tree is known by its own fruit.

I would encourage you to go through the other Gospels and see many other similar things in the doctrine and teaching of Christ. This is true teaching of the Word. Stay with and abide in the doctrines (and instructions) of Christ. And again, we believe every scripture that is in the Word about God's grace and righteousness, but we also believe that every warning is certain. It *all* harmonizes. God through the Word has made known to us the *"mystery of His will."* Put it *ALL* together and you have a clear, *complete* picture, and the whole counsel of God (Acts 20:27). If He says repent of and confess any sin, we'd better do it, for God doesn't waste words and make statements for naught; nor can He alter what He said, nor treat people differently from what's written. *"My covenant will I not break, nor alter the thing that is gone out of my lips"* (Ps. 89:34). *"For ever, O Lord, Thy Word is settled in heaven"* (Ps. 119:89).

Hebrews 13:8

"Jesus Christ the same yesterday, and to day, and for ever."

God was the God of all grace in history past and yet Cain, Saul, Judas, Korah, the Canaanites, and so on, all died and were lost when they lived contrary to Him. His love was just as great then toward any of them, seeing He is no respecter of persons and never changes, but the consequences resulted anyway. There is no grace or love that can automatically protect a person from the consequences of rebellion, or living contrary to God's own moral law. If they persist in what's wrong, they will *"eat the fruit of their own ways."* Whatever the Word says is the penalty that will be paid; it will be paid, except a person repent. (Examples: 1 Cor. 3:16-17; Gal. 5:19-21.)

Is God's Kingdom a Lawless Society?

Now let's look at some things that Christ taught in the Epistles.

In 1 Corinthians 14:37-38 Paul wrote,

*"If any man think himself to be a prophet, or spiritual, let him acknowledge that the things that I write unto you **are the commandments of the Lord**. But if any man be ignorant, let him be ignorant."* (See also Col. 3:16.)

Those who say that grace teaches that you need not keep the Lord's commandments, are rejecting the Lord Himself, for He and His Word are one (John 12:48-49; 1 John 2:4). Now, we know we need not keep Israel's laws of holy days, circumcision, dietary laws, civil laws, ceremonial laws, carnal ordinances, and animal sacrifices. For we are never told to do these works of the law in the New Covenant. We are freed from the law of types and shadows for Christ ended these things, but the Lord's moral laws are forever, and were in existence before man was ever created. Paul, in Galatians, never stated that obedience to God or His moral law was legalism, but rather, going back to circumcision, holy days, and Sabbath days, and so on, to try and be justified or made holy, was. These things are not of faith, but works. Paul himself said that although he was no longer under the Mosaic law, he was still under the law of God and Christ (1 Cor. 9:21). We must still keep the *"royal law"* of love (James 2:8).

Paul, in his writings, revealed that if you put away a good conscience, you'll make shipwreck of your faith. We are not free to go contrary to God's moral law, for in this New Covenant He's written His laws in our hearts and minds so that we will live according to His will. Paul said we hold *"the mystery of the faith in a pure conscience"* (1 Tim. 3:9).

*"And herein do I exercise **myself, to have always** a conscience void of offence toward God, and toward men"* (Acts 24:16). Faith only functions right when the conscience is freed from sin. *"For if our heart condemn us, God is greater than our heart, and knoweth all things. Beloved, if our heart condemn us not, then have we confidence toward God"* (1 John 3:20-21).

Second Peter 2:1-2

*"Wherefore **laying aside** all malice, and all guile, and hypocrisies [professing one thing, but living another], and envies, and all evil speakings, as newborn babes, desire **the sincere milk** of the Word, that ye may grow thereby."* Don't allow any mixture of the poison of hypocrisy in from the old serpent. Remember, only Satan works to okay or promote evil. He doesn't want you to believe in all the scriptures, just the ones he picks out for his own end. His interest is always to get people to disobey God so that they choose the wrong path and reap death and corruption (Gal. 6:7-9). Remember that the scripture calls him *"the deceiver of the whole world."* To yield to sin is to yield to Satan. His excuses and disguises are many and widespread as he tries to lead people to rebel against God's moral government. His goal is always the same, "rebellion," so that people will eventually reap God's judgment against evil by living contrary to God's moral law (Eph. 5:5-7). For *"rebellion is as the sin of witchcraft, and stubborness as idolatry."*

Some think, well, if grace could save us out of sin, why can't it save us IN our sins? Paul said, *"God forbid."* Grace makes it so you don't have to return to the vomit you came out of, nor back to wallowing in the mire (2 Pet. 2:21-22). Grace included you in Christ's death to sin and Satan and broke their hold upon you. Peter taught that a Christian who has walked with the Lord and come out of the pollutions of the world by the grace of God, but then goes back willingly into those same pollutions doing, "*despite to the Spirit of Grace,*" lives unholy, and stays there until he's overcome and bound up by them, will be worse off in the end than if he never knew the Lord. He, by going back and living in the things he once lived in as a sinner, is now responsible for rejecting more light than before he ever knew the Lord. Before it may have been in much ignorance, but now it's outright rebellion and he will be judged accordingly. "*And that servant, which knew his lord's will, **and prepared not himself,** neither did according to his will, shall be beaten with many [more] stripes*" (than someone who didn't know at all, Luke 12:47).

Those who feel they have this special grace revelation (which permits a life of sin and a following after Satan, and which makes them one of God's special or predestined ones, see Ephesians 2:2) while taking certain secluded scriptures out of context, become very critical of ministers and ministries who don't agree with them. And actually get very aggressive in a very ungraceful way in their attempts to get others to agree with them; neither considering the damage they may be causing born again churches or Christians, while at the same time, saying they are full of grace and love. The reason they manifest this way when confronted with the real truth, is because the worldly spirit that has bound and misled them with this doctrine, seeks to keep them captive to this false concept of grace. Not only that, but it seeks to lead others into this false belief also, through them. And sadly, when one's deceived, they don't even know it (Matt. 6:23). For it is a fact that probably 99.9% of all *full Gospel* ministers and ministries do not believe in such a "sinning saint" religion as this, that is the product of grace. As though grace now is an automatic cloak for a life of sin. This is because through the Holy Spirit Baptism (Acts 2:4) the truth is revealed concerning this. The Holy Spirit is the great teacher (John 16:12-14,26). To think one can now do the very same things he had repented of before, turn back again and follow the course of this world, follow the prince of the power of the air, live in the pollutions of this world and pleasures of sin, grieving the Holy Spirit and hurting others, and that God's own grace will automatically cover for these works of darkness, and thereby permit the willing offender into heaven, is absurd (Matt. 7:21). It is a doctrine of devils

(Eph. 5:11-12). Did God work out a plan so that man can now freely sin, rebel against Him, and follow Satan? Does God build again what He Himself, sent Jesus to destroy? (1 John 3:8) Is He transgressing His own nature and law? By no means! All who repent will receive mercy. All, who don't, will be judged.

A soul that is morally loose because of believing wrong teachings loses its conviction of the awfulness of sin. People need to see sin as a work of the devil (1 John 3:8) and not just as a little behavior problem. *"Wherein in time past ye walked according to the course of this world, **according to** the prince of the power of the air, **the spirit that now worketh in the children of disobedience"*** (Eph. 2:2). *"He that [habitually] committeth sin [John said], is of the devil."* They are on the devil's side.

Where there is sin, there is the spirit of disobedience at work, and when it's yielded to, it quenches and grieves the Holy Spirit. This false teaching on grace gets Christians to once again yield themselves over to this spirit of disobedience they once were delivered from, who then deceives them into thinking everything is alright (2 Thess. 2:10-12). But in reality, all disobedience and works of the flesh bring spiritual blindness and corruption (2 Pet. 1:9-10). If you sow to the flesh, Paul said, you'll reap corruption. Would God ever give you grace then to reap corruption? Can a good tree produce evil fruit? Did He not say in 2 Peter 1:4, *"Whereby are given unto us exceeding great and precious promises: that by these ye might be partakers of the divine nature, **having escaped the corruption** [moral pollution] that is in the world through lust"* (Unlawful desires).

Notice, God's provision is that you escape moral corruption and the pollutions of this world, not so that you can live in them. *"**According as His divine power hath given unto us all things that pertain unto life and godliness, through the [true] knowledge of him** that hath called us to glory and virtue"* (2 Pet. 1:3).

His Spirit and power frees us from the spirit of disobedience who is now at work in disobedient people. God said, *"And I will put my Spirit within you, **and cause you** to walk in my statutes, and ye shall keep my judgments, and do them"* (Ezek. 36:27).

"That the righteousness of the law might be fulfilled in us, who walk not after the flesh, but after the Spirit" (Rom. 8:4). For he whom the Son sets free from a life of sin, is free indeed. For us to follow after Satan and live for the world, would vex God's Holy Spirit. "Vex" means "to torment;

grieve; afflict; cause sorrow; provoke; and trouble." Would God give a Christian grace to vex His own Holy Spirit? Listen to this scripture, *"But they rebelled and vexed his holy Spirit: therefore he was turned to be their enemy, and he [God] fought against them"* (Isa. 63:10).

In 2 Peter 2:7-8 it says, *"And [God] delivered just Lot, vexed with the filthy conversation of the wicked (For that righteous man dwelling among them, in seeing and hearing, [what they did]* **vexed his righteous soul from day to day with their unlawful deeds.)"**

If Lot's soul was vexed with their filthy conversation and *unlawful deeds,* how much more the Holy Spirit? There is *not one scriptural example* of anyone living in rebellion against God, going to heaven or having God's favor or blessings. But there are many about them being judged and cast down to hell. Let's heed David, a man after God's own heart that said, *"Blessed are the undefiled in the way, who walk in the law of the Lord. Blessed are they that keep his testimonies, and that seek him with the whole heart. They also do no iniquity: they walk in his ways. Thou hast commanded us to keep thy precepts diligently"* (Ps. 119:1-4). Obviously, David was a man of faith; a man, God said, after God's own heart, and he kept God's testimonies, obeyed God, and repented when he did wrong. This is faith, and without this kind of faith, it's impossible to please God (Heb. 11:6).

Let me ask this; does God not see what we do? Are His eyes blinded by grace? Hear God's Word: *"Yet they say, The Lord shall not see, neither shall the God of Jacob regard it. [Pay any attention to the way we live.] Understand, ye brutish among the people: and ye fools, when will ye be wise? He that planted the ear, shall he not hear? He that formed the eye, shall he not see?"* (Ps. 94:7-9).

Psalm 50:16-22

*"But unto the wicked God saith, What hast thou to do to declare My statutes, or that thou shouldest take my covenant in thy mouth? Seeing thou hatest instruction, and casteth my words behind thee. When thou sawest a thief, then thou consentedst with him, and hast been partaker with adulterers. Thou givest thy mouth to evil, and thy tongue frameth deceit. Thou sittest and speakest against thy brother; thou slanderest thine own mother's son. **These things hast thou done, and I kept silence; thou thoughtest that I was altogether such an one as thyself: but I will reprove thee,** and set them in order before thine eyes. Now consider this, ye that forget God [and His ways], lest I tear you in pieces, and there be none to deliver."*

So, Heed the Word of the Lord.

Certainly mercy is available to every repentant person, even if he sins 490 times a day (Matt. 18:21-22) and turns and repents, but not to the unrepentant, for the repentant person humbly turns to receive mercy and grace but the other does not. *"God resists the proud but gives grace to the humble."*

And we know that sin first destroys or hinders fellowship with God before it destroys the relationship. And we know a sin, or sins, do not automatically cut a person off from his relationship with God, just his fellowship (1 John 1:5-9). Not until a person becomes so hardened through sin that they become unwilling to turn and receive of God's grace any longer. Their soul then releases its commitment to *"live by faith,"* for the will of God. (You'll know them by their fruits if this has happened.) They then willingly turn from *"the way of righteousness,"* back into things they once were delivered from. It's a will and a heart thing. It's different from a person struggling with the flesh and falling temporarily into sin, but being willing to repent and go on with God. With faith in our heart, we used our will and we turned from Satan to Jesus (Rev. 22:17; Rom. 10:9-10). But people can get back into sin and unbelief (Heb. 3:12-14), and willingly, once again, depart from God and turn aside after Satan (1 Tim. 4:1, 5:8,12,15). For those who turn back to a life of willful sinning, Titus 1:16 says, *"They profess that they know God; but in works [behavior] they deny him, being abominable, and disobedient, and unto every good work reprobate."* *"For if we sin willfully [returning to our former ways of life] after that we have received the knowledge of the truth [that we needed to repent of a life of sin and follow the Lord], there remaineth no more sacrifice for sins. [There is no sacrifice that will cover for willful rebellion.] But there is [just] a certain fearful looking for of judgment and fiery indignation, which shall devour the adversaries"* (Heb. 10:26). So, the sacrifice is not automatically applied to those who live their lives willingly in sin. It is there only for the repentant soul. We had to come to the cross as the basis for our first cleansing from sin, and so it continues this way (1 John 1:9).

First Corinthians 3:1-3

"And I, brethren, could not speak unto you as unto spiritual, but as unto carnal, even as unto babes in Christ. I have fed you with milk, and not with meat: for hitherto ye were not able to bear it, neither yet now are ye able. For ye are yet carnal: for whereas there is among you envying, and strife, and divisions, are ye not carnal, and walk as men?"

Babes *in Christ*. Christians that are involved in these things such as strife, debate, and quarreling, are carnal and carnality hinders spiritual perception. They can only digest spiritual milk and not meat. These Corinthians were zealous for God, and continuing in church and still seeking to walk in the Lord's ways, so their will was to continue on with God, but yet their actions caused them to be carnal. (See also 2 Peter 1:5-10.) So you sure don't want to be instructed by those who live in these things and teach that these things are okay and are thereby either deceivers or spiritually dull and carnal people. *"As the priest, so are the people."* Jesus revealed that, everyone that's taught shall be as his teacher. Whoever you accept as your teacher, you'll become like them. Their teaching will affect you. It's up to you to discern between a true teacher and a false one. Peter and Jude pointed out that false teachers teach that you can live in morally loose and evil ways and be automatically covered by God's grace and love. True teachers teach as Paul, that grace is given so you'll deny ungodliness and worldly lusts; and so you'll live soberly, righteously, and godly in this present world (Titus 2:11-14). So take heed that no man deceive you with their same old teachings which misled many in times past. Hear, instead, the apostles and let us heed these scriptures:

2 Corinthians 5:11

*"Knowing therefore the **terror of the Lord**, we persuade men [to turn from Satan to God]; but we are made manifest unto God; and I trust also are made manifest in your consciences."*

1 Timothy 1:19

*"Holding faith, and a good conscience; **which some [Christians] having put away** concerning faith have made shipwreck"* (of their faith life). A ship that is wrecked sinks, unless it is patched. Paul said *some have* made shipwreck of their faith life because they put away a good conscience and would no longer listen to it (1 Tim. 3:9).

They evidently would no longer listen to the *"law written in their hearts,"* but hardened their hearts by continually overriding it. When faith sinks, the person no longer lives by faith for the will of God.

Hebrews 3:12-14

*"Take heed, [then] brethren, lest there **be in any of you an evil heart of unbelief,** in departing from the living God. But exhort one another daily, while it is called today; lest any of you be hardened through the deceitfulness of sin. **For we are made partakers of Christ [eternal life, 1 John 1:1-3], if [on this condition] we hold the beginning of our confidence steadfast unto the end"*** (to

the end of our lives, so fight the good fight, lay hold on eternal life). Receive, as Peter said, the final goal of your faith, *"even the salvation of your souls."* Jesus said, *"In your patience [and endurance] possess ye your souls."*

Paul points out that people who once committed their lives to live for God by faith, can, afterwards, become hardened by repeated sinning without repentance and finally decide to no longer live for God. If that happens, they are no longer keeping the faith, for unbelief has led them astray. *"So, we see that they could not enter in because of unbelief"* (Heb. 3:19).

Romans 11:21-22

"For if God spared not the natural branches, **take heed** *[Christian, Rom. 1:7] lest he also spare not thee. Behold therefore the goodness and severity of God: on them which fell, severity; but toward thee, goodness,* **if thou continue** *in his goodness:* **otherwise** *thou also shalt be cut off."* (Just like Israel was, who was also God's elect.)

Grace does not nullify these, or the many other scriptures like these.

CHAPTER TWELVE

ELECTION, FOREKNOWLEDGE, PREDESTINATION, AND THE BOOK OF LIFE

Words such as election, predestination, foreknowledge, and the Book of Life, as found in the scriptures, do not do away with the free moral agency of man as some think. Let me give a brief explanation of these phrases, which we will possibly cover more extensively elsewhere in another treatise.

ELECTION: The elect are simply those who cast in their vote to follow Jesus. The same is true with the "elect angels" (1 Tim. 5:21). Two thirds remained faithful; one third rebelled (Rev. 12:9). They all had their own free wills (Isa. 14:12-14; Luke 11:24). The elect is whosoever chooses to side in with God. Lucifer was not predestined to be the devil. If so, he'd have a right to be upset, but scripture reveals that he used his own will to go contrary to God's will. The nonelect are those beings (men or angels) who choose to follow after Satan (Eph. 2:2-3; John 8:12, 10:9). Jesus said, *"Preach the Gospel to **every creature**."* (For the choice is for all.) *"He that believeth shall be saved"* (Mark 16:15-16) and *"Except ye repent [of following Satan], ye shall all likewise perish"* (Luke 13:3). Paul and Barnabas preached the Word to some Jewish people who were called God's elect (Isa. 45:4), to give them God's Word about salvation and how they must turn from Satan to God, but they contradicted and blasphemed. *"Then Paul and Barnabas waxed bold, and said, It was necessary that the Word of God should first have been spoken to you: but seeing ye put it from you, and **judge yourselves unworthy** of everlasting life, lo, we turn to the Gentiles"* (Acts 13:46). If people refuse Jesus, God will refuse them (Gal. 6:7). Notice they rejected God's invitation to accept His Son who is truly His elect, and therefore they judged themselves unworthy of eternal life (Isa. 42:1). Then, if you do accept Christ as Lord and you cast in your vote to follow Jesus, you must continue to side in with Him to the end, as Peter said, in order to *"make your calling and **election sure**"* (2 Pet. 1:8-11; Col. 1:21-23). So, Israel was His elect, but when they rebelled, God fought against them, and they were cut off (Rom. 11:19-23).

God has chosen as His elect, anyone who repents of following Satan and chooses to make Jesus Lord of their life (2 Pet. 3:9; 1 Tim. 2:4). It's on the basis of mercy, not on a previous track record, nor a keeping of the works of the law. Election is always unto *obedience* (1 Pet. 1:2; Heb. 5:9). Who you live for is who you've elected to side in with. Jesus said, *"He that gathers not with me is against me"* (2 Thess. 1:7-8). Truly Jesus is called *"the elect of God"* (Isa. 42:1), and all who repent and enter into Him become "elect" in Him, provided that they continue to ***abide*** *"in Him"* (1 John 15:6, 2:28).

Outside of Jesus, we are not promised anything. No man can serve two masters (Rom. 6:16). You've elected to follow one or the other by submission of your will and actions; and nothing is more prideful than a man to imagine himself to be one of the elect and others the nonelect of God without obedience to God, as if God just chose him and rejected others. Paul said, *"There is no respect of persons with God."* How dare anyone pridefully say God predestined some to heaven and some to hell, and then say they are one of the ones predestined to heaven, and they don't even need to love or obey God to get there. It is the prideful, fallen nature of man, still trying to exalt itself that does so. But God has promised to resist the proud, such as these, and give grace to the humble. (See Luke 18:9-14.) Besides that, if this were the case, there would be no security at all, for no one would really know if they were one of the elect or predestined ones until they actually entered heaven. What if they really were predestined to be deceived, or to be another Judas at the last hour of their life? What if their being a predestined one was all an illusion in their own mind, and they were self deceived? Then where does that docrtine leave them? Christ is the only chosen one, and all who repent of their ties with Satan and accept Christ, become chosen *in Him* who was the Lamb slain from before the foundation of the world (Matt. 12:18; 1 Pet. 2:4). Everything hinges on being in Him and abiding in Him. This alone makes us His chosen and His elect. So the elect are those who have repented of a life of sin and abide in Christ by living for God (John 15:10). We are only *"chosen and elect in Him"* (John 15:6).

FOREKNOWLEDGE: has to do with the fact that God can see what happens in the future when He chooses to. It does not interfere with the free moral agency of man, but simply sees their own free decisions and the final outcome of things before it happens in the realm of time. God is not limited by time (Isa. 57:15). He can see what He wants to; and what He chooses not to, He doesn't know until it happens in the realm of time. *"And God saw [in time] that the wickedness of man was great in the earth, and that every imagination of the thoughts of his heart was only evil continually,* **And it repented the Lord that he had made man on the earth** *[when* **He saw** *the extent of man's wickedness], and it grieved him at his heart. And the Lord said, I will destroy man whom I have created from the face of the earth; both man, and beast, and the creeping thing, and the fowls of the air;* **for it repenteth** *me that I have made them"* (Gen. 6:5-7). (See also Gen.11:5,18:20-22.) If God ever did choose to see a free moral agent in the future (such as Judas), He only sees what the free moral agent himself freely decides to do. (Judas, God's Word says, *"by transgression fell."*) God's foreknowledge does not interfere with our decisions (Deut. 30:19). God then, when He chooses to do so, only foresees what the free moral agent chooses to do. *"And we know that all things work together for good to them that love God, to them who are the called according to his purpose.* **For whom he did foreknow,** *he also did predestinate to be conformed to the image of his Son, that He might be the firstborn among many brethren"* (Rom. 8:28-29). His purpose was to bring many sons and daughters to glory (Heb. 2:10). We see here that His promise is only to them that love Him and keep His commandments (John 15:10, 14:21-23; 1 John 2:4-6; Rev. 22:14). These are the ones who abide in Christ (John 15:1-10). He foreknew that some would repent of a life of sin, make Jesus Lord, and obey Him (Heb. 5:9); and those who *have* willingly done so, and *are* doing so, are the ones He foresaw, who are now a part of the predestined plan of God, and they will be His glorified sons and daughters. But what they've done, they've done willingly (Rev. 22:17). We become His elect and stay His elect, then, by obeying Jesus as Lord (Heb. 5:9; Matt. 7:21). God placed Saul as king because of his humility at one time; and later removed him because of his pride. God deals, then, with each person in the realm of time and where they are at today, regardless of His foreknowledge (2 Cor. 6:1-2).

PREDESTINATION: This has to do with Christ. He was the only individual predestinated beforehand to do a specific thing. It was by the determinate counsel of God and therefore He's called the Lamb that was slain from the foundation of the world. Even this He did willingly (John

6:38). God has chosen and predestined all who are *in Christ* to be His sons and daughters, but *"whosoever will "* (Rev. 22:17) can enter in if they choose to. Jesus said, *"I am the door, by me **if any man enter in** he shall be saved."* (John 10:9). If a man enters into Christ, they are then predestined in Him to obtain all that the predestined plan reveals, *provided* they continue to abide in Christ. (See John 15:6; 1 John 2:6, 3:5-8.) It's like, He's the envelope destined for glory and we all are the letters that get into the envelope. If we get in and stay in, we are then predestined to reach the predetermined destination, and the glory that is set for all that are in Him and abide in Him. The Gospel is for *"all the world,"* *"every creature,"* and *"whosoever will,"* as the scriptures clearly teach, and God wills all men to be saved (1 Tim. 2:4). He's not willing that any perish but that all repent and enter into Christ (2 Pet. 3:9). His predestined plan is to save all who are in Christ; but He will not override the human will and make people receive Christ, for He sovereignly made man with a free will. God sovereignly gave us a free will, so we must willingly get into Christ by repentance and faith, and stay in Him by continuing in the faith in order to remain predestined IN Him for glory (Acts 14:22). In the fullness of time, He's going to gather everything that's in Christ together (Eph. 1:10). The apostle John exhorted us then to continue to abide *"in Him"* for only *"in Him is life"* (1 John 2:28). God foreknew that some would accept Christ and some would not. Those who would accept Christ, fight the good fight of faith, and continue in Him until the end of their earthly lives, He also predestined to obtain glory. But it is up to you to continue in the faith (Rev. 22:14; Rom. 11:22), and to continue to abide in Him (Rom. 2:1-11). All is ours *in Christ* but apart from Him nothing is promised. *"If a man **abide not in me**, he is cast forth as a branch, and is withered; and men gather them, and cast them into the fire, and they are burned"* (John 15:6).

There is much more we will say about these things perhaps in another treatise, but let me conclude here by referring to the Book of Life.

THE BOOK OF LIFE: Everyone's names were originally written in it from the foundation of the world. The psalmist said, *"Thine eyes did see my substance, yet being unperfect; and **in thy book** all my members were written, which in continuance were fashioned, **when as yet there was none of them"*** (Ps. 139:16).

God told Jeremiah that before he was formed in the womb, God knew him (Jer. 1:5). God is the Father of all spirits (Heb. 12:9) and gives spirit *to all* men on the earth (Zech. 12:1; John 1:9). He doesn't give dead spirits, for *"in Him is life."* But, people went astray from Him into trespasses and sins and died spiritually. Romans 3:23 says, *"For all have sinned, and come short of the glory of God." "Therefore to **him** that knoweth to do good, and doeth it not, to him it is sin"* (James 4:17). Paul wrote in Romans 7:9, *"I was **alive** without the law once: but when the commandment came, sin revived, and I died"* (not physically but spiritually). *"And the Lord said unto Moses, Whosoever hath sinned against me, him will I blot out of my book"* (Exod. 32:33). Children then that die before the age of accountability or are aborted, are still written in the book. Christ's salvation includes them. *"Therefore as by the offence of one judgment came upon all men to condemnation; even so by the righteousness of one the free gift **came upon all men unto justification of life"*** (Rom. 5:18). No sin is imputed against them before they know to choose the good and refuse the evil (Isa. 7:15-16). So we received a spirit which was alive from God, but sinful flesh subject to the power of darkness from Adam. But we don't bear punishment for Adam's transgression, but our own.

*"Wherefore, as by one man sin entered into the world, and death by sin; and so death passed upon all men, **for that all have sinned"*** (Rom. 5:12). *"The soul that sinneth, it shall die. The son shall not bear the iniquity of the father, neither shall the father bear the iniquity of the son: the righteousness of the righteous shall be upon him, and the wickedness of the wicked shall be upon him"* (Ezek. 18:20). *"So then every one of us shall give account of himself to God"* (Rom. 14:12).

Our personal sin and going astray from God is what caused our individual names to be blotted out of His book (Isa. 53:6; Rom. 3:23). Then when people repent of a life of sin and turn to God for mercy and follow Him, He, because of His great mercy and grace, forgives them, blots out their sins, and writes their names in His book again. To those who choose to repent and follow Him, Jesus said, *"Notwithstanding in this rejoice not, that the spirits are subject unto you; but rather rejoice, because your names are written in heaven"* (Luke 10:20). *"And Jesus said unto him, **This day** is salvation come to this house, forsomuch as he also is a real son of Abraham"* (Luke 19:9). Notice, *"this day;"* not in eternity past. But if people turn back and rebel against God again, God warns them that He will blot their names out again if they persist in sin without repentance (Rom. 11:22; James 5:19-20).

This He did with Israel, His elect (those who, at one time, elected to follow Him). He said if they turned aside to follow other gods, He'd blot them out of the book, but He said that if they'd believe, receive, and follow Christ, He is able to graft them in again.

The Lord's warning to those in the church that rebel without repentance is the same. Jesus says, *"He that overcometh [the world and its moral pollutions], the same shall be clothed in white raiment; and I will not blot out **his name out** of the book of life, but I will confess his name before my Father, and before his angels. He that hath an ear, let him hear what the Spirit saith **unto the churches"*** (Rev. 3:5-6). What then about those who don't overcome?

Concerning those who rejected Christ in Israel, David writes in Psalm 69:22-23,28, *"Let their table become a snare before them: and that which should have been for their welfare, let it become a trap. Let their eyes be darkened, that they see not; and make their loins continually to shake.... Let them be blotted out of the book of the earth, and not be written with the righteous."*

Paul wrote about the same things in Romans chapter 11. God's elect became blinded because they rejected the Messiah, went into unbelief, and were then cut off (Rom. 11:19-23).

See then, God is no respecter of persons. They were cut off because they didn't continue in God's plan. You were grafted in because you repented, believed, and made Jesus Lord of your life. You, by faith, entered then into the predestined plan of God; they, by unbelief and disobedience, missed it. Your sins were blotted out and your name was written in when you repented and believed. (See Luke 19:9.) Paul says, behold, God cut them off when they didn't continue in His goodness even though they were His elect and the natural olive branches. And He will do the same to you and cut you off if you don't continue in it. *"And if some of the branches be broken off, and thou, being a wild olive tree, were grafted in among them, and with them partakest of the root and fatness of the olive tree; Boast not against the branches. But if thou boast, thou bearest not the root, but the root thee. Thou wilt say then, The branches were broken off, that I might be grafted in. Well; because of unbelief they were broken off, and thou standest by faith. Be not high-minded [then Christian], but fear: For if God spared not the natural branches, take heed lest he also spare not thee. Behold therefore the goodness and severity of God: on them which fell, severity; but toward thee, goodness, if thou continue in his goodness: otherwise **thou also** [like them] shalt be cut off"* (Rom. 11:17-21). In other words, you too, can have your name blotted out if you refuse to live for Him.

Now, only those who live for God are the just. Romans 1:17 says, *"The just shall **live** by faith"*; and God says, *"But the path of the just is as the shining light, that shineth more and more unto the perfect day"* (Prov. 4:18). But verse 19 says, *"The way of the wicked is as darkness: they know not at what they stumble."* *"The just,"* those who live by faith, are children of the light and can see. They go on from glory to glory, and their names are in the Book of Life, but those who live in sin are blind. Peter said, *"For if these things [all these good virtues] be in you, and abound, they make you that ye shall neither be barren nor unfruitful in the knowledge of our Lord Jesus Christ. But he that lacketh these things is blind, and cannot see afar off, and hath forgotten that he was purged from his old sins. **Wherefore the rather, brethren, give diligence to make your calling and election sure:** for if ye do these things, ye shall never fall"* (like those who were God's elect and fell away, as recorded in Romans 11:22, and were cut off, 2 Pet. 1:8-10). Now, the devil is against God, and God's Word says, *"And all that dwell upon the earth shall worship him, whose names are not written in the book of life of the Lamb slain from the foundation of the world. If any man have an ear, let him hear"* (Rev. 13:8-9). These are those who are blinded by their sins and separated from God, because of following the course of this world (Eph. 2:2-3).

Only those who have repented and made a decision to live for God (as well as those who haven't reached the age of accountability) have their names in God's book, although they may have some struggles with the flesh (1 John 2:1). Their name was written in once again when they were born again (that is, made spiritually alive again), or, as it is also called, "regeneration" (Titus 3:5); and sin's controlling power was also broken over the flesh. These will not follow the devil nor the course of this world, but follow the good shepherd in paths of righteousness. *"And the dragon was wroth with the woman, and went to make war with the remnant of her seed, which keep the commandments of God, and have the testimony of Jesus Christ"* (Rev. 12:17).

Revelation 20:15 says, *"And whosoever was not found written in the book of life was cast into the lake of fire."* Now God wants everyone to have their name in the Book of Life (Heb. 2:9; 1 John 2:2; Matt. 28:19-20; Acts 17:30; John 1:29; Mark 16:15; 2 Pet. 3:9; 1 Tim. 2:4), but only those who repent of a life of sin, and make a decision to follow the Lord and His ways, have their names in there. (Along with infants, small children, and mentally handicapped people, John 1:9; 2 Cor. 8:12.)

Revelation 22:14 goes on to say, *"Blessed are they that do his commandments, that they may have right to the tree of life, and may enter in through the gates into the city."* We, who have been saved out of the pollutions of the world are now to obey God's commandments and continue to walk in His ways. *"Here is the patience of the saints: here are they **that keep the commandments of God, and the faith of Jesus**. And I heard a voice from heaven saying unto me, Write, Blessed are the dead **which die in the Lord** [in Christ] from henceforth: Yea, saith the Spirit, that they may rest from their labors; and their works do follow them"* (Rev. 14:12-13). *"He that overcometh, the same shall be clothed in white raiment; and I will not blot out his name out of the book of life, but I will confess his name before my Father, and before his angels. He that hath an ear, let him hear what the Spirit saith unto the churches"* (Rev. 3:5-6).

Now, God also warns that those whose names are in the book, not to intentionally add to, or take away from, His words. Listen to what He says in Revelation 22:18-19, *"For I testify unto every man that heareth the words of the prophecy of this book, **If any man** shall add unto these things, God shall add unto him the plagues that are written in this book: and **if any man** shall take away from the words of the book of this prophecy, **God shall take away his part out of the book of life**, and out of the holy city, and from the things which are written in this book."* He couldn't warn them He'd take their name out of the book if He predestined them to be in it. If He warned them that He'd blot their name out if they intentionally changed His book, then He couldn't have just Himself predestinated certain individuals to be in there before the foundation of the world as a set thing, as some have presumed. So it's obvious He didn't just "predestinate" certain individuals to be in His book and other poor souls to not be in it, for *"God is no respecter of persons."* The Bible says, *"If ye fulfil the royal law according to the scripture, Thou shalt love thy neighbor as thyself, ye do well: But if ye have respect to persons, ye commit sin, and are convinced of the law as transgressors"* (James 2:8-9). God won't transgress His own law, therefore those who accept, follow, and obey Christ, He will reward with eternal life. Those who refuse and rebel, will, according to Paul, receive tribulation and wrath (Rom. 2:4-11). The decision is yours. So people whose names are in the book can, in certain situations, have their names blotted out of it. This has always been the case.

I hope you can see now that God wrote everyone's name in it from the foundation of the world. But sin and going astray after the age of accountability (Isa. 53:6), caused their names to be blotted out. *"Wherefore, as by one man sin entered into the world, and death by sin; and so [spiritual] death passed upon all men, for that all have sinned"* (Rom. 5:12). We *all*, the Bible says, were children of wrath even as the rest of mankind because of our sins and following the course of this world, but Christ then came, bore our sins, and shed His blood so that our sins might be washed away. So when we repent, believe, and turn to follow Christ, our sins are blotted out and our names are written once again in the Book of Life. He then promised that if we'd keep living for Him He'd not blot our names out again. But Jude spoke of people who turned away from living for Him because of a counterfeit idea of grace as being twice (spiritually) dead and blotted out of His book both times because of choosing a life of sin (2 Pet. 2:20-21). All who are in Christ and abide in Him by keeping His commandments of love (John 15:10) are predestined to obtain the glory of God's predestined plan to have glorified sons and daughters (1 John 2:6). Those who don't enter into Christ or don't remain in Him will enter into the judgment for their sins. This too, was determined beforehand (Eph. 5:5-7). Each individual must make His own choice (Deut. 30:19-20), not only to start in the race, but to continue in it and finish it. (See 1 Thessalonians 1:8-9.) Don't depart, then, back into a life of sin. Fight the good fight of faith, lay hold on eternal life (1 Tim. 6:12).

1 Timothy 4:1

"Now the Spirit speaketh expressly, that in the latter times some shall depart [go astray] **from the faith,** *giving heed to seducing spirits, and doctrines of devils."* **Some shall** *make shipwreck of their faith.* **Some shall** *depart from the faith (***some shall depart** *from the living God) the love (agape) of many shall wax cold.* The possibility in scripture is clear. Scripture warns us not to *"draw back to perdition."* And no one can depart from something he never was a part of. And remember, Peter said there would be "many" false teachers in the church teaching a lawless way of salvation saying, don't worry, you can't be lost no matter how you live and whether you repent or not. These, Peter said, are damnable heresies. For they will damn those deceived by them if they return back to a life of sin, for by returning back to living like the world, they make themselves the enemy of God (James 4:4). *"For some are already turned aside after Satan"* (1 Tim. 5:15).

A Look At Hebrews

Hebrews 10:19-23

"Having therefore, **brethren,** *boldness to enter into the holiest by the blood of Jesus, by a new and living way, which he hath consecrated for us, through*

*the veil, that is to say, his flesh; and having an High Priest over the house of God; **Let us** draw near with a true heart in full assurance of faith, having our hearts sprinkled from an evil conscience, and our bodies washed with pure water. **Let us** hold fast the profession of our faith without wavering; (for he is faithful that promised)."*

Notice then, by saying over and over again, "us" and "our," that Paul is clearly writing to born-again Christians. Now he goes on to strongly warn them against going back into a life of sin, drawing back to perdition, or returning back to old, wrong beliefs about Christ. Again what's true for the Jewish Christian is also true for the Gentile, for in Christ there is neither Jew nor Gentile. *"There is neither Jew nor Greek, there is neither bond nor free, there is neither male nor female: for ye are all one in Christ Jesus"* (Gal. 3:28).

Now in Hebrews 10: 26-30 he says:

*"**For if we** [Christians] **sin willfully** [go back to a life of willful sinning against the truth we've received without repentance] **after that we have received the knowledge of the truth** [after we have known and accepted the truth that we needed to repent of a life of sin and follow Christ], there remaineth no more sacrifice for sins [there is no automatic cloak for sins that will cover for this], but [there is] just a certain fearful looking for of judgment [nothing but a terrible outlook of doom] and fiery indignation [and a fury of fire], **which shall devour** the adversaries. [That will consume the rebellious that live in opposition to God.] He that despised Moses' law [anyone who set at naught Moses' law as insignificant] **died without mercy** under two or three witnesses [no mercy was shown to him]: **Of how much sorer punishment suppose ye, shall he be thought worthy**, who hath trodden under foot the Son of God, and hath counted the blood of the covenant, **wherewith he was [at one time] sanctified**, an unholy thing, and hath done despite unto **the Spirit of grace?** [By rejecting His conviction and His help to live righteously.] For we know Him that hath said, Vengeance belongeth unto Me, I will recompense [pay back], saith the Lord. And again, The Lord shall judge his people." "It is a fearful thing to fall into the hands of the living God"* (when you've lived contrary to Him). God will judge Christians that do this (Jew or Gentile), and not just see them then through some kind of unrealistic grace or imputed righteousness. He gave us all we'd need to live right and to whom much is given, of him is much required. It says they died *without mercy.* Why? Simply because they would not turn to Him for mercy, despised His provisions, and went their own way. They, like others, chose death for themselves.

Just as a person chooses life by turning from Satan to God, they can again choose death by turning away from God to Satan (Acts 26:16-18).

So, sin then can bring a person to the place where it destroys their faith and their commitment, and it can eventually move them to make a reverse decision and choose to no longer live the Christian life nor obey the Gospel. Yet, they may, after this, make an empty profession before others. Jesus said, *"Even so ye also outwardly appear righteous unto men, but within ye are full of hypocrisy and iniquity"* (Matt. 23:28). *"And he said unto them, Ye are they which justify yourselves before men; **but God knoweth your hearts:** for that which is highly esteemed among men is abomination in the sight of God"* (Luke 16:15).

Man looks on the outward appearance, but the Lord looketh upon the heart (1 Sam. 16:7). *"Neither is there any creature that is not manifest in his sight: but all things are naked and opened unto the eyes of him with whom we have to do"* (Heb. 4:13; Matt. 7:13-21). To keep our name in His book, all we need to do is to keep living for Him, repent, and confess our sin if we do stumble and transgress.

For every real thing in the scriptures, Satan has his counterfeit, and this includes a counterfeit grace and a counterfeit righteousness. We give scripture after scripture; the ultra gracists give reasoning after human reasoning with a few scriptures privately interpreted and twisted as though their seemingly "proof texts" are the whole counsel of God. Together with what God has said *throughout* the New Testament, they are true, but pulled out by themselves while ignoring the other scriptures, brings forth unscriptural doctrines. If the truth must be rightly divided, then it can also be wrongly divided. No one scripture is an island to itself. God gave us the whole Bible so we'd believe it all (2 Tim. 2:15). *"**All scripture** is given by inspiration of God, and is profitable for doctrine, for reproof, for correction, for **instruction in righteousness:** That the man of God may be perfect, **thoroughly furnished unto all good works**"* (2 Tim. 3:16-17). Nothing contradicts; all of what Christ taught in the Gospels agrees with *all* of what the apostles taught in the Epistles, and what was revealed in the book of Revelation. Remember, Satan will use some scriptures in order to twist their meaning and deceive, but he will never use all of the scriptures.

Where then do ultra gracists go to get this "super grace" they speak of? Not from God or His Word. It is simply something that has *captured* their imagination. Most people that teach it obtained these theories from a seminary of some kind. The devil has persuaded them to take a

Bible truth, give it a human definition, and stretch it way past its real God-given boundaries. Satan knows the effect unrighteous living has on faith and the soul's perception of things, and his aim is always only to kill, steal, and destroy. The doctrine of false grace is a killer in disguise, which seeks to deceive people to death!

Galatians 5:19-21

*"Now the **works** of the flesh are manifest, which are these; Adultery, fornication, uncleanness, lasciviousness, idolatry, witchcraft, hatred, variance, emulations, wrath, strife, seditions, heresies, envyings, murders, drunkenness, revellings, and such like: of the which I tell you before, as I have also told you in time past, that they which do [practice] such things **shall not inherit the kingdom of God.**"* *"Shall **not!**"* Could it be any clearer? As we've abundantly shown, the *"Kingdom of God"* and the *"Kingdom of Heaven"* are the same (Matt. 7:21).

Paul wrote: *"Who knowing the judgment of God, that they which commit such things are worthy of death, not only do the same, but have pleasure in them that do them"* (Rom. 1:32). Should we not heed the words of the apostle in his doctrine? This warning is not an empty threat, it means exactly what it says. *They who do* (present tense) *such things shall not inherit the Kingdom of God!* Why? Because they are living for selfish, sinful desires and not for God. God must eventually judge all evil that's not repented of. And if people continue in this course without repentance, God said He'd blot them out of His book.

Ephesians 5:1, 3-7

*"Be ye therefore followers of God, as dear children…. But fornication, and all uncleanness, or covetousness, **let it not be once named among you, as becometh saints;** neither filthiness, nor foolish talking, nor jesting, which are not convenient: but rather giving of thanks. **For this ye know** [you understand clearly], that no whoremonger, nor unclean person, nor covetous man, who is an idolater, **hath any inheritance [at all] in the kingdom of Christ and of God. Let no man deceive you with vain words [empty promises to the contrary]: for because of these things cometh the wrath of God** upon the children of disobedience. **Be not ye therefore partakers with them.**"* It's obvious, then, that Christians can partake of the wrath of God if they go back into disobedience. Paul also knew that deceived men would come along and make empty promises saying that you, as a Christian, couldn't possibly partake of God's wrath towards evil even if you did these things the children of disobedience did, so Paul warned, *"Let no man deceive you,"* concerning these things.

In James 2:12-13, James writes in the doctrine of the Lord, Therefore, *"So speak ye, and so do, as they that shall be judged* the law of liberty. *For he shall have judgment without mercy, that hath showed no mercy; and mercy rejoiceth against judgment."*

To Have Life We Must Not Continue In Sin

It is inexcusable for a person to tell others that they need to repent and turn to Christ to be forgiven of their sins because of breaking God's laws and commandments, and then turn right around and say that Christ has provided that you could then go back, live in sin, break His commandments, and be covered over by His grace automatically. This is absolute ignorance of the truth.

Is Christ then the minister of sin? God forbid! Does He now okay, or build again, the thing He came to destroy and free us from? Has He come to cooperate with the devil, or to destroy the works of the devil, which includes the bondage and slavery to sin?

Romans 6:1-2, 17-19

"What shall we say then? Shall we continue in sin, that grace may abound? [In other words, "Can't grace then save us while we live in sin?"] God forbid. How shall we, that are dead to sin, live any longer therein? *[Grace brought about our death to sin.] But God be thanked, that ye were the servants of sin,* **but ye have obeyed** *from the heart that form of doctrine which was delivered you.* **Being then made free from sin** *[by obeying the Word], ye became the* **servants of righteousness.** *I speak after the manner of men because of the infirmity of your flesh: for as ye have yielded your members servants to uncleanness and to iniquity unto iniquity; even so now yield your members servants to righteousness unto holiness."*

Righteousness, as Paul pointed out, is not only our standing in Christ after we've repented. The other side of the coin is that it is something we live because of what He has done in us. We become servants of righteousness and *"to whom you yield yourselves servants to obey,* **his servants ye are to whom you obey,"** whether of sin (and Satan) unto (spiritual and eternal) death, or of obedience unto righteousness. The point is this, if you're obedient to and obey sin as your course of life, you're sin's servant and not God's, and the wages sin pays is still death. No man can serve two masters. Sin is still sin, even for the Christian. Listen to these scriptures for some ignorantly imply that sin is not accounted as sin for the Christian, for we are not under law, but let's hear the Word.

*"***My little children,*** these things write I unto you, that ye sin not. And if any man [Christian] sin, we have an advocate with the Father, Jesus Christ the*

righteous" (1 John 2:1). We see a Christian, then, can sin, and needs to repent when he does. Paul, in writing to the Corinthian church said, *"And lest, when I come again, my God will humble me among you, and that I shall bewail many [in the church] which **have sinned already, and have not repented** of the uncleanness and fornication and lasciviousness which they have committed"* (2 Cor. 12:21). But Paul said, *"Sin is not imputed where there is no law."* If there was no law for us as Christians there would be no sin. But sin is still recognized as sin, so there is still law. The apostle John wrote, *"Whosoever committeth sin transgresseth also the law: for sin is the transgression of the law"* (1 John 3:4). This is the moral law. *"If ye fulfill the **royal law** according to the scripture, Thou shalt love thy neighbor as thyself, ye do well: But if ye have respect to persons, **ye commit sin**, and are convinced of the law as transgressors"* (James 2:8-9). And as Paul said, *"The sting of death is sin; and the strength of sin is the law"* (1 Cor. 15:56). So, it is obvious that the moral law still exists for us as Christians. If we follow His law written in our hearts as the course of our life, all is well, even if you have some struggles at times as you're trying to overcome and learn the ways of God. But if you willingly rebel and turn from Him, all is not well until you repent. The Lord says, *"If ye be willing and obedient, ye shall eat the good of the land: but if ye refuse and rebel, ye shall be devoured with the sword: for the mouth of the Lord hath spoken it"* (Isa. 1:19-20). We are still under God's law but not the Old Covenant works of the law.

Paul said God gave us the gift of the Holy Spirit, *"That the righteousness of the law might be fulfilled in us, who walk not after the flesh, but after the Spirit"* (Rom. 8:4). So Christians need to *"awake to righteousness and sin not."*

Romans 2:1-11

*"Therefore thou art inexcusable, O man, whosoever thou art that judgest [that passes judgment on sinners]: for wherein thou judgest another, thou condemnest thyself; for thou that judgest **doest the same things. But we are sure that the judgment of God is according to truth against [and rightly falls on] them which commit [and practice] such things. And thinkest thou this, O man, that judgest them [and tells them they are sinners and worthy of judgment] which do such things, and doest the same [and live in the same kind of immoral practices], that thou shalt escape the judgment of God?** Or despisest thou the riches of His goodness and forbearance and longsuffering; **not knowing that the goodness of God leadeth thee to repentance? [God leads you to repent of those things] But after thy hardness and impenitent [unrepentant] heart treasurest up unto thyself wrath against the day of wrath and**

revelation of the righteous judgment of God; Who will render to [and repay] *every man according to his deeds* [behavior]: *to them who by* **patient contin-** **uance in well doing** *seek for glory and honor and immortality [He will reward them with], eternal life: But unto them that are contentious, and* **do not obey** *the truth,* **but obey unrighteousness [He will give], indignation and wrath, tribulation and anguish, upon every soul of man that doeth evil,** *of the Jew first, and also of the Gentiles; but glory, honor, and peace, to every man that worketh good, to the Jew first, and also to the Gentile:* **For there is no respect of persons with God.**" Notice, Paul said that if we have patient continuance in welldoing God will then reward us with eternal life. Get it? He's talking about obtaining eternal life! Would Paul say one thing here about eternal life and then teach something directly opposite in chapters 4 and 5? No! In Galatians 6:8-9 Paul writes, *"For he that soweth to his flesh shall of the flesh reap corruption; but he that soweth to the Spirit shall of the Spirit* **reap life everlasting.** *And* **let us [then] not be weary in well doing:** *for in due season we shall reap [eternal life], if we faint not"* (if we don't give up). Then Peter says in First Peter 4:19, *"Wherefore let them that suffer according to the will of God* **commit the keeping of their souls to him in well doing,** *as unto a faithful Creator."*

Now God said His people *are destroyed* for a lack of knowledge. Sad to say, some who think they are covered by grace while they take the broad road to destruction living contrary to God's moral law only deceive themselves and give themselves a false peace and a false security. They will be in for an awful awakening at the end of this life except they repent. Christ will say, *"Depart from Me, ye that work iniquity."* Why? Because they lived their lives contrary to Jesus and sided in with Satan. (To side in with Satan is to live the way this world lives, with no regard for the will of God.)

Therefore Jesus, the author of our faith says, *"Strive to enter in at the strait gate: for many, I say unto you,* **will seek to enter in, [thinking that they are going to] and shall not be able.** *Then shall ye begin to say, We have eaten and drunk in thy presence, and thou hast taught in our streets. But He shall say, I tell you, I know you not whence ye are;* **depart from me, all ye workers of iniq-** **uity. There shall be weeping and gnashing of teeth, [and bitter regret] when ye shall see Abraham, and Isaac, and Jacob, and all the prophets, in the king-** **dom of God, [kingdom of Heaven, Matt. 8:12] and you yourselves** *(who work iniquity) thrust out"* (Luke 13:24, 26-28).

CHAPTER THIRTEEN

TAKING THE RIGHT WAY

T he Bible says, *"There is **a way** which seemeth right unto a man but the end thereof are the **ways** of death."*

God, speaking about Abraham and his faith, said, *"For I know him, **that he will command** his children and his household after him, and they shall **keep the way of the Lord, to do justice and judgment**; that the Lord may bring upon Abraham that which he hath spoken of him"* (Gen. 18:19). Notice, *"the way of the Lord."* There is *a way* that leads to life and there is *a way* that leads to death; a true way and a counterfeit way.

Let's see some other scriptures that show us the true way of the Lord. It is also called, *the "**way** of truth."*

*"But there were false prophets also among the people, even as there shall be false teachers among you [coming in to the church], who privily shall bring in [to the church] damnable heresies, even denying the Lord that brought them, and bring upon themselves swift destruction. **And many shall follow their pernicious [lawless, deadly, and immoral] ways;** by reason of whom **the [real] way of truth** [which is according to godliness] shall be evil spoken of"* (2 Pet. 2:1-2). False teachers teach that immoral ways are okay and bring reproach upon the way of truth. Those who follow these false teachers get upset with those who teach the real way of truth and that godliness is necessary, saying that it's legalistic to say we have to obey God.

The way *of peace.* *"Destruction and misery are **in their ways:** And the **way of peace** have they not known"* (Rom. 3:16-17). *"Blessed are the peacemakers for they shall be called the children of God."* We must follow the way of peace to be His children.

The way of good men. *"That thou mayest walk **in the way of good men**, and keep the paths of the righteous"* (Prov. 2:20). Good men walk in the paths of righteousness; evil men walk in unrighteous paths.

The way of righteousness. *"For it had been better for them not to have known **the way of righteousness**, than, after they have known it, to turn from the holy commandment delivered unto them"* (2 Pet. 2:21). God has commanded us to follow the Spirit and walk in the way of righteousness. We must never turn from His holy commandment. *"He leadeth us in paths of righteousness for his name's sake"* (Ps. 23:3).

The narrow ***way***. *"Enter ye in at the strait gate: for wide is the gate, and **broad is the way, that leadeth to destruction**, and many there be which go in thereat: Because strait is the gate, and **narrow is the way which leadeth unto life**, and few there be that find it"* (Matt. 7:13-14). The narrow way is living for the will of God (1 John 2:17). This is the only road grace has provided. The broad way is living for selfish lusts just as Satan did with no regard for God's will.

The way of life. *"**The way of life** is above to the wise, that he may depart from hell beneath"* (Prov. 15:24). *The way* of the wise is righteousness (Dan. 12:3).

The straight ***way***. *"Lead me, O Lord, in thy righteousness because of mine enemies; make Thy way straight before my face"* (Ps. 5:8).

The word "way" means "the road, street, or path, which heads in a direction towards a certain destination." You cannot head in two opposite directions and end up in the same place.

*"Wait on the Lord, and **keep His way**, and [then] he shall exalt thee to inherit the land: when the wicked [who don't keep His way] are cut off, thou shalt see it"* (Ps. 37:34). There is no such thing as a grace given by God that covers for us while we walk in the way of sinners (Ps. 1:1-3).

*"Our heart is not turned back, neither have our steps declined from **thy way**."* Never let your steps and the direction of your life turn from the right way of the Lord. It's only when people's hearts turn away from God that they turn away and no longer obey the truth.

*"What man is he that feareth the Lord? **Him** shall he teach in **the way** that he shall choose"* (Ps. 25:12). Never lose the fear of the Lord, or you shall not receive His teaching and guidance.

*"I will instruct thee and teach thee in **the way** which thou shalt go: I will guide thee with mine eye"* (Ps. 32:8). His instructions are given to us New

Testament believers through the apostles. *"But thou, O man of God, flee these things; **and follow after** righteousness, godliness, faith, love, patience, meekness. Fight the good fight of faith, lay hold on eternal life, whereunto thou art also called, and hast professed a good profession before many witnesses"* (1 Tim. 6:11-12). This is *the way* we should go. Walk ye in it.

*"Teach me **thy way**, O Lord; I will walk in thy truth: unite my heart to fear thy name"* (Ps. 86:11). *The way* of the Lord is to walk in truth. All sin is yielding to, or acting like, the father of lies.

"Blessed are the undefiled in the way, who walk in the law of the Lord" (Ps. 119:1). *The right way* is to walk in the *law of the Lord;* these are the ones who are blessed (Rev. 22:14).

*"Wherewithal shall a young man cleanse **his way?** By taking heed thereto according to thy word"* (Ps. 119:9). God's Word *always* cleanses from sin and helps us to live holy (John 15:3). (See also 1 John 2:14.)

*"I have chosen **the way of truth:** Thy judgments have I laid before me"* (Ps. 119:30). You must choose the way of truth over the way of evil. He has called us out of darkness to live in His marvelous light.

*"I will run **the way of thy commandments,** when thou shalt enlarge my heart, Teach me, O Lord, **the way of thy statutes; and I shall keep it** unto the end"* (Ps. 119:32-33). *"Turn away mine eyes from beholding vanity; and quicken thou me in thy way"* (Ps. 119:37). *"I have refrained my feet from every evil way, that I might keep thy word"* (Ps. 119:101). To keep God's true Gospel is to turn from every evil way, for the *"face of the Lord is [still] against them which do evil"* (1 Pet. 3:12).

*"Through thy precepts I get understanding: therefore I hate every **false way"*** (Ps. 119:104). The concept of false grace is a *false way*; it is not the way of the Lord, nor the way of understanding. It should therefore, be rejected by us. It has a religious form but denies the power to really live it. From those who teach such things, the Bible says, *"turn away."*

*"Therefore I esteem all Thy precepts concerning all things to be right; and I hate every **false way"*** (Ps. 119:128). Certainly, God doesn't give grace for us to walk in a false way. All the ways of godliness, holiness, righteousness, love, and so on, are truth. *Anything* then, that is opposite to them must be a false way. If godliness is truth, any ungodliness must be false; and if righteousness is truth, then sin is always a false way. If holiness is truth, then to think that the truth says you can live unholy and it's okay, is to be deluded by the angel of light.

*"Search me, O God, and know my heart: try me, and know my thoughts: and see if there be **any wicked way** in me, and lead me in **the way** everlasting"* (Ps. 139:23-24). To take any path of wickedness is a wicked way, but the way of everlasting life is the right way.

*"Cause me to hear thy lovingkindness in the morning; for in thee do I trust: cause me to know **the way** wherein I should walk; for I lift up my soul unto thee"* (Ps. 143:8). If you sincerely pray to the Lord about which way to take, He will always show you the pathway of righteousness (James 1:5).

*"The Lord preserveth the strangers; he reliveth the fatherless and widow: **but the way of the wicked** he turneth upside down"* (Ps. 146:9). God will never bless those who walk in the ways of wickedness. (That is, in the ways of the world whose behavior is contrary to God.) *"Wherein in time past ye walked according to the course of this world, according to the prince of the power of the air, the spirit that now worketh in the children of disobedience"* (Eph. 2:2-3). God only promises to judge those who continue in that way and calls them *"the children of wrath"* because of these things.

*"I have taught thee in **the way of wisdom**; I have led thee in right paths"* (Prov. 4:11). The way of wisdom is the way of following what is right in God's sight. *"For the commandment is a lamp; and the law is light; and reproofs of instruction are **the way of life**"* (Prov. 6:23). The way of life is to let God's Word purge you from every evil way, to follow the light of truth, and adjust our lives accordingly.

*"The fear of the Lord is to hate evil: pride, and arrogancy, and **the evil way**, and the froward mouth, do I hate…. I lead in the way of righteousness, in the midst of the paths of judgment: that I may cause those that love me to inherit substance; and I will fill their treasures"* (Prov. 8:13, 20-21). God hates the evil way and would never provide a grace that would okay people walking in it. Wisdom here says that it leads in the way of righteousness and it causes those that love this way to inherit substance and their treasures will be filled. Peter taught that God sent Jesus to bless us by turning us all away from the way of sin. *"Unto you first God, having raised up his Son Jesus, sent him **to bless you, in turning away every one of you from his iniquities**"* (Acts 3:26).

*"Forsake the foolish, and live; and go in **the way of understanding**"* (Prov. 9:6). *"Fools make a mock at sin: but among the righteous there is favor"* (Prov. 14:9).

***"He is in the way of life that keepeth [obeys] instruction:** but he that refuseth reproof erreth…. **The way of the Lord** is strength to the upright: but* *destruction shall be to the workers of iniquity"* (Prov. 10:17, 29). *Working iniquity is always opposite of the true way of life in the scriptures.*

"Working iniquity" means "evil behavior and deeds" (Rom. 1:28-32).

"The righteousness of the perfect shall direct his way: but the wicked shall fall by his own wickedness.... They that are of a froward heart are abomination to the Lord: but such as are upright in their way are his delight" (Prov. 11:5,20). If people live wickedly, the scriptures call them wicked regardless of what label they think they have.

*"**The way** of a fool is right in his own eyes: but he that hearkeneth unto counsel is wise.... **In the way of righteousness is life**; and in the pathway thereof there is no death"* (Prov. 12:15,28). But if people turn from the way of righteousness and go another direction, there is death and no life, unless they repent and turn around. (See 2 Pet. 2:20-21.)

*"Righteousness keepeth him that is upright in the way: but wickedness overthroweth the sinner.... Good understanding giveth favor, but the **way of transgressors is hard**"* (Prov. 13:6,15). Those who transgress God's ways will not find blessings, but cursings (Amos 3:3). Their way will become hard.

"The way of the wicked is an abomination unto the Lord: but he loveth him that followeth after righteousness" (Prov. 15:9). *"Correction is grievous unto him that forsaketh **the way**: and he that hateth reproof shall die"* (Prov. 15:9-10). If you loved truth, righteousness, goodness, and God's will, you wouldn't want to believe a false concept of grace. But correction in the Word grieves those who leave the right path because they love darkness more than light.

*"**The highway of the upright is to depart from evil**: [behavior] he that keepeth his way preserveth his soul"* (Prov. 16:17). Do you want to preserve your soul? Then take the way of the upright and depart from evil. *"Receiving the end of your faith, even the salvation of your souls"* (1 Pet. 1:9).

"Every way of a man is right in his own eyes: but the Lord pondereth the hearts" (Prov. 21:2).

*"An unjust man is an abomination to the just: and he that is upright in **the way** is abomination to the wicked"* (Prov. 29:27).

If people want to continue in their evil ways, or want to follow teachers who teach that you can walk in an immoral way, they don't like those who say you must live for the will of God and obey Him. They don't want that responsibility because they don't want to do what's right. People hear what they *want* to hear. Let's heed the Lord's warnings and instructions. *"But whoso hearkeneth unto me shall dwell safely, and shall be quiet from fear of evil"* (Prov. 1:33). *"Wherefore lift up the hands which hang down, and the feeble knees; And make straight paths for your feet, lest that which is lame be turned out of the way; but let it rather be healed. Follow peace with all men, and holiness, without which no man shall see the Lord"* (Heb. 12:12-14).

The Wrong Path

Now let's look further at the wrong path to take.

Broad is **the way** that leads to destruction. *"Enter ye in at the strait gate: for wide is the gate, and **broad is the way**, that leadeth to destruction, and many there be which go in thereat"* (Matt. 7:13). Most people take the broad road to destruction. The narrow way is living for God's will and not self-will (1 Pet. 4:2). The broad way is living the way you want apart from the will of God (1 John 2:15-17).

The way *of sinners:* *"Blessed is the man **that walketh not** in the counsel of the ungodly, nor standeth in **the way of sinners** [that is the way of those who sin] nor sitteth in the seat of the scornful"* (Ps. 1:1). You can't live like a sinner and be called a saint (James 5:19-20).

The way *of Cain:* *"Woe unto them! For they have gone in **the way of Cain**, and ran greedily after the error of Balaam for reward, and perished in the gainsaying of Core"* (Jude 11). Cain killed his brother because his own *works were evil* and his *brother's works were righteous* (1 John 3:12). Cain's evil way was to kill his brother who lived right in God's sight. There is also the brother who goes back into sin and goes back into *the way of error* (James 5:20). Don't take the way of Cain and persecute those who say you must live right.

The way *of Balaam*, who compromised what was right for the sake of selfish temporal gain. *"Which have forsaken the right way, and are gone astray, following **the way** of Balaam the son of Bosor, who loved **the wages of unrighteousness**"* (2 Pet. 2:15). The wages of sin is always death (Rom. 6:23). Peter said this is what false teachers in the church have done, they have forsaken the right way. *"They are all gone out of **the way**, they are together become unprofitable; there is none that **doeth good**, no, not one"* (Rom. 3:12). To depart from the way of the Lord is to stop doing good.

The way *of the ungodly:* *"For the Lord knoweth **the way** of the righteous: but **the way** of the ungodly shall perish"* (Ps. 1:6). The ungodly are those who do not live godly the way the Lord wants them to live. *"My son, **walk not thou in the way with them**; refrain thy foot from their path"* (Prov. 1:15).

God said, *"They would none of my counsel: they despised all my reproof. Therefore shall they eat of the fruit of **their own way, and be filled with their own devices**"* (Prov. 1:30-31). All will get a harvest from their own life's actions and from what they are doing and have been sowing, and according to whether or not they have repented.

The truth is given to you, *"To deliver thee from **the way** of the evil man, from the man that speaketh froward things"* (Prov. 2:12). The evil man is the man that lives to do evil and do wrong in the sight of the Lord.

*"**Enter not into the path of the wicked**, and go not in the way of evil men. Avoid it, pass not by it, turn from it, and pass away"* (Prov. 4:14-15). Hear God's instructions!

*"**The way** of the wicked is as darkness: they know not at what they stumble"* (Prov. 4:19). Any immoral behavior contrary to righteousness will cause spiritual darkness (2 Pet. 1:9-10).

These false teachers and this false concept of grace has caused many to respond negatively to this real way of the truth and has caused a great darkness in their souls and in the lives of numerous Christians. Peter said, *" ... by reason of whom [these false teachers] the way of truth shall be evil spoken of."* By listening to these teachers, many fight for their right to live in sin, but as shown, that is *the way* of death, and they have greatly persecuted the Lord's true way down through the centuries.

If people want to get by with living in lusts and sinful pleasures, it is grievous to them to hear the truth. But if they want to live for God, then their heart rejoices when instruction in righteousness is given. *"Blessed are they which do hunger and thirst after righteousness: for they shall be filled"* (Matt. 5:6).

*"The man that wandereth out of **the way** of understanding shall remain in the congregation of the dead"* (Prov. 21:16). If you leave the way of the Lord and live among the dead, you too will die. Paul wrote, *"She that liveth in [sinful] pleasure is dead while she liveth"* (1 Tim. 5:6).

*"Thorns and snares are in **the way** of the froward: he that doth keep [guards] his soul shall be far from them"* (Prov. 22:5). Notice, it doesn't say blessings and prosperity, but thorns and snares. "Froward" means "willfully stubborn and unruly."

"Whoso [whatever person] **causeth the righteous to go astray in an evil way**, *he shall fall himself into his own pit: but the upright shall have good things in possession"* (Prov. 28:10). Never say that grace means you can leave the narrow path of God's will. If you teach such things, you also will fall into a pit and become blinded as to God's true way. Notice also that it is the upright that will have good things in their possession. *"For the Lord God is a sun and shield: the Lord will give grace and glory: no good thing will he withhold from them* **that walk uprightly"** (Ps. 84:11).

It should be obvious to all that can read that God plainly reveals there is a right way and a wrong way. One way leads to life and blessings, the other leads to death and cursings. So don't listen to those who say you can walk in evil ways and be blessed of the Lord or find life, for such is not the case unless you repent and get on the right path. *"I call heaven and earth to record this day against you, that I have set before you life and death, blessing and cursing: therefore choose life, that both thou and thy seed may live"* (Deut. 30:19). And if you're going to choose life, you're going to have to choose to live for, and be obedient to, the will of God (John 8:12, 6:38). Note that He said, men have to choose.

Look at these scriptures to see the way we should "walk."

"As for me, behold, my covenant is with thee, and thou shalt be a father of many nations" (Gen. 17:4).

"Then said the Lord unto Moses, Behold, I will rain bread from heaven for you; and the people shall go out and gather a certain rate every day, that I may prove them, **whether they will walk in my law, or no"** (Exod. 16:4).

"And if ye will not be reformed by me by these things, **but will walk contrary unto me; Then will I also walk contrary unto you,** *and will punish you yet seven times for your sins"* (Lev. 26:23-24).

"Ye shall walk in all the ways *which the Lord your God hath commanded you, that ye may live, and that it may be well with you, and that ye may prolong your days in the land which ye shall possess"* (Deut. 5:33).

"And it shall be, if thou do at all forget the Lord thy God, **and walk after other gods**, *and serve them, and worship them, I testify against you this day that* **ye shall surely perish"** (Deut. 8:19).

"And now, Israel, **what doth the Lord thy God require of thee, but to fear the Lord thy God, to walk in all his ways,** *and to love him, and to serve the Lord thy God with all thy heart and with all thy soul"* (Deut. 10:12).

*"They kept not the covenant of God, **and refused to walk in his law**"* (Ps. 78:10).

*"For the Lord God is a sun and shield: the Lord will give grace and glory: no good thing will he withhold **from them that walk uprightly**"* (Ps. 84:11).

*"**Blessed are the undefiled** in the way, **who walk in the law of the Lord** .... They also do no iniquity: they walk in his ways"* (Ps. 119:1,3).

*"He layeth up sound wisdom for the righteous: He is a buckler **to them that walk uprightly**"* (Prov. 2:7).

*"Who is wise, and he shall understand these things? prudent, and he shall know them? for the ways of the Lord are right, **and the just shall walk in them**: but the transgressors shall fall therein"* (Hosea 14:9).

*"But in the last days it shall come to pass, that the mountain of the house of the Lord shall be established in the top of the mountains, and it shall be exalted above the hills; and people shall flow unto it. And many nations shall come, and say, Come, and let us go up to the mountain of the Lord, and to the house of the God of Jacob; and he will teach us of his ways, **and we will walk in his paths**: for the law shall go forth of Zion, and the word of the Lord from Jerusalem. And he shall judge among many people, and rebuke strong nations afar off; and they shall beat their swords into plowshares, and their spears into pruninghooks: nation shall not lift up a sword against nation, neither shall they learn war any more"* (Micah 4:1-3). Even in the Millennium, people must obey the *"Law of the Lord."*

*"Therefore we are buried with him by baptism into death: that like as Christ was raised up from the dead by the glory of the Father, even so we also **should walk in newness of life**"* (Rom. 6:4).

*"There is therefore now no condemnation to them which are in Christ Jesus, **who walk not after the flesh, but after the Spirit**.... That the righteousness of the law might be fulfilled in us, who walk not after the flesh, but after the Spirit"* (Rom. 8:1,4).

*"**Let us walk honestly**, as in the day; not in rioting and drunkenness, not in chambering and wantonness, not in strife and envying"* (Rom. 13:13).

*"This I say then, **Walk in the Spirit, and ye shall not fulfil the lust of the flesh**"* (Gal. 5:16).

*"For we are his workmanship, created in Christ Jesus unto good works, which **God hath before ordained that we should walk in them**"* (Eph. 2:10).

*"I therefore, the prisoner of the Lord, beseech you that ye **walk worthy of the vocation wherewith ye are called**.... This I say therefore, and testify in the*

Lord, that ye henceforth **walk not as other Gentiles walk**, in the vanity of their mind" (Eph. 4:1,17).

"**And walk in love**, as Christ also hath loved us, and hath given Himself for us an offering and a sacrifice to God for a sweetsmelling savour .... For ye were sometimes darkness, but now are ye light in the Lord: **walk as children of light:** For the fruit of the Spirit is in all goodness and righteousness and truth" (Eph. 5:2,8-9).

"**See then that ye walk circumspectly, not as fools, but as wise**" (Eph. 5:15).

"Brethren, be followers together of Me, **and mark them which walk so as ye have us for an ensample. For many walk**, of whom I have told you often, and now tell you even weeping, that they are the enemies of the cross of Christ: Whose end is destruction, whose God is their belly, and whose glory is in their shame, who mind earthly things" (Phil. 3:17-19).

"For this cause we also, since the day we heard it, do not cease to pray for you, and to desire that ye might be filled with the knowledge of his will in all wisdom and spiritual understanding; **That ye might walk worthy of the Lord unto all pleasing, being fruitful in every good work**, and increasing in the knowledge of God" (Col. 1:9-10).

"As ye know how we exhorted and comforted and charged every one of you, as a father doth his children, That ye would **walk worthy of God**, who hath called you unto his kingdom and glory" (1 Thess. 2:11-12).

"Furthermore then we beseech you, brethren, and exhort you by the Lord Jesus, that as **ye have received of us how ye ought to walk and to please God, so ye would abound more and more**. For ye know what commandments we gave you by the Lord Jesus" (1 Thess. 4:1-2).

"The Lord knoweth how to deliver the godly out of temptations, and to reserve the unjust unto the day of judgment to be punished: **But chiefly them that walk after the flesh** in the lust of uncleanness, and despise government. Presumptuous are they, selfwilled, they are not afraid to speak evil of dignities. Whereas angels, which are greater in power and might, bring not railing accusation against them before the Lord. But these, as natural brute beasts, made to be taken and destroyed, speak evil of the things that they understand not; and shall utterly perish in their own corruption; And shall receive the reward of unrighteousness, as they that count it pleasure to riot in the day time. Spots they are and blemishes, sporting themselves with their own deceivings while they feast with you; Having eyes full of adultery, and that cannot cease from sin; beguiling unstable souls: an heart they have exercised with covetous *practices; cursed children: Which have forsaken the right way, and are gone astray, following the way of Balaam the son of Bosor, who loved the wages of unrighteousness"* (2 Pet. 2:9-15).

*"**If we say that we have fellowship with him, and walk in darkness, we lie**, and do not the truth: **But if we walk in the light**, as he is in the light, we have fellowship one with another, and the blood of Jesus Christ his Son cleanseth us from all sin"* (1 John 1:6-7).

*"**He that saith he abideth in him ought himself also so to walk, even as he walked"*** (1 John 2:6).

*"But, beloved, remember ye the words which were spoken before of the apostles of our Lord Jesus Christ; How that they told you there should be mockers in the last time, **who should walk after their own ungodly lusts**. These be they who separate themselves, sensual, having not the Spirit. But ye, beloved, building up yourselves on your most holy faith, praying in the Holy Ghost, keep yourselves in the love of God, looking for the mercy of our Lord Jesus Christ unto eternal life"* (Jude 17-21).

*"And unto the angel of the church in Sardis write; These things saith he that hath the seven Spirits of God, and the seven stars; I know thy works, that thou hast a name that thou livest, and art dead. Be watchful, and strengthen the things which remain, that are ready to die: for I have not found thy works perfect before God. Remember therefore how thou hast received and heard, and hold fast, and repent. If therefore thou shalt not watch, I will come on thee as a thief, and thou shalt not know what hour I will come upon thee. Thou hast a few names even in Sardis which have not defiled their garments; **and they shall walk with me in white: for they are worthy**. He that overcometh, the same shall be clothed in white raiment; and I will not blot out his name out of the book of life, but I will confess his name before my Father, and before his angels"* (Rev. 3:1-5).

Keeping God's Commandments

Let's look now at the words "keep," "kept," and "keepeth," and see their definition and what the Lord has to say about this in the New Covenant. The word "keep" means "to do," "to persevere in," "to continue doing and persist in."

The apostle Paul wrote in 1 Corinthians 7:19, *"Circumcision is nothing, and uncircumcision is nothing, but [what really matters is] **the keeping** of the commandments of God."* John wrote, quoting Christ in Revelation 22:14, *"**Blessed are they that do** his commandments, that they may have right to the tree of life, and may enter in through the gates into the city."* We see then that to keep is to do and continue doing. Now let's look at the words "keep," "kept," and "keepeth" in the New Covenant and see how they are used (James 1:22).

Matthew 19:17

*"And he said unto him, Why callest thou me good? There is none good but one, that is, God: but **if thou wilt enter into life, keep the commandments.**"* Here is the way to life regardless of what any man says (John 5:25-29).

Luke 11:28

*"But he said, yea, rather, blessed are they that hear the word of God, **and keep it.**"* Here we see who Christ pronounced special blessing upon; those who do the commandments.

John 8:51,55

*"Verily, verily, I say unto you, **If a man keep my saying**, he shall never see death…. Yet ye have not known him; but I know him: and if I should say, I know Him not, I shall be a liar like unto you: but I know Him, **and keep His saying.**"* What about those who refuse to keep His sayings? (See 1 John 2:3-4.) Jesus, the author of faith, kept His Father's sayings. This, then, is faith. To disobey is unbelief and displeasing to God. It doesn't honor God in the least to willfully disobey and say, "Oh, His grace will cover for it." A person that says such a thing is only repeating what the devil has said.

John 14:14-15,21,23-24

*"If ye shall ask anything in my name, I will do it. If ye love me, **keep my commandments**…. He that hath my commandments, **and keepeth them**, he it is that loveth me: and he that loveth me shall be loved of my Father, and I will love Him, and will manifest myself to him…. Jesus answered and said unto him, **If a man love me, he will keep my words:** and my Father will love him, and we will come unto him, and make Our abode with him. **He that loveth me not keepeth not my sayings:** and the word which ye hear is not mine, but the Father's which sent me."* His words are His commandments. The only way to show Him that you love Him, and are on His side, is to keep His words and commandments.

"Keep yourselves in the love of God, looking for the mercy of our Lord Jesus Christ unto eternal life" (Jude 21). How? *"**If ye keep my commandments, ye shall abide** in my love; even as I have kept my Father's commandments, and abide in his love"* (John 15:10). Christ is our example. He was, and is, full of grace and truth, and He said to keep His commandments.

In John 15:14 Christ says:

*"Ye are my friends, **if ye do** whatsoever I command you."*

First Timothy 6:13-14

*"I give thee charge in the sight of God, who quickeneth all things, and before Christ Jesus, who before Pontius Pilate witnessed a good confession; that thou **keep this commandment without spot**, unrebukeable, until the appearing of our Lord Jesus Christ."*

1 John 2:3-4

*"And hereby we do know that we know him, **if we keep his commandments**. He that saith, I know him, **and keepeth not** his commandments, is a liar, and the truth is not in him."* Don't listen to liars who say that you don't have to keep His commandments.

1 John 3:22

*"And whatsoever we ask, we receive of him, **because we keep his commandments**, and do those things that are pleasing in His sight."* Faith pleases God. Faith keeps His commandments and does what's pleasing in His sight. Whoever doesn't obey Him is a sinner.

1 John 5:2-3

*"By this we know that we love the children of God, when we love God, **and keep his commandments. For this is the love of God, that we keep his commandments:** and His commandments are not grievous."* To love God is to keep His commandments.

Revelation 12:17

*"And the dragon was wroth with the woman, and went to make war with the remnant of her seed, **which keep the commandments of God**, and have the testimony of Jesus Christ."* He's not concerned about those who don't keep God's commandments. He's already got them.

Revelation 14:12

*"Here is the patience of the saints [the separated ones]: **here are they that keep the commandments of God, and the faith of Jesus.**"* The faith of Jesus is *all* that is in the Gospels, Epistles, and the book of Revelation. Godly saints obey it. Keeping the faith and keeping the commandments, as are recorded in the New Covenant, is one and the same thing. This is *"the faith"* that was once delivered to the saints. Contend for it.

Revelation 22:7-9

*"Behold, I come quickly: **blessed is he that keepeth** the sayings of the prophecy of this book. And I John saw these things, and heard them. And when I had heard and seen, I fell down to worship before the feet of the angel, which*

*showed me these things. Then saith he unto me, See thou do it not: for I am thy fellow servant, and of thy brethren the prophets, **and of them which keep the sayings of this book**: worship God."*

1 Peter 4:19

"Wherefore let them that suffer according to the will of God commit the keeping of their souls to him in well doing, as unto a faithful Creator."

It is obvious by these scriptures that not just hearing God's Word brings blessing but the doing of it (James 1:22-25). Keeping His commandments is not just saying you believe. In Matthew 7:24-27, Christ says, *"Therefore whosoever heareth these sayings of Mine, and doeth them [acts accordingly], **I will liken him unto a wise man**, which built his house upon a rock: and the rain descended, and the floods came, and the winds blew, and beat upon that house; and it fell not: for it was founded upon a rock. And every one that heareth these sayings of mine, **and doeth them not** [does not adjust his life accordingly], **shall be likened unto a foolish man**, which built his house upon the sand: and the rain descended, and the floods came, and the winds blew, and beat upon that house; and it fell: and great was the fall of it."* To just say that you believe and not do it, is foolish, and your life will eventually crash.

Let us then be wise and continue to live, obeying His commandments. And if you do sin, go to your advocate Jesus Christ the righteous and He will cleanse you from all unrighteousness (1 John 2:1).

Paul wrote in his first letter to Timothy in 1 Timothy 6:12, *"Fight the good fight of faith, lay hold on eternal life, whereunto thou art also called, and hast professed a good profession before many witnesses."* You have to fight to continue in the faith to the end (Rev. 2:10).

In 2 Timothy 4:6-8 he later wrote concerning his own departure from this world, *"For I am now ready to be offered, and the time of my departure is at hand. **I have fought a good fight**, I have finished my course, **I have kept the faith**: Henceforth [because of this] there is laid up for me a crown of righteousness, which the Lord, the righteous judge, shall give me at that day: and not to me only, but unto all them also that love [and look forward to] His appearing."*

To Paul, keeping the faith was keeping God's commands and the teachings of Christ (1 Cor. 7:19). And it was to him, a fight and a race to the finish line (Heb. 12:1-2).

Ultra Grace

So grace never has been, nor ever will be, a cloak for sin in such a way as the ultra gracists erroneously think. There is no "all covering" grace that keeps one saved no matter how they willfully act. If one acts and lives consistently contrary to God's will with no repentance, he reveals by his fruit that he is not one of the elect and chooses not to be.

Certainly we know the blood of Jesus washes away all sin when it's confessed and repented of, and a person turns back to the right way (1 John 1:9). Go to God. He will instantly, abundantly pardon all wrong doing if you confess it, but then He wants you to stay on the right road.

This is what mercy and grace have truly provided. Grace clauses in any contract only go as far as the one who made the contract has written. Any presumptions beyond it will not stand up in any court of law. You have to go by what is actually written, there is no room for reasoning and rationalization.

If repentance or confession of sin was no longer necessary, as some caught up in this ultra grace teaching say, then a person could repent for one second when first saved, receive Christ, and then go on living the way they did (or even worse), and would still be saved.

Is this repentance? Is this the great salvation we are told not to neglect? Is this the narrow way that leads to life? Is this what being under the Lordship of Christ means? Did Jesus come to save us *from* our sins, or *in* our sins? Is holiness and righteousness then just old fashioned and only for the early church and no longer needed? Or is righteousness just a label that's put on us when we say a few words in prayer; a label that will never be removed, regardless of how wicked one becomes, and whether or not they choose the world once again over God? (James 4:4). Is this the "*most holy faith,*" Jude told us to earnestly contend for? It is, because we live in an instant, push-button society that we want an instant push button salvation. But God only does things His way.

*"Again, the devil taketh him up into an exceeding high mountain, and showeth him all the kingdoms of the world, and the glory of them; and saith unto him, **All these things will I give thee, if thou wilt fall down and worship me.** Then saith Jesus unto him, Get thee hence, Satan: for it is written, thou shalt worship the Lord thy God, and him only shalt thou serve"* (Matt. 4:7-10). Has Christ now provided that we can fall down and worship the devil by choosing to live for the ungodly things of the world over God's will? God

forbid! For Christ is our example and we are to rebuke any such temptations that come to us and live for the will of the heavenly Father.

This "ultra (false concept of) grace," which is not Bible grace, tries to make anything that doesn't agree with its worldly, ungodly, and loose, moral standards look legalistic, including the statements made by Christ and the apostles themselves in their doctrine. Like any other wrong doctrines, it searches for proof texts, which it can twist and manipulate and it overexaggerates and emphasizes them, while ignoring numerous other clear scriptures to the contrary. It causes people to not want to endure sound doctrine, and if received, it will even drive them from the presence of the true Word, for light always drives away darkness. While it promises them liberty, it's really a bondage which leads people into further corruption and it can cause a Christian to become lukewarm, or even shipwrecked in their faith (See Rev. 3:16.), and finally move them to depart from God once again. Christ said if a person is lukewarm in their faith, He will spit them out of His mouth.

Remember, "Evil communications corrupt good behavior." Never let anyone persuade you that you could leave the right way and still have eternal life, for such is not the case (Rev. 22:14). *"Let no man deceive you!"* *"And Enoch also, the seventh from Adam, prophesied of these, saying, Behold, the Lord cometh with ten thousands of his saints, to execute judgment upon all, and **to convince all that are ungodly among them of all their ungodly deeds which they have ungodly committed**, and of all their hard speeches which ungodly sinners have spoken against him. But, beloved, remember ye the words which were spoken before of the apostles of our Lord Jesus Christ; How that they told you there should be mockers in the last time [mocking God, thinking they could sow evil and reap good, Gal. 6:7], **who would walk after their own ungodly lusts**…. But ye, beloved, building up yourselves on your most holy faith, praying in the Holy Ghost, **keep yourselves** in the love of God [by keeping His commandments, John 15:10], looking for the mercy of our Lord Jesus Christ [given to repentant sinners] unto eternal life. And of some [of these misled people] have compassion, making a difference: And others save with fear, pulling them out of the fire [of hell]; hating even the garment spotted by the flesh"* (Jude 14-15,17-18,20-23).

2 Peter 2:19-21

"While they [these misguided teachers in their great discourses] promise them [Christians] liberty [and freedom], they themselves are the servants of corruption [and sin]: for of whom a man is overcome, of the same is he brought in bondage. [A man is a slave to whatever overcomes him.] For if after they have

*escaped the pollutions of the world through the knowledge of the Lord and Savior Jesus Christ, they are again entangled therein [back in the same pollutions], and overcome, the latter end is worse with them than the beginning. **For it had been better for them not to have known the way of** righteousness, than, after they **have known it, to turn** from the holy commandment delivered unto them.*" There is no way to misinterpret this clear passage unless it's intentional.

Ultra gracists reject this part of the Apostles' Doctrine and teach this warning isn't so, or they ignore it. They will water down all such clear statements made by the apostles and also try and get others to not believe these clear warnings. The meaning of clear passages such as these are deliberately twisted so that they are not taken for what they actually say. Let us continue to walk close to Jesus and examine all things with a sincere heart in the light of God's Word. Can two walk together except they be agreed? (Amos 3:3) Let's take the right way.

John 10:27

Jesus said, "*My sheep hear my voice, and I know them, **and they follow me**.*" His sheep follow Him and those who "follow Him," cannot be plucked out of His hand. What about those who don't "follow Him," but head in another direction doing their own thing? (Isa. 53:6)

Psalm 23:3 says,

"*The Lord is my shepherd. He restoreth my soul: **he leadeth me in the paths of righteousness** for his name's sake.*" If we are following Him, we are walking inthe paths of righteousness (1 John 3:7-8).

1 John 2:6

"***He that saith he abideth** in him **ought himself** also so to **walk**, even as He walked.*" "*Let that therefore abide in you, which ye have heard from the beginning. If [on this condition] that which ye have heard from the beginning shall remain in you, **ye also shall continue** in the Son, and in the Father*" (1 John 2:24). "*And this is the record, that God hath given to us eternal life, and this life is in his Son*" (1 John 5:11). Notice, this life is in His Son. You have to continue *in Christ* to continue to have this life as a son of God (John 15:6). Those who abide in Christ walk the walk and not just talk the talk. "*In Him is life*" and "*whosoever abideth in Him sinneth not,*" for "*in Him is no sin.*" Adam was a son of God but lost life through sin (Luke 3:38; Rom. 5:12).

Acts 3:19-20

You must then, "***Repent** [turn from a life of sin] ye therefore [and turn to God], and be **converted, that your sins may be blotted out** [so that the record of your sins may be cancelled out], when the times of refreshing shall come from* *the presence of the Lord; and he shall send Jesus Christ, which before was preached unto you."* This is the faith of Jesus; the message He came to bring. Peter preached, *"Save yourselves from this crooked generation."*

To be really free is to want to serve the Lord from our hearts. It is to want to keep His commandments because He is working in us to do so (Heb. 13:20-21). We understand that Christians sometimes have struggles with the flesh in this world and they fall into sin at times; but if they are serving the Lord, they turn to Him in repentance and faith. *"Watch and pray, that ye enter not into temptation: the spirit indeed is willing, but the flesh is weak"* (Matt. 26:41). He didn't say run and play, but watch and pray. From the time sin entered the universe and iniquity was found in Lucifer, God's attitude toward sin has always been the same; He's against it. Sin, which is behavior that is contrary to His moral law, is what has caused all the destruction and ruin in His creation. Is He not then concerned about behavior? Isn't that what the sin problem is all about, wrong and evil behavior? God is not to blame for sin (James 1:13; 1 John 1:5).

"Be ye not unequally yoked together with unbelievers: for what fellowship hath righteousness with unrighteousness? and what communion hath light with darkness? And what concord hath Christ with Belial? or what part hath he that believeth with an infidel?" (2 Cor. 6:14-15).

Men and devils have willfully transgressed God's moral law and therefore are guilty. Not because God willed it but because they willed it (Rom. 3:23). God creates everything good in its original state (Gen. 1:31). *"Lo, this only have I found, that God hath made man upright; but they have sought out many inventions"* (Eccl. 7:29). *"Moreover the word of the Lord came unto me, saying, Son of man, take up a lamentation upon the king of Tyrus [the devil], and say unto him, Thus saith the Lord God; thou sealest up the sum, full of wisdom, and perfect in beauty. Thou hast been in Eden the garden of God; every precious stone was thy covering, the sardius, topaz, and the diamond, the beryl, the onyx, and the jasper, the sapphire, the emerald, and the carbuncle, and gold: the workmanship of thy tabrets and of thy pipes was prepared in thee in the day that thou wast created"* (Ezek. 28:11-13).

"Thou art the anointed cherub that covereth; and I have set thee so: thou wast upon the holy mountain of God; thou hast walked up and down in the midst of the stones of fire. ***Thou wast perfect in thy ways from the day that thou wast created****, till iniquity was found in thee"* (Ezek. 28:14-15).

"Do not err, my beloved brethren. Every good gift and every perfect gift is from above, and cometh down from the Father of lights, with whom is no variableness, neither shadow of turning" (James 1:16-17).

1 John 2:4-6

Listen again to this New Testament scripture:

*"He that saith, I know him, **and keepeth not his commandments, is a liar, and the truth is not in him.** But whoso keepeth his word [he that does what God says], in him verily is the love of God perfected: hereby know we that we are in Him. [By this we can be sure we are in union with God.] He that saith he abideth [continues] in him [in Christ] ought himself also so to walk, even as he walked."* (Must live like He lived for the will of God, John 6:38.) Those who say that you don't need to obey God or keep His commandments do not have the truth in them. Jesus said that Satan *"abode not in the truth."* Jesus said if we keep His commandments, *then* we will abide in the truth (John 17:17; 15:10).

This is the real love of God that we want to keep His commandments and not want to make excuses for *our bad behavior* and the breaking of His commandments. This false teaching on grace says, or implies, that you can live your whole life contrary to God's Word (just like the devil), and still abide in Christ and be the elect. Sadly, these misguided people think this is love and grace and so they spend their whole time learning these false things about grace, ever learning but never coming to the knowledge of the truth which then digs them deeper and deeper into their bondages and false teaching. But the scriptures teach just the opposite of what they say (1 John 3:3-8). Who then is the source of that other teaching? Realize this, faith, if it's Bible faith, is a commitment of the heart and soul to live for the will of God. This is the main direction of that person's life. This is what Paul preached as he preached *"obedience to the faith"* (Rom. 1:5). Faith does what the written Covenant says. Paul said, *"But they have not all obeyed the Gospel"* (Rom. 10:16).

In John 15:6,10 Jesus said,

*"If a man abide not (continues not) in me [in Christ], he is cast forth as a branch, and is withered; and men gather them, and cast them into the fire, and they are burned. **If ye keep my commandments, ye shall abide** [continue] in my love; even as I have kept My Father's commandments, and abide [continue] in his love."* In verse 10 notice it says, *"IF."*

But the ultra gracists really want to do away with having to obey any commands of the Lord saying it's legalism and humanistic to have to follow Jesus' example, or to have to obey Jesus, the author of faith. What they are doing by saying such things is rejecting the New Covenant. They are like the rebellious that came out of the land of Egypt by God's power, who refused to continue to obey Him and walk in His ways, but wanted to go back to Egypt and its bondages. God was grieved with that generation for they erred in their hearts; they knew not His ways. Those who teach such things as an immoral grace are following the angel of light and don't even know it. He tells them that they can take the broad road to life and blessings, and that there is no need *to really abide* in Christ, just profess you are and you're eternally safe and secure. But Jesus, the light of the world said, *"Enter ye in at the strait gate: for wide is the gate, and broad is the way that leadeth to destruction, **and many** there be which go in thereat: because strait is the gate, and **narrow is the way**, which leadeth unto life, and few there be that find it"* (Matt. 7:13-14). Sin must be left at the gate. Who will you believe, Jesus or Satan?

Sin Is to the Soul What Sickness Is to the Body

Jesus, in talking about sinners said, *"They that be whole need not a physician, but they that are sick"* (Matt. 9:12).

One person said rightly, "It is better to be sick *of* sin than sick *with* sin." In the scriptures sin is called a great debt which we owed God. It is compared to a scorpion's sting (1 Cor. 15:56), and scripture reveals that it will soon destroy the whole man unless an antidote is taken. In Leviticus 13:2-6, it is compared to a plague upon the human race and leprosy. There is no disease more gruesome, or painful as it eats away at the whole life, causing weakness, feebleness, pain, and torment until final death is the result. In Romans 3:13 it's compared to poison; to vomit (2 Pet. 2:22); to pollution (2 Pet. 2:20); to wallowing in a pigpen. It is called uncleanness (Ezek. 36:29; Zech. 13:1). It originated with the father of lies, the wicked one (John 8:44; Eph. 2:2; 1 John 3:8). Sin made God's angel a devil. It is also called an abomination, a reproach, and the fruit of the wicked. Jesus said, *"whosoever commits sin is a slave of sin."* The Bible says that as true Christians we are dead to sin, freed from sin, that sin's dominion is broken over us, and from henceforth, we should not serve sin. For the wages of sin is (always) death (James 1:13-15). Romans 1:28-32 shows a clear picture of the kind of sin God hates and yet some would say these things are just a little behavior problem. By doing so, they side in with the devil.

In John 15:14 Listen to what Jesus says:

*"Ye are my friends, **if ye do whatsoever I command you**"* "IF" (on this condition). For a friend will not hurt another friend by going contrary to what's right and be constantly grieving the other. Jesus takes us down

the narrow road of His Father's will. He leads us in paths of righteousness (Ps. 23). Which road are you following?

Hebrews 5:9

"And being made perfect, he became the author of eternal salvation unto all them that obey him." He's either our Lord in reality, or He's not our Lord at all. He will not accept empty professions while hearts and lives are willingly lived contrary. He understands people's struggles with the flesh and temptation, but He who knows all hearts also knows when one is struggling as they are striving against sin, and when one is willingly rebellious and has willingly gone astray in their heart, back into a life of sin because of choosing the pleasures of sin over living for the will of God (Heb. 12:4).

In Mark 7:6

"He answered and said unto them, Well hath Esaias prophesied of you hypocrites, as it is written, This people honoreth me with their lips but their heart is far from me." He went on to say if that's all the commitment you have, your worship of Him is in vain. We must worship God in Spirit and in truth (John 4:23-24). He is the same yesterday, today, and forever. Therefore this is still what He thinks of such people. So, yes, He understands struggles with the flesh. He understands that Christians need to grow, that sanctification is a progressive thing as more light is received, and He will perfect that which concerns us, pruning us to bring forth more good fruit. But with more light comes more responsibility. *"To whom much is given, of him is much required"* (2 Cor. 8:12). We must go on from faith to faith, and walk in the light we have. No man turning back *"is fit for the Kingdom of God"* except he repent.

Some want to believe this ultra grace teaching in order to protect loved ones they know are not living for God, as though their thinking this way will make a difference on the Day of Judgment. It may provide a temporal false peace concerning loved ones, but that which is not founded upon the real truth of God's Word will not stand. It will actually hinder them from praying, believing for them, and trying to restore them, for "they think" they are already okay. This is just what Satan wants.

Of course we know there is an abundance of mercy and that the blood of Jesus can wash away every confessed sin. We understand that God will welcome back and instantly forgive every prodigal son who repents and returns, and provide all blessings immediately by His grace.

We understand that there is an abundance of mercy given to those who don't know better and are ignorant, such as the elderly or babes in Christ. But we are mainly focusing on those who should know better, are willingly living contrary to God's way of righteousness, and are exposing the counterfeit teaching on grace that Satan has sown into the church, for Satan gets some to think that they can live any way they please and they are yet the predestined ones. Really, as we've said, how would they know they are? *"My little children, let us not love in word, neither in tongue; but in deed and in truth. **And hereby we know that we are of the truth**, and shall assure our hearts before him"* (1 John 3:18-19).

Here is true Bible grace. It's bountiful, beautiful, changing us into the image of Christ from glory to glory, from faith to faith, enabling us to put off the old man and put on the new man in Christ. It's available to cleanse away all manner of sin when we go to the Lord and acknowledge it, giving us power to live an overcoming life as sons of God. Is not God's true grace sufficient enough? Do we have to make up excuses and believe the false doctrine concerning grace that was revived again hundreds of years ago by an intellectual (non-Spirit-filled) man, just after the Dark Ages and Reformation who implied, and taught in an indirect way that we can still follow Satan and still be okay with God? And that God's own grace would cover automatically for us because we are the chosen ones? Although he may not have said it in those terms, it is what his doctrine implies. Regardless of how many large volumes of theology one has written and how great and intellectual their arguments, they are carnally minded if they teach that you can follow the flesh and still be OK and secure with God. As Paul said, if they don't agree with the words and the teachings of Jesus Christ, *"they are proud, knowing nothing."* Volumes and volumes filled with a lot of reasoning that amounts to nothing! The disciples, on the other hand, were considered ignorant and unlearned men, but they taught the way of God in truth. *"In that hour Jesus rejoiced in Spirit and said, I thank thee, O Father, Lord of heaven and earth, that thou hast hid these things from the wise and prudent, and hast revealed them unto babes: even so, Father; for so it seemed good in thy sight"* (Luke 10:21). Having a great ability to use *"enticing words of man's wisdom"* does not mean one is spiritual or really knows the truth, but many Christians, like wandering sheep, just follow whatever sounds intellectual without proving all things by God's Word. There is so much Bible illiteracy in the church even among many leaders.

God says in Proverbs 28:13, *"He that covereth his sins shall not prosper: but whoso confesseth and forsaketh them shall have mercy."* So, let us never presume things about the grace of God that are not clearly written in the Word, or you are liable to be following a man's opinion or a doctrine of devils and not the Lord. And what could be worse? Remember that God's Word is His instructions to us concerning the true way of life.

Men's strong opinions and great intellectual arguments clothed in spiritual phraseology mean nothing, and many times it is only the old serpent's corrupted wisdom being made manifest through them coming clothed in many disguises. He, too, has many apostles and teachers disguised as ministers of God (2 Pet. 2:1; 2 Cor. 11:13-15). According to the Word, they are most definitely among us. They are a test to the true people of God: *"By their fruits"* gathered from their teachings, ye shall know them. Satan has sown tares among the wheat and only the real harvest at the end will show the difference. *"The field is the world; the good seed are the children of the kingdom; but the tares are the children of the wicked one; The enemy that sowed them is the devil; the harvest is the end of the world; and the reapers are the angels. As therefore the tares are gathered and burned in the fire; so shall it be in the end of this world. The Son of man shall send forth his angels, and they shall gather **out of his kingdom all things that offend, and them which do iniquity; And shall cast them into a furnace of fire**: there shall be wailing and gnashing of teeth. Then shall the righteous shine forth as the sun in the kingdom of their Father. Who hath ears to hear, let him hear"* (Matt. 13:38-43).

Remember, God said, *"the fruit of the wicked is sin."* If they tell you that grace automatically covers a life of sin, then you know its source; SATAN! Regardless of how nice or how smiley the person seems to be, flee from them.

<u>In Romans 16:17-18 Paul writes:</u>

*"Now I beseech you, brethren, **mark them which cause divisions and offenses contrary to the doctrine [of godliness, Titus 1:1] which ye have learned; and avoid them**. For they that are such serve not our Lord Jesus Christ, **but their own belly;** [their own selfish desires] and by good words and fair [flattering] speeches deceive the hearts of the simple"* (unsuspecting people). As one preacher said, this extreme grace doctrine, is held together by adjectives, pronouns, verbs, and adverbs, but not by God's Word.

Whereas the apostles have said that we are to avoid those that cause division in Christ's body and offenses contrary to the doctrine of Christ which is always according to godliness, yet multitudes flock to those very people because of their good sounding words, fair speeches, and great intellectual arguments and promises. A thing is not true just because it tickles our ears, sounds easier, or it's the way we personally want it to be. It's not true just because the person is, or seems to be, a nice person with a flamboyant personality, or is a great orator who has a great ability to use words. The Bible says, *"prove all things, hold fast to that which is **good**."* Some though, chase every wind of doctrine that sounds fluffy and nice. Everyone everywhere is always looking for the easy way out rather than the true way out. Many want to follow Satan in this life and then spend eternity with God in heaven. Some of these doctrines suit these types of people just fine.

"Again, the kingdom of heaven is like unto a net, that was cast into the sea, and gathered of every kind: Which, when it was full, they drew to shore, and sat down, and gathered the good into vessels, but cast the bad away. So shall it be at the end of the world: the angels shall come forth, and sever the wicked from among the just, And shall cast them into the furnace of fire: there shall be wailing and gnashing of teeth" (Matt. 13:47-50).

Be not found in that category. Obey God's clear warnings. Give no place to the devil, and follow after godliness. Whatever path Jesus took is the right way. When Phillip asked Jesus the way to heaven, *"Jesus said unto him, I am the way, the truth, and the life: no man cometh unto the Father, but by me"* (John 14:6). *"**He that followeth me** shall not walk in darkness but shall have the light of life."* Only by the way He pointed out will we go to the Father. His life is our example (Phil. 1:21).

CHAPTER FOURTEEN

THE GOSPEL REVEALED IN ROMANS

Romans 1:5

*"By whom we have received grace and apostleship, **for obedience to the faith** among all nations, for his name."*

Paul preached obedience to the faith. He preached a faith that produces obedience, not merely saying we have faith (Titus 1:16). His commission as an apostle was to win men to an obedience to God that springs from faith in one's heart to turn them from darkness to light; from Satan to God (Acts 26:18). This is a forsaking of sin (Rom. 6). This was Paul's theology. As we've already stated from God's Word, a faith that doesn't work to purify the heart is not Bible faith at all (Acts 15:9). God says, *"And the word of God increased; and the number of the disciples multiplied in Jerusalem greatly; and a great company of the priests were **obedient to the faith**"* (Acts 6:7). This is the true faith that saves. It saves a person from the broad road that leads to destruction; it produces obedience to God. *"But God be thanked, that ye were the servants of sin, but ye have obeyed from the heart that form of doctrine which was delivered you. Being then made free from sin, ye became the servants of righteousness"* (Rom. 6:17-18). (See also Rom. 15:18; Heb. 5:9.) Faith without actions is dead (James 2:14-26). This is what Paul believed.

Romans

The book of Romans was written by Paul, who himself was a Jew, mainly to Jewish believers and proselytes in Rome. It was written to show them that the Gentiles can now be equal heirs with them of God's divine plan and he explains why, even though they didn't keep all the legalistic codes of the law with all its carnal ordinances. This was always God's plan. God first came to Abram and said He'd make of him a great nation, and through him he would bless all the nations (Gen. 12:1-3, 17:1-7; Gal. 3:6-9). In Ephesians 3:4-7, Paul says, *"Whereby, when ye read, ye may understand my knowledge in the mystery of Christ, which in other ages was not made known unto the sons of men, as it is now revealed unto his holy apostles and prophets by the Spirit; that the Gentiles [all the other nations] should be fellow heirs, and of the same body, and partakers of his promise in Christ by the gospel: Whereof I was made a minister, according to the gift of the grace of God given unto me by the effectual working of His power."*

In Romans, Paul was simply showing them that no one could be justified nor cleanse away their own sins by all the tedious works of the law or by such works as circumcision (Rom. 2:28-29). For the Jews had thought that outward circumcision and their outward observing of the carnal ordinances of the law automatically marked them out as God's chosen and elect above all the other nations (Rom. 2:28-29); *"for by the works of the law shall no flesh be justified"* (Gal. 2:16). But Paul pointed out that both Jew and Gentile were all under the power of sin and that sin's wages was death for them both, regardless of their keeping the works of the law or not. He says, *"What then? Are we better than they? No, in no wise: for we have before proved [concerning] both Jews and Gentiles, that [regardless of these ceremonies] they are all under [the power of] sin"* (Rom. 3:9). Both Jew and Gentile needed a way of deliverance from the sin problem, which led them down the road to death and hell, and Paul clearly showed them that the works of the law couldn't provide it. He revealed that the law only showed how all had sinned and fallen short of the glory of God, and how *"all the world is guilty before God"* (Rom. 3:19), for breaking God's moral law. He made it clear that God wasn't the God of the Jews only, but, also, of the Gentiles, for all were just one race right up to the Tower of Babel. Abraham was just called out because he had faith and God would use him to bless all the families of the earth.

The works of the law were just added over 400 years later to keep Israel occupied until the Savior of the world came. It also provided the blood of animals which couldn't take away sin but covered over their sin if they repented and did certain things in faith according to God's Word. It was all a temporal setup. He then reveals to these believers that God had made a plan before the foundation of the world, that if anyone repented of a life of sin (Acts 17:30) and accepted His Son as Lord of their life calling on His name (Rom. 10:9-13), they would be justified and delivered from sin's condemnation and sin's power by faith, mercy, and grace, without the works of the Mosaic law with its circumcision, Sabbath Days, and other rituals. Paul had to make their condition clear, for their thinking that keeping circumcision and animal sacrifices would justify them and make them right in God's sight, had so long been ingrained into them (Heb. 10:1). But Paul proved that just as the Gentiles didn't keep the law of conscience so the Jews didn't keep the righteousness of the Law of Moses. He also showed them that Abraham was justified by his living faith before the Mosaic law with its carnal, outward ordinances existed, and if he could be justified by faith and live for God without the works of the law, so could the Gentiles. *"Know ye therefore that they which are of faith, the same are the children of Abraham...."* Paul says, *"Wherefore then serveth the law? It was added because of transgressions [to show them what sin was], till the seed should come to whom the promise was made; and it was ordained by angels in the hand of a mediator.... There is neither Jew nor Greek, there is neither bond nor free, there is neither male nor female: for ye are all one in Christ Jesus"* (Gal. 3:7,19,28). So the law was given to expose sin for what it is, but it didn't deliver them at that time from spiritual death, nor from Satan and the power of sin. This was something only the life and grace of God entering a person's life, could do.

In the Gospel, God revealed that He willed for all people to return to a life of faith. It is faith alone that enables us to receive from Him, the sustaining power of His grace (Eph. 1:19; 2 Cor. 12:9), and it is only grace that can deliver us from sin and the evil one. *"For sin shall not have dominion over you: for ye are not under the law, but under grace"* (Rom. 6:14). Paul was simply pointing out to the Jews that now that the grace to obey has come, they no longer needed all the works of the law. *"We know that whosoever is born of God sinneth not; but he that is begotten of God keepeth himself, and that wicked one toucheth him not"* (1 John 5:18). *"For what the law could not do, in that it was weak through the flesh, God sending his own Son in the likeness of sinful flesh, and for sin, condemned sin [dealt with the sin problem], in the flesh [and broke its power over us and our flesh] that the righteousness of the law might [now] be fulfilled in us, who walk not after the flesh, but after the Spirit"* (Rom. 8:3-4). Paul's point was this, under the law all there was, was death and a future promise. For God could not yet, at that time, come back by the Holy Spirit into the hearts and lives of His people, and make their lives complete, as He was with Adam in Eden; but now Christ may again *"dwell in your hearts by faith,"* and therefore we *"can do all things through Christ which strengthens us."* Paul said, *"I do not frustrate the grace of God: for if righteousness [living morally right] come by the law, [and its rituals] then Christ is dead in vain"* (Gal. 2:21). *"If ye know that he is righteous, ye know that every one that doeth righteousness is born of him"* (1 John 2:29).

Paul points out that we can now live, once again, *"by the faith of the Son of God,"* and only by His Spirit and grace can people now fulfill the righteousness of the law. He says to these Jewish believers, *"Do we then make void the [moral] law through faith? God forbid: yea, we establish the law"* (what the law was truly aiming at, Rom. 3:31). *"Now the end [the aim] of the commandment is charity out of a pure heart, and of a good conscience, and of faith unfeigned"* (1 Tim. 1:5). Notice the three things God was aiming at: (1) a pure heart; (2) a good conscience void of offense; (3) a sincere faith. He asks the Galatians, *"Are ye so foolish? Having begun in the Spirit, are ye now made perfect by the flesh? [By keeping Sabbath days and circumcision and Jewish dietary laws] Have ye suffered so many things in vain? If it be yet in vain. He therefore that ministereth to you the Spirit, and worketh miracles among you, doeth he it by the works of the [Jewish] law [and its rituals], or by the hearing of faith?"* (Gal. 3:3-5) Of course, only faith can receive the miracle-working, life-changing power of God (Heb. 11:11; 1 Pet. 1:5).

Paul went on to point out that the great need of both Jew and Gentile was that we receive the gift of the Holy Spirit by faith. *"That the blessings of Abraham might come on the Gentiles through Jesus Christ; that we might receive the promise of the Spirit through faith"* (Gal. 3:14). The Holy Spirit would then free us from the law of sin and death, mortify the deeds of the body, enable us to fulfill righteousness, crucify the works of the flesh, and produce the fruits of righteousness in us (Rom. 8:1-12; Gal. 5:22-23), a thing which the old, outward law could never do, for the people were weak because of the sinful flesh. What we needed, whether we were labeled Jew or Gentile, was to have God back in our lives. Paul wrote, *"For it is God which worketh in you both to will and to do of his good pleasure"* (Phil. 2:13). His strength, Paul wrote, is to be made perfect in our weakness. And we also needed Satan's operation in us legally cancelled (Col. 1:13, 2:12-15). God did this by crucifying our old self (who was under Satan's authority) with Christ (Gal. 2:20).

"Knowing this, that our old man was crucified with him, that the body of sin might be destroyed, that henceforth we should not serve sin. For he that is dead is freed from sin" (and Satan, Rom. 6:6-7; Col. 1:13).

Some of these Jews then said, *"Shall we sin then?"* if we are no longer under the law with its condemnation? Paul said, God forbid. *"Know ye not, that to whom ye yield yourselves servants to obey, his servants ye are to whom ye obey: whether of sin unto death, or of obedience unto righteousness?"*

(Rom. 6:16) In other words, sin, as it has always done, still produces death. You may be delivered from the legalistic law but not from the moral law. He says, *"Therefore, brethren, we are debtors, not to the flesh, to live after the flesh. For if ye live after the flesh, ye shall [still] die: but if ye through the Spirit do mortify the deeds of the body, ye shall live"* (Rom. 8:12-13). *"This I say then, Walk in the Spirit, and ye shall not fulfill the lust of the flesh. For the flesh lusteth against the Spirit, and the Spirit against the flesh: and these are contrary the one to the other: so that ye cannot do the things that ye would. But if ye be led of the Spirit, [then] ye are not under the law [with its curse]. Now the works of the flesh are manifest, which are these; Adultery, fornication, uncleanness, lasciviousness, idolatry, witchcraft, hatred, variance, emulations, wrath, strife, seditions, heresies, envyings, murders, drunkenness, revellings, and such like: of the which I tell you before, as I have also told you in time past, that* **they which do such things shall not inherit the kingdom of God.** *But the fruit of the Spirit is love, joy, peace, longsuffering, gentleness, goodness, faith, meekness, temperance:* **against such there is no law.** *And they that are Christ's have crucified the flesh with the affections and lusts"* (Gal. 5:16-24; 1 Pet. 4:1-2).

Grace, Paul revealed, doesn't mean that you can live in sin and automatically escape the consequences of it, but that you now are freed from a life of sin by grace, and thereby escape. For *"he whom the Son sets free by his grace [from a life of sin], is free indeed"* (John 8:34-36). This is the provision of the New Covenant, a Savior that delivers us from sin's power (Acts 3:26). Again, no man can serve two masters. It's either sin or Jesus. Jesus said, *"And why call ye me, Lord, Lord, and do not the things which I say?"* (Luke 6:46) And again, *"Not every one that saith unto me, Lord, Lord, shall enter into* **the kingdom of heaven;** *but he that doeth the will of my Father which is in heaven"* (Matt. 7:21). So we have now received the Spirit of Grace to enable us to live the way man was supposed to live back in the garden (Ezek. 36:27). Only now, because of the blood of Jesus, if you do sin, you have an advocate with the Father, who will plead your case if you will repent and confess your sin (1 John 1:9). Then in Hebrews 10:19-31, He says, *"Having therefore, brethren, boldness to enter into the holiest by the blood of Jesus, by a* **new and living way,** *which He hath consecrated for us, through the veil, that is to say, his flesh; and having an high priest over the house of God; let us draw near with a true heart in full assurance of faith, having our hearts sprinkled from an evil conscience, and our bodies washed with pure water. Let us hold fast the profession of our faith without wavering; (for He is faithful that promised) and let us consider one another to provoke unto love and to good works: not forsaking the assembling of ourselves together, as the* *manner of some is; but exhorting one another: and so much the more, as ye see the day approaching. For if we [brethren] sin wilfully [go back to a life of wilful sinning] after that we have received the knowledge of the truth, [that we needed to turn from darkness to light, and from Satan to follow God, Acts 26:18] there remaineth no more sacrifice for sins, but [just] a certain fearful looking for of judgment [for such people] and fiery indignation, which shall devour the adversaries. [For you remember how] he that despised Moses' law died **without mercy** under two or three witnesses: of how much sorer [and worse] punishment, suppose ye, shall be thought worthy, who hath trodden under foot the Son of God and hath counted the blood of the covenant, wherewith he **was [at one time] sanctified, an unholy thing, and hath done despite unto [and resisted the work of] the Spirit of Grace? [Who came to free us from a life of sin.] For we know him that hath said, 'Vengeance belongeth unto me, I will recompense, saith the Lord.' And again, The Lord shall judge his people. It is a fearful thing to fall into the hands of the living God"* (Heb. 2:1-3).

This means that if we go back and turn aside after Satan again, following the course of this world, and withdraw our allegiance from God (1 Tim. 5:15), all that's left is certain judgment which will devour all of God's adversaries (James 4:4). So, yes, all is by grace, but a grace that gives us the ability to obey and live for God and His will (Heb. 12:28). This was Paul's message to these Romans and others. That only grace (the free, unmerited power of God) can save us from the broad road that leads to destruction. There is not a religious or human work in the entire world that can do it, and the works of the law were foreseen to never be able to do it. So, salvation is by God's grace and not by human strength.

So, the only works Paul rejected now that we have a New Covenant, were Jewish legalistic works, heathenish works, and any works of the unregenerate. *"Because the carnal mind is enmity against God: for it is not subject to the [moral] law of God, neither indeed can be. So then they that are in the flesh cannot please God"* (Rom. 8:7-8). But as Christians, he said that we are to *"be careful to maintain good works"* (Titus 3:8); and to *"provoke one another to good works,"* for Paul said God hath *"before ordained that we should walk therein"* (Eph. 2:10). Paul was never against the works of a true believer, but encouraged them and rebuked those who professed faith in God, but whose works and lives were lived contrary (Titus 1:16).

Paul, therefore, simply said that as an unregenerate, you, whether Jew or Gentile, couldn't be saved by your works but only by faith in God's redemption. But he clearly pointed out that once you are saved and regenerated, you must then continue living right by His grace, and showing forth your faith by your actions and life, and never go back to the world and live like them, or you will die (Rom. 8:12-13).

"Whereupon, O king Agrippa, I was not disobedient unto the heavenly vision: But shewed first unto them of Damascus, and at Jerusalem, and throughout all the coasts of Judaea, and then to the Gentiles, that they should repent and turn to God, and do works meet for repentance. For these causes the Jews caught me in the temple, and went about to kill me. Having therefore obtained help of God, I continue unto this day, witnessing both to small and great, saying none other things than those which the prophets and Moses did say should come: That Christ should suffer, and that he should be the first that should rise from the dead, and should shew light unto the people, and to the Gentiles" (Acts 26:19-23). Paul then wrote in his theology, *"For we are made partakers of Christ, if we hold the beginning of our confidence steadfast unto the end"* (of our lives, Heb. 3:14). Abide then in the calling, and remain in Christ. His whole message was that God had provided salvation for the whole world and no man (neither Jew nor Gentile) could obtain it by himself. And to the Jew He said, *"No man is justified [or made righteous] by the works of the law, it is evident."*

A Look At Romans

Chapter 1
Summary:

Paul was called to be an apostle and preach *obedience* to the faith. He said the Gospel, concerning God's Son, was the power of God for every one who will believe it and be changed by it (2 Cor. 3:18). He said the Gospel reveals that men need to return to live the life of faith and that the Gospel reveals God's wrath towards those who live in sin and suppress righteousness (Matt. 7:21,24, 12:50; John 14:21, 15:10; Isa. 1:19). God said they are worthy of death if they live in those things. He said that men have enough light to let them know there is a God, and if they weren't suppressing what they knew was right they could search for Him and find Him (Acts 17:27). But if they want to reject the light and knowledge of God, then God would reject and give them up also (Gal. 6:7; John 3:19-20).

The Gospel is given to return men to the one true worship and reverence of God, that man should have kept in Eden (Rev. 22:14). But if men don't want the truth about God and His righteousness, He will turn them over to a reprobate mind to do the ungodly works of the flesh and to judgment, and they will end up believing a lie (2 Thess. 2:11).

"The Lord knoweth how to deliver the godly out of temptations, and to reserve the unjust unto the day of judgment to be punished" (2 Pet. 2:9).

Chapter 2
Summary:

Men are inexcusable when they say they know what's right, condemn others for their wrong, but then practice the same things as they whom they condemn (Rom. 1:32). Paul knew the Jews who did the works of the law were just as much sinners as the Gentiles. He knew the law pointed out sin, but they couldn't keep the law in their fallen condition.

He says God's goodness leads men to repent, and that if they live for God and for what's good, God will reward them with eternal life; but if they are stubborn and unrepentant and they live for sin and evil, He will give them tribulation and wrath. And he says there is no respect of persons with God. Jew, Gentile, and Christians will all be judged only according to the light that they have and whether or not they have repented of the evil done in the day when God will judge the secrets of men according to the Gospel. He tells men not to rest with a label they've given themselves, but to obey what they know is right. He says that this is what matters (1 Cor. 7:19). A real Jew (Abraham's real seed) is one who lives for the praise of God (vv. 28-29).

Chapter 3
Summary:

If some don't believe God's Word and plan, it is true anyway. Some say, "Why can't we sin and God get the glory for being so gracious, it will just show how wonderful His grace is." Paul said, *"Their damnation is just,"* who say such things.

He then says the Jew is the same as the Gentile; all are under the power of sin; all are guilty. No one can justify himself by the law or human works for all have sinned and are under the power of darkness. All therefore need God's mercy provided for us in Christ, the Lamb of God. Everyone is guilty before God, but now God has provided a new way of righteousness through faith. It is available for everyone. By this new and living way of righteousness we don't do away with the moral law, we really establish it. It is God's work in us. Our part is to repent and willingly yield to God's work in us (Heb. 13:20-21). *"Wherefore, my beloved, as ye have always obeyed, not as in my presence only, but now much more in my absence, work out your own salvation with fear and trembling. For it is God which worketh in you both to will and to do of his good pleasure"* (Phil. 2:12-13). So, none of us can boast that we are saved because of our own doing, but if we are saved, we are saved by God's grace from a life of sin.

Chapter 4
Summary:

Abraham, as a heathen, wasn't justified by his past works. He didn't deserve what God offered, but by faith he believed and obeyed God. He left his old way of life and turned to God for mercy and God freely gave it to him. His willing obedience and faith in God, then, moved him to obey and live for God and leave his past behind (Heb. 11:8). This kind of faith, that moved him to leave his past life behind and obey and follow God (Gen. 18:18-19) was imputed to him as righteousness. And it is also imputed to any other whether he be Jew or Gentile, if they have this kind of living faith that turns from their old self-centered way of life and live for God and His will like Abraham's faith moved him to (Acts 10:34; John 8:39; Gen. 18:19). Abraham's faith was not a mere profession without action; his words and actions agreed. This alone is the kind of faith that God accepts (James 2:14-26). *"They answered and said unto him, Abraham is our father. Jesus saith unto them, If ye were Abraham's children, ye would do the works of Abraham"* (John 8:39). God said that He blessed Abraham, *"Because that Abraham obeyed my voice, and kept my charge, my commandments, my statutes, and my laws"* (Gen. 26:5).

Chapter 5
Summary:

Repentance is the first action of saving faith (Luke 13:3, 24:47).

"Repent ye therefore, and be converted, that your sins may be blotted out, when the times of refreshing shall come from the presence of the Lord" (Acts 3:19). (See also Acts 2:36-38.) God then gives grace to the humble, repentant sinner. Jesus, after His resurrection, told His disciples, *"That repentance and remission of sins should be preached in his name among all nations, beginning at Jerusalem"* (Luke 24:47). You must have the kind of faith that leaves the past life behind.

We are made in right standing with God by an obedient faith and stand now by the power of His grace, and we rejoice in the hope of the glory that will come to us who live for Him (Rom. 8:17). Salvation centers around Christ and His redemptive work. By man, sin and death entered the world. By man, also, came back life and righteousness. By grace, we can now reign over a life of sin. We were made sinners by Adam's act of disobedience and inherited sinful flesh from him, but we are made righteous by Christ's saving work, when we repent of a life of sin and accept His Lordship over us. He then regenerates our dead spirits and imparts grace. Where sin abounded in one's life, grace to overcome it does much more abound; for Christ's strength is made perfect in our weakness (2 Cor. 12:9). Just look around at the changed lives of Christians everywhere. That is grace (Col. 1:6).

Chapter 6
Summary:

Someone might say, "If grace could save us instantly out of all that sin, isn't it only logical that it could then save us while we live in sin?" Paul said, "*God forbid*," or "You're mistaken!"

Grace doesn't mean that you can continue in sin. Grace means you're freed from sin. We should now walk in the new life God has given us. So we should no longer serve sin, for that is the old master we died to. Christ has freed us from its controlling power. We therefore don't have to live a life of sin any longer. Sin's dominion has ended because of the power of God's grace at work within us to will and to do God's good pleasure. So we are free of being sin's slave and are now the servants of righteousness. If you serve sin, you will die spiritually again. These are the wages it pays, but God will grant eternal life to those who now bring forth fruit unto Him. We have simply changed masters and the yoke of bondage has been destroyed (Isa. 10:27); but now we are yoked to Jesus (Matt. 11:28-30). Whatever master you serve will pay your wages (2 Pet. 2:1,15).

Chapter 7
Summary:

Christ fulfilled all the types of Jewish law contained in carnal ordinances. We are dead to these things and joined to Christ, the True Vine, that we might now produce His fruits of righteousness. When we were bound by the flesh, sin at work within us worked in our members and moved us to break God's moral law, and spiritual death was the result. But now we are freed from the law because Christ has come and fulfilled all the shadows and types, and now we can serve in newness of spirit. The law was only written for the disobedient (Gal. 5:7-24; 1 Tim. 1:9-11). Sin was a power at work within us. It was the prince of the power of the air holding us captive under his power. We were slaves chained to bodies under sin's control. We couldn't deliver ourselves from this body of death, which headed us like slaves toward death and hell. The answer, therefore, was not in us, but thank God, Christ came to save us and set us free from the shackles of sin and break its power over our flesh (1 John 3:4-8). Let us never then, return to legalism or to a life of sin, for we are freed from both. One brought bondage, the other, death.

Chapter 8
Summary:

There is now no coming judgment to those who abide in Christ Jesus *and walk after the Spirit*, for the Holy Spirit can now enable us to do what the law couldn't. Now we can fulfill the righteousness of the law and mortify the sinful deeds of the body by the Spirit. For the Holy Spirit of grace has freed you from the law of sin and death that, at one time, controlled you. If you choose to return to follow after the sinful flesh, you again will die spiritually. But if you mortify the old way of life, you will live forever with Christ. If we do this and suffer with Him taking our flesh to the cross, we will also live with Him as a joint heir (Rom. 8:17; Gal. 5:24; 1 Pet. 4:1-2). God will make things work out for those who love and obey Him (v. 28).

Now God foreknew some would repent, accept Christ, and choose to follow and live for Him, and those who would use their free will to do so. He also did predestinate to become glorified sons when the full salvation is revealed in the last time. Nothing in all of creation except our own willful life of sin can separate God and us (Rom. 5:12; Eph. 4:17-18; Isa. 59:2; Heb. 3:12-14). As stated, He only makes everything work out for those who love Him (v. 28), and they who love Him, keep His words and commandments (1 John 5:3, 2:3-6; John 14:21-24, 15:10). Those who do so are predestined in the final plan to be glorified (James 1:12). *"Here is the patience of the saints: here **are** they that keep the commandments of God, and the faith of Jesus. And I heard a voice from heaven saying unto me, Write, Blessed are the dead which die in the Lord from henceforth: Yea, saith the Spirit, that they may rest from their labors; and their works do follow them"* (Rev. 14:12-13).

Chapter 9

For Romans chapters 9 and 11, because many have used them to teach predestination of individuals to heaven and hell, it is necessary that we cover some important scriptural principles in more detail to more clearly understand Paul's mind in the matter. So think over what we say. Remember, he was explaining how the Gentiles could be heirs by faith in the Messiah regardless of their past, and their not keeping the legalistic works of the law, and that the Jews couldn't expect special treatment because of the works of the law. All need the mercy and grace of Christ; for there is no respect of persons with God. There is neither Jew nor Gentile. There is only the human race which the last Adam came to save. The Jews with that whole legalistic process was only for a time (Matt. 16:15, 24:14, 28:20).

Summary:

Paul here reveals that nothing in the flesh or natural realm, regardless of the ceremonies, makes you a real Jew to whom the promises were made.

A real Jew is one whose circumcision is in the heart, just like Abraham's, not in the flesh. He reveals that God chooses to have mercy on those who have faith in His Son over those who don't have faith (Mark 16:15-16). If He planned to save the repentant Gentiles even though they didn't keep the works of the law, He can do so. The Jews had a real hard time with this.

Paul points out that God is no respecter of persons. He is the God of the Gentiles as well as the Jews, even if the Jews didn't think the Gentiles could be saved (Acts 11:18). The Jews had a Covenant with God, but didn't keep it, so God was not obligated to keep Covenant with them. *"Know therefore that the Lord thy God, he is God, the faithful God, which keepeth covenant and mercy **with them** that love him and keep his commandments to a thousand generations"* (Deut. 7:9).

Watch God's law of sowing and reaping in these following passages, for there are literally dozens of such passages that reveal God responds to those who respond to Him (Matt. 6:14-15; James 4:8; Mal. 3:7). *"And the Lord said unto Moses, Behold, thou shalt sleep with thy fathers; and this people will rise up, and go a whoring after the gods of the strangers of the land, whither they go to be among them, and will **forsake me**, and break my covenant which I have made with them. Then my anger shall be kindled against them in that day, **and I will forsake them**, and I will hide my face from them, and they shall be devoured, and many evils and troubles shall befall them; so that they will say in that day, Are not these evils come upon us, because our God is not among us? And I will surely hide my face in that day for all the evils which* *they shall have wrought, in that they are turned unto other gods"* (Deut. 31:16-18).

God said to Israel, *"And if ye will not be reformed by me by these things, but will walk **contrary unto me**; Then will I also walk **contrary unto you**, and will punish you yet seven times for your sins"* (Lev. 26:23-24).

*"My people are destroyed for lack of knowledge: **because thou hast rejected knowledge, I will also reject thee**, that thou shalt be no priest to me: **seeing thou hast forgotten** the law of thy God, **I will also forget** thy children"* (Hosea 4:6).

*"For rebellion is as the sin of witchcraft, and stubbornness is as iniquity and idolatry. **Because thou hast rejected** the word of the Lord, **he hath also rejected thee** from being king"* (1 Sam. 15:23).

Paul, knowing this unchangeable working of God, warns the Galatian Christians, *"Be not deceived; God is not mocked: for whatsoever a man soweth, that shall he also reap"* (Gal. 6:7).

"Bring forth therefore fruits worthy of repentance, and begin not to say within yourselves, We have Abraham to our father: for I say unto you, That God is able of these stones to raise up children unto Abraham. And now also the axe is laid unto the root of the trees: every tree therefore which bringeth not forth good fruit is hewn down, and cast into the fire" (Luke 3:8-9). Professing Christian, take warning for the same thing is true today. God changes not.

But there were always some (a remnant) that did obey God, and had the same kind of faith that Abraham had.

Romans 9:11: If God didn't elect to call us by His Gospel to salvation none of us would be saved. Now, He didn't call us because of our works but because of His mercy. This was the case with everybody. Jacob obviously wasn't saved because of his works, but only because he preferred spiritual things over natural. If God had to bring the promise through either Esau or Jacob, He chose Jacob because he had faith and God knew faith would later change him.

Romans 9:13: The word hated here is "preferred." God didn't just hate (or, rather, prefer) Esau for no reason, for God is no respecter of persons. God always responds to people depending on **their** response. God preferred Jacob, not because of works, but because of his love for spiritual things. God said to Jeremiah, *"Before I formed thee in the belly **I knew thee**; and before thou camest forth out of the womb I sanctified thee, and I ordained thee a prophet unto the nations"* (Jer. 1:5).

In Hebrews chapter 12, Paul points out that none of us Christians should be like Esau, who preferred the natural over the spiritual, and lost his birthright. God says, *"I love them that love me"* (Prov. 8:17); but scripture says that He *"scorns the scorner"* (Prov. 3:34). Esau scorned his birthright and blessing, so was scorned by God. God loved Jacob more than Esau because Jacob loved God more than Esau did. God saw this even before they were born. Now Jacob who was a deceiver at first, reaped from his own actions and was himself deceived a number of times, but faith in his heart later brought about a change in him and his name was changed to Israel. (To prove that God only chose Jacob over Esau and didn't hate Esau, see the same word in Luke 14:26; Matt. 10:37; and then see John 15:12.) This word "hate" here only means "prefer" for we are commanded to love one another. Election then is not by past works but by a life-changing faith; when we choose spiritual things over natural. *"He that loveth his [natural sinful] life shall lose it; and he that hateth his life in this world shall keep it unto life eternal"* (John 12:25; 1 John 2:15-17). Like Jacob and Esau, the Gentiles came along later than the Jews, but they had faith in the Messiah when the Jews didn't. And so, if God prefers those who have faith whether Jew or Gentile over those who don't, it's up to God regardless of their works or past track record; He can have mercy on whomever He wants to have mercy on.

Romans 9:14: There is no unrighteousness in God.

Romans 9:15: God shows mercy on whom He wants to show mercy. Who does God give mercy to? He will have mercy on the merciful. The Lord says, *"Blessed are the merciful: for they shall obtain mercy"* (Matt. 5:7).

He will have mercy on the repentant. *"Repent ye therefore, and be converted, that your sins may be blotted out, when the times of refreshing shall come from the presence of the Lord"* (Acts 3:19). *"For I will be merciful to their unrighteousness, and their sins and their iniquities will I remember no more"* (Heb. 8:12).

He is merciful to those who endeavor to keep His commandments. *"And shewing mercy unto thousands of them that love me, and keep my commandments"* (Exod. 20:6).

He gives mercy to those who love Him and keep His Covenant. *"Know therefore that the Lord thy God, he **is** God, the faithful God, which keepeth covenant and mercy with them that love him and keep his commandments to a thousand generations"* (Deut. 7:9).

He gives mercy to those who trust in Him. *"Many sorrows shall be to the wicked: but he that trusteth in the Lord, mercy shall compass him about"* (Ps. 32:10).

He gives mercy to those who devise good. *"Do they not err that devise evil? but mercy and truth shall be to them that devise good"* (Prov. 14:22).

He that confesses and forsakes his sin, shall find mercy from God. *"He that covereth his sins shall not prosper: but whoso confesseth and forsaketh them shall have mercy"* (Prov. 28:13).

Brethren, we could go on and on and show you He doesn't just randomly give mercy to certain people and reject others. Paul is just saying in Romans 9:15 that if He wants to show mercy to the Gentiles, who never did the works of the law, when they repent and accept the Messiah as Lord, God is righteous to do so. Paul said, He *"will have compassion on whom He will have compassion."* God says, if people return to obey Him, He will have compassion on them (Deut. 30:1-3). If the Gentiles repent and return to God in faith, and He wants to have mercy on them, He can. He is God. The Jews have no right to complain about this.

He sometimes has compassion on people for a while for the sake of others (2 Kings 13:23). His compassion is on people for a long time because He remembers they are but dust (Ps. 78:38, 86:15). God, Paul said, can have compassion on anyone whom He pleases. No one should argue with God, for He does all things according to perfect righteousness, and, as Paul stated, God is *"no respecter of persons,"* and there is coming a revelation of the righteous judgment of God.

Romans 9:16: No man could decide to save himself, whether Jew, with their outward works, or Gentile. It all depended on God's mercy.

Romans 9:17-18: Why did God harden Pharaoh's heart? *"Be not deceived; God is not mocked: for whatsoever a man soweth, that shall he also reap"* (Gal. 6:7).

It was because Pharaoh had hardened his heart against the Israelites over and over again, made slaves of them, and ordered their male children killed. God had promised Abraham, *"And I will bless them that bless thee, and curse him that curseth thee: and in thee shall all families of the earth be blessed"* (Gen. 12:3). In other words, depending on how other people treat Abraham's seed, they would reap what they have sown. Pharaoh showed no mercy to Israel's children, but had them put to death. God's Word says, God *"shall have judgment without mercy [on them], that hath shewed no mercy; and mercy rejoiceth against judgment"* (James 2:13). Now again, God is no respecter of persons. *"Then Peter opened his mouth, and said, Of a truth I perceive that God is no respecter of persons: But in every nation he that feareth him, and worketh righteousness, is accepted with him"* (Acts 10:34-35).

"Say unto them, As I live, saith the Lord God, I have no pleasure in the death of the wicked; but that the wicked turn from his way and live: turn ye, turn ye from your evil ways..." (Ezek. 33:11).

God didn't just will Pharaoh's destruction, God just simply responded to Pharaoh how He responded to others. God knew what Pharaoh was like and that when He gave His word to Pharaoh, Pharaoh would resist and thereby become harder. In this sense only, God hardened his heart; for the Bible also says that Pharaoh hardened his own heart. As Paul said in Romans chapter 2 concerning people, Pharaoh's unrepentant heart became harder and stored up wrath for itself, for God resists the proud. God then raised him up to demonstrate His power in judging those who are hard-hearted and unrepentant, that all the earth may fear the Lord (Rom. 2:4-11). Paul preached, *"And the times of this ignorance God winked at; but now commandeth all men every where to repent: Because he hath appointed a day, in the which he will judge the world in righteousness by that man whom he hath ordained; whereof he hath given assurance unto all men, in that he hath raised him from the dead"* (Acts 17:30-31). And he taught that those who don't repent at the Word of the Lord, will store up wrath for themselves.

God says, *"Wherefore then do ye harden your hearts, as the Egyptians and Pharaoh hardened their hearts? when he had wrought wonderfully among them"* (they refused to yield to God's Word and let His people go, 1 Sam. 6:6). This is what hardened their hearts, so in a sense, it was God's Word that did it, but only because of the way they responded to it.

The Bible says, *"Happy is the man that feareth alway: but **he that hardeneth his heart** shall fall into mischief"* (Prov. 28:14).

"He, that being often reproved hardeneth his neck, shall suddenly be destroyed, and that without remedy" (Prov. 29:1).

God then has mercy on those who repent, and those who won't obey the light He gives, He hardens, but only in the sense that if they harden themselves against His Word and refuse His reproof, they get harder. *"And this is the condemnation, that light is come into the world, and men loved darkness rather than light, because their deeds were evil. For every one that doeth evil hateth the light, neither cometh to the light, lest his deeds should be reproved"* (John 3:19-20). *"Take heed, brethren, lest there be in any of you an evil heart of unbelief, in departing from the living God. But exhort one another daily, while it is called To day; **lest any of you be hardened through the deceitfulness of sin**"* (Heb. 3:12-13). *"Jesus answered them by saying, My teaching is not My own, but His Who sent Me. If any man desires to do His will (God's pleasure), he will know (have the needed illumination to recognize, and can tell for himself) whether the teaching is from God, or whether I am speaking from Myself and of My own accord and on My own authority"* (John 7:16-17, Amplified). Concerning Pharaoh the scripture reveals, *"He that exalts himself shall be humbled."* Pharaoh brought this on himself. *"For the ways of man are before the eyes of the Lord, and he pondereth all his goings. His own iniquities shall take the wicked himself, and he shall be holden with the cords of his sins"* (Prov. 5:21-22). Paul never contradicts himself, but his theology is the same in all of his epistles. He points out that if people repent of evil, God will have mercy; but if they harden their hearts, they will receive judgment (Rom. 2:4-11). *"Because sentence against an evil work is not executed speedily, therefore the heart of the sons of men is fully set in them to do evil"* (Eccl. 8:11).

Romans 9:19: He said the ignorant would ask this question about resisting God.

Obviously, multitudes have resisted His will and will be judged for it. Multitudes do resist Him who wills all men to be saved (1 Tim. 2:4). *"And the times of this ignorance God winked at; but now commandeth **all men every where** to repent"* (Acts 17:30). If they don't, they will have to face Him as judge. Even multitudes of Christians resist God's holy will and get into sin; they don't tithe, are prayerless, don't witness as they should, etc.

Stephen under inspiration of the Holy Spirit preached to those who wouldn't listen. *"Ye stiff-necked and uncircumcised in heart and ears, **ye do always resist** the Holy Ghost: as your fathers did, so do ye"* (Acts 7:51).

Paul, knowing people could resist God's plan warns, *"Let every soul be subject unto the higher powers. For there is no power but of God: the powers that be are ordained of God. Whosoever therefore resisteth the power, resisteth the ordinance of God: and they that resist shall receive to themselves damnation"* (Rom. 13:1-2).

God told us to pray, His *"will be done on earth even as it is in heaven."* Also, *"The Lord is not slack concerning His promise, as some men count slackness; but is longsuffering to us-ward, not willing that any should perish, but that all should come to repentance"* (2 Pet. 3:9), but multitudes resist and fail to repent. So, Paul cannot be saying, all that happens is the will of God. It would be foolish for Paul to go out everywhere and command all men to repent if it wasn't God's will for them to do so. He said he was sent "*to make all men see.*"

Paul knew his message was for "all" "whosoever" "every man" "any," and "everyone that believes," as he clearly stated in his doctrine throughout his epistles, so no one can take a passage from Romans 9 or 11 and make it an island to itself, and say that what he said in those passages is the complete picture of what he was saying. Everything must be looked at and compared. Some things are written in such a way so as to expose people's views. This reveals their real heart attitudes about God and will be clearly seen at the judgment when He "*makes manifest the counsels of the hearts*" (1 Cor. 4:5).

Romans 9:20-21: If a vessel refuses to be molded into a vessel of honor, then that clay lump will be thrown back into the furnace. Paul himself tells us how we can become a vessel of honor if we will to.

He said, "*Nevertheless the foundation of God standeth sure, having this seal, The Lord knoweth them that are [really] his. And, Let every one that nameth the name of Christ depart from [a life of] iniquity. But in a great house there are not only vessels of gold and of silver, but also of wood and of earth; and some to honor, and some to dishonor. If a man therefore purge himself from these, he shall be a vessel unto honor, sanctified, and meet for the master's use, and prepared unto every good work*" (2 Tim. 2:19-21).

Notice, if a man purges himself from a life of sin he will be a vessel of honor. If he doesn't, he won't. So man's will is still shown to be free and God is shown to be innocent of making some eternal souls just for the purpose of their being a vessel of destruction (Deut. 30:19). Read Matthew 25:34-46.

"*Again, the kingdom of heaven is like unto a net, that was cast into the sea, and gathered of every kind: Which, when it was full, they drew to shore, and sat down, and gathered the good into vessels, but cast the bad away. So shall it be at the end of the world: the angels shall come forth, and sever the wicked from among the just, And shall cast them into the furnace of fire: there shall be wailing and gnashing of teeth. Jesus saith unto them, Have ye understood all these things? They say unto him, Yea, Lord*" (Matt. 13:47-51). Good vessels and bad vessels will be separated. The bad will be cast away, for many are called but few are chosen. Peter said, live in such a way as to "*make our calling and election sure*" (2 Pet. 1:10-11).

See also the parable of the five wise virgins and the five foolish. The foolish didn't keep their vessels full of the Holy Spirit's oil and light, but the wise did (Matt. 25:1-14). (See also Matt. 7:24-27.) There is human responsibility. There is a God-ward side and a man-ward side in all of the teaching of the scriptures, for man's will is free to choose; therefore, all will be judged by their works.

Romans 9:22-24: God before prepared a place for the devil, his angels, and his followers. We were all children of wrath, *"Wherein in time past ye walked according to the course of this world, according to the prince of the power of the air, the spirit that now worketh in the children of disobedience: Among whom also we all had our conversation in times past in the lusts of our flesh, fulfilling the desires of the flesh and of the mind; and were by nature the children of wrath, **even as others**"* (Eph. 2:2-3). (Just the same as everyone else.) He also prepared a kingdom from before the foundation of the world for the righteous who would repent and follow Him.

"Then shall the King say unto them on his right hand, Come, ye blessed of my Father, inherit the kingdom prepared for you from the foundation of the world.... Then shall he say also unto them on the left hand, Depart from me, ye cursed, into everlasting fire, prepared for the devil and his angels" (Matt. 25:34, 41). And He said the righteous were those who did good, and the evil were those who lived selfishly.

Jesus said, *"Marvel not at this: for the hour is coming, in the which all that are in the graves shall hear his voice, And shall come forth; **they that have done good**, unto the resurrection of life; **and they that have done evil**, unto the resurrection of damnation"* (John 5:28-29). Paul said that destruction was prepared for those who don't obey the Gospel, whether they be Jew or Gentile (2 Thess. 1:7-8; Rom. 21:1-11). But a heavenly city is prepared for those vessels who fight the good fight of faith and live for the will of God (1 Tim. 6:12; 1 John 2:15-17). So, those who refuse to obey God's Gospel are the vessels of wrath filled for destruction. *"For the time is come that judgment must begin at the house of God: and if it first begin at us, what shall the end be of them that obey not the gospel of God?"* (1 Pet. 4:17)

*"And to you who are troubled rest with us, when the Lord Jesus shall be revealed from heaven with His mighty angels, In flaming fire taking vengeance on them that know not God, **and that obey not the Gospel of our Lord Jesus Christ**"* (2 Thess. 1:7-8). Those who obey the Gospel are vessels of honor.

Romans 9:25

"As he saith also in Osee, I will call them my people, which were not my people; and her beloved, which was not beloved." Paul was showing them

that the Gospel call went out to the Gentiles as well as the Jews (vv. 26-27), and that this was before predicted for God had before promised Abraham that through him all nations would be blessed (Matt. 28:19-20; Mark 16:15).

Romans 9:27: Paul points out that Isaiah predicted by the Spirit that although there were many Jews as the sand of the sea, only a remnant shall be saved who would receive the Messiah. *"He was in the world, and the world was made by him, and the world knew him not. He came unto his own, **and his own [Covenant people] received Him not.** But as many as received Him, to them gave he power to become the sons of God, even to them that believe on his name"* (John 1:10-12). This explains to them why so many Jews turned against Christ. God had shown before in scripture that *"in His name would the Gentiles trust."* But false religious leaders had forsaken the Word of God and substituted human tradition and opinions, just as it is today. It was the blind leading the blind.

Romans 9:28-29: And Isaiah said, except the Lord had intervened when He did (Gal. 4:4), all of Israel would have become like Sodom and Gomorrah, so they have no reason to exalt themselves.

Romans 9:30-33: He concludes this chapter by showing that it was always God's plan to restore man through faith in Christ, the chief cornerstone, not by the works of the law. The Gentiles received Him while most Jews rejected Him, and they stumbled at the stumbling stone. But *whosoever* believes and puts their trust in the Messiah, shall not be ashamed.

Men are either vessels of honor or dishonor, depending on their faith and actions (2 Tim. 2:19-21). If they believe and follow the Lord, their sins and iniquities will He remember no more, but he that believes not, shall be damned. God has mercy on those who turn to Him for mercy, but He resists the proud. Whoever repents and believes in His Son, He accepts, regardless of their past. Here's God's principle, *"The soul that sinneth, it shall die. The son shall not bear the iniquity of the father, neither shall the father bear the iniquity of the son: the righteousness of the righteous shall be upon him, and the wickedness of the wicked shall be upon him. But if the wicked will turn from all his sins that he hath committed, and keep all my statutes, and do that which is lawful and right, he shall surely live, he shall not die. All his transgressions that he hath committed, they shall not be mentioned unto him: in his righteousness that he hath done he shall live. Have I any pleasure at all that the wicked should die? saith the Lord God: and not that he should return from his ways, and live? But when the righteous turneth away from his righteousness, and committeth iniquity, and doeth according to all the abominations that the wicked man doeth, shall he live? All his righteousness that he hath done shall not be mentioned: in his trespass that he hath trespassed, and in his sin that he hath sinned, in them shall he die"* (Ezek. 18:20-24). Righteousness comes to us through faith when we repent of a sinful life, and mercy was provided by God for all who repent. It is not by religious, carnal or outward works; and salvation is only given to all who turn from their evil ways (Heb. 13:9).

Chapter 10
Summary:

Paul prayed for Israel that they might be saved. He didn't believe they were predestined to be lost. He said that they didn't recognize God's true way of righteousness through faith in the Messiah and are trying to establish their own righteousness. Christ ended the law of types and shadows, Sabbaths and circumcision.

Righteousness comes when a person believes and obeys the Gospel (vs. 16). It is for *whosoever.* God reached out to Israel but they refused, while the Gentiles responded. Those who refuse God, God refuses. Those who accept God, God accepts (John 1:10-12). A person must allow Jesus to reign over them and make Him Lord and believe in His saving work in order to be saved. *"For there is no difference between the Jew and the Greek: for the same Lord over all is rich unto all that call upon him. For whosoever shall call upon the name of the Lord shall be saved"* (Rom. 10:12-13; Luke 6:46, 19:13,27; Matt. 7:21).

He goes on to say that the Gospel must be preached to everyone (Rom. 1:15-16), for this is how people, if they are receptive, get faith to be saved (v. 17). God says that for a long time He stretched out His hands to a disobedient people. *"O Jerusalem, Jerusalem, thou that killest the prophets, and stonest them which are sent unto thee, how often would I have gathered thy children together, even as a hen gathereth her chickens under her wings, **and ye would not!** Behold, your house is left unto you desolate. For I say unto you, Ye shall not see me henceforth, till ye shall say, Blessed is he that cometh in the name of the Lord"* (Matt. 23:37-39). He was willing and desirous to help them, but they weren't willing.

Chapter 11
Summary:

The Jews thought that they were automatically God's elect because of being Abraham's natural seed, but Paul points out that it is only those who God foreknew would obey, who are the real elect. Israel disobeyed in the past and God judged those who did. But there was always a remnant who obeyed by faith (Heb. 11:6). Even so, there is now a remnant who have put their faith in the Messiah and have become the true elect by grace (v. 5). And if it is by grace that Jews and Gentiles are saved, then it no longer depends on all the carnal, outward ordinances and sacrifices. And if it is by grace then it is not by the outward works of the law (v. 6). Therefore the Gentiles do not have to keep the Jewish law, only the moral law. The elect who elected to repent and accept God's Son have obtained salvation, but those who refused the light of the Messiah were blinded. (vv. 7-23). (See Prov. 1:23-33.)

The election of grace is not by what we have done in the past or how we lived before He saved us. It is not by our own works as Gentiles which we produced while in our sinful, polluted condition, but by His provision and our faith in it; nor is it by Israel's works of the law. Israel, to a great degree, became blinded because of getting into unbelief and they, for the most part, fell away from their election to be God's chosen. They were as branches broken off because of this and, Paul points out, you Gentiles who have faith were grafted in, but don't boast. They were broken off because of unbelief. You were grafted in because of faith, and only living faith pleases God (Heb. 11:6). Don't be high minded though, for if God spared not the natural branches, then neither will He spare you if you go back into unbelief and disobedience (Jude 3-12). When Christ comes, they will look on Him who they have pierced and will repent and wail that their forefathers had rejected their Messiah and so a nation shall be saved and born in a day. God's wisdom is great in how He deals righteously with all things. God then is fair with both the Jews and the Gentiles. Both will be judged or receive mercy depending on their response to Christ and His salvation.

Chapter 12

Summary:

In view then of the mercy God gave you in blotting out all of your past sins, and providing you the ability by His grace to overcome a life of sin, you should now therefore present your bodies as a living sacrifice. Don't let sin reign in it any longer. This is your reasonable service. Don't be conformed any longer to this world's ungodly system, but be transformed, putting on the new man by the renewing of your mind. Grace is given to us all to give us divine ability to serve God and man and we should cooperate with it. In view of what God has done for us, your reasonable response should be as it is written in verses 9-21.

Chapter 13
Summary:

Submit to the good authorities that are over you and God ordained (Acts 5:29). The moral law is fulfilled now by love, for love works no ill towards God or man. So cast off all works of darkness. Do not seek to satisfy sensual earthly cravings but put on the Lord Jesus Christ. God says, *"If ye fulfil the royal law according to the scripture, Thou shalt love thy neighbor as thyself, ye do well: But if ye have respect to persons, ye commit sin, and are convinced of the law as transgressors"* (James 2:8-9).

Chapter 14
Summary:

Don't judge one another, but live with your whole heart for the Lord. Be moved by faith towards God and what's pleasing to Him. Be careful not to make a brother stumble and sin, for we all have to stand before Christ's judgment seat and give an account of what we've done (2 Cor. 5:9-10).

We are called to no longer live for ourselves, but for the Lord. Whatever we can't do in faith towards Him, is sin. This is living by faith. *"And whatsoever ye do in word or deed, do all in the name of the Lord Jesus, giving thanks to God and the Father by him"* (Col. 3:17).

Chapter 15
Summary:

We need to help one another and encourage one another in the faith. Be like-minded, all believing the whole doctrine of Christ. Grace was given to Paul so he'd have the ability to preach to the Gentiles, that their lives, too, might be purified by the working of the Holy Ghost. Paul was sent to make the Gentiles obedient to the faith.

Chapter 16
Summary:

Mark the people that cause divisions contrary to the apostle's teachings and instructions and avoid them. They are not serving the Lord, but their own selfish lives and desires, and they lead others astray also, by good sounding words and fair speeches. *"Brethren, be followers together of me, and mark them which walk so as ye have us for an ensample. (For many walk, of whom I have told you often, and now tell you even weeping, that they are the enemies of the cross of Christ: Whose end is destruction, whose God is their belly, and whose glory is in their shame, who mind earthly things,"* Phil. 3:17-19). The fame of your obedience to the Lord and His Gospel has spread everywhere. Now, God has the power to strengthen and establish you in the faith, as you believe His message. At God's command, the light of His truth is to be made known to all nations to win them, also to obedience to God that springs from a sincere faith. To God be all the glory through Jesus Christ for ever. Amen.

Living Faith, Living Grace

James 2:14,20,26

*"What doth it profit [then], my brethren, **though a man say** he hath faith, and have not works? Can (that kind of) faith save him? But wilt thou know, O vain man, that faith without works is dead?...For as the body without the spirit is dead, so faith without works [actions that correspond to what's professed] is dead also."* *"Thou believest that there is one God; thou doest well: the devils also believe, and tremble"* (James 2:19). Even the demons confess that Jesus is the Christ, and was the Son of God (Luke 4:41), but they won't live under His Lordship. The point is, that if professing you believed was all that was needed, the demons too would be saved. Paul, James, and Christ, perfectly agree concerning faith. Listen to Christ in these scriptures concerning those who refused to obey Him in this earthly part of His creation: *"But his citizens hated him, and sent a message after him, saying, We will not have this man **to reign over us** ... (then the Lord said) But those mine enemies, which would not that I should reign over them, bring hither, and slay them before me"* (Luke 19:14,27; Matt. 7:21). James and Paul also do not contradict the Lord, nor do they contradict one another *if* you rightly divide the Word and accept all of what it says. It's just more pieces to the same puzzle.

Some things in scripture seem paradoxical until you investigate them further to rightly divide the Word (2 Tim. 2:15). And some things look on the surface like they may be saying a certain thing until you investigate them further.

Paul was saying, You weren't saved by any works you did without faith or grace. None of those things done by a child of wrath could be accepted by God. Grace and faith were gifts you received when you used your God-given will and repented of a life of sin and turned to God (Rom. 12:3; Eph. 4:7). Without them you were in the flesh, a corrupt tree, a child of wrath and couldn't save yourself ... God made the provision by grace to save you out of that lost, spiritually dead condition. He delivered you out of the authority of darkness and broke sin's dominion over you. Grace was His gift to you.

James then was saying that once you've received grace and faith, it would always change your life and focus, and move you to produce good fruit and good works. It is not just a profession, it's real! So he said, *"Faith without works is dead."* Paul believed the same, that faith would cause a change of works (Titus 1:16).

Works and Grace

One denomination, and some cults emphasize, "works only," even before faith and grace, as if you (a spiritually dead person) could, by dead, defiled works, deliver yourself from Satan's domain and earn your way to a new birth or free yourself from sin's control by works. It's obvious that religious works cannot produce these results. Many fundamentalists say "grace only," as if you didn't have to obey God after salvation and you could still be saved. Both are wrong.

The one needs to realize you can't be saved by your own efforts or works, out of your lost, spiritually dead condition; but you need to repent of dead works, turn to God, and be saved by the power of His grace through faith out of the old, corrupt way of life (Matt. 7:21). And then faith and grace given to you at salvation will bring about the true inward change that God desires and will move you to produce good fruit and show forth by works what's now in your heart, if this change has really occurred in you (Eph. 2:8-10). This is the true New Testament way of righteousness. This grace and faith in one's heart then can be seen by the changed life (Acts 11:23).

Fundamentalists need to realize that, yes, we are saved by grace through faith, but this means being saved out of an old, corrupt lifestyle and enslavement to sin, so that empowered by God's grace, Spirit, and faith, we can now fulfill a walk of righteousness (Rom. 8:4). They must realize that God expects this of us (Rom. 8:12-13). We, then, who are saved and empowered by grace are now to keep His commandments (1 Cor. 7:19; 1 John 2:2-6; Rev. 22:14), and we are exhorted to let grace have its way in us and produce good works. Read these scriptures above and it should make this clear to you, for if someone speaks contrary, *"the truth is not in him"* (1 John 2:4).

So, it's all by His mercy and grace that saves us from sin's condemnation and sin's power, and enables us to live for the will of God and not for the will of Satan any longer, and we thereby obtain life. So no one was saved by their own works or because they deserved it, but by mercy and grace. No one can live the Christian life except by grace, but "live it" we are required to do, and to not receive the grace of God in vain (2 Cor. 6:1). Therefore at the resurrection, they who have done good will enter into life (John 5:28-29), and they who have done evil, into judgment, just as Jesus taught (John 5:25-29; Rom. 2:1-11).

So, a faith that doesn't produce action, or a change in life, is dead. Paul, again, taught the same things (Titus 1:16). Words can be cheap. Sometimes actions speak louder than words. It all starts with faith, and once we've begun in faith, if we really have Bible faith, it produces good fruit in us. *"The just shall **live** by faith."* This is the purpose and design of faith. Everything is promised to us on this condition, *"If ye continue in the faith,"* living for the will of God (Col. 1:23). Peter said *"His divine power"* has given you the ability to do so. But grace never operates automatically without the cooperation of the human will (Heb. 2:9; Rev. 22:17).

Anytime a person leaves God to return to live the way they did before they met Christ, they have departed from the faith and grace. They are no longer living by faith or continuing in grace. Their faith is dead, or shipwrecked (Jude 12). They are not considered, then, *"the just,"* but a sinner once again (James 5:19-20).

Hebrews 5:9

*"And being made perfect, he became the author of eternal salvation unto all them **that obey him**."* Obedience then is faith (Rom. 1:5). Disobedience is unbelief (Heb. 3:12-19).

To obey means to "submit to," "to comply with the commands given," "to be under the rule or government of someone," "to be under the control of another," "to carry out the instructions of another." The author of our faith is also the author of salvation. He reveals that you must obey Him if you want salvation.

1 Peter 2:25

"For ye were as sheep going astray; but are now returned unto the Shepherd and Bishop of your souls." Returned means that "you've returned to follow Him and to walk in the truth and in the light;" and to "not go astray again." We are to *"walk in the light as He is in the light,"* and have *"no fellowship with the unfruitful works of darkness."*

John 19:27

*"My sheep hear my voice, and I know them, **and they follow me**."*

His real sheep follow Him in paths of righteousness and He gives to those who follow Him, eternal life (Ps. 23:1-6).

John 8:12

"Then spake Jesus again unto them, saying, I am the light of the world: **he that followeth me shall not walk in darkness** *[sin], but shall have the light of life" (1 John 1:5-7).* Only those who follow Him daily shall have light. To follow is more than just saying, *"I believe."* You could say that you believe someone and still not follow them.

Matthew 16:24-25

"Then said Jesus unto his disciples, **If any man will come after me, let him deny himself, and take up his cross, and follow Me.** *For whosoever will save his [sinful] life shall lose it: and whosoever will lose his [ungodly, worldly] life for My sake, shall find it."* (Life that lasts forever.) To follow means, "to walk in the same direction," "to pursue or accompany," "to imitate or follow as a guide," "to have your goal as the same definite object as another." So then, *His sheep* do follow Him, and only those who follow Him shall not be plucked out of His hand. If you try and save the old life of living in this world and its lusts, operating under the law of sin and death, you will lose eternal life. There are two worlds but only one choice, which one are you living for? *"What does it profit a man if he gain the whole world and lose his own soul?"* (1 John 2:15-17)

Did the apostles in their teaching on grace say then that obeying the Lord's commands or commandments were unnecessary? By no means! A faith that doesn't obey God's commandments is not faith at all (1 John 2:1-6), and grace was given so we'd be able to fulfill them. He was just saying that without faith and grace it could never be accomplished, but we must not receive the faith and grace of God in vain (Gal. 2:20-21). So religious works cannot save you, but if there is faith and grace, then there is also deliverance from Satan and a life of sin. God made the provision but we must willingly cooperate (Rev. 22:17). You'll know who has faith by how they live, for by *"their fruits"* ye shall know them. So, the scripture says, *"And now, little children, abide in him; that, when he shall appear, we may have confidence, and not be ashamed before him at his coming"* (1 John 2:28).

Obey the Truth

Hear ye the Apostles' Doctrine!

Galatians 5:7

"Ye did run well; **who did hinder you that ye should not obey the truth?"**

Romans 2:8,11

Paul says, *"But unto them that are contentious, and **do not obey the truth**, but obey unrighteousness, [God will give] indignation and wrath. For there is no respect of persons with God."*

Second Thessalonians 1:8

*"In flaming fire taking vengeance on them that know not God, **and that obey not the gospel of our Lord Jesus Christ**."*

Romans 10:6

*"But they have not all **obeyed the gospel**. For Esaias saith, Lord, who hath believed our report?"* To really believe, then, is to obey (1 John 3:3; Heb. 11:7). Disobedience is a result of unbelief.

So then they have not all submitted to the faith, nor complied with the commands and demands of the Gospel. Real faith always brings about a response to God's Word. (See Heb. 11.)

What did Paul say about the Lord's commandments?

Obeying God's Commandments

1 Corinthians 14:37-38

*"If any man think himself to be a prophet, or spiritual, let him acknowledge that the things that I write unto you are the **commandments** of the Lord. But if any man be ignorant, let him be ignorant."*

Commandment means the same thing in the New Testament as in the Old.

1 Corinthians 7:19

*"Circumcision is nothing, and uncircumcision is nothing, **but the keeping of the commandments of God**."* This is faith. Paul was a man of faith who taught that faith, once received, produced action and the keeping of God's commandments. He stated that this is what matters. He pointed out that it all starts with faith and then faith taps into the power of God which enables us to keep God's commandments (1 Pet. 1:5). The same faith and grace that justifies and gives us the new birth also sanctifies if it's continued in. Therefore it is faith that taps us into grace (God's unmerited power) which enables us all to live the way God desires. So, yes, we fully believe it's all by faith and grace, but not a false grace or faith which produces nothing.

Romans 13:9-10

*"For this, Thou shalt not **commit** adultery, Thou shalt not kill, Thou shalt not steal, Thou shalt not bear false witness, Thou shalt not covet; **and if there**

*be any other commandment, it is briefly comprehended in this saying, namely, Thou shalt love thy neighbor as thyself. Love worketh no ill to his neighbor: therefore love is **the fulfilling of the law**."*

We don't do away with the moral law or the demands of God's moral law. We fulfill them by love and walking after the Spirit. For if we love God, we keep His commandments. His true, moral law is now written in our hearts. This is true New Covenant theology.

If we live in the fruit of the Spirit, against such there is no law (Gal. 5:22-24). But there is still a law against the works of the flesh no matter who lives in them. We are free from the curse of the law because we are free to walk in the fruit of the Spirit. *"But **if** ye be led of the Spirit [then] ye are not under the law"* (Gal. 5:18). And if ye be led of the Spirit, *"ye shall **not fulfill** the lusts of the flesh."* If you live after the flesh, the curse is still out there (Rom. 8:12-13; Gal. 5:19-21; Eph. 4:27). *"Do we then make void the law through faith? God forbid: yea, we establish the law"* (Rom. 3:31). But thank God the blood of Jesus which provided mercy instantly cleanses anyone who will avail themselves to it by confessing their sin. With the sin then erased away the curse loses its legal hold (1 John 1:9), and you stand in Christ's perfect garment of righteousness.

The Righteous Garment

"I will greatly rejoice in the Lord, my soul shall be joyful in my God; for he hath clothed me with the garments of salvation, he hath covered me with the robe of righteousness, as a bridegroom decketh himself with ornaments, and as a bride adorneth herself with her jewels" (Isa. 61:10).

*"Let us be glad and rejoice, and give honor to him: for the marriage of the Lamb is come, and **his wife hath made herself ready**. And to her was granted that she should be arrayed in fine linen, clean and white: for the fine linen is the righteousness of saints. And he saith unto me, Write, Blessed are they which are called unto the marriage supper of the Lamb. And he saith unto me, These are the true sayings of God"* (Rev. 19:7-9). Here it says, *"The bride hath made herself ready."*

"And every man that hath this hope in him purifieth himself, even as he is pure" (1 John 3:3).

"And when the king came in to see the guests, he saw there a man which had not on a wedding garment: And he saith unto him, Friend, how camest thou in hither not having a wedding garment? And he was speechless. Then said the king to the servants, Bind him hand and foot, and take him away, and

cast him into outer darkness; there shall be weeping and gnashing of teeth. For many are called, but few are chosen" (Matt. 22:11-14).

Jude said, *"And others save with fear, pulling them out of the fire; hating even the garment spotted by the flesh"* (Jude 23).

"Wherefore, beloved, seeing that ye look for such things, be diligent that ye may be found of him in peace, without spot, and blameless" (2 Pet. 3:14).

"That he might present it to himself a glorious church, not having spot, or wrinkle, or any such thing; but that it should be holy and without blemish" (Eph. 5:27).

"Thou hast a few names even in Sardis which have not defiled their garments; and they shall walk with me in white: for they are worthy. He that overcometh, the same shall be clothed in white raiment; and I will not blot out his name out of the book of life, but I will confess his name before my Father, and before his angels. He that hath an ear, let him hear what the Spirit saith unto the churches" (Rev. 3:4-6).

Oh, friends, we get a clean garment when we are saved, and keep it clean by living righteously and confessing any sin we may have committed.

"Little children, let no man deceive you: he that doeth righteousness is righteous, even as he is righteous. He that committeth sin is of the devil; for the devil sinneth from the beginning. For this purpose the Son of God was manifested, that he might destroy the works of the devil" (1 John 3:7-8).

1 John 5:3

"For this is the love of God, that we keep his commandments: and His commandments are not grievous." Loving God is willingly keeping His commandments. He has put this desire in us as a seed. If anyone doesn't want to live for God, then neither do they love God. To love is to fulfill the law, not to excuse people while they break it. That would not be love at all but it would be siding in with the devil that has always wanted people to rebel and break God's commandments and choose selfishness instead.

Romans 8:3-4

"For what the law could not do, in that, it was weak through the flesh, God sending his own Son in the likeness of sinful flesh and for sin, condemned sin in the flesh: **that the righteousness of the law** *might be fulfilled in us, who walk not after the flesh, but after the Spirit"* (Ezek. 36:27). Notice he said, fulfilled in us, not rejected by us. *"So speak ye, and so do, as they that shall be judged by the law of liberty"* (James 2:12).

So then, the righteousness of God's law is not done away with in the New Covenant, it's just that we are now empowered by His Spirit (the Spirit of Grace) to keep the righteousness of the law. *"For the law of the Spirit of life in Christ Jesus **hath made me free** from the law of sin and death"* (Rom. 8:2). It's a new and living way, which He has given to us, not in oldness of letter and outward carnal ordinances, but in newness of Spirit. He broke sin's power over our flesh in the New Covenant (Col. 1:13). Now faith taps us into God's power and by it we overcome and conquer the world and its lusts (Eph. 2:2-3; 1 John 5:3-4).

"In whom also ye are circumcised with the circumcision made without hands [not a physical act], in putting off the body of the sins of the flesh [but by being set free from the power of sin which controlled the flesh] by the circumcision of Christ" (Col. 2:11). God condemned sin's operation in our flesh when we died with Christ to sin on the cross (Gal. 2:20; 2 Cor. 5:14; Rom. 6:4; Eph. 2:5-6; Col. 2:12-13). He that is dead is freed from sin. Our relationship with sin has ended.

Thank God we were set free of sin's control over the flesh by the work of Christ. His work didn't supply grace so that you could continue in the works of the flesh, but rather, just the opposite (Rom. 6:14).

Romans 8:13

"For if ye live after the flesh [in unrighteousness], ye shall [spiritually] die [again]: but if ye through the Spirit do mortify the deeds of the body, ye shall live" (reap life everlasting, Gal. 6:7-8).

Romans 3:31

"Do we then make void the law through faith? [Does faith overthrow then God's moral law?] God forbid: yea, [by it] we establish the law."

(We uphold the law.) It's a new and living way empowered by faith and grace that enables us to live holy, keep His commands in the New Testament, and to please Him. *"What shall we say then? That the Gentiles, which followed not after righteousness, have attained to righteousness, even the righteousness which is of [and produced by] faith. But Israel, which followed after the law of righteousness, hath not attained to the law of righteousness. Wherefore because they sought it not by faith, but as it were, by the works of the law [their religious ceremonies]. For they stumbled at that stumblingstone;* to establish the righteousness of the law in our lives, not certain rituals or religious works done in people's own strength, and it's faith that taps us into this. Then the same grace and faith that saved us out of the world which is under Satan's influence and blotted out our past, also continues its work to sanctify us and keep us free from Satan and sin if it's really continued in. We are then changed more and more into Christ's image from glory to glory.

Jesus said in John 17:14-17, *"I have given them thy word; and the world hath hated them, because they are not of the world, even as I am not of the world. I pray not that thou shouldest take them out of the world, **but that thou shouldest keep them from the evil.** They are not of the world, even as I am not of the world. **Sanctify them through thy truth: thy word is truth.**"* To sanctify means "to separate from Satan and the world's pollutions." God wants a separated people. *"Wherefore come out from among them, and be ye separate, saith the Lord, and touch not the unclean thing; and I will receive you, And will be a Father unto you, and ye shall be my sons and daughters, saith the Lord Almighty"* (2 Cor. 6:17-18). He says, *"We then, as workers together with him, beseech you also that ye receive not the grace of God in vain. For he saith, I have heard thee in a time accepted, and in the day of salvation have I succored thee: behold, now is the accepted time; behold, now is the day of salvation"* (2 Cor. 6:1-2). He'd never provide a grace that would encourage us to live in an evil, worldly way. Such would be the case if it all were automatically ours by some kind of irresistible grace without our cooperation with grace. But God says every branch that abides not in Christ withers away and loses the fruit it once had (John 15:6). That is, if they no longer cooperate with His plan, they will go back into their former pollutions and produce evil fruit. Most Christians know someone like this. Jesus says, *"Sin no more lest a worse thing come upon you"* (John 5:14). Again He says, *"When the unclean spirit is gone out of a man, he walketh through dry places, seeking rest, and findeth none. Then he saith, I will return into my house from whence I came out; and when he is come, he findeth it empty, swept, and garnished. Then goeth he, and taketh with himself seven other spirits more wicked than himself, and they enter in and dwell there: **and the last state of that man is worse than the first.** Even so shall it be also unto this wicked generation"* (Matt. 12:43-45). Hopefully they will repent before the end of their life on earth and turn back to the Lord. These people have left the sustaining power of the grace of God (1 Pet. 1:5). They have left the Lord's table and have returned to the table of demons. *"Ye cannot drink the cup of the Lord, and the cup of devils: ye cannot be partakers of the Lord's table, and of the table of devils"* (1 Cor. 10:21).

Romans 16:25-26

*"**Now to him that is of power to stablish you** according to my gospel, and the preaching of Jesus Christ, according to the revelation of the mystery, which*

*was kept secret since the world began, but now is made manifest, and by the scriptures of the prophets, **according to the commandment of the everlasting God**, made known to all nations **for the obedience of faith**"* (obedience to the faith). *God's command under this dispensation* is that all obey the faith, for He's provided the power to do so if we are willing, so all can obey. Therefore men are *"without excuse,"* and on this basis will be judged (John 3:19-20).

Further Evidence on Obedience

Ephesians 6:1-2

*"Children **obey** your parents in the Lord: for this is right. Honor thy father and mother; which **is the first commandment with promise.**"*

Did Paul imply these commandments which reveal God's universal moral laws are not relevant today? No, he said it still has an effect today the same as it ever did. If a Christian honors his father and mother, it will be well with him. If not, it won't be. God doesn't suggest that you can now dishonor your parents and He will still honor you, because His grace makes Him see you as though you were honoring them. This would be ridiculous indeed. Again, any command of the Old Covenant that's included in the New Covenant is now a part of the New Covenant and for us today.

He freed you so that you can walk pleasing to Him and this is what He expects. *"For we are his workmanship, created in Christ Jesus unto good works, which God hath before ordained that we should walk in them"* (Eph. 2:10). James said you will be judged by the law of liberty. You are now free to serve God. All excuses are cancelled out.

1 Timothy 6:13-14

*"I give thee charge in the sight of God, who quickeneth all things, and before Christ Jesus, who before Pontius Pilate witnessed a good confession; that thou **keep this commandment** without spot, unrebukeable, until the appearing of our Lord Jesus Christ."*

But this ultra idea of grace, contrary to Paul, wants to make you think that the words Paul used in his theology such as "obey," "commandment," and "holiness," are legalism, and that therefore Paul himself who gave us the revelation of grace, was then legalistic and didn't know what he was talking about when he said such things. What gospel are they then left with? With no real gospel at all, for the real Gospel is the power of God unto salvation, saving us from the fall. It's a new way of righteousness through the Spirit. Legalism only basically has to do with the outward Jewish or religious ceremonies and other rules made up by men that don't affect a person morally; but the keeping of God's commandments is faith and love in action, not legalism. There is a fine line, they say. And the truth is, it is they that have jumped across a broad line from truth to error concerning this. They have bought Satan's counterfeit.

Concerning those who stop living for the Lord's will Peter said, *"For it had been better for them not to have known the way of righteousness, than, after they have known it, to turn from **the holy commandment** delivered unto them"* (2 Pet. 2:21). Which word does the ultra gracist teacher not understand? Or, will they run back to some commentary written hundreds of years ago to prove their theory. Who are you following, Jesus or a man?

2 Peter 3:1-2,17-18_

*"This second epistle, beloved, I now write unto you; in both [of them] which I stir up your pure minds by way of remembrance, that ye may be mindful of the words which were spoken before by the holy prophets, **and of the commandment of us the apostles of the Lord** and Savior.... Ye therefore, beloved, seeing ye know these things before, beware [be warned] **lest ye also, being led away [led astray] with the error [wrong teachings]** of the wicked, fall from your own steadfastness [in Christ]. But grow in grace, and in the knowledge of our Lord and Savior Jesus Christ. To him be glory both now and for ever. Amen."*

Don't let any teaching cause you to fall from your own steadfastness in the things of God. If you willingly lose ground by believing a false doctrine, it's harder to regain ground once again unless you wholeheartedly repent.

2 John 3-6

*"Grace be with you, mercy, and peace, from God the Father, and from the Lord Jesus Christ, the Son of the Father, in truth and love. I rejoiced greatly that I found of thy children walking in truth, **as we have received a commandment from the Father**. And now I beseech thee, lady, not as though I wrote a new commandment unto thee, but that which we had from the beginning, that we love one another.*

***And this is love that we walk after his commandments. This is the commandment**, that, as ye have heard from the beginning, **ye should walk in it.**"* Do you see what real Christian love is? Reread this passage.

To obey Christ's word, keep His commandments, be doers of the Word, keep the faith, awake to righteousness and sin not, keep oneself unspotted from the world, holiness, and good works, acting on what the written Word says, and so on, are all New Testament teachings as well as grace. It is the Covenant we have with God and *the faith that was once delivered to the saints.* No part of it may be ignored nor cancelled out. As a matter of fact, it is all *the Word of His grace.* They all harmonize with one another. There is no conflict as some extreme gracists imply, between works and grace, or obedience and grace, but only between grace and the works of the law. James and Paul believed the same thing (2 Tim. 2:15). God is neither the author of confusion, nor does He contradict Himself. Grace, good works, serving God, obedience, prayer, walking righteously, generosity in giving, and so on, are all the products of true grace and faith once they have been received (2 Cor. 9:8; 1 Cor. 15:10; Heb. 12:28-29). Jesus, the author of faith, walked in all of these things and He was full of grace. These things then are neither legalism nor dead works in the least. The ultra gracists really don't know what they are talking about when they say such things. They have wrongly divided the Word in this area and have accepted Satan's counterfeit. Grace may be contrary to religious works such as keeping certain days, circumcision (eat this, don't eat that, or, listen to this style of Christian music, but not that style), but it is never contrary to holiness or right living but rather, grace produces right living. And, as we've said, any time we obey what God has said through His Son, or the apostles, it is faith, and that kind of faith pleases God (James 1:22).

Jesus, Peter, Paul, James, and John were not into religious legalism but truly understood the real grace of God and the whole counsel of God concerning these things. They understood that grace, God's divine influence in the heart, moves and empowers us to live the way God desires, but that without this grace we couldn't be saved, and none of the apostles contradicted each other or Christ. The whole New Testament, as we've shown, is the "faith" that was once delivered to the saints, which Jude said we are to contend for. It is a "holy" faith.

Commandments

Now that we can clearly see that we are to obey His commandments and that this is love, and all of His promises are to them that love Him, let's see what the word "commandment" really means. Then we'll see if just profession with the mouth is all that's necessary, or if it's obedience that matters. Commandment means "a command for others to obey"; "an order given"; "an injunction or charge given by an authority"; "a law given by God"; "to obey Him who has the power or right of governing."

Well the word is very clear: to obey or not to obey. We will obey our Father's Word and walk by faith, keeping His commandments as Paul also did (1 Cor. 7:19). He said, *"Those things, which ye have both learned, and received, and heard, and seen in me, do: and [then] the God of peace shall be with you"* (Phil. 4:9). Just saying that you believe is not obedience. It's easy to honor Him with your lips and yet have your heart far from Him (Mark 7:6).

Romans 1:18,32

*"For the wrath of God is revealed [in the Gospel] from heaven **against** all ungodliness and unrighteousness of men, who hold [suppress] the truth in [or by their] unrighteousness.... Who knowing [clearly] **the judgment [and decree] of God, that they which commit such things are worthy of death, not only do the same, but have pleasure in them that do them.**"* (One translation says, *"yet they went right ahead and did them anyway."*)

Read that italicized part again. We dare not put ourselves in that category.

Romans 2:1-2, 9-11

*"**Therefore thou art inexcusable [and have nothing to say in your own defense], O man, whosoever thou art** that judgest: for wherein thou judgest another, thou condemnest thyself; for thou that judgest **doest the same things.** But we are sure that the judgment of God is according to truth against them, which **commit such things....** Tribulation and anguish, upon every soul of man that doeth evil, of the Jew first, and also of the Gentile: but glory, honor, and peace, to every man that worketh good, to the Jew first, and also to the Gentile: For there is no respect of persons with God."* God's judgment, we see, is against them *that commit such things.* Their behavior is contrary to the Gospel.

"Saying" Is Not Enough

These extreme gracists think that because they say they are Abraham's seed or just say they belong to Christ that they need not obey the Gospel. Again their reasoning is the same as the Pharisees was.

Matthew 3:7-9

John the Baptist boldly proclaimed the truth to them. *"But when he saw many of the Pharisees and Sadducees come to his baptism, he said unto them, O generation of vipers, who hath warned you to flee from the wrath to come? Bring forth therefore fruits meet for repentance: [That is, changed lives revealing that you've really repented.] And **think not to say within yourselves,***

We have Abraham to our father [therefore we are God's special chosen people]: for I say unto you, that God is able of these stones to raise up children unto Abraham."

It is a religious, deceiving spirit that causes people to believe they will be accepted just because they say it, but yet won't obey it. Some think that if they just say they belong to a certain denomination, they will be saved. But no denomination can save. There is only one mediator between God and man and that is Christ Jesus. And He is the *"author of eternal salvation unto all them that obey Him"* (Heb. 5:9).

Besides, if we really were following Abraham, we would do the works of Abraham. These were works of faith and pertain to the actions and deeds of his life. His faith was not merely a profession with the mouth. *"And the LORD said, Shall I hide from Abraham that thing which I do; seeing that Abraham shall surely become a great and mighty nation, and all the nations of the earth shall be blessed in him?* **For I know him, that he will command his children and his household after him, and they shall keep 'the way' of the** LORD, **to do justice and judgment**; *that the* LORD *may [because of this] bring upon Abraham that which he hath spoken of him"* (Gen. 18:17-19). God said that the reason He'd bless Abraham is because Abraham's faith moved him to obey God's commands and that he'd keep the way of the Lord. This is the kind of faith that saves.

John 8:39_

"They answered and said unto him, Abraham is our Father. Jesus saith unto them, If ye were Abraham's children, **ye would do the works of Abraham.**" If you really are a Christian you'll do as a Christian does and live for God's will. What did Abraham do? *"And I will make thy seed to multiply as the stars of heaven, and will give unto thy seed all these countries; and in thy seed shall all the nations of the earth be blessed; Because that Abraham obeyed my voice, and kept my charge, my commandments, my statutes, and my laws"* (Gen. 26:4-5).

Hebrews 11:8

"By faith Abraham, when he was called to go out into a place which he should after receive for an inheritance, **obeyed**; *and he went out, not knowing whither he went."* He obeyed. Was that legalism or faith? FAITH! He obeyed God's commands and walked in God's ways and God said that that was faith. And if we are God's children, we too would walk in paths of righteousness for His name's sake (Gal. 3:6-9).

Genesis 14:18-20

*"And Melchizedek king of Salem brought forth bread and wine: and he was the priest of the most high God. And he blessed him and said, Blessed be Abram of the most high God, possessor of heaven and earth: and blessed be the most high God, which hath delivered thine enemies into thy hand. **And he [Abram] gave him tithes of all.**"*

He freely gave tithes of all to God, and he commanded his children to obey the Lord and do the same.

Was that legalism or faith? Faith (Gen. 18:17-19)! This was hundreds of years before the legalistic law was given to the children of Israel. God had to give them this outright because they were so hard-hearted and would have kept what belongs to God and brought a curse on themselves (Mal. 3:6-10). The Lord said Abraham would obey Him and keep His commands, *and that therefore* God would bring upon him all that was said. God recognized all this as living faith in action. Those who say one needs only to believe but not obey, do not have the same kind of faith Abraham had, for decades later, Abraham was even willing to offer his son upon the altar for the Lord's sake. The Lord then said to Abraham, *"**And in thy seed shall all the nations of the earth be blessed; because thou hast obeyed my voice**"* (Gen. 22:18). Abraham's actions and obedience pleased God and passed God's test, and without faith it's impossible to please Him, so his keeping God's commands, his tithing, his obedience all were faith, real faith. Get it?

James 2:22-23

"Seest thou how faith wrought with his works, and by works was faith made perfect? And [then] the scripture was fulfilled which saith, Abraham believed God, and it was imputed unto him for righteousness: and he was called the Friend of God." He was called God's friend *because he did* whatever God asked him to do. His faith always moved him to action. God wants to see our faith, to see that it is real (Matt. 9:2).

In John 15:14 Jesus said,

"Ye are My friends, if ye do whatsoever I command you."

Abraham was no hypocrite. He showed God his faith by the way he lived and it was imputed to him for righteousness. Jesus said and required the same thing from His followers, and said the Father *"gave me a commandment what I should say, and what I should speak."* So then, God has not changed, nor is He a respector of persons.

Galatians 3:9

*"So then they which be of faith [and obey God's commands like Abraham did] are blessed with **faithful** Abraham."*

Faithful means reliable (Prov. 25:19, 28:20). Works and actions prompted by faith are different from dead, religious, ceremonial works without faith, although some have not figured this out yet. Just look at Hebrews 11 and you will see God's definition of faith. If there isn't obedience to the Word connected with it, then it's not faith or real believing at all (Matt. 9:2). Faith, in other words, is not merely saying you have faith while your actions are contrary. Faith is revealed by actions. *"Show me thy faith without thy works and I will show thee my faith **by** my works."* This too is the doctrine of Christ. He simply is saying that profession is part of it but by itself it is not enough. If the life is lived contrary, then they can confess to know God, but by works [actions] deny Him (Titus 1:16). Both what a person says he believes and his actions and life must agree or he has not yet met the qualifications for Bible faith and believing. And if there's no real faith, there is no tapping into the provisions of grace. And if one is in grace, they are then under God's divine influence and power, are overcoming a life of sin (Rom. 6:14), and keeping His commandments (1 John 2:3-4).

The gift of righteousness includes the gift and ability of being able to live righteously because of being grafted into Christ, the true vine, and partaking of His righteous nature and grace. This is the practical side of it. We are no longer corrupt trees having to bring forth corrupt fruit. We are now *"trees of righteousness,"* the planting of the Lord that He might be *"glorified,"* and the Father is glorified that we *"bring forth much [good] fruit,"* and good works (Matt. 5:16). But Paul that said if they [these Christians] served sin and didn't continue in the grace of God, spiritual death would be the end result. (See also Ephesians 2:10.)

Therefore the apostle of grace states, *"Therefore brethren, we are debtors, not to the flesh, to live after the flesh. For 'if' ye live after the flesh [the works of the flesh] ye shall die [spiritually]: **but if ye through the Spirit [of grace] do mortify [and put to death] the deeds of the body, ye shall live.** For as many as are led by the Spirit of God [out of a walk of being dominated by the flesh], they are the [true] sons of God .... And if children, then heirs; heirs of God, and joint heirs with Christ; **if so be that we suffer with him**, [taking up our cross also], that we may be also glorified together"* (Rom. 8:12-14,17), just like He experienced glorification after the cross (Gal. 5:24).

This suffering is taking the narrow way that leads to life. It is picking up our cross daily and following Him (1 Pet. 4:1). *If we suffer with Him we shall (then) be also glorified.* If we go back to live in the pleasures of sin, we shall not. Concerning Moses and his faith, scripture says, *"Choosing rather to suffer affliction with the people of God, than to enjoy the pleasures of sin for a season; esteeming the reproach of Christ greater riches than the treasures in Egypt: for he had respect unto the recompense of the reward"* (Heb. 11:25-26). Do you choose by faith to walk the narrow way with the people of God, or to go down the broad road choosing to enjoy the pleasures of sin for a season? Remember that grace empowers us to walk down the narrow road. Sin takes people down the broad road. Each road is taking you somewhere.

*"Who his own self bare our sins in his own body on the tree, that **we, being dead to sins** [abandoning a life of sin], **should live unto righteousness: by whose stripes ye were healed"*** (1 Pet. 2:24).

Our relationship with sin and Satan has ended at the cross. We now live unto righteousness, taking up our cross and following Jesus. The old sinful self that was under Satan's authority was crucified with Christ. We show God now that ignorance was the cause of our former lifestyle (1 Pet. 1:13-17).

Concerning the Christian, Peter writes:

"That he no longer should live the rest of his time in the flesh to the lusts of men, but to the will of God" (1 Pet. 4:2).

Whether it be angels, men, or the pre-Adamite creation (demons), God dealt with and judged them when they left the paths of faith and righteousness. God changes not, but under this dispensation of grace, thank God we have the blood of Jesus which will cleanse us if we confess our unrighteousness and sin. It is a time of great mercy and grace, but never can we presume that God won't judge those *who continue* in rebellion against Him by living a life of sin. God's warnings are abundantly clear. In the Old Testament, one sin of adultery brought death by stoning. In the New Covenant, there is great mercy for the repentant, because the blood of Jesus can now wash away sins and the person can be delivered from any evil spirits that had made entrance into his life. This is because of this dispensation of grace that we are in. But it doesn't go so far as to say you can do anything without repentance and still be okay with God. Grace doesn't work in the life of any free moral agent without their willing cooperation.

CHAPTER FIFTEEN

THINGS GRACE CANNOT DO

Grace doesn't automatically set aside judgment on future sins (John 5:14; Gal. 5:17-21; 1 Cor. 11:30-32; 2 Pet. 2:20-21).

Grace cannot automatically excuse disobedience to the Gospel (2 Thess. 1:7-9; 1 Pet. 3:10-12, 4:17-19; James 5:19-20; 2 Pet. 2:20-21; Jude 3-12).

Grace cannot override the free will of man (Rev. 22:17; Rom. 6:16, 8:12 13; John 5:6).

Grace cannot keep people saved if they willingly turn back to a life of sin (Heb. 10:26-31; 2 Pet. 2:20-21; Rom. 11:22; James 5:19-20; John 15:6).

Grace doesn't automatically do away with the death penalty if people choose to follow the flesh and live after its sinful passions (Rom. 6:16, 8:12-13; James 1:15, 5:19-20).

Grace cannot forgive known sins before confession of them is made to God and before a person judges themselves (1 John 1:9; Rev. 2:5, 2:21-23,29; Prov. 28:13; 2 Tim. 2:24-26; 1 Cor. 11:21).

Grace is not responsible if people use their free wills and depart from the faith (2 Pet. 2:21-22; James 5:19-20; Heb. 3:12-14, 12:14-15; 1 Tim. 4:1).

Grace cannot force men to take the narrow road which leads to life (John 3:16; Heb. 2:9; Rev. 22:17; Rom. 6:16, 8:1-13; 2 Pet. 3:9; Luke 13:3).

Grace cannot automatically protect anyone from the wrath of God if they continue in disobedience (Rev. 2:21-24,29; Eph. 5:5-8; Col. 3:25; 1 Cor. 10:5-12; 2 Thess. 1:7-8).

Grace cannot operate in the life of a free moral agent without that person's consent (Gen. 2:7; Mark 16:15-16; Rev. 22:17; 2 Pet. 3:9; John 1:12; Rom. 10:13).

Grace cannot give eternal life to anyone who serves sin and Satan (Rom. 2:1-9, 6:16, 8:12-13; James 4:4; 1 Cor. 2:9; 1 John 2:15-17; 1 Tim. 6:11-12).

Grace cannot automatically cancel out the law of sowing and reaping (Gal. 6:7-8; Heb. 2:1-3). It cannot give unconditional, eternal security (2 Pet. 1:10). It cannot move God to lay aside the conditions He's already laid out in the New Covenant (John 12:48). It cannot automatically wash away sins, keep men from falling away if they don't want to be kept, accept rebels, or guarantee heaven for anyone who wants to live in sin.

*"The night is far spent, the day is at hand: let us therefore cast off the works of darkness, and let us put on the armor of light. Let us walk honestly, as in the day; not in rioting and drunkenness, not in chambering and wantonness, not in strife and envying. But put ye on the Lord Jesus Christ, **and make not provision for the flesh, to fulfill the lusts thereof**"* (Rom. 13:12-14). *"Fight the good fight of faith, lay hold on eternal life, whereunto thou art also called, and hast professed a good profession before many witnesses"* (1 Tim. 6:12).

These scriptures reveal the limitations of grace because of God dealing with us as free moral agents.

If one walks hand in hand with the devil, he will be judged with the devil. Whoever you're walking with reveals whom you are really willing to receive from and serve. It shows whom your master is that you have chosen. You either follow the Good Shepherd down paths of righteousness, or the devil down paths of unrighteousness! Christ's sheep follow Him. Are you one of His sheep?

Romans 15:18 The apostle said, *"For I will not dare to speak of any of those things which Christ hath not wrought by me, **to make the Gentiles obedient, by word and deed.**"* But today when a preacher, inspired by God, puts forth the same truth as the apostles to make the people obedient by word and deed, they are condemned by extreme gracists as legalistic. They call God's minister's, Jesus's, and the apostles' teaching legalistic. Who are they planning on being saved by? These gracists who themselves many times are hard, unyielding, and legalistic towards others in many ways as those in Jude 3, are indeed following a philosophy and the spirit of this world rather than the Bible, and then don't even know it. There are legalists who are in a ditch on one side of the road with religious ceremonies, Jewish ordinances, and manmade rules and traditions, and the extreme gracists who are in the ditch on the other side. Both pervert the Gospel. They really are saying you could follow the serpent and go to heaven; although they may not put it in those words, it is what they teach (Eph. 2:2-3). Persistently walking in the paths of unrighteousness will never lead to heaven. If sin reigns, the result is death. If grace reigns, it produces righteousness in one's life and the result is eternal life through Jesus Christ our Lord (Rom. 5:21).

Let's Go Now to Corinthians and See What Paul Wrote to the Christians at Corinth

Grace cannot protect you from judgment if you follow the flesh.

Paul, in his theology, wrote in 1 Corinthians 3:16-18,

*"Know ye not that ye are the temple of God, and that the Spirit of God dwelleth in you? [Only Christians are the temple of God.] If any man defile the temple of God [by going back to live in the pollutions of the world], **him [that Christian] shall God destroy**; for the temple of God is holy (it is to be consecrated to God and to His service), which temple ye are. Let no man deceive (mislead) himself. If any man among you seemeth to be wise in this world, let him become a fool, that he may be wise."*

Does it sound as though God just continues to see the person the same way regardless of how they act even if they continue on in a course of sin? No, if they return back to their old, former life following Satan once again without repentance, God said He would destroy them. They make themselves then a vessel fitted for destruction (2 Tim. 2:19-22). It all depends on whom they've committed to live their lives for. This determines whose servants they are. God's warnings are sure. He destroyed millions in the Old Covenant who rebelled and were idolaters. He said in the New Covenant that these things were written down as a warning to us.

Certainly, where known sin is confessed, the blood of Jesus washes away all unrighteousness and you stand complete in Christ, in His perfect righteousness. But sin defiles the garment of salvation, and to be cleansed, there must be confession of it to God. Confession is an act of faith, not a dead work (Heb. 11:13). Anything God tells us to do in the New Covenant, if we do it, it is faith. *If we don't do it, it's unbelief.* Faith always moves a person to respond to God's written Word. Faith responds to the truth, and God's Word is truth (Matt. 4:4; Rom. 1:17).

Grace Can't Save People Who Won't Serve God

Jude 22-23

"And of some have compassion, making a difference: And others save with fear, pulling them out of the fire [of Ghenna]; hating even the garment spotted by the flesh." We are to serve God either by love or fear, but by all means serve and obey God. We are to flee the wrath to come to escape the fire. The fear of the Lord is the beginning of wisdom (Prov. 1:7). But thank God, the blood of Jesus washes away the stains of sin and the garment is then perfectly clean when confessed. And as we've shown, a sin doesn't instantly break relationship, just fellowship, but it can make one carnal and hinder spiritual perception. If it's continued in without repentance, the scripture warns that it will harden the heart, sear the conscience, shipwreck faith, and will cause a person to depart from God with an evil heart of unbelief. There are no two ways about it, it *will* cause this. When they return to live the way they used to live before meeting Christ, they then apostatize. They abandon the faith and the grace of God (Heb. 11:15), and grace cannot save such a person unless they return to God. This is sin's effects in the human soul and why Peter admonished us to *"abstain from fleshly lusts which war against the soul."* So although God wouldn't depart from us, we still have free wills and can choose to depart from Him, and then He must let us go. Then if we depart from Him He will depart from us (Deut. 31:16-17; Gal. 6:7; John 6:66; Heb. 10:26-31).

Hebrews 3:12-14

"Take heed [then], brethren, lest there be in any of you an evil heart of unbelief, **in departing from the living God.** *But exhort one another daily, while it is called today;* **lest any of you be hardened through the deceitfulness of sin.** *For we are made partakers of Christ, if we hold the beginning of our confidence steadfast unto the end."* To depart from God is to no longer keep His commandments. Listen to this scripture and see clearly what we say. *"For he clave to the Lord, and departed not from following him, but kept his commandments, which the Lord commanded Moses"* (2 Kings 18:6). David said, *"Depart from me, ye evil doers: for I will keep the commandments of my God"* (Ps. 119:115). David was a man of faith.

Grace Can't Save Those Who
Refuse to Obey God's Commandments

Revelation 14:12 says, *"Here is the patience [the endurance] of the saints: here are they that keep the commandments of God, and the faith of*

Jesus." (That is, the teaching and instructions of Jesus in the Gospels and Epistles.) Then see again, Revelation 22:14: "*Blessed are they that do his commandments, that they may have right to the tree of life, and may enter in through the gates into the city.*"

This is why Paul wrote 1 Corinthians 7:19: "*Circumcision is nothing, and uncircumcision is nothing, but the keeping of the commandments of God.*" After he lived a life of obedience to God and His commandments and didn't allow Satan to draw him back to his old way of life, he said, "*I have fought a good fight, I have finished my course, I have kept the faith: henceforth there is laid up for me a crown of righteousness, which the Lord, the righteous judge, shall give me at that day: and not to me only, but unto all them also that love His appearing*" (2 Tim. 4:7-8). To depart from God then is to no longer live in such a way as to keep His commandments. John wrote in 1 John 2:3-4, "*And hereby we do know that we know him, if we keep his commandments.* **He that saith, I know him, and keepeth not his commandments, is a liar, and the truth is not in him.**"

"*But the fearful, and unbelieving, and the abominable, and murderers, and whoremongers, and sorcerers, and idolaters, and all liars, shall have their part in the lake which burneth with fire and brimstone: which is the second death*" (Rev. 21:8). It's obvious then that grace is given so you can keep His commandments, while a false counterfeit concept of grace teaches that you need not keep His commandments implying that it's legalism to have to do so when really it is faith. Is not the deceiver of the whole world a crafty creature? He even has duped some who once accepted Christ to fight for their right to continue to follow the serpent. He promises them life with God while they lead a life of sin and rebellion, but be not ignorant of his devices. Put on the whole armor of God that you may be able to stand against "*the wiles*" of the devil (Eph. 6:10-17).

If you allow sin into your life without repentance, looking at it as insignificant, it will work to deceive you and begin its hardening effect on the conscience. There is no escaping it. If you follow after a life of sin, you are no longer the just, but a sinner, for "*The just shall live by faith,*" and faith and sin are opposites. The very reason people go back into sin or make up doctrines such as ultra grace is because of their unbelief, lack of commitment to God, or desire to sin (Rom. 14:22-23). They don't believe or don't want to obey all the scriptures, so they just accept the ones they want to believe that have nothing to do with obedience or a change of behavior. (See John 3:20-21.) And they shout, "grace, grace," not even knowing what it is.

Israel believed and kept the Passover (a type of Christ's sacrifice), and was delivered from Egypt (a type of the world), and they were protected from *the death angel* (a type of Satan who had the power of death) by the blood. But when they later departed in their hearts, the epistle of Jude warns that God *"afterwards destroyed them"* because they departed from Him with an evil heart of unbelief. This departing was not saying that there is no God, but a departing from obedience to Him. There is not one scripture in all the Bible that says "once saved, always saved," regardless of how one lives, but numerous scriptures that reveal how God dealt with those that rebelled against Him. However, you can always have assurance as long as you are willing to live for Him, and you confess and repent of your sins if you do sin.

I have been saved for over twenty-eight years and have never doubted my salvation, nor my security in Christ. So if you live for God, you can always be assured of your position in Christ. If you sin, repent of it and confess it, then Jesus washes it away (1 John 2:1).

*"My little children, let us not love in word, neither in tongue; but in deed and in truth. **And hereby we know** that we are of the truth, and shall assure our hearts before him. For if our heart condemn us, God is greater than our heart, and knoweth all things. Beloved, if our heart condemn us not, then have we confidence toward God"* (1 John 3:18-21). The only way you can really tell if you are of the truth is if you live what you say you believe. Tares look like wheat but are different by nature. They don't produce the same thing. At the end of the world they will be gathered and burned, and there will be weeping and gnashing of teeth (2 Thess. 1:8).

Grace Can't Save an Unwilling Soul Who Refuses to Continue in the Race

"Then Paul and Barnabas waxed bold, and said, It was necessary that the word of God should first have been spoken to you: but seeing ye put it from you, and judge yourselves unworthy of everlasting life, lo, we turn to the Gentiles" (Acts 13:46).

"Behold therefore the goodness and severity of God: on them which fell, severity; but toward thee, goodness, if thou continue in his goodness: otherwise thou also shalt be cut off" (Rom. 11:22).

1 Timothy 1:19

"Holding faith, and a good conscience; which some [Christians] having put away concerning faith have made shipwreck (of their Christian walk."

Ephesians 6:12 Be like Paul (Fellow Christian), *"Fight the good fight of faith, **lay hold** on eternal life, whereunto thou art also called, and hast professed a good profession before many witnesses."* Stay willing right to the finish line.

*"Know ye not that they which run in a race run all, but one receiveth the prize? So run, that ye may obtain. And every man that striveth for the mastery is temperate in all things. Now they **do it** to obtain a corruptible crown; but we an incorruptible"* (1 Cor. 9:24-25).

"Brethren, I count not myself to have apprehended: but this one thing I do, forgetting those things which are behind, and reaching forth unto those things which are before, I press toward the mark for the prize of the high calling of God in Christ Jesus" (Phil. 3:13-14).

"Wherefore seeing we also are compassed about with so great a cloud of witnesses, let us lay aside every weight, and the sin which doth so easily beset us, and let us run with patience the race [to heaven] that is set before us, Looking unto Jesus the author and finisher of our faith; who for the joy that was set before him endured the cross, despising the shame, and is set down at the right hand of the throne of God. For consider him that endured such contradiction of sinners against himself, lest ye be wearied and faint in your minds (and give up the race). Ye have not yet resisted unto blood, striving against sin" (Heb. 12:1-4).

God won't forsake us but we can forsake Him (Deut. 31:16-17). No *other* creature can separate us from the love of God which is in Christ Jesus, our Lord (Rom. 8:38). But *our own* unconfessed sins and iniquities can bring this about (Isa. 59:2; Hab. 1:13; Rom. 5:12). No other man can pluck you out of His hand, but you can walk out. God says, *"And if ye will not be reformed by me by these things, but will walk contrary unto me; Then will I also walk contrary unto you, and will punish you yet seven times for your sins"* (Lev. 26:23-24).

God doesn't remove the free will of man after a man is saved. We don't suddenly become robots. The will is either willing to receive from God, or unwilling. People can be willing for awhile and then become unwilling (John 5:34-35). If God's grace was irresistible as some foolishly believe, all the world would be saved (Heb. 2:9), holy (1 Pet. 1:15-16), and fulfilling all of God's will in every area (Matt. 6:10). But it's obvious if you just look and think for a moment, that all Christians still have free wills and free action, and the Bible does reveal that people can believe for awhile and in time of temptation fall away from following Christ (Luke 8:13). So if God just forced His will on all Christians, they would all be holy, powerfully anointed, preaching the Gospel to every creature, fasting, praying, tithing, living holy, and doing many other good things, for this is His perfect will (Eph. 2:10), but they then would not have free wills. There would be no exhortations then in scripture for Christians to continue, or people to obey, for all would be doing so. So it's obvious even Christians exercise their wills many times contrary to God's perfect will. Why would we have to pray His will be done on earth if it all was already being done? So then it's obvious the will is still free. Each will be judged by their life's actions, and by whether or not they repented of sin, or refused to repent. *"And I saw a great white throne, and him that sat on it, from whose face the earth and the heaven fled away; and there was found no place for them. And I saw the dead, small and great, stand before God; and the books were opened: and another book was opened, which is the book of life: and the dead were judged out of those things which were written in the books, according to their works. And the sea gave up the dead which were in it; and death and hell delivered up the dead which were in them: and they were judged every man according to their works. And death and hell were cast into the lake of fire. This is the second death. And whosoever was not found written in the book of life was cast into the lake of fire"* (Rev. 20:11-15). *"So then every one of us shall give account of himself to God"* (Rom. 14:12). *"Wherefore we labor, that, whether present or absent, we may be accepted of him. For we must all appear before the judgment seat of Christ; that every one may receive the things done in his body, according to that he hath done, whether it be good or bad. Knowing therefore the terror of the Lord, we persuade men; but we are made manifest unto God; and I trust also are made manifest in your consciences. For we commend not ourselves again unto you, but give you occasion to glory on our behalf, that ye may have somewhat to answer them which glory in appearance, and not in heart"* (2 Cor. 5:9-12).

The Lord says, speaking of a woman named Jezebel in the church who refused to repent, *"And I will kill her children with death; and all the churches shall know that I am he which searcheth the reins and hearts: and I will give unto every one of you according to your works.… And he that overcometh, and keepeth my works unto the end, to him will I give power over the nations.… He that hath an ear, let him hear what the Spirit saith unto the churches"* (Rev. 2:23, 26, 29). And of course, God will instantly accept back by mercy and grace any prodigal son who comes to himself and uses his will to turn back to God. So run back to Him if need be (Heb. 4:16).

Why would we have to fight the good fight of faith to lay hold on eternal life if we've already, automatically, laid hold on it, no matter how we live? Yes, we have it now, but it's not permanently ours. It becomes permanently ours when we, as overcomers, partake of the tree of life (Rev. 2:7, 22:14; Gen. 3:22). This is why it's called the "hope" of eternal life (Titus 1:1-2). Any gift once received can later be rejected. Paul said, "**Hold fast** *to that which is good.*" The gift of eternal life is not a part of us, it's God's life given to a person. So, eternal life is something separate from the individual. It is something that we are blessed with as we continue on in Christ; for, *"in Him is life."* (See John 1:4.)

But if *"any man abide not"* in Christ, he is cast forth as a branch and is burned (John 15:6). He then forfeits life. He's broken off or pruned off from the true vine. So grace cannot save an unwilling soul (1 Pet. 2:11). (See also James 5:19-20.)

The Prodigal

Luke 15:17-20 Concerning the prodigal (wayward son) who ended up back out into the pollutions of the world: *"And when he came to himself, he said, How many hired servants of my father's have bread enough and to spare, and I perish with hunger!* **I will arise** *and go to my father, and will say unto him, Father,* **I have sinned** *against heaven, and before thee, and am no more worthy to be called thy son: make me as one of thy hired servants. And he arose, and came to his father. But when he was yet a great way off, his father saw him, and had compassion, and ran, and fell on his neck, and kissed him."* And the Father said, *"For this my son was dead, and is* **alive again; he was lost, and is found.** *And they began to be merry"* (v. 24).

God loves us and rejoices at the return of every prodigal, but it isn't until the prodigal comes home out of living in the pollutions of the world and uses his own will to do so, that he is restored. Mercy and grace then instantly gives him the best robe, the fatted calf, and the ring of inheritance. It's not by the prodigal's own merits that he deserves it; it's because he became willing to return and receive the forgiveness that mercy and grace were offering to him (Heb. 4:16). In other words, he "repented." He turned from Satan to God; from the pollutions of the world back to the Father. Mercy forgave him and grace gave him power to continue and to receive the blessings.

If we'd only believe all of the Word and the whole counsel of God, we'd clearly understand these things, but people many times express what they think, rather than say what the Word of the Lord actually says. They build their doctrines on what they prefer, taking certain scriptures out of context rather than looking at the *"whole counsel of God"*; they think that just because they believe it that way, it is so. Paul wrote, *"Beware lest any man spoil you through philosophy [intellectual reasonings and theories] and vain deceit [a hollow sham or delusive speculations], after the tradition [the instructions] of men, after the rudiments of the world [following the world's way of looking at things], and not after Christ"* (instead of what Christ has said and taught, Col. 2:8).

So, again, relationship with God isn't instantly broken by a sin, or certain sins committed, but if the sin (or sins) goes unconfessed, they will produce hardness of heart in a person, war against the will, and eventually lead them back to lukewarmness, the world, and its pollutions. Again, the Bible says, *"abstain from fleshly lusts which war against the soul,"* or, what Peter so clearly stated would come to pass if a person continues in unconfessed sin. It can cause the heart to depart from living for the will of God (1 Tim. 4:1).

Grace Cannot Keep a Person Saved
Who Wills to Live Like the World

2 Peter 2:20-21

*"For **if after they have escaped the pollutions of the world through the knowledge of the Lord and Savior Jesus Christ, they are again entangled therein, and overcome [conquered again by them], the latter end is worse with them than the beginning. For it had been better for them not to have known the way of righteousness, than, after they have known it, to turn from the holy commandment** delivered unto them."*

Why is it worse? Because they are responsible for more light and God's own righteousness must deal with it accordingly. We can confess it and instantly find abundant mercy and pardon or we can continue in it and find judgment.

It's our choice. But God prefers that we turn to Him for mercy.

"If we would judge ourselves, we'd not be judged," but if we don't, God's Word shows that we will be judged by God for following Satan. He gives space to repent but then someone must pay; either we ourselves, or we must turn to, and take advantage of, the blood of Christ and confess our

sin (John 1:9). But sin will eventually deceive a person and lead a person to continue in a wrong direction. If they continue in that course, they will be judged, for God is against all wrongdoing, and His righteousness and wrath must deal with evil, unless the individual repents (Eph. 5:1-17). Their being judged then, is not God's fault, but the person's.

"Love not the world, neither the things that are in the world. If any man love the world, the love of the Father is not in him. For all that is in the world, the lust of the flesh, and the lust of the eyes, and the pride of life, is not of the Father, but is of the world. And the world passeth away, and the lust thereof: but he that doeth the will of God abideth for ever" (1 John 2:15-17).

Acts 3:26

"Unto you first God, having raised up his Son Jesus, sent him to bless you, in turning away every one of you from his iniquities."

Blessings only come as we willingly yield to the influence of God's grace and obey the Word. They don't come automatically, they come only by obedience (Isa. 1:19-20); and God's grace gives us the power to obey. So it is by grace and our cooperation with it.

There is a battle going on for the will of man. Fleshly lust, the scripture says, *"Wars against the soul,"* to try and conquer it once again. Would God ever then provide something that would cover for us so we could live in those ungodly things that work to draw us away from God to Satan? Of course not! Such doctrines are preposterous. People that teach such things just don't know their Bible. I've read books by the ultra gracists and it's all philosophy and human reasoning with a few scriptures taken out of context and mixed in for good (or rather bad) measure. If they didn't put some scripture in there, no one would believe what they had to say. But many are misled by these great humanistic, intellectual arguments that contradict the clear, plain teaching of the scriptures. Read the whole New Testament, believe it all to be safe and secure, and if you can't believe *everything* that Christ and the apostles taught and wrote then your beliefs are wrong.

Grace Cannot Automatically Protect an Evil Doer from Judgment

"For he that will love life, and see good days, let him refrain his tongue from evil, and his lips that they speak no guile: Let him eschew evil, and do good; let him seek peace, and ensue it. For the eyes of the Lord are over the righteous, and his ears are open unto their prayers: but the face of the Lord is against them that do evil" (1 Pet. 3:10-12).

"*But he that doeth wrong shall receive for the wrong which he hath done: and there is no respect of persons*" (Col. 3:25).

"*Therefore we ought to give the more earnest heed to the things which we have heard, lest at any time we should let them slip. For if the word spoken by angels was steadfast, and every transgression and disobedience received a just recompense of reward; How shall we escape, if we neglect so great salvation; which at the first began to be spoken by the Lord, and was confirmed unto us by them that heard him*" (Heb. 2:1-3).

1 Corinthians 5:1-5

"*It is reported commonly that there is fornication among you, and such fornication as is not so much as named among the Gentiles, that one should have his father's wife. And ye are puffed up,* **and have not rather mourned, that he that hath done this deed** *might be taken away from among you. For I verily, as absent in body, but present in spirit, have judged already, as though I were present, concerning him* **that hath so done this deed.** *In the name of our Lord Jesus Christ, when ye are gathered together, and my spirit, with the power of our Lord Jesus Christ,* **to deliver such an one unto Satan** *for the destruction of the flesh, that the spirit may be saved in the day of the Lord Jesus.*" This is *the Lord's response* to such a man. Why? Because the Lord loved him and desired that he use his will to repent and turn back to Him for mercy. It wasn't God's best, but as one preacher said, "It sure beats going to hell." Always remember that even though God's love is great and He's not willing that any should perish, yet contrary to His love, His grace, and His will, people are perishing by the multitudes and going to hell every day. Why? Because they are not using their wills to come to Him and to receive what He, by mercy and grace, offers to them and has provided for them. They have to turn from Satan and turn to God (Acts 26:18-20) to receive (Mark 16:15-16). Their unwillingness is what will send them to hell.

Revelation 22:17

"*And the Spirit and the bride say,* **Come.** *And let him that heareth say,* **Come.** *And let him that is athirst* **come. And whosoever will,** *let him take the water of life freely.*" Yes, it's free, but it must always be willingly received. A person must willingly go to the Lord for grace and for forgiveness (Heb. 4:16).

Here is His great promise. Jesus said, "**Whosoever cometh to ME** I will *in no wise cast out.*" "*Then Peter opened his mouth, and said, Of a truth I perceive that God is no respecter of persons*" (Acts 10:34).

John 1:12

*"But as many **as received him, to them** gave he power to become the sons of God, even to them that believe on His name."* So the human will is always involved, both to come and to continue.

And why did Paul say some would *depart* from the faith and *depart* from the living God?

(1) Because of being deceived by wrong, religious doctrines started by devils (1 Tim. 4:1).

(2) Because of becoming hardened through sin and being overcome by the world once again (Heb. 3:12-13).

Both things can cause a person to leave the life of faith. Again it's a "will" issue. The human will is always free to chart its own course either down the broad road that leads to destruction, or to cooperate with grace down the narrow road that leads to life. As the will goes, so goes the man. Men are heading the way they "will" to go. They themselves are either choosing life or death (Deut. 30:19).

"For this ye know, that no whoremonger, nor unclean person, nor covetous man, who is an idolater, hath any inheritance in the kingdom of Christ and of God. Let no man deceive you with vain words: for because of these things cometh the wrath of God upon the children of disobedience. Be not ye therefore partakers with them" (Eph. 5:5-7).

It's God's desire that all choose the narrow road and He has provided the necessary grace and power for us to take it (2 Peter 3:9; 1 Tim. 2:4). *"Come unto me, all ye that labor and are heavy laden, and I will give you rest. Take my yoke upon you, and learn of me; for I am meek and lowly in heart: and ye shall find rest unto your souls. For my yoke is easy, and my burden is light"* (Matt. 11:28-30). At the narrow gate you must lay down all sin and pick up your cross to enter this narrow gate and road. *"Wherefore seeing we also are compassed about with so great a cloud of witnesses, let us lay aside **every weight, and the sin** which doth so easily beset us, and let us run with patience [endurance to the end of this life] the race that is set before us"* (Heb. 12:1).

Deuteronomy 30:15-20

*"**See,** I have set before thee this day life and good, and death and evil; in that I command thee this day to love the* Lord *thy God, to **walk in his ways,** and to keep his commandments and his statutes and his judgments, that thou mayest live and multiply: and the* Lord *thy God shall bless thee in the land*

*whither thou goest to possess it. **But if thine heart turn away, so that thou wilt not hear, but shalt be drawn away, and worship other gods, and serve them; I denounce unto you this day, that ye shall surely perish**, and that ye shall not prolong your days upon the land, whither thou passest over Jordan to go to possess it. I call heaven and earth to record this day against you, that I have set before you life and death, blessing and cursing: **therefore choose life**, that both thou and thy seed may live: That thou mayest love the* Lord *thy God, and that thou mayest obey his voice, and that thou mayest cleave unto him: for he is thy life, and the length of thy days...."*

These principles never change but are revealed in both Covenants. Each individual must choose. Who are they going to serve, God or Satan; the lusts of this world, or heaven? Whoever they serve as their course in life is their lord (Luke 6:46). Adam fell because he changed masters, and by this he lost eternal life (Eph. 4:18; Rom. 5:12). Our salvation again is also a change of masters and a regaining of eternal life as long as we serve God (Rom. 6:16). Whatever world a person chooses to live for is the decision they've made (John 12:25; 1 John 2:15-17; James 4:4). What they do is their fruit that shows what they are living for (Matt. 3:10,12:13). Everyone will eat the fruit of their own ways. Both Covenants also show that people can, in faith, turn to live for God for awhile but then later turn away (2 Pet. 2:20-21; John 6:66; Heb. 3:12-13). The decision is always left up to the person, and God in His sovereignty chose it to be this way (Rom. 11:22). This is why the scripture constantly exhorts that they that begin in this life of faith, are to continue in it to the end (Rev. 2:10-11). It's not how you start a race that counts, it's how you finish. It's up to you as to whether or not you will continue (1 Tim. 6:12; 2 Tim. 4:7-8). If you're willing to continue, God is always there willing to supply the ability to live the Christian life (Col. 1:22-23).

If a person decides to go back to *a life* of disobedience in the world, they then yield themselves to follow the evil spirit of disobedience. They do despite to the Spirit of Grace, and all that's left for them is certain judgment (Heb. 10:26-31).

1 Corinthians 5:11

*"But now I have written unto you not to keep company, **if any man that is called a brother** be a fornicator, or covetous, or an idolater, or a railer, or a drunkard, or an extortioner; with such an one no not to eat."* (If any is walking according to the course of this world, don't even eat with him, but try to restore him.)

Why shouldn't you have fellowship with him? *So that he may be ashamed of himself and turn back to what's right.* If you treat him as though he's not doing wrong, you are encouraging him in his sin and he may therefore go to hell because of you. This is not love to do so.

James 5:19-20

*"Brethren, **if any of you** do err [go astray or are seduced away] from the truth, and one convert him [bring him back once again]; let him know, that he which converteth [turns] **the sinner** from the error of his way [his misguided course] shall save a soul [that person's soul] from death, and shall hide a multitude of sins."* The brother who turns away to live in sin without repentance is heading towards eventual spiritual death once again, and is once more called a sinner. The scripture still stands. *"The soul that sinneth, it shall die."* Anyone who lives a life of sin is called a sinner by the Word of God. *"The just shall live by faith."* Real faith purifies the heart and takes us on from glory to glory in paths of righteousness (1 John 3:3). We are, as Paul said, to *"press on to perfection."*

1 Corinthians 6:7-10

*"Now therefore there is utterly a fault among you, because ye go to law one with another. Why do ye not rather take wrong? Why do ye not rather suffer yourselves to be defrauded? Nay, ye do wrong, and defraud, and that your **brethren. Know ye not** that the unrighteous [the sinful and those who live for wrongdoing] shall **not** inherit the kingdom of God? **Be not deceived:** [misled] [fellow Christian] neither fornicators, nor idolaters, nor adulterers, nor effeminate, nor abus-ers of themselves with mankind, nor thieves, nor covetous, nor drunkards, nor revilers, nor extortioners, shall inherit (nor share in) the Kingdom of God."*

Evidently the Ultra Gracists *Know It Not and Have Been Deceived*!

Paul points out that the unrighteous are those that live unrighteously. James said *the sinner* is the one who lives in sin, whether he was once called a brother or not. So sin eventually leads the will back to the old lifestyle and the pollutions of this world which is the work of the devil and will bring a person to judgment. God will judge all evil, but, *"If we would judge ourselves, we would not be judged."* When a person makes a decision to depart from God and from living as a Christian, they've departed from the faith and from life. You can tell if they've then made the decision by whether or not they are now living for the world and its pollutions, or for God and the way of righteousness (1 John 2:3-4). Yes, by the fruit of their lives ye shall know them.

Grace Couldn't Even Keep a Preacher Saved if
He Chose Later to Follow After the Ways of the Flesh.

"There salute thee Epaphras, my fellow prisoner in Christ Jesus; Marcus, Aristarchus, Demas, Lucas, my fellow laborers" (Philem. 23-24).

"For Demas hath forsaken me, having loved this present world, and is departed unto Thessalonica; Crescens to Galatia, Titus unto Dalmatia" (2 Tim. 4:10).

"But if any man love God, the same is known of him" (1 Cor. 8:3).

"Love not the world, neither the things that are in the world. If any man love the world, the love of the Father is not in him" (1 John 2:15).

"Hearken, my beloved brethren, Hath not God chosen the poor of this world rich in faith, and heirs of the kingdom which he hath promised to them that love him?" (James 2:5).

1 Corinthians 9:27

Even Paul the Apostle said, *"But I keep under my body, and bring it into subjection: lest that by any means, when I have preached to others [and called them to enter the race], I myself should be a castaway"* (fall away and fail to obtain the prize at the end of the race). He said, *"for if you live after the flesh, ye shall die"* (spiritually). The word "cast away" in the Greek means "a reprobate; to be rejected and become worthless." Jesus said to His disciples, *"Ye are the salt of the earth: but if the salt have lost his savor, wherewith shall it be salted? it is thenceforth good for nothing, but to be cast out, and to be trodden under foot of men"* (Matt. 5:13; Luke 14:34-35).

1 Corinthians 10:1-13

Listen as Paul, in his theology, uses Old Testament examples to warn New Testament believers (thereby) revealing that God's dealing with man is the same in both Covenants when it comes to His moral law.

"Moreover, brethren, I would not that ye should be ignorant, how that all our fathers were under the cloud, and all passed through the sea; and were all baptized unto Moses in the cloud and in the sea; and did all eat the same spiritual meat; and did all drink the same spiritual drink: for they drank of that spiritual Rock that followed them: **and that Rock was Christ. But with many of them God was not well pleased** *[most of them lost the favor of God]: for they were overthrown [and died] in the wilderness.* **Now these things were our examples, [written as warnings to us] to the intent we should not lust after evil things, as they also lusted.** *[To teach us not to lust after evil and forbidden things as they also did.] Neither be ye idolaters, as were some of them; as it is*

written, *The people sat down to eat and drink, and rose up to play.* **Neither let us** *commit fornication, as some of them committed, and fell in one day three and twenty thousand.* **Neither let us tempt Christ, as some of them also tempted, and were destroyed** *of serpents. Neither murmur ye, as some of them also murmured, and were destroyed of the destroyer. Now all these things happened unto them for ensamples:* **and they are written for our admonition** *[our warning and our caution], upon whom the ends of the world are come.* **Wherefore let him that thinketh he standeth [so securely] take heed lest he fall.** *There hath no temptation taken you but such as is common to man: but God is faithful, who will not suffer you to be tempted above that ye are able; but will with the temptation also make a way to escape, that ye may be able to bear it."* So then, anything that comes to you, you can overcome it rather than yield to it. God is faithful. There is goodness we see towards those who live a good life and follow Him by faith, but Paul reveals terror towards evil doers. (Remember, God Himself is the one who made the lake of fire for all rebels.) That is, all free moral agents who refuse to live for His will. His judgment is that this is what evil deserves; seeing it is the opposite of good, it deserves the opposite of blessings.

So grace cannot automatically protect anyone from judgment. (See also Rev. 2:20-29.)

Grace Cannot Save Those Who Serve Satan

1 Corinthians 10:21-22 Listen to Paul:

*"***Ye cannot*** drink the cup of the Lord, and the cup of devils: ye cannot be partakers of the Lord's table, and of the table of devils. Do we provoke the Lord to jealousy? Are we stronger than he?"* It is *not possible* for a person to partake of the Lord's blessings and partake with demons at the same time. You cannot be a partaker of the Lord's table and of the devil's table also (1 Cor. 10:21).

"Ye cannot" serve two masters; *"a good tree* **cannot** *bring forth evil fruit"; "and if a kingdom be divided against itself, that kingdom* **cannot** *stand."* God sent Jesus and the Holy Spirit to lead us back into paths of righteousness. How then can some say we can walk in the paths of the evil one, and that God set it up that this would be okay? Is God divided against Himself? Is He the author of confusion? By no means, for Jesus was manifested to destroy the devil's work of sin in our life and to free us so we could walk in the light as He is in the light, not so we could walk in darkness. Jesus said, *"And whosoever doth not bear his cross, and come after me, cannot be my disciple.... Or what king, going to make war against another*

king, sitteth not down first, and consulteth whether he be able with ten thousand to meet him that cometh against him with twenty thousand? Or else, while the other is yet a great way off, he sendeth an ambassage, and desireth conditions of peace. **So likewise whosoever he be of you that forsaketh not all that he hath** *[that's contrary to Me], he cannot be my disciple. Salt is good; but if the salt have lost his savor, wherewith shall it be seasoned? It is neither fit for the land, nor yet for the dunghill; but men cast it out. He that hath ears to hear, let him hear"* (what Christ is saying, Luke 14:27, 31-35). Jesus further said, "*the scripture* **cannot be broken**." All must be exactly as it is written. The judgment is set. There will be no variation from what is taught in the New Covenant regardless of people's opinions or the carefully worded philosophies of men (Heb. 2:1-3), whether that person be some well known theologian of the past, whose written volumes and volumes of books reasoning against the truth, or anyone else. The Word will judge us in the last day.

You're either living for this world or the next world, for Jesus or for Satan, for sin or for righteousness, for "**no man**" can serve (nor follow) two masters.

"If any man serve me, let him follow me; and where I am, there shall also my servant be: if any man serve me, him will my Father honor" (John 12:26).

Grace Cannot Automatically Excuse Evil Behavior

1 Corinthians 11:23-34 Listen again to Paul's warnings:

"For I have received of the Lord that which also I delivered unto you, That the Lord Jesus the same night in which he was betrayed took bread: And when he had given thanks, he brake it, and said, Take, eat: this is my body, which is broken for you: this do in remembrance of me. After the same manner also, he took the cup, when he had supped, saying, This cup is the new testament in my blood: this do ye, as oft as ye drink it, in remembrance of me. For as often as ye eat this bread, and drink this cup, ye do show the Lord's death till He come. Wherefore, **whosoever shall eat this bread, and drink this cup of the Lord, unworthily,** *shall be guilty of the body and blood of the Lord. But* **let a man examine himself,** *and so let him eat of that bread, and drink of that cup. For he that eateth and drinketh* **unworthily, eateth and drinketh damnation to himself,** *not discerning the Lord's body. For this cause many are weak and sickly among you and many sleep. For if we would judge ourselves, we should not be judged. But when we are judged, we are chastened of the Lord, that we should not be condemned with the world. Wherefore, my brethren, when ye come together to eat, tarry one for another. And if any man hunger, let him eat*

at home; that ye come not together unto condemnation. And the rest will I set in order when I come."

Paul didn't presume they could stand in their positional righteousness while doing evil and escape God's displeasure and judgment. He never said that grace would be a cloak for evil, He said to the contrary, God will judge those who do wrong in the body of Christ except they repent. He said many are sick and die before their time because of disobedience and because of the Lord's judgment (Deut. 28:45-47); for everyone reaps what they sow. No one should take the Lord's supper unless they are committed to obey Him, for it is a Covenant meal between two totally committed parties (1 Thess. 4:6-7).

Be Not Deceived

1 Corinthians 15:33-34

*"**Be not deceived** [be not led astray by false reasonings]: evil communications corrupt good manners [good character]. Awake to righteousness [understand what real righteousness is], **and sin not** [stop sinning]; for some have not the knowledge of God [some of you don't have the real knowledge of God that teaches this]: I speak this to your shame."*

*"**Be not deceived**; God is not mocked: for whatsoever a man soweth, that shall he also reap"* (Gal. 6:7).

*"Know ye not that the unrighteous shall not inherit the kingdom of God? **Be not deceived**: neither fornicators, nor idolaters, nor adulterers, nor effeminate, nor abusers of themselves with mankind"* (1 Cor. 6:9).

*"For this ye know, that no whoremonger, nor unclean person, nor covetous man, who is an idolater, hath any inheritance in the kingdom of Christ and of God. **Let no man deceive you** with vain words [empty promises]: for because of these things cometh the wrath of God upon the children of disobedience. Be not ye therefore partakers with them"* (Eph. 5:5-7).

*"**Little children**, let no man deceive you: he that doeth righteousness is righteous, even as he is righteous"* (1 John 3:7).

*"Now I beseech you, brethren, mark them which cause divisions and offences contrary to the doctrine which ye have learned; and avoid them. For they that are such serve not our Lord Jesus Christ, but their own belly; **and by good words and fair speeches deceive the hearts of the simple**"* (Rom. 16:17-18).

The true knowledge of God will truly show you both the deadliness of sin and the deception of sin. It is not a small thing. To deal with the sin problem is the reason Christ came. Sin (evil behavior) works to stop a person from living by faith (Rom. 1:17). Those who say you can live in sin and that grace will cover for you are deceived and don't have the true knowledge of God. *"And for this cause God shall send them strong delusion, that they should believe a lie: That they all might be damned who believed not the truth, but had pleasure in unrighteousness"* (2 Thess. 2:11-12). Ultra gracists preach a corrupt, perverted Gospel, which cannot save if followed. The legalistic Jewish believers perverted it by adding Jewish ceremonies, saying you still need to keep the outward works of the law, or their own traditions and commands; the ultra gracists perverted it by turning (perverting) the grace of God into lasciviousness. Be not deceived by either of those camps.

Christ died for our sins and endured tremendous pain to free us from sin's condemnation, deception, and its power. *"All unrighteousness is sin." "Sin is transgression of the [moral] law"* (1 John 3:4). The knowledge of God will never condone sin nor provide any type of a cloak for people to transgress His *"moral law,"* for *"in Him is **no** sin."* God is good; sin is evil. Sin is only to be judged, not condoned. God hates sin, for sin is people yielding to the devil. Christ's blood, though, will wash it away if it's confessed. This is how we partake of His blood's cleansing power. This is the provision of grace. Awake then to (real God-given) righteousness and sin not. For grace frees us from a life of sin (Rom. 6:14), and is only given to the willing soul (Rev. 22:17; 2 Cor. 8:12; John 5:35; Acts 27:43; Heb. 13:18).

So there are many things grace cannot do for an individual without their willing cooperation. *"Let us therefore come boldly unto the throne of grace, that we may obtain mercy, and find grace to help in time of need"* (Heb. 4:16).

Jesus said, *"Wilt thou be made whole?"* Grace doesn't remove free will, this is God's sovereign design, and this is the way it is.

THE FEAR OF THE LORD

L isten to the wisdom of God speak.

Proverbs 2:1-22

"My son, if thou wilt receive my words, and hide my commandments with thee; So that thou incline thine ear unto wisdom, and apply thine heart to understanding; Yea, if thou criest after knowledge, and liftest up thy voice for understanding; If thou seekest her as silver, and searchest for her as for hid treasures; **Then shalt thou understand the fear of the** LORD**, and find the knowledge of God.** *For the* LORD *giveth wisdom: out of his mouth cometh knowledge and understanding. He layeth up sound wisdom for the righteous: he is a buckler to them that walk uprightly. He keepeth the paths of judgment, and preserveth the way of his saints.* **Then shalt thou understand righteousness, and judgment, and equity; yea, every good path. When wisdom entereth into thine heart, and knowledge is pleasant unto thy soul; Discretion shall preserve thee, understanding shall keep thee:** *To deliver thee from the way of the evil man, from the man that speaketh froward things;* **Who leave the paths of uprightness, to walk in the ways of darkness; Who rejoice to do evil, and delight in the frowardness of the wicked; Whose ways are crooked, and they froward in their paths:** *To deliver thee from the strange woman, even from the stranger which flattereth with her words;* **Which forsaketh the guide of her youth, and forgetteth the covenant of her God.** *For her house inclineth unto death, and her paths unto the dead. None that go unto her return again, neither take they hold of* **the paths of life. That thou mayest walk in the way of good men, and keep the paths of the righteous. For the upright shall dwell in the land, and the perfect shall remain in it. But the wicked shall be cut off*

from the earth, and the transgressors [who transgress the moral law] shall be rooted out of it." It would do you good to look clearly at what is said here. Go back and thoughtfully read it again.

Proverbs 3:7-8

*"Be not wise in thine own eyes [don't pride yourself in your own human wisdom or philosophy about these things]: **fear the Lord**, and depart from evil. It shall be health to thy navel, and marrow to thy bones."*

Proverbs 8:13-14

"The fear of the LORD **is to hate evil:** *pride, and arrogancy, and the evil way, and the froward mouth, **do I hate**. Counsel is mine, and sound wisdom: I am understanding; I have strength."* Jesus loves righteousness and *hates iniquity* (*evil doing*, Hebrews 1:9). Jesus hates the *deeds* and *the doctrine* of the Nicolaitanes which taught that people could sin, eat things sacrificed to idols, and commit fornication and still be okay with God. They taught that just the human body was evil and it was going to go to the grave anyway, so it didn't matter what you did in it now. In other words, like the ultra gracists, they taught that sin was okay to live in now and that it wouldn't really affect your relationship with God. God says, *"Rebellion is as the sin of witchcraft."* And *"if you live after the flesh, ye shall die"* (spiritually, Rom. 8:12-13). You are either rebelling or submitting. There is no gray area.

If Jesus hated the deeds and the doctrine of the Nicolaitanes, then (Rev. 2:6,15-17) He must also hate the wrong teaching of the ultra gracists which can produce the same effect as the Nicolaitanes doctrine now. Jesus told the Pergamos church, *"I have a few things **against you** because you have there those who hold the doctrine of Balaam"* (which caused people to commit sexual immorality; and He said, *"You also have those who hold the doctrine of the Nicolaitanes which thing **I hate**"*). (See Hebrews 1:8-9.) So ultra gracists, WAKE UP, for you are promoting a doctrine which Jesus hates, but which Satan loves. Your teaching is very similar to the doctrine of the Nicolaitanes. So, if you want wisdom, godly counsel and understanding, turn from evil behavior.

Proverbs 9:10

"The fear of the Lord is the beginning of wisdom [true wisdom begins with this kind of reverence for the Lord]: and the knowledge of the Holy [one] is understanding." We should never lose the fear of the Lord. This means "awesome respect" for who He is and the power He has as the Almighty. Jesus said, *"And fear not them, which kill the body, but are not able to kill the soul: but rather fear him which is able to destroy both soul and body in hell."*

Proverbs 10:27,29

*"The fear of the LORD prolongeth days: but the years of the wicked shall be shortened.... The way of the LORD is strength to the upright: but destruction [downfall and misery] shall be to **the workers of iniquity.**"* God's truth concerning these things *"endureth to all generations." "Dead works"; "evil deeds"; "workers of iniquities,"* all have to do with behavior. God said there is only destruction for all those who are involved in those things and continue on in that course. Remember, the wonderful thing about our Covenant is that His grace gives us supernatural ability to live the way He wants us to live (Heb. 12:28).

Proverbs 14:26-27

*"In the fear of the Lord is strong confidence: and **his children shall have a place of refuge.** The fear of the LORD is a fountain of life, to depart from [escape from and avoid] the snares of death."*

Do not think Satan has no more snares of death (2 Tim. 2:26-27). He's always trying to snare Christians with death and doctrines of death (1 Tim. 4:1). His tactics are many. His ways of presenting his lies are manifold. Remember, he, at one time, *"sealed up the sum of wisdom"* (Ezek. 28). So unless you stay right with the Word, he will outreason you if you allow him to. Look closely at the "once saved, always saved" doctrines and you'll see they are all philosophy and not just Bible. They emphasize phrases, which the Bible never speaks of; teach doctrines which the Bible doesn't teach; imply things the Bible never actually says; and people ignorantly swallow it hook, line, and sinker, because it sounds a little spiritual.

Proverbs 15:16

"Better is little with the fear of the LORD than great treasure and trouble therewith."

Proverbs 16:5-6

*"**Every one** that is proud in heart **is an abomination to the LORD:** though hand join in hand, **he shall not be unpunished.** By mercy and truth **iniquity is purged:** and by the fear of the LORD men depart from evil."* If there is truth and mercy, people are being more and more set free from iniquity, never going back into it once again. We see also again that God resists the proud but gives grace to the humble.

No wonder Satan wants to remove the fear of the Lord from people, for by the fear of the Lord men depart from evil and the ways of death.

Sin, evil behavior, and iniquity will always lead one to cursings, corruption, and down the road to death (Gal. 6:7-8). Satan knows this so he gets men to promote doctrines which make people think that sin is okay now in this age of grace, and then there is no fear of God before their eyes (Rom. 3:17-18).

Proverbs 19:23

"The fear of the L*ord* *tendeth to life: and he that hath it shall abide satisfied; he shall not be visited with evil."* What a promise!

Proverbs 23:17

"Let not thine heart envy sinners [as they continue in sinful pleasures]: but be thou in the fear of the L*ord* *all the day long."*

We would further encourage you to study all of Proverbs, which reveals the wisdom of God and shows clearly how He deals with man according to how they behave and live. Grace, remember, is sure to change our behavior and enable us to put on the *"new man"* who is created in righteousness and true holiness. Living as a new creature is what causes us to be blessed (James 1:25), and God commands us to obey because He's given us grace to obey.

Paul wrote that all these things which were written before time were written for our learning and for our admonition, to instruct us concerning God's dealing with man. But are we still supposed to fear God? Yes, not with a terrified fear, but a reverential fear, a godly fear; understanding who He is and how He has dealt with the rebellious in times past. Hundreds of millions of people just like us have been eternally lost because they lived contrary to God and wouldn't turn to Him for mercy. Now they await the great judgment of fire. Don't be one more in that great number, but follow the Lord at all times, ye people.

Hebrews 12:28-29

*"Wherefore we receiving a kingdom which cannot be moved, **let us have grace, whereby we may serve God acceptably with reverence and godly fear: For our God is a consuming fire."*** Knowing how God will judge evil and wrongdoing that's not repented of because His nature is such to do so, we serve Him then with godly fear. And here is another problem with this false grace teaching: It removes this godly fear that Paul said we should have, for it implies "all is well with my soul," regardless of what I do. It seems to imply that there is no need for the fear of God any longer, but what does the Word say? Jude said those who misinterpret grace take its meaning way too far, and stop living by faith for the will of

God, that, *"These are spots in your feasts of charity [Christian gatherings], when they feast with you, **feeding themselves without fear:** clouds they are without water, carried about of winds; trees whose fruit withereth, without fruit, twice dead [spiritually], plucked up by the roots"* (Jude 12).

He also stated that these people who believe these false doctrines lose the fear of God and respect for authority. Then some become so misled that no God-ordained authority can say anything to them for they feel they need not obey God nor anyone else. They are still covered by their idea of some unconditional love; while all the time God says, *"Obey them that have the rule over you, and submit yourselves: for they [like watchmen] watch for your souls, as they that must give account, that they may do it with joy, and not with grief: for that is unprofitable for you"* (Heb. 13:17). And make sure you're following a real pastor, anointed by God to stand in that position. No little home group without a real God-called pastor is ordained of God, unless perhaps, where people are in a foreign country where there is no access to any real churches and pastors (Acts 20:28).

Here are more New Testament scriptures about the fear of the Lord. In the mouth of two or three witnesses let every word be established. We'll give you many (Eph. 5:21; Phil. 2:12-13; 1 Pet. 2:17; Rev. 14:6-7).

In Romans 3:18 Paul pointed out the fallen condition of the Gentiles. *"There is no fear of God before their eyes."* This is the problem with humanity and this is why there is so much lawlessness. Ultra gracists bring about the same result in many of their listeners. This is what happened in our public schools. When they took the consciousness of God out, young people began to sneak around more and more and do evil. They need to know, *"The eyes of the Lord are in every place, beholding the evil and the good"* (Prov. 15:3). Remember, Paul, in his theology, wrote, *"Knowing the terror of the Lord we persuade men"* (to turn from evil).

2 Corinthians 7:1

*"Having therefore these promises, dearly beloved, let us **cleanse ourselves** from all filthiness of the flesh and spirit, perfecting holiness **in the fear of God.**"*

Paul, although he was a man who knew true grace, also understood the fear of the Lord and the boundaries of grace. Grace is for the humble, repentant, willing soul, never for the prideful or rebellious. It is a provision but it does not operate automatically without the cooperation of the individual (2 Cor. 6:2; 1 Pet. 4:10).

Acts 2:43

*"**And fear came upon every soul:** and many wonders and signs were done by the apostles."*

Acts 5:5,11-13

*"And Ananias [a believer who thought he could get away with a planned out deception in the church] hearing these words fell down, and gave up the ghost: and great fear came on all them that heard these things.... **And great fear came upon all the church**, and upon as many as heard these things. And by the hands of the apostles were many signs and wonders wrought among the people; and they were all with one accord in Solomon's porch. And of the rest durst no man join himself to them: but the people magnified them."*

Even during this dispensation of grace, judgment fell upon these church members who tried to deceive the church of that time. Because of this, no one would dare join them unless they were really sincere about their faith in the Lord. Before the coming of the Lord, as God's power is turned up, people once again will not be able to do such things and get away with it. *"But who may abide the day of his coming? And who shall stand when he appeareth? For he is like a refiner's fire, and like fuller's soap: And he shall sit as a refiner and purifier of silver: and he shall purify the sons of Levi, and purge them as gold and silver, that they may offer unto the Lord an offering in righteousness"* (Mal. 3:2-3).

Acts 9:31

*"Then had the churches rest throughout all Judaea and Galilee and Samaria, and were edified; and walking **in the fear of the Lord**, and in the comfort of the Holy Ghost were multiplied."*

Acts 19:17

*"And this was known to all the Jews and Greeks also dwelling at Ephesus; **and fear fell on them all, and the name of the Lord Jesus was magnified."***

Ephesians 5:21

*"Submitting yourselves one to another **in the fear of God**."* For God will deal with those who overstep proper boundaries.

Ephesians 6:5

*"Servants, be obedient to them that are your masters according to the flesh, **with fear and trembling**, in singleness of your heart, as unto Christ."* Because what you do, you do in His sight, and He deals with all without partiality. No one can escape His dealings.

Philippians 2:12

"Wherefore, my beloved, as ye have always obeyed, not as in my presence only, but now much more in my absence, work out your own salvation with fear and trembling." (Knowing that it's a matter of eternal life or eternal damnation.)

1 Peter 2:17

"Honor all men. Love the brotherhood. **Fear God.** *Honor the king."* *"Wherefore gird up the loins of your mind, be sober, and hope to the end for the grace that is to be brought unto you at the revelation of Jesus Christ; As obedient children, not fashioning yourselves according to the former lusts in your ignorance: But as he which hath called you is holy, so be ye holy in all manner of conversation; because it is written, Be ye holy; for I am holy. And if ye call on the Father, who without respect of persons judgeth according to every man's work, [their behavior] pass the time of your sojourning here [your time upon the earth]* **in fear"** (1 Pet. 1:13-17).

Revelation 14:7

The angel cried out, *"Saying with a loud voice,* **Fear God,** *and give glory to him; for the hour of his judgment is come: and worship him that made heaven, and earth, and the sea, and the fountains of waters."* You must also worship Him in Spirit and in truth (reality), or He will not accept it (Mark 7:6-7).

Revelation 19:5

"And a voice came out of the throne, saying, Praise our God, all ye his servants, **and ye that fear him,** *both small and great."* Don't ever let anyone talk you out of this cleansing fear of the Lord. *"No good thing will He withhold from them that walk uprightly";* but *"it's a fearful thing to fall into the hands of the living God,"* if you forsake Him and His ways (Isa. 66:1-2).

Understand Also How the Lord Hates Iniquity

Ultra gracists teach that you could be a worker of iniquity living in all manner of evil behavior without repentance and still be eternally secure and okay with God, but what does the Word say? *"The foolish shall not stand in thy sight: thou hatest all workers of iniquity"* (Ps. 5:5). (No matter who they are, Acts 10:34.) Workers of iniquity are those who live in sinful, evil behavior with no regard for the will of God. *"Draw me not away with the wicked, and with the workers of iniquity, which speak peace to their neighbors, but mischief is in their hearts"* (Ps. 28:3).

"There are the **workers of iniquity** *fallen: they are cast down, and shall not be able to rise"* (Ps. 36:12).

"A Psalm of David. Fret not thyself because of evil doers, neither be thou envious against the **workers of iniquity.** *For they shall soon be cut down like the grass, and wither as the green herb"* (Ps. 37:1-2). *"Hide me from the secret counsel of the wicked; from the insurrection of the* **workers of iniquity"** (Ps. 64:2). (That is, those who rebel against God's authority.)

*"When the wicked spring as the grass, and when all the **workers of iniquity** do flourish; it is that they shall be **destroyed for ever**"* (Ps. 92:7). Don't be deceived because it looks like the wicked flourish for awhile, and it seems like all is well for a time. The clock is ticking and their hour glass is running out. The Word of God says,

"Because sentence against an evil work is not executed speedily, therefore the heart of the sons of men is fully set in them to do evil. Though a sinner do evil an hundred times, and his days be prolonged, yet surely I know that it shall be well with them that fear God, which fear before him: But it shall not be well with the wicked, neither shall he prolong his days, which are as a shadow; because he feareth not before God."

"How long shall they utter and speak hard things? And all the workers of iniquity boast themselves?" (That everything is fine with them, Ps. 94:4.)

*"Incline not my heart to any evil thing, to practice **wicked works** with men that **work iniquity**: and let me not eat of their dainties"* (Ps. 141:4).

*"The way of the Lord is strength to the upright: but destruction shall be to the **workers of iniquity**"* (Prov. 10:29).

*"It is joy to the just to do judgment: but destruction shall be to the **workers of iniquity**"* (Prov. 21:15).

But He (Jesus) shall say at the great judgment seat, *"I tell you, I know you not whence ye are; depart from me, all ye **workers of iniquity**"* (Luke 13:27).

The Lord shall say, *"depart from me **all ye workers of iniquity**."*

What are the works of iniqity? *"And even as they did not like to retain God in their knowledge, God gave them over to a reprobate mind, to do those things which are not convenient; being filled with all unrighteousness, fornication, wickedness, covetousness, maliciousness; full of envy, murder, debate, deceit, malignity; whisperers, backbiters, haters of God, despiteful, proud, boasters, inventors of evil things, disobedient to parents, Without understanding, covenantbreakers, without natural affection, implacable, unmerciful: Who knowing the judgment of God, that they which commit such things are worthy of death, not only do the same, but have pleasure in them that do them"* (Rom. 1:28-32).

These works of iniquity are dead works and evil behavior, also called works of darkness, evil deeds, and unrighteousness, and works of the flesh in the scripture. It is sin and a work of the devil. All who live for such things rather than for God's will, will not be blessed and go to heaven, but will hear Christ say, *"depart from Me"* ye cursed; ye that have lived for sinful, selfish pleasures and not for God. For no man can serve sin and serve God also. So you see in this aspect it hasn't changed from the Old Testament to the New. God still hates sin and iniquity (Heb. 1:9), and still expects people to serve and obey Him.

*"And to you who are troubled rest with us, when the Lord Jesus shall be revealed from heaven with his mighty angels, in **flaming fire taking vengeance on them** that know not God, and **that obey not the gospel of our Lord Jesus Christ"** (2 Thess. 1:7-8).

The word "iniquity" means "lawlessness"; "moral wickedness"; "evil behavior"; "unrighteousness"; or "those who transgress the moral law." Those who willingly do these things and live this way side in with Satan and the antichrist. This is why Paul said, *"Now the **works** of the flesh are manifest, which are these; Adultery, fornication, uncleanness, lasciviousness, idolatry, witchcraft, hatred, variance, emulations, wrath, strife, seditions, heresies.... Envyings, murders, drunkenness, revellings, and such like: of the which I tell you before, as I have also told you in time past, that **they which do such things shall not inherit the kingdom of God"** (Gal. 5:19-21). It further means injustice and wrongdoing. I tell you, ultra gracists, be even more afraid of the works of the flesh than the works of the law. Paul said that those who live in such behavior shall not inherit the Kingdom of God.

*"For the mystery [secret power] **of iniquity** doth already work: only he who now letteth will let, until he be taken out of the way.... That they all might be damned who believed not the truth [which Paul said is always according to godliness], but had pleasure in unrighteousness"* (evil behavior, 2 Thess. 2:7,12).

It should be getting clear to you by now, dear Reader, that anyone who chooses to live that way, makes himself the *"enemy of God"*; and that there is no grace that saves an unrighteous person who chooses to live in the pollutions of the world and not for God.

"For the vile [impious] person will speak villainy [foolishly], and his heart will work iniquity [work ungodliness], to practice hypocrisy [saying one thing but doing another], and to utter error against the Lord [and His ways], to make empty the soul of the hungry, and he will cause the drink of the thirsty to fail" (Isa. 32:6). Causing people to think that the way of unrighteousness can somehow coincide with the way of grace and the way of the Lord, and bring any kind of fulfillment (teaching a false peace and a false security). These teachers are really *"empty wells"* and *"clouds without rain."* The Spirit is not in their teaching, but sadly, people follow them anyway,

because they give a good talk: and so many don't know their Bibles. Peter said, "***Many*** *shall follow their pernicious ways.*"

Again in Matthew 7:23, it is recorded that Christ will say to those who practice lawlessness, "*depart from me ye that work iniquity.*" Those who teach that you could go back and live in iniquity and still be okay with God, really are telling people it's okay to yield to the spirit of antichrist, to the wicked one. And they imply that you can go back now to dead works and the works of darkness and God will cover for you and even bless you in this willful rebellion. This the apostle Paul never taught in his doctrine on grace (Eph. 5:11-12,15), but all the apostles warned against such things. Those who teach such things teach a subtle form of Satanism, for "*rebellion is as the sin of witchcraft.*" Paul spoke of Satan having ministers and doctrines (2 Cor. 11:14-15; 1 Tim. 4:1).

Please, dear Reader, consider these things and do not yield yourself to the wicked one, and do not become his mouth piece and teach such things (James 3:1). Jesus said, "*Why do ye not understand my speech? even because ye cannot hear my word. Ye are of your father the devil, and the lusts of your father ye will do. He was a murderer from the beginning, and abode not in the truth, because there is no truth in him. When he speaketh a lie, he speaketh of his own: for he is a liar, and the father of it. And because I tell you the truth, ye believe me not*" (John 8:43-45). Your only real protection is *exactly* what God's Word says, and believing *ALL* of what He said (John 12:48). His truth is your shield and buckler.

Now Let's See the Apostles' Doctrine in 2 Corinthians.

2 Corinthians 5:9-11

"***Wherefore 'we labor, [strive to live right] that, whether present or absent, we may be accepted of him. For we must all appear before the judgment seat of Christ; that every one may receive the things done in His body, according to that he hath done, whether it be good or bad. Knowing therefore the terror of the Lord, we persuade men*** (to turn to the Lord and live right); ***but we are made manifest unto God; and I trust also are made manifest in your consciences.***"

Now we know all is ours in Christ as we continue to be willing to walk with Him, imperfect as we may be at times. But again, remember, it's the willingness of heart that counts. "*For where your treasure is, there will your heart be also.*" And "*no man can serve two masters*" (Rom. 6:16).

Are we willing to walk with Him or not? One may be struggling and trying to live for Him, and "*if there's first a willing mind, it's accepted according to what a person hath and not according to what he hath not"* (2 Cor. 8:12). But one who is willfully rebelling and going in the opposite direction is in another class that God will resist and eventually judge, and He has shown us clearly in His Word that He will do so (2 Pet. 2:4-6). God knows the *"counsels of the hearts"* and the *"secrets of men."* So, live accordingly in His sight.

Isaiah 1:19-20

"If ye be willing and obedient, ye shall eat the good of the land: **But if ye refuse and rebel**, *ye shall be devoured with the sword: for the mouth of the Lord hath spoken it."* For rebellion is as the sin of witchcraft. God's truth endures forever and these things were written for our learning. If you're going to willingly rebel and not live for God, it's the same as being involved in witchcraft. Then you're following Lucifer's example; the leader of all rebels. Lucifer's fall came about when he rebelled and refused to obey God any longer. He refused to allow God to rule over him; and what he tries to do through his schemes and carefully twisted false doctrines, is to get other free moral agents to do as he did. That's why you can tell the source of a doctrine, by what fruit it produces. Does it teach that you need to submit to and obey God, or does it say rebellion against God is permissible? Does it imply that God's love and grace will cover for you as you join in the devil's revolution? That's just what the serpent wants you to believe. Satan will never tell you to obey God and His commandments. He will never encourage you to believe *all of* the Word of God (just certain scriptures he can twist). He will never tell you that you need to submit to Jesus' Lordship, nor to confess your sins so that the blood of Christ may wash it away. He will always craftily teach just the opposite of these scriptural things. He will use phrases the Bible never uses such as *"unconditional"* love, or *"irresistible"* grace, in order to get people to continue to live wrong, thinking it's okay. He is a mastermind at using such phrases, which are neither from God, nor are they scriptural. For neither God's love nor grace can, nor will, save a person, or bless them without their cooperation. And God Himself set it up to be this way. *"And Simeon blessed them, and said unto Mary his mother, Behold, this child is set for the fall and rising again of many in Israel; and for a sign which shall be spoken against; (Yea, a sword shall pierce through thy own soul also,) that the thoughts of many hearts may be revealed"* (Luke 2:34-35). Your thoughts and words reveal you, and on the Day of Judgment God will make manifest the counsels of the heart (1 Cor. 4:5). *"But they hearkened not, nor inclined their ear, but walked in the counsels and in the imagination of their evil heart, and went backward, and not forward"* (Jer. 7:24). His

love and grace provided all we'd need if we'd cooperate to go on. His grace leads us to repentance, opens our eyes to believe, and gives us power to obey; but in each step, the scriptures reveal that man has a part to play. We must still *"press on."*

James 1:22

"But **be ye** *doers of the word, and not hearers only, deceiving your own selves."* Now we understand that there are some of those who have embraced an unbalanced, ultra grace message. They are not planning on departing from God, but yet they've gotten caught up in a philosophy that has caused them to not want to hear sound doctrine, and the scriptures we've been declaring from the doctrine of Christ. And we know there are sincere, God-fearing men who are our brothers, who also have been led wrong into this belief, and our prayer is that your eyes will be opened. But contrary to Christ's doctrine, some have even gone so far as to think they do not have to be *"doers of the word"* and obey God's instructions to be blessed, for they think that, that too, would be works. James said it's those who do the work of the Word by the grace in their hearts that are blessed (James 1:25). James showed that this is faith. (Works here simply means "actions and deeds.") So how could faith be legalistic works?

Some who have not rightly divided the Word think that the word "works," always means legalism when really it is used numerous times to show forth a person's faith and grace at work in their heart. **Works without faith are dead. They are works done by those who are "dead in trespasses and sins,"** but faith without works is dead faith; it's hypocritical faith; but the Word reveals that works with faith, and faith with works is alive and is accepted by God (Rev. 14:12-13). The scripture reveals, *"Was not Abraham our father justified by works, when he had offered Isaac his son upon the altar? Seest thou how faith wrought with his works, and by works was faith made perfect? And [then] the scripture was fulfilled which saith, Abraham believed God, and it was imputed unto him for righteousness: and he was called the Friend of God. Ye see then, how that by works a man is justified, and not by faith only. Likewise also was not Rahab the harlot justified by works, when she had received the messengers, and had sent them out another way? For as the body without the spirit is dead, so faith without works is dead also"* (James 2:21-26). So then, faith and works can go hand in hand. Many ultra gracists have thought that faith means you *just* need to say it or think it, but as shown, if there are not actions, too, that correspond to what is professed, then all they have is dead faith; it is not scriptural believing at all. Although it starts with a confession, it then becomes *"obedience to the faith"* (Rom. 1:5). *"But God be thanked, that ye were the servants of sin,* **but ye have obeyed from the heart** *that form of doctrine which was delivered you. Being then made free from sin, ye became the servants of righteousness"* (Rom. 6:17-18). This obedience is faith.

Anytime we reject God's full counsel, we will suffer for it to some degree as a consequence of not believing the whole truth. Satan always uses partial truths in his deceptions. To kill a wild animal, you'd never use just poison. He'd never go for it. You would use a lot of meat and a little poison, just enough to kill it. And so does Satan! A little leaven of wrong doctrine can change a person's whole attitude about life completely. Can you then ignore this multitude of scriptures we've given you? Dear Ultra Gracist, will you yet hold on to a false concept of grace even in view of the truth? God said that His people were destroyed for *"a lack of knowledge."* This is the case with the ultra gracists also sometimes called, unconditional, eternal securityists. There is no unconditional covenant given to man by God, and there never has been. Any covenant is based on conditions, and if you'd carefully read this New Covenant the way you'd read any legal document, rather than through religious eyeglasses, you'd easily see what we are saying.

A false perception of grace has already uprooted some from their steadfastness and commitment to all the Word of God, their commitment to any local church, and has even gotten some to be aggressive in spreading their wrong teaching which encourages unrighteousness. They then are critical and judgmental of those that are in the Lord's work promoting godliness and good deeds of faith, and are called of God to do so. They think they are in grace and promoting grace, but yet don't understand grace. They say it's all by faith, but don't understand faith. They are simply "caught up" in a doctrine of Satan's counterfeit grace and do not grasp it or discern it. Satan, who's the deceiver of the whole world, is a master at forming and disguising doctrines. But remember if any scripture clearly contradicts it, it is wrong! When Satan said to Christ, *"It is written,"* and quoted a scripture out of context, Jesus said to him, *"It is written again,"* or, also written ... and overcame him. Let us do the same with this false concept of grace that Satan has sown as a tare into the body of Christ (Matt. 13:24-30).

This is the effect of any false revelation in religious circles. They confidently attack in an aggressive manner, boldly stating what they understand not, but their conscience is not affected because of their wrong belief, not because of a godly revelation from the Word. And their aggression is motivated by a wrong spirit and they don't even know it. And by "*good words and fair speeches they deceive the hearts of the simple*," and lead good people away from the real truth of God (Acts 9:1-3).

Is it wrong to make this clear because we love God's people? Would God that all believers would just believe all of His Word and do what it says, for this is all we tell anyone. Just do what God says to do and obey what He wants you to obey, and repent if that's needed, and then all is safe and secure. There is conditional, eternal security. All one must do is to "*continue in the faith*" living for God, not going back to the pollutions they were once delivered out of. This is simple enough and it's obvious that the New Covenant reveals that the better you live, the more blessed you will be. (See 1 Pet. 3:10-12; Matt. 5:6-8; Eph. 6:1-3,8; 1 Thess. 4:1-2; 1 John 3:22.) And we could give you probably at least 100 more New Testament scriptures that prove this. For grace is given to change our behavior so that we can live the way God wants us to and thereby be blessed and have life.

Acts 5:29

"*Then Peter and the other apostles answered and said, **We ought to obey God** rather than men.*" Get it? Obey God's Word rather than any instruction given by a man to the contrary. This is the only way to blessings and life.

And in writing this, I have obeyed what the Holy Spirit has led me to do, for the whole main outline of this treatise was written in one sitting as the Spirit of God had me write. All we desire is that the reader believes all of God's Word concerning this and every other subject. We don't ask you to believe us but to believe God's Word. Try this: Forget all you've been taught and reread the New Testament like a contract. Agree with it, heed its warnings, and then just live accordingly. Believe it is all the faith that was once delivered to the saints, and believe it's all for us today because it is (Matt. 28:20).

1 Thessalonians 4:7-9

"***For God hath not called us unto uncleanness, but unto holiness. He therefore that despiseth, despiseth not man, but God**, who hath also given unto us his Holy Spirit. But as touching brotherly love ye need not that I write unto you: for ye yourselves are taught of God to love one another.*" Do not ever despise the teaching of holiness for it is God's doctrine. You have not been called to live in uncleanness, but holiness. The more filled with *the*

Holy Spirit you are, the more holy, more free from sin, and more godly you become. Carnal people want to excuse carnal behavior. Any preacher that says it's okay to live in sin is known by his own fruit. That is, what he's really like is known by what he's teaching others to do. For *"out of the abundance of the heart the mouth speaks."*

Keep the Unity of the Faith

Listen to Paul: Galatians 4:16 *"Am I therefore become your enemy, because I tell you the truth?"*

He told the Galatians: Verse 15

"Where is then the blessedness ye spake of? For I bear you record, that, if it had been possible [When I first preached the truth to you, to repent, turn from a life of sin and turn to God and accept His Son, Acts 26:19-20.], ye would have plucked out your own eyes, and have given them to me." This was so when he first brought the true Gospel message to them. But then they were influenced by false teachers and were no longer receptive to him because of the bad seeds and tares sown against him by the mouths of these misled teachers who wanted them to return to circumcision and Sabbath days. But the more he loved them, the less they loved him. Sadly, ignorant people will be moved by many things rather than remaining true and steadfast in the pure, plain, simple Word of God. Legalism is in a ditch on the one side of the road, trying to get people to keep outward things such as circumcision, or manmade commandments, which can never make one better morally; as Jude and Peter expounded, a grace excusing lawlessness is in the other ditch on the other side. Let's just believe all the Word and there is then no need for legalism or lasciviousness. There would then be no need for such theological, intellectual arguments by men which cause division among brethren, but all would just steadfastly stay on the pathway of righteousness following Jesus, the author and the finisher of our faith, neither being legalistic nor lascivious.

Why don't we just do and believe all of what the Word says? This will please the Father. This is faith. And if all the body of Christ would just believe all of the New Testament just as it's written, there would then be great unity and not all this division caused by the carnal and religious minds of individual men who pose as being spiritual but really are promoting their philosophical views. How can there be only *"one Lord,"* and *"one faith,"* and yet be hundreds and hundreds of denominations. It's because almost all of the sects only believe certain parts of the new Testament and their sect emphasizes that part while rejecting the rest. My brethren, these things ought not be.

Psalm 133:1

"A song of degrees of David. Behold, how good and how pleasant it is for brethren to dwell together in unity!"

Ephesians 4:3

"Endeavoring to keep the unity of the Spirit in the bond of peace." The Holy Spirit will always lead us to believe all of God's Word. This is what will cause unity (John 16:13, 17:17).

Let's go on. 2 Corinthians 6:14-18

*"Be ye not unequally yoked together with unbelievers [don't have unsuitable connections with unbelievers]: for **what fellowship hath righteousness [good] with unrighteousness** [evil]? And what communion hath light with darkness? And what concord hath Christ with Belial? [the evil one] or what part hath he that believeth with an infidel? And what agreement hath the temple of God with idols? For ye are the temple of the living God; as God hath said, I will dwell in them, and walk in them; and I will be their God, and they shall be My people. Wherefore come out from among them, and be ye separate, saith the Lord, and touch not the unclean thing* (separate yourselves from them); *and I will receive you, and will be a Father unto you, and ye shall be My sons and daughters, saith the Lord Almighty."*

There is no fellowship, communion, concord, or agreement between these opposites. Can we touch unclean things, live in the world's pollution, and still have favor in the eyes of God? Will God just impute light to darkness and then have fellowship with darkness? Satan told Eve, disobey God to become more like God. He still teaches similar things (that God gives grace so you can do evil), or let us do evil that good may come. He says, "That God's grace may be magnified." Should we all then study to be like Judas Iscariot that God will be magnified? This is what Satan would have you do.

Listen to what Peter says in Christ's doctrine:

1 Peter 3:10-12

*"**For he that will love life, and see good days**, let him refrain his tongue from evil, and his lips that they speak no guile: Let him eschew [shun all] evil, and do good; let him seek peace, and ensue [pursue] it. **For the eyes of the Lord** are over the righteous [upright men and women], and his ears are open unto their prayers: **but the face of the Lord is against them that do evil."** Those who do evil, Peter says, are not the righteous, and if people do evil, the Lord's face is against them, at least until they repent. John said, *"He that doeth righteousness is righteous...."* But he went on to say if you do

unrighteousness, you're following the devil. Neither Peter nor any of the apostles implied that blessings will come automatically because of grace. Reread that passage again. If you change the way you act, then you'll get to love life and see good days.

And if you do evil without repenting of it, then the Lord's face is against you (Col. 3:25). Why? Because you're following the Lord's adversary and the Lord said that curses would come upon you and overtake you (Deut. 28). The Lord will graciously try and lead a person to repentance and give them space to repent, because He is rich in mercy. But if people refuse and rebel and continue to follow Satan, they will suffer their own consequences, eat the fruit of their own ways, and will not see good days. God's Word guarantees it.

Revelation 3:18,21-22

To those in one lukewarm church the Lord said, *"**I counsel thee** to buy of me gold tried in the fire [pure faith, 1 Pet. 1:7], that thou mayest [really] be rich; and white raiment [a righteous life, Rev. 19:8], that thou mayest be clothed, and that the shame of thy nakedness do not appear [as with Adam after he sinned and lost the covering of glory, Rom. 3:23; 1 John 2:28]; and anoint thine eyes with eyesalve, that thou mayest see.... **To him that overcometh** [the evil one] will I grant to set with Me in My throne, even as I also overcame (the evil one and this world), and am set down with My Father in His throne. He that hath an ear, let him hear what the Spirit **saith unto the churches**"* (Heb. 12:1-4).

Proverbs 1:25-33

Listen to what the Lord says to those who won't heed Him (and remember He is the same *"yesterday, today and forever"*).

*"But ye have set at naught all my counsel, and would none of my reproof; **I also will laugh at your calamity; I will mock when your fear cometh**; when your fear cometh as desolation, and your destruction cometh as a whirlwind; when distress and anguish cometh upon you. **Then shall they call upon me, but I will not answer**; they shall seek me early, but they shall not find me: For that they hated knowledge, and did not choose the fear of the LORD; They would none of my counsel: they despised all my reproof. **Therefore shall they eat of the fruit of their own way, and be filled with their own devices. For the turning away of the simple shall slay them**, and the prosperity of fools shall destroy them. But whoso hearkeneth unto me shall dwell safely, and shall be quiet from fear of evil."* (See also Matt. 7:24-27.)

Proverbs 28:13-14

"He that covereth his sins shall not prosper: but whoso confesseth and forsaketh them shall have mercy. Happy is the man that feareth [God] alway: but he that hardeneth his heart shall fall into mischief" (Heb. 3:12).

Proverbs 29:1

"He that being often reproved hardeneth his neck, shall suddenly be destroyed, and that without remedy." This is God's wisdom expressed through Solomon. These scriptures further show that the Lord will not just automatically overlook sin in the believer; sin must be confessed (1 John 1:9). The Bible reveals the mind of God in these matters. He is the only true God. The devil will try and get you to believe the opposite though through carefully manipulated words and craftily reasoned out doctrines. He has set many snares for the unsuspecting and the high minded (1 Cor. 3:18). God's grace is given to enable us to obey, not to automatically cover for disobedience. So be not deceived about the true purpose of grace. Be especially wary of this false concept of grace promoted by the adversary through many avenues.

Concerning Finances and Material Blessings

The Lord says in His doctrine in 2 Corinthians 9:6-11:

"But this I say, He which soweth sparingly [wanting to hold back] shall reap also sparingly; and he which soweth bountifully shall reap also bountifully. *Every man according as he purposeth in his heart, so let him give; not grudgingly, or of necessity [not with reluctance or a sense of compulsion]: for God loveth a cheerful giver. And God is able to make all grace abound toward you; [and to supply you richly with all that you need] that ye, always having all sufficiency in all things, may abound to every good work: [so that you can have plenty to give for every good cause], [As it is written, He hath dispersed abroad; he hath given to the poor: his righteousness remaineth for ever. Now he that ministereth seed to the sower both minister bread for your food, and multiply your seed sown, and increase the fruits of your righteousness;] Being enriched in every thing to all bountifulness, which causeth through us thanksgiving to God."*

We cannot reap what we have not sown and we will not reap what we have not sown. Some have thought grace means that you don't have to be a doer of the Word and you'd still be blessed. Not so! You still have to act in faith on the Word to be blessed. Faith is action. (See Hebrews 11.) Faith responds in obedience to the written Word. Only living faith taps you into grace's operations and blessings (Rom. 5:2).

Galatians 6:7-10

*"Be not deceived [make no mistake about it]: God is not mocked: **for whatsoever a man soweth, that** shall he also reap. [A man's harvest depends entirely on what he has sown.] For he that soweth to his flesh shall of the flesh reap corruption [decay and ruin]; **but he that soweth to the Spirit shall of the Spirit reap life everlasting.***

*And let us not be weary in well doing: for in due season we shall reap [eternal life], if we faint not. [The ultimate harvest in both cases is sure.] **As we have therefore opportunity, let us do good** unto all men, especially unto them who are of the household of faith."* Do you not then see it is a life which is sown to the Spirit that reaps everlasting life and blessings? A life sown to the flesh reaps corruption and death. *"And many of them that sleep in the dust of the earth shall awake, some to everlasting life, and some to shame and everlasting contempt. And they that be wise [that fear the Lord and depart from evil] shall shine as the brightness of the firmaments; **and they that turn many to righteousness** as the stars for ever and ever"* (Dan. 12:2-3). *"Knowing that whatsoever good thing any man doeth, the same shall he receive of the Lord, whether he be bond or free"* (Eph. 6:8). God blesses those who do good.

What you sow, God then sees to it that you reap. He is not mocked. The apostle also then wrote to his fellow believers, *"But he that doeth wrong shall receive for the wrong which he hath done: and there is no respect of persons"* (Col. 3:25). For God is always against wrongdoing. He will never bless it, but blesses people who walk uprightly and do what's pleasing in His sight (Ps. 84:11; 1 John 3:22).

Notice that this is contrary to the false interpretation of grace which thinks a person can sow to the flesh and still reap blessings, life, or favor from God without their cooperation. But this is not so, you'll only reap corruption and death. *"For to be carnally minded is death; but to be spiritually minded is life and peace"* (Rom. 8:6). Grace simply means that God has provided a redemption that no man by human effort, could have supplied or provided. It never says that you don't have to cooperate with it, but to the contrary, it teaches that *you must willingly* cooperate. Paul said you could,

"Receive the grace of God in vain" (2 Cor. 6:1).

"Frustrate the grace of God" (Gal. 2:21).

"Fall from the grace of God" (Heb. 12:15).

"Do despite to the Spirit of Grace," and resist Him (Heb. 10:29); and that men must *"continue in the grace of God"* (Acts 13:43).

Some even go so far as to say "tithing is legalism." No, Abraham tithed by faith over 400 years before the law. It was an act of his faith honoring God. (See also Hebrews 11:4.) Giving to God is our faith and love in action. *"My little children, let us not love in word, neither in tongue; but in deed and truth"* (1 John 3:18). Even keeping God's commandments, statutes, and laws is not legalism but faith. Jesus did these things and He is the author of faith (John 15:10). Abraham, too, was a man of faith and the father of our faith. Listen now to this scripture, *"And I will make thy seed to multiply as the stars of heaven, and will give unto thy seed all these countries; and in thy seed shall all the nations of the earth be blessed; **because that Abraham obeyed my voice, and kept my charge, my commandments, my statutes, and my laws"*** (Gen. 26:4-5). The Bible says, *"by faith ... Abraham obeyed...."*

Abraham wouldn't have been the father of our faith if he just said he believed, but stayed in Ur and didn't obey God. Faith only shows itself by what it does. Abel, also, wouldn't have been accepted if he just said he believed, but didn't give his best to God. Faith lives only for God, therefore, *"the just shall live by faith"* (Rom. 1:17).

Would Enoch have been translated if he said he believed but didn't live his faith? Certainly not! Would David have been a man after God's own heart if he just said that he believed, and then lived contrary to God? God said that if we don't obey His Word we deceive ourselves (James 1:22-25) and are foolish people (Matt. 7:24-27). What man of faith would have been recorded in Hebrews eleven, the faith chapter, if he never lived his faith? God will never excuse nor promote evil, nor cover over it automatically, but by mercy and grace He will forgive all evil that truly is repented of. Then if we are doers of the Word, we can be blessed. This is the kind of faith that pleases God.

It is Satan who wants to deceive people away from God; who promotes a false security just as he did with Eve, saying go ahead, disobey God, *"you'll not surely die."* Grace covers for evil. "Do evil that good may come." "Isn't God wonderful? He even let's you join my rebellion and you can still go to heaven. HISSSSS!"

Satan will say God is too good; God is too loving; God is so gracefull. But listen to the Lord, *"Woe unto them that call evil good, and good evil; that put darkness for light, and light for darkness; that put bitter for sweet, and sweet for bitter."* Some come against righteousness, good works, obeying the Lord, and then call it legalism, almost implying that it's evil and contrary to God and His redemption when it is actually the word of the Lord and faith. Their kind of faith denies the Lord, the author of faith. Heed the Lord's warning you who do such things. Read it again.

True, God is good. God is loving and God is the God of all grace, but He is the one who sets the rules, not us. And you cannot operate in faith and sin at the same time. Adam found this out and he died, just like God's Word said he would regardless of what he thought, and so will anyone else who lives contrary to what God has said. (Neither any form of unconditional love nor grace automatically saved him.)

Real faith in God then always moves one to obedience to God, *never* disobedience. It's an obedience that springs from faith, and real Bible grace gives victory over sin, not an excuse to live in it (Rom. 6:14; 1 John 5:4).

Adam and Eve were heirs of the grace of life. They didn't deserve or earn life and yet died spiritually, contrary to God's love, will, and grace, because they used their wills to depart from Him. He tried to get them to confess it, but instead, they passed the blame off themselves and on to others. Adam even tried to use God as an excuse for his disobedience. Ultra gracists use God's grace in the same way. They hold His grace responsible for covering their actions. Over 4000 times in scripture God speaks of man's will, man's choices. Men must choose. Joshua said, ***"Choose** ye this day whom ye will serve.... as for me and my house we **WILL** serve the LORD"* (Josh. 24:15). (See aslo Heb. 12:28.) Jesus said, *"If any man serve me, let him follow me; and where I am, there shall also my servant be: if any man serve me, him will my Father honor"* (John 12:26). But remember, *"No man can serve two masters."* If you're saying that Jesus is your Lord, you must take up your cross daily and follow Him. Jesus said, *"My [real] sheep follow Me."*

CHAPTER SEVENTEEN

WHAT ABOUT GOOD WORKS?

IS IT FAITH AND GRACE, OR LEGALISM?

Jesus, the author and finisher of our faith, said to the religious lead-ers, *"Many **good works** have I showed you from my Father; for which of those works do ye stone me?"* (John 10:32). Some ultra gracists, like the Pharisees, would also stone Him for good works, if not with stones, with their mouths. Jesus also kept His Father's commandments and revealed that **this was faith** (John 8:29, 15:10; Heb. 11:6).

2 Corinthians 9:8

*"And **God is able to make all grace abound toward you; that ye,** always having all sufficiency in all things, **may abound to every good work.**"* Grace, then, causes good works (deeds and religious actions). You didn't have any that God could accept as payment for sin. You were, at that time, a corrupt tree, a child of wrath by nature, a wild olive branch, and a cor-rupt tree that could not bring forth the good fruit of faith as God desired. *"So, then, they that are in the flesh cannot please God; 'for' without faith it is impossible to please God."*

For what the law could not do, in that it was weak through the flesh, God sending his own Son in the likeness of sinful flesh, and for sin, condemned sin in the flesh; that the righteousness of the law might be fulfilled in us, who walk not after the flesh, but after the Spirit" (Rom. 8:3-4). God will not accept the dead works of those who are still spiritually children of the devil and dead in sin, as a means of salvation. But if you, as a Christian, and as God's child, willingly serve the Lord, you'll be rewarded for good works, which are now prompted by faith, at the judgment seat of Christ. His grace then empowers you to do good works. The two are not contrary to each other. He's ordained that now that you're saved from your ties with Satan that you should maintain good works and actions, and walk in them (Eph. 2:10). Now you're free to do good. Now you can do the *"work of faith,"* and *"labor of love."* Paul said in 2 Timothy 3:16-17 that all scripture is given by inspiration of God so that we have instruction as to how to live righteously; and that the man of God may *be equipped for every good work.*

Note that good works are different from godliness in this respect. Godliness is living for the Father's will and moral law, empowered and influenced by His grace. This makes us secure in God for without pursuing holiness, *"no man shall see the Lord."* Good works are also produced by grace, but are specific deeds done which earn the believer eternal rewards. Both are the product of grace in one's life and their cooperation with it (1 Cor. 15:10,58).

Matthew 5:16

Jesus said, *"Let your light so shine before men, that they may see your good works, and glorify your Father which is in heaven."* Good works are just as Jesus said, *"Good."*

Matthew 16:27

"For the Son of man shall come in the glory of his Father with his angels; and then he shall reward every man according to his works" (deeds and actions).

Again Paul said, *"Where upon, O king Agrippa, I was not disobedient unto the heavenly vision, but showed first unto them of Damascus, and at Jerusalem, and throughout all the coasts of Judaea and then to the Gentiles, that they should repent and turn to God, **and do works** [actions] meet for repentance"* (Acts 26:19-20).

Do you hear Paul's instruction? He wanted to see a change of life proving that they had repented and had Bible faith. This kind of works is the fruit of faith and of a changed life. There are numerous kinds of "works" referred to in the Bible, but only one kind of legalistic works. We must rightly divide the Word here. There are dead works, works of the law, works of the devil, the works of God, works of faith, good works, works of darkness, mighty works, evil works, works proving repentance, works of iniquity, works revealing a person's faith, works of the flesh, being fruitful in every good work, wicked works, the work of the ministry, and, Paul said, some deny God by their works (Titus 1:16). So it is necessary to qualify which works we are to do and which we are not to do. Just as we must understand what kind of suffering in scripture is according to God's will, and which is not. You cannot just take the word "works" and say that it's all legalistic. If so, God Himself would be legalistic, for the heavens are the "works" of His hands, but this is not the case. Jesus said, *"If Abraham were your father, you would do the works of Abraham."* Some works, then, are the product of grace, faith, and of a changed life, while some types of works are lifeless, outward ceremonies which really benefit no one. These are dead works.

Ephesians 2:10_

*"For we are his workmanship, created in Christ Jesus unto good works, which **God hath before ordained that we should walk in them.**"*

God certainly wouldn't have ordained that we, of the New Covenant, walk in Old Testament legalism now that Christ has fulfilled all those shadows and types. So these works are works of faith and the product of God's grace working in one's heart. *"Now the God of peace, that brought again from the dead our Lord Jesus, that great shepherd of the sheep through the blood of the everlasting covenant, **make you perfect in every good work to do his will, working in you** [by His grace, Heb. 12:28] that which is well pleasing in his sight, through Jesus Christ; to whom be glory for ever and ever. Amen"* (Heb. 13:20-21). These works are the result of what's in one's heart by the grace of God, not legalism. Legalism has to do only with Jewish and religious ceremonies that cannot really affect people spiritually or morally. Living holy and righteously is not legalism but a product of being in Christ if one really is abiding in Him. (See 1 John 3:3-10.)

Paul said, *"God is not unrighteous to forget your work of faith and labor of love which you have showed towards his name"* (Heb. 6:10). God is pleased with good works and says that everyone will be rewarded according to His own labor.

1 Timothy 2:10

Paul pointed out that it's not the outward appearance that's important, *"But (which becometh women professing godliness) [to be adorned] with good works."* Let others see the grace in your heart (Heb. 12:28). It expresses itself through what you do (1 Pet. 4:10).

1 Timothy 5:10,25_

*"**Well reported of for good works;** if she have brought up children, if she have lodged strangers, if she have washed the saints' feet, if she have relieved the afflicted, **if she have diligently followed every good work....** Likewise also*

the good works of some are manifest beforehand; and they that are otherwise cannot be hid." (See also Acts 9:36.) God is not against people doing good works but tells us to provoke one another to good works, to be careful to maintain good works, and that we should walk in good works. God is against ungodly living, evil behavior, and the works of the flesh, a thing that the ultra grace doctrine deceptively permits.

1 Timothy 6:18:

Charge the rich. " ...*That they do good, that they **be rich in good works**, ready to distribute, willing to communicate.*" So, good works come forth from us if we have faith and have grace in our hearts. Good works acceptable to God, then, are the product of His grace (1 Cor. 15:10). If we yield to grace, we'll do good works. How then, could grace and these kinds of works be in conflict?

2 Timothy 3:16-17

*"All scripture is given by inspiration of God, and is profitable for doctrine, for reproof, for correction, for instruction in righteousness: **That the man of God** may be perfect [become mature], thoroughly furnished **unto all good works**."* Notice the reason for the scriptures: (1) instruction on how to live in righteousness; (2) to be equipped for every good work. Ultra grace denies the need for both, and in some cases, even tries to imply it's wrong if you mention either showing they don't know the scriptures, or how to rightly divide the Word. Dead works before grace are different than living works AFTER grace. *"And Jesus answering said unto them, Do ye not therefore err, because ye know not the scriptures, neither the power of God?"* (Mark 12:24).

So, there are works that are inspired by faith and love. Once you're a Christian, this is how you show forth your faith and love, by how you live and what you do. Dead works and bad and sinful behavior are works motivated by unbelief and selfishness. They are contrary to faith and love.

Hebrews 9:14

"How much more shall the blood of Christ, who through the eternal Spirit offered himself without spot to God, purge your conscience from dead works [the deadness of your former sinful life of ignorance] to serve [render obedience to] the living God?" Dead works then are works produced by people who are still "in the flesh" and spiritually children of the devil. It is the dead works of the flesh that we are purged from (Gal. 5:19-21). *"And they that are Christ's have crucified the flesh with the affections and lusts"* (Gal. 5:24).

They are also called the *"unfruitful works of **darkness**"* (Eph. 5:11). Again, God will not accept what's not done because of faith in God (Heb. 11:6; Rom. 8:8-9). But as for us Christians, we are to abound to every good work and God will give us grace to do it if we desire it (2 Cor. 9:8). The Bible says, Jesus wants a people *"zealous of good works,"* so ultra gracists, if you don't want dead works, don't go back to the works and sins of the flesh, for those are the kinds of works that God hates.

Hebrews 10:24

*"And let us consider one another to **provoke unto love and to good works.**"* It doesn't say provoke one another to not walk in love and refuse to do good works. Remember, real love *"fulfills the law"* (Rom. 13). It is not passive concerning evil. God is love and love hates iniquity. In view of the fact that in almost every New Testament book, the Bible exhorts us to do good works, to walk in them, that it's our fruit and our faith energized by grace, and so on, I'm surprised that so many are afraid of saying anything about "good works" as though it's contrary to the New Testament or contrary to grace. Good works prompted by faith and love are not legalism but a manifestation of grace, faith, and love, as is holiness. The "works" of the law such as Sabbaths, holy days, to eat or not eat meats, and other carnal ordinances are legalism, but not good works. And know this also, that Paul, in writing to the Galatian Christians, wasn't saying that the moral law was legalism, but that some Jewish Christians tried to mix Jewish ceremonies such as circumcision and Sabbath days in with the Gospel. He never said, nor implied, that keeping God's moral law and commandments were legalistic. Listen again to this apostle of faith and grace in his own teaching, *"Circumcision is nothing, and uncircumcision is nothing, but [what counts is] **the keeping of the commandments of God**"* (1 Cor. 7:19).

Revelation 14:12-13 says:

*"Here is the patience [endurance] of the saints: here are they **that keep the commandments of God**, and the faith of Jesus [the two are directly connected]. And I heard a voice from heaven saying unto me, Write, Blessed are the dead which die in the Lord from henceforth: Yea, saith the Spirit, that they may rest from their labors; **and their works do follow them.**"* Your works are your investment in eternity. If you have faith, you'll have these kinds of works. Jesus said, *"**Labor not** for the meat which perisheth, but for the meat which endureth unto everlasting life, which the Son of man shall give unto you: for him hath God the Father sealed"* (John 6:27). It is really more scriptural, then, to work for God and do good works, than to work a job to obtain

material comforts (Matt. 6:19-21). This is the way to eternal rewards (Luke 19:17). And your picking up your cross and following Jesus daily, obeying God's moral law, is the way to eternity with God (Matt. 16:24-25; Heb. 5:9). (See also Matt. 28:20.)

Works (actions) without faith cannot save, as Paul said, no matter how many works a person has done. And as James said in our same Bible, faith without works (actions) also cannot save (James 2:14). Faith must be lived; *"the just shall live by faith."* Living faith produces a changed life and behavior and good works, which is involvement in *"the work of the ministry."* Works here, as James used it, does not mean ceremonial works adding up a certain amount of good deeds or dead works by the number of ceremonies one does, but the actions of a life moved by faith. Faith gives itself to God and lives for His will. This is what it means when it says, *"The just shall live by faith."* It has to do with morally fulfilling the righteousness of the law by a walk of faith in the Spirit (Rom. 3:21, 8:4). If a person understands faith and grace, then they, as Paul did, will both live for the will of God and abound always in the work of the Lord (1 Cor. 15:58).

1 Corinthians 3:6-8

Paul said, *"I have planted, Apollos watered; but God gave the increase. So then, neither is he that planteth any thing, neither he that watereth; but God that giveth the increase. Now he that planteth and he that watereth are one: and every man shall receive his own reward **according to his own labor.**"* This means their work of faith and labor of love. Works with faith and faith with works are a work of faith, not legalism. The Jews trusted that circumcision would save them, just like the ultra gracists think that a mere profession, by itself, will save them; but it won't (Matt. 7:21; Luke 6:46; Rom. 2:28-29). The works of the law were not of faith, they were ceremonies. Their system of "do's" and "don'ts" were done religiously, but not necessarily because of faith and love towards God; nor could they provide a new birth or deliverance from Satan and his kingdom, and someone's profession is not necessarily faith. If they don't live it, it is mental assent and not faith. It's a counterfeit and God doesn't accept counterfeits (Mark 7:6-7).

First Corinthians 3:13-15 says, *"**Every man's work** shall be made manifest: for the day [we stand before the Lord] shall declare it, because it shall be revealed by fire; and the fire shall try **every man's work** of what sort it is. [What was the motive behind it?] If any man's work abide which he hath built thereupon, **he shall receive a reward.** If any man's work shall be burned, he shall suffer loss: but he himself shall be saved; yet so as by fire."*

So, good works are to bless God's work, to bless others, and to earn rewards in heaven, and are a product of faith in one's heart. God certainly does give reward according to what we do here on earth and the labor put forth. We are to respond to the leading, prompting, influences, and inspirations of the Spirit. And good works, it is obvious, please God, so they must be in agreement with faith and grace. *"And let us not be weary in well doing: for in due season we shall reap, if we faint not"* (Gal. 6:9). Listen to the apostle Paul. *"But by the grace of God I am what I am: and His grace which was bestowed upon me was not in vain; but **I labored more abundantly than they all: yet not I, but the grace of God which was with me**"* (1 Cor. 15:10). He labored and worked because of grace.

Grace, faith, and love, then, *move a person* to serve and obey God and work for Him abundantly (Heb. 12:28). This is God's plan of grace. Even in the Old Testament, Abraham, by faith, tithed; Abel, by faith, gave God a more excellent sacrifice; Moses, by faith, kept God's ordinances; and Noah, by faith, worked preparing the ark. Faith is the same in both Covenants. We too, must live by faith, and if we do, there will be a change of life and works showing forth both our repentance from a life of sin and dead works and our living faith in His Word. As we've shown, if there's no faith, works are dead. If there are no works, faith is dead. We could never be saved nor justified by dead works while we were yet in our sins, but rather, only by faith and grace. Now that we're saved from our old corrupt lives and way of living by grace, and have become new creatures, God expects us to walk in the faith and grace that He's given us, and produce the good fruit of a changed life, or He Himself said that we'd eventually be cut off (John 15:1-2). So, your good, holy fruit is your changed life. Your works are for rewards. And every tree is known by its own fruit of what sort it is (Matt. 7:16-17). People of faith and grace, then, serve God and do good (Heb. 12:28). People of unbelief serve self and live according to the course of this sinful world.

Back to Rewards

Let's look at some New Covenant scriptures concerning rewards. *"Blessed are ye, when men shall revile you, and persecute you, and shall say all manner of evil against you falsely, for my sake. Rejoice, and be exceeding glad: **for great is your reward** in heaven: for so persecuted they the [holy] prophets which were before you (2 Tim. 3:12). For if ye love them which love you, **what reward have ye?** Do not even the publicans the same?"* (Matt. 5:11-12,46).

Matthew 6:3-4,6,16-18

"But when thou doest alms, let not thy left hand know what thy right hand doeth: that thine alms may be in secret: **and thy Father which seeth in secret shall reward thee openly**.... *But thou, when thou prayest, enter into thy closet, and when thou hast shut thy door, pray to thy Father which is in secret; and thy Father* **which seeth in secret** *shall reward thee openly.... Moreover when ye fast, be not, as the hypocrites, of a sad countenance: for they disfigure their faces that they may appear unto men to fast. Verily I say unto you, They have their reward. But thou, when thou fastest, anoint thine head, and wash thy face; that thou appear not unto men to fast, but unto thy Father which is in secret: and thy Father, which seeth in secret,* **shall reward thee openly.**"

Again, the Father sees all things and understands all the motives and intents of the heart and rewards accordingly (1 Sam. 16:7). Can Christians' motives vary? Most certainly, yes, and God deals with each accordingly (Rom. 2:11).

Matthew 16:27

"For the Son of man shall come in the glory of his Father with his angels; **and then he shall reward every man according to his works**" (deeds and actions) and the counsels of each man's heart (1 Cor. 4:5).

Jesus said to the churches in Revelation: *"And, behold, I come quickly; and* **my reward** *is with me, to give every man according as his work shall be"* (Rev. 22:12).

What we do for His Kingdom is what we do from our own heart willingly. God doesn't predestine what we do. We decide what we do. Hundreds of times in scripture he tells us to choose. He tells us to *"have faith in God"* (Mark 11:22). He tells us to be *"doers of the word and not hearers only"* (James 1:22).

Hebrews 11:6

"But without faith it is impossible to please him: for he that cometh to God must believe that he is, and that he is a **rewarder of them that diligently seek him.**" He clearly states the qualifications for rewards. Seeking Him also has to do with seeking to please Him and living the way He wants us to live. The Bible says, *"As long as they sought the Lord, God caused them to prosper." "Furthermore then we beseech you, brethren, and exhort you by the Lord Jesus, that as ye have received of us* **how ye ought to walk [conduct your lifestyle] and to please God, so ye would abound more and more**" (1 Thess. 4:1). It is walking according to the truth and pleasing God that causes us

to abound more and more in all things (3 John 4). There is no grace that will automatically cause you to abound more and more (James 1:22).

Psalm 19:7-11

"The law of the LORD is perfect, converting the soul: the testimony of the LORD is sure, making wise the simple. The statutes of the LORD are right, rejoicing the heart: the commandment of the LORD is pure, enlightening the eyes. The fear of the LORD is clean, enduring forever: the judgments of the LORD are true and righteous altogether. More to be desired are they than gold, yea, than much fine gold: sweeter also than honey and the honeycomb. Moreover by them is thy servant warned: and **in keeping of them there is great reward."** His moral law still has all these same effects and we should desire to walk in it more than we desire silver or gold. There is great reward in the keeping of God's commandments. There always has been and there always will be.

Proverbs 25:21-22

The Lord through Solomon says, *"If thine enemy be hungry, give him bread to eat; and if he be thirsty, give him water to drink: For thou shalt heap coals of fire upon his head,* **and the LORD shall reward thee."**

Mark 9:41

"For whosoever shall give you a cup of water to drink in my name, because ye belong to Christ, Verily I say unto you, He shall not lose his reward." Every action of the free moral agent is taken into account and rewarded justly, as well as every disobedience. *"Therefore we ought to give the more earnest heed to the things which we have heard, lest at any time we should let them slip. For if the word spoken by angels was steadfast, and every transgression and disobedience received a just recompense of reward: How shall we escape, if we neglect so great salvation; which at the first began to be spoken by the Lord, and was confirmed unto us by them that heard him"* (Heb. 2:1-3).

Luke 6:35

"But love ye your enemies, and do good, and lend, hoping for nothing again; **and your reward shall be great***, and ye shall be the children of the Highest: for he is kind unto the unthankful and to the evil."* Paul wrote in Ephesians 6:8, *"Knowing that whatsoever good thing any man doeth, the same shall he receive of the Lord, whether he be bond or free."*

These things then are not legalistic works but love and faith in action. Those who say, imply, or teach, that such things are legalistic or wrong in the least, haven't rightly divided the Word of Truth, but are hung up on a wrong perception of these things. It is living a life of faith that pleases God, not just saying something. It's not just a mental decision but a new life. *"My little children, let us not love in word, neither in tongue; but in deed and in truth…. And whatsoever we ask, we receive of him, **because we keep his commandments, and do those things** that are pleasing in his sight"* (1 John 3:18,22).

The more we put on the new man and put off the old man, the better off we will be. Faith moves us to walk in such a way that we please God. *"And every man that hath this hope in him purifieth himself, even as he is pure"* (1 John 3:3). This is the whole plan of faith. Faith makes us aware of God all the time and so we live accordingly. Jewish ceremonies just caused them to focus on doing something, which just kept them busy until the full revelation of faith should clearly come. But faith now taps us into grace's power which frees us from a life of sin (Rom. 6:14), and moves us to want to serve God and work for Him. It is unbelief in the Word that brings about doctrines such as unconditional, eternal security, or that tells people they can receive the blessings without the heart following after God. God never said such things; men did. The Bible says, *"Let no man deceive you."*

Matthew 6:19-21

"Lay not up for yourselves treasures upon earth, where moth and rust doth corrupt, and where thieves break through and steal: But lay up for yourselves treasures in heaven, where neither moth nor rust doth corrupt, and where thieves do not break through nor steal: For where your treasure is, there will your heart be also." Abounding in the work of the Lord is how you store up treasure in heaven (1 Cor. 15:58; Rev. 14:13). This we are greatly encouraged to do, but God won't make you; it's your decision. This is the whole basis of His reward system (Heb. 2:1-3). The Bible states, *"As we have therefore opportunity let us do good."* To act on this is faith. To not act on it is foolish (Matt. 7:24-27).

Philippians 4:15-17

"Now ye Philippians know also, that in the beginning of the gospel, when I departed from Macedonia, no church communicated with me as concerning giving and receiving, but ye only. For even in Thessalonica ye sent once and again unto my necessity. Not because I desire a gift: but I desire fruit that may abound to your account" (in heaven).

Paul, in his teaching said, because they gave to his need, now God would supply all of their needs (Phil. 4:19). Giving is the fruit of a righteous person. It is a wok of faith (Heb. 11:4). Unbelief and false doctrines will lead a person to do what the devil wants, and to not give to God and His work in the earth. Deuteronomy 8:18 says, *"But thou shalt remember the Lord thy God: for it is he that giveth thee power to get wealth, that He may establish his covenant which he sware unto thy fathers, as it is this day."*

Note: If we are willing to work for the Lord and give for the Lord's cause in the earth, what we do goes into our heavenly account. All will not receive the same eternal reward in heaven, but it will be according to their works on the earth; their giving, their prayers, their obedience, and so on, will all affect this. God then responds to all people according to what they do, and then also, according to their repentance and faith, both in this life and the life to come (1 Pet. 1:17; John 5:28-29). Howbeit, no one could be saved from sin's condemnation and power if it wasn't for the Lord and His redemption. It took His power to regenerate us, His blood to cleanse us, and only He can impart eternal life and wash people's sins away. He does this when people repent of their sinful lives and believe the Gospel. So no one is saved by their own works, for dead works don't have the supernatural power to regenerate anyone, but we are saved unto good works (Eph. 2:10). Once we are saved by grace out of the pollutions of the world, the scripture admonishes us to abound in good works and walk in love, fulfilling the righteousness of the law (Rom. 13:9-11).

1 Corinthians 15:58

*"Therefore, my beloved brethren, be ye steadfast, unmovable, always abounding **in the work of the Lord**, for as much as ye know that your labor is not in vain in the Lord."*

Sometimes "works" means "evidence of a changed life." Sometimes the word "works" means "a person's labor." Works done by faith are not dead works. Noah worked and built an ark by faith and became the heir of righteousness by faith. His faith was shown to be real by what he did, and by his work of faith he condemned the unbelieving world that continued to live in their sins. Those who live a life free of sin by grace, will be a testimony against those who believe and make up doctrines that say you can sin and still be okay with God, even without repentance. As Peter said, *"For the time is come that judgment must begin at the house of God: and if it first begin at us, what shall the end be of them that obey not the gospel of God? And if the righteous scarcely be saved, where shall the ungodly and the sinner appear?"* (1 Pet. 4:17-18). A person with much faith will work much (Acts 11:24). Paul did, and he encouraged everyone else to do so.

Keep Your Garment Clean

Those, then, who are moved to live right and prepare themselves by faith will expose the shallowness of the understanding of those who say that we can live in sin and that we don't need to prepare ourselves. *"By faith Noah, being warned of God of things not seen as yet, moved with fear, prepared an ark to the saving of his house; by the which he condemned the world, and became heir of the righteousness which is by faith"* (Heb. 11:7).

*"And every man that hath this hope in him **purifieth himself**, even as he is pure"* (1 John 3:3). *"Let us be glad and rejoice, and give honor to him: for the marriage of the Lamb is come, and his wife hath **made herself ready. And to her** [who made herself ready] was granted that she should be arrayed in fine linen, clean and white for the fine linen **is the righteousness of the saints"*** (Rev. 19:7-8). *"Wherefore, beloved, seeing that ye look for such things, **be diligent that ye may be found of him in peace, without spot, and blameless.**... Ye therefore, beloved, seeing ye know these things before, beware lest ye also, being led away with the error [wrong beliefs] of the wicked, fall from your own steadfastness"* (2 Pet. 3:14,17). The wicked, Peter said, are those who twist the scriptures and teach that you could go back and live ungodly and never be lost again, and they thereby cast aside their wedding garments. Listen to these scriptures. *"Thou hast a few names even in Sardis which have not defiled their garments; and they shall walk with me in white: **for they are worthy.**... He that hath an ear, let him hear what the Spirit saith unto the churches"* (Rev. 3:4,6). *"Behold, I come as a thief. Blessed is he that watcheth, **and keepeth his garments**, lest he walk naked [because of sin], and they see his shame"* (Rev. 16:15). *"And when the king came in to see the guests, he saw there a man which had not on a wedding garment: and he saith unto him, Friend, how camest thou in hither not having a wedding garment? And he was speechless. Then said the king to the servants, Bind him hand and foot, and take him away, and cast him into outer darkness; there shall be weeping and gnashing of teeth. For many are called, but few are chosen* (Matt. 22:11-14). Remember, the wedding garment is the righteousness of the saints. John wrote, *"If ye know that he is righteous, ye know that every one that doeth righteousness is born of him"* (1 John 2:29). *"Little children, let no man deceive you: he that doeth righteousness is righteous, even as He is righteous. He that committeth sin is of the devil; for the devil sinneth from the beginning. For this purpose the Son of God was manifested, that he might destroy the works of the devil.... In this the children of God are manifest, and the children of the devil: whosoever doeth not righteousness is not of God, neither he that loveth not his brother"* (1 John 3:7-8,10).

In Colossians 1:10 Paul reveals in his theology, that grace was given, *"That ye might walk worthy [live lives worthy] of the Lord unto all pleasing [fully pleasing Him by your conduct], being fruitful in every good work [being a branch with much good fruit, glorifying your Father], and increasing in the knowledge of God"* (Rom. 7:4).

As we've stated before, we didn't work for our salvation and obtain it by a certain amount of good deeds done, for all of our works as sinners were defiled and contaminated. Salvation from the condemnation and power of sin is a gift, when we turn from Satan and turn to God. God owed it to no man. We simply turn and willingly receive it, and then walk in the Spirit, keep the righteousness of the (moral) law by His grace, and thereby have life. Freely we receive and freely we cooperate with God and His Spirit. We then willingly continue in it, but if we really continue in it, we continue to change from glory to glory into the image of Christ (2 Cor. 3:18). We continue to bring forth more and more good fruit in our lives as time goes on, if we are indeed grafted into the true vine. Now as Christians, though, we do good works out of love for God and for our fellow man, and for rewards that the Lord has promised to those who work for Him. This takes faith. The works of His children are well pleasing to Him just as Abraham's were (John 8:39). See that our works are also our fruit, and the Father is glorified that you bear much fruit (Matt. 5:16). So our obedience to His moral law makes us secure in Him (Heb. 5:9), and our good works prompted by faith, bring us rewards.

Rewards Because of Yielding to Grace

1 Corinthians 15:10

"But by the grace of God I am what I am: and his grace which was bestowed upon me was not in vain; but I labored more abundantly than they all: yet not I, but the grace of God which was with me."

Grace empowers and equips you to work for God and to live right, as does faith and love. True grace gives power to do good works. A false grace gives excuses to shun good works. Guess which one of these two is from the devil?

1 Corinthians 9:17

"For if I do this thing willingly, I have a reward: but if against my will, a dispensation of the gospel is committed unto me." If he wasn't willing, the same responsibility was upon him anyway. If he did it willingly, he'd receive a reward.

2 John 8

"**Look to yourselves,** *that we lose not those things which we have wrought, but that we receive a full reward.*" If it were all just by grace without our cooperation, we'd all receive a full reward no matter what.

Revelation 11:18

"*And the nations were angry, and thy wrath is come, and the time of the dead, that they should be judged,* **and that thou shouldest give reward unto thy servants the prophets, and to the saints, and them that fear thy name, small and great; and shouldest destroy them which destroy the earth.*"*

Revelation 22:12-13

"*And, behold, I come quickly; and* **my reward is with me, to give every man according as his work shall be.** *I am Alpha and Omega, the beginning and the end, the first and the last.*"

Those who aren't born again or those who are no longer willingly following the Lord will also be rewarded according to their evil works (2 Thess. 1:8).

Matthew 23:14

"*Woe unto you, scribes and Pharisees,* **hypocrites!** *for ye devour widows' houses, and for a pretence make long prayer: therefore* **ye shall receive the greater damnation.**" Their hypocritical actions will bring them even greater judgment. They spoke it but didn't obey God's Word. It's the same today for all hypocrites who only honor the Lord with their lips while their heart is far from Him. This is still so for anyone who just plays a religious game in the sight of men. Hypocrites who just say they believe and know God's will but don't live it, will receive a greater damnation than those who don't know.

Matthew 23:1-3

"*Then spake Jesus to the multitude, and to his disciples, Saying, The scribes and the Pharisees sit in Moses' seat: All therefore whatsoever they bid you observe, that observe and do; but do not ye after* **their works: for they say, and do not.**" "Works" here means "corresponding actions," as it does in many places in the New Testament.

2 Corinthians 11:14-15

"*And no marvel; for Satan himself is transformed into an angel of light. Therefore it is no great thing if his ministers also be transformed as the ministers of righteousness;* **whose end shall be according to their works.**" (But their end will be according to what they have done and how they have lived, whether they lived according to God's moral law or not.) There must be some of these men around then, teaching what Satan wants them to teach. Notice what their end will be according to. Actually, there are many (1 John 4:1).

Revelation 20:12-15

*"And I saw the dead, small and great, stand before God; and the books were opened: and another book was opened, which is the book of life: and the dead were judged out of those things which were written in the books, **according to their works**. And the sea gave up the dead which were in it; and death and hell delivered up the dead which were in them: **and they were judged every man according to their works**. And death and hell were cast into the lake of fire. This is the second death. And whosoever was not found written in the book of life was cast into the lake of fire."* All are judged by their works. Read what the Lord said to the churches in Revelation. Their works were the things produced by their lives. And He dealt with all accordingly. John, the Baptist, declared in Matthew 3:10, *"And now also the ax is laid unto the root of the trees: therefore every tree which bringeth not forth good fruit is hewn down, and cast into the fire."* Jesus also said, *"Every tree that bringeth not forth good fruit is hewn down, and cast into the fire. Wherefore by their fruits ye shall know them"* (Matt. 7:19-20). The apostle Paul declared in his teaching, *"But I showed first unto them of Damascus, and at Jerusalem, and throughout all the coasts of Judaea and then to the Gentiles, that they should [1] repent, and [2] turn to God, and [3] **do works meet** for [revealing the reality of their] repentance [and faith]"* (Acts 26:20). God wants to see your faith, not just an empty profession. Paul, remember, in Romans 2 said that God will reward with eternal life, those who patiently continue in well doing. This is what faith moves us to do and what living by faith is all about.

The Gospel message clearly then, emphasizes works, and that the good works that God accepts are a product of true grace, and the faith of the individual.

CHAPTER EIGHTEEN

THE FREE WILL OF MAN

*"**If ye be willing** and obedient, ye shall eat the good of the land: But if ye refuse and rebel, ye shall be devoured with the sword: for the mouth of the Lord hath spoken it"* (Isa. 1:19-20).

*"And the Spirit and the bride say, Come. And let him that heareth say, Come. And let him that is athirst come. **And whosoever will**, let him take the water of life freely"* (Rev. 22:17).

Salvation is something either willingly received, or willing rejected. And because the human will stays free even after the the initial salvation, Paul's warning to the Christians is to not let sin harden you to the point where you willingly reject it and forfeit the grace of God, and choose the world over God once again. Be not like Demas, Esau, Judas, or Lot's wife. You continue in the faith by continued obedience to the faith (Rom. 1:5). God in His gift to us has supplied all that we need to continue (1 Pet. 1:5; 2 Pet. 1:2-3).

But it's your choice. It always is. *"Life or death," "blessing or cursing."* Therefore, God says *"choose life"* (Deut. 30:15-20). Paul said, *"but they have not all **obeyed** the gospel."* Yet God commands *ALL men everywhere* to repent (Acts 17:20-21), because, Paul said, He hath appointed a time in which He will judge the world in righteousness. Now, *"The Lord is not slack concerning his promise, as some men count slackness; but is longsuffering to us-ward, **not willing** that any should perish, but that all should come to repentance"* (2 Pet. 3:9). But not all will to repent and obey the Gospel, so all do not receive salvation (John 1:12). Men, then, can choose to not allow God's will in their lives (Matt. 6:9). *"Yea, they turned back and tempted God, and limited the Holy One of Israel"* (Ps. 78:41). Grace, too, is willingly received or willingly rejected. Yes, it is God's unmerited provision and power, and yes, it's a gift. No, you can't earn it, don't deserve it, or can't merit it, but you can receive or reject God's provision at any time according to your choice by continuation or by turning from God and turning back to Satan and the world (1 Tim. 5:15). This is the deciding factor and this is what Satan and sin want from a person, that they use their will to either reject it in the first place, or reject it later (Luke 8:13). Nothing in all of creation can cast you out of Christ regardless of your struggles with sin and the flesh, but you can choose to walk out and forsake Him (John 6:66). As the will goes, so goes the man.

Example: Some refuse the Gospel when they hear it (Mark 16:15; Heb. 2:9; 1 Tim. 2:4).

Acts 13:46

"Paul and Barnabas waxed bold, and said, It was necessary that the word of God should first have been spoken to you: **but seeing ye put it from you, and judge yourselves unworthy of everlasting life**, *lo, we turn to the Gentiles."* Some reject it afterwards with their will. *"Love not the world, neither the things that are in the world. If any man love the world, the love of the Father is not in him"* (1 John 2:15). Paul said, *"For Demas hath forsaken me, having loved this present world, and is departed unto Thessalonica; Crescens to Galatia, Titus unto Dalmatia"* (2 Tim. 4:10).

Demas, as we before pointed out, was before a fellow laborer in the Gospel with Paul (Philem. 24), but yet forsook the Gospel for this temporal world. Paul wrote, *"For some are already turned aside after Satan"* (1 Tim. 5:15). So, give no place to the devil.

Grace is always willing to provide for all who are willing regardless of their condition. But the will, my friend, has everything to do with it. Let no one tell you otherwise. As we've stated, God refers to man's will over 4000 times in scripture. A person is walking with the Lord or not. They cannot head in two directions at the same time. If they are walking with God they are obeying His moral commandments. The apostle wrote, *"And hereby we do know that we know him, if we keep his commandments. He that saith, I know him, [present tense] and keepeth not his commandments,* **is a liar**, *and the truth is not in Him"* (1 John 2:3-4). If we are following the Lord we are keeping His commandments. If a person is walking with Satan, they are following the course of this world. *"Wherein in time past ye walked according to the course of this world, according to the prince of the power of the air, the spirit that now worketh in the children of disobedience"*

(Eph. 2:2). To depart from His commandments, then, as revealed in the New Covenant, is to depart from God and not keep the faith.

Genesis 2:7

*"And the Lord God formed man of the dust of the ground, and breathed into his nostrils the breath of life; and man became **a living soul**."* (A being with freedom of choice.)

Why do you think God mentions us "choosing" over 4000 times in scripture? God clearly holds men responsible for their decisions and if anyone contradicts this statement, it shows how biblically illiterate they are.

God has revealed that He wants His will to be done on earth *even as* it is in heaven, but His will is never automatically carried out in the life of any individual without that person's willing cooperation. Just look at all that's happening in the earth. Do you want salvation? Then do what He says. Do you want to continue to abide in Christ? Then do what He says. Do you want to end up in heaven? Then do what He says. His conditions are simple and He's provided all you would need to keep them (Ezek. 36:27; Heb. 13:20-21) if you are willing, and therefore as He has stated over and over again, all will be judged according to their works. It has to be this way, friend, because He said it and His Word cannot change. All you need to do is to keep living for God and let Him perfect that which concerns you. Walking by faith is responding to His Word (Heb. 11). This is the work and walk of faith.

So yes, certainly we know salvation is a gift. It is God's deliverance from sin and its power. And yes, we also know according to the scriptures, the effect sin has on the will and soul to work on it to try and get it to either willingly reject God's grace in the first place, or to release what God has given after it was once received (Heb. 12:15). Paul said, you must *"hold fast to that which is good."* Jesus said, *"They on the rock are they, which, when they hear, receive the word with joy; and these have no root, which for awhile believe, and in time of temptation fall away"* (they recant, Luke 8:13). Just look at all the changed lives of Christians. This change for the better is the real work of grace. So if one is continuing in God's sustaining grace, then they are continuing to live right and obey His commandments going from glory to glory into more and more freedom from the pollutions of the world. By this, John said, you can tell if a person is continuing in Christ or not. Are they continuing in the light they have received? This is the question. So the change doesn't just take place for a month or two after receiving Christ and then it's back into the world as usual. No, it goes on from glory to glory if we are willing, pressing past the hard times, overcoming sin, and resisting the devil. *"The law and the prophets were until John: since that time the kingdom of God is preached, and every man presseth into it"* (Luke 16:16). *"Blessed is the man that endureth temptation: for when he is tried, he shall receive the crown of life, which the Lord hath promised to them that love him"* (James 1:12).

"Confirming the souls of the disciples, and exhorting them to continue in the faith, and that we must through much tribulation enter into the kingdom of God" (Acts 14:22).

"That the trial of your faith, being much more precious than of gold that perisheth, though it be tried with fire, might be found unto praise and honor and glory at the appearing of Jesus Christ.... Whom having not seen, ye love; in whom, though now ye see him not, yet believing, ye rejoice with joy unspeakable and full of glory: Receiving the end of your faith, even the salvation of your souls" (1 Pet. 1:7, 9; 1 Thess 3:1-8).

1 Peter 2:11

*"Dearly beloved, I beseech you as strangers and pilgrims, abstain from fleshly lusts, **which war** (battle and wage military operations) against the soul."* Satan's and sin's strategy and desire is to move the will to eventually, over time, make a reverse decision and to go back and follow the course of this world and the prince of the powers of the air, and to no longer *"live by faith"* for the will of God. They are at war with the soul, which contains the will.

So, in view of man's free will, the Bible "only" teaches conditional, eternal security. It's a life of living for God, empowered by His Spirit to do so. We couldn't do it at all without His grace, but He won't give grace to the rebellious. Humble yourself therefore under the mighty hand of God, for He resists the proud but gives grace to the humble.

In Hebrews 3:7-14 Paul wrote to Jewish Christians:

*"**Wherefore** (as the Holy Ghost saith, Today if ye will hear his voice, **harden not your hearts**, as in the provocation, in the day of temptation in the wilderness: When your fathers tempted me, proved me, and saw my works forty years. Wherefore I was grieved with that generation, and said, **They do alway err in their heart; and they have not known my ways.** So I sware in my wrath, They shall not enter into my rest.) Take heed, [beware then] brethren, [fellow Christian] **lest there be in any of you an evil heart of unbelief**, [an unfaithful heart] **in departing from** [falling away from and deserting] the living God. [Just like them.] **But exhort one another daily**, [warn each other daily and help one*

*another to stand firm in the faith] **while it is called today; lest any of you be hardened** [so that none of you be hardened into rebellion like Israel was] **through the deceitfulness** [and wiles] of sin. For we are made partakers of Christ, [and continue to share in all He has for us] if [on this condition that] we hold the beginning of our confidence steadfast unto the end"* (and continue to live for the living God). Paul taught that you had to continue with Christ in order to continue to partake of Him who is called eternal life (1 John 1:1-2).

Hebrews 4:6, 11-13

*"Seeing therefore it remaineth that some must enter therein, and they to whom it was first preached entered not in because of unbelief.... **Let us labor therefore to enter into the rest, lest any man** (among you Christians) **fall after the same example of unbelief** [and disobedience] [As Israel did who couldn't enter the Promised Land]. For the Word of God is quick and powerful, and sharper than any twoedged sword, piercing even to the dividing asunder of soul and spirit, and of the joints and marrow, and is a discerner of the thoughts and intents of the heart. Neither is there any creature that is not manifest in His sight: but all things are naked and opened unto the eyes of him with whom we have to do."* (No creature can escape the sight of God.)

The false concept of grace also has this deceptive effect on the soul, implying that sin and faith can walk hand in hand; that good and evil can mix; that light can fellowship with darkness; that God doesn't really mind if we walk with the evil one; that you can sit at the table of the Lord and the table of demons also; that you can have the label of righteousness while willingly living unrighteously. It is this that the apostle Peter called a *"damnable heresy,"* because of the great danger of such teachings and the souls that will be damned if they follow it and go back into the world and its ways. Paul warned Christians not to fall into the same pattern of unbelief as the Israelites who, by faith, were delivered from Egypt, but went back again into rebellion and unbelief. They therefore couldn't enter the Promised Land but their carcasses fell in the wilderness of sin. Peter, too, said for us also to not be led away from the way of righteousness by *"the error of the wicked"* who taught once saved, always saved, regardless of how one lives. (See 2 Pet. 2:1-22.) Many of these also deny the need of the Baptism with the Holy Ghost (Acts 1:4-5; Jude 17-21).

1 Timothy 4:1

*"Now the Spirit speaketh expressly, **that in the latter times some shall depart** from [Greek: "to fall away from and rebel against"] **the faith,** giving*

heed to seducing spirits, and doctrines of devils" (doctrines made up by devils). A false concept of grace can get the will to release its commitment to obey God. And if Satan can somehow get a person to go back into unbelief and to believe that they don't *need* to repent after they've sinned, believe that they don't *need* to go to church or be under a pastor as the Lord said (Heb. 13:17), or to obey the Lord, he has them in his clutches. Beware of the doctrine of devils that says you can live contrary to God and His Word or moral law and still be in God's favor. You are not in God's favor if you live contrary to God. ***"But Noah found grace in the eyes of the Lord.*** *These are the generations of Noah:* ***Noah was a just man*** *and perfect in his generations, and* ***Noah walked with God….*** *And God looked upon the earth, and, behold, it was corrupt; for all flesh had corrupted his way upon the earth"* (Gen. 6:8-9,12). Those who find grace are those who live right and walk with God. Those whom God destroyed were those who lived in moral corruption. What should we then do concerning those who have believed the doctrine of false grace?

2 Timothy 2:25-26

"In meekness instructing those that oppose themselves [by going against the truth]; if God peradventure will give them repentance to the acknowledging of the truth; And that ***they may recover themselves*** *[and come to their senses and come] out of the snare of the devil, who are taken captive by him at his will."* (They've been caught by him and are doing his will.) Anyone going contrary to the truth which is according to godliness is in the devil's snare and doing his will (Titus 1:1).

"Finally, my brethren, be strong in the Lord, and in the power of his might. Put on the whole armor of God, that ye may be able to stand against ***the wiles*** *of the devil. For we wrestle not against flesh and blood, but against principalities, against powers, against the rulers of the darkness of this world, against spiritual wickedness in high places. Wherefore take unto you the whole armor of God, that ye may be able to withstand in the evil day, and having done all, to stand. Stand therefore,* ***having your loins girt about with truth***, *and having on the breastplate of* ***righteousness***; *and your feet shod with the preparation of the gospel of peace; above all, taking* ***the shield of faith***, *wherewith ye shall be able to quench all the fiery darts of the wicked. And take the helmet of salvation, and the sword of the Spirit, which is the word of God:* ***Praying always*** *with all prayer and supplication in the Spirit, and watching thereunto* ***with all perseverance*** *and supplication for all saints"* (Eph. 6:10-18). Here is our armor. Walking in truth, righteousness, peace, faith, love, hope, taking the sword of the Spirit, which is the Word of God, and prayer. Satan's

scheme is always to get people to live contrary to these things so that they reap both corruption and wrath, and eventually lose the fight of faith.

1 Timothy 1:3

"As I besought thee to abide still at Ephesus, when I went into Macedonia, that thou mightest charge some that they teach no other doctrine." (Tell them to give no other instructions or teachings other than what is actually contained in the Word, Matt. 28:20.)

1 Timothy 4:16

"Take heed unto thyself, and unto the doctrine; **continue in them: for in doing this thou shalt both save thyself, and them that hear thee.**" Wasn't he already saved? Yes and he would continue to be saved provided that he continue in the truth of the Gospel.

"Let that therefore abide in you, which ye have heard from the beginning. If that which ye have heard from the beginning shall remain in you [then], ye also shall continue in the Son, and in the Father. And this is the promise that he hath promised us [if we continue], **even** *eternal life"* (1 John 2:24-25; Col. 1:21-23; Heb. 3:14).

"For Moses truly said unto the fathers, A prophet shall the Lord your God raise up unto you of your brethren, like unto me; him shall ye hear in all things whatsoever he shall say unto you. And it shall come to pass, that every soul, which **will not** *hear that prophet, shall be destroyed from among the people"* (Acts 3:22-23).

Be willing *"But* **we will give ourselves** *continually to prayer, and to the ministry of the word"* (Acts 6:4).

"For if there be first a **willing mind**, *it is accepted according to that a man hath, and not according to that he hath not"* (2 Cor. 8:12).

"Then Joseph her husband, being a just man, and **not willing to** *make her a publick example, was minded to put her away privily"* (Matt. 1:19).

"He was a burning and a shining light: and **ye were willing** *for a season to rejoice in his light"* (John 5:35).

"We are confident, I say, and **willing rather** *to be absent from the body, and to be present with the Lord"* (2 Cor. 5:8).

"Pray for us: for we trust we have a good conscience, **in all things willing to live honestly**" (Heb. 13:18).

Dear Reader, we could go on and on with hundreds and hundreds of scriptures proving that God sovereignly created man with a free will and not as a preprogrammed puppet. So, God commands free moral agents to repent and obey, or suffer the consequences.

You can see then, that if a doctrine comes along that teaches you that grace gives a cloak for living in sin and ungodliness and says that you're still safe and secure while living in these things, it *cannot* be of God. God would never will this. It must be the devil who is trying to uproot people from sound doctrine and to get them to relax on their stand of righteousness; to get their consciences to where they will neither respond to conviction from the Holy Spirit, nor will they feel condemned, or have godly sorrow when they do wrong, feeling that there is no need for either. Then if a true preacher of righteousness speaks that you need to live right and obey God as the scriptures teach, in order to protect your heart and your faith (Prov. 4:23), they will believe that he is legalistic, and they will fight off the very means of their own deliverance from Satan. Oh, the wiles of the devil. His schemes are many. His traps are numerous. This is the power of deception. It catches people without them even being aware of what's going on. So they fight for their right to be in the devil's snare and go to hell, and try to encourage others to join them. It is a deceptive battle for their will. Those who have fallen into a sinning saint religion have the form, outward show, and verbal profession of being a Christian but are no longer living right, and have fallen into the snare of Satan. What's needed is repentance and faith and then mercy and grace will totally restore the person. They need to come back and "do" God's commandments (Rev. 22:14). *"Having a form of godliness, but denying the power [to live godly] thereof:* ***from such turn away****"* (2 Tim. 3:5). Notice that it doesn't say to gather around them and listen to them, but to turn away from them.

"That they all might be damned who believed not the truth [which Paul said is always according to godliness], but had pleasure in unrighteousness" (2 Thess. 2:12). Hear the warning?

A Fight to the Finish

1 Timothy 6:11-12

"But thou, O man of God, flee these things; ***and follow after righteousness****, godliness, faith, love, patience, meekness [by these things].* ***Fight the good fight of faith****, lay hold on [keep your grip on] eternal life, whereunto thou art also called, and hast professed a good profession before many witnesses."*

It is a fight. A fight to the finish! It is necessary to stay strong in the Lord and strong in His grace that enables us to live right. This is no small matter. This false grace doctrine is a doctrine made up by the devil himself, to get the human will to make wrong decisions to go contrary to God's commandments and break the soul's commitment of faith to really live by faith for the will of God (James 1:22). He knows the end result! If he can get them to believe wrong or believe that they are the predestined ones with no chance of being lost no matter how they live, he will lure them back into unrighteous ways and the latter end will be worse with them than the beginning. Sadly, Satan knows more about these things than some who are called "preachers."

Sincerity, No Guarantee of Safety

Adam and Eve sincerely believed the devil that they wouldn't die, but they died anyway when they disobeyed God's command. God's love didn't automatically somehow cover for them and automatically protect them from their disobedience. It's truth that sets people free from sin and its destructive paths. In John 17:17 Jesus said, *"Sanctify them through thy truth: thy word is truth."* The true Word will always separate you from sin, the ungodly world system, and Satan (1 John 3:8-10); and any doctrine that sympathizes with sin, sympathizes with the devil. It only took *one sin* for Adam and Eve to bring vast destruction to all their future offspring. What's wrong with eating one little piece of fruit, you say? Everything, if the devil is the one behind it. Some ultra gracists perhaps, would have sided in with Satan back in the garden and told Eve, "You shall not surely die just for disobeying God's command. God loves you more than that"; "His grace is bigger than a piece of fruit"; "Can a piece of fruit stop the grace of God?" Sure, He loves man, but His Word cannot be broken. If you side in with the devil, you have chosen whom you will serve. The way you live your life reveals whose side you're on (Matt. 12:30). And Satan and all that show by their lives that they are his followers will be judged and cast into hell, for God must judge evil and He will judge all rebels (Eph. 2:2; James 4:4). It's God's will or Satan's. There is no in-between. There are only two kingdoms; a kingdom of light and a kingdom of darkness. God will judge evil and anyone involved willingly and persistently in it. Either that or we must judge ourselves, confess our sin, and partake of Christ's sacrifice who bore the wrath towards sin (1 John 1:9; Eph. 5:6-7). None of it is automatic but it is there and available waiting for the response of faith for all who are willing to partake of it. If it were automatic, the whole world would be saved, but they aren't; and yet, Jesus *"by the grace of God, tasted death for every man"* (Heb. 2:9). And forgiveness based on Christ's finished work, wasn't automatically applied to us when we first came to the Lord (for it was necessary for us to repent and believe). It's the same now if we need forgiveness (Luke 13:3; Rev. 2–3).

Yes, all is well as long as your will is set to follow the Lord even in the midst of the battles Satan brings out against you. It is then possible for the Christian to be in heaviness through manifold temptations as he continues to learn to walk in this new way of life. He may even stumble, be tempted and sin, but soon afterwards he repents because he truly wills to go on with God. If a person is in Christ, his heart will move him to live for the will of God. This is very different from one who has lost the fight and now chooses to willingly go back to their former life and conduct he had once been delivered out of. *He then* turns back to follow Satan (1 John 2:3-6). He has surrendered the fight and given in to the enemy and quit the race. His only hope, then, is repentance and getting back in the race.

The words *"fall away"* here, mean to revolt: depart from, or withdraw themselves from, the former way they believed or lived; to no longer believe or obey the good truths of the Gospel they once believed and walked in.

This is the devil's aim with temptation. His aim in deception, temptation, and false doctrine is to mislead the will into a state of false security or rebellion, while at the same time getting them to think, "all is well" (1 Tim. 4:1). He furthermore brings persecution and affliction against your faith to try and get you to give up (Mark 4:13-17). But, onward Christian soldier. *"Thou therefore, my son, be strong in the grace that is in Christ Jesus. And the things that thou hast heard of me among many witnesses, the same commit thou to faithful men, who shall be able to teach others also. Thou therefore endure hardness, as a good soldier of Jesus Christ"* (2 Tim. 2:1-3).

Grace Given To Reign

Grace is given to us to enable us to reign over Satan and sin. *"For sin shall not have dominion over you: for ye are not under the law, but under grace"* (Rom. 6:14). Sin once reigned over us, but now grace should reign.

"For if by one man's offence death reigned by one; much more they which receive abundance of grace and of the gift of righteousness shall reign in life by one, Jesus Christ." (Rom. 5:17).

Just to show you that you can fail of the grace of God, if you choose to go back to unrighteous living, let's go to Hebrews 12:12-17: *"Wherefore lift up the hands which hang down, and the feeble knees; And make straight paths for your feet [keep your feet on the straight path], lest that which is lame be turned out of the [narrow] way; but let it rather be healed.* **Follow peace with all men, and holiness,** *[down this narrow way]* **without which no man shall see the Lord:** *Looking diligently lest any man fail of the grace of God [that none of you lose out on the grace of God]; lest any root of bitterness springing up [in you] trouble you, and thereby many be defiled [poisoned]; Lest there be any fornicator, or profane [immoral] person, as Esau, who for one morsel of meat sold his birthright. For ye know how that afterward, when he would have inherited the blessing, he was rejected: for he found no place of repentance, though he sought it carefully with tears."*

In verse 15, the Greek word for "fail," means to "fall from" or "forfeit" the grace of God. Right after this warning in verse 28 the apostle shows us that grace is given to us to empower us to serve God and obey Him. Don't have any wrong ideas about what grace is. Don't let anyone turn you off the right path with their cleverly crafted doctrines. There are only two paths. The narrow road which is the highway of holiness, which leads to eternal life, and the broad road of unrighteous living, which leads to destruction. One leads to life eternal, one leads to everlasting punishment. You are heading down one or the other depending on which way your will is set. Listen to what God says about this highway of holiness: *"And an highway shall be there, and a way, and it shall be called, the way of holiness; the unclean shall not pass over it; but it shall be for those: the wayfaring men, though fools, shall not err therein. No lion shall be there, nor any ravenous beast shall go up thereon, it shall not be found there; but the redeemed shall walk there: and the ransomed of the* LORD *shall return, and come to Zion with songs and everlasting joy upon their heads: they shall obtain joy and gladness, and sorrow and sighing shall flee away"* (Isa. 35:8-10). (The redeemed that walk down the highway of holiness shall obtain everlasting joy.)

Paul says, *"What fruit had ye then in those things whereof ye are now ashamed? For the end of those things is death. But now being made free from sin, and become servants to God, ye have your fruit unto holiness and the end [result is] everlasting life"* (Rom. 6:21-22).

In Hebrews 12:17 it shows that Esau couldn't obtain the blessing, for he came to consider a bowl of pottage of greater value than spiritual things and his covenant rights, and now he found himself in a horrible condition. It was too late, he had crossed the line. The blessing that was rightfully his, was gone.

"He, that being often reproved hardeneth his neck, shall suddenly be destroyed, and that without remedy" (Prov. 29:1).

Please, brethren, understand that my heart's desire is to help God's people see the evil of doctrines that mislead people away from the true ways of the Lord and deceive them. They come as an angel of light, clothed in beautiful sounding words, but by their fruit ye shall know them. What do they get people to do? What is implied, or the end result? Huge organizations are set up and labeled "the church," and deceive multitudes. I understand some people's intentions may be good when they teach such things contrary to the truth because of their ignorance, but that doesn't change what God said in His Word. Satan will still use the good intentions of men who have zeal without knowledge as he did with Saul (Paul). Beware minister, for the devil will even try to use you in the pulpit to destroy souls (James 3:1). Neither God's warnings about sin, nor His commandments can be changed. What is written is our only protection against the enemy of men's souls, for the only thing we "really" know about God and how He deals with things is by what is written. Satan brings many teachings wrapped in many pretty (seemingly beautiful spiritual) packages. He always comes in some form as an angel bringing a false light, seemingly bringing a more wonderful love or a more gracious grace, but he really brings darkness, and he will always persecute those who promote real righteousness (2 Tim. 3:12). He has been deceiving people for almost 6,000 years and is a master at it. (See Rev. 12:9,17.) He has succeeded in deceiving the whole world at one time or another. You and I, and Paul included (Titus 3:3). Only God's truth and counsel can enable us to see.

God's written Word rightly divided is our only defense (2 Tim. 2:15).

Grace is given to us to strengthen us against the enemy's onslaughts to keep us from the pathway of death, not so we could go back and live under his influence. By grace, *we overcome* Satan and the effects of the fall as good soldiers of Jesus Christ (2 Pet. 1:3; 1 John 5:4).

2 Corinthians 6:1-2

"We then, as workers together with him, beseech you also that ye receive not the grace of God in vain. [Don't fail to cooperate with it.] For he saith, I have heard thee in a time accepted, and in the day of salvation have I succored

thee [and saved you by grace from your ties with Satan]: behold, now is the accepted time; behold, now is the day of salvation.")

Grace can be received in vain. It is by no means irresistible, as some have erroneously taught. Grace is given so that we would have the strength to live for God. But if you believe wrong things about it, you cannot tap into its power. This is why doctrines such as false grace exist. Let me explain. In many cases, they don't know about the sustaining power of the Holy Spirit, or what true grace is. Their leaders have taught them wrong. They then must make up things to comfort themselves. True grace is power to live holy and walk with God. A false grace is nothing but excuses to live unholy and walk with Satan. Sadly, some cannot see through his obvious disguise, just as the Pharisees, blinded by their wrong beliefs, couldn't even see the Messiah when He stood right in front of them.

In Acts 14:22 the apostles went about,

*"Confirming the souls of the disciples, **and exhorting them to continue in the faith**, and that we must through much tribulation enter into the kingdom of God."* This, too, is an exhortation to continue. Why? *"For we wrestle not against flesh and blood, but against principalities, against powers, against the rulers of the darkness of this world, against spiritual wickedness in high places"* (Eph. 6:12).

And Satan with his wiles is always up to his trickery including twisting scriptures to serve his own ends. (See Matthew 4:5-6.) Why would the apostles exhort them to continue in the faith and in grace if they couldn't do anything but that? Such exhortations would, then, as we've said, have no meaning.

Let's go back now to Paul's doctrine in Second Corinthians.

2 Corinthians 11:3, 13-16

*"But I fear, lest by any means, as the serpent beguiled Eve through his subtlety, so your minds should be corrupted [drawn and seduced away] from the simplicity that is in Christ [from its pure devotion and faithfulness to Christ].... For such are **false apostles, deceitful workers, transforming themselves** into the apostles of Christ. And no marvel; for Satan himself is transformed into an angel of light. Therefore it is no great thing if **his ministers** [Satan has ministers] also be transformed as the ministers **of righteousness** [they come in sheep's clothing]; whose end shall be according to their works."* (What they produce in their hearers.) Satan has ministers who come clothed as ministers of righteousness whose teaching really promotes unrighteousness. They,

in their cleverly disguised teachings, actually lead people away from *pure* devotion to Christ. Their end will be according to their works (their behavior, their deeds done and the fruit of their teaching). Jesus said, *"But whoso shall offend one of these little ones which believe in Me, it were better for him that a millstone were hanged about his neck, and that he were drowned in the depth of the sea"* (Matt. 18:6). The word "offend" here means "cause to stumble and sin." So then, there are those who will come with an unscriptural interpretation of righteousness saying, it doesn't matter how you live, you're still righteous. But really they are promoting not the work of God but the work of Satan; they are wolves in sheep's clothing or else very deceived and carnal Christians. They say they believe in righteousness but promote unrighteousness through the message they bring. But God's command is *"Be ye holy for I am holy"*; and without following after holiness *"no man shall see the Lord."* And, by the way, nowhere in scripture is there any such thing as infant baptism regeneration. Even if there was (which there is not), these people would still have to live their lives by faith after this, focused on obeying the will of God *to continue* in the Covenant. So, the important thing is not how things were last year between a person and God, but how things are right now. Real faith is a lifelong decision to live for the will of God (1 Pet. 4:2; Matt. 12:50). You must, as Christ taught, lose your life in this world to gain the next. Jesus said, *"Be thou faithful unto death and I will give thee a crown of life. He that hath ears, let him hear what the Spirit saith unto the churches. **He that overcometh** shall not be hurt by the second death"* (Rev. 2:10-11). *"Blessed and holy is he that hath part in the first resurrection: on such the second death hath no power, but they shall be priests of God and of Christ, and shall reign with him a thousand years.... And death and hell were cast into the lake of fire. This is the second death"* (Rev. 20:6,14).

CHAPTER NINETEEN

GRACE AND WORKS IN GALATIANS

Galatians 1:6-7

"I marvel that ye are so soon removed from him that called you into the grace of Christ unto another gospel: Which is not another; but there be some that trouble you, and would pervert add to or take away from the gospel of Christ." Paul was speaking of legalistic Judaizers who wanted the Gentiles to be circumcised and keep their holy days.

Ultra gracists though, under the devil's influence, blow certain scriptures, such as this passage in Galatians, way out of proportion, and take the extreme opposite view of the legalistic Jewish believers. They pervert the Gospel in another direction, to another extreme, not really agreeing with all we've shown that Paul has said in his other epistles. They too preach *"another Gospel,"* as Jude pointed out in his epistle (Jude 3-4).

Paul, in Galatians, wasn't speaking of obedience to God or righteousness being legalism, but was speaking of people trusting in Sabbath days, new moons, circumcision, and so on. (Paul said in 1 Corinthians 9:21, that he himself was not without law to God.) He also said that love *fulfills* the law, and that faith doesn't nullify the moral law but establishes it (Rom. 3:31). In Galatians then he was speaking of people mixing Jewish ceremonies with the Gospel. We are all supposed to be *"doers of the Word"* (James 1:22), and obey the Gospel. He Himself taught that we need to obey, and said that all who don't obey will receive everlasting destruction (2 Thess. 1:7-8; Heb. 5:9).

So listen to what He's really speaking of in this letter to the Galatians. Galatians 4:9-11:

"But now, after that ye have known God, or rather are known of God, how turn ye again [back] to the weak and beggarly elements, where unto ye desire again to be in bondage? **Ye observe days, and months, and times, and years.** *I am afraid of you, lest I have bestowed upon you labor in vain."* (They began to think that perhaps these things justified them.)

In Galatians 5:1-4,7 Paul writes:

*"Stand fast therefore in the liberty wherewith Christ hath made us free, and be not entangled again with the yoke of bondage. Behold, I Paul say unto you, that **if ye be circumcised**, Christ shall profit you nothing, for I testify again to every man that is circumcised, that he is a debtor to do the whole [Jewish ceremonial] law. Christ is become of no effect unto you, whosoever of you are justified [or trying to be made righteous] by the [Jewish ceremonial] law; ye are fallen from grace. Ye did run well; who did hinder you that ye should not obey the truth?"*

Obeying the truth and following the Spirit is the true way of righteousness, not Jewish ceremonies, Sabbaths, new moons, circumcision, and carnal ordinances (Gal. 6:17-24). Paul never, ever, implied that obedience to the Gospel, obedience to the truth, or living in righteousness was self-righteousness or legalistic. As a matter of fact, he showed that it was faith and that it was the result of following after the Holy Spirit. But ultra gracists, contrary to Paul, try and say that if a person says we have to live right, that that's legalism. No, it's the result of Bible grace and the fruit of righteousness. Holiness, right living, morality, doing good, and so on, is not Jewish law, it's following the Spirit of God into the fruit of the Spirit and really *living* by faith. *"Do we then make void the law [of God] through faith? God forbid: yea, we establish the law"* (Rom. 3:31). Anyone who continues in the faith and in grace will go from righteousness to righteousness, and glory to glory as they are changed by the Gospel. Legalism has to do with going back to outward religious ceremonies to be justified, which are not of faith. Outward things such as Sabbaths, dietary laws, carnal ordinances, and rules made up by men, and so on, don't make a person morally better, nor could they regenerate a person and make them spiritually alive. It is the new birth that empowers us, as new creatures, to live right and live the way God wants us to live. *"For in Christ Jesus neither circumcision availeth any thing, nor uncircumcision, but a new creature. And **as many as walk** according to this rule, peace be on them, and mercy, and upon the Israel of God"* (Gal. 6:15-16). Live according to the fact that you're a new creature and that all the bondages of sin and Satan are passed away and then God's peace will be on you (Phil. 4:9; 2 Cor. 5:17).

1 Peter 1:22

"Seeing ye have purified your souls in obeying the truth through the Spirit unto unfeigned love of the brethren, see that ye love one another with a pure heart fervently." Here Peter speaks of an obedience of faith which purifies the soul (1 John 3:3).

Circumcision, carnal washings, Sabbaths, and so on, do not change a person inwardly. So again, Paul like Peter, was simply telling them that these things of the Old Testament such as Jewish ceremonies, don't matter. It's obeying God's moral commands that matters, and we are empowered by His Spirit and grace to do so. God gave us a new heart and spirit. Let us walk accordingly. If we live by the work of the Spirit, let us also walk in the Spirit (Gal. 5:16-25).

Listen to Paul in 1 Corinthians 7:19:

"Circumcision is nothing, and uncircumcision is nothing, but [what matters is] the keeping of the commandments of God." Paul simply taught that the Spirit of Grace was given for us to overcome the flesh and to obey God's moral commandments, but the carnal ordinances like circumcision couldn't help at all. They were only pictures of coming spiritual realities (Col. 2:11). God is our source and our victory. His Spirit of Grace empowers us to live right, to work for God, to have victory over sin and Satan, and to serve God acceptably (Ezek. 36:27). Paul wrote, *"And what is the exceeding greatness of his power to us-ward who believe, according to the working of his mighty power, Which he wrought in Christ, when he raised him from the dead, and set him at his own right hand in the heavenly places"* (Eph. 1:19-20).

Paul then went on to say in Galatians 5:16-23:

*"This I say then, Walk in the Spirit, and **ye shall not** fulfill the lust of the flesh. [This is the real way to walk in righteousness.] For the flesh lusteth against the Spirit, and the Spirit against the flesh: and these are contrary the one to the other: so that ye cannot do the things that ye would. But **if ye be led of the Spirit [into the fruit of the Spirit then] ye are not [no longer] under the law.** Now the works of the flesh are manifest, which are these: Adultery, fornication, uncleanness, lasciviousness, idolatry, witchcraft, hatred, variance, emulations, wrath, strife, seditions, heresies, envyings, murders, drunkenness, revellings, and such like: of the which I tell you before, as I have also told you in time*

past, **that they which do such things shall not inherit the kingdom of God.** *But the fruit of the Spirit is love, joy, peace, longsuffering, gentleness, goodness, faith, meekness, temperance:* **against such there is no law.**" Anyone who goes back and yields to the flesh *is not* walking in the Spirit and if that's their course in life, they shall not inherit the Kingdom of God, but rather, destruction (Gal. 6:7-9). In other words, no one who lives after the flesh without repentance will inherit heaven (Matt. 7:21), and the Kingdom of God (Rev. 22:14). You cannot walk in the flesh and in the Spirit at the same time. They are contrary to one another. If you're involved in the works of the flesh, you're walking after the flesh and you'll reap corruption. For there still is, and always has been, a law against the works of the flesh. But he said, "**IF ye be led of the Spirit,** *then* *ye are not under the law,*" nor its curse. So, can you not simply see that he was teaching these Galatians that now we must obey the Spirit and not a bunch of outward rituals, and if we obey the Spirit, we are led into the fruit of a changed life and are then the sons of God?

And to show there is a universal moral law Paul writes, *"Now we know that what things soever the law saith, it saith to them who are under the law: that* **every mouth** *may be stopped, and all the world may become guilty before God"* (Rom. 3:19). The whole world was never under Jewish ceremonial law, but men originally had God's moral law written in their hearts. *"For when the Gentiles, which have not the law, do by nature the things contained in the law, these, having not the law, are a law unto themselves: Which show* **the work of the law written in their hearts,** *their conscience also bearing witness, and their thoughts the mean while accusing or else excusing one another"* (Rom. 2:14-15). So, those who continue following the works of the flesh and suppress what they know is right without repenting of these things *will not* inherit the Kingdom of God. They have put themselves once again under the curse.

So then, this is Paul's statement: We have a new and living way. He said *"if ye be led of the Spirit"* into living in the fruit of the Spirit, then you are not under the law nor its curse, for against such fruit there is no law and no curse attached to them. But you cannot use the book of Galatians to prove that grace is contrary to moral uprightness. No, grace, and the Spirit of Grace, he said, causes you to not fulfill the lusts of the flesh and moves you to walk in the fruit of the Spirit, and thereby live a life pleasing to God. *"Herein is my Father glorified, that ye bear much fruit; so shall ye be my disciples"* (John 15:8).

Again, against such fruit there is no law. It's a new spiritual way that we walk in righteousness and not by keeping certain days and rituals. It's in newness of Spirit and not in oldness of letter. But the fact is, we do *fulfill the righteousness* of the law (Rom. 8:4), and we are to keep God's moral commandments (1 Cor. 7:19). If people aren't moved in this direction, then they either really don't know God, have been taught wrong, or they aren't continuing in grace and in the faith (1 John 2:2-6).

Remember that grace saved us from sin and keeps us from a life of sin. Christ died to make this available to us. Righteousness doesn't come by religious works keeping rituals, but grace alone produces in us a changed life and the fruit of righteousness. If people depart from grace, either because of going back to religious ceremonies or back to a life of sin, they will find that they are just as weak as any other sinner. They will fall from the sustaining power of grace. They will come under bondage to the works of the flesh once again, and if continued in, will once again incur the death penalty (Jude 12) and not inherit the Kingdom of God (Rom. 1:32). *"For the wages of sin is death ..."* (Rom. 6:23).

Philippians 1:11

Paul wrote, *"Being filled with the fruits [results] of righteousness, which are by Jesus Christ, unto the glory and praise of God."* Righteous living is the result of having Jesus in our lives. Willingly living wickedly is a result of having the devil in one's life (Eph. 2:2; John 8:44). Righteous living brings glory to God and His grace. *"To appoint unto them that mourn in Zion, to give unto them beauty for ashes, the oil of joy for mourning, the garment of praise for the spirit of heaviness; that they might be called trees of righteousness, the planting of the Lord, that he might be glorified"* (Isa. 61:3).

Romans 8:4

"That the righteousness of the law might be fulfilled in us, who walk not after the flesh, but after the Spirit."

First Timothy 1:9-11

Paul wrote, *"Knowing this, that the law is not made for a righteous man [who walks after the Spirit],* **but for the lawless and disobedient, for the ungodly and for sinners** *[for all who follow the flesh and its works], for unholy and profane, for murderers of fathers and murderers of mothers, for manslayers, for whoremongers, for them that defile themselves with mankind, for menstealers, for liars, for perjured persons,* **and if there be any other thing that is contrary to sound doctrine;** *according to the glorious gospel of the blessed God, which was committed to my trust."*

Here Paul reveals a righteous man is a man who fulfills the moral law written in the heart and who lives right. (The just shall live by faith committed to the will of God.) So again *if ye be led of the Spirit*, then only are ye not under the law, for the law was made for all those who walk in unrighteousness following the flesh. We must listen to all that the apostle Paul said, if we really want his revelation on grace. So if everyone lived righteously, there would have been no need for God to write down for us what is righteousness and what is sin.

In Galatians 6:7-10 Paul warns the Galatian Christians:

"Be not deceived; God is not mocked: for whatsoever a man soweth, that shall he also reap. For he that soweth to his flesh shall of the flesh reap corruption; but he that soweth to the Spirit shall of the Spirit reap life everlasting. And let us not be weary in well doing: for in due season we shall reap [eternal life], if we faint not [don't give up]. As we have therefore opportunity, let us do good unto all men, especially unto them who are of the household of faith" (Eph. 6:8).

Ultra gracists need to heed Paul's warning here. In Galatians 5:7-9 He said, *"Ye did run well; who did hinder you **that ye should not obey the truth? This persuasion cometh not of him that calleth you.** A little leaven leaveneth the whole lump."*

What some people have done is to push the truth on grace presented by Paul in the book of Galatians, way too far to the other side of the road, to where it is no longer the truth, or what Paul taught. It is then just as destructive, if not more so, than legalism. Ultra gracists only preach half-truths, which by themselves are not true. They have added their own brand of leaven to the Gospel, and have perverted it.

No wonder Jude wrote to the church to contend for our *"most holy faith."*

2 Timothy 2:15

"Study to show thyself approved unto God, a workman that needeth not to be ashamed, rightly dividing the word of truth." Study to rightly divide the Word of Truth. So then it can be wrongly divided if you don't interpret scripture with scripture and take the whole counsel of God (2 Tim. 3:16-17). *All scripture* is given by inspiration of God. *All of what God said* is important in order to get the full and clear picture. It is a shame that Christians will listen to what Dr. so and so says, or Pharisee so and so, just because they have a title or degree given to them by men rather than the pure, simple Word of God. Learn to believe the Bible more than

what men say about the Bible. Learn to look at it all and take it at face value. So, in the book of Galatians, Paul was simply telling Christians not to go back into any religious activities which are not clearly revealed as a part of our New Covenant to be justified. Whether it be circumcision, or saying a repetitive prayer over and over again as some do (Matt. 6:7).

Ephesians

"For by grace are ye saved through faith; and that not of yourselves: it is the gift of God: Not of works, lest any man should boast" (Eph. 2:8-9). Remember, to be saved is to be made spiritually alive, that is, regenerated (Eph. 2:5; Titus 3:5). Works could never do that.

Again, certainly, it all is by grace; by the true Bible definition of grace, that is. When we are willing we can receive it. If we turn away in our hearts and are unwilling, we do not receive, although the gracious Holy Spirit will work on a person for a long time trying to persuade them to turn back to God (Rom. 2:4). To God be all the glory and honor. We fully believe in His wonderful grace, but the *true* grace of God, which the will can accept or reject (Rev. 22:17), which you can receive in vain or take advantage of (2 Cor. 6:1). *"But we see Jesus, who was made a little lower than the angels for the suffering of death, crowned with glory and honor; that he by the grace of God should taste death for every man"* (Heb. 2:9). *"For the grace of God that bringeth salvation hath appeared to all men"* (Titus 2:11). It's there for all, but not all willingly receive it. To receive from God we must always turn from Satan (Acts 26:18).

Ephesians Chapter One

Everything is elect in Him, predestined in Him, chosen in Him, and God is going to gather together all things in Christ. We get into Christ by repenting (Luke 13:3) and believing (John 3:16, 10:9), and we continue in Him by living for Him (John 15:6; Jude 22; 1 John 2:28). *"Let that therefore abide in you, which ye have heard from the beginning. If that which ye have heard from the beginning shall remain in you, ye also shall [then] continue in the Son, and in the Father. And this is the promise that he hath promised us [who continue], **even** eternal life"* (1 John 2:24-25).

If we continue to abide in Him, we are predestined in Him for glory. In Him we are elect; outside of Him we are not. *"Wherefore the rather, brethren, **give diligence to make your calling and election sure**: for if ye do these things, ye shall never fall: For so an entrance shall be ministered unto you abundantly into the everlasting kingdom of our Lord and Savior Jesus Christ"* (2 Pet. 1:10-11).

In Him we are chosen; outside of Him we are not (Matt. 20:16). In Colossians, which is a twin epistle to Ephesians, Paul said, *"And you, that were sometime alienated and enemies in your mind by wicked works, yet now hath He reconciled in the body of his flesh through death, to present you holy and unblameable and unreproveable in his sight:* **If ye continue in the faith** *grounded and settled, and be not moved away from the hope of the Gospel, which ye have heard, and which was preached to every creature which is under heaven; whereof I Paul am made a minister"* (Col. 1:21-23). Notice, you must continue *in Him*. *"In Him was life"* (John 1:4). To abide in Him you must simply be willing to live for His Father's will.

"For whosoever shall do the will of my Father which is in heaven, **the same** *is my brother, and sister, and mother"* (Matt. 12:50).

"Not every one that saith unto me, Lord, Lord, shall enter into the kingdom of heaven; but he that doeth the will of my Father which is in heaven" (Matt. 7:21).

He said that if we keep His commandments then we will abide in Him (*in Christ*, John 15:1-10).

"He that saith he abideth **in him** *ought himself also so to walk, even as he walked"* (1 John 2:6).

"Behold, what manner of love the Father hath bestowed upon us, that we should be called the sons of God: therefore the world knoweth us not, because it knew him not. Beloved, now are we the sons of God, and it doth not yet appear what we shall be: but we know that, when he shall appear, we shall be like him; for we shall see him as he is. **And every man that hath this hope** *in him purifieth himself, even as he is pure. Whosoever committeth sin transgresseth also the law: for sin is the transgression of the law. And ye know that he was manifested to take away our sins; and* **in him is no sin**. *Whosoever abideth* **in Him** *sinneth not: whosoever sinneth hath not seen him, neither known him. Little children, let no man deceive you: he that doeth righteousness is righteous, even as he is righteous. He that committeth sin is of the devil; for the devil sinneth from the beginning. For this purpose the Son of God was manifested, that he might destroy the works of the devil"* (1 John 3:1-8).

Paul stated that it's *in Him* that we have an inheritance (Eph. 1:11). To abide or not abide is once again up to you. Do you will to live for God or not? *"And the world passeth away, and the lust thereof: but he that doeth the will of God abideth for ever"* (1 John 2:17). If you do abide in Christ, you will abide with God forever. So there is no sense in one saying that they are one of the predestined ones unless they abide in Christ, living their lives in obedience to Christ and the Father's will. So, being in God's pre-destined plan has everything to do with your will. The will remains free. If you repent of your ties with Satan, submit to Jesus' Lordship and obey Him, you then are predestined in Him. Only then can you say that you're predestined in Him to be glorified. God foresaw some would enter and abide, and some would not. Those who abide, He predestined to be glo-rified. His plan to have glorified sons is predestined, but not who is a part of it (Rev. 22:17; Heb. 2:9; Matt. 16:15; John 1:29, 3:16). God will gather all things *in Christ*, and they will be changed in the twinkling of an eye (Eph. 1:10). Listen now, to His teaching, *"As therefore the tares are gathered and burned in the fire; so shall it be in the end of this world. The Son of man shall send forth his angels, and **they shall gather out of his kingdom all things that offend, and them which do iniquity; And shall cast them into a furnace of fire**: there shall be wailing and gnashing of teeth. Then shall the righteous shine forth as the sun in the kingdom of their Father. Who hath ears to hear, let him hear"* (Matt. 13:40-43).

Titus 2:11-15

*"For the [true] grace of God that bringeth salvation hath appeared to **all men**, teaching us [and instructing us] that, denying ungodliness and worldly lusts, **we should live soberly, righteously, and godly** [and no longer follow Satan], in this present world [as we are]; looking for that blessed hope, and the glorious appearing of the great God and our **Savior Jesus Christ; who gave himself for us, that he might redeem [deliver] us from all iniquity [wrongdo-ing], and purify [and make holy] unto Himself a peculiar people, zealous of good works.** These things speak, and exhort, and rebuke with all authority. Let no man despise thee."*

God will never force anyone to believe, receive, or do anything; it's up to you. You have power over your own will; to receive or not receive; to continue or not continue; to cooperate or not cooperate with the grace of God. None of it is automatic. God sovereignly chose it to be this way. It was the only way if He was to have man in His image and likeness and not just a robot. All is ours if we willingly abide in Him.

Ephesians chapter 2 reveals that God made us alive again when we turned from sin and Satan. Living in sin made us children of wrath just like others. He saved us by the power of His grace out of bondage to sin and Satan, and it was not by our past merits. The blood of Christ cleansed us. He goes on to use the words, "in whom," showing what's ours in Him. We are to be a holy temple for the Lord. *"If any man defile* the temple of God, him shall God destroy; for the temple of God is holy, which temple ye are" (1 Cor. 3:17).

Ephesians 4:1-3

"*I therefore, the prisoner of the Lord, beseech you **that ye walk worthy** of the vocation wherewith ye are called, with all lowliness and meekness, with longsuffering, forbearing one another in love; endeavoring to keep the unity of the Spirit in the bond of peace.*" If God's life-changing grace was irresistible, it would automatically change everyone to be as God wants them to be, and make them all abound in good works for this is His will (1 Cor. 15:10,58), but it takes human cooperation.

"*Be ye therefore followers of God, as dear children; And walk in love, as Christ also hath loved us, and hath given himself for us an offering and a sacrifice to God for a sweet smelling savor. But fornication, and all uncleanness, or covetousness, let it not be once named among you, as becometh saints; Neither filthiness, nor foolish talking, nor jesting, which are not convenient: but rather giving of thanks. **For this ye know**, that no whoremonger, nor unclean person, nor covetous man, who is an idolater, hath any inheritance in the kingdom of Christ and of God. Let no man deceive you with vain words [empty promises]: for because of these things cometh the wrath of God upon the children of disobedience. **Be not ye** therefore partakers with them*" (Eph. 5:1-7).

Those who think they have a special revelation on some super grace, unwisely compare themselves with others whom they perceive don't see. Yet it is they who have gone out of balance in their doctrine, and those staying with the whole Word will never see it their way nor agree with them. Why, because the ultra gracists are not accepting the whole counsel of God on the subject. We know their doctrine by its fruit. True grace gives a person power to live right. This is what gives security.

This counterfeit grace is similar to what Satan said at the tree of knowledge of good and evil. God said, If you eat of that tree, "*Ye shall surely die*"; and the devil said, "*Ye shall not surely die.*" The devil, in his doctrine, still says, "Those who say "ye shall die," are just legalistic." "God's love will save you from the consequences when you eat of this tree." "Nothing bad will happen. His grace is more powerful than your disobedience." "Go ahead, eat, it's OK." "Can your behavior stop God's grace?" "SSSS!" Isn't he saying the same things today? It all just comes in different packages (good words and fair speeches). But it's still the same old devil with the same old lies and reasonable sounding arguments, *but he still contradicts what God has actually said.* Get it?

God Hates Sin

The one thing that God hates the most is sin. When God told Adam if you sin *"you shall surely die,"* He meant it. When God tells a Christian, *"if you live after the flesh ye shall die,"* He means it. Because of God's Word, God was obligated to judge Adam worthy of death (Rom. 1:32). He *couldn't* change it once He said it; the Bible says, *"The scriptures **cannot** be broken."*

Satan though, has always promoted a false teaching that has said, "You can be disobedient to God's Word," and "Ye shall not surely die." "God is too nice you know." "God didn't *really* mean what He said." But God meant it when He said it to Adam. Does He still mean it today? Why didn't He tell Adam He was just kidding?

If sin has no effect on Christians or their destiny, why then did God say to Christians in scripture, If you yield yourself to sin to be its servant, the end of that is death (Rom. 6:16)

That the wages of sin *is death* (Rom. 6:23).

That if you live after the flesh *you shall die* (Rom. 8:12).

That if a brother goes astray, his soul is heading for death (James 5:19-20).

That those who live in the works of the flesh will not inherit the Kingdom of God (Gal. 5:19-21).

That those who live unrighteously shall not share in the inheritance (1 Cor. 6:9-10).

And those who commit such things without repentance are worthy of death (Rom. 1:32). Why did he say through Peter that if you turn back to the pollutions of the world after knowing Christ, you'll be worse off than if you had never known the way of truth? (2 Pet. 2:20-21).

That if a man didn't abide in Christ, he'd spiritually wither up and be cast forth as a dead branch and be burned (John 15:6).

That only those who do His commandments shall enter into heaven and partake of the tree of life (Rev. 22:14).

That only those who overcome this world are promised eternal life and eternity with Him (Rev. 2: 3).

That if you make yourself the friend of the world, you make your stand as the enemy of God (James 4:4).

That if you don't continue, you'd be cut off (Rom. 11:22).

And many other numerous warnings in the New Covenant (this new contract).

Death by Sin

Spiritual death is separation from God and His Kingdom (Rom. 5:12; Eph. 2:1).

What Does God Say About Sin and Death?

He says:

That death enters by sin (Rom. 5:12).

That the end of a life of sin is death (Rom. 6:21).

That sin brings forth fruit unto death (Rom. 6:21).

To be carnally minded is death (Rom. 8:6).

The sting of death is sin (1 Cor. 15:56).

People could be twice dead (Jude 12).

That sin when it's finished brings forth death (James 1:13-15).

That if a person hates his brother he abides in death (1 John 3:4).

That there are sins that can lead Christians back to spiritual death (1 John 5:16-17).

That we are to be faithful unto the end of our lives and then He will give us a crown of life (Rev. 2:10).

He told Adam he'd surely die if he sinned (Gen. 2:17). Did Adam die? Yes! Who told Eve, "ye shall not surely die"? The serpent. Did she die? Yes! Whose telling Christians now "ye shall not surely die" even if they return back to a life of sin? The *SAME* serpent!

If God didn't really mean these things, why did He say them? Again, did He mean it when He said to Adam he would surely die? Yes! If so, doesn't He mean it today?

Doesn't His Word say:

That we are to be dead in our relationship to sin (Rom. 6:2).

That we are now freed from sin (Rom. 6:7).

That people who live in sinful pleasures are dead while they live (1 Tim. 5:6).

That people are dead when they are in their sins (Col. 2:13).

Furthermore, why has God revealed in the New Covenant that people can turn aside and follow Satan once again; depart from the faith; desert the living God; go back to a life of willful sinning and incur certain fiery judgment; love this world more than God and forsake the right way? Or, turn from the way of righteousness; endure only for awhile; that they must do certain things to make their calling and election sure? That He'll say, *depart from Me all ye workers of iniquity*; that all hypocrites will be cast into the lake of fire; that only those who do the Heavenly Father's will, will enter heaven; that saying you have faith is dead if your actions don't correspond; that those who do not obey the truth will receive indignation and wrath; that if you try and save your life in this world, you'll lose it; that His promises are only to those who love Him, and if we love Him, we'll keep His commandments; that if we didn't continue in His goodness, we'd be cut off; that men could forfeit the grace of God; close their ears to the truth and turn to follow teachers who will tickle their ears and teach that they can follow their lusts? Why did He warn against false teachers who'd bring in damnable heresies; and that if we suffer with Him that only then we'd be glorified together with Him; that all have not obeyed the Gospel; and that He will bring everlasting punishment to those that obey not the Gospel? Why did He say Jesus is the author of eternal salvation to all them *that obey Him*?

Why did God have Paul preach obedience to the faith and tell him that he was to turn people from darkness to light, from the power of Satan unto God, and that they should bring forth works proving their faith and repentance? Why did He say they must continue in the faith and continue in grace; plus reveal that some could fall from grace if no one could? Why warn us not to be like Esau who gave up his birthright for something natural? Why was Paul concerned that the tempter had tempted some and his labor be in vain concerning them. Why warn Christians not to be partaking of the wrath of God because of disobedience? Why did Paul say that he cried over some in the church that had sinned and not yet repented? Why warn us that we should not be like Israel who committed fornication and 23,000 fell dead in one day, or, that we shouldn't tempt Christ as some of them did and were destroyed of serpents; that we should not murmur as some of them did and were destroyed of the destroyer? Why did Paul say the same thing could happen to us?

Why did Jude use as examples what happened to rebels in time past to warn the church concerning rebellion and a false concept of grace now, implying that God still deals with rebellion against Him the same as always? Why does God say that if Timothy continued in the true doctrine of Christ, he'd save both himself and those who heard him; that profession is not enough; that He only promises mercy to the repentant and never to rebels; that we are to endure hardness, and fight the good fight of faith in order to lay hold on eternal life? That *the saints are those* that keep the commandments of God and the faith of Jesus; that we are to pass the time we have here on the earth with godly fear, knowing God is no respecter of persons; that in the last time people would follow their own ungodly lusts instead of the Lord? That they'd be lovers of pleasure more than lovers of God and despise those who are good and godly? Why are all of Christ's promises only to overcomers in the churches of Revelation, and nothing is promised to those who turn back to follow the course of this world and the prince of the power of the air? That only those who overcome this world's sinful ways will not be hurt by the second death? Why did He say if people take away from, or add to, His book, He'd take their name out of the Book of Life? If He warned them He'd take it out, it had to be in there, and they had to be saved at one time; and if He warned them that He would blot it out, then He didn't automatically predestine it to be in there, why did He say that those who live for earthly things and walk contrary to the cross of Christ that their end is destruction? Shall we go on? We could, with dozens and dozens and dozens of other scriptures and clear warnings from the New Covenant.

One statement from God was enough for Adam. God has given us hundreds of warnings and told us the penalty. I think what we have said is sufficient for any honest person to even see by these few pages above, that there are no such things in scripture such as just professing Christ and then being saved or staying saved, regardless of how one lives afterwards. Grace changes our lives (Col. 1:6). That's the whole purpose of it. There is no irresistible grace; no predestined individual aside from Christ; no unconditional love that automatically forgives.

Adam had one sentence from God about dying. Adam disobeyed and died just as God said. God meant it. We have hundreds of scriptures that show this truth and the scriptures cannot be broken. Dare anyone nullify all this and remove it from God's Word implying that all of these warnings are insignificant gibberish?

Funny then why God said all these things and yet never once said "once saved, always saved"; or "once a son, always a son;" or "once in grace, always in grace." If this is the case, then those who say such things believe men and not God at all, who are saying things God didn't say. This false concept of grace is a work and a doctrine of men and of devils. But they continue to compare real Word teachers with their false concept, and so they denounce what's true, and they are led astray by their own misunderstandings. (See 2 Pet. 3:14-18.) You can have a Doctor of Divinity degree and still be unstable as far as the truth goes, and twist the scriptures to your own destruction. You can fill volumes full of unscriptural teachings and use million dollar words to convince people to follow you, yet still not know what you're talking about.

2 Corinthians 10:12

But Paul said, *"For we dare not make ourselves of the number, or compare ourselves with some that command themselves: but they measuring themselves by themselves, and comparing themselves among themselves, are not wise."* If these ultra gracists measure others by their own false, taken-out-of-context doctrine, they are truly deceived (Matt. 6:23). We need to measure everything by the whole counsel of God. By what God *actually said.* We need to continue steadfastly in the Apostles' Doctrine (Acts 2:42) and not Calvin's, nor any other man, that contradicts the apostles. Calvin was not an apostle. The foundation of the church is not built in him. *"On Christ the solid rock I stand, all other ground is sinking sand."*

Furthermore, the apostle in his doctrine said, we are to walk worthy of our calling. Is this self-righteousness? Not so, it's living the real Christian life as a real Christian.

Listen also to Peter:

"And beside this, giving all diligence, add to your faith virtue [moral and noble character]; and to virtue knowledge; and to knowledge temperance [self control]; and to temperance patience [perseverance]; and to patience godliness [pure devotion to God]; and to godliness brotherly kindness; and to brotherly kindness charity. For if these things [these qualities] be in you, and abound, they [will] make you that ye shall neither be barren nor unfruitful in the knowledge of our Lord Jesus Christ. **But he that lacketh these things [these qualities] is blind,** *and cannot see afar off, and* **hath forgotten** *that he was purged from his old sins [when he at first repented of them]. Wherefore the rather, brethren, give diligence to make your calling and election sure [certain]:* **for if ye do these things, ye shall never fall:** *[As long as you live according to and practice these things, you will never fall away from God.] For so an entrance shall be ministered unto you abundantly [you will then be given an abundant and rich admission] into the everlasting kingdom of our Lord and Savior Jesus Christ."* Is it wrong then to teach these virtues and the wonderful blessing and

results of them? Many ultra gracists would have you think so, saying that it takes away from grace. How duped can a person be?

The apostle said, "But he that lacketh **these things** *is blind!*" He further said, if you *do these things* you will be fruitful in your understanding and you shall never fall, and you will be abundantly welcomed into the kingdom. What then if you don't do these things? You will become blind and you will eventually fall. Furthermore He said to be diligent in living this way to "*make your calling and election sure*" (certain). *"Many are called, but few are chosen."* The elect, then, are simply those who, like the elect angels, have elected to follow God instead of Satan. But Satan keeps working to get you to change your mind and cast your lot back in again with him (2 Pet. 2:20-21). And remember, we are only "*chosen in Him*" (Christ), so, in Him we must abide.

Ephesians 4:2

"With all lowliness and meekness, with longsuffering, forbearing one another in love." Again, the fruit I've seen from many who have been involved in this ultra grace teaching is not lowliness and meekness, forbearing one another in love when it comes to discussing these things, but rather, resistance, getting upset, and high mindedness when others won't agree with them in this lawless doctrine. Yet, on the other hand, they say their teaching on grace makes them more loving towards others. But what it really does is make them more tolerant of sin and of the devil's work in the lives of people. (And this they think is acting in love.) Sin, you know, is the operation and work of Satan (1 John 3:7-8). So they tolerate and agree with the devil and teach that there's no real need to obey God or His commandments. A fine doctrine that is! It is not love to mislead people, nor is it right to resist that which is holy, just, and good (John 14:15, 20-24).

What is the fruit then of this idea of righteousness or grace? Yes, by their fruits ye shall know them. Some of them might be seemingly nice people but their attitude towards sin, Satan, and evil, changes when misled by this doctrine. Then contrary to Paul, they become tolerant of evil and excuse it as mere, insignificant behavior, and they, then, following Cain's example, attack what is good (1 John 3:10). They get upset if you don't believe it their way. Why should we? It's not scriptural! We will choose God's way.

Blessed Are the Peacemakers

Ephesians 4:3

"Endeavoring to keep the unity of the Spirit in the bond of peace."

Colossians 3:15

"And let the peace of God rule in your hearts, to the which also ye are called in one body; and be ye thankful."

Instead of being thankful and endeavoring to keep the unity of the Spirit in the bond of peace, some, getting caught up in a false, counterfeit grace doctrine, have done just the opposite. They even sometimes knowingly do not care if they cause problems in a local church, vigorously attacking any who do not agree with them and their morally loose doctrine, not seeing themselves as a source of division. And because of how they believe, feeling that they are right and God's real truth is wrong, they feel no need to repent about what they've done, for they think grace has done away with the need of repentance. So why feel remorse? Why not reject conviction? Who can tell them anything? This produces a false peace and boldness in them, which only works to harm themselves and others who they persuade to follow this *"pernicious"* way. And if they receive not the love of the truth, the Bible says, they will receive a strong delusion and believe a lie to be the truth. *"That they all might be damned who believed not the truth, but had pleasure in unrighteousness"* (2 Thess. 2:12).

This brethren, is not the grace of God at all which causes people to be and act as such. *"God is not the author of confusion but of peace as in all the churches of the saints." "But the wisdom that is from above **is first pure, then peaceable**, gentle, and easy to be entreated, full of mercy and good fruits, without partiality, and without hypocrisy. And the fruit of righteousness is sown in peace of them that make peace"* (James 3:17-18). If this then, is a picture of God's wisdom, any thing contrary is of the devil.

The scripture says, *"Obey them [real pastors] that have the rule over you, and submit yourselves: for they [as watchmen on the wall] watch for your souls [and are called and anointed of God to do so], as they that must give account, that they may do it with joy, and not with grief: for that is unprofitable for you"* (Heb. 13:17; Acts 20:28; 1 Pet. 5:1-2; Eph. 4:11-13). And it is the Baptism with the Holy Ghost that equips a minister to stand in this office (Acts 1:4-5, 2:4). And yes, it is accompanied by speaking in tongues just like the Bible teaches. All one needs to do is look up tongues in a concordance, and then believe it all exactly as it is written to see this is true.

But some of these people have fallen into just what Paul said *not* to fall into. In Ephesians 4:14, *"That we henceforth be no more children, tossed to and fro, and carried about with every wind of doctrine, by the sleight of men, and cunning craftiness, whereby they lie in wait to deceive."* They've been carried away from the Word in this area and others, by winds of doctrine made up by the cunning craftiness of men and their skill in inventing errors and making them seem like truth. No wonder Christ told us to watch their fruit, for sooner or later you will see what kind of a tree it is by what kind of fruit it produces and what is said, or implied, by them (Matt. 12:33-37). By this, and this alone, you know who's who. For fruit eventually shows up on a tree.

Ephesians 4:28-30

"Let him that stole steal no more: but rather let him labor, working with his hands the thing which is good, that he may have to give to him that needeth. Let no corrupt communication proceed out of your mouth, but that which is good to the use of edifying, that it may minister grace unto the hearers. **And grieve not the holy Spirit of God,** *whereby ye are sealed unto the day of redemption."*

God can be grieved by our wrong doing as the apostle clearly states. The Holy Spirit too, who dwells within us is grieved by any unrighteousness. Would God give you permission then by grace to grieve the Holy Spirit and to hurt others? His grace is not a magic blanket that stops Him from seeing and knowing all of our actions. To the contrary Paul said, *"All things lie naked and exposed before the eyes of him with whom we have to do"* (Heb. 4:13); and Peter said, *"The face of the Lord is against them that* **do evil"** (1 Pet. 3:12).

God Sees and Knows All

"For the ways of man are before the eyes of the Lord, and he pondereth all his goings" (Prov. 5:21).

"The eyes of the Lord are in every place, beholding the evil and the good" (Prov. 15:3).

"All the ways of a man are clean in his own eyes; but the Lord *weigheth the spirits"* (Prov. 16:2).

Psalm 139:1-12

"To the chief musician, A Psalm of David, O Lord, thou hast searched me, and known me. **Thou knowest my downsitting and mine uprising, thou understandest my thoughts afar off. Thou compassest my path and my lying down, and art acquainted with all my ways, for there is not a word in my tongue, but, lo, O** Lord**, thou knowest it altogether.** *Thou hast beset me behind and before, and laid thine hand upon me. Such knowledge is too wonderful for me; it is high, I cannot attain unto it. Whither shall I go from thy*

spirit? or whither shall I flee from thy presence? If I ascend up into heaven, thou art there: if I make my bed in hell, behold, thou art there. If I take the wings of the morning, and dwell in the uttermost parts of the sea; even there shall thy hand lead me, and thy right hand shall hold me. **If I say, Surely the darkness shall cover me; even the night shall be light about me. Yea, the darkness hideth not from thee; but the night shineth as the day: the darkness and the light are both alike to thee.***"*

Genesis 6:56

*"**And God saw** that the wickedness of man was great in the earth, and that every imagination of the thoughts of his heart was only evil continually. And it repented the Lord that he had made man on the earth, **and it grieved him at his heart.***"* God saw what they were doing and the imaginations of their hearts, and He was grieved.

To say as ultra gracists do, that God only sees us one way even in rebellion and sin, is not so. He is a person; He knows about us; He gets grieved (Eph. 4:30); He is real; His warnings are plenteous; and He has promised to deal with all rebels (1 Cor. 10:5-11). There is no acceptance by God when one persists in willful rebellion against His ways. *"Wherefore (as the Holy Ghost saith, To day if ye will hear his voice, harden not your hearts, as in the provocation, in the day of temptation in the wilderness: When your fathers tempted me, proved me, and saw my works forty years. Wherefore I was grieved with that generation, and said, **They do alway err in their heart; and they have now known my ways.** So I sware in my wrath, **They shall not** enter into my rest)"* (Heb. 3:7-11). When we abide in Christ, He sees us that way, and all that's in Christ is ours. If we rebel He sees that too and deals with each person accordingly (1 John 3:6), until they repent. According to John the Apostle, anyone who says they are abiding in Christ, has to walk the walk and not just talk the talk (1 John 2:4-6), or, he says, they are lying. Those who believe in unconditional, eternal security, err in their hearts and *do not know* the righteous ways of the Lord.

Ephesians 5:1-7

*"Be ye therefore followers of God, as dear children; **and walk in love,** [fulfilling the law, Rom. 13:9-10] as Christ also hath loved us, and hath given himself for us an offering and a sacrifice to God for a sweet smelling savor. But fornication, and all uncleanness, or covetousness, let it not be once named among you, as becometh saints; Neither filthiness, nor foolish talking, nor jesting, which are not convenient: but rather giving of thanks.* **For this ye know** [clearly and understand]*, that no whoremonger, nor unclean person, nor covetous*

man, who is an idolater, **hath any inheritance** *[whatsoever] in the kingdom of Christ and of God.* **Let no man deceive you with vain words** *[with groundless arguments and empty promises saying that God won't deal with such things]:* **for because of these things cometh the wrath of God upon the children of disobedience. Be not ye therefore partakers with them**" (therefore don't throw your lot in with them). Anyone who breaks God's moral law without repentance will eventually be judged as Paul said (Heb. 10:26-30).

Let no man deceive you, Christian or not. Paul stated that you can partake of the wrath of God if you live contrary to what's right, for God's wrath impartially strikes against evil. Paul wrote in Romans 1:18, *"For the wrath of God is revealed from heaven* **against all** *ungodliness and unrighteousness of men."* All the works of the flesh are still under the curse and give place to the devil, and eventually, the wrath of God (Eph. 5:5-7). Sin is sin, whether it is committed by the Christian or the person of the world. And if there is sin, there must be law, for sin is not imputed where there is no law. But the apostles taught that there still was law (1 John 3:4-8; Rom. 8:2, 3:31; 1 Cor. 9:21; James 2:12). To speak to the contrary is to reject the words of God. To live contrary is to face certain judgment (Heb. 10:26-31). But there is no judgment if you walk after the Spirit and not the flesh. *"There is therefore now no condemnation to them which are in Christ Jesus, who walk not after the flesh, but after the Spirit"* (Romans 8:1). Do ultra gracists know that people who choose to live in ungodliness have no inheritance in the Kingdom of Christ; that wrath is due them, not blessings? Again they speak contrary to Paul who had the true scriptural revelation of grace, *"But I certify you, brethren, that the gospel which was preached of me is not after man. For I neither received it of man, neither was I taught it, but by the revelation of Jesus Christ"* (Gal. 1:11-12).

Ephesians 5:15

"See then that ye walk circumspectly [conduct your lifestyle with a sense then of responsibility], not as fools, but as wise" (men).

Ephesians 6:1-3,7-8

"Children obey your parents in the Lord: for this is right (the right thing to do in God's sight). Honor thy father and mother; **which is the first commandment with [a] promise;** *that it may be well with thee, and thou mayest live long on the earth."* Again we say, did you not notice that Paul didn't do away with this moral commandment, but revealed that it's still in force? Paul said that all he wrote were the *"commandments"* of the Lord. It reveals God's moral law. We, again, state that we are not under legalistic Jewish

ceremonies. But, anything from the Old Covenant (which has passed away), which is now in the New Covenant, is now a part of the New Covenant and is for us today! Who can deny this?

*"With good will doing service, as to the Lord, and not to men: Knowing that whatsoever good thing **any man doeth**, the same shall he receive of the Lord, whether he be bond or free"* (Eph. 6:7-8).

God will bless those that do good, but the *"face of the Lord is still against [all] them which do evil."* Good and evil are still good and evil even in this dispensation, and God still judges righteously. The God of the Old Covenant is still the same God in the New Covenant. He has just given us the grace and power to obey Him in the New Covenant, and mercy through the blood of Jesus, on the condition that we repent and confess it, so now there is no excuse to live in sin (James 2:12; John 8:34-36).

In Colossians 3:25 Paul wrote to Christians:

*"**But he** that doeth wrong **shall receive for the wrong** which he hath done: and **there is no respect of persons**."* God is dealing with each of us according to our behavior and actions, which proceed from our wills. He deals with us as to whether or not we keep His commandments, and whether or not we repent. There is no denying it unless you deny all that's taught by the apostles, the prophets, and Jesus Christ Himself; and if you reject them you reject Christianity and all it stands for. Real grace influences us to do right and then empowers us to do right. It is by grace then and by our obedience and cooperation with it, that we are saved and blessed.

Philippians 2:12

*"Wherefore, my beloved, **as ye have always obeyed**, not as in my presence only, but now much more in my absence, work out your own salvation with fear and trembling."* (Why? Because we are dealing with our eternal existence.) *"And whatsoever we ask, we receive of him, because we keep his commandments, **and do those things** that are pleasing in his sight"* (1 John 3:22). Yet even this is by the work of God as we yield to His working in us what's well pleasing in His sight (Heb. 13:20-21).

Philippians 3:13-19

*"**Brethren, I count not myself to have apprehended**: but this one thing I do, forgetting those things which are behind, and reaching forth unto those things which are before. I press toward the mark for the prize of the high calling of God in Christ Jesus. Let us therefore, as many as be perfect, be thus minded: and if in any thing ye be otherwise minded, God shall reveal even this unto you. Nevertheless, whereto we have already attained, let us walk by the same*

rule [walk in the freedom and light you've already received], let us mind the same thing.

***Brethren, be followers together of me,** [follow my example on how you are to live] **and mark them which walk so as ye have us for an ensample.** [And keep your focus on those who are living this way and teaching you to live this way, Matt. 5:19]. **(For many walk,** [live] of whom I have told you often, and now tell you even weeping, that they are the enemies of the cross of Christ [they practice living for the world just like enemies of the cross of Christ and they behave as though they hated the cross and what it stands for]: **Whose end is destruction** [eternal loss and doom], whose God is their belly [only following selfish desires], and whose glory is in their shame [proud of what they should be ashamed of], who mind earthly things.)"*

Many willingly walk contrary to God, and contrary to the cross. This means they conduct their lifestyle contrary (in opposition) to the will of God. They refuse to pick up their cross daily any longer, but have chosen ungodly, earthly things over the heavenly (Luke 9:23). They no longer keep God's commandments (Heb. 12:16-17). Paul said, *"even weeping,"* that their end is destruction, their God is not God but their own selfishness, who glory in their own shamefulness, whose mind is set on this world and its lusts. *"These are murmurers, complainers, walking after their own lusts; and their mouth speaketh great swelling words, having men's persons in admiration because of advantage. But, beloved, remember ye the words which were spoken before of the apostles of our Lord Jesus Christ; How that they told you there should be mockers in the last time, **who should walk after their own ungodly lusts.** These be they who separate themselves, sensual, having not the Spirit. But ye, beloved, building up yourselves on your most holy faith, praying in the Holy Ghost, keep yourselves in the love of God, looking for the mercy of our Lord Jesus Christ unto eternal life"* (Jude 16-21). Paul said in 2 Corinthians 12:21, that he bewailed many (Christians) that had sinned and not yet repented. To bewail means "to lament"; "weep"; "mourn over and beat the breast." Why? His concern was for their eternal well being, and all his labor in bringing them to Christ, being for nothing (1 Thess. 3:5-8).

Warning after warning, exhortation after exhortation, scripture after scripture, but with the stroke of a humanistic, theological pen the ultra gracists erase it all. They give carnal excuses made up by the crafty minds of men and substitute devilish reasonings for the Word of God, pulling secluded passages of scripture out of context, twisting their meanings, and multitudes like wandering sheep aimlessly follow them.

Oh brethren, God says we are to *"prove all things and hold fast to that* **which is good."** *"Beloved, follow not that which is evil, but that which is good.* ***He that doeth good is of God: but he that doeth evil hath not seen God"*** (doesn't understand, or perceive God, 3 John 1:11).

Time and again the apostles make the Gospel clear, and our responsibilities in it. As Paul said he preached obedience to the faith; not just a dead faith that merely says something. He realized as Jesus said, *"Not every one that saith unto me, Lord, Lord, shall enter into the kingdom of heaven; but he that doeth the will of My Father which is in heaven."* Just saying you believe is not good enough; hypocrites do that (Matt. 7:21; Mark 7:6-7). At conversion you were justified by faith. At the judgment you will be justified by whether or not you lived by faith from that point on, and whether or not you confessed your sins when you did sin (1 John 1:9; James 2:14-26; Titus 1:16; 1 Cor. 7:19).

Luke 6:46

"And **why call ye me, Lord,** *Lord, and do not the things which I say?"*

When Paul called Jesus, Lord, in Acts 9, he, like Abraham, surrendered his whole life to Christ and obeyed Him from then on. This is what he meant when he said in Romans 10:9, *"That if thou shalt confess with thy mouth the Lord Jesus, and shalt believe in thine heart that God hath raised him from the dead, thou shalt be saved."*

We may not be perfect, but we are willing to go on to perfection and walk in the light we've received. *"For to this end Christ both died, and rose, and revived, that he might be Lord both of the dead and living"* (Rom. 14:9). *"And that he died for all, that they which live should not henceforth live unto [and just for] themselves, but unto him which died for them, and rose again"* (2 Cor. 5:15). *"Who his own self bare our sins in his own body on the tree,* ***that we, being dead to sins, should live unto righteousness:*** *by whose stripes ye were healed"* (1 Pet. 2:24).

Colossians

Colossians 1:9-10

"For this cause we also, since the day we heard it, do not cease to pray for you, and to desire that ye might be filled with the knowledge of his will in all wisdom and spiritual understanding; ***That ye might walk worthy of the Lord unto all pleasing, being fruitful in every good work, and increasing in the knowledge of God.***

Here is God's desire. That you, by grace, walk worthy of the Lord fully pleasing Him by your life, *being fruitful in every good work,* and increasing in the true knowledge of God. Only when you walk pleasing to Him, can you increase in the true knowledge of God in spiritual wisdom and understanding. Anyone who lives in sin is spiritually blind and carnal (2 Pet. 1:8-9). And Paul said anyone teaching contrary to Christ and the doctrine, which is according to godliness, is *proud, knowing nothing!* If anyone teaches you that you need not live holy, he is a man full of pride and doesn't understand anything about God, or God's ways.

"This then is the message which we have heard of him, and declare unto you, that God is light, and in him is no darkness at all. If we say that we have fellowship with him, and walk in darkness, we lie, and do not the truth: But if we walk in the light, as he is in the light, we have fellowship one with another, and the blood of Jesus Christ his Son cleanseth us from all sin" (1 John 1:5-7).

Colossians 1:28

*"Whom we preach, **warning every man, and teaching every man in all wisdom**; that we may present every man perfect in Christ Jesus."*

Colossians 3:5-10

*"Mortify therefore your members which are upon the earth; fornication, uncleanness, inordinate affection, evil concupiscence, and covetousness, which is idolatry: **For which things' sake** the wrath of God cometh on the children of disobedience: In the which ye also walked some time, when ye lived in them. **But now ye also put off all these**; anger, wrath, malice, blasphemy, filthy communication out of your mouth. Lie not one to another, **seeing that ye have put off the old man with his deeds; and have put on** the new man, which is renewed in knowledge after the image of him that created him."* Man was originally created in the moral likeness of God, created to live for, and in, the will of God. This is given back to us by the Spirit in redemption (Titus 3:5), and it's for whosoever will (Rev. 22:17; Rom. 10:13; 2 Pet. 3:9; 1 John 2:1; Heb. 2:9, etc.).

"For whosoever shall do the will of my Father which is in heaven, the same is my brother, and sister, and mother" (Matt. 12:50).

1 Thessalonians 2:10

*"**Ye are witnesses, and God also, how holily and justly and unblameably we 'behaved' ourselves** among you that believe."*

God also was a witness of how they lived and of their behavior. God sees and knows all things.

Philippians 4:9

"Those things, which ye have both learned, and received, and heard, and seen in me, do: and [then] the God of peace shall be with you." Do.

Ultra gracists would tell Paul they need not do anything and the God of peace would still be with them. That there is no real need to live for God's will. Their version of grace then, exceeds God's version, but it's not so just because they say it is, or just because they want it this way. They may have their own religious beliefs but they are not faithfully holding fast to the Word of God. No one who has been duped into believing a tradition of men or doctrine of devils wants to believe it's them. Multitudes of seemingly intelligent people have been deceived by the devil in this area. Satan is a formidable foe, and only the whole counsel of God's truth can set people free. Was Paul teaching fleshly works in these above scriptures? I think not!

1 Thessalonians 2:11-12

*"**As ye know how we exhorted and comforted and charged every one of you,** as a father doth his children. **That ye would walk [live lives] worthy of God,** who hath called you unto his kingdom and glory."*

*"Thou hast a few names even in Sardis **which have not defiled their garments** [Jude 23]; and they shall walk with me in white: **for they are worthy.** He that overcometh, the same shall be clothed in white raiment; and I will not blot out his name out of the book of life, but I will confess his name before my Father, and before his angels. He that hath an ear, let him hear what the Spirit saith unto the churches"* (Rev. 3:4-6).

1 Thessalonians 3:1-8

*"Wherefore when we could no longer forbear [we were anxious to know your spiritual condition]; we thought it good to be left at Athens alone; and sent Timotheus, our brother, and minister of God, and our fellow laborer in the gospel of Christ, to establish you, and to comfort you concerning your faith: That no man should be moved [away from God] by these afflictions [and let them uproot your faith, Mark 4:17]: for yourselves know that we are appointed there unto [Matt. 5:10-12]. For verily, when we were with you, we told you before that we should suffer tribulation (Mark 4:16-17); even as it came to pass, and ye know. For this cause, when I could no longer forbear, I sent to know your faith, **lest by some means the tempter have tempted you [away from God), and our labor (in having won you to the Lord] be in vain** [and have no lasting result]. But now when Timotheus came from you unto us, and brought us good tidings of your faith and charity, and that ye have good remembrance*

of us always, desiring greatly to see us, as we also to see you: Therefore, brethren, we were comforted over you in all our affliction and distress by your faith: For now we [you], [Christians] live, if [on this condition] ye stand fast in the Lord."

So, Paul told those of Thessolonica, you now live if you stand fast in the Lord. What was Paul saying? He was concerned lest the tempter had gotten them to fall away from Christ, and his labor in the Gospel work in that area be in vain (v. 5). For the souls that remain steadfast in the Lord, Paul said, were his crown and rejoicing (vv. 7-8).

"Moreover, brethren, I declare unto you the gospel which I preached unto you, which also ye have received, and wherein ye stand; By which also ye are saved, if ye keep in memory what I preached unto you, unless ye have believed in vain" (1 Cor. 15:1-2). You must continue to believe and stand.

"Watch ye, stand fast in the faith, quit you like men, be strong" (1 Cor. 16:13).

"Put on the whole armour of God, that ye may be able to stand against the wiles of the devil" (Eph. 6:11).

"Therefore, my brethren dearly beloved and longed for, my joy and crown, so stand fast in the Lord, my dearly beloved" (Phil. 4:1).

Paul knew what the tempter was up to. He works to get people to deny Christ by living contrary to Him and to depart from Him (Titus 1:16). He works to get people to go back to their former ways of life and thereby depart from the faith. And remember as a safe guard, Paul said that the true doctrine of Christ is always according to godliness. Let no man persuade you otherwise. Godliness only has the promise of the life which is to come (1 Tim. 4:8).

Titus 1:1

*"Paul, a servant of God, and an apostle of Jesus Christ, according to the faith of God's elect, and **the acknowledging of the truth which is after godliness.**"* (The true elect acknowledge that we must live for God.) Truth will never condone, cover for, excuse, nor willingly permit ungodliness, nor sin (which is life outside of God's will), in any form. Truth is good, sin is evil, but evil repented of will be totally blotted out by God's abundant mercy. That's because a person then willingly turns back to the truth and the good will of God. Satan's doctrines always give excuses for ungodliness, saying that you can live in sin contrary to God's Word and live for Him. That God will cover for you, when God neither said nor promised any such thing, but gave severe and strong warnings against a person

going back into a life of sin outside of His will. God said, for such a person there is only a *"**certain** fearful looking for of judgment."* They have put themselves in the war zone where God's wrath must fall. God is simply telling us that it's our responsibility to stay out of the war zone, where God's wrath must fall on evil.

Romans 11:16

"For if the firstfruit [Christ] be holy, the lump [the rest] is also holy: and if the root be holy, so are the branches." Any doctrine contrary to the holiness of God is not from God. *" … No fountain can yield both salt water and fresh"* (James 3:11-12).

Matthew 7:15-20

*"Beware [then] of false prophets, which come to you in sheep's clothing, but inwardly they are ravening wolves. Ye shall know them by their fruits. Do men gather grapes of thorns, or figs of thistles? **Even so every good tree bringeth forth good fruit;** but a corrupt tree bringeth forth evil fruit. A good **tree cannot bring forth evil fruit. Every tree that bringeth not forth good** [moral] fruit is hewn down, and cast into the fire. Wherefore by their fruits ye shall know them."* A tree produces fruit that comes from its own inward nature. The doctrine of unconditional security produces corrupt fruit and therefore cannot come from a good root and righteous source.

Always look at *the final fruit* of what the doctrine is teaching. What's being gathered from them? Is it teaching godliness? Does it glorify Jesus? Does it cause unity? Is it exhorting people to live soberly, righteously, and godly in this present world? Does it give them the same warnings that Christ and the apostles did? Corrupt fruit such as a "sinning saint religion," cannot come from a good source; it comes from a corrupt, diseased source: Satan. Anything that says or implies sin is okay in any form, or that sin cannot have any affect on you even if you don't repent, is from a corrupt source. It cannot possibly come from God in whom is no darkness *at all* (1 John 1:5).

Second Timothy 3:12

"Yea, and all that will live godly in Christ Jesus shall suffer persecution."

If you preach godliness and follow after it to live it, you will receive persecution from those who don't want to believe that it is necessary. People don't like it when you mess with their corrupt, religious theories, especially if they want to continue in evil deeds and behavior. *"And this is the condemnation, that light is come into the world,* **and men loved darkness rather than light, because their deeds were evil. For every one that doeth evil hateth the light,** *neither cometh to the light,* **lest his deeds should be reproved. But he that doeth truth cometh to the light, that his deeds may be made manifest, that they are wrought in God"** (John 3:19-21). ("Deeds" means "behavior, lifestyle, and actions.")

Those who want to continue in evil behavior and deeds hate the light. But those who do truth want to come to the light. To walk in darkness and to go after sin is to walk as a fool. For God says, only *"fools make a mock of sin,"* as if it's insignificant.

1 Timothy 6:11

"But thou, O man of God, flee [and run from] these things; and follow after righteousness, godliness, faith, love, patience, meekness." Here's what people of God do and teach. Paul said to flee all forms of corruption, and flee from those who only have the form of godliness, but tell you it's not really necessary. *"Having a form of godliness, but denying the power thereof: from such turn away"* (2 Tim. 3:5).

2 Peter 1:3-11

"According as **his divine power hath given [granted] unto us all things that pertain unto life and godliness** *[everything we need to live a godly life], through the [true] knowledge of him that hath called us to [share His] glory and virtue [moral uprightness]: Whereby are given unto us exceeding great and precious promises: that by these ye might be partakers of the divine nature, having escaped the corruption [moral decay] that is in the world through lust [wrong human sensual desires and passions, Gal. 5:24]. And beside this, giving all diligence, [make every effort to] add to your faith virtue; and to virtue knowledge; and to knowledge temperance [self control]; and to temperance patience; and to patience godliness; and to godliness brotherly kindness; and to brotherly kindness charity [the God kind of love]. For if these things be in you, and abound [if these qualities are yours and increase in your life], they (will) make you that ye shall neither be barren nor unfruitful in the [true] knowledge of our Lord Jesus Christ.*

But he that lacketh these things [these qualities] is blind, [again] and cannot see afar off, and hath forgotten *that he was [once] purged from his old sins [the sins of the past].* **Wherefore the rather, brethren, give diligence [be very earnest] to make your calling and election sure [certain and beyond all doubt]: for if ye do these things, ye shall never fall [away]:** *For so an entrance* *shall be ministered unto you abundantly into the everlasting kingdom of our Lord and Savior Jesus Christ."*

First Timothy 4:7-10

*"But refuse profane and old wives fables, and **exercise thyself rather unto godliness** [stay spiritually fit]. For bodily exercise profiteth little: but **godliness is profitable** unto all things, **having promise of the life that now is, and of that which is to come.** [Godliness holds the promise of blessing the life we now live, and leads to eternal life as well.] This is a faithful saying and worthy of all acceptation. For therefore we both labor and suffer reproach, because we trust in the living God, who is the Savior [deliverer] of all men, specially of those that believe."* For it is they who truly believe what the scriptures teach who are delivered from the broad road that leads to destruction (Heb. 11:7).

Romans 2:6-8

Concerning God, Paul said, He *"will render to every man according to his deeds: To them who by patient continuance in well doing seek for glory and honor and immortality, [He will grant] eternal life: But unto them that are contentious, and do **not obey the truth, but obey unrighteousness,** he will give indignation and wrath."* We trust that God's grace empowers us to live victoriously over the devil. Grace is stronger than Satan. Christ's grace is His strength. In the New Covenant we can live the way He wants us to and keep His commandments because He has put His Spirit into us to cause us to keep His statutes and judgments (Ezek. 36:27).

Do you who believe in the ultra grace teaching, really believe the Gospel message is telling us that Christ provided a cloak for us so we can still continue to yield to, and submit to, Satan as before and join in his rebellion, and yet still remain in God's favor? Jesus said, *"Now you have **no cloak** for your sin"*; so is there really a sinning saint religion in the plan of God? There may be certain sects in professing Christendom that believe this way, but it's not Bible Christianity.

Is this the grace message? Can you really believe in a grace that says we who know God's will can willingly rebel and turn away from God and His provision? Can we now follow the course of this world following Satan again and it will really be okay, because grace made this provision? Like, I'm okay, you're okay, we're all okay? Does the whole world's sinful behavior then mean nothing to God? If so, why did Christ come and die because of it? A behavior problem, is a sin problem for *"all unrighteousness is sin."* Did Christ come so we could continue to do what the rest of the world is doing? Is grace then just a blinder for God's eyes, but makes no changes in us. Or does this glorious redemption really free us from the authority of darkness so that we can now walk as children of light and really be new creatures? Yes! A thousand times, yes!

This wrong philosophy of grace in so many books these days, comes from some teachers in the non-Spirit-filled Christian section of the body of Christ, and also from some who've come out of that camp, but have received the Holy Ghost. And it is really the *spirit* of this world and of this age at work, and it is not a product of the Holy Spirit at all, but they just don't recognize it.

Dear ultra gracists, provide us with clear scriptures that don't contradict other scriptures, if you can. The truth is, you can't. You have to twist the meanings of clear verses and water down others, and other scriptures you overemphasize or ignore. Do you suppose that the same ones who merely profess faith in His grace, but live worse than other people, will go to heaven, while they who don't even know God's will will go to hell? Is this justice? One doesn't know and lives in sin because he's still blind and bound. The other knows, was once freed, but now has directly chosen a path of rebellion against God and His will, and lives in sin. The truth is that both will be judged for their sins. (The latter greater than the former.)

Obeying the Gospel

Watch these two groups in this next verse, 2 Thessalonians 1:7-8:

*"And to you who are troubled rest with us, when the Lord Jesus shall be revealed from heaven with his mighty angels. In flaming fire **taking vengeance on them that [1] know not God, and, [2] that obey not [refuse to obey and submit to] the Gospel of our Lord Jesus Christ."***

1 Peter 4:17-18

*"For the time is come that judgment must begin at the house of God: and if it first begin at us, **what shall the end be of them that obey not the gospel of God?** And if the righteous [those living right] scarcely be saved, where shall the ungodly and the sinner appear?"* James called *the brother* that's gone back into sin a *"sinner"* (James 5:19). John said the righteous are those who, empowered by God's grace, now live righteously. Now read the scripture again.

1 Thessalonians 4:1

*"Furthermore then we beseech you, brethren, and exhort you by the Lord Jesus, that as ye have received of **us how ye ought to walk and to please God,***

so ye would abound more and more." Walking worthy and pleasing God, causes people to abound more and more. This is not the message of some of the ultra gracists who say, what you do doesn't change God's response to you. You cannot walk contrary to God and still be receiving His blessing, nor please Him, nor increase in the true knowledge of God. You will instead receive His wrath. *"For the wrath of God is revealed from heaven against all ungodliness and unrighteousness of men, who hold [and suppress] the truth [they know] in [and by their] unrighteousness"* (Rom. 1:18). It's not that God is mean, but His nature must deal with wrongdoing. He's against evil and will judge it, and so He tells men to repent so He won't have to judge them. If they repent, then yes, many times, as with the prodigal, He does show His goodness to them immediately for He rejoices over the sinner's repentance; but as the apostle taught, *"the face of the Lord is against them that do evil"* (Rev. 2:18-23).

Let's continue.

1 Thessalonians 4:2

"For ye know what commandments we gave you by the Lord Jesus."

"Commandments" is that word shunned by this ultra grace teaching. Some of them say that there are no commandments for us in the New Testament. At least not any you really have to keep. Why then did He give them? Was He just wasting His words? They are not suggestions, but *commandments*. And we've already shown numerous scriptures that if a person says they know God but does not keep His commandments, they are a liar. Shall we then listen to liars?

Here are more scriptures that show that God responds to us according to how we respond to His royal law of love.

1 Thessalonians 4:6

"That no man go beyond and defraud his brother in any matter: because that the Lord is the avenger of all such, as we also have forewarned you and testified."

1 Thessalonians 3:13_

"To the end he may stablish your hearts unblameable in holiness before God, even our Father, at the coming of our Lord Jesus Christ with all his saints." This holiness he speaks of here is not just an imputed holiness, but being holy. It's not just a word (Heb. 12:14). The true doctrine of Christ works to establish a Christian's heart unblameable in holiness (2 Pet. 3:14).

2 Thessalonians 2:9-11

Paul then talks of Satan's man of sin. *"Even him, whose coming is after the working of Satan with all power and signs and lying wonders, and **with all deceivableness of unrighteousness** [with all the delusions that unrighteousness brings] in them that perish; [and are doomed to destruction] **because they received not the love of the truth, that they might be saved. And for this cause God shall send them strong delusion, that they should believe a lie."** God changes not. (He will send them what they want.) Notice, "all deceivableness of unrighteousness." All wrong living has deception attached to it as well as any doctrine that says you can live unrighteously, or that it's okay because it's just the flesh, or just a little behavior problem. All such suggestions are the work of the old serpent, the devil.

Notice also that because they wouldn't receive the love of the truth (which Paul said was according to godliness) and because they chose to have pleasure in unrighteousness, God sent them what they wanted. He allowed them to believe a lie and believe false doctrine, and to be deceived by unrighteousness. This is what they wanted. People are free moral agents. If people want unrighteous doctrines even though God wills them to know the truth (1 Tim. 2:4), *God will still allow them to believe the lies connected with them* if it's what they choose. Remember the doctrine of Christ is always according to godliness. It always promotes and increases godly living, never any form of evil or sin or returning to the old lifestyle. Jesus, the Shepherd and Bishop of our souls, always leads us in "paths of righteousness" if we follow Him. We were as sheep gone astray, doing what's right in our own eyes, but now we are following the Good Shepherd and doing what's right in His eyes (2 Chron. 16:9). Anyone who misleads you and says you can walk a different way and do not need to obey God's commands should not *ever* be heeded or listened to. Depart from that person. *"Now I beseech you, brethren, **mark them which cause divisions and offenses contrary to the doctrine** [of godliness] **which ye have learned; and avoid them.** For they that are such **serve not our Lord Jesus Christ**, but their own belly; and by good words and fair speeches deceive the hearts of the simple"* (Rom. 16:17-18). This is what the Word of the Lord tells you to do! They are *not* servants of the Lord, no matter how nice they look or sound, but rather, tools of the devil.

*"And Simeon blessed them and said unto Mary his mother, Behold, **this child is set for the fall and rising again of many** in Israel; and for a sign which shall be spoken against (Yea, a sword shall pierce through thy own soul also); **that the thoughts of many hearts may be** [clearly] **revealed"*** (Luke 2:34-35).

Who will you really follow? Your heart and thoughts are revealed by your actions and response to Him and His will (Heb. 5:9); and God will *"bring to light the hidden things of darkness, and will make manifest the counsels of the hearts"* (1 Cor. 4:5), at the *"revelation of the righteous judgment of God"* (Rev. 2:5), when He judges the secrets of men (Rom. 2:16) according to truth. *"But we are sure that the judgment of God is according to truth against them which commit such things"* (Rom. 2:2).

2 Thessalonians 3:6,14-15

"Now we command you, brethren, in the name of our Lord Jesus Christ [by His command and authority], **that ye withdraw yourselves** *[and keep away] from every brother that walketh disorderly, and not after the tradition which he received of us [who doesn't live in agreement with the teaching we gave you]....* **And if any man obey not** *our word by this epistle [and doesn't give heed to what we've written in this letter], note that man [mark him], and have no company with him, that he may be ashamed. [Until he is ashamed of how he is living.] Yet count him not as an enemy, but admonish [caution and warn] him as a brother."*

Notice, you are to withdraw yourself from such people, mark them, and have no company with them (at least until they repent). You are not to follow such teachers, nor listen to what they have to say (1 John 4:1).

1 Timothy 1:3

"As I besought thee to abide still at Ephesus, when I went into Macedonia, that thou mightest **charge some that they teach no other doctrine.***"* Paul himself would have strongly warned and rebuked the ultra gracists for their false theories and how they have twisted his words. Ultra gracists teach another doctrine different than Paul's. This treatise is written to charge them to get back to the truth and to help others to remain steadfast in their walk with the Lord.

CHAPTER TWENTY

MORE SCRIPTURES THAT REVEAL THE TRUTH

1 Timothy 4:1

*"Now the Spirit speaketh expressly, that in the latter times **some shall depart from the faith** [they once had walked in] giving heed to seducing spirits, and doctrines of devils."*

Christians can depart from the faith for you cannot depart from something you never were in. The faith referred to is the "Christian faith." Why did they end up departing? Because of believing doctrines made up by devils, but promoted through men (1 John 4:1-2; 2 Pet. 2:1). No one would want to think they were the ones deceived, but it's obvious that some *must* fall into this category. They then no longer *contend for* and *keep* the holy faith that was once delivered to the saints.

1 Timothy 4:16

*"Take heed unto thyself, and unto the doctrine; **continue in them:** for **in doing this** thou shalt both save thyself, and them that hear thee."* Wasn't he already "saved"? Yes, but he needed to continue in the truth so as not to be deceived away from God. So by rightly dividing the Word, he would not only keep himself secure, but also keep them saved that heard him preach the truth.

1 Timothy 5:6,11-12,15

*"But she that liveth in [sinful] pleasure is [spiritually] dead while she liveth. …But the younger widows refuse: for when they have begun to wax wanton against Christ, they will marry; **having damnation, because** they have cast off*

*their first faith.... **For some [who once were in the faith] are already turned aside after Satan.***"

1 Timothy 6:17-19

"*Charge them that are rich in this world, that they be not highminded, nor trust in uncertain riches, but in the living God, who giveth us richly all things to enjoy; **that they do good**, that they be **rich in good works**, ready to distribute, willing to communicate; laying up in store for themselves a good foundation against the time to come, **that they may lay hold on eternal life.**" **That they may** *...* (Matt. 25:34). And in verse 46 of Matthew 25, you will see that He is speaking of eternal life and eternal damnation.

2 Timothy 2:1-3

"***Thou therefore, my son, be strong in [by means of] the grace that is in Christ Jesus.** And the things that thou hast heard of me among many witnesses, the same commit thou to faithful men, who shall be able to teach others also [the same exact things]. **Thou therefore endure hardness (share in the hardships), as a good [loyal and true] soldier of Jesus Christ.**" Faithful men stay right with the Gospel, which is according to godliness, and they endure hardness as good soldiers of Jesus Christ. They don't throw down the weapons of their warfare and run off with the enemy living contrary to Jesus, their own Commander-in-Chief. Peter warned us not to be like a dog that returns to its own vomit, or like a pig that goes back into the mud. Grace is given to stand strong against the evil one, not so you can follow after him back into the vomit and pollutions of the world and still be okay with the Lord (Jude 23). If one chooses to go back and follow Satan, this world, and its pollutions once again, he commits high treason (a breach of faith) just as Adam did. He then rejects the will of God and accepts the will of Satan for his life (Eph. 2:2-3). God will never compel people but gives grace to those who are willing to go on in righteousness.

"*And if it seem evil unto you to serve the* LORD, *choose you this day whom ye will serve; whether the gods which your fathers served that were on the other side of the flood, or the gods of the Amorites, in whose land ye dwell: but as for me and my house, we will serve the Lord*" (Josh. 24:15).

2 Timothy 11-13_

"*It is a faithful saying: For if we be dead with him (to a life of sin, 1 Pet. 2:24), we shall [then] also live with him [forever]: If we suffer [persevering onward, 1 Pet. 4:1-2] we shall also reign with him [in eternity]: if we deny [disown] him, he also will deny [disown] us: If we believe not, yet he abideth faithful: he cannot deny himself.*" This is God's law of sowing and reaping. In other words, you can't change Him, but you can change your relationship with Him (Isa. 59:2). (See also, Lev. 26:23-24; Deut. 31:16-17; 2 Chron. 15:2).

2 Timothy 14-19

"Of these things put them in remembrance, charging them before the Lord that they strive not about words to no profit, but to the subverting of the hearers. Study to show thyself approved unto God, a workman that needeth not to be ashamed, rightly dividing the word of truth. **But shun profane and vain [unholy and empty] babblings: for they will increase [and lead people] unto more ungodliness. And their word [false teachings] will eat as doth a canker** *[cancer and gangrene]: of whom is Hymenaeus and Philetus; who concerning the truth have erred [and gone astray],* **saying that** *the resurrection is past [and over] already; and* **by this [what they taught and said with their mouths] overthrow [and destroy] the faith of some."** (This is the potential of these false doctrines. They eat away at godliness as a cancer and even overthrow the faith of some.)

"Never the less, the [true] foundation of God standeth sure, **having this seal** *[this inscription], The Lord knoweth them that are [really] his.* **And, Let every one that nameth the name of Christ depart from iniquity."** (Everyone who says they are a Christian, must depart from, forsake, and give up, all evil and unrighteousness.) This is the seal. The Lord seals us to keep us from the wicked one. *"We know that whosoever is born of God sinneth not; but he that is begotten of God keepeth himself, and that wicked one toucheth him not"* (1 John 5:18). Notice, John did not say we are to believe we can live in sin and that grace will cover. Paul never, ever, made any such statement as the ultra gracists do; Nor did he ever say or imply, "once saved, always saved"; or "once in grace, always in grace"; but he did exhort his converts to, *"continue in the faith"; "to continue in His [God's] goodness";* and that now they would *"live," "if ye stand fast in the Lord."* So, Paul said to shun anything that promotes ungodliness, and he further spoke of some people's faith being overthrown by wrong teachings. Faith, then, can be overthrown and people can give up living the right way. Paul further said, those who say such things as, let us do evil that good may come (that God's grace may be magnified), he said *"their damnation is just"* (Rom. 3:8). Paul would tell us to turn and flee from those who persist in teaching, once in grace always in grace, regardless of how one lives.

2 Timothy 2:21 **"If** *a man therefore* **purge himself from these, he shall be a vessel unto honor, sanctified, and meet for the master's use, and prepared unto every good work."** So then, your usefulness or not, in the

kingdom also depends on whether or not you purge yourself from iniquity. Sounds as though God responds to us according to our lives and our behavior which should be *changed* by grace, not according to a humanistic view of grace.

Isaiah 52:11

*"Depart ye, depart ye, go ye out from thence, touch no unclean thing; go ye out of the midst of her; be ye clean, that bear the **vessels** of the Lord."*

2 Corinthians 4:7

"But we have this treasure in earthen vessels, that the excellency of the power may be of God, and not of us." "Wherefore come out from among them, and be ye separate (from the sinners and unbelievers), saith the Lord, and touch not the unclean thing [and don't follow their unclean paths]; and I [then] will receive you, and will be a Father unto you, and ye shall [then] be My sons and daughters, saith the Lord Almighty" (2 Cor. 6:17-18). (See also Rev. 21:7-8.)

We, as saints, are not to touch the unclean things of this world system which is following Satan (Eph. 2:2). Satan is the ruler over all those who live in lawlessness (Eph. 5:3-7). We are not saying that you cannot watch television or a movie, or go to a sporting event once in a while, but we are to stay away from seductive, vulgar, and perverse activities and things which war against the soul (Heb. 12:14). Anything that affects you that way, avoid it (Gal. 5:19-21).

2 Timothy 3:10-12

*"But thou hast fully known my doctrine, **manner [behavior] of life**, purpose, faith, longsuffering, charity, patience, persecutions, afflictions, which came unto me at Antioch, at Iconium, at Lystra; what persecutions I endured: but out of them all the Lord delivered me. Yea, and all that will live godly in Christ Jesus shall suffer persecution."*

But not those who live like the world. A religion that lives like the world is no threat to Satan. He already has them and uses them to get sinners to accuse our Christian faith. For I've heard over and over again that sinners and cults say, "you Christians think you can just say you believe and then live any way you want." I tell them no, I'm not in that category. I believe we must live for the will of God. Even sinners and cults know that the ultra gracists are wrong. They have pushed the doctrine of grace so far even the unregenerate can tell it cannot be right, but yet they, like the Pharisees, cannot. What a shame. *"Am I therefore become your enemy, because I tell you the truth?"* (Gal. 4:16). *"And the dragon was wroth with the woman, and went to make war with the remnant of her* seed, which keep the commandments of God, and have the testimony of Jesus Christ" (Rev. 12:17).

Sound Doctrine

2 Timothy 4:1-4

"I charge thee therefore before God, *and the Lord Jesus Christ, who shall judge the quick and the dead [everyone] at his appearing and his Kingdom;* **preach the word** *[not men's opinions or philosophies about it];* **be instant in season, out of season; reprove, rebuke, exhort with all longsuffering and doctrine. For the time will come [a time is coming] when they will not endure sound doctrine [the real truth]; but after their own lusts [their own selfish, sinful inclinations] shall they heap to themselves teachers [and they will accumulate for themselves teachers], having itching ears; [who will teach them what they want to hear] and they shall turn away their ears from the truth [refuse to listen to the real truth about godliness any longer], and shall** be *turned unto fables"* (fictitious doctrines, stories, and teachings made up by men and demons).

Sound doctrine will never say that you can live in lust, but people that desire to will heap and accumulate to themselves teachers that teach such things, searching high and low for those who will teach them what they want to hear, gathering their tapes and books, and seeking to spread it to others like a cancer or gangrene. There can be a spiritual spread of disease just as there is a natural spread of contagious diseases (Matt. 9:12; 2 Tim. 2:16-17).

Titus 1:1-2

"Paul, **a servant of God,** *and an apostle of Jesus Christ, according to the faith of God's elect, and the acknowledging of the truth which is [always] after godliness; [Every true servant of God will teach truth which is always according to godliness, and false teachers will teach that you can live ungodly. They are ignorantly or knowingly, a tool of the devil.]* **in hope of eternal life,** *which God, who cannot lie, promised before the world began."* Notice too, it's the hope of eternal life. It continues to be ours if we continue in the faith. *"Blessed are they that do his commandments so that they may have right to the tree of life, and may enter in through the gates into the city"* (Rev. 22:14). Ever since Adam it has been the same, and the serpent is still up to his same old tricks. He is still trying to deceive people to not obey God's commandments that they might not partake of the tree of life (Gen. 2:16-17, 3:4). He was kicked out of heaven for his sin, disobedience, and rejection of God's will, and doesn't want anyone else now to be eternally blessed in

heaven. His deadly deceptions are very crafty and very real. He has deceived multitudes. Multitudes are in hell right now, having believed in their hearts religious sounding lies.

Colossians 1:21-23

*"And you, that were sometime alienated and **enemies in your mind by wicked works** [in the past you lived in evil deeds and behavior and were God's enemy], yet now hath he reconciled [you], in the body of his flesh through death, to present you holy and unblameable and unreprovable in His sight: IF [provided that] **ye continue** in the faith, grounded and settled, and be not moved away from [nor abandoning] the hope of the gospel, which ye have heard, and which was preached to every creature which is under heaven; whereof I Paul am made a minister."* Notice the condition is, *"if ye continue"* in the faith. So then, it must be possible to decide to depart from the faith and go back to the world. It is a fight of faith to lay hold on eternal life and keep the faith. The serpent still promises many things if you just refuse God and follow him. He still is promising people the world and the glory of it, if they will just follow and worship him (Luke 4:5-8). But understand this, if the things you did before you repented and came to Christ were called *"wicked works,"* then how can some now think that you can once again return to those wicked works and not be God's enemy if they were what caused you to be His enemy in the first place? (Rom. 1:18). Paul says, *"Therefore thou art inexcusable, O man."*

Hebrews 3:14

*"For we are made partakers of Christ, **if we hold** the beginning of our confidence steadfast unto the end."* (We are to hold on until the end of our life to the faith that we had at the start of our walk with the Lord.) What about those who don't? The opposite must then be true. They will not be partakers of Christ and eternal life. You cannot have both worlds.

John 12:25-26

"He that loveth his life shall lose it; and he that hateth his life in this world shall keep it unto life eternal. If any man serve me, let him follow me; and where I am, there shall also my servant be: if any man serve me, him will my Father honor."

Revelation 2:7

*"He that hath an ear, let him hear what the Spirit saith unto the churches; **to him that overcometh [Satan and this world, 1 John 2:14, 5:4] will I give to eat of the tree of life, which is in the midst of the paradise of God."** To whom? God wants all to see where your loyalty is.

Revelation 3:5-6

*"**He that overcometh [a life of sin], the same** shall be clothed in white raiment; and I will not blot out his name out of the book of life, but I will confess his name before my Father, and before his angels. He that hath an ear, let him hear what the Spirit **saith unto the churches**."* If He threatened to blot their name out, it must have been in there. (For further proof see Rev. 22:18-19.) And the very fact that He threatened, in these passages, to take them out, shows there is no such thing as "once saved, always saved." And you that believe in predestination, how would you know that you were predestined to make it all the way to heaven? What if then you're really predestined to be another Judas? He was called, anointed, and ordained. He was a preacher. He, like the others, had his name in the book (Luke 10:20). He was an apostle of Christ and shared that ministry. He healed the sick, walked with Jesus, and so on. But, *"by transgression, fell"* away. There is no security in the teaching of predestination, for no one would really know for sure if they were truly one of the predestined ones until they actually got into heaven. So away with those carnal reasonings and doctrines of men and doctrines of devils!

Notice, these messages in Revelation are to the churches. What about those that go back to the pollutions of the world and are overcome by it? Or, as Peter said, *"What shall the end be of them that **obey not the gospel of God**?"* We understand that at any point a person like the prodigal, can come to themselves, use their will, repent, and instantly be restored by the mercy and grace of God; but they must be willing to do so. The problem is that some go so far, they are no longer willing to return. They are conquered once again by sin and bondage. Herein is the danger and deception of sin and false doctrines like those which we are discussing. For God will not give grace to an unwilling soul.

First Timothy 6:11-12

*"But thou, O man of God, flee these things; and follow after righteousness, godliness, faith, love, patience, meekness. **Fight the good fight of faith, lay hold on eternal life**, whereunto thou art also called, and hast professed a good profession before many witnesses."* (If they had already laid hold on it as a permanent possession, then there would be no real need to *"fight the good fight of faith,"* and remain steadfast to lay hold on it, for they'd already have laid hold on it permanently.)

Titus 2:1-5

"But speak thou the things which become sound doctrine: That the aged men be sober, grave, temperate, sound in faith, in charity, in patience. The aged

women likewise, **that they be in behavior as becometh holiness**, *not false accusers, not given to much wine, teachers of good things; that they may teach the young women to be sober, to love their husbands, to love their children, to be discreet, chaste, keepers at home, good,* **obedient to their own husbands**, *that the word of God be not blasphemed."* Godliness is a protection for us; sin blinds. *"But the path of the just is as the shining light, that shineth more and more unto the perfect day. The way of the wicked is as darkness: they know not at what they stumble"* (Prov. 4:18-19). If a person goes back into moral darkness, their path doesn't get brighter, but darker, so they can't be the *"just"* whose light gets brighter. They've left the *"assembly of the upright."* For the just shall live by faith, going on to perfection from glory to glory. And in those who are willing to go on even though they are weak and may stumble at times, God will perfect that which concerns them.

Titus 2:7-8,10-15

"In all things showing thyself a pattern of good works [be an example of doing good deeds]: in doctrine showing uncorruptness [moral purity], gravity, sincerity, sound speech, that cannot be condemned; that he that is of the contrary part may be ashamed, **having no evil thing to say of you**.... *[If you lived though, according to false grace, they could have many evil things to say about you.] Not purloining, but showing all good fidelity; that they may adorn the doctrine of God our Savior in all things. For* **the grace of God that bringeth salvation hath appeared to all men, teaching us** *that, denying [disowning and turning away from] ungodliness and worldly lusts [evil cravings], we should live soberly, righteously, and godly, in this present world; looking for [while we await] that blessed hope, and the glorious appearing of the great God and our Savior Jesus Christ.* **Who gave himself for us, that he might redeem us from all iniquity** *[all wrong doing], and purify unto Himself [and secure for Himself], a peculiar people, zealous of good works [who live good lives filled with good deeds].* **These things speak, and exhort, and rebuke with all authority** *[continue to boldly teach and proclaim these things].* **Let no man despise thee."**

There is a constant exhortation in the Word to live right and to deny all ungodliness, to *"awake to righteousness and sin not."* Should we not teach the same? This is the true way of righteousness and the real pathway of eternal security; the narrow way which leads to life, the true Gospel. A person *cannot go back* to live in the pollutions of the world and go back to live willingly contrary to God's commandments and end up in heaven *unless* they repent. Jesus said, *"I tell you, Nay: but, except ye repent, ye shall all likewise perish"* (Luke 13:3). All the Lord's instructions on living right, and His warnings both through His teachings in the Gospels and all through the writings of the apostles mean nothing, if we don't *really* have to keep them. Let it be known that the disobedient will not eat the good of the land (Isa. 1:18-19; 1 Pet. 3:8-12). They will rather, be devoured, *"for the mouth of the Lord hath spoken it"* (Isa. 1:19-20).

"My covenant will I not break, nor alter the thing that is gone out of my lips" (Ps. 89:34).

Titus 3:1-2,8-11

*"Put them in mind to be subject to principalities and powers, to obey magistrates, **to be ready to [perform] every good work**. To speak evil of no man, to be no brawlers, but gentle, showing all meekness unto all men.... This is a faithful saying, and these things **I will that thou affirm constantly, that they which have believed in God might be careful to maintain good works. These things are good** and profitable unto men. [For the faithful doing these things, determines eternal positions and rewards.] But avoid foolish questions, and genealogies, and contentions, and strivings about the law; for they are unprofitable and vain. A man that is an heretic after the first and second admonition reject. Knowing that he that is such is subverted [self-deceived], and sinneth, being condemned of himself."*

The word "subverted" means that their foundation has been overthrown. (Good works, in the above passage, are works that are motivated by faith and love.) The foundation of the Christian faith are repentance (turning from Satan and evil); faith towards God (living righteously by faith in His sight); and eternal judgment for those who refuse to obey God. (See Heb. 6:1-2.) These are the very basics every Christian should know. If they don't, they don't even have a proper foundation to build on. Ultra gracists have left these foundational doctrines.

To strive and fight over the Old Testament ceremonial law is unprofitable and vain. This is the big issue with ultra gracists. They have made mountains out of molehills and oceans out of a bucket of water, for we don't believe in any legalistic code of works as a means of justification. We're not telling people to get circumcised, keep Sabbath days, or festival days, and so on. It is not a matter of grace versus legalism, but rather, is grace contrary to holiness? The answer is no! Grace produces holiness and right living. This is why our lives changed when we accepted Christ, so we don't believe in Old Testament legalism, but we do believe in doing what the Word says to do in the New Covenant. Yet it's made to seem as though we are going under the Old Covenant *because we quote the New Covenant* and say, *"by love serve one another"*; that we ought to *"walk worthy and please God"* and keep God's commandments as Paul said

(1 Cor. 7:19). It's really they who don't understand which laws are done away with in Christ, and which eternal law we are to keep; nor do they really understand grace and faith. For it is the power to obey, given to those who are willing to change. *"Jesus answered and said unto them, Ye do err, not knowing the scriptures, nor the power of God"* (Matt. 22:29).

These false teachers have, so to speak, thrown the baby out with the bath water because of wrongly dividing the Word. God's moral government is still intact and operating under this new contract. Those who live contrary to it will all still suffer the consequences of breaking it, be they Christian or not (Heb. 2:1-3). Faith causes obedience. Unbelief causes disobedience. Only faith pleases God while all unbelief displeases God, and He will not bless what He's not pleased with. There are numerous scriptures that prove we must cooperate with God by doing something in order to be blessed. For example: *"But be ye doers of the word, and not hearers only, deceiving your own selves …. But whoso looketh into the perfect law of liberty, and continueth therein, he being not a forgetful hearer, **but a doer of the work, this man shall be blessed** in his deed"* (James 1:22,25). We are commanded to love, pray, do good works, tithe, live holy, purge ourselves, cleanse ourselves, deny ourselves, turn ourselves from sin, repent, have faith, fast, let peace rule in our hearts, not to speak evil, not to think evil, not backbite, or commit fornication. We are to judge ourselves when we do wrong, confess our sins, examine ourselves, edify ourselves, prepare ourselves, walk in the light, follow that which is good, walk as Christ walked, and numerous other things that are our responsibility. These actions of faith are what put us in position to receive the blessings (1 John 3:18-22). *"So then every one of us shall give account of himself to God"* (Rom. 14:12). This is also *"the faith that was once delivered to the saints."*

Realize that we believe no more or no less than what the scriptures actually do say. We accept the *"whole counsel of God"* that Paul taught, not just certain secluded or twisted texts to fit a pet doctrine, as do the ultra gracists.

Concerning any church or ministry, people should be able to just read every scripture the apostles or Jesus said, and say after that, "Our pastor (minister) believes this, and believes it is for us today." (See Matt. 28:18-20.) Can the ultra gracists do this? No, they cannot! And all I want to accomplish by this treatise is to feed God's people the true manna from heaven so that they are strong in these last days, stay in the race, and stay true to the Lord. There will come a dividing of the ways between those who will serve the LORD and those who will not in these days. *"And if it seem evil unto you to serve the Lord, choose you this day whom ye will serve; whether the gods which your fathers served that were on the other side of the flood, or the gods of the Amorites, in whose land ye dwell: but as for me and my house, we will serve the LORD"* (Josh. 24:15). Concerning these last days Christ said, *"And because iniquity shall abound, the love [agape, Christian love] of many shall wax cold. [Zeal for the Lord and His house will be lost.] But he that shall endure unto the end, the same [that is the person that] shall be saved"* (Matt. 24:12-13). Don't let the spirit of disobedience in society lead you astray and quench your love for God. And remember, to love God is to keep His commandments (1 John 5:3, 2:4). And His Kingdom is promised to them that love Him (James 1:12; 1 Cor. 2:9).

Hebrews

Again let's see Hebrews 2:1-3:

"Therefore we [Christians] ought to give the more earnest heed [pay close attention] to the things which we have heard, lest at any time we should let them slip [or we will drift from them]. For if the word spoken by angels was steadfast [proved to be binding and true], and every transgression and disobedience received a just recompense of reward [every transgression of it or refusal to obey it met with just retribution and penalty]; **how shall we** *[Christians] escape [What makes you think you can escape?]; if* **we neglect** *[and ignore the warnings of] so great salvation;* **which at the first began to be spoken by the Lord***, and was confirmed unto us by them that heard him."* (The ultra gracists would say, "Paul don't you know we escape by grace?") I tell you, the ultra gracist's doctrine is a work of the cunning craftiness of men who have listened to the serpent. It is not the teaching of the Word. It sounds nice, at least for those who pridefully think they are the special elect, but it's not true. All counterfeits and imitations look like they could be the real things until they are investigated. The broad road never leads to heaven; and every tree is known by its own fruit.

Can Satan's version of grace save a person? Certainly not! The Lord will judge all who obey not the Gospel (2 Thess. 1:8). Multitudes are on their way to hell, thinking they will go to heaven. *"Strive to enter in at the strait gate: for many, I say unto you, will seek to enter in, and shall not be able"* (Luke 13:24).

Israel's Example to Us

Listen to the apostle as he speaks concerning these Hebrew Christians:

Hebrews 3:1

*"Wherefore, **holy brethren, partakers of the heavenly calling**, consider the Apostle and High Priest of our profession, Christ Jesus; who was faithful to him that appointed him, as also Moses was faithful in all his house."* (Note who He's speaking to, to brethren!)

Hebrews 3:7–4:2

*"Wherefore [as the Holy Ghost saith], Today **if ye** will hear his voice, **harden not your hearts**, as in the provocation, in the day of temptation in the wilderness: When your [fore] fathers tempted me, proved me, and saw my works forty years. Wherefore I was grieved [displeased] with that generation, and said, They do alway err [and go astray] in their heart; and they have not known My ways [Nor recognized My paths]. So I sware in my wrath, They shall not enter (be admitted) into my rest. **Take heed, brethren** [so be careful fellow Christians], lest there be in any of you an evil heart of unbelief, **in departing from the living God.** [A heart of unbelief that shows itself by turning away from the living God, just like those who fell away before.] But exhort [and warn] one another daily, while it is called Today; lest any of you be hardened through the deceitfulness of sin. **For we are made partakers of Christ**, if [on this condition that] we hold the beginning of our confidence steadfast unto the end; while it is said, **Today if ye will hear His voice, harden not your hearts**, as in the provocation. For some, when they had heard [the message God gave], did provoke: howbeit not all that came out of Egypt by Moses. **But with whom was he grieved forty years? Was it not with them that had sinned** [and gone astray], whose carcasses fell in the wilderness? And to whom sware he that they should not enter into his rest, but to them that believed not? [and proved to be unfaithful]. So we see that they could not enter in because of unbelief. **Let us therefore [have godly] fear**, lest, a promise being left us of entering into his rest, **any of you** [Christians] should seem to come short of it. For unto us was the gospel preached, as well as unto them: but the word preached did not profit them, not being mixed with (real) faith in them that heard it.*

*[We are to surrender our hearts and lives to the finished work of Christ and let it work in us.] **Let us labor [and be diligent] therefore to enter into that rest** [of giving up all of the dead works and ways of our old life], **lest any man** [among you Christians] **fall after the same example of unbelief"** (as Israel did because of disobedience).*

Israel left Egypt in faith, and were delivered by the blood of the Lamb and the power of God, and were all baptized in the sea; but then they rebelled in the wilderness, went back into unbelief, and their carcasses eventually fell in the *"Wilderness of Sin."* They never did enter the

Promised Land. Paul said for Christians to be diligent lest they fall after the same example of unbelief and die in sin, or depart from the living God in their hearts like those Israelites did and incurred the wrath of God. Remember, God being good, His wrath is against evil and He will devour it, for our God is a consuming fire.

Hebrews 5:8-9

Concerning Jesus, *"Though he were a Son, yet learned he obedience by the things which he suffered; and being made perfect, he became the author of eternal salvation **unto all them that obey him.**"*

To all that what? That obey Him, comply with His commands, and are subject to His government. Lucifer's fall came when he left the boundaries set by God's Word, no longer submitted himself to God's government and will, but chose a path of selfishness and independent self-will. And it's the same for all other free moral agents.

How clear the Word is. Don't just jump at every interpretation just because someone gives it, or writes it in a book and puts a fancy cover on it, or brashly criticizes the true way of the Lord. *"Prove all things, **hold fast to that which is good.**"* And prove it all by the Word. Let the Word speak for, and interpret, itself. Read all the scriptures that pertain to a subject and then obey them. This is the way to true security.

Paul's Warning

Hebrews 6:4-8

Now he speaks concerning those who were mature Christians and have fallen away. *"For it is **impossible** for those who were once enlightened [by the work of the Holy Spirit], and have tasted of the heavenly gift [the gift of eternal life from heaven], and were made partakers of the [Baptism with the] Holy Ghost, and have tasted [experienced] the good word of God, and the powers of the world to come, **if they shall fall away** [and commit apostasy], to renew [or bring] them [back] again unto repentance; seeing they crucify to themselves the Son of God afresh [labeling Him an imposter in the sight of the world], after their open confession and witness of him, and put him to an open shame [by their actions]. For the earth which drinketh in the rain that cometh oft upon it, and bringeth forth herbs meet for them by whom it is dressed, receiveth blessing from God: But that which [later] beareth thorns and briers is rejected, and is nigh unto cursing; **whose end is to be burned.**"*

These Christian people he speaks of:

(1) Were enlightened as to the truth.

(2) Tasted of the heavenly gift (salvation, Rom. 6:23).

(3) Were filled with the Holy Ghost.

(4) Operated in the gifts of the Spirit.

Paul said, if they apostatize and turn from obedience back to what they once believed and lived in, and produce thorns and briers rather than good fruit, it is impossible for them to come back because they have crossed certain boundaries. Not that God wouldn't accept them back if they repented, but that they would not return, because to get to this point, they had to constantly go against the light they had and override their conscience, and the effect was, and is, devastating. Their conscience became seared as with a hot iron (1 Tim. 4:1-2). They had at one time, drunk in the blessings of God and produced good herbs, but now were producing thorns and briars *"**whose end** (Paul said) is to be burned."*

God's warnings are sure. *"He, that being often reproved hardeneth his neck, shall suddenly be destroyed, and that without remedy"* (Prov. 21:1). This is what happened to Pharaoh (Gal. 6:7).

Philippians 3:17-19

"Brethren, be followers together of me, and mark them which walk so as ye have us for an ensample. (For many walk, of whom I have told you often, and now tell you even weeping, that they are the enemies of the cross of Christ."

Let us continue.

Hebrews 10:15-19 says:

*"Whereof the Holy Ghost also is a witness to us: for after that he had said before, this is the covenant that I will make with them **after those days**, saith the Lord [in this New Covenant], **I will put my laws into their hearts, and in their minds will I write them**; and their sins and iniquities will I remember no more. Now where remission of these is, there is no more offering for sin. Having therefore brethren, boldness to enter into the holiest by the blood of Jesus."*

God's laws are now written in our hearts by the Spirit of God, not done away with.

Notice in Hebrews 10:15-19, he is speaking to brethren who have been cleansed by the blood of Jesus and have God's laws written in their hearts by the Spirit of God. Listen now to the apostle's warning and exhortation to these Christians.

Hebrews 10:26-31

*"For if **we** [as Christians who have God's law written in our hearts] sin willfully [go back to a life of willful and persistent sinning and living contrary to God and His laws or go back to a religion that would deny Christ's divinity and salvation] after that we have received the knowledge of the truth [that to be*

*saved we needed to repent, believe, and follow Jesus], there remaineth no more sacrifice for sins [for it's available only to the repentant, so there is no sacrifice that will automatically cover a life of willful sinning], but [there is only] **a certain** fearful looking for of judgment and fiery indignation (a fury of fire), which shall devour [and consume] **the adversaries** [all those who oppose God, James 4:4]. He that despised [looked down on as insignificant] Moses' law died without mercy under two or three witnesses: Of how **much sorer** [more severe] **punishment, suppose ye, shall he be thought worthy**, who hath trodden under foot the Son of God, and hath counted the blood of the covenant, **wherewith he was [at one time] sanctified**, an unholy thing, and hath done despite unto the Spirit of grace? [Who had come to free him from the works of the flesh, Rom. 8:4, 12-13]. For we know Him that hath said, Vengeance [retribution] belongeth unto Me, I will recompense, saith the Lord. And again, The Lord shall judge his people. It is a fearful [dreadful and terrifying] thing to fall into the hands of the living God."*

If we "sin willfully": This must mean to go back to a life of persistent, willful sinning *without repentance* for John said in 1 John 2:1, *"My little children, these things I write unto you, that ye sin not, and if any man sin, we have an advocate with the Father, Jesus Christ the righteous."* There is always forgiveness for all manner of sins, if we confess them to God and judge ourselves. The great High Priest will then cleanse us with His blood.

But for those who have received the knowledge and understanding of the truth (Heb. 10:26), and turn from it by choice because of the pleasures of sin, and are not willing to return, there is only certain judgment awaiting them. It is not a matter of love as to whether God loves man or not; it's a legal issue. God loves the whole world, but tens of thousands go to hell every day regardless, because they will not come to God for mercy. They are in the war zone where the wrath of God is judging evil. Don't live there. God doesn't will any of them to perish, but wants *all* to come to repentance (2 Pet. 3:9) so He can have mercy on them all. But multitudes go to hell regardless of God's grace, God's love, and God's provision of mercy. God's great, unmerited love made provision and a way of escape, but He still always needs the cooperation of the free moral agent's will (Rev. 22:17). He sovereignly chose it to be this way, for He works all things after the counsel of His own will.

So remember, the will sets the direction either down the broad road of destruction, or the narrow road that leads to life. You cannot travel down both roads at the same time.

If the people willingly go astray from God following the pleasures of sin, serving various lusts, or return to a false, religious view of Christ after they had already escaped these pollutions through the knowledge of our Lord and Savior Jesus Christ, then they will receive the reward of unrighteousness as Peter also said. It is just that way and it cannot be changed.

Hebrews 10:29

*"**Of how much sorer punishment** (worse punishment), suppose ye, shall he [that Christian] be thought worthy, who hath trodden under foot the Son of God, and hath counted the blood of the Covenant, **wherewith he was [once] sanctified**, an unholy thing, and hath done despite unto the Spirit of grace?"* Greater is the judgment that will fall on a Christian who turns from God back to Satan, than those under the Old Covenant who turned from, and rebelled against, Moses' law. Jesus said, *"Woe unto thee, Chorazin!... For if the mighty works, which were done in you, had been done in Tyre and Sidon, **they would have repented** [turned from their lives of sin] long ago in sackcloth and ashes .... But I say unto you, That **it shall be more tolerable** for the land of Sodom in the day of judgment, than for thee"* (Matt. 11:21, 24). Because they were responsible for more light that they refused to obey.

So evidently, a person can get to the place where they count the blood of the Covenant that had sanctified them, to be a common thing, and continually resist the Spirit of Grace who was sent to help them live right. If this be the case, all that's left for them is the fruit of their own ways. (See Prov. 1:23-32.) For God's Spirit will not always strive with a man but will let them take their own course if it's what they really want. (As it says in Romans chapter one, if they give God up He will give them up to a reprobate mind.) *"And even as **they did not** like to retain God in their knowledge, **God gave them over** to a reprobate mind, to do those things which are not convenient [that is to improper and indecent conduct]; Being filled with all **unrighteousness**, fornication, wickedness, covetousness, maliciousness; full of envy, murder, debate, deceit, malignity; whisperers, backbiters, haters of God, despiteful, proud, boasters, inventors of evil things, disobedient to parents, without understanding, covenantbreakers, without natural affection, implacable, unmerciful: **Who knowing the judgment of God, that they which commit such things [as these] are worthy [and deserving] of death, not only do the same, but have pleasure in them that do them"** (Rom. 1:28-32). (Notice that this is a list of unrighteousness.) God says that anyone who lives in these things as a way of life, is worthy of death; and those who consistently live like that have a reprobate mind.

Hebrews 10:31

"It is a fearful [terrifying] thing to fall into the hands of the living God."

Hebrews 12:12-17

"Wherefore lift up the hands which hang down, and the feeble knees; **and make straight paths for your feet, lest that which is lame be turned out of the way** *[cause you to turn from the path of righteousness]; but let it rather be healed. Follow peace with all men, and [follow] holiness, without which* **no man** *shall see the Lord:* **Looking diligently** *lest any man [among you Hebrew Christians] fail of [Greek: forfeit or fall from] the grace of God; lest any root of bitterness springing up trouble you, and thereby many be defiled;* **lest there be any fornicator** *[among you Christians], or profane [immoral] person, as Esau, who for one morsel of meat* **sold his birthright** *[gave up his own firstborn* **rights]. For ye know how that afterward, when he would have inherited the blessing, he was rejected** *[and refused]: for he found no place of repentance [no way to repair what he had done], though he sought it carefully [and pleaded for it] with tears"* (to get it back after it was too late). Again, it's possible to fall away from, or forfeit, the grace of God by habitually choosing the wrong over the right and coming to a place where you are no longer willing to repent. Never put away a *"good conscience"* (1 Tim. 1:19). Don't play on thin ice for at some point you may fall through. And in hell, God says, *"Repentance shall be hid from Mine eyes"* (Hosea 13:14; Heb. 9:27).

Hebrews 12:28-29

"Wherefore we receiving a kingdom which cannot be moved, let us **have grace, whereby we may serve** *God acceptably* **with reverence and godly fear:** *For our God is a consuming fire."* (Grace is given to serve God, not to serve sin; to keep God's commandments, not to break them.) Ultra gracists have everything backwards. Their false doctrine sends multitudes to hell by the decree of God, and then makes them the elect and blessed ones regardless of how they live. Thank God their doctrine is wrong (James 1:16-17).

"For I have no pleasure in the death of him that dieth, saith the Lord God: wherefore turn yourselves, and live ye" (Ezek. 18:32).

Follow the Right Way

Hebrews 13:7-9

"Remember them which have the rule over you who have spoken unto you the word of God: **whose faith follow,** *considering the end of their conversation [way of life]. Jesus Christ the same yesterday, and today, and forever. Be not carried about with divers and strange doctrines. For it is a good thing that the heart be established [and made stable in the things of God] with grace; not with meats [Jewish ceremonial ordinances], which have not profited them that have*

been occupied therein." Grace establishes the heart in the things of God, not outward rituals or not eating certain things.

1 Thessalonians 5:15

*"See that none render evil for evil unto any man; but ever **follow** that which is good, both among yourselves, and to all men."*

1 Timothy 6:11

*"But thou, O man of God, flee these things; and **follow** after righteousness, godliness, faith, love, patience, meekness."*

2 Timothy 2:22_

*"Flee also youthful lusts: but **follow** righteousness, faith, charity, peace, with them that call on the Lord out of a pure heart."*

2 Timothy 3:1-5

*"This know also, that in the last days perilous times shall come, for men shall be lovers of their own selves, covetous, boasters, proud, blasphemers, disobedient to parents, unthankful, unholy [not consecrated to God], without natural affection, trucebreakers, false accusers, incontinent, fierce, despisers of those that are good [they will look down upon those who are good], traitors [they will betray their friends and those who have blessed them], heady, highminded [inflated with self importance], lovers of pleasures more than lovers of God [they will put selfish pleasures in the place of God and His will]; **having a form of godliness, but denying the power thereof: from such turn away."***

Hebrews 12:14

*"**Follow** peace with all men, and (follow) holiness, **without which no man shall see the Lord."*** It is obvious when Paul spoke of legalism and works of the law he spoke of the outward, carnal ordinances, not heart righteousness and godliness. If living righteously and godly were at all legalism, Paul then never ceased to tell people to be legalistic. Paul furthermore, preached *"obedience to the faith,"* never just a verbalizing of it as some erroneously supposed he did.

2 Peter 2:21-24

*"For even hereunto were ye called: because Christ also suffered for us, leaving us an example, that ye should **follow his steps: Who did no sin,** neither was guile found in his mouth: Who, when he was reviled, reviled not again; when he suffered, he threatened not; but committed himself to him that judgeth righteously: Who his own self bare our sins in his own body on the tree, **that we, being dead to sins, should live unto righteousness:** by whose stripes ye*

were healed." Our relationship with sin is dead. We no longer fellowship with it as before. For, *"he that is dead, is freed from sin."* It is not *just* imputed righteousness, but, *"live unto righteousness."* We are *"kept by the power of God through faith"* from a life of sin. For Jesus came to *"save us **from** our sins"* (not in them); and He whom *"the Son sets free is free indeed."* People who teach that grace means you can now live in sin, teach just the opposite of the Bible. If you're saved from drowning, you're pulled out of the water. If you're saved from a fire, you're pulled out of the fire. If you're saved from a car wreck, you're pulled from the wreck. If you're saved from sin, you're pulled out of a life of sin. *"For by grace are ye saved through faith; and that not of yourselves: it is the gift of God"* (Eph. 2:8). Grace pulled you out of sin's power. He saved us *"from our sins."* *"For the law of the Spirit of life in Christ **Jesus hath made me free from the law of sin and death"*** (Rom. 8:2). *"And of some have compassion, making a difference: and others save with fear, **pulling them out** of the fire; hating even the garment spotted by the flesh"* (Jude 22-23). ***"Who hath delivered us from the power of darkness,*** *and hath translated us into the kingdom of his dear Son"* (Col. 1:13). Our deliverance is not while we live like those in the kingdom of darkness, but a deliverance from darkness and a life of sin. He has *"called us **out of** darkness into His marvelous light."* This is what leads to life. This is salvation; saved from sin (Matt. 1:21); saved from spiritual death and Satan (Eph. 2:1-8); saved from the pollutions of the world (2 Pet. 2:20-21), and so on. There is no such thing as once saved from drowning, always saved from drowning. Especially if the man who was saved throws himself back into the very thing that caused his dilemma in the first place. (See also, Matt. 24:13; 1 Cor. 15:1-2; 2 Thess. 2:10-11; 1 Pet. 4:18; 2 Pet. 2:5; Jude 6).

2 Peter 2:1-2

*"But there were false prophets also among the people, even as **there shall be false teachers** [who teach false doctrines] among you [Christians], who privily [secretly unnoticed] shall bring in damnable heresies [cunningly bringing into the church fatal heresies], even [to the point of] **denying the Lord that bought them**, and bring upon themselves swift destruction [and ruin]. **And many [people] shall follow** their pernicious [morally loose] ways; by reason of whom the way of truth shall be evil spoken of"* (and discredited). The professing church that doesn't really live and obey the faith, is a great part of the reason why the world isn't saved. Many do not believe in Christianity after seeing the lives of those who profess to be religious but do not "obey the faith." It is then discredited by this, just as the Jews also caused God's name to blasphemed. *"And art confident that thou thyself art*

a guide of the blind, a light of them which are in darkness, An instructor of the foolish, a teacher of babes, which hast the form of knowledge and of the truth in the law. Thou therefore which teachest another, teachest thou not thyself? thou that preachest a man should not steal, dost thou steal? Thou that sayest a man should not commit adultery, dost thou commit adultery? thou that abhorrest idols, dost thou commit sacrilege? Thou that makest thy boast of the law, through breaking the law dishonourest thou God? For the name of God is blasphemed among the Gentiles through you, as it is written" (Rom. 2:19-24). Some of these false teachers will even say that you can deny the Lord that bought you and still be saved. But Peter said they bring destruction on themselves and many will follow their lawless ways. Pernicious means, thinking they can live in unbridled passions and uncleanness and that they are still okay with God. These lose all sense of shame. Read on and see what Peter says in 2 Peter, chapter 2. True grace is what we need. Not a product, as Paul said, of *"the cunning craftiness of men whereby they lie in wait to deceive."* Combining a few translations this scripture says, that we should be *"no longer like infants tossed to and fro and carried about by every wind of doctrine through the trickery of men with their ingenuity in inventing error and their crafty presentation of error as truth."*

Hebrews 13:17,20-21

*"**Obey** them that have the rule over you, and submit yourselves [to those God called and set in the church as shepherds and leaders]: for they watch for your souls [they are watchmen standing guard over your souls], as they that must give an account."* (Pastors who are born again, filled with the Holy Ghost, and God-called, have a supernatural anointing to guard the sheep from the wolf's many disguises. They stand in a position as shepherd of the flock. Sheep shouldn't just go feed on any pasture, eating anything they find.) (See Acts 20:28-32.) Obey God anointed leaders. *"That they may do it with joy, and not with grief: for that is unprofitable for you [you will lose much reward if you cause them grief].... Now the God of peace, that brought again from the dead our Lord Jesus, that great shepherd of the sheep, through the blood of the everlasting covenant, **make you perfect in every good work to 'do' his will, working in you that which is well pleasing in his sight**, through Jesus Christ; to whom be glory for ever and ever. Amen."* God's work in you is to move you to live right in His sight, not to excuse evil; to do good works, not to condemn good works.

The Truth in the Book of James

One ultra grace teacher says that you neither need to love God, nor submit to Jesus' Lordship to be saved. This is an actual thing that was said. This person is teaching outright lies in the name of the Lord. Woe to the man that goes about uprooting people from good churches and causes God's children to stumble back into sin. *"But whoso shall offend [cause to stumble] one of these little ones which believe in me, it were better for him that a millstone were hanged about his neck, and that he were drowned in the depth of the sea"* (Matt. 18:6). (See Luke 6:46; 1 Cor. 2:9.)

James 1:12

*"Blessed is the man that endureth temptation [remains firm in his living by faith]: for when he is tried [when he has stood the test], he shall receive the crown of life, which the Lord hath **promised to them that love Him.**"* To whom is the crown of life promised? *To them that love Him.* And John said, if we love Him we will keep His commandments (2 John 1:6).

1 Corinthians 2:9

*"But as it is written, Eye hath not seen, nor ear heard, neither have entered into the heart of man, the things **which God hath prepared for them that love him.**"* *"My little children, let us not love in word, neither in tongue; but in deed and in truth"* (1 John 3:18). The Lord is not going to say, "Well *said* thou good and faithful servant," but rather, "*well done.*"

It's obvious then that that teacher doesn't know what he's talking about when he says that you don't need to love God. Does he think, as the Nicolaitanes, that the death of his physical body will bring about a change of heart? If we don't love God now and live for Him here, we wouldn't want to live for Him in heaven either. *"Choose you **this day** whom you will serve."* *"As for me and my house we will **serve** the Lord."*

Now James' letter is written to brethren (to Christians).

James 1:1-2

*"James, a servant of God and of the Lord Jesus Christ, to the twelve tribes which are scattered abroad, greeting. **My brethren,** count it all joy when ye fall into divers temptations."* Notice: "brethren."

James 2:1

"My brethren, have not the faith of our Lord Jesus Christ, the Lord of glory, with respect of persons."

James 2:8

*"**If ye** [My brethren] fulfill **the royal law** according to the scripture, Thou shalt love thy neighbor as thyself, ye do well."* This royal law is directly taken from what God said in the Old Testament. It still stands. God included it in the New Covenant. This law is part of the Gospel.

Notice: "*if ye brethren*." What then if you don't fulfill the royal law? Then you don't do well.

James 2:9

"*But if ye* have respect to persons, *ye commit sin, and are convinced of the law as transgressors.*" Christians can still transgress God's moral law and commit sin, and when they do they still must confess it (1 John 1:9). The wages of sin is still death, for going unconfessed, if you serve it long enough, it will always lead a soul down a wrong pathway towards destruction (Rom. 6:23).

James 2:10-12 James, in writing to brethren says,

"*For whosoever shall keep the whole law, and yet offend in one point, he is guilty of all. For he that said, Do not commit adultery, said also, Do not kill. Now if thou commit no adultery, yet if thou kill, thou art become a transgressor of the law. So speak ye, and so do, as they that shall be judged by the law of liberty.*" But clearly see that the moral law continues to exist with all of its consequences if broken, unless one repents.

James is saying that Christ has freed you from the law of sin, death, and Satan, by His grace, so that you can now live right, so speak and act accordingly. ("*That we being dead to sin should live unto righteousness.*") Notice James, like Paul, shows that the law, as far as the moral law goes, is still intact. Christians have no permission to think they can now live contrary to it. Instead, they are freed from the power of sin and lawlessness and can now walk in the Spirit and in love, and as Paul said, "*fulfill the law.*"

1 Peter 4:2

"*That he no longer should live the rest of his time in the flesh to the lusts of men, but to the will of God.*" Why? Because the Lord has set us free from the old life and made us new creatures (Eph. 2:10). His anointing destroyed the yoke of bondage and freed us from sin's slavery.

James 2:13

"*For he shall have judgment without mercy, that hath showed no mercy; and mercy rejoiceth against judgment.*"

So again He does respond to us depending on our response, not according to a presumed idea of grace which implies grace will cover over for works of darkness and somehow mysteriously make you look righteous in God's sight while you live in sin. You have Christ's perfect righteousness if you confess your unrighteousness and continue to walk with Him. Listen to the apostle Paul. Ephesians 5:11-12: *"And have no fellowship with the unfruitful works of darkness, but rather reprove them. For it is a shame even to speak of those things which are done of them in secret."* So, "works" here means behavior.

Reread the verse.

If it's a shame to even speak of those things, certainly He never taught of a grace that gives a person a license to live in them.

Ephesians 2:2:

*"Wherein **in time past** [before you were a Christian] ye walked according to the course of this world, according to the prince of the power of the air, **the spirit that now worketh in the children of disobedience.**"* Where there is disobedience, there is another spirit at work, and God doesn't bless us when we yield to the spirit of disobedience. Whenever anyone says or teaches that you're now free to sin or not sin because of grace, it is the spirit of disobedience working through that person, not the Holy Spirit. The Holy Spirit will always say, *"be ye holy for I am holy."*

James 2:14,26

*"What doth it profit [then], **my brethren**, though a man say he hath faith, and have not works [Corresponding behavior]? Can [that kind of] faith save him? For as the body without the spirit is dead, so faith without works [corresponding behavior and actions] is dead also."*

So, James says that those people who just say, I have faith, and don't live it, have dead faith. Yes, it takes repentance and faith, not the dead works of the polluted sinner, to justify a person. But then after a person is justified and becomes a new creature saved by grace, faith frees them from their old way of life, and their actions express if their faith is genuine or not. If they say they have faith and are not saved from the old way of life, that kind of faith cannot save them (James 2:14-26). Saving faith shows itself in a person's behavior. It saves us from our old way of life. This was James' declaration. (See also 1 John 3:3-7.) You cannot be saved without it, but if you are saved and have it, you're saved from your old sinful way of life. James 2:19-20: *"Thou believest that there is one God; thou doest well: the devils also believe, and tremble. But wilt thou know, O vain man, that faith without works [corresponding behavior] is dead?"* If saying that you believe was all that was necessary to be saved, the demons too would be saved, for they believe and even confess Jesus is the Son of God (Luke 4:41). Faith justifies at conversion, but works, which is the result of the faith in the heart, which simply means deeds and actions of one's life, prove that you have saving faith. *"But wilt thou know, O vain man, that faith without works is dead? Was not Abraham our father justified by works, when he had offered Isaac his son upon the altar? Seest thou how faith wrought with his works, and by works was faith made perfect? And the scripture was fulfilled which saith, Abraham believed God, and it was imputed unto him for righteousness: and he was called the Friend of God. Ye see then how that by works a man is justified, and not by faith only. Likewise also was not Rahab the harlot justified by works, when she had received the messengers, and had sent them out another way? For as the body without the spirit is dead, so faith without works is dead also"* (James 2:20-26).

James 4:4_

"Ye adulterers and adulteresses [unfaithful people], know ye not that the friendship of the world is enmity with God? **Whosoever therefore** *will [go back and] be a friend of the world is the enemy of God."* (In other words he takes his stand as God's enemy.)

The only two things Christ taught that could break a marriage Covenant was, (1) adultery (Matt. 19:9), and (2) If an unbelieving spouse depart, let him depart (Heb. 3:12-13; 1 Cor. 7:15). And so it is with our union and walk with Christ (John 6:66).

This too is spoken to brethren. Jesus said, *"Ye are my friends **IF** ye do whatsoever I command you."* He said, *"He that loveth me not, keepeth not my words, but he that hath my commandments and keepeth them,* **he it is** *that loveth me."* Jesus said, *"He that loveth his life shall lose it; and he that hateth his life in this world shall keep it unto life eternal. If any man serve me,* **let him follow me***; and where I am, there shall also my servant be:* **if any man serve Me, him** *will my Father honor"* (John 12:25-26). Paul said that whoever you obey, his servant you are. Again, Jesus obeyed His Father and kept all His commandments and He is the author of faith, so obedience to God and His commandments is faith.

James 4: 6

"But he giveth more grace [to those who love Him, Eph. 6:24]. Wherefore He saith, God resisteth the proud, but giveth grace unto the humble."

Here James reveals that if you're proud and want to go your own way God, then, won't give you more grace, but He will resist you. He will respond to you according to your heart (Acts 10:34). He resists the proud just as He did Pharaoh, who wouldn't obey or yield to His Word. Therefore His response is according to each individual heart; and we all know it is possible for any free, moral agent to be prideful and that being so, God would then resist that person rather than give them grace in that area of their life. At least until they repent or come to Him for deliverance from their pride (Heb. 4:16).

James 4:8,10

"Draw nigh to God, and [then] He will draw nigh to you. Cleanse your hands, ye sinners; and purify your hearts, ye double minded.... Humble yourselves in the sight of the Lord, and he shall lift you up."

James was obviously speaking to those who believed in the Lord. If you don't humble yourself, neither will He lift you up. If you don't draw near to Him then neither will He draw near to you. God responds then to both individuals differently depending on their actions and behavior (Gal. 6:7).

James 5:19-20

*"**Brethren, if any of you** do err [are led astray] from the truth, and one convert him [turning him back to the narrow road which leads to life]; let him know, that he which converteth the sinner [the brother that's gone astray] from the error of his way shall save **a soul from death**, and shall hide a multitude of sins."*

Note: *"brethren."* A brother that goes astray and goes back into a life of sin is once again called a sinner, and is again headed for eventual spiritual death if he doesn't turn around. At some point, it is possible for people to give up walking and living by faith for the will of God, and return once again to their former lives, to quit the race, and no longer fight the good fight, but surrender back to the enemy (John 6:66).

1 Peter 1:13

*"Wherefore gird up the loins of your mind, be sober, and **hope to the end for the grace that is to be brought unto you at the revelation of Jesus Christ."***

More grace will be given at the end of your life or when Jesus comes, provided you've responded to what's already given. Grace is given for different things. It's called *"the manifold grace of God."* If you've been faithful with what's given, more grace will be given at the revelation of Jesus Christ. But remember the five virgins whose lamps went out couldn't enter in, while the five wise ones were ready and went out to meet the bridegroom. Then the door was shut. Jesus also said in His warning, *"remember Lot's wife,"* whose heart strings were still attached to Sodom and she received the same judgment as Sodom because in her heart she turned back. *"Where your treasure is, there will your heart be also."*

Continue On

1 John 2:28

"And now, little children, abide in him [continue to live your life in union with Him]; that, when he shall appear, we may have confidence, and not be ashamed [and draw back and hide yourself like Adam did after he sinned] before him at his coming." Why exhort them to abide in Him (Christ) if they couldn't do anything but abide?

Romans 11:22_

*"Behold therefore the goodness and severity of God: on them, which fell severity but toward thee, goodness, **if thou continue** in His goodness: otherwise thou also (like millions of others who chose their own way) shalt be cut off."* We must all willingly continue on in His goodness.

1 Peter 1:14-17

"As obedient children, *not fashioning yourselves according to the former lusts in your ignorance: But as he which hath called you is holy, so be ye holy in all manner of conversation [behavior]; because it is written, Be ye holy; for I am holy. And if ye call on the Father,* **who without respect of persons judgeth according to every man's work, [behavior]** *pass the time of your sojourning here in [reverent] fear."* (Knowing quite clearly how He has dealt with rebels in ages past.) (See Christ's message to the church in Rev. 2:23.)

1 Peter 2:7-8,11

"Unto you therefore which believe [and obey] he is precious: **but unto them which be disobedient**, *the stone which the builders disallowed, the same is made the head of the corner, and a stone of stumbling, and a rock of offense,* **even to them which stumble at the word, being disobedient:** *[to it] where unto also they were appointed [because as Peter said, they loved the wages of unrighteousness] …. Dearly beloved, I beseech you as strangers and pilgrims,* **abstain from fleshly lusts, which [wage] war against the soul."**

This is what the Divine Word teaches; not a false grace which implies that a person can live a disobedient life and live in all manner of fleshly lusts and still be spiritually okay with God. Those who go back to lead a disobedient life *stumble and fall into the devil's snare. The thoughts of their hearts are revealed by their actions, and their attitude toward Christ is revealed by whether or not they are obeying Him.* Whom you yield yourself a servant *to obey* His servants ye are; whether to Jesus or Satan, whether this present sinful world or the world to come. It shows whose side you want to be on.

1 Peter 4:17-19_

"For the time is come that judgment must begin at the house of God: and if it first begin at us, what shall the end be of them that obey not the gospel of God? [Ultra gracists ignorantly would say, "heaven".] And if the righteous [who live righteously, 1 John 2:29, 3:7-8] scarcely be saved, where shall the ungodly [man] and the sinner [the person who lives a sinful life] appear? Wherefore let them that suffer according to the will of God commit the keeping of their souls to him in well doing, as unto a faithful Creator" (Rom. 2:6-10). You commit the keeping of your soul to Him in living well before Him, just as you keep yourself in the love of God looking for His mercy and eternal life by obeying Him (Jude 21; John 15:10,14). Grace has given us the ability to do so. This is the true Bible grace.

I'd like to repeat 2 Peter 1:2-11

*"Grace and peace be multiplied unto you through the knowledge of God, and of Jesus our Lord, **according as his divine power hath given unto us all things that pertain unto life and godliness**, [all we need to live and behave godly] through the knowledge [as we advance in the knowledge] of Him that hath called us to glory and virtue (moral excellence): Whereby are given unto us exceeding great and precious promises: that by these ye might be partakers of the divine nature, **having escaped the corruption** [moral decay] that is in the world through [sinful] lust. And beside this, giving all diligence, add to your faith virtue [moral excellence]; and to virtue knowledge; and to knowledge temperance; and to temperance [self-control] patience [perseverance in what's right]; and to patience godliness; and to godliness brotherly kindness; and to brotherly kindness charity. For if these things be in you, and abound, they make you that ye shall neither be barren nor unfruitful in the knowledge of our Lord Jesus Christ. **But he that lacketh these things is blind**, and cannot see afar off, and hath forgotten that he was purged [set free] from his old sins [which caused him to be blind in the first place]. Wherefore the rather, brethren, give diligence to make your calling and election sure: [certain] for if ye do these things [then], ye shall never fall: for so an entrance shall be ministered unto you abundantly into the everlasting kingdom of our Lord and Savior Jesus Christ."* His divine power has freed us from sin's power and the authority of darkness. He has given us all we need to live a life of godliness. The longer we follow Him the more godly, and like Him, we become. Notice He said for you to do these things to *"make your calling and election sure."* (Secure, and something that can be relied upon.) If you don't *do these things* and live right you're *"blind"* and not secure.

What then if someone refuses to continue in these things but chooses the pollutions of the world once again? For certainly such a thing is possible as long as a human being has a free will? For them then there is no eternal security. They don't make their calling and election "*sure.*" The only thing certain then Paul said, is a "*certain fearful looking for of judgment.*"

2 Peter 2:20-21 Listen again to the Apostles' Doctrine:

"*For **if after they have escaped** the pollutions [the moral contaminations] of the world through the knowledge of the Lord and Savior Jesus Christ, they are [once] **again entangled therein**, [back in a life of immorality] and overcome, [conquered again by it] **the latter** end is worse with them than the beginning. [Their condition is worse than it was before.] For it had been **better for them not to have known the [Lord's] way of righteousness**, than, after they have known it, to turn [away] from the holy commandment delivered unto them.*"

Righteousness then is not just standing it is a way. We are to follow after righteousness. The righteousness of the law is to be fulfilled in us "*who walk not after the flesh but after the Spirit*" (Rom. 8:4). "*Little children, let no man deceive you: he that doeth righteousness is righteous, even as he is righteous*" (1 John 3:7). But those who live for sin are following the devil. Paul said, "*Awake to righteousness and sin not.*" John also stated that the one who lives unrighteously committing sin, is of the devil. (See also Acts 10:35; Rom. 2:26; 1 Cor. 15:34; 2 Cor. 6:14; Eph. 6:14; Ps. 23:3.) When Peter said that God will make "*new heavens and a new earth wherein dwelleth **righteousness**,*" it is obvious He didn't mean that people would just have the label of righteousness, but be living the way sinners do now. If so, the new heavens and the new earth would be in the same condition they are now, but righteousness means right living. Christ being our righteousness means that He is our life (Col. 3:4). As He lives His life out through us, we walk as He walked. He, the True Vine we've been grafted into, is the source of our strength. We are the branches producing His fruit.

1 John 2:6

"*He that saith he abideth in him ought himself also so to walk, even as he walked.*"

Again notice in verse 6 of 2 Peter chapter 2, that God let His judgment fall upon Sodom and Gomorrah and burnt them (thousands of people) to ashes to make them an example unto those *"WHO SHOULD AFTERWARDS **LIVE UNGODLY**."*

Where do such statements in the Apostles' Doctrine leave ultra gracists? I can hardly believe they can be so ignorant of so many scriptures. They just conveniently overlook all these scriptures and cling to their own personal false concept of grace, pulling a few scriptures out of context and twisting their meaning. They systematically leave out all the scriptures that show man's responsibility to obey God and cooperate with His grace. So then, what about their interpretation of grace that says, God looks through grace and doesn't see our behavior? What about Ananias and Sapphira? What about the man in 1 Corinthians chapter 5, who was delivered to Satan for the destruction of his flesh because of sin? He most certainly does deal with sin in the church if it's not repented of. He is abundantly clear on this subject. Howbeit we know He is longsuffering and gives space to repent, but we must never interpret this as Him closing His eyes to it (Eccl. 8:11). (See also Revelation chapters 2 and 3.)

2 Peter 2:9, 15

*"The Lord knoweth how to deliver **the godly** out of temptations, and to reserve the unjust [those who don't live by faith for God's will] unto the day of judgment to be punished ... which have **forsaken the right way, and are gone astray**, following the way of Balaam the son of Bosor, who **loved the wages of unrighteousness**."* Sin's wages is still death, and if people choose the way of unrighteousness and forsake the right way, they will be judged and paid the wages of unrighteousness. It must be so for the scriptures cannot be broken, and this New Covenant declares it.

The godly are those who live godly. The ungodly and unjust are those who live ungodly. Now we are not talking about those that slip and then quickly repent, but about those who choose to persistently live contrary to the will of God. The weakest Christian with all his struggles with the flesh, will make it to heaven provided he is *willing* to go on with God and repents when he sins. For Jesus made it clear that even if a person sinned numerous times a day, he would be forgiven *IF* (on this condition) he repented and asked for forgiveness. *"Take heed to yourselves: **IF** thy brother trespass against thee, rebuke him; and **IF** he repent, forgive him. And **IF** he trespass against thee seven times in a day, and seven times in a day turn again to thee, **saying, I repent**, thou shalt forgive him"* (Luke 17:3-4). The Word alone is true.

2 Peter 3:11,14,17-18

"Seeing then that all these things shall be dissolved, what manner of persons ought ye to be in all holy conversation [behavior] and godliness. Wherefore, beloved, seeing that ye look for such things, **be diligent that ye may be found of him in peace, without spot, and blameless** *.... Ye therefore, beloved, seeing ye know these things before,* **beware lest ye also, being led away** *[from walking in righteousness] with the error of the wicked [you], fall from your own steadfastness [in Christ], but grow in [real] grace, and in the knowledge of our Lord and Savior Jesus Christ. To him be glory both now and for ever. Amen."*

Don't let anybody lead you into compromise or lukewarmness. Such a teacher does wickedly and leads people away from steadfastness in Christ. It produces a false peace, and eternal insecurity, or as one president of a well-known full Gospel Bible school called this wrong teaching, "infernal security."

The Epistle of 1 John

Now let's see what the apostle John has to say in 1 John 1:5-10:

"This then is the message which we have heard of him, and declare unto you, that God is light, and in him is no darkness [no sin or evil] at all. **If we say that we have fellowship with him, and walk in darkness** *[sin and evil behavior]* **we lie, and do not [really have] the truth:** *But if we walk [live our lives] in the light, as he is in the light, we have fellowship one with another, and the blood of Jesus Christ his Son cleanseth us from all sin.* **If we say** *that we have no sin [because He removed all future sin], we deceive ourselves, and the truth is not in us.* **If we** *[brethren] confess our sins, he is faithful and just to forgive us our sins, and to cleanse us from all unrighteousness. If we say that we have not sinned [when we have transgressed His laws], we make Him a liar, and his word is not in us."*

Some ultra gracists believe in their made up doctrine that all future sins are also *automatically* washed away, therefore God always sees us the same. It is a wild speculation not founded upon scripture. They think God provided that you can now live unholy and contrary to His commandments and still be called righteous. Come now, even common sense would tell a person this isn't so. And according to God's Word this is not so.

If you sin but say it's not sin, you're a liar. If you say you have fellowship with God while committing sin, you're lying. If you say you're intimate with God and know Him while not keeping His commandments, you're a liar.

1 John 2:3-4

"And hereby we do know that we know him, if we keep his commandments. **he that saith, I know him, and keepeth not his commandments, is a liar, and the truth is not in him.**" This is the Holy Spirit's commentary on it. Then let God be true and every one who contradicts Him be a liar.

If you say you have no sin to confess even though you're sinning and doing unrighteous things, you deceive yourself and the truth is not in you. You have fallen into the *"deceivableness of unrighteousness."*

Now if you sin and you confess it, you'll find abundant and plentiful mercy.

1 John 1:9

"If we confess our sins, he is faithful and just to forgive us our sins, and to cleanse us from all unrighteousness." *"He that covereth his sins shall not prosper: but whoso confesseth* **and forsaketh them** *shall have mercy"* (Prov. 28:13). Notice who will find mercy.

1 John 2:6,14

"He that saith he abideth in him [in Christ] *ought himself also so to walk, even as he walked [that is, live like He lived for the will of God].... I have written unto you, fathers, because ye have known him that is from the beginning. I have written unto you, young men, because ye are strong, and the word of God abideth in you,* **and ye have overcome the wicked one.**"

If the true Word is really living in you, you're overcoming the wicked one and his lusts and temptations. We're not saying you cannot possibly sin nor that a Christian does not ever fall into sin at times. God knew they would, so He tells us that if we judge ourselves, repent of it, and confess it, we'll have mercy, and the blood of Jesus will cleanse us of all unrighteousness. But anyone who says that they are abiding *"in Christ"* must walk like He walked. That means, live right. The real Word of God will always enable you to overcome the wicked one, not to walk with the wicked one.

1 John 2:1

"My little children, these things write I unto you, that ye sin not. And if any man sin, we have an advocate [who will plead your case] with the Father, Jesus Christ the righteous." If you do sin go to the Lord and confess it and He will instantly forgive you and cleanse you. He is very merciful.

But sin's ruling power has been broken over you by God's grace. You don't *have to* live after sin nor be under its control. *"There is therefore now* no condemnation *[no coming judgment] to them which are in Christ Jesus, **who walk not after the flesh but after the Spirit***". *"Who hath delivered us from the power of darkness, and hath translated us into the kingdom of his dear Son"* (Col. 1:13). Contrary to what some say, no one has to sin every day. There is no scripture that says that we have to submit to Satan every day, but there are those scriptures that say, *"give no place to the devil,"* and, *"sin not."*

1 John 2:15-17

*"Love not the world, neither the things that are in the world. **If any man love the world, the love of the Father is not in him.** For all that is in the world, the lust of the flesh, and the lust of the eyes, and the pride of life, is not of the Father, but is of the world. And the world passeth away, and [those involved in] the lust thereof: **but he that doeth the will of God abideth forever."***

Notice: He That Doeth the Will of God Abides Forever.

What about those that willingly go back into sin, back into self-will, and that which is knowingly contrary to the will of God? There is no promise for them except they repent, come back, and willingly receive of God's mercy and grace, and live for God. If they do, He will always abundantly pardon. So then, they need to once again make a commitment of faith to live for the will of God (Rom. 1:17), for the scriptural prerequisite for salvation is to be born again and then live for the will of God (Matt. 7:21).

1 John 2:28-29

*"And now, little children, **abide in him**; that, when he shall appear, we may have confidence, and not be ashamed before him at His coming. If ye know that he is righteous, ye know that every one that **doeth** righteousness is born of him."*

To obey or not obey; to abide or not to abide. Is it automatic? If so, there would be no need of such an exhortation for us to abide. And remember, *in Christ* is where all of our blessings are and our righteousness. Notice, to that John said, *"Every one **that** doeth righteousness is born of him."* This is their fruit if they are really born of Him and continue in Him, for they continue to draw from His strength and righteousness. *"Being filled with the fruits of righteousness, which are by Jesus Christ, unto the glory and praise of God"* (Phil. 1:11).

John 15:6

Jesus said, *"If a man abide not **in me [in Christ]**, he is cast forth as a branch [broken off], and is withered [and dies]; and men gather them [branches* *that once were alive but are now dead], and cast them into the fire, and they are burned"* (Jude 12).

It is possible for a man to abide or not abide. It's always their choice. If they continue to abide (living for the Father's commandments, v.10), He continues to prune them from all evil that they might bring forth more good fruit. If they abide not, choosing to no longer live for the will of God, their good fruit they once had begins to wither away. And Christ revealed that if they continue in this state without repentance, their end is to *"be burned."* Not because He wills it, but because of their own free choice. All evil will be judged but, *"If we would judge ourselves, we would not be judged"* (Matt. 13:41-42).

1 John 3:2-8

"Beloved, now are we the sons of God, and it doth not yet appear what we shall be: but we know that, when he shall appear, we shall be like him; for we shall see him as he is. **And every man that [truly] hath this hope in him purifieth himself,** *even as He is pure.* **Whosoever committeth** *sin [and willingly lives sinfully]* transgresseth *also the law [is living in violation of God's moral law]:* **for sin is the transgression of the [moral] law.** *And ye know that he was manifested to take away our sins; and* **in him is no sin [no transgressing of God's moral law]. Whosoever abideth in him sinneth not** *[no one who abides in him lives a life of sin]: whosoever sinneth [continues in sin breaking God's laws] hath not seen him, neither known him [he has not really known what God is like and what He stands for] Little children, let no man deceive [or mislead] you: he that* **doeth** *righteousness is righteous, even as he is righteous.* **He that committeth [practices or lives in] sin is of the devil;** *for the devil sinneth from the beginning. For this purpose the Son of God was manifested, that he might destroy the works of the devil."* That is, that He might set us free from sin's control, for sin is a work of the devil. It's one of His works and operations. We are now *"dead to sin,"* and *"free from sin,"* and no longer *"a servant of sin,"* because we have been delivered from the authority of darkness. Whoever sins and transgresses the moral law regardless of who does it, Christian or sinner, will suffer the consequences unless it's repented of. This is a statement of the New Covenant. It's in our contract. Whatever is in the New Covenant we are obligated to obey, but the Old has passed away. But the curse is still here. Faith frees you from the curse and the devil (See Ephesians 6:16.), but only as you submit to God. In order to overcome Satan who brings the curse, you must first submit to God (James 4:7). Then you can resist the devil and the curse steadfast in the

faith (1 Pet. 5:8-9). If you're living in sin you're resisting God and submitting to the devil, and the curse can then begin to legally operate in your life (Eph. 4:27). Therefore neither you nor God can do anything about it until you repent and turn from Satan back to God. Then through faith you can overcome (2 Tim. 2:25-26).

Was John self-righteous or a legalist because he said these things? No, John, like Paul and the Lord's other apostles, knew the true message and meaning of grace and the true Gospel, which is that grace is given to empower you to keep the moral law and God's commandments and thereby be blessed (Acts 3:26). Nevertheless, some in the ultra grace camp would have you to believe that John either didn't know what he was talking about or that he was lying about it. For they choose their own manmade, or devil-made, version of the Gospel over the Apostles' Doctrine. (Real grace in the heart causes a person to purify themselves.) John said this is true with "every man" *that really* has this hope in him. This is what the New Covenant actually reveals. Forget all those books that have a few little taken-out-of-context scriptures, and then page after page of human reasoning. They are the ones that don't take the Word by faith. They are the ones' reasoning against God and His revelation.

What John said was a mouthful. Let no man deceive you and say that you could live a life of sin and continue to be in the grace of God. Those who willingly practice a life of sin, he said, are really of the devil (tares sown among the wheat, John 8:44). In other words, they are in union with the father of all rebels not in union with God (Amos 3:3). Do you really want their perspective on grace? There is no security in it!

1 John 3:10

"In this the children of God are manifest [revealed], and the children of the devil: [It is clear by this who the children of God are and who the devil's children are.] Whosoever doeth not righteousness **is not** *of God, neither he that loveth not his brother."* Now remember, John said, *"If you do sin you have an advocate with the Father, Jesus Christ the righteous,"* but the truth is, if one is following Christ he is following Him in paths of righteousness. A Christian can backslide for a short while and commit sin, but his heart stirs him to repent and to come to the throne room of grace and mercy to find mercy and grace to help in his time of need, for God's law is written in his heart (Heb. 4:16). He is still in Christ (1 Cor. 3:1-3). But if he persists in sin, he will eventually sear his conscience, shipwreck his faith, and he then stands the chance that he won't come back to *"live by faith."* This can take place if he continues in unrepented of sin choosing the

pleasures of it and the pollutions of the world over obedience to God's will. If he does so, he then departs from God and from Christ by his own will, and joins himself to the devil (Eph. 5:5-6).

It's a dangerous thing to play with fire. *"Can a man take fire in his bosom, and his clothes not be burned? Can one go upon hot coals, and his feet not be burned?"* (Prov. 6:27-28)

1 John 3:22

"And whatsoever we ask, we receive of him, **because** *we keep his commandments, and do those things that are pleasing in his sight."*

Because why? Many of the ultra gracists don't want you to believe in God's conditions for eternal life or answered prayer. They cannot endure the sound teaching of John the Apostle and the New Covenant, as though they had a better understanding of grace than he did, who was one of our Lord's apostles. David said, *"If I regard iniquity in my heart, the Lord will not hear my prayer."* (See also 1 Peter 3:12.) If anyone lives the way the ultra grace message permits, they will not have their prayers answered. God has clearly shown He won't answer their prayers.

1 John 3:21

John wrote, *"Beloved, if our heart condemn us not, then have we confidence toward God."* But your heart will condemn you if you do wrong, unless it's been hardened. John said, *"God is greater than our hearts and knoweth all things."* He's not ignorant of how we live; He knows, but He will forgive and forget if you repent.

1 John 5:2-3,16-17_

"By this we know that we love the children of God, when we love God, and keep his commandments. **For this is the love of God, that we keep his commandments:** *and his commandments are not grievous.... If any man see* **his brother** *[in Christ] sin a sin, which is not unto death, he shall ask, and he shall give him life for them that sin not unto death. There is a sin [a brother can sin] unto death: I do not say that he shall pray for it. All unrighteousness [evil behavior] is sin: and there is a sin not unto death."* Some sins, if persisted in, carry the death penalty and some don't. (See Gal. 5:19-21; Rom. 1:29-32.)

The sin unto death is the sin of willingly being persistent in resisting the Holy Ghost's convictions and the dealings of God. It is a decision of a free moral agent to not want to come back to God, to no longer want to walk the faith life. God will finally let people have their own way just as He did with Israel, who persisted in wanting a king like the other nations. He finally let them have their way and they had many problems because of it. Neither you nor God can override another person's will. God ordained this to be so (Gen. 2:7). It wouldn't be that way unless God willed it, but this was done by his own counsel. Notice also, that John is talking about *a brother;* and John, in his epistle, is speaking of spiritual death. If you want to be a Christian and live for Christ, you need never fear this, regardless of your struggles with the flesh or this world, for this speaks of a person who has used his will to turn away from God. Their actions reveal their decision (Titus 1:16).

The only sin that cannot be forgiven is the one of turning away from God and no longer being willing to come back, repent, and ask for forgiveness. God respects a person's decision to choose death if they want to (Deut. 30:19-20). Persistent sinning and hardening of the heart, which sears the conscience and gets a person deeper and deeper into unbelief, bondage, and darkness, can bring this about.

Seared flesh is when all the nerve endings have been burned and there is no more feeling. *"This I say therefore, and testify in the Lord, that ye henceforth walk not as other Gentiles walk, in the vanity, of their mind.... **Who being past feeling** have given themselves over unto lasciviousness [which Jude said some ultra gracists have done, Jude 4], to work all uncleanness with greediness"* (Eph. 4:17,19). This is the effect that sin has on the unrepented conscience, but you can intercede and pray for those who have not made that decision, but have sinned and *are ignorant,* and God will continue to try and *"lead them to repentance"* (Rom. 2:4). He will evidently even give life for the ignorant concerning some sins. Here is a great hope. But the fact is, a brother can sin a sin unto spiritual death, or John would never have mentioned it. That is the sin of unbelief, which means to depart from living for the living God, and to stop abiding in Christ (Heb. 3:12-14).

2 John 4,6,9

*"I rejoiced greatly that I found of thy children walking in truth **as we have received a commandment from the Father .... And this is love that we walk after his commandments.** This is the commandment, that, as ye have heard from the beginning, **ye should walk in it....** Whosoever transgresseth, and abideth not in the doctrine [the teachings and instructions] of Christ [who taught that you needed to repent, believe and obey Him to be saved], hath not God. He that abideth in the doctrine (the teachings and instructions) of Christ, he hath both the Father and the Son."* The doctrine of Christ is to repent of a life of sin, believe, obey, and follow Him, being faithful unto death to

have eternal life. These are the basic foundational truths of His teaching (Rev. 2:10).

Jude said our faith is a most holy faith. We must contend for it and stand in defense of it. For similar things as this false-type grace, crept into the early church until finally, for centuries, the church fell asleep in a time of great darkness and spiritual depravity and lukewarmness, and then much of it got legalistic and bound up in outward rituals. The professing church lived just like the world. Isn't this just what the ultra gracists imply can be done now?

Worldliness was hand in hand with the church. Religion had the outward form and profession but no power to live it, by reason of whom the way of truth was evil spoken of. This false teaching on grace is a worldly, religious spirit that motivates a Laodicean church, having the form of words and outward appearance but denying the power to live right.

To the ultra gracists I say no more than Jude. I quote the apostles. If you can bring forth as many *scriptures* clearly showing your belief without contradicting all those scriptures, I will listen. But I will not heed human opinions, philosophy, or good sounding speeches contrary to the Apostles' Doctrine and the *"whole counsel of God."* My concern is for the multitudes that have been led astray by this false teaching, people that started on the pathway of life, but then were taught a false grace doctrine.

I trust that all who have read this will know my heart is not just to scold, but to explain the truth so that we all overcome the adversary of our souls, and that we all live lives pleasing to God and enter into heaven. This is what Christ has freed us to do. The battle continues to rage; light against darkness, truth against error, good against evil, all for the souls of men. Let us not play with sin (with fire), and we won't get burned. Let us not so quickly believe the wrong accusations against truth and true righteousness, for Satan's deceptions come clothed in so many different ways and in so many disguises, and God says that Satan is waging war against those *"which keep the commandments of God and have the testimony of Jesus Christ"* (Rev. 12:17). And *"Yea, and all that will live godly in Christ Jesus shall suffer persecution"* (2 Tim. 3:12). So, let us not be as Cain who was of the wicked one and slew his brother and wherefore slew he him? Because his own works were evil and his brother's righteous (1 John 3:12). All that's good is from God while all that's evil is from Satan.

Let us walk hand in hand to that eternal city following Jesus, the Shepherd and Bishop of our soul, in paths of righteousness, and let us, as Paul said, *"have grace whereby we may serve God acceptably with reverence and godly fear."*

Brethren, I have written the main outline of this in one sitting, stirred in my heart for the care of the flock, wanting only the best in Christ for all. Wanting those under our care to be cared for, that we all continue to *really* follow Him who is the light of the world, to that glorious city whose builder and maker is God (John 8:12). Heed the Word of the Lord.

Revelation 22:14

"Blessed are they that do his commandments, that they may have right to the tree of life, and may enter in through the gates into the city."

Revelation 2:7

"He that hath an ear, let him hear what the Spirit saith unto the churches; To him that overcometh will I give to eat of the tree of life, which is in the midst of the paradise of God."

"Let us hear the conclusion of the whole matter: Fear God, and keep his commandments: for this is the whole duty of man" (Eccl. 12:13).

"He hath shewed thee, O man, what is good; and what doth the LORD *require of thee, but to do justly, and to love mercy, and to walk humbly with thy God?"* (Micah 6:8).

*"The foundation of God stands sure **having this seal.**"* (This true inscription.) *"The Lord knows them that are His."* (And who really belongs to Him.) And let everyone that names the name of Christ (and claims to be His) depart from (a life of sin and) iniquity (2 Tim. 2:19), for *"they that are Christ's [and really belong to Him]* **have crucified the flesh** *with the [evil] affections and lusts"* (Gal. 5:24). If we stay in the seal of the Holy Spirit, we don't follow after a life of sin and Satan. There is so much more that could be said, but I will end here with this statement from Paul: Hebrews 13:22, *"And I beseech you, brethren, suffer the word of exhortation."*

Stay right with the Bible and believe *all* of it. Contend for the faith which was once delivered to the saints. May God's true grace be with you all! Amen. If you have believed the false concept of grace, ask God to forgive you, now.

Prayer

"Dear Lord, please forgive me for believing things contrary to Your Word. Cleanse me and free me from sin and all the deceiving effects of false doctrine. I choose to live for You and Your will. Thank You for forgiving and cleansing me now. Jesus, I acknowledge that You are the Lord of my life, and I now choose to believe all of the New Testament. In Jesus' name. Amen."

If you have never been saved, pray this scriptural prayer to God right now, and commit your life to Him. This prayer is according to God's own Word.

Pray this prayer out loud:

"Dear God, I realize that without Jesus I would be lost and separated from You because of my life of sin. But I believe that Jesus Christ is Your Son; that He died on the cross for my sins and rose again from the dead. God, with Your help, I now repent and turn from a life of sin. Please forgive me of all my past sins. I now confess that I accept Jesus Christ as the Lord of my life and I invite and receive Him into my heart and life right now. Thank You, Lord, that I am now, according to Your own Word, born again and Your child. I am saved from judgment to come, and will follow You for the rest of my life. In Jesus' name. Amen."

If you have not already received, you should also seek information on the biblical experience of the "Baptism with the Holy Spirit" which will greatly empower your Christian walk (Acts 1:8, 2:4, 8:14-17, 19:1-6). If you don't have a church home that teaches you clearly concerning these basic, fundamental things, and you live in the Milwaukee, Wisconsin area, you are welcome here at:

Faith's Creation Christian Fellowship, 4400 North Mayfair Road, Wauwatosa, Wisconsin 53225

We are a church that is *"Excited About Jesus."* Our services are held Sundays at 8.00 a.m., 10:00 a.m., and 7:00 p.m. Please feel free to call us for more information or if you would like to hold special meetings with Reverend Ted Rouse on this topic or on others, please call us at: (414) 461-8770, or go to our website and send us an invitation by email, www.faithscreation.org.

And remember that
Jesus is Lord!

ACKNOWLEDGEMENTS

Some gleanings about "grace" have been received from the teachings of Finis Dake. Some of the aspects about "sin" have been seen from an old book entitled, "Sin" written hundreds of years ago, and a few nuggets about repentance have blessed me from an old, old book called, "Repentance."

ABOUT THE AUTHOR

Ted Rouse has been married over thirty two years and has been in full-time ministry since 1981. Having had a life-changing experience with Jesus Christ when calling on the name of the Lord in his bedroom in the mid seventies, Ted went on to receive the Baptism with the Holy Spirit after reading a book called *This Awakening Generation* by former Baptist minister, John Osteen.

Ted has written a number of books and booklets such as *Faith and the Pharisees; Why Suffering Cannot Be God's Will; Dear Mr. Evolutionist, Please Answer Me This; What Hell Is Like, Who Must Go There and Why; Have You Received the Holy Ghost Since You Believed; The Importance of Continuing in the Faith;* and *The Thirty Minute Presentation of God's Plan to Save Man From Hell.*

Having had a supernatural call to the ministry after being filled with the Holy Spirit, Pastor Ted Rouse was led by the Lord into the wonderful message of faith in God's Word that has revolutionized his life. Having learned about the absolute integrity of God's written Word, he has founded his ministry solidly upon it (Luke 1:2).

Ted has traveled overseas on various occasions and has seen hundreds filled with the Holy Ghost at one time, just like the meetings in the book of Acts.

Presently, Pastor/Bible Teacher Ted Rouse is pastor of a lively faith-filled church in the Milwaukee, Wisconsin area called *Faith's Creation Christian Fellowship*. He has four children, and together with his wife, Doreen, are all serving and walking with the Lord.

Pastor Rouse has the following life-changing books and tape messages available. To order any of the following, please contact us: 414-461-8770.

Books and Tape Sets by Ted Rouse

Faith and the Pharisees

What Is Hell Like?

Who Must Go There and Why?

Continuing On in the Faith

A Two Step Journey Back to God

The Key to the Mystery of Life

Have You Received the Holy Ghost Since You Believed?

Dear Mr. Evolutionist, Please Answer Me This

Witnesses to the Truth (book for Jehovah's Witnesses)

The One Thing You Must Do to Enter Into Heaven (tract)

Why Suffering Cannot Be God's Will

Tape Sets

The Creator and His Word

Grace Is Given

Reality of Life After Death

Freedom From Satan and His Works

The Will of Man and the Will of God

Please check our website for more books and tapes:
www.faithscreation.org